HONORABLE
TREACHERY

HONORABLE TREACHERY

A History of U.S. Intelligence,
Espionage, and Covert Action from
the American Revolution to the CIA

G. J. A. O'Toole

Grove Press
New York

Published simultaneously in Canada
Printed in the United States of America

FIRST GROVE PRESS PAPERBACK EDITION

ISBN 978-0-8021-2328-2
eISBN 978-0-8021-9202-8

Grove Press
an imprint of Grove/Atlantic, Inc.
154 West 14th Street
New York, NY 10011

Distributed by Publishers Group West

www.groveatlantic.com

14 15 16 17   10 9 8 7 6 5 4 3 2 1

For Mary Ann

A Note on Sources

To satisfy the legal requirements of the secrecy agreement that binds every former employee of the Central Intelligence Agency, I submitted the manuscript of this book to the CIA's Publications Review Board. In this case the security review was a formality; the portions of the narrative that cover the CIA and other recent intelligence matters are based entirely on my research of the books, articles, and other publicly available materials I have cited in the source notes, and are not drawn from confidential or classified materials. The CIA's *nihil obstat* permitting the publication of this book means only that it contains no classified information; it should not be construed as a confirmation or endorsement of the accuracy of its contents.

G. J. A. O'Toole

Our spy was not long in returning from St. Catherine's with a dispatch which was also allowed to pass unopened upon his assurance that it contained nothing of importance. In this way he went back and forward from Richmond to St. Catherine's once or twice. We supplied him with money to a limited extent, and also with one or two more horses. He said that he got some money from the Confederates, but had not thought it prudent to accept from them anything more than very small sums, since his professed zeal for the Confederate cause forbade his receiving anything for his traveling expenses beyond what was absolutely necessary. . . .

All his subsequent dispatches, however, whether coming from Richmond or from Canada, were regularly brought to the War Department, and were opened, and in every case a copy was kept. As it was necessary to break the seals and destroy the envelopes in opening them, there was some difficulty in sending them forward in what should appear to be the original wrappers. . . . At any rate, the confidence of the Confederates in our agent and in theirs never seemed to be shaken by any of these occurrences. . . .

He was one of the cleverest creatures I ever saw. His style of patriotic lying was sublime; it amounted to genius.

—*Charles A. Dana*, Recollections of the Civil War

Contents

PART FIVE
THE ROAD TO CENTRAL INTELLIGENCE:
1920–1962

Introduction

To understand American intelligence, its history, and the consequences of its use and abuse by policymakers, politicians, and the military, one can read scores of recent books on these subjects, or one can try to locate the definitive but long out-of-print *Honorable Treachery* by G. J. A. O'Toole, a search that was rarely successful, until now.

While others have written about George Washington's many successful intelligence operations during the War of Independence, which the British credited for Washington's victory, O'Toole goes back to Washington's youth to explain the intelligence lesson learned as a twenty-one-year-old adjutant in the Virginia militia under British General Edward Braddock during the French and Indian Wars, and the consequences of going into battle without intelligence.

Many books on intelligence history have been written by historians or academic scholars, and some by former intelligence officers, usually with backgrounds and experience in operations, based on open or newly declassified documents. The problem faced by these writers is the many interrelated and connected facets of intelligence—collection, analysis, counterintelligence, covert action, warning—intertwined and interacting like an expanding, multilevel Rubik's Cube. O'Toole, instead, shows us the clear interconnections with exceptional finesse.

Much has been written on one or more of the facets of intelligence and its role in war and peacetime. One of the more difficult issues writers face, and therefore often ignore, is the preconceived view each new president has on the intelligence functions he inherits. O'Toole covers, for example, Roosevelt's relationship with Britain's Winston Churchill, an ally, and the Soviet Union's Joseph Stalin, also an ally but, in reality, an adversary bent on world domination. Roosevelt not only favored Stalin, but essentially ordered his counterintelligence service, the FBI, to cease their anti-Russian counterintelligence efforts. The Roosevelt administration went further by closing down the nation's only intelligence organization, the Department of State's Division of Eastern European Affairs, which was keeping an intelligence eye on the Soviets. The United States was now blind to Stalin's machinations. O'Toole explains the consequences, which subsequent presidents would have to counter by establishing new, effective intelligence methods and organizations.

From his experience as a producer of finished intelligence, O'Toole objectively describes the key differences between intelligence producer and consumer, including the many intelligence failures as well as successes. He shows that President Wilson's Inquiry, a forerunner of producing a National Intelligence Estimate (NIE), was ignored and never seriously read, since it was attacked by our Department of State. The State department thought they should be the only producers of "finished intelligence"—something the fading president was unable to prevent. O'Toole's assessment of why so many highly skilled and competent intelligence analysts failed to predict Pearl Harbor becomes obvious when he points out the incredible volume of intelligence data they face, most of which is useless, blatantly skewed, or deceptive, a fact that makes analysis akin to finding a thread in a haystack. Trying to predict things yet to happen is an even greater challenge. From his own experience, O'Toole understood that presidents not only have the authority to declassify intelligence, but may choose to ignore it entirely, since they might have other information or hidden reasons for alternative actions they choose to take. But history has shown that more often than not, these decisions were made more out of political expedience than for the benefit of the nation or our allies.

Others have written extensively about intelligence failures and successes and the consequences of good intelligence, bad intelligence, and no intelligence. O'Toole, on the other hand, examines why such failures occurred, their often disastrous consequences, and, more important, the lessons learned, if any. His chapter 25, which could readily be the subject of an entire book, uniquely covers the U.S. Army's disastrous incursion into Russia ordered by President Wilson in the aftermath of World War I. O'Toole assesses the performance of several presidents who had no prior experience with intelligence, making comparisons with those like George Washington, Ulysses S. Grant, and Dwight Eisenhower, all of whom had a military background and intimate knowledge of the critical importance of the field.

O'Toole takes the reader from the period before the American Revolution up through the peacetime intelligence successes that turned the tide of World War II, as in the Battle of Midway, through the intelligence that prevented nuclear war, as in the Cuban Missile Crisis. He traces the then recent changes in American intelligence surrounding the introduction of high-tech intelligence collection systems such as the U-2, still active today a half century later, which foretold of the drones and the sophisticated satellites we have today, changing forever the way intelligence and warfare are conducted forever. He gives the reader the who, what, where, when, and why of every intelligence-related event from the beginning of this nation up to the close of the twentieth century. While most readers get their intelligence education from spy movies, TV series, James Bond novels, and Jason Bourne, *Honorable Treachery* provides the realities that underpin all of these fictional incarnations and provides an ideal foundation any historian or intelligence officer or scholar should have in his educational arsenal.

Present-day professors teaching intelligence courses will find O'Toole's *Honorable Treachery* an indispensable bible and ideal basic text for students. As an intelligence professional and professor teaching in this field, I long searched for a book that covered not only the history of the United States, but our hidden history: the use and abuses intelligence has had on that history. When I discovered O'Toole's *Honorable Treachery*, I used it widely and urged students to locate it, until its elusive out of print status made it a punishing course requirement. With this fresh edition putting it back in print where it belongs, I am pleased to recommend it again to all readers and intelligence scholars.

S. Eugene Poteat, former CIA science and technology officer; current president, Association of Former Intelligence Officers

HONORABLE
TREACHERY

Foreword

Intelligence is information. Specifically, it is information about an adversary that is useful in dealing with him. This was the sense of General George Washington's observation to one of his lieutenants in July 1777: "The necessity of procuring good intelligence is apparent and need not be further urged." It is also the meaning of the Central Intelligence Agency's middle name.

To call information *intelligence* implies the existence of an adversary. In war the adversary is, of course, the enemy. But war, as Clausewitz pointed out, is simply the continuation of international relations by violent means. Conversely, diplomacy is a kind of nonviolent warfare; it may be unfashionable to say so, but in diplomacy all nations are adversaries, if only in the sense that no two of them share a total commonality of interest. Thus, the information one nation must have in its dealings with another is intelligence.

Much of what one nation would know about another is readily available in the latter's books, newspapers, government publications, and electronic media. But other information is closely held and can be obtained only through subtle and usually secret methods, such as espionage and code breaking.

Secret intelligence is as old as warfare and diplomacy. It has been said, with some reason, that it is the missing dimension of history. Both foreign policy in peacetime and command decision in wartime are driven by intelligence, much of which has necessarily been obtained by covert means. Obviously, such sources and methods must be protected by a cloak of secrecy if they are to continue to supply needed intelligence. But even after the intelligence itself has long since ceased to be of anything but historical interest, governments tend to hold secret the means used to acquire it.

During the Revolutionary War, when Dr. Benjamin Franklin was our ambassador to the French court, his trusted secretary was an agent of the British Secret Service, a penetration that enabled King George III to know all that passed between the Continental Congress and Versailles soon after the fact. The man's treachery went unsuspected until, a full century later, the British government made public some of its archives.

General Thomas Gage, a British governor of colonial Massachusetts, ran a network of agents that spied on the preparations of the Patriots in Boston and the surrounding countryside before the battles of Lexington and Concord. Their very existence was confirmed only when Gage's personal papers became public in the 1930s, and the identities of most of them are still unknown.

The Confederate Secret Service was active in the Northern states during the Civil War, and recent scholarship indicates that it may have had a hand in the assassination of President Lincoln. The facts may never be known with certainty, for the agency's records disappeared—perhaps were destroyed—when the Confederate leaders fled Richmond in April 1865.

Today, a half century after the outbreak of the Second World War, most of the records of the Office of Strategic Services—America's wartime secret intelligence agency—remain classified and are held in the closed archives of the Central Intelligence Agency.

Because such material is obscure and inaccessible, the role of intelligence has largely been ignored by diplomatic and military historians, especially those who have chronicled American history. Furthermore, Americans are quite ambivalent on the matter of intelligence, for there has long been a sense among us that secret undertakings, especially espionage, were, if not dishonorable, at the very least un-American. Thus, while we find in Woodrow Wilson's five-volume history of the American people a lengthy account of the treason of Benedict Arnold, there is not a word of our own Revolutionary spy, Nathan Hale.[1] Wilson, who was a historian and university president before his ascent to the presidency, revealed his own innocence of the entire subject in a post–World War speech:

> Let me testify to this, my fellow citizens, I not only did not
> know it until we got into this war, but I did not believe it
> when I was told that it was true, that Germany was not the

only country that maintained a secret service. Every country in
Europe maintained it, because they had to be ready for Germany's spring upon them, and the only difference between the
German secret service and the other secret services was that the
German secret service found out more than the others did and
therefore Germany sprang upon the other nations unawares,
and they were not ready for it.[2]

Secret service was the term for such things until late in the nineteenth
century, when it became the misnomer of a United States government
agency that pursues counterfeiters and protects the president. The term
was especially useful in that it referred not only to espionage but to a range
of other covert activities usually carried out by the same people who collect
secret intelligence, using many of the same methods. Most of these other
activities can be conveniently lumped together under the pejorative word
subversion and include such things as sabotage, psychological warfare, and
even paramilitary operations. They have more recently been called *covert
action*, *special operations*, or *special activities*. In the most general sense, they
comprise all actions that are calculated to achieve foreign-policy objectives and are covert, or at least not openly attributable to the governments
sponsoring them.

A knowledgeable student of such matters has observed that "the attitude of Americans toward intelligence and espionage is similar to their attitude toward monarchy: they approve the institution only for others. . . ."[3]
In fact, American attitudes toward the subject have often exemplified the
theme invoked so often in the novels of Henry James: American innocence
contrasted with European subtlety and corruption. Americans are blunt,
forthright, direct, ingenuous—all qualities acquired on the frontier and permanently incorporated in the American national character. Deviousness,
secretiveness, indirection, and duplicity are, literally, foreign. Americans
believe that "gentlemen do not read other people's mail," in the words of
the secretary of state who shut down the State Department's code-breaking
unit in 1929.[4] Even in these pragmatic final years of the twentieth century,
American politicians and commentators regularly profess their indignation
over the discovery that the United States government may actually have
some secrets or may even have undertaken some covert operations. Secrecy

is alien to the spirit of a free people, they say, and espionage is incompatible with the American character. But the facts tell a different story.

American gentlemen have read other people's mail at every major turning in our national career. What is more, American gentlemen have proved to be very good at it.

If there is one figure from American history who may be said to personify the veraciousness and openness of our national character, it is George Washington. But the historical Washington was far different from the guileless little boy of the cherry-tree myth. Washington was in fact the most important intelligence officer of the American Revolution, the chief American spy master. He recruited spies, instructed them in their treacherous craft, sent them out, welcomed them back, and paid them off.

Paul Revere, another nearly mythical figure of American tradition, is immortalized in the mind of every schoolchild for his famous midnight ride. But few children ever learn that that ride was part of an American intelligence operation or that Revere belonged to a Boston secret intelligence network.

Such forgotten threads can be found everywhere in the fabric of American history. During the Civil War the chief of the Confederate Secret Service in Europe was an uncle of Theodore Roosevelt. Grenville Dodge is best known to history as the railroad builder who linked California to the East Coast by rail in 1876, but he was also one of the most important Union intelligence officers of the Civil War, running an espionage network that penetrated deep into the Confederacy. Socialite Vincent Astor ran a private intelligence service for President Franklin D. Roosevelt. Arthur Goldberg, sometime secretary of labor, Supreme Court justice, and ambassador to the United Nations, ran espionage operations against the Axis powers while serving in the Office of Strategic Services, the predecessor of the CIA. Other prominent Americans who served in the OSS include the filmmaker John Ford, Arthur Schlesinger, Jr., Ralph Bunche, and Julia Child. And the civil rights activist and antiwar leader Rev. William Sloane Coffin, Jr., served as a CIA intelligence officer and recruited, trained, and dispatched CIA agents to the Soviet Union during the Korean War.

Even our folklore and literature are steeped in spying. The spy novels and films so popular around the world today are examples of a genre that had its beginning in what students of literature regard as the first American novel to explore a native American theme: *The Spy* by James Fenimore Cooper. Set in the Revolution, it is the story of Harvey Birch, a peddler who suffers the scorn of his Patriot neighbors, who believe him to be a Tory while in fact he is a secret agent for General Washington. First published in 1821, *The Spy* was not purely a product of Cooper's imagination; it was based on the actual secret services of Enoch Crosby, an itinerant shoemaker who operated as a Patriot counterespionage agent throughout Westchester County, New York, during the Revolution.

Like secret intelligence, covert action has also been an instrument of American foreign policy since the birth of the Republic and before. The phrase "the shores of Tripoli" in the Marine Corps hymn refers to an 1805 paramilitary operation ordered by President Thomas Jefferson to topple the ruler of that Near Eastern nation—today's Libya—and free the American hostages he held. President James Madison and Secretary of State James Monroe—with the approval of Congress—mounted a covert political and paramilitary operation aimed at acquiring the Spanish colony of East Florida in 1811. In the 1830s and 1840s several presidents launched covert political action operations aimed at acquiring Texas and California. During the Civil War covert propaganda agents of both the Union and the Confederacy fought a secret war for the hearts and minds of Europe.

Secret service is the hidden subplot of the American story, yet scarcely a word about it is to be found in our history books. On the other hand, spies and secret agents hold a certain allure that has caused them to be celebrated in popular literature. There have even been several attempts to compile histories of American secret service. But such "true spy stories" neglect historical background. They are replete with the details of tradecraft—the dead drop, the microdot, the double or triple agent—but they almost completely ignore the ultimate reasons for the derring-do. It is as though secret service had some existence separate from other things, like the smile that remained after the Cheshire cat vanished.

In this work I have tried to supply that missing nexus, to put secret service within its historical context in order to understand the events that gave rise to a particular covert operation, and to discover what effect, if any, such operations had on subsequent history. Here, then, is an unfamiliar story: the honorable treachery of secret servants and the roles they have played in America's hidden history.

PART ONE

TRIUMPH OF THE AMATEURS:

The American Revolution

Chapter One

Liberty Boys and British Moles

It is a commonplace that the struggle for American independence, which began at Lexington and Concord in April 1775, had as one of its root causes the Stamp Act, imposed on the American colonies by Parliament ten years earlier. Less familiar, however, is the fact that this same act led to the creation of the first American intelligence service. And it is virtually unknown that the shots fired that April morning on Lexington Green marked the culmination of a secret war between British and American intelligence.

The ultimate ancestor of all American intelligence services is the Sons of Liberty, a federation of dissident political groups formed in colonial America in 1765 in reaction to the Stamp Act. The act, which required the colonists to use tax stamps on virtually all printed matter, had the effect of unifying colonial resistance to British rule; earlier revenue measures had fallen more heavily on some colonies than on others, but the Stamp Act burdened all more or less equally. The Sons of Liberty provided the means for this unification.

The organization took its name from Major Isaac Barré's impassioned speech against the passage of the act in the House of Commons. In Boston the fiery Samuel Adams transformed the Caucus Club, a political club that had been in existence for a half century, into the Sons of Liberty. In Charleston, South Carolina, the Fireman's Association—a local volunteer fire company—followed suit, as did the Ancient and Honorable Mechanical Company of Baltimore and the Heart and Hand Fire Company in Philadelphia. Within a short time similar organizations in each of the thirteen colonies had adopted the name and joined the network of secret political groups to resist enforcement of the Stamp Act.

The Sons of Liberty, or the Liberty Boys, as they were sometimes called, employed a variety of tactics, most of them violent and illegal—for example, rioting, seizing and destroying the hated stamps, and attacking the appointed stamp agents. The New York chapter of the Liberty Boys entered into a mutual defense pact with its Connecticut and New Jersey counterparts, providing for military resistance should the British government attempt to enforce the act with troops. In North and South Carolina local Liberty Boys actually stormed British forts and garrisons but met no armed resistance.

Within a year the Sons of Liberty had achieved its immediate goal: Parliament repealed the Stamp Act. The federation did not go out of existence, however, but continued to operate as a Patriot underground from New Hampshire to South Carolina, but especially in Boston and New York.

In 1772 the Patriots began to establish Committees of Correspondence, a more formal structure for the coordination of resistance to Britain's colonial policies. While the Liberty Boys were composed largely of artisans and tradesmen of the colonial towns and cities, the committees were organized in the countryside as well, thus uniting rural Patriots with their urban brethren. In addition to disseminating anti-British propaganda, the committees sometimes exercised judicial, legislative, and executive functions, becoming in effect a Patriot shadow government or underground. The intercolonial communication network established by the committees was instrumental in the convening of the First Continental Congress in 1774.

The committees did not completely replace the Sons of Liberty, however, although the membership of the two groups overlapped to a great extent. The Liberty Boys continued to exist as a less formal organization in parallel with the Committees of Correspondence until the outbreak of the war made them superfluous.

In the terms of modern revolutionary warfare, the Sons of Liberty and the related committees comprised the insurgent infrastructure of Patriot America in the decade before the Revolution; they were a cadre of dedicated revolutionaries who propagandized against British rule, indoctrinated the uncommitted, organized the Whigs, terrorized the Tories, procured arms and munitions, trained farmers and tradesmen in the military arts, and generally prepared for an armed conflict with the British government. And this, of course, included espionage.

In Boston some thirty members of the Sons of Liberty met regularly at the Green Dragon Tavern on Union Street during the winter of 1774–75. They had constituted themselves as a committee for the purpose of watching the activities of the British troops and the Tories in and around the city. Boston had been occupied by British troops under the command of General Thomas Gage since late in 1768, following the sporadic incidents of mob violence and other public disorders in that city in resistance to the Townshend Acts, yet another of the onerous taxation measures Parliament imposed on the Americans. Clashes between soldiers and civilians heightened tensions—in the so-called Boston Massacre of March 1770, troops fired into an angry mob, killing five—and the British responded by further strengthening the Boston garrison. By the beginning of 1775, there were some forty-five hundred British troops in the city.[1] Meanwhile, the Patriot underground had raised and drilled militia units throughout Massachusetts and continued to accumulate arms, ammunition, and other military stores at secret depots in the countryside.

General Gage, who was by then both commander in chief of British forces in the colonies and colonial governor of Massachusetts, had a network of informers among the Patriots and knew in great detail of some of their military preparations. On September 1, 1774, his troops raided a supposedly secret military depot the Patriots had established at Cambridge, the existence of which he had learned from one of his agents the previous March.[2] This raid probably was the reason the surveillance committee of the Sons of Liberty began meeting at the Green Dragon in the fall of 1774; members of the group regularly patrolled the streets of Boston during the night to observe British military preparations and other activity. Their purpose was to obtain early warning of any further British raids into the countryside so that the military stores could be moved to new hiding places before the troops arrived. In December 1774 they learned that Gage planned to reinforce a British arsenal at Portsmouth, New Hampshire, with two regiments, intelligence that prompted the Sons of Liberty to raid the installation before the fresh troops arrived and carry off about a hundred barrels of gunpowder and several cannons.

The leadership of the Mechanics, as the Green Dragon group is now some times called,[3] consisted of Samuel Adams, John Hancock, Dr. Joseph Warren, Dr. Benjamin Church, and one or two others. Warren, a prominent

Boston physician and later a major general who was killed at Bunker Hill, may have been the chairman of the group. Church, another physician and political leader, was also a member of the Boston Committees of Correspondence and of Safety, the latter a body responsible for control of the militia. A minor poet as well as a medical man, he was a prolific author of Patriot propaganda and was famous for the oration he delivered in commemoration of the Boston Massacre on the third anniversary of that event.[4]

Dr. Church was also one of General Gage's informers, a British mole, in modern espionage jargon, and probably the most valuable spy the British had in America at that time.[5]

Benjamin Church, a native of Newport, Rhode Island, graduated from Harvard in 1754 and then went to England to study medicine at the London Medical College. He returned to America with an English wife and began practicing medicine in Raynham, Massachusetts, in about 1768. Apparently, he acquired a taste for high living while in London, and he managed to continue to indulge it in colonial Boston, at least to the extent of keeping a mistress and building an elaborate summer home. The doctor's free-spending habits outstripped his ability to produce income through his medical practice. It was probably for this reason that he took up a second and older profession in exchange for British gold.[6]

One member of the Mechanics realized the group had been penetrated. Paul Revere, the well-known Boston silversmith and a member of the surveillance committee, had his own penetration agent within the ranks of the Tories and had learned from him (his name is lost to history) in November 1774 that the proceedings of at least one meeting at the Green Dragon were known to General Gage within twenty-four hours thereafter. But Revere did not learn the identity of the traitor.[7]

"We did not then distrust Dr. Church," he later remembered, "but supposed it must be some one among us."[8]

Unable to devise any other security measure, each of the Mechanics would swear on a Bible at every meeting at the Green Dragon that he would not divulge the group's secrets. While this was certainly a laudable measure, it was scarcely the whole of counterintelligence.

Ironically, Dr. Church may have done an unintended service for the Patriots in spying on them for Gage. According to his reports to the British commander in chief, the Patriot cause was losing support.[9] This, and the effectiveness of Gage's espionage network in keeping track of the Patriots' preparations, may have caused the general to become complacent.

On April 14, 1775, Gage received secret instructions from Lord Dartmouth, secretary for the colonies, urging him to take some forceful action against the Patriots, such as arresting the Patriot leaders, before the situation in Massachusetts reached "a riper state of Rebellion."[10] Gage ignored the instruction and decided instead to content himself with seizing the Patriot military stores that he knew—from the reports of Dr. Church and his other agents—to be located in the town of Concord. Indeed, Gage's intelligence was so complete he knew the precise location of the military stores within the town.[11]

Preparations for the operation began on April 15, when the troops were relieved of their regular duties and a large number of boats were assembled during the night for use in ferrying men and materials across the Charles River on the first leg of the march from Boston to Concord.

The Mechanics had not failed to notice these preparations, of course, and on April 16 Dr. Warren sent Revere to Lexington to warn Samuel Adams and John Hancock that the object of the coming expedition might be their arrest. On his way back to Boston, Revere stopped in Charlestown and arranged a visual signaling system with Colonel William Conant, a prominent local citizen and a member of the Sons of Liberty: when the British began to launch their expedition, Revere would signal by means of lanterns hung in the steeple of Boston's Old North Church, which was visible from Charlestown; one lantern would mean the British were marching across Boston Neck, the narrow strip of land to the west of Boston; two lanterns would mean they were coming by water—that is, across the harbor to Charlestown.[12]

This, then, is the little-known intelligence and espionage background of the events that marked the beginning of the Revolutionary War. The stories of Paul Revere's midnight ride and the Battles of Lexington and Concord are too familiar to need retelling here, but there is a postscript to the account of Dr. Church's treachery.

Dr. Church's espionage continued undetected in the wake of Lexington and Concord. On April 21, after the Patriots had driven the British troops back into Boston, he passed through the Patriot lines at Cambridge into the besieged city to meet with Gage, probably to work out arrangements for future secret service. He had disarmed Patriot suspicion by boldly declaring at a meeting of the Committee of Safety that he was going to undertake a risky trip into the city on behalf of the committee in order to obtain needed medicines. He was back in Cambridge in a few days with a harrowing tale of having been arrested, taken before Gage, and then held for several days for investigation.[13]

On May 13 Dr. Church wrote to Gage that the Patriots planned to reinforce Bunker Hill, a strategic point on the Charlestown peninsula, which was then occupied by neither the British nor the Patriots. This was a month before the Patriots actually fortified Breed's Hill on the same peninsula, thereby triggering the Battle of Bunker Hill.[14]

On May 24 Gage received yet another letter from Dr. Church, this time reporting that the Massachusetts Provincial Congress (a body established by the Patriots in the autumn of 1774 to supersede the royal government of the colony and whose members generally belonged to the local Committees of Correspondence) was sending the doctor to confer with the Continental Congress in Philadelphia. The purpose of this mission was to ask the Continental Congress to adopt the various New England militias that were laying siege to Boston as its own army—that is, to take charge of (and responsibility for) this bold and rebellious step. Dr. Church seems not to have seen the opportunities for mischief presented him by the Provincial Congress in entrusting a British mole with this important and sensitive assignment, for he expressed only his "vexation" to Gage that he would be prevented from reporting to him for some time.[15]

In June he returned to Cambridge, where the militias laying siege to Boston were soon to be transformed into the Continental army under the command of General George Washington. The members of the Continental Congress were so impressed with Dr. Church that they appointed him director general of the army's hospital at Cambridge and chief physician of the Continental army at a salary of four dollars per day and granted him the authority to hire four surgeons and other medical staff. Although the title had not yet been created and American nationhood was yet a year away, Dr. Benjamin Church, British spy, had in effect been made the first surgeon general of the United States.[16]

Dr. Church's treachery might have gone undetected for the duration of the war, with unimaginable consequences, but for one of those absurd little incidents that so often bring about the downfall of the covert operator. Soon after returning from Philadelphia, he received a letter in cipher from his brother-in-law, John Fleming, a Boston printer and bookseller. Fleming, apparently unwitting of Dr. Church's secret service, had written to urge him to repent his rebellion against the British government and come to Boston, where he would undoubtedly be pardoned for his transgressions. If Dr. Church was unwilling to do that immediately, Fleming continued, might he at least reply? Fleming asked him to write in cipher, address the letter in care of Major Cane—one of General Gage's aides—and send it by the hand of Captain Wallace of the H.M.S. *Rose*, a British warship then stationed near Newport, Rhode Island.

Dr. Church did indeed reply, but it is not clear whether he believed he was writing to his brother-in-law or to General Gage. Gage had not had a report from his spy since Church's departure for Philadelphia, and the doctor may have seen in the channel proposed by Fleming—via the master of the H.M.S. *Rose*—a secure means of resuming his profitable correspondence with the British commander in chief. In any case, Church's letter to Fleming contained some exaggerated reports of American military strength and some inaccurate reports of military plans, all framed within an impassioned plea to the British to adopt a more reasonable colonial policy ("For the sake of the miserable convulsed empire, solicit peace, repeal the acts, or Britain is undone"). Whether these were the sincere words of a repentant traitor or clever camouflage to guard against the chance that the letter might be intercepted and deciphered cannot be known; but if it was the latter, Dr. Church had badly miscalculated.

He dispatched the letter to Newport by the fair hand of his mistress. Unable for some reason to contact Captain Wallace of the *Rose*, the young woman entrusted the letter to Godfrey Wenwood, a local baker she mistakenly believed to be a Tory, before returning to Cambridge.[17] Wenwood seems to have put aside the letter and forgotten about it until sometime in September, when he received an urgent inquiry from the woman expressing her concern that "you never Sent wot you promest to send." Realizing that word of his failure to forward the letter could have originated only in British-occupied Boston and remembering that the letter was in cipher,

Wenwood became suspicious. He took the letter to Cambridge and turned it over to General Nathanael Greene, commander of the Rhode Island contingent of the Continental army. Greene promptly passed it along to General Washington.[18]

"I immediately secured the woman," Washington reported in a letter to the president of the Continental Congress on October 5, "but for a long time she was proof against every threat and persuasion to discover the author. However, at length she was brought to a confession and named Dr. Church."[19]

Dr. Church readily admitted that he had written the letter and said that it was intended for his brother-in-law, but he had no explanation of why he had attempted to send it to Boston by way of a British warship off Rhode Island when it could have been sent more easily into the city from Cambridge under a flag of truce, nor could he say why it happened to be in cipher. Furthermore, Church declined to provide Washington with the key that would enable him to decipher the message.

Washington reported to the Continental Congress that he had had Dr. Church's papers searched but found neither the key nor anything else incriminating among them but added that he had reason to suspect that an unknown accomplice of Dr. Church had gotten to them first and removed all incriminating items. He turned his attention to finding the key to the cipher letter.

An amateur cryptanalyst stepped forward in the person of the Reverend Samuel West, who happened to have been a Harvard classmate of Church. While West set to work on the cipher, a second and a third code breaker, working as a team, attempted an independent solution: Elbridge Gerry, member of the Massachusetts Provincial Congress and the Committee of Safety, and Colonel Elisha Porter of the Massachusetts militia.[20]

Church had used a type of cipher known as a monoalphabetic substitution,[21] one of the easiest ciphers to solve (Edgar Allan Poe explains the technique in his short story "The Gold Bug"), and it was only a matter of time before both West and the Gerry-Porter team had made identical translations of Church's letter.

Confronted with the text of his letter, Church claimed he had sought only to impress the British with the strength and determination of the Patriots and so to discourage General Gage from pursuing further military action. The letter was certainly not an intelligence report, he insisted. General Washington was not impressed by this explanation. He probably noticed Church's closing line: "Make use of every precaution, or I perish."

Yet Dr. Church was not to perish, at least not on the gallows. After the court-martial that Washington had convened found him guilty of criminal correspondence with the enemy, the general discovered that the articles of war had no provision for a penalty commensurate with the crime. On orders of the Continental Congress, Church was confined at Norwich, Connecticut.[22] Within a year or two—there is some confusion over the date in the record—he was released and permitted to depart on a schooner for the West Indies. Neither the ship nor the doctor was heard from again. Presumably both were lost at sea.

Washington and the other Patriot leaders never learned the full extent of Church's treachery; as far as they knew, the intercepted letter could have been the beginning and end of it. The full story emerged only in the twentieth century, when historians found his earlier reports among General Gage's papers.

General Gage's intelligence network continued to function despite the loss of its star agent. In Woburn, Massachusetts, Benjamin Thompson, the twenty-two-year-old husband of a wealthy former widow fourteen years his senior, reported on American military matters to General Gage by means of letters written in invisible ink. Thompson, an unabashed opportunist, was soon to abandon both wife and country for twin careers as soldier and scientist in Europe; he is known to history as Count Rumford, a distinguished physicist of his time.[23] But most of Gage's informers were plainer men, Tories prepared to risk their life for their king or traitors who found in General Gage the highest bidder. The following March it all passed into history: the British army and an assortment of Tory refugees sailed out of Boston Harbor, bound for Halifax, Nova Scotia, to regroup and prepare for an invasion of New York. The British agents who stayed behind found refuge in their continuing anonymity. For most of them the war was over.

The Revolution was a war of divided loyalties. The two sides shared the same language, culture, customs, and—until 1776—even the same government. Whenever such ingredients are present—as in Civil War America or post–Second World War Berlin—there is an abundance of potential espionage agents.

The development of the Sons of Liberty as a dissident element in colonial America and its eventual involvement in intelligence operations against the British were natural consequences of the general displeasure of the colonists with British rule, not a deliberate policy; indeed, there would have been no institution to work out such a policy before the Stamp Act brought the Liberty Boys into being. It is therefore not surprising that the Patriots were rank amateurs in the cloak-and-dagger business, just as they were in the more conventional forms of warfare. What little military experience they possessed had been gained in the French and Indian War, a conflict in which military intelligence went no further than the fairly obvious task of reconnaissance in the field.

The Liberty Boys had little comprehension of the principles of counterespionage and security and were therefore vulnerable to the sort of high-level penetration exemplified by Benjamin Church. Neither had they learned the espionage tradecraft that might have enabled them to establish agent networks within the British occupation forces and colonial government. They were reduced to creeping along the streets of nocturnal Boston to peek around corners at the British troop movements and to swearing their allegiance on a Bible at the Green Dragon. And yet they provided effective early warning at Concord. Like the farmers and tradesmen who laid siege to General Gage's regular troops in Boston, they awaited the professional leadership that would tell them what to do and how to do it properly. And when General Washington finally organized his secret service, he found many of his agents among those who had been Sons of Liberty.

For their part the British were not without their own intelligence assets in the colonies. It is estimated that up to one third of the population of the colonies were loyal to Great Britain during the Revolution,[24] and many of the Loyalists were ready to serve the British as secret intelligence agents. The British government, however, refusing to see the shadows of coming events, failed to exploit these assets in any organized way before the Revolution. The same arrogance toward and contempt for the colonials that was at the root of England's American troubles bred a fatal complacency among those with the responsibility for taking such precautions.

Although General Gage had an effective network of informers for keeping track of Patriot military stores in Massachusetts, he failed in the matter of political intelligence. His most valuable agent, Dr. Church, seems
to have been a walk-in or a defector in place, a gift of fate rather than
the reward of a careful recruitment operation. And Gage failed to exploit
Church fully; a man who sat at the meetings of the Committees of Correspondence and Safety, who even served briefly as liaison with the Continental Congress, was used mainly to collect military intelligence, never
for political reporting or political sabotage.

Gage's tenure as commander in chief was soon to come to an end, but
his successor, General Sir William Howe, had even less regard for intelligence. It was not until Howe was succeeded by General Sir Henry Clinton
in 1778 that the British forces established a true Secret Service in North
America, and by then many opportunities had been lost.

And so, as the curtain rose on the great armed struggle for the American
colonies, the combatants of the secret war waited in the wings: bumbling
amateurs on one side, complacent professionals on the other.

Chapter Two

The Education of an Intelligence Officer

The forty-three-year-old farmer whom the Continental Congress unanimously elected commander in chief of the army had not borne arms in sixteen years. He had never attended a military academy and had little formal education. What he knew of soldiering he had learned from experience in the French and Indian War.

One of the lessons he had learned that way was the value of surprise. He had learned it the hard way, in a ravine just past the Monongahela River on a July day twenty years earlier. A British column commanded by General Edward Braddock stumbled into an ambush by a much smaller force of French and Indians. Washington, then a lieutenant colonel of provincial troops and Braddock's aide-de-camp, saw his commander mortally wounded and had his own horse shot out from under him in the three-hour action. Sixty-three British officers and 914 of their men were killed or wounded; the French lost only 43 men. Most of the British column turned and fled. Twenty years later it still remained the worst British military debacle on the North American continent.

If General Washington reflected on the value of surprise as he took command of the Continental army in Cambridge on July 2, 1775, he knew that the British commander in chief across the Charles River in Boston understood the principle equally well: Thomas Gage had been the lieutenant colonel in command of Braddock's three-hundred-man advance guard on that bloody July day, leader of the point unit that was supposed to contact any enemy forces along the route, thereby preventing a general ambush. If any officer had learned the bitter lesson of surprise better than Washington, it was Gage.

The situation at Boston was a military stalemate. Washington had sufficient forces to lay siege to the city but not enough to capture it. Gage had three options: attack the Continentals and attempt to lift the siege, evacuate Boston by sea, or simply sit tight and await reinforcements from England. Time was not on his side, however, for the siege had cut off his food supply. Nonetheless, he chose to wait and do nothing.

Under these circumstances, neither side was to take the military initiative, and therefore both assumed defensive postures. Consequently, intelligence was put at a premium by both Washington and Gage: one must learn where and when the blow may fall if one is to defend against it. Gage already had his network of informers in place; they managed to forward their reports to the British commander in spite of the siege. Washington was forced to start from scratch, however. On July 15, 1775, less than two weeks after taking command of the army, he recorded in his accounts a payment of $333.33 to an unidentified person "to go into the town of Boston to establish secret correspondence for the purpose of conveying intelligence of the Enemys movements and designs."[1]

In October Gage was relieved as commander in chief and summoned back to London. His successor, William Howe, was another veteran of the French and Indian War. Howe's aristocratic background and links to the royal family (his grandmother had been the mistress of George I, a liaison that made him and his two brothers illegitimate uncles of George III)[2] did not prevent him from being a Whig in politics with a sympathetic disposition toward the American colonials.

By January Washington's spies in Boston reported British preparations for an expeditionary force.[3] The following month Howe's deputy, General Henry Clinton, sailed with some fifteen hundred men in an unsuccessful expedition to capture Charleston, South Carolina. Washington and his staff had expected Clinton's destination to be New York; they needed no spies within the British councils of war to know that New York would be Howe's destination when he left Boston. Howe had, in fact, spent the winter working out a plan in which occupation of New York would be the crucial first step. As both he and Washington understood, control of the port of New York and the Hudson River would permit British land and sea power to split the colonies in two. British forces could move up the easily navigable river and meet their comrades striking south from

Canada along Lake Champlain. Howe planned to wait in Boston for supplies and reinforcements to arrive from England. Then, in the spring, he
would remove his forces to New York.

Howe's plans were disrupted in January by the arrival in Cambridge of
General Henry Knox with more than fifty pieces of heavy artillery captured
by the Patriots at Fort Ticonderoga the previous May. Washington placed
these siege guns on Dorchester Heights, where they threatened both the city
of Boston and its harbor, as well as the military stalemate that had existed
since April. Faced with this development, Howe abandoned his plans for
the orderly removal of his forces to New York in the spring and gave the
order to evacuate Boston on March 7. But Halifax, not New York, became
his destination. The British commander decided that the Nova Scotia port
would be a safer place to regroup his debilitated forces and await reinforcements from England before launching his Hudson-Champlain campaign.

Convinced that New York was Howe's final destination, Washington
quickly moved his army there after Howe's departure from Boston and
prepared for the British landing. He arrived in New York on April 13 and
began to survey the tactical problems involved in defending the place,
which, in the face of British control of the rivers and coastal waters, were
formidable. The city lay at the southern tip of an island whose surrounding
waterways, with the exception of the short, narrow Harlem River separating Manhattan from the mainland to the north, were easily navigable by
British warships. Furthermore, the nearby shores of Long Island, Staten
Island, and New Jersey provided convenient points where the British force
could land unopposed and stage an attack on the city. To complete the
dismal picture, the population of the city included a large percentage of
Tories, a ready-made fifth column of British spies and saboteurs. Although
Washington seems not to have realized it,[4] capture of the city by the British was inevitable, and the only question remaining was whether it was to
be accomplished with or without a fight.[5]

Whatever Washington may have understood at this time of the importance of intelligence in war, he was about to have his awareness heightened
considerably by the events that lay ahead in the balance of 1776.

Howe arrived off Sandy Hook, New Jersey, late in June with a task force
of 130 vessels. Despite Washington's steps to prevent it—posting troops
along the shores of Long Island and New Jersey and patrolling the coastal

waters with armed whale boats—many Tories managed to slip through and board the British warships, bringing with them up-to-date reports on the military situation in the city. On July 2 the British landed unopposed on Staten Island. On the twelfth Howe's brother, Admiral Lord Richard Howe, arrived with 150 more ships carrying reinforcements from England. Shortly thereafter, shiploads of German mercenaries and yet more British troops arrived from Europe. On August 12 General Clinton and his expeditionary force, sent to Charleston in January, returned from the South. In all, the force arrayed against Washington consisted of more than thirty-one thousand British troops and a naval force that included ten ships of the line, twenty frigates, and numerous transports, all manned by some ten thousand British seamen. It may now have been apparent to Washington that holding New York would not be possible. The Continental Congress had ordered him to do so, however, and he prepared to make the attempt.

By August 24 a large British force had crossed from Staten Island, landed in Brooklyn, and pushed the Continental lines several miles inland. The defenders' lines now ran several miles eastward, from Gowanus Bay, along Long Island Heights, a densely wooded ridge running east-west and screening the two opposing forces from each other. Three main north-south roads traversed the heights through gaps in the high ground and were well guarded by the Continentals. A fourth gap, however, the Jamaica Pass, lay several miles to the east of the troop concentrations and was only lightly guarded by the Continentals.

Washington was about to fight his first battle of the war and to suffer his first defeat. The day was to be lost because of an American intelligence failure.

On the night of August 26–27, Howe made a diversionary attack on the Continental forces at the western end of Brooklyn. Meanwhile, a larger British force advanced up the Gowanus Road, which went through the Jamaica Pass. Unaware of this flanking movement, Washington reinforced the western end of his lines and met the British diversionary assault there. At about nine in the morning he heard the sound of cannon from his left flank. A British force of ten thousand men and twenty-eight cannons was advancing from the east. Too late, he realized that a second British column had marched throughout the night and managed to arrive undetected at his rear while he had been preoccupied by the diversionary action.

The ensuing battle was a total disaster for the Continentals. At a cost of 377 men, the British inflicted over 1,400 casualties on the Americans.[6] Washington and remnants of the Continental force were driven back to Brooklyn Heights. Howe's victory would have been complete if he had attacked the Heights immediately, but he hesitated, and Washington evacuated his force across the East River to Manhattan under cover of night and fog two days later.

Washington now fully comprehended the dangerous situation of his army, trapped on an island little more than a dozen miles in length and two miles in width, surrounded by a large part of the Royal Navy, and facing a much larger foe across the narrow waters of the East River. And the lesson of Howe's surprise flanking maneuver was not lost on him. One of his first acts after evacuating to Manhattan was to summon Lieutenant Colonel Thomas Knowlton, a seasoned veteran of the French and Indian War who had also distinguished himself at Bunker Hill, and direct him to form a company of hand-picked volunteers to carry out reconnaissance missions and other special operations "either by water or by land, by night or by day."[7] The establishment of Knowlton's Rangers, as the company was called, marked the birth of United States Army intelligence (and is the reason the year 1776 appears in the army's Military Intelligence emblem).

Knowlton's Rangers' first assignment was to patrol possible British landing sites along the shores of Manhattan and Westchester (the latter including today's borough of the Bronx). Useful as these missions were, they were no substitute for direct observation of Howe's activity.

"As everything, in a manner, depends upon obtaining intelligence of the enemy's motions," Washington wrote on September 5 in a letter to General William Heath,

> I do most earnestly entreat you and General [George] Clinton to exert yourselves to accomplish this most desirable end. Leave no stone unturned, nor do not stick at expense, to bring this to pass, as I was never more uneasy than on account of my want of knowledge on this score. . . .[8]

Heath commanded a detachment at King's Bridge on the northern extremity of Manhattan, and Clinton was in charge of the defense of the Hudson Highlands, even farther north. These were strategically important areas; if Howe cut the roads running north through Westchester, Washington would have no remaining avenue of retreat. But as to what Howe actually intended to do, that question could be answered only by sending a spy into the British lines on Long Island. On September 10 Washington asked Colonel Knowlton to find a volunteer for the mission among his Rangers.[9] Knowlton summoned his officers and put the proposition to them. At first none stepped forward; the Rangers did not fear for their lives but for their honor, and stealing into the enemy camp in the guise of a civilian struck them as being most dishonorable. But finally, Captain Nathan Hale volunteered for the mission, a form of treachery he judged was made honorable by its purpose, a "peculiar service" demanded by his country.

Hale, twenty-one, was a native of Coventry, Connecticut, and a member of the Yale class of 1773. He had taught school for two years, and in June 1775 he sought and received a commission as lieutenant in the Connecticut militia. His unit took part in the siege of Boston that summer, and he thereby became an officer in the newly established Continental army. He was promoted to the rank of captain in January 1776 and arrived in New York on April 30 with his regiment.

In mid-May Hale had taken part in the capture of a sloop loaded with supplies for the *Asia*, a British man-of-war lying in the harbor beyond the power of Washington's land forces and the waterborne refuge of William Tryon, the royal governor of New York.[10] It may have been this exploit that led Knowlton to recruit him as one of his company commanders when he formed his elite unit. Hale was, however, completely ignorant of espionage tradecraft and ill suited for the job of agent. He was, first of all, not a man who could easily avoid attention, being above average height and bearing facial scars acquired in a gunpowder explosion. And he was a particularly bad choice for this mission because his cousin, Samuel Hale, was a Tory, General Howe's deputy commissary of prisoners, and at this very moment with Howe's forces.

Colonel Knowlton's understanding of the kind of espionage mission Washington had ordered was obviously nil. He arranged no cover story to account for Hale's absence from the Rangers, most of whom already knew what Hale was to do in any case. The possibility that the British might have their own spy in the American camp seems not to have occurred to him.

Hale set out on his mission on about September 12 (the exact date is disputed),[11] accompanied by Sergeant Stephen Hempstead, a close friend from New London, Connecticut, where Hale had taught school. The pair traveled to Norwalk, Connecticut, by a circuitous route, a trip that probably took two or three days. There they boarded the *Schuyler*, a sloop captained by Charles Pond, a fellow officer from Hale's Connecticut regiment.[12] The trio crossed to Huntington, Long Island, where Hale, now dressed in a "plain suit of citizen's brown clothes, with a round brimmed hat," disembarked. Sergeant Hempstead returned to Norwalk to await some pre-established date when he would arrange to exfiltrate the officer from Long Island.

Hale set out toward the British encampment in Brooklyn. His cover story was that he was a schoolmaster, which of course he had been, and he took along his Yale diploma to support the story. His movements during the following week are not known. If he landed on September 15, as is generally supposed, he must soon have discovered that Howe had chosen that same day to make his move across the East River to Manhattan. The British had landed at Kip's Bay (which lies at the eastern end of today's Thirty-fourth Street), surprising the Continentals and meeting virtually no resistance. Units of Washington's army positioned to the south were nearly cut off from the main Continental force but succeeded in escaping the trap and joining their comrades at Harlem Heights (a rocky plateau north of the western end of today's 125th Street).

It seems likely that Hale followed the British to Manhattan, hoping to observe their strength and disposition on the island before returning to the American lines and reporting to Washington. In any case, nothing more is known of his mission until its disastrous end. On September 22 Captain John Montressor, an aide-de-camp to General Howe, appeared under a flag of truce at an American outpost near Harlem Heights carrying a letter from Howe to Washington concerning a prisoner exchange. He mentioned in passing to the two Continental officers who met him—Captains Alexander Hamilton and William Hull—that an American officer, one Captain Hale, had been hanged that morning as a spy. The news came as a shock to Hull, who had been one year ahead of Hale at Yale.[13] When Montressor returned to the Continental outpost two days later to receive Washington's reply to Howe, Hull made a point of being there to find out from the British officer more about Hale's mission and death.

Hale had been captured on the twenty-first while trying to return to the American lines. He had been taken before Howe together with some evidence of his espionage mission, perhaps notes and sketches he had made of the British force on Manhattan. He readily admitted that he was an officer in the Continental army. Without further deliberations, Howe ordered him executed the following day. He was denied the comfort of a clergyman or even a Bible. He wrote two letters, but these were apparently destroyed. He died with a bravery grudgingly acknowledged by his captors after declaring that his only regret was that he had but one life to give for his country. The place of his death was the artillery park near the Dove Tavern (which stood near today's intersection of Third Avenue and Sixty-sixth Street). His body was left hanging as an example to other rebels. He was probably buried nearby later.

That is all of what Hull learned from Montressor, and it is nearly all that is known. Where he was captured, and, more to the point, why, remain matters of speculation. But the general reason for the failure of his mission is obvious—it was a thoroughly amateurish undertaking in a business that permits few mistakes.

We may assume Washington realized that the life of a fine soldier had been wasted by the general ineptness of his superiors in running secret operations. While Washington probably blamed himself in any case, Colonel Knowlton was not around to share any part of the responsibility: he had been killed and his Ranger unit destroyed in an indecisive battle with the British below Harlem Heights on the sixteenth.

Everything depended upon intelligence, Washington had told his commanders. And yet he had permitted himself to be caught by surprise twice in a period of two weeks, each time seeing parts of his army nearly trapped by the British. He may have shared the opinion of later military historians that his survival of the New York campaign owed as much to General Howe's sluggishness in following up his victories as to anything he himself may have done.

The period of September–December 1776 was the darkest time of the war. In mid-October Howe's forces landed on the eastern shores of

Westchester, forcing Washington to withdraw from Manhattan and pull back to White Plains. After temporarily stopping the British at White Plains, he withdrew farther, to North Castle in upper Westchester. Howe did not pursue him but instead returned to Manhattan and captured the garrisons Washington had unwisely left behind at Fort Washington and, across the Hudson River, at Fort Lee.[14]

Washington crossed the Hudson and withdrew southward through New Jersey with the British hard on his heels. The British entered Princeton barely an hour after Washington's rearguard departed the town. They poured into Trenton as the last of the Continentals rowed across the Delaware River to Pennsylvania. Howe may have held back in the hope of a psychological victory: that the prospect of the fleeing Continentals would demoralize those who witnessed it.

Howe was right. Many of the American troops deserted during the retreat, and with the losses sustained in New York, Washington now had a force of only some two thousand men. To prevent the British from coming any farther, Washington seized or destroyed all the boats he could find, but he doubted that this would prove to be an insurmountable obstacle.

The spectacle of the Continental army in full retreat rapidly eroded local popular support for the Revolution. The New Jersey legislature had disbanded so that each member could save himself; the Continental Congress had fled from Philadelphia to Baltimore; some Patriot leaders had recanted and urged their compatriots to do likewise; across New Jersey citizens lined up to swear renewed allegiance to the British king and receive pardons; and farmers refused Continental money when commissaries tried to buy provisions. On December 18 Washington wrote his brother, John Augustine, "I think the game is pretty near up. . . . No man, I believe ever had a greater choice of difficulties and less means to extricate himself from them."

Sometime during the following week Washington changed his mind and took heart, however. At least one of the causes, if not the only one, was the sudden appearance on December 22 of John Honeyman, a suspicious character who claimed to be a cattle dealer and who had been apprehended by Washington's pickets near the western bank of the Delaware River.

Washington dismissed the guard in order to be alone with Honeyman, with whom he was well acquainted. He had first met him in Philadelphia a year and a half earlier, when the Irish-born weaver proposed to the newly elected commander in chief that he serve as Washington's spy. Washington had accepted, and Honeyman moved himself and his family to Griggstown, a village a few miles southwest of New Brunswick, New Jersey, and there became known as an ardent Tory. He abandoned the weaver's trade for that of a cattle dealer and butcher, which enabled him to pass freely within the British lines. And that is what he had recently been doing in British-occupied Trenton on orders he had received personally from Washington at Hackensack in mid-November. Now he had come across the Delaware to report.[15]

There is no record of what Honeyman told Washington, but if the agent had just come from Trenton, he probably knew that the main British army had returned to New York to go into winter quarters and that the Hessian commander left to occupy Trenton, Colonel Johann Rall, although a fine officer in battle, had several fatal flaws. First, he was complacent and down-right arrogant when it came to American fighting men, whom he regarded as "country clowns." Second, he had disregarded British orders to construct fortifications and send out scouts. ("Let them come," he is quoted as having said. "We want no trenches. We will go at them with the bayonet".)[16] And finally, Honeyman may have reported, the Hessian colonel was a bit too fond of the juice of the barley; he was, in fact, a drunkard.

Whatever Honeyman may have told him, Washington knew that this was probably his last chance to turn the tide that had been running against him since the disaster on Long Island. The enlistments of many of his troops were due to expire on December 31, after which he would be left with a mere twelve hundred regulars. And he knew that soon the Delaware River would freeze so hard the enemy could cross it on foot, while his possession of the only boats in the area gave him for this brief moment an advantage almost unknown among those who challenged the British—naval superiority. In any case, he organized his weary army, and on Christmas afternoon he crossed the Delaware to the Jersey bank with twenty-four hundred troops and eighteen guns. Some three thousand other troops under two of Washington's commanders failed to take part in the action owing to problems in crossing the ice-filled river. Nonetheless, Washington's assault on Trenton early the following morning was a resounding and much-needed victory for the American side. Colonel Rall, awakened from an alcoholic slumber, was killed in the action, along with four of his officers and seventeen of his men. The Continentals suffered no battle fatalities,[17] withdrawing across the river after the battle with their prisoners. In military terms Trenton was a minor victory for the Continentals; in the psychological dimension, however, the battle restored American morale, and the cause, which so recently had been called hopeless, was given new life.

The tide had begun to turn, at least in part through Honeyman's intelligence report. But Honeyman had been a walk-in, a small island of good luck in the midst of a sea of adversity. He may have been an augury that God had taken the side of the Patriots. He was certainly a confirmation of the lesson Washington had learned in New York—that the difference between victory and defeat is often timely intelligence. And as the year 1777 dawned, General Washington took this lesson to heart.

Chapter Three

Poor Richard's Game

The first American government agency formally established to collect foreign intelligence was the Committee of Secret Correspondence, a panel created by the Continental Congress on November 29, 1775 "for the sole purpose of Corresponding with our friends in Great Britain, Ireland and other parts of the world." The original committee consisted of five members, but it was dominated by Benjamin Franklin, the only member with experience in foreign affairs.[1] Franklin had only recently returned from eighteen years in London, where he had served as colonial agent for Pennsylvania, Georgia, and Massachusetts.

Franklin saw clearly that the Revolution had already become an important factor in European international politics. France, prostrated by Britain in the Seven Years' War (of which the French and Indian War had been the North American theater), had been compelled to give up her colonial ambitions and accept a secondary role in European affairs. Franklin realized that France would see the Revolution as a means of splitting the British Empire, thereby weakening Britain to the benefit of French international aspirations. In short, he saw that a Franco-American alliance promised great mutual benefits, and he made the bringing about of such an alliance a matter of the highest priority.

Franklin began with a few tentative feelers, inquiries with trusted friends on the Continent—Dr. Jacques Barbeu-Duborg in Paris and Charles W. F. Dumas in The Hague—who were in a position to sound out the political climate in Versailles and the other European capitals.[2] Before he could receive replies to these initiatives, however, an unofficial emissary of France arrived in Philadelphia in the person of Julian Achard de Bonvouloir.

Bonvouloir,[3] a mysterious figure, was a native of Normandy who had served as an officer in the French army in Saint-Domingue (now Haiti) before visiting the American colonies in 1774. The following year he turned up in London, where he reported to the French ambassador, the Count de Guines, on the situation in America. He stated that he had developed sources of information there and offered to return to America on behalf of the French foreign ministry.

Bonvouloir's proposal was most welcome to the French foreign minister, the Count de Vergennes, who was aware of Franklin's inquiries with Barbeu-Duborg. He had been thinking along similar lines himself, but he required extensive intelligence of the political situation in America before he'd consider the possibility of a Franco-American alliance against Britain.

In September Bonvouloir had sailed for America posing as a merchant of Antwerp on a private commercial errand. He arrived in Philadelphia late in December and met with Franklin and other members of the committee. On Vergennes's instructions he disclaimed any official connection with the French government, but he added that he did have powerful friends at Versailles and would be pleased to serve as an informal channel between them and the committee. Franklin understood that this was a pose and the reason for it and proceeded to explore with him the conditions for a French alliance.

Bonvouloir stated that France had no plan to recover Canada, which had been lost to Britain as a result of the Seven Years' War, nor did she wish to entangle America in political or military ties. If she could be assured that there was a real commitment to independence among the Americans, however, and that they had a reasonable chance of winning it, France was prepared to help. She would open her ports to American ships, sell the Americans arms in exchange for agricultural commodities, and even send two military engineers to advise on the construction of fortifications. After listening to Franklin's reassurances regarding American commitment and strength, Bonvouloir sent off a glowing report to the French foreign ministry.[4]

As the next step toward securing French assistance, the Committee of Secret Correspondence dispatched an agent to France. Silas Deane, a Connecticut delegate to the Continental Congress, departed on the mission in April 1776. Deane was a lawyer who had graduated from Yale in 1758 and earned a master of arts degree from that institution two years later.

A leader of the Connecticut Patriots, he had been secretary of the local Committee of Correspondence. Deane went to France not only as an agent of the Committee of Secret Correspondence but also as a representative of the Secret Committee, a panel established to procure arms and other supplies for the Continental Army.[5]

Soon after his arrival in Paris, Deane was met by Pierre-Augustin Caron de Beaumarchais, playwright, merchant, and, as it happened, a secret agent of the French foreign ministry.[6]

Beaumarchais had been instructed by the Count de Vergennes to work with Deane and arrange a secret channel through which French arms and supplies could be traded for American farm produce without openly involving the French government: France was not yet ready to take the step of an open alliance with America, which would mean war with Great Britain. To this end, Beaumarchais established what in today's intelligence jargon would be called a proprietary company or a devised facility—that is, a dummy corporation created to provide cover for a clandestine operation. Beaumarchais formed Hortalez et Compagnie, an import-export firm, which was capitalized by loans from France and Spain, as well as by Beaumarchais and his business associates. Hortalez et Compagnie acquired a fleet of forty ships and after some initial difficulties began shipping the military stores to America.

Some of the initial difficulties encountered by Beaumarchais and Deane originated with the British Secret Service, which had not remained unaware of Deane's mission and Beaumarchais's proprietary company. Lord Stormont, the British ambassador to Versailles and head of the Secret Service within France (chief of station in today's espionage jargon), had learned of Hortalez et Compagnie and its arms dealings through his agents. When he confronted Vergennes with the evidence, the foreign minister of course disavowed any official responsibility for the firm's activities, but the French government was forced to go through the motions of issuing ordinances against the smuggling of military supplies. At first, some minor French officials did not get the word and actually enforced these laws. It was then Beaumarchais's turn to complain to Vergennes, who replied that he would just have to proceed with more discretion.[7]

Just how Stormont managed to learn of Hortalez is not clear, but neither is it surprising. If the British had been tardy and complacent about developing intelligence assets in the colonies, they were not equally embarrassed on the Continent, where their Secret Service had been active for centuries. British naval intelligence, directed at this time by Sir Philip Stephens, the permanent undersecretary of the admiralty, ran its own extensive networks in European seaports out of a bookshop in Rotterdam. Frouw Marguerite Wolters, a Dutch widow, was both the proprietor of the shop and the chief of the Rotterdam station.[8] This apparatus, established for the specific purpose of collecting maritime intelligence, may well have been the means by which the British discovered the Hortalez operation. It is also possible, however, that the source was much closer to Silas Deane.

When Deane sailed for France he carried with him a letter of introduction to one Dr. Edward Bancroft of London, signed by Franklin, Bancroft's longtime friend and mentor.[9] (Deane really needed no introduction to Dr. Bancroft; the young man had been his pupil in Connecticut when Deane had been a schoolteacher some years before.) Franklin, who had met Bancroft during his years as colonial agent in London, had early recognized in the young man a talent for espionage and had used him as his personal spy in some of the many intrigues of colonial politics in which he was then involved.

But Franklin was not alone in seeing Bancroft's gift for intrigue. It was also recognized by Paul Wentworth, the colonial agent for New Hampshire and one of the London agents of the Committee of Secret Correspondence. When Wentworth learned that Bancroft had accepted an invitation to visit Silas Deane in Paris, he found this fact to be of particular interest. Wentworth had recently been recruited by the British Secret Service and was, in fact, the right-hand man to William Eden, an ambitious undersecretary of state and the chief of the intelligence service.[10]

When Bancroft returned from France, Wentworth induced him to meet with Lords Suffolk and Weymouth, the secretaries of state, and report everything he had learned from Deane, which may well have included the operations of Hortalez et Compagnie. At Wentworth's urging Bancroft made several more trips to France and also opened a regular correspondence with Deane, who may have naively believed he now had a secret intelligence source in London.[11]

Meanwhile, Franklin and his associates on the Committee of Secret Correspondence waited impatiently for reports from Deane of progress toward a formal alliance with France. In September 1776 the Continental Congress appointed a formal diplomatic commission to represent the newly established United States of America in the French court. Deane, Franklin, and Arthur Lee (an American-born lawyer living in London who had served as a confidential correspondent for the committee) were named to the commission. Franklin departed Philadelphia late in October and arrived in France on December 3.

Wentworth saw the opportunity to place Bancroft inside the American mission as a British penetration agent, and he convinced the Secret Service that the penetration was worth the investment of the money it would take to persuade Bancroft. This was, initially, five hundred pounds down, plus four hundred more per year.[12] In February Lord Suffolk also promised the young man a life pension of two hundred pounds per year commencing the previous Christmas for the services he had already rendered the Crown; if Bancroft would go to Paris as Wentworth's agent within the American ministry, the pension would be increased to five hundred pounds per year commencing either when the American rebellion ended or when an open break of Anglo-French diplomatic relations occurred. All together, this proved to be an offer Dr. Bancroft couldn't refuse, and he was soon on his way across the Channel once more.[13] He went immediately to Passy, a suburb of Paris, and the Hotel de Valentinois, where the American ministry was situated. There he was reunited with his old friend Franklin, who promptly hired him as secretary and adviser to the American diplomatic commission.

Wentworth followed his recruit to France. He established his cover as a wealthy businessman (which he was), man-about-town, and bon vivant. He took a mistress and used her house in the rue Traversière to entertain a wide circle of French and American notables whom he found useful in one way or another, including Vergennes and Beaumarchais. The main reason for his presence in France was, of course, his agent Dr. Bancroft.

Bancroft had been instructed in the means to be used to communicate secretly with Wentworth and Lord Stormont. He was to compose letters on the subject of gallantry addressed to a Mr. Richards and signed by Edward Edwards. He was to write his reports in invisible ink between their lines and conceal the letters in a bottle placed within a hole in the roots of a certain box tree in the garden of the Tuileries "every Tuesday evening after half past nine." Stormont's secretary, Thomas Jeans, would service the drop sometime thereafter, retrieving the bottle by means of a string Bancroft had tied to it, removing Bancroft's reports, and leaving the doctor's new instructions.[14] (A classic dead-letter box, the technique is still commonly used today.)

William Eden, the Secret Service chief, wanted to know all about French aid to the rebels. He wanted to know whether Spain or any other European court was supplying aid or trading with them. He wanted to know how the Americans were obtaining credit. In fact, he had a long list of things for Bancroft to report on. But most of all, he wanted to know of the progress toward a Franco-American treaty of alliance.

Bancroft had soon forwarded copies of hundreds of documents to the Secret Service, including instructions from the Continental Congress to the American commissioners to send agents to Spain, Portugal, Berlin, and Tuscany; lists of military stores required by the Continental army; and the draft of a proposed Franco-American treaty of alliance and commerce.[15]

Franklin and Deane sent Bancroft on frequent secret intelligence missions across the Channel, which provided him welcome opportunities for relaxed meetings with Eden and other British officials—including members of the Privy Council—within the security of Secret Service headquarters at 17 Downing Street. Lest the ease with which he passed through the scrutiny of British security raise suspicions in Passy, Bancroft contrived to have himself arrested on one of these journeys.

"This worthy man is now confined in the Bastile of England," Deane lamented. But Bancroft was soon back at Passy with a plausible tale to account for his miraculous release.[16]

Bancroft added a nice touch to his imposture when he threatened to quit as secretary to the diplomatic commission after its cash-flow problems caused his salary to be delayed. He seems to have fooled everyone except Arthur Lee, the querulous and irascible third member of the commission. Lee suspected him of being a British spy. He had heard of Bancroft from a sea captain who was acquainted with him and had learned of his meetings with the Privy Council in London.[17] This accusation made little impression in Passy, however, because Lee suspected everyone of being a British spy; everyone, that is, except his personal secretary, Major John Thornton. After Thornton was exposed by Franklin as actually being a

British spy—Franklin had learned this from some of his own agents in London—the French foreign minister demanded that Lee be sent back to Philadelphia. With Lee gone, Bancroft was free to continue his espionage undisturbed.

If Bancroft overcame suspicion in France, he did not do as well in England, where George III looked upon both Wentworth and his agent with a skeptical eye. The king knew that both men were dabbling heavily in the London stock market, and he wondered whether the intelligence he was getting from them might be calculated to manipulate events in a way that would benefit their speculations.

"The two letters from Mr. Wentworth are certainly curious," the king told his prime minister, Lord North, in reference to Wentworth's reports in mid-1777 that a Franco-American alliance was imminent,

> but as *Edwards* [Bancroft's pseudonym] is a stockjobber [i.e., stock speculator] as well as a double spy no other faith can be placed in his intelligence but that it suits his private views to make us expect the French Court to mean War, whilst undoubtedly there is good ground to think that Event is more distant than we might suppose Six months ago. Mr. Wentworth I suspect is also a dabbler in the Alley [i.e., Exchange Alley, site of the London stock exchange] and as such may have views, I am certain he has one, the wish of getting some Employment.[18]

The king was half-right. Wentworth and Bancroft were indeed mixing their espionage and their stock speculation. For example, when Bancroft learned of the defeat of Burgoyne's forces at Bennington, Vermont, in August 1777—information that had not yet reached London—he immediately sent instructions to his London broker, although he did not promptly report the news to the Secret Service. The intelligence reached the king nonetheless, when Bancroft's letter was opened and read by another of Eden's agents.

But Wentworth and Bancroft were simply using their inside information to guide their speculation and were not doctoring their reports to manipulate events. The intelligence they supplied was highly accurate. Eden, however, apparently had no way of confirming it through a collateral source. Faced with uncertainty, the king chose to believe more congenial reports than the ones sent by his spy in Passy, thereby wasting the enormously valuable penetration his Secret Service had achieved. (The situation has countless parallels in the history of espionage; some of the greatest intelligence coups have been in vain simply because the end product was judged incredible by the decision makers who needed it.)

Whatever progress Franklin and his fellow commissioners were making toward achieving a military alliance, it was obvious to all that the prospects of a Franco-American treaty depended heavily upon events in America. In the late spring of 1777, the British had renewed their plan to bisect the colonies by taking control of the Hudson and Lake Champlain. In June General John Burgoyne led a British force southward across Lake Champlain while a second column, under Lieutenant Colonel Barry St. Leger, moved down the Mohawk Valley to join Burgoyne at Albany. St. Leger was stopped at Fort Stanwix, New York, however, and Burgoyne suffered a major defeat at Bennington. The campaign ended in complete disaster on October 17, when Burgoyne, after a series of defeats around Saratoga, was forced to surrender his army to the Continental commander General Horatio Gates.

The news of Saratoga reached Passy on December 4. An exultant Franklin dashed off reports to Vergennes and to the American representatives at Madrid and other European courts. The news that a force of some five thousand British and German regulars had surrendered to the "rabble in arms," as the Continental army had been characterized, struck the French and British courts like a thunderclap. Eager to press his advantage immediately, Franklin formally proposed the Treaty of Amity and Commerce, which included provisions for a military alliance with France and Spain against Britain.

Bancroft dashed for London, not to report to Eden but to take a direct hand in his speculations before the London market could plummet in reaction to the news. But Wentworth, who had been in London when the news arrived there, rushed back across the Channel on an important errand for William Eden. The Secret Service chief now wished to learn whether the Americans were prepared to settle for "anything short of unqualified independence" and if so, to find out "their sentiments both as to the grounds of an accommodation and the mode of negotiating it."

Wentworth met with Deane on December 17, but he was not able to arrange a meeting with Franklin until sometime later. It suited the shrewd Sage of Philadelphia to keep Wentworth at arm's length while he pursued his negotiations with Vergennes. The French knew why Wentworth was seeking an interview with Franklin. Beaumarchais had reported it to Vergennes the same day Deane had met with the man. Franklin knew they knew this; he also knew that the French had made their alliance with the Americans dependent upon Spain's joining in the pact. On December 31 it was learned in Versailles and Passy that Spain would not join. On January 6 Franklin consented to meet with Wentworth, ostensibly to discuss old times when both were colonial agents in London. They quickly got down to business, however.

Franklin began by declaring that America would consent to no peace without independence, that he had no authorization to negotiate peace with Britain anyway, and even if he had, he could have nothing more than polite conversation with an unofficial representative of the British government. Wentworth then read aloud a letter Eden had given him, without disclosing the identity of the author. The letter was full of conciliatory sentiment and flattery of Franklin and inquired whether the Americans might settle for something "short of unqualified independence." When Wentworth had finished, Franklin was noncommittal. The meeting ended without result. Wentworth departed for London nine days later carrying the additional disquieting news, reported by Bancroft, now back from London, that the Americans hoped soon to negotiate a treaty of independence with the Opposition, which would certainly succeed Lord North's government when the British grew weary of the sort of thrashing they had received at Saratoga.

But Franklin knew that that thrashing had been administered by troops armed, clothed, and paid with French aid. An open alliance with France would permit French troops and, even more important, French sea power to be put into action against Britain. If the alliance were not to be, perhaps some accommodation "short of unqualified independence" would be the best America could hope for. Yet Franklin realized that to deal with the British now might rupture the fragile informal alliance that already existed with the French and doom any chance of a treaty, and he also understood that this might well have been the true object of Wentworth's mission. America, on her own once again, would have no chips with which to bargain for any concessions at all from the British.

The solution, then? Somehow to use the British overtures as a lever on the French without going so far as to jeopardize the prospects of a treaty. The French, who of course knew of Franklin's meeting with Wentworth, responded to this gentle pressure. On January 7, the day after the meeting, a royal council decided to negotiate an alliance with the Americans without the involvement of the Spanish. The following day an official representative of the foreign ministry visited the commissioners.

"What is necessary to be done to give such satisfaction to the American Commissioners as to engage them not to listen to any propositions from England for a new connection with that country?" he formally inquired. The answer was simple: a treaty of alliance.[19]

The treaty was signed on February 6. France had openly entered the war on the American side.

Franklin's job was not finished, of course. There remained the task of keeping the alliance whole in the face of such Francophobic Americans as John Adams, whom the Continental Congress had sent to replace Lee. And then, when the English king was finally reconciled to the inevitable, there were more secret peace feelers for Franklin to deal with, another narrow and treacherous pathway that would end only in 1783, when the Treaty of Paris brought the war to an end and permanently established American independence.

In the meantime, Bancroft remained in his position with the American ministry at Passy. (He later claimed to have arranged for the delivery of a copy of the treaty to Eden's London office within forty-two hours of the signing ceremony, a remarkable undertaking considering that the usual time for mail to get from Paris to London was five days.[20]) The terms of his original recruitment by the Secret Service specified that he would not have to stay beyond the open rupture of Anglo-French relations, but the offer of additional emolument induced him to remain, a British mole at the heart of the alliance.[21] In 1779 Franklin and the Marquis de Lafayette sent him to Ireland to assess the possibility of fomenting a revolt among the Presbyterian Ulstermen, who were sympathetic to the American Revolution; he reported that the time was not ripe, and the project was scrapped. In 1781 he and Wentworth induced the disgruntled Silas Deane—who meanwhile had been charged by the Continental Congress with collaborating with Beaumarchais to profiteer on the Hortalez operation—to write a series of letters to important Americans stating his failing confidence in the American cause and urging some accommodation with Britain short of independence. These letters were, of course, delivered to the Secret Service and were published in a New York Tory newspaper. The extent of Deane's involvement with the Secret Service is unclear, and one historian has compiled a case that Bancroft murdered him some years later to cover up the matter.[22]

Bancroft's treachery apparently went undiscovered during his lifetime, which lasted until 1821. He returned to England and resumed his scientific work, specializing in the chemistry of dyes. His role as a British spy emerged in the 1880s, when the British government opened some of its official archives to the American researcher B. F. Stephens. Bancroft's grandson, a British general, reacted to the discovery with a horror of espionage worthy of an American and destroyed the greater part of his grandfather's papers, which might have shed interesting additional light on some of the doctor's intrigues.[23]

Chapter Four

George Washington, Spy Master

It has been suggested that intelligence is more critical to defense than to offense, that it is far more important for the defender to know where his enemy's blow is to fall than it is for the aggressor to know the best place at which to strike.[1] Put another way, the underdog can use intelligence to make up for his relative weakness. General Washington's predicament during the first half of 1777 provides strong support for the thesis.

Howe not only had a larger, better trained, and better equipped army, but his brother's fleet gave him control of the coastal waters. In a day in which roads were primitive or nonexistent, in a war that was to be fought along the eastern seaboard, this meant he also had superior mobility—he could move his army far more quickly than Washington could move his.

In the face of superior British strength and mobility, Washington had already resolved "that on our side the war should be defensive: it has even been called a War of Posts [i.e., fortified defensive positions]. That we should on all Occasions avoid a general Action, or put anything to the Risque, unless compelled by a necessity, into which we ought never to be drawn."[2]

Washington's strategy, then, was to keep the British between himself and the sea, moving when they moved, hitting them only when the situation gave him some temporary advantage, and hoping that time would prove to be on the side of the Americans. Obviously, timely intelligence of British moves was basic to this strategy.

After his victory at Trenton the day after Christmas, Washington again employed surprise and deception, crossing once more into New Jersey, then slipping out of a British trap by leaving his campfires burning brightly through the night of January 2–3 to trick distant British pickets into believing his army slept, and marching through the winter darkness on the lightly defended town of Princeton. After inflicting heavy losses on the surprised British regulars there and driving them in disarray toward New Brunswick, he moved north to Morristown, where the woods and hills provided natural protection against British attack, and went into winter quarters. General Howe, stunned by the sudden turn of events at Trenton and Princeton, withdrew most of his army to New York. But given the defensive posture forced upon him by British military superiority, Washington could do little but bide his time and try to guess what Howe would do next.

Washington realized that Howe might well decide to venture into New Jersey once again if he learned that desertions and the expiration of enlistments had reduced the Continental army to fewer than four thousand men. He therefore distributed his troops so thinly through the various hamlets around Morristown that the local inhabitants believed there were forty thousand American troops under Washington's command. When one of his officers requested authority to arrest a spy he had detected in one of the American camps, Washington told him to befriend the man, instead, and invite him to dinner. The commander in chief then contrived to give the British agent a chance to steal a document he had specially prepared that gave the Continental army's strength as twelve thousand.[3]

At about the same time, Washington did what he undoubtedly regretted not having done a year earlier: he organized a real intelligence service. He began by initiating a system of direct correspondence with the principal Committees of Safety that were functioning throughout each of the colonies.[4] The committees were, of course, made up of Sons of Liberty and other Patriots, most of whom had not hidden their political sympathies before the outbreak of hostilities and were therefore now of limited potential for undercover espionage work. But they did provide a network for the prompt and systematic reporting of what was generally known of British and Tory activities in their localities.

To recruit those individuals whose lack of pre-war political activity now made them most useful as spies, Washington saw that he would probably have to offer the inducement of money; even some of those who had lately acquired a degree of Patriot ardor required some monetary inducement to risk the gallows. He turned to Robert Morris, a successful Philadelphia merchant and congressman (who became known as the Financier of the Revolution), and asked for some "hard money to pay a certain set of people."[5] Morris quickly came through with a bag of silver coins, and Washington wasted no time in putting the money to work to hire the agents he needed.

Washington's accounts during the winter and spring of 1777 reflect his new emphasis on intelligence. Among the several large sums he paid out for intelligence collection during this period was the $238 he gave Lieutenant Colonel Joseph Reed, an officer on his staff, to purchase the information on which he based his second foray across the Delaware and his successful attack on Princeton. And in February he gave $500 to Nathaniel Sackett of Westchester County to hire agents and send them into New York City to collect "the earliest and best Intelligence of the designs of the Enemy."[6]

New York and British-occupied Long Island and Staten Island were, of course, the foci of Washington's intelligence interest. He now had reason to regret not having planted stay-behind agents in Manhattan to report to him on British military activity and preparations. While he was not completely without intelligence assets in New York, those we know of seem to have been walk-ins, Patriot New Yorkers who spied on their own initiative but were already marked as suspicious persons by the British and, therefore, of limited potential.

Haym Salomon may have been such a one. Salomon, a Jew, had fled persecution in his native Poland and settled in New York about 1773. There he opened a brokerage and mercantile business. He became a close friend of Alexander McDougall, a leader of the New York Sons of Liberty, and a member of the Sons himself.[7] On September 22, 1776—perhaps, coincidentally, the day Nathan Hale was hanged—he was arrested by the British and charged with espionage.[8] He escaped the gallows when his captors discovered his linguistic skills: he spoke Polish, French, Russian, Italian, English, and German. The last-named language made him too valuable to hang, and he was assigned to serve as an interpreter between the British commanders and the Hessian troops. Whether the conditions of his parole allowed him to pass on to Washington the military intelligence he learned in this capacity is unknown, but he did exploit the opportunity to persuade some of the German troops to defect to the American side.[9] (In

August 1778 Salomon was again arrested and charged with conspiracy to burn the British fleet and destroy British storehouses and was sentenced to death, but he managed to escape and make his way to Philadelphia, where he resumed his business activities and became an important financier of the American war effort.)

Hercules Mulligan, another member of the New York Sons of Liberty, was more successful as a spy—or, as he liked to put it, as a confidential correspondent—for Washington. A native of Ireland, Mulligan was brought to New York by his parents at the age of six. He became a tailor and opened a haberdashery on Queen (now Pearl) Street. He was active in colonial politics and was a member of both the Sons of Liberty and the New York Committee of Correspondence. In 1772 Mulligan, then thirty-two, befriended the young Alexander Hamilton, who had just arrived in New York from his native West Indies to pursue a higher education. Hamilton lived with the Mulligan family during his early years in New York and acquired a Patriot view of colonial politics from Hercules. Mulligan was arrested by the British in the general roundup of Patriots in New York soon after Howe landed at Manhattan in September 1776, but he was released about a month later.

In March 1777, when Washington was well on his way toward developing a true intelligence service, he appointed as his secretary and aide-de-camp Captain Alexander Hamilton, who had by that time distinguished himself as commander of an artillery company that took part in all the battles following Howe's landing on Long Island the previous August. Hamilton had had at least one clandestine meeting with Mulligan in New Jersey after the retreat from New York and by March may already have been receiving intelligence reports on the situation in New York from the tailor. In any case, Mulligan then became Washington's "confidential correspondent."[10]

As a notorious member of the Sons of Liberty, Mulligan may have seemed an unlikely candidate to collect any important military intelligence in New York. He had three means of spying on the British, however, and they seem to have been fairly effective. The first and probably the most important was his brother, Hugh, who owned the New York banking and importing firm of Kortright and Company. The firm had done considerable business with the British commissariat in New York before the Revolution, and despite Hercules's notoriety as a Patriot, the British continued to deal with Hugh Mulligan during the occupation of New York, and he was on friendly terms with many of the British officers. The considerable amount of intelligence he was able to collect through this situation he promptly passed on to his brother, who relayed it to Washington.[11]

Hercules Mulligan was also able to pick up bits and pieces of useful information from the British officers who were billeted in his home. But he may have learned even more from the many others who patronized his haberdashery. Whig he may have been, but the British dandies who served under Howe did not let that stand between them and the services of "the fashionable clothier" of Queen Street, and as they preened before the mirrors in his shop, they may have let slip more than a few interesting tidbits that did not escape the tailor's ears.

Washington understood the necessity of developing many separate sources and channels of intelligence in New York in order to be able to confirm the reports of his spies by cross-checking them and of not putting all his intelligence eggs in a single basket that might suddenly fall into British hands. In addition to the agents reporting through Sackett in Westchester and through Mulligan, he established at least one more network, the Mersereau Spy Ring.

During his withdrawal through New Jersey the previous fall, Washington had recruited Joshua Mersereau, a Patriot refugee from Staten Island, to serve as a secret intelligence agent. Mersereau sent his son, John LaGrange Mersereau, back to Staten Island to observe and report on the British force there and in New York City.[12]

Sackett's agents, Mulligan, Mersereau, perhaps Salomon, and probably others whose names are lost were Washington's intelligence assets in New York during the spring and early summer of 1777. On March 28 one of Sackett's agents, the wife of a Tory, left the city for Westchester to report to Sackett that the British were building a large number of flat-bottomed boats, which they intended to use in an expedition against Philadelphia "to subdue that city."[13] Early in April Washington received a report, perhaps from Mulligan, that the British intended to embark three thousand troops on the transports then anchored in the harbor and that they were probably bound for the Delaware.[14]

The intelligence indicating that Howe planned an expedition against Philadelphia seemed to Washington too good to be true and, therefore, to be received with great skepticism. He saw four possible courses open to Howe. The British commander in chief could return to New Jersey in the hope of forcing the general engagement that Washington intended to avoid. He could sail up the Hudson and attack the small command Washington had left on the highlands near West Point. He could sail down the coast and then march inland to capture the American capital, Philadelphia. Or he could take what Washington considered the most logical step—strike north up the Hudson to meet another British force striking south from Canada, thereby splitting the colonies and isolating New England—the Hudson-Champlain strategy Howe himself had devised two years earlier. And if Howe chose the last option, Washington could do nothing but march his army northward over difficult terrain with little chance of preventing the larger British force from achieving its aim. Therefore, intelligence that Howe intended something other than this was most welcome to the American commander in chief, if a little doubtful.

In June Howe led his army from Staten Island into New Jersey in an attempt to force a general engagement on Washington. After considerable maneuvering and some skirmishing by the two armies, Howe abandoned the plan and returned to Staten Island, where, late in June, he began loading a force of fifteen thousand men aboard the transports standing in the bay, leaving only a small garrison under General Sir Henry Clinton to occupy New York. The entire force had embarked by early July, but the ships just swung at anchor under the sweltering summer sun as days passed into weeks. Washington had no clue to their intended destination, but reports that a large British force under General Burgoyne was striking south along Lake Champlain confirmed fears that Howe would soon sail up the Hudson to Albany as part of a Hudson-Champlain operation. Additional evidence supporting this theory arrived early in July in the form of the distressing news that the American force at Fort Ticonderoga, on the southern end of the lake, had withdrawn from the fort on the night of July 5–6, abandoning it to Burgoyne. Anticipating the need to follow Howe north along the Hudson, Washington moved his army out of Morristown in mid-July and positioned it in the Clove, a rugged gorge running north through the Hudson Highlands.

On July 23 the 230 British ships in New York Harbor set sail and stood out to sea, leaving the mouth of the Hudson in their wake. Howe, in the meantime, had contrived to have a letter signed by him and addressed to General Burgoyne fall into Washington's hands. Although the letter announced a plan for the two British commanders to launch a joint attack against Boston, Washington was too much a master of military deception to be taken in by the ruse.[15] Nonetheless, he remained in doubt about Howe's true destination, which now seemed to be Philadelphia. The possibility remained that the fleet's departure was also a ruse.

Reports from Washington's spies in New York continued to indicate that Philadelphia was Howe's destination; nonetheless, the American commander in chief wanted more independent reports on the military situation Howe had left behind him, perhaps to be assured that the largest part of the British force was indeed aboard the transports. On July 26—three days after Howe sailed—he instructed Colonel Elias Dayton, one of his regimental commanders, to send "trusty persons to Staten Island in whom you can confide, to obtain Intelligence of the Enemy's situation & numbers—what kind of Troops they are, and what Guards they have—their strength & where posted."[16]

Dayton's agents' reports may have convinced Washington that the southward course of Howe's fleet was not a ruse to draw him away from New York, for two days later he led his army on a rapid march southward through New Jersey, reaching the banks of the Delaware River at Coryell's Ferry by July 30. But the apparent senselessness of Howe's move continued to disturb him. "Genl. Howe's, in a manner, abandoning Genl. Burgoyne, is so unaccountable a matter," he wrote, "that till I am assured it is so, I cannot help casting my Eyes continually behind me."[17]

Washington's doubts were quite the reverse of the more familiar situation in which a commander tends to discount confirmed intelligence. The usual reason intelligence is rejected is because the facts are unwelcome, but Washington suspected his spy's reports because they seemed too good to be true. Yet he would have comprehended the situation had his intelligence been good enough to inform him that the British command in North America had, in effect, become divided: during the winter of 1776–77, Lord George Germain, the British colonial secretary in London, had failed to knock together the heads of his generals and had approved both

Burgoyne's plan to move down the Champlain-Hudson line and Howe's plan to capture Philadelphia. Howe, who saw capturing the rebel capital as a major psychological blow to the Revolution, believed he was also supporting Burgoyne by drawing Washington away from the Hudson. For his part, Burgoyne would probably have understood Washington's astonishment and skepticism.

Washington's uncertainty was temporarily relieved on July 31, when he received word that the British fleet had been spotted off the mouth of Delaware Bay, but the following day he had a new report that the ships were not entering the bay, as he expected, but standing off to the east. The possibility that Howe, having drawn Washington to central New Jersey, was now returning to New York to sail up the Hudson was obvious. But the British fleet was spotted moving south off the Delmarva Peninsula on August 9, and on the twenty-second Washington received word that the fleet was well up the Chesapeake Bay. Obviously, Philadelphia was Howe's object.

Washington now abandoned his resolution to avoid a general engagement; for psychological and political reasons he felt he could not abandon the American capital to the British without a fight. He placed his army athwart Howe's probable route from the Chesapeake Bay to Philadelphia, making his stand at Chad's Ford on Brandywine Creek on September 11. Unfortunately, he did not have an accurate map of the area and relied on erroneous information that there was no ford across the creek immediately to the north of his position (inaccurate basic intelligence, in today's jargon, and a particularly embarrassing lapse in a commander who had once been the official surveyor of Culpeper County, Virginia). He also placed unwarranted trust in the local militia to scout the British advance. The combination of these two lapses led to an unpleasant surprise reminiscent of Long Island—Howe again managed to get his main force to Washington's rear.

Of some eleven thousand troops Washington lost between twelve hundred and thirteen hundred at Brandywine Creek (including about four hundred who were taken prisoner).[18] He did not stop Howe, of course, who captured Philadelphia on September 26. After an indecisive battle at Germantown, Pennsylvania, on October 4, Howe again declined to press his advantage and withdrew to Philadelphia.

In spite of this unhappy turn of events, Washington could at least now console himself with the foresight he had demonstrated in April, when against the possibility that Howe might occupy Philadelphia, he had ordered General Thomas Mifflin to establish stay-behind agent networks in that city. He had instructed Mifflin to "look out for proper persons for this purpose, who are to remain among them under the mask of Friendship." Regarding secret inks and the other tradecraft of the spy, he told Mifflin, "Give the persons you pitch upon, proper lessons."[19]

Mifflin delegated the task of setting up the stay-behind networks to a subordinate, Major John Clark. Like Mifflin, Clark was a Pennsylvanian who had grown up in the Philadelphia area and therefore knew which of the local citizens could be relied upon as spies. After Howe occupied Philadelphia, running the networks became Clark's full-time job. This consisted for the most part of daily clandestine meetings with his couriers—the farmers and tradesmen who traveled in and out of the city to sell their goods to the British, a trade officially prohibited by Washington's order but secretly permitted in the interest of agent communications.[20]

Clark was taken ill in January 1778 and forced to give up his work and return to his home in York, Pennsylvania. His networks remained in place, of course, and were now serviced by several other officers. Even General Washington personally managed at least one agent, Jacob Bankson, who passed through the British lines around Philadelphia with such ease that the general for a time suspected the man was a double agent. Washington assigned the task of checking the man's background to his aide-de-camp, Alexander Hamilton, who gave Bankson a clean bill of health.[21]

The names of most of the Philadelphia stay-behind agents and their couriers are unknown. A few are to be found in local tradition but not among the records of Washington or the Continental army, and the stories relating to them may be no more than the folklore that so frequently attaches to espionage activities.[22] While the stay-behind networks in Philadelphia were undoubtedly useful to Washington during the winter of 1777–78,[23] there was little likelihood that Howe would leave the comfort of Philadelphia to attack the well-fortified Continental camp twenty miles away at Valley Forge, where Washington's army had gone into winter quarters in mid-December. Howe had already tendered to London his resignation as commander in chief—in the wake of Burgoyne's defeat at Saratoga, it was immediately accepted—and he remained in Philadelphia only until his successor, General Sir Henry Clinton, could come down from

New York and take charge. In the meantime, he presided over a program of balls, theatrical performances, horse races, cockfights, drinking bouts, and similar diversions. This culminated on May 18 in the Mischianza, a 4:00 P.M.–to–4:00 A.M. extravaganza complete with fireworks, a mock medieval tournament, a regatta of decorated barges on the Delaware, and a banquet, all to give a hearty send-off to the popular General Howe. The celebration was organized by a young officer who was soon to play a major role in the secret war—Captain John André.[24]

The stay-behind networks had already discovered and reported the plans of Howe's successor. General Clinton, who had arrived in Philadelphia on May 8, carried with him orders from London to evacuate Philadelphia and bring the British force back to New York. A new factor had been introduced into the military equation by the Franco-American treaty of alliance that had been executed in February: French sea power. William Eden's agents in France had learned that the Count d'Estang, admiral of the French navy, departed for America from the port of Toulon on April 10 with a fleet boasting twice the number of warships Howe's brother commanded in American waters. In anticipation Lord North had decided in March to evacuate Philadelphia.

Clinton chose to move his army to New York by land, thereby avoiding the unpleasant prospect of encountering the French fleet en route. The land route, however—a network of narrow roads blocked by destroyed bridges and other obstructions calculated to slow British progress—was going to force him into a very vulnerable situation: his army was strung out in a thin line many miles long that was exposed to attack from either flank.

Washington now found himself, as he had at Brandywine, faced with an intelligence problem that could not be solved by spies and requiring the services of swift, long-range reconnaissance units. After the retreat from New York, he had not created a unit equivalent to the lost Knowlton's Rangers, and his prejudice against using cavalry—he regarded them as ineffective in the terrain of the Northeast and with the horses' mouths to feed an added burden—now denied him the mounted scouting capability cavalry units could provide.[25] He therefore lacked the reconnaissance resources to determine which of two obvious routes through New Jersey Clinton would follow. This was intelligence that would have enabled him to strike a mighty blow against the British column, perhaps delivering a major defeat to Clinton, which, only months after Saratoga, would force the North ministry to end the war. Instead, he found himself attacking a large portion of the British force concentrated around Monmouth Court House on June 28.

The Battle of Monmouth, fought in extreme summer heat that hampered the British and Americans equally, turned out to be a tactical draw. Although suffering heavy losses, Clinton managed to remove his army to New York. For Washington the intelligence failure resulted in a lost opportunity but not defeat.

The Battle of Monmouth was the last major action in the North. For the British the scale of the strategic map had suddenly enlarged to include the West Indies, where their extremely valuable possessions were now threatened by the French and, potentially, the Spanish. They had been forced to abandon Philadelphia because a large part of Clinton's command—a detachment of fifty-eight hundred men under General James Grant—was soon to be sent south to the Caribbean. But Clinton's task as the new British commander in chief in the colonies was no longer to attempt to destroy Washington's army in the North but to contain it until he could receive reinforcements. In the meantime, his offensive action was to be limited to a series of raids in the area around New York City.

Having for the most part lost the strategic initiative and been placed by events in a semidefensive situation, Clinton now found that intelligence had taken on increased importance. In the British military organization secret service came under the direction of the adjutant general, and Clinton's AG was Francis Rawdon-Hastings, or Lord Rawdon, as he was then called (he was created the first marquess of Hastings in 1817). Lord Rawdon had assigned the actual running of the Secret Service—such as it was—to his deputy, Lieutenant Colonel Stephen Kemble, a New Jersey native who had served in the British army since 1757 and had had the Secret Service assignment under both of Clinton's predecessors, Gage and Howe, since 1772. Kemble, something of a plodder, had been first given the job by General Gage on the strength of being the general's brother-in-law and probably continued to hold it under Howe simply because that gentleman was not greatly dependent on intelligence. In September 1779

Clinton arranged for Kemble to be replaced by his energetic and engaging young aide-de-camp, Captain John André.[26] André was promoted to the grade of brevet major as part of the move.

After Clinton withdrew to New York in June 1778, Washington deployed his army in a rough semicircle around the city, quartering troops at Middlebrook, Elizabeth, and Ramapo in New Jersey; West Point and Fishkill in New York; and Danbury, Connecticut. Although the reduction in the size of Clinton's force had taken the strategic initiative away from the British commander, it had not been handed to Washington. Count d'Estang took the French fleet to the Caribbean late in the year, returning control of the coastal waters around New York to the British and thereby precluding Washington from challenging Clinton's possession of Manhattan, a move for which he did not have the numerical strength in any case. The strategic situation in New York settled down to a prolonged stalemate.

The secret war went on. Washington's spies continued to operate in the city. Hercules Mulligan still reported what he could learn from his brother of British preparations, and during this period he is credited with warning Washington of two British plots to kidnap the general.[27]

Just because his New York secret agents were proving so valuable may have been the reason Washington wanted to have more of them. Or it may be that his experience with the Philadelphia stay-behind nets had shown him the proper way secret intelligence operations should be organized and run, and he was now eager to apply these lessons. In any case, in the summer of 1778, Washington ordered Major Benjamin Tallmadge to establish, in Tallmadge's words,

> a private correspondence with some persons in New York . . .
> which lasted through the war. How beneficial it was to the
> Commander-in-Chief is evidenced by his continuing the same
> to the close of the war. I kept one or more boats constantly
> employed in crossing the Sound on this business.[28]

This was the beginning of the Culper Spy Ring, the most professional of Washington's espionage operations on record.

While far more details of the Culper Ring have survived than have the details of any of the other New York agents and networks, it is not clear just how Major Tallmadge managed to set it up. Tallmadge, a Yale classmate of Nathan Hale, had been superintendent of a high school in Wethersfield, Connecticut, before receiving a commission in a Connecticut regiment in June 1776. Later he was assigned to the Connecticut Second Dragoons. He saw action at Long Island, White Plains, Brandywine, Germantown, and Monmouth, but nothing in the record indicates that he had been entrusted with an espionage assignment before the Culper project.

Tallmadge was a native of Brookhaven, on the South Shore of eastern Long Island, and his acquaintance with the locals was probably what led him to recruit Abraham Woodhull of Setauket, a nearby town on the North Shore, as his principal agent. Woodhull, about twenty-eight, had served briefly in the New York militia early in the war but resigned to work the family farm on British-occupied Long Island. A naturally cautious and timorous man, he was in a constant state of suppressed terror as he carried on his espionage under the eyes of the British.[29] On October 31, two months after his recruitment, he reported to Tallmadge using his pseudonym, Samuel Culper:

> Since my last have explored Long Island, City of New York and island unto the ten mile stone to Tryons [i.e., William Tryon, at this time a major general of Loyalist provincial forces] Quarters where I received his threats for comeing their that made me almost tremble knowing my situation and business but blessed be God have been prosperd and particularly successful in ingaging a faithful friend and one of the first characters in the City to make it his business and keep his eyes upon and meet and consult weekly in or near the city. I have the most sanguine hopes of great advantage will acrue by his assistance. . . .[30]

The faithful friend Woodhull recruited as his New York City agent was Robert Townsend, a partner in Oakman and Townsend, a dry-goods business at 18 Smith Street, at the corner of William Street. Townsend, a Quaker, had not been outspoken in his Patriot views before the war and so more easily passed as a Tory in New York. His cover was further enhanced by his sideline: contributing bits of society news to the pages of the *Royal Gazette*, a newspaper published by James Rivington. Townsend made his cover even stronger in 1780 by enlisting in the British Provincials, the local Tory militia.[31] With the recruitment of Townsend, Woodhull became Culper Sr., while Townsend was Culper Jr.

Through his dry-goods business and newspaper work Townsend collected intelligence directly on the British in New York, and he received additional information from several subagents, including his brother-in-law, Amos Underhill, who kept a boardinghouse with his wife on Queen Street; and his common-law wife, a woman known to history only by the code number the Culpers used in reference to her, 355.

The number was part of an extensive code developed for the Culpers by Major Tallmadge for their agent communications. Townsend himself was 723; Woodhull, 722; Washington, 711; Long Island, 728; Setauket, 729; and so on.[32] Townsend's coded reports were further secured against discovery through the use of invisible ink, a special type of which was developed for Washington by Sir James Jay, the brother of John Jay.[33]

Although Washington had appointed Tallmadge the case officer for the Culper Ring, he was not always satisfied to leave the minute details of espionage tradecraft to him. In fact, it seems that Tallmadge contributed only his knowledge of Long Island and his acquaintance with its residents, while Washington relied entirely on his own hard-won knowledge of espionage tradecraft in running the network. Here, for example, are his very specific instructions on the method Townsend was to employ in writing in invisible ink:

> One thing appears to me deserving of [Culper Jr.'s] particular consideration . . . he should occasionally write his information on the blank leaves of a pamphlet, on the first, second, and other pages of a common pocket book, or on the blank leaves at each end of registers, almanacks, or any new publication or book of small value. He should be determined in the choice of these books principally by the goodness of the blank paper, as the ink is not easily legible unless it is on paper of good quality. . . .
>
> I would add a further hint on this subject. Even letters may be made more subservient to this communication, than they have

yet been. He may write a familiar letter on domestic affairs, or on some little matters of business, to his friend at Setauket or elsewhere, interlining with the stain [i.e., the invisible ink] his secret intelligence, or writing it on the opposite blank side of the letter. But that his friend may know how to distinguish these from letters addressed solely to himself, he may always leave such as contain secret information without date or place (dating it with the stain), or fold them up in a particular manner, which may be concerted between the parties. This last appears to be the best mark of the two, and may be the signal of their being designated for me. The first mentioned mode, however, or that of the books, appears to me the one least liable to detection.[34]

Here we see a measure of just how sophisticated Washington had become in intelligence tradecraft. Evidence of such close attention to the details of spying is not often found among his collected papers, but it survives here in one of the letters preserved by Major Tallmadge. We can only guess how often he issued the same instructions to other agents.

Washington agreed to let Woodhull keep to himself the identity of Culper Jr., "whose name I have no desire to be informed of provided his intelligence is good, and seasonably transmitted,"[35] but he urged that the agent "should endeavour to hit upon some certain mode of conveying his information quickly, for it is of little avail to be told of things after they have become matter of public notoriety, and known to every body."[36]

Tallmadge, Woodhull, and Townsend established a swift and secure means of getting the latter's reports to Washington. Austin Roe, a Setauket tavern keeper, made frequent trips to New York City to purchase supplies for his establishment and carried back to Long Island the coded reports penned in invisible ink by Townsend. He concealed them in a dead drop—for example, in a hollow tree trunk or beneath a rock—on Woodhull's farm. Woodhull then conveyed the dispatch to Caleb Brewster, a local blacksmith and boatman, who carried it across Long Island Sound to Tallmadge or one of his couriers.

Washington never wearied of the details of the Culper Ring's operations. Here, for example, are his detailed instructions for the ring, found among Tallmadge's papers:

C—— Junr, to remain in the City, to collect all the useful information he can—to do this he should mix as much as possible among the officers and Refugees, visit the Coffee Houses, and all public places. He is to pay particular attention to the movements by land and water in and about the city especially.

How their transports are secured against attempt to destroy them—whether by armed vessels upon the flanks, or by chains, Booms, or any contrivances to keep off fire Rafts.

The number of men destined for the defence of the City and Environs, endeavoring to designate the particular corps, and where each is posted. . . .[37]

And so on, at great length and in more painstaking detail:

These are the principal matters to be observed within the Island and about the City of New York. Many more may occur to a person of C. Junr's penetration which he will note and communicate.

C—— Senior's station to be upon Long Island to receiv and transmit the intelligence of C——Junior. . . .

Proper persons to be procured at convenient distances along the Sound from Brooklyn to Newton whose business it shall be to observe and report what is passing upon the water, as whether any Vessels or Boats with troops are moving, their number and which way they seem bound.

And he closed with a detailed admonition regarding security:

There can be scarcely any need of recommending the greatest Caution and secrecy in a Business so critical and dangerous. The following seem to be the best general rules:

To intrust to no one but the persons fixed upon to transmit the Business.

To deliver the dispatches to none upon our side but those who shall be pitched upon for the purpose of receiving them

and to transmit them and any intelligence that may be obtained
to no one but the Commander-in-Chief.[38]

Washington had come a long way from the amateur intelligence officer
who sent Nathan Hale on his ill-conceived mission to Long Island and his
lonely death. Two years of maneuvering against a more powerful British
force, of running the Philadelphia stay-behind nets, and of dispatching a
host of nameless spies behind the enemy's lines had taught him far more
than the basic principles of the Great Game of spying. He had developed
his native shrewdness, his respect for secrecy, and his talent for deception
into the expertise of a professional intelligence officer. His biographer
James Thomas Flexner observed: "Washington had a passion for intelligence that would enable him to foresee, and, as far as his possibilities
went, he was an excellent spymaster."[39]

And the intelligence skills and assets he had developed during the
previous two years were to stand him in good stead in the final phase of
the war for independence.

Chapter Five

Endgames

"I am destitute of information with respect to the present state of European politics," Washington complained,[1] thereby putting his finger squarely on a major defect in the American intelligence apparatus of the Revolution. Before the Franco-American alliance was established, foreign political intelligence was of minimal use to the commander in chief of the Continental army, but with the entry of France into the war, the strategic map had suddenly changed scale; the war was no longer purely a land conflict to be fought in a zone bounded by Maine and South Carolina. It now involved military and commercial factors on both sides of the Atlantic and in the Caribbean.

The American who best understood the new, larger strategic situation was, of course, Benjamin Franklin, the commander in chief of the diplomatic side of the war (the Continental Congress had made Franklin American minister plenipotentiary—the sole American diplomatic representative in France—in September 1778). But Franklin and Washington had no direct channel of communication. Franklin reported to the Committee of Secret Correspondence (which had become the Committee on Foreign Affairs in 1776) of the Continental Congress, but Congress thought to pass on to Washington little of what he told them.

On June 29, 1779, Culper Jr. reported the psychological climate in New York in a paragraph with a surprisingly Tory tone: "We are much alarmed with the prospect of a Spanish war—Should that be the case, I fear poor old England will not be able to oppose the whole but will be obliged to sue for peace."[2] Washington must certainly have been bemused by his spy's turn of phrase; he heartily wished for an alliance with Spain, which he—along with Culper Jr.—believed would bring the British to the bargaining table.[3] And he would soon be pleased to discover that Spain had indeed entered the war just eight days before Culper Jr. had written his report. Spain had not entered into an alliance with the United States—she feared the American fever for independence might prove contagious in her own colonies in the New World—but she had declared war against Great Britain to pursue her own global objectives: the recovery of Gibraltar and the acquisition of new footholds along the Mississippi and the Gulf of Mexico. In some ways, Spain's policy in the war was more rational than that of France, and it was guided by a systematic intelligence operation in North America that Spain had undertaken several years earlier.

The story of Spanish espionage in North America is an almost unknown chapter in the history of the American Revolution. It actually began fifteen years before the Revolution, when the governor general of Cuba organized a secret service to report on affairs in British America, using such assets as the Cuban fishing fleet that operated out of Havana, Cuban merchants who traded in the colonies, and pro-Spanish residents of East Florida. The governor general also kept tabs on British activity along the Mississippi through his military subordinate, the governor of Louisiana.

With the outbreak of the Revolution in the British colonies, Spain enlarged her intelligence activities in North America in order to assess possible threats against her nearby territories and to be aware of any opportunities to profit from Britain's troubles. In February 1776 the minister of the Indies—Spain's chief colonial officer—ordered the Marquess de la Torre, the Cuban captain general, to establish a new espionage network to report on the American Revolution.[4] Torre took several immediate measures to increase intelligence collection in the Caribbean, including the placing of a secret agent in Jamaica, and then turned his attention to improving his assets on the North American mainland.

One of his first steps was to activate an agent already in place in East Florida, a territory of particular interest because it had been ceded to Britain as a consequence of the Seven Years' War, had not been extensively settled by the British since then, and might be the price the Spanish court would accept in exchange for entering the war on the American side. Torre's agent was Luciano de Herrera, who had been born in Saint Augustine in 1736, when it was Spanish territory. Herrera stayed on in Saint Augustine after Florida changed hands and on his own initiative began reporting covertly on the local situation to the captain general of Cuba. These reports were largely ignored in official circles, however, until the events of 1775–76 focused Spanish interest on North American affairs.[5]

Although Saint Augustine was far from the scenes of the conflict to the north, East Florida soon became a haven for a continuous stream of Tory refugees, who brought with them recent news of events in the colonies, and Herrera, with the aid of another agent sent from Havana, promptly forwarded this information to Captain General de la Torre and Don Diego Joseph Navarro, who succeeded Torre late in 1777. Navarro, however, was anxious to place an agent at the political hub of events, the Continental Congress, and he therefore dispatched to Philadelphia Don Juan de Miralles Trailhon, a Spanish-born merchant of Havana who spoke excellent English, which he had learned during many years of trading with the British at Saint Augustine.[6]

Miralles arrived in Philadelphia in the summer of 1778. In the guise of a merchant seeking to purchase flour, he ingratiated himself by dispensing Havana cigars liberally around the Revolutionary capital.[7] He quickly gained the confidence of many of the Revolutionary leaders, including Washington, and during the next two years dispatched hundreds of secret reports to Captain General Navarro. These reports furnished informed descriptions of life in the rebellious colonies and presented character sketches of the Revolutionary leaders.[8]

Miralles's reports were optimistic regarding American prospects, and they may have encouraged the relatively minor financial aid Spain gave the United States in the form of loans and subsidies, but the Spanish foreign ministry stuck to a policy of cynical self-interest in its dealings with all of the belligerents. The Count de Floridablanca, the Spanish foreign minister, first proposed a deal to the British: in exchange for Spain's mediating the conflict between Britain and the Franco-American allies, Britain would return Gibraltar to Spain. When King George III turned down the proposal, Spain allied herself with France against Britain but did not go so far as to recognize American independence. On June 21, 1779, Spain declared war against Britain, but for the then-foreseeable future her military efforts were to be concentrated on recovering Gibraltar.

Spanish entry into the war had one salutary effect for the American military situation: it revived centuries-old British fears of a Spanish invasion of England, and thereby kept a large part of Britain's sea power on the eastern side of the Atlantic.

An invasion of England was actually in the planning stage by the French during 1779 but was abandoned in October as impractical. The political momentum the plan had gathered forced the French to the reluctant step of sending a large expeditionary force to America to fight under Washington's command, however. On July 10, 1780, General Rochambeau landed at Newport, Rhode Island, with a force of seventy-six hundred French troops.

The prospect of the arrival of the French expedition, of which Washington had learned only sometime in May, awakened hopes that the war in the North would move beyond the stalemate that had existed for the past two years. Washington now regretted the impatience that had led him virtually to discharge the Culpers. Townsend, for some reason lost to history, had withdrawn from the network. On May 19 Washington had expressed his annoyance to Tallmadge:

> As C. junior has totally declined and C. Senior seems to wish to
> do it, I think the intercourse may be dropped, more especially
> as from our present position the intelligence is so long getting
> to hand that it is of no use by the time it reaches me.[9]

The delay in reporting was not the fault of the Culper Ring. Washington was at this time making his headquarters at Morristown, New Jersey, and to the usual time required to carry dispatches from Townsend in New York to Woodhull in Setauket, thence across Long Island Sound to Connecticut and westward to White Plains or West Point, was added the delay of relaying them across the Hudson and southward into New Jersey, a mere twenty miles from where Culper Jr. had penned them. In any case, the Culper Ring was inactive until July 11, when Washington, realizing he had been too hasty, wrote to Tallmadge again:

> As we may every moment expect the arrival of the French Fleet
> [Washington did not then know that it had arrived the previous

day] a revival of the correspondence with the Culpers will be of a very great importance. If the younger cannot be engaged again, you will endeavor to prevail upon the older to give you information of the movements and position of the enemy upon Long Island....[10]

It may have been one of Washington's most fortunate decisions. Tallmadge received the letter three days later in Westchester and set out the following morning for Fairfield, Connecticut, where he located Caleb Brewster, the boatman of Setauket, and sent him across the Sound with instructions for the Culpers. Woodhull sent his courier, Austin Roe, into New York on July 18, the same day General Clinton received word of Rochambeau's arrival off Rhode Island.[11]

"In the hope that I might yet be in time to undertake something offensive against the enemy," Clinton reported later to London,

> ... I determined as speedily as possible to put a body of troops afloat in the Sound, ready for operation to the eastward, if further information should warrant it, and not too distant to return rapidly, and act against the rebel army, should they, in my absence, form an enterprize against these posts.[12]

Clinton hesitated to detach too large a force from his New York stronghold lest he tempt Washington, but he could not resist the attractive possibility of catching Rochambeau's expedition debilitated from the two-month sea voyage and perhaps with some men, horses, and equipment still aboard the transports at Newport. He began preparations to embark a detachment of eight thousand men aboard transports at Whitestone, on the North Shore of western Long Island, and send it to Rhode Island to attack the French.

"Many causes conspired to retard the arrival of transports at Frog's-neck," he reported, "from which place my embarkation was only effected the 27th."[13] The delay in embarking the British troops gave the Culpers time to report the move to Washington. Townsend, who had rejoined the Culper Ring for reasons as obscure as his motive for leaving it, sent Roe back to Setauket with detailed accounts of the embarkation and a British naval force that had already left for Newport. The intelligence reached Washington's headquarters on July 21.[14]

Alerted to Clinton's move against Rochambeau, Washington understood that he could not move his army overland to Newport in time to help the French, but he also realized that if the force Clinton had sent to Newport was really strong enough to endanger Rochambeau, he must have weakened his defenses at New York. The American commander in chief therefore crossed the Hudson and marched southward through Westchester toward Manhattan. The feint succeeded; Clinton promptly recalled his troops to New York, leaving the French force unmolested.

"I am very much pleased the Correspondence with the C—— is again opened," Washington told Tallmadge on August 11. "I have the greatest dependence in his good intentions and I am persuaded when he pleases to exert himself he can give the most useful intelligence."[15]

With the Culper Ring reactivated, Tallmadge made his headquarters at New Canaan, Connecticut, ready to receive the dispatches carried across the Sound by Caleb Brewster and forward them to Washington by means of a chain of express couriers. On the evening of September 21, however, he chanced to be in North Castle, a Continental stronghold in northern Westchester.

"Soon after I halted, and disposed of my detachment," he recalled, "I was informed that a prisoner had been brought in that day by the name of John Anderson."[16]

He learned that three local militiamen had stopped and searched the man, whom they encountered near Tarrytown, New York, and found some suspicious papers concealed in his boots. Their suspicions were further aroused when he tried to buy his freedom, so they brought him to North Castle and turned him over to Lieutenant Colonel John Jameson of the Light Dragoons. Jameson had written a report of the matter and sent it and Anderson, under guard, to General Benedict Arnold, the commander at West Point. At the same time he sent the papers that had been found on Anderson to Washington, who was then en route to West Point from a meeting with Rochambeau at Hartford, Connecticut.

Upon learning all this, Tallmadge immediately tried to persuade Jameson to turn the whole affair over to him. Failing in this, he prevailed on the officer to send a messenger after Anderson and have him brought back to North Castle. Jameson insisted that his report of the matter should continue on to Arnold, however.

Tallmadge does not adequately explain the reasons for his interference in the matter. His suspicions of Arnold might have been aroused if he had heard of the general's recent attempt to pry the identities of the Culpers from Washington[17] or if he had been shown Arnold's letter of August 5 to one of Washington's commanders:

> As the safety of this Post and garrison [i.e., West Point] in a great measure depends on having good intelligence of the movements and designs of the enemy, and as you have been fortunate in the agents you have employed for that purpose, I must request, with their permission, to be informed who they are, as I wish to employ them for the same purpose.[18]

Fortunately, Arnold was refused the information in both instances. But if Tallmadge had begun to develop the instincts of a good case officer, he must have made a sharp mental note of Arnold's inquiries. And Tallmadge must certainly have also wondered whether the John Anderson with the suspicious papers in his boot was the same man Arnold had named in his orders to Tallmadge of September 13:

> If Mr. James Anderson, a person I expect from New York should come to your quarters, I have to request that you will give him an escort of two Horse to bring him on his way to this place, and send an express to me that I may meet him.[19]

"As soon as I saw Anderson, and especially after I saw him walk (as he did almost constantly) across the floor, I became impressed with the belief that he had been *bred* to *arms*."[20]

Anderson soon admitted to Tallmadge that he was indeed "Major John André, Adjutant General to the British Army."[21] Tallmadge saw that his suspicions of Arnold had been well-founded, but it was now the afternoon of the twenty-fourth, three days after Lieutenant Colonel Jameson had sent his report of Anderson's arrest to Arnold.

"I knew it must reach him before I could possibly get to West Point," he recalled.[22]

Arnold received Jameson's report at breakfast the following morning, a meal he would have been sharing with Washington had the commander in chief not been delayed. Washington was virtually on his doorstep when Arnold galloped off toward the Hudson River and the British ship that would take him to the safety of New York. The reason for his subordinate's abrupt departure became clear to Washington later in the day, when the rider Jameson had sent to meet him with André's incriminating papers finally arrived, having earlier missed him on the road from Hartford.

Although Tallmadge may have suspected Arnold, Washington had not, and he was stunned. The man was an American hero. It was he who, together with Ethan Allen, led the daring expedition to capture Fort Ticonderoga in the first months of the war. It was he who captured the British fort at Saint Johns, Quebec, who led the expedition against Quebec, who rushed to Danbury to drive off and harass the numerically superior force that had raided that Patriot arsenal, who had lifted the British siege of Fort Stanwix, and who had distinguished himself and been severely wounded at Saratoga.

Arnold's treachery remains an enigma, but apparently it had its roots in the ingratitude of the Continental Congress, the jealousy of rivals, and the resultant quarrels and grievances that marked his later career. Or it may have had something to do with his Tory wife, Peggy Shippen, whom he met while in command at Philadelphia after the British evacuation of that city in 1778. It was only a month after his marriage the following year that he first offered to sell military information to General Clinton. His secret correspondence with the British was handled by Clinton's Secret Service chief, Major André, and culminated in Arnold's proposal to surrender the American fortress at West Point and several nearby American strongholds to Clinton for the sum of twenty thousand pounds. And it was to finalize this bargain that André had made his dangerous trip behind American lines, the trip from which he was returning when he was apprehended at Tarrytown.

Washington was almost equally stunned to discover that a senior officer on Clinton's staff had entered his lines in disguise, an act he characterized as "an unaccountable deprivation of presence of mind in a man of the first abilities."[23] But André had worn his British regimentals when he disembarked from the British ship to meet Arnold at Haverstraw. It was only when he was unable to return to the ship and was forced to travel back to New York City overland through Westchester that he made the fatal mistake of exchanging his uniform for civilian clothes.

At first André seemed not to appreciate his situation. He asked Tallmadge what he might expect from the military tribunal he had been told awaited him, and the dragoon asked him whether he remembered Nathan Hale and what General Howe had done to him.

"Surely you don't consider his case and mine alike," André exclaimed.

Tallmadge said they were "precisely similar," and added, "Similar will be your fate."[24]

In the Anglo-American scheme of things, spying was a necessary repugnance, a thing the lowborn were paid to do. It was difficult for Major André to grasp the idea that a British officer and gentleman could be called a spy, even if he had been caught behind enemy lines in civilian clothes with stolen information in his shoes.

Under the rules of warfare recognized by both sides, Washington was entitled to hang André after the same sort of summary hearing General Howe had granted Hale. The commander in chief elected to refer the matter to a fourteen-member board of general officers, however, which convened at Tappan, New York, on September 29. With great dignity André admitted the facts in the case but insisted that he did not regard himself as a spy. The board found otherwise and recommended the death penalty. Washington sentenced André to hang at five o'clock in the afternoon of October 1 and notified General Clinton of his decision.

Clinton was thunderstruck. The charming young officer was more than his friend and protégé; he was his alter ego, almost his son. He quickly wrote to Washington, arguing that André had gone to meet Arnold under a flag of truce and at the invitation of Arnold, who, after all, had been a general in the Continental army at the time. This tortured logic failed to persuade Washington, but he agreed to postpone the execution for a day and sent a representative to hear further arguments from a deputation of three British officers at Dobbs Ferry. But the arguments were simply variations on the theory Clinton had already ventured: André had gone forth under a flag of truce.

The major's case was probably not helped by an unctuous and insolent letter from Arnold to Washington in which he stated that André had crossed the lines "at my particular Request" under a flag of truce, "and as Commanding Officer in the Department, I had an undoubted right to transact all these Matters, which if wrong Major André ought by no means to suffer for them." Then Arnold switched from wheedles to threats:

> But if after this just and candid Representation of Major André's Case, the Board of General Officers adhere to their former Opinion, I shall suppose it dictated by Passion and Resentment, And if that Gentleman should suffer the Severity of their Sentence, I shall think myself bound by every Tie of Duty and Honor to retaliate on such unhappy Persons of your Army as may fall within my Power—that the respect due to Flags and the Law of Nations may be better understood and observed.[25]

Washington let it be known that there was but one way in which André could escape the gallows: if Clinton traded Arnold for him. This, of course, Clinton could not consider, and the offer certainly only increased his anguish.

André had resigned himself to his fate, but not the means prescribed for carrying it out. He sent a letter to Washington:

> ... I trust that the request I make of your Excellency at this serious period, and which is to soften my last moments, will not be rejected. Sympathy towards a soldier will surely induce your Excellency, and a military tribunal, to adapt the mode of my death to the feelings of a man of honour. Let me hope, Sir, that if aught in my character impresses you with esteem towards me, if aught in my misfortune marks me as the victim of policy and not of resentment, I shall experience the operation of these feelings in your breast by being informed that I am not to die on the gibbet.[26]

Washington ignored the request. André was hanged at midday on October 2. Just like Nathan Hale.

"I am happy to think that Arnold does not know my name," Townsend wrote to Woodhull on October 20. "However, no person has been taken up on his information."[27] To complete his treachery and perhaps justify the painful price Clinton had paid for his defection, Arnold now appointed himself chief British counterspy in New York. He seems not to have known the identity of any of Washington's small army of secret agents in the city, but he had his suspicions, and some of them centered on Hercules Mulligan. At Arnold's insistence Mulligan was arrested and accused of spying, but no evidence was produced, and the wily tailor talked his way out of the situation.[28] Unabashed, Arnold now contrived the one sure method of catching Washington's spies: he tried to persuade Major Tallmadge to defect. Reaching new heights of audacity, he wrote to the dragoon:

> As I know you to be a man of sense, I am convinced you are by this time fully of opinion that the real interest and happiness of America consists of a reunion with Great Britain. To effect which happy purpose I have taken a commission in the British army, and invite you to join me with as many men as you can bring over with you. If you think proper to embrace my offer, you shall have the same rank you now hold, in the cavalry I am about to raise.[29]

Arnold's courier made a much more accurate assessment of Tallmadge's character, and he therefore hesitated for more than a month before delivering the letter. Tallmadge, "mortified that my patriotism could be even suspected by this consummate villain," did not reply, but turned the letter over to Washington.[30]

Arnold's readiness to believe that his former comrades were no better than himself led him to accept the story of Sergeant Major John Champe, a Virginia cavalryman, when he showed up in New York on October 23 claiming to have deserted from the Continental army. Arnold welcomed him and gave him a post in his brigade, which was composed of deserters and Tories.

Champe had actually been sent on a twofold undercover mission by Captain Light-Horse Harry Lee of the Light Dragoons: first, to learn whether other American officers were dealing with the enemy and, second, to organize the kidnapping of Benedict Arnold. He was successful in the first instance, sending back to Lee word that he had found no evidence of other highly placed traitors, but his unit was shipped off to Virginia on the eve of the planned kidnapping. Champe later managed to rejoin the Continental forces in the Carolinas.[31]

Arnold led his brigade on several raids into Virginia in December and burned New London, Connecticut, the following September. Shortly thereafter he, his wife, and his son went to England, where he lived on a military pension and entered into several unsuccessful commercial ventures. The British seemed to like the treason better than the traitor, and although they kept their part of their bargain with Arnold, he felt himself the victim of scorn and neglect. After the war he moved to Saint John's, Newfoundland, but he found that the Tory refugees who had settled there had only hostility for the former American general. He returned to London in 1791 and died there ten years later, perhaps regretting that the British musket balls that felled him at Saratoga had not sent him on to glory then, securing forever his place in the sacred ranks of American heroes.

The Arnold affair, written indelibly in American Revolutionary lore,[32] soon passed from military view, eclipsed by the coming strategic climax of the war at Yorktown. Paradoxically, the Yorktown campaign began as a planned Franco-American assault on New York involving the armies of Washington and Rochambeau and augmented by an additional French force to be moved from the Caribbean war theater to New York aboard a French fleet commanded by Admiral de Grasse. On August 14, 1781, however, word reached Washington that de Grasse was on his way not to New York, but to the Chesapeake Bay with three thousand troops and twenty-nine warships to confront a force under General Cornwallis that was establishing a new British stronghold on the Yorktown peninsula in Virginia.

Washington immediately changed his plans and moved to join in the campaign against Cornwallis. Leaving a small force to defend his stronghold on the Hudson Highlands, he and Rochambeau moved southward through New Jersey. To forestall the possibility of Clinton sending reinforcements to Cornwallis, he took several deceptive measures to delude the British commander in chief into believing that New York was still his objective and that he planned to approach it across Staten Island.

He stopped at Chatham, New Jersey, and established a camp, including a large bakery, knowing that Clinton's secret service would report it and the British general would take it to be Washington's headquarters for a New York campaign. Once again, he resorted to the hoary but effective ruse of letting fabricated dispatches containing disinformation fall into the hands of Clinton's spies. He assembled boats along the Jersey shore as if in preparation for a crossing to Staten Island. And he arranged an ostentatious display of French troops along the Jersey Palisades, their distinctive white uniforms easily visible across the river in New York. All of this confirmed what Clinton had learned from genuine American dispatches he had captured before Washington's change of plans—that New York was the Continentals' objective.[33] He was so thoroughly convinced of this that even when his secret service learned from an American woman who was the mistress of Colonel Donatien Rochambeau—General Rochambeau's son and his assistant adjutant general—that the French army was marching to the Chesapeake, he refused to believe it.[34]

Clinton learned of Washington's true plans only on September 1, when the French and Continental armies had already reached Philadelphia and de Grasse had two days earlier arrived at the mouth of the Chesapeake and landed the French troops on the Yorktown peninsula. Cornwallis and his army of seventy-four hundred British and German troops could no longer withdraw inland without a fight, and they were blockaded in Yorktown by de Grasse's fleet. A second French squadron was on its way from Newport bringing siege artillery and provisions. The three thousand French troops that de Grasse had landed would soon be joined by the armies of Washington and Rochambeau, which French transports were preparing to carry down the Chesapeake from Baltimore and Annapolis, bringing the total allied force Cornwallis faced to 16,650.

Clinton realized the only way to extricate Cornwallis's army from the trap was to use his sea power to lift de Grasse's blockade and take control of the

Chesapeake, thereby preventing the Franco-American force from moving down the bay to Yorktown, and then reinforcing or evacuating Cornwallis. On September 5 a British fleet of nineteen ships under Admiral Thomas Graves arrived off the mouth of the Chesapeake. De Grasse's larger squadron—twenty-four ships—sailed out to engage it. The two-and-a-half-hour engagement that ensued was indecisive, but after several days of maneuvering, the British departed for New York, leaving Cornwallis to his fate.

The French advantage in what is known as the Battle of the Chesapeake Capes may have been more than numerical. Admiral de Grasse may have benefited from an intelligence coup achieved by one of Washington's New York spies.

James Rivington was notorious as one of the most ardent Tories of New York. A London printer, he had moved to America in 1760 on the advice of the author and lexicographer Dr. Samuel Johnson, and he opened bookstores in Philadelphia, New York, and Boston. In 1773 he started a newspaper, *Rivington's New York Gazetteer*, which was decidedly Tory in its editorial policy. The paper earned him the enmity of the New York Sons of Liberty, who wrecked his printing shop in 1775. Rivington sailed for England but returned to British-occupied New York two years later with a royal commission as the king's printer for the province. He resumed publication of his newspaper, which he now called *Rivington's New York Loyal Gazette* and, later, the *Royal Gazette*.

The *Gazette* reported American defeats in great detail, ignored American victories, and published anti-American satires, sketches, and doggerel, as well as the poetry of General Clinton's young intelligence officer, Major André. It was Rivingtort's *Gazette* that published the seditious letters Silas Deane wrote at the behest of Dr. Bancroft, which the doctor had delivered to his Secret Service chiefs. Indeed, Rivington and his paper had such a solidly Tory reputation that they provided excellent camouflage for Robert Townsend, who used his role as gossip columnist to cover his activities as Culper Jr.

After the war Rivington stayed on in New York, the target of Patriot assaults and death threats. He was eventually driven out of business and into debtor's prison; he died in poverty in 1802. It was only in 1860 that anyone suspected he might have been one of Washington's spies, a conjecture that was confirmed in 1959 by Catherine Snell Crary of Finch College.[35]

It is not known when Rivington began working for Washington, but the fact that in 1779 he and Townsend became partners in a coffee shop a few doors away from Rivington's newspaper office strongly suggests that he became part of the Culper Ring in that year. British military personnel, anxious to see their names in Townsend's gossip feature, understood that the route to such celebrity was patronage of the coffee shop. It may be presumed that the proprietors' unquestioned devotion to the king removed any inhibition about loose talk regarding British plans and operations, and the establishment was therefore an excellent listening post for Townsend, and probably for Rivington as well.

There is only one specific piece of intelligence for which Rivington is known to have been the source, however. This came to light when Crary discovered a memoir among the papers of Major Allan McLane, an intelligence officer Washington had sent on a liaison mission to de Grasse in the Caribbean and who had accompanied the French fleet back to the Chesapeake. McLane's memoir states:

> After I returned in the fall was imployed by the board of war to repair to Long Island to watch the motion of the Brittish fleet and if possible obtain their Signals which I did threw the assistance of the noteed Rivington. Joined the fleet Under the Count D Grass with the Signals.[36]

What part, if any, possession of the British naval signals played in de Grasse's success in driving off Admiral Graves's fleet remains to be discovered.[37] If it did make a significant contribution, then Rivington's espionage may well have been the most important secret service of the war. Had de Grasse lost control of the Chesapeake to the British, the Yorktown trap could not have been sprung, and the history of the war thereafter would have been much different from what it was.

Cornwallis's decision to remain in his Yorktown fortress after de Grasse's arrival late in August was based on his absolute confidence that he would be relieved by sea. By mid-September, when he realized Graves's squadron had been driven off by the French fleet, the first elements of the

Franco-American column had arrived from the North. It was now apparent to him that retreat inland would be very costly, if not impossible. On September 17 he sent a dispatch to Clinton warning that if he were not relieved soon, the British commander in chief should be prepared to hear "the worst." By September 30 he had word from Clinton that a relief expedition of more than five thousand troops would be on its way from New York about October 5. This was but the first of a series of dispatches from Clinton, however, announcing delays in the relief expedition; Graves's fleet was ill prepared to undertake another engagement with de Grasse, and it was taking longer than Clinton had foreseen to make it ready.

The departure date was slipped to October 8, and then to the twelfth. The expedition did not actually weigh anchor until the seventeenth, and then it waited in the harbor for a favorable wind and tide until the nineteenth. Washington was probably kept abreast of the situation by the Culpers and his other New York agents, but his best information regarding the situation within the British redoubt at Yorktown may have been that which came from Cornwallis himself by way of the code-breaking talents of James Lovell, a member of the Continental Congress.

Lovell, who had been a member of the Committee of Secret Correspondence, was an accomplished linguist and mathematician who dabbled in cryptology. In mid-September the Congress, meeting in Philadelphia, received some of the dispatches that had been sent by Cornwallis to his officers before the British general occupied Yorktown and had been intercepted by the Continental forces in the South. Lovell quickly solved the cipher but found that the dispatches were too old to provide any useful military intelligence. He sent the cipher system used in the messages to Washington at Yorktown, however, correctly guessing that Cornwallis would use the same method to protect his communications with Clinton. By October 6 an officer on Washington's staff had used the cipher to read a captured dispatch from Cornwallis to Clinton, a message that probably gave Washington an accurate picture of the desperate situation within the British fortress.[38]

Several of the dispatch boats Clinton sent to Cornwallis were captured off the New Jersey coast by the Americans. On October 14 Lovell was given an intercepted dispatch that was a duplicate of one Clinton had sent Cornwallis two weeks earlier. Upon deciphering it, he read:

Your Lordship may be assured that I am doing every thing in my power to relieve you by a direct move, and I have reason to hope, from the assurances given me this day by Admiral Graves, that we may pass the bar by the 12th of October, if the winds permit, and no unforeseen accident happens: this, however, is subject to disappointment, wherefore, if I hear from you, your wishes will of course direct me, and I shall persist in my idea of a direct move, even to the middle of November.[39]

It is likely that Washington already had more recent intelligence of Clinton's relief preparations from the Culpers or from some of his other New York agents. In any case, this intercept did not reach Washington until October 20, when the intelligence it contained must have come somewhat as an anticlimax. Cornwallis had surrendered the day before. Clinton and Graves, learning of the loss of Yorktown from a boatload of British refugees as the relief expedition rounded Cape Charles four days later, came about and returned to New York.

"Oh God! It is all over!" Lord North is said to have exclaimed when he heard of the British defeat at Yorktown. The event did indeed mark the end of major military engagements in North America, and it triggered the chain of political events in England that would lead, two years later, to the Treaty of Paris, peace, and American independence. In the meantime, however, the secret war went on.

With the return of de Grasse to the Caribbean in November, Washington was again deprived of the sea power necessary for an assault on New York. Seeking another way to bring the war to a swift end, he looked north to Canada and considered a second invasion of Quebec. He wondered whether a force of eight thousand troops could conquer the province.[40] The same question was in the mind of Sir Frederick Haldimand, the British governor general of Canada. He turned to his own secret service for the answer.

The British Secret Service, Northern Department[41] was established by Haldimand in June 1781—months before Yorktown—to provide early warning of an American invasion and to assess public opinion in Vermont during what has since become known as the Haldimand Negotiations.[42]

The status of Vermont was unique during the Revolution; long before the war the territory was claimed by New York, but it had been settled by holders of land grants issued by New Hampshire, which regarded the area as the western part of that province. To secure their holdings, the settlers established themselves as the Republic of Vermont in 1777 and applied for representation as the fourteenth state in the Continental Congress. The Vermonters were rebuffed by the Congress, however, which was unwilling to meddle in the dispute. The British seized the opportunity to fish in these troubled New England waters and began secret negotiations with the Vermont leadership for reunion of the state with Great Britain as a self-governing British dominion. The proposition held no great appeal for most Vermonters, but resentment of their rejection by the Continental Congress kept them negotiating with the Canadian governor general Sir Guy Carleton and his successor, Haldimand, for the duration of the war. And keeping his finger on the pulse of public opinion in Vermont was one of the reasons Haldimand established his secret service in June 1781.

Haldimand appointed Captain Justus Sherwood of the Loyal Rangers, a Vermont Tory militia, as chief of the secret service. Sherwood was a disaffected Patriot and former member of Ethan Allen's Green Mountain Boys who had taken part in Allen's raid and capture of Fort Ticonderoga in 1775. He soon had second thoughts, however, and switched allegiances, becoming a scout for General Burgoyne. In 1780 Haldimand appointed him his representative in the negotiations with the Vermonters—one of the representatives of the Vermont side was Sherwood's former comrade Ethan Allen—and the following year the Canadian governor general ordered him to establish a secret service in the Champlain Valley.[43]

In the wake of Yorktown, rumors spread throughout the region that a Franco-American expedition would soon move on Quebec. Haldimand called upon his Secret Service for verification and early warning. In February 1782 his military secretary told Sherwood: "I am commanded by His Excellency to acquaint you [with] the indispensable necessity of procuring authentic intelligence of the Enemy's preparations and motions in every quarter [which] is such that no pains, no trouble or expense must be spared to effect it."[44]

Sherwood, in turn, canvassed all his resident agents throughout the Champlain Valley and Connecticut. He already had reports that Washington was raising a new army of twenty-five thousand for a spring offensive against either Canada or New York. He ordered his networks to learn "Washington's particular objective in reinforcing his army with so large a number of new levies," repeating Haldimand's order to spare no expense.[45] This carte blanche approach to the problem boomeranged, however, as it has so often done, tempting informers and subagents to furnish prodigious quantities of that which Sherwood was apparently prepared to pay handsomely to hear.

By the end of February, the Secret Service chief had reports of eight thousand stands of arms and as many suits of military clothing deposited at Claverack on the east bank of the Hudson south of Albany; British cannon captured at Yorktown transported to Hartford, Connecticut; seven thousand French troops with some American support marching northward through the Mohawk and Connecticut valleys; a Franco-American force of ten thousand gathering in Albany; and news of de Grasse's imminent return to northern waters from the Caribbean. One may imagine the distress such intelligence caused Haldimand, who had estimated a few months earlier that he could muster no more than twenty-five hundred troops to defend Canada against an invasion.[46]

There was not a word of truth in any of this, of course. Washington, having put aside his daydreams of a Canadian expedition, had returned to New York and once again settled down to invest the city. Rochambeau and his troops were wintering in Williamsburg, Virginia, preparing for their departure from North America later in the year; and de Grasse, having captured the British West Indian island of Saint Kitts, was shortly to be captured himself by the British. By March Sherwood had received more reliable reports, realized his service had managed to see monsters in the dark, and learned that lesson so familiar to seasoned intelligence officers: reports confirming one's worst fears or fondest hopes ought to be given the closest scrutiny.

The invasion scare having evaporated, Sherwood turned his attention once again to the negotiations with the Vermonters, who, fearing that Congress might suppress their republic after the war, had made new overtures to Haldimand. By this time, however, the handwriting on the wall had become quite legible in London, and the Canadian governor general was ordered to break off his negotiations with Vermont. Annexing the little republic seemed a bit ludicrous now: in Paris Franklin had responded to preliminary British peace feelers with the view that Britain ought to hand over Canada to the Americans, just as the French did to the British as part of the price of peace at the close of the Seven Years' War. The wily Sage of Philadelphia may not have expected the king ever to agree to such a thing, but he surely saw that it was a wonderful bargaining chip.

It took another year to complete the bargaining, and on September 3, 1783, the peace treaty was signed by the British, the French, and the Americans. The historian Richard B. Morris observed: "The peacemaking began as an encounter between innocence and guile, but the Americans rapidly acquired a measure of sophistication sufficient for the task at hand. Neophytes in the arts of secret diplomacy at the start, they were peers of their Old World counterparts at the finish."[47]

And neophytes as well in the arts of secret intelligence, Washington, Franklin, and a host of other American gentlemen quickly overcame their innocence, studied guile, and mastered that which has been called the world's second oldest profession. Amateurs in espionage, they had beaten the British at a game Englishmen had first learned to play in the days of Elizabeth I. Or they had at least won the first round.

On November 25, 1783, the British evacuated New York City under the eyes of the Continental army. Tories and redcoats crowded beneath the forest of masts in the harbor. The Union Jack came down, and the flag of the new republic was raised over the Battery at the tip of Manhattan. Washington spent that night in Fraunces Tavern in the midst of a city he had not seen in seven years. In the morning he arose and breakfasted with Hercules Mulligan and his family, then ordered a complete suit of civilian clothes from the tailor. This was all the reward Mulligan desired for his secret service, and thereafter his shop proudly proclaimed that he was "Clothier to Genl. Washington."[48]

The commander in chief's next stop was the offices of the *Royal Gazette*, much to the astonishment of scandalized New York Patriots. There he met in private with the notorious James Rivington. His aides, waiting in an anteroom, heard "the chinking of two heavy purses of gold" as Washington paid off his spy.[49]

Where else Washington may have gone that day to reward or recompense his New York agents has not been recorded; we know that he must have passed by the dry-goods store of Oakman and Townsend. Washington never knew Townsend by any name other than Culper Jr., but there were certainly many other agents whose identities he knew, although he faithfully withheld their names from the official records.

But there were yet other agents in New York unknown to Washington, men and women whose loyalty remained to the Crown. As the British flotilla passed into the Lower Bay and stood out to sea, one man looked back at the spires and chimneys of New York and recalled their names. Major George Beckwith, a subordinate of the late Major André and of André's successor, Major Oliver De Lancey, had been deeply involved in the Arnold affair. In July 1782 he had become chief of the Secret Service for Clinton's successor, Sir Guy Carleton, and he continued to direct British intelligence in New York until the very day he boarded the ship that was to return him to England. And during those sixteen months his expenditures for secret service operations amounted to almost one fifth of the total spent by Clinton for the same purpose between 1778 and 1782.[50]

As Major Beckwith gazed back at New York over the taffrail of the British warship, he may have reflected that the stay-behind network was not an exclusively American espionage institution.

Part Two

Americans at the Great Game:

1783–1860

Chapter Six

Intrigue in the
New Republic

With independence and peace, the citizen-spies of Washington's Secret Service returned to their shops and farms, but the activities of foreign intelligence services in America did not also cease. Britain, Spain, and France continued to conduct espionage and covert political operations in the United States. In some cases during the three decades following independence, these foreign secret services managed to penetrate the United States Senate, the highest level of the United States Army, and even President Washington's cabinet. The British had by far the most extensive intelligence apparatus, reaching into almost every corner of the new Republic and deep into the national government.

In the immediate postwar years Britain viewed the loss of her American colonies as a temporary state of affairs and was content to wait for the disintegration of the United States through internal, regional conflicts and the voluntary return of each of them to the British fold. To hasten this process, Britain tried to isolate the United States both politically and economically, refusing to exchange diplomatic representatives with the new Republic and denying American ships entry to British ports in Canada and the West Indies.

Essential to Britain's American policy was intelligence of American internal affairs, not military intelligence—the United States had no navy and only a skeletal army—but political and economic intelligence. Such information and occasional covert political action to hasten the disintegration of the United States were given the highest priority by the British Secret Service in America.

Most British intelligence operations against the American target were run out of Quebec and were under the overall authority of the governor general of that province.[1] But the wartime Secret Service that had been run by Justus Sherwood for Governor Haldimand was not the kind of apparatus that could collect the political and economic intelligence London now needed, and it had in any case been shut down at the end of the war; Sherwood and many of his agents had resettled in Canada. It fell to Haldimand's successor, Lord Dorchester, to establish a new intelligence service south of the Canadian border, and he happened to be especially well qualified to accomplish this.

Dorchester had been created a baron shortly before he left England to assume the Quebec governorship in August 1786. Before that he had been simply General Sir Guy Carleton, the same officer who had served as the British commander in chief in America during the last year and a half of the war. This was Dorchester-Carleton's second tour as governor of Quebec, a post he had held from January 1775 to July 1778.

Dorchester brought with him several officers who had served on his staff in New York, including Lieutenant Colonel George Beckwith, the young officer who had helped Major Oliver De Lancey reorganize General Clinton's Secret Service after the capture and execution of Major André. In July 1782 Beckwith had become chief of the Secret Service under the new commander in chief, General Carleton (i.e., Dorchester).[2] Thus, for the final three years of the war, he had been at the nerve center of British intelligence activities in America. With that experience he was the logical choice to head Dorchester's new Secret Service.

Beckwith lost no time in activating some of his dormant assets south of the border. In March 1787—only a few months after his arrival in Quebec with Dorchester—he traveled to New York, which was then the capital of the United States and the seat of the Continental Congress. There he was welcomed by many familiar and friendly faces, for the city had been a center of Toryism during the war and many Tories chose to remain there afterward.[3] Even among some of those who had taken the Patriot side and now held positions of power or influence, Beckwith found a warmly pro-British sentiment. While most did not wish for a reunification with the mother country, they hoped to establish a form of government similar to the British constitutional monarchy. One of his informants told the British agent that there was not a gentleman from New Hampshire to Georgia "who does not view the present government with contempt, who is not convinced of its inefficiency, and who is not desirous of changing it for a Monarchy."[4] As to the upcoming Constitutional Convention, to be held that spring and summer in Philadelphia, Beckwith found few people of influence who held great expectations for it.

With the help of Tory refugees in Canada and England, Dorchester and Beckwith soon spread their intelligence networks far and wide in the United States, especially in such sensitive areas as Vermont, the borders of Florida and Louisiana, and the territories of Kentucky and Tennessee.[5] The western territories, isolated from the East by the then-formidable barrier of the Appalachian Mountains, were alienated from the rest of the American confederation by the insensitivity of the eastern states to the particular problems arising from their topography and location. Alerted by his sources to the political discontent in the region, Dorchester dispatched a secret agent to Kentucky with a plan for splitting the territory from the United States.

Dorchester's agent was John Connolly, a Pennsylvania-born Tory whose intrigues had caused him to spend much of the war confined in American prisons. After the war he went to England and, in 1787, to Quebec. The following year Dorchester sent him to Louisville supplied with funds and authority to offer the Kentuckians British troops and equipment to open the Mississippi River as a commercial route between the frontier and world markets (Spain, which then owned Louisiana, refused the United States navigation rights to the river). In exchange for this aid, Kentucky was to leave the American confederation and bear allegiance to Britain.

Connolly did not succeed in bringing off this covert political operation for Dorchester.[6] He may have failed because of inadequate security. Far from being covert as intended, his activities were well-known in official circles in New York.[7]

Beckwith returned to New York in the autumn of 1788. By then the Constitutional Convention had done its work, and the Constitution had been ratified by enough states to have become effective. The British agent reported to Dorchester that monarchical sentiment had become low-key but was still prevalent and that pro-British feeling continued to be strong. A few months later he traveled to London and gave a full briefing on his observations to the British cabinet.

In his travels in the United States, Beckwith did not operate under cover, nor did he disguise either his identity or the fact that he was a

British army officer. This would have been impossible in any case, since he was well known in New York from his wartime service there, and even President Washington remembered him as the British officer who had served as liaison between himself and General Carleton during the British evacuation of New York in 1783. When he first appeared in New York, he was viewed simply as a British army officer on a casual personal tour, but when he continued to reappear at more or less yearly intervals, it became understood that he was now the unofficial representative of Lord Dorchester and, perhaps, higher levels of the British government. Of course, as the United States government as yet had nothing like a security or counter-intelligence service, his intelligence activities remained unknown. Meanwhile, his overt role as a sort of diplomat without portfolio gave him entrée to the highest levels of the new national government of the United States, including Congress and even the cabinet.

On his third mission to New York, in the late summer and autumn of 1789, he had private interviews with Dr. William Samuel Johnson, president of Columbia College and senator from Connecticut; Philip Schuyler, senator from New York; Henry Knox, the secretary of war; and Senator Schuyler's son-in-law, Secretary of the Treasury Alexander Hamilton. Of these, Hamilton was by far the most forthcoming.

Hamilton actually sought out Beckwith. At their first meeting he outlined a proposal for a commercial treaty between the United States and Britain that would permit American trade with the British West Indies. He also brought up the critical problem of Spain's denial of Mississippi River navigation rights to the United States and suggested that it might be in Britain's own interest to help bring about a solution. France might be of assistance, he said, but if America were forced to rely upon her in that area, the dependence "might become important to West India possessions." Or, in other words, the United States might have to take the French side in any Anglo-French contest for the rich colonies of the British West Indies.

"I have always preferred a connection with you [i.e., Britain] to that of any other country," Hamilton explained. "We think in English and have a similarity of prejudices and predilections."[8]

Hamilton was careful to make it clear that he was not speaking on behalf of the United States government and that he was not authorized to do so: "These are my opinions," he told the British agent.

They are the sentiments which I have long entertained, on which I have acted, and I think them suited to the welfare of both countries. I am not sufficiently authorized to say so, it is not in my department, but I am inclined to think a person will soon be sent to England to sound out the disposition of your court upon it.

Hamilton knew that President Washington had already decided to send an unofficial diplomatic agent to London to test the waters on the questions of a commercial treaty and the forts in the American Northwest Territory that, contrary to the terms of the peace treaty, were still occupied by British troops.[9]

Beckwith may have been startled by such a direct overture from the American secretary of the treasury. He was cautious.

"Pray what use do you intend me to make of [the proposal]?" he inquired. "Is it with a view to my mentioning it to Lord Dorchester?"

"Yes, and by Lord Dorchester to your Ministry, in whatever manner His Lordship shall judge proper," Hamilton answered. "But I should not choose to have this go any further in America."

Just what Hamilton was actually up to remains something of a mystery, or at least a matter of controversy among historians. Apparently, neither Washington nor any member of his cabinet was aware of Hamilton's proposal to the British through Beckwith. While Hamilton had clearly stated that the proposal was his own and that he lacked the authority to make it as an official government initiative, Beckwith quite likely regarded this disclaimer as the necessary paraphernalia of a diplomatic trial balloon. It seems, then, that through his astute manipulation of the British agent, Hamilton managed to establish his own secret channel to the British government, unknown to Washington and in parallel to the overt, if unofficial, channel to London the president was about to inaugurate in the person of Gouverneur Morris.

The recently created post of secretary of state had not yet been filled when Hamilton first met with Beckwith, and it was to be six months before Thomas Jefferson would return from France to fill the vacancy. Meanwhile, John Jay held down the job of acting secretary of foreign affairs, a position temporarily held over from the old confederation government.

Thus, American foreign affairs were in the hands of a caretaker during this period of transition from a confederation to a central federal government, and it therefore may have been somewhat less inappropriate than it might seem for the secretary of the treasury to have meddled in them. Whatever his justification or lack thereof, Hamilton was not acting out of any sentimental Anglophilia; he firmly believed that trade with Britain was crucial to American national interests, a view that was not shared by everyone else in the new government. He seems to have set up his secret channel to London for the sole purpose of helping to bring about a commercial treaty.[10]

The British government became especially interested in Hamilton's overture a few months later, in the spring of 1790, when there threatened to be war with Spain. At issue were the conflicting claims to Nootka Sound, a small inlet on the west coast of Vancouver Island, which was the center of the flourishing fur trade on the Pacific coast of North America. The crisis was triggered when the Spanish seized a British expedition sent there to claim possession of the inlet. The situation offered great potential diplomatic advantages to the United States, which was strategically situated between British Canada and Spanish Louisiana and had outstanding problems with both countries: British occupation of the northwestern forts and Spanish refusal of navigation of the Mississippi River. From London Gouverneur Morris offered Washington his opinion that the British would "give us a good Price for our Neutrality, and Spain I think will do so too. . . ."[11]

The British government, however, by using the secret channel the American secretary of the treasury had so conveniently established, sought to find a cheaper way of ensuring American neutrality. Morris might have been talking tough in London, perhaps even implying the possibility of a Spanish-American alliance in his unofficial negotiations with the foreign ministry, but Hamilton had sounded a far softer note in his private chats with Beckwith, and London had reason to believe the secretary of the treasury was speaking for the United States government, his disclaimers notwithstanding. Instead of negotiating the matter of the forts with Morris, Lord William Wyndham Grenville, the British secretary of state for home affairs (a post that included responsibility for Canada and other British colonies), directed Dorchester to send Beckwith back to New York with the additional role of what today would be called an agent of influence.[12]

Beckwith arrived in New York in June 1790, his second visit to the American capital that year. He carried with him Dorchester's orders to assess American attitudes toward the impending Anglo-Spanish conflict and to collect extensive intelligence of any military preparations the United States might be making. He also carried the governor general's instructions to dangle before Hamilton the prospect of British help in opening the Mississippi to American use, with the caveat that the agent was to represent the idea as his "own opinion."

Hamilton must have been left extremely uncomfortable by this unexpected turn of events. His relatively minor subterfuge aimed at furthering an Anglo-American trade agreement had suddenly become something beyond his control, undercutting the president's own agent, Gouverneur Morris, in his dealings with the ministry in London while misleading the British government into forming the idea that it had a discreet means of whispering in Washington's ear. Hamilton could hardly pass on to the president Beckwith's trial balloon without disclosing the extent of his unauthorized and ill-advised venture in conducting American foreign policy.

He was rescued by events, however. The Nootka Sound crisis evaporated when the Spanish gave in, and British urgency for some sort of rapprochement with the United States vanished along with it. A treaty with Britain covering both trade and the northwestern forts was not completed until five years later (Jay's Treaty), and the secret Beckwith-Hamilton channel had little to do with it.

While the Beckwith-Hamilton channel had not worked out to be the instrument of secret diplomacy that Dorchester and his London superiors had hoped, the British agent's penetration of President Washington's cabinet was an immensely valuable intelligence coup and was especially useful during the Anglo-American negotiations leading to the treaty. Hamilton was in no sense a British agent, of course, but since his own personal agenda made him most forthcoming with Beckwith and with the diplomatic minister sent to the United States at Beckwith's urging in 1791, he could be characterized as a British Secret Service asset, to use a modern espionage term. Beckwith's access to the secretary of the treasury and, through him, to the innermost councils of the United States government, was so valuable that the agent ceased his annual travels between Quebec and New York and took up residence in the American capital in the summer of 1790. When the capital was moved to Philadelphia shortly thereafter, he followed, re-establishing his residence. In all, Beckwith remained in the United States continuously for nineteen months, departing only well after George Hammond, the British diplomatic minister, had established himself in Philadelphia and taken over Beckwith's confidential relationship with Hamilton.[13]

The declaration of war on Great Britain by revolutionary France in February 1793 polarized American politics and led to further intrigue by European secret services in the United States. Federalists, such as Hamilton, who admired the British form of government were horrified by the French Jacobins, while Democratic Republicans, epitomized by Thomas Jefferson (although he did not join the party until 1795, after he had left the cabinet), esteemed the ideals of the French Revolution, if not its terror and bloodshed. President Washington held to a middle course, however, and maintained a policy of strict neutrality regarding the two belligerents.

In an effort to undermine American neutrality, Edmond Genet, the minister sent to Philadelphia by the new French government, commissioned privateers in American ports and secretly organized military expeditions against the Spanish possessions of Louisiana and the Floridas (Spain was now allied with Britain in her war with France).

Washington had no choice but to demand Genet's recall. The French government acceded, but due to the advent of a new regime in Paris that promised to prosecute and perhaps execute the diplomat should he return, Genet elected to stay in the United States and become an American citizen.

Washington's refusal to tilt American policy toward France did nothing to reduce Anglo-American tensions, which actually increased as a consequence of the British war with the French. Each of the belligerents seized American merchant ships trading with their enemy, but in this the British far outstripped the French and virtually closed the profitable trade between the United States and the French West Indies. To exacerbate Anglo-American relations further, Lord Dorchester delivered an inflammatory speech the following February to an assemblage of Indian chiefs forecasting that Britain would soon be at war with the United States and inviting them to take the British side. As evidence that he meant what he told the Indians, he ordered another fort built on the Maumee River, some fifty miles southwest of Detroit, an act that amounted to an invasion of the United States.

War was averted, however, when Washington sent Chief Justice John Jay to London to try to resolve the crisis through negotiation. The treaty that Jay brought home early in 1795 contained many concessions to the British and was something of a disappointment to Washington. Although the president eventually signed it, he had not yet done so when, early in August, he was suddenly made aware of an apparent French penetration of his cabinet.

Late in March the British warship *Cerberus* captured the French corvette *Jean Bart*, which was carrying dispatches to France from J. Fauchet, who had succeeded Genet as the French minister to the United States. One of these—Dispatch No. 10, dated October 31, 1794—was a report by Fauchet of a conversation with Edmund Randolph, the new secretary of state. If Fauchet's account of this conversation was accurate, Randolph had been at the very least indiscreet and possibly guilty of corruption and even treason.

The document was turned over to Lord Grenville, now the British foreign minister, who transmitted it to George Hammond in Philadelphia. In late July Hammond turned it over to Oliver Wolcott, Hamilton's successor as secretary of the treasury. Wolcott forwarded the dispatch to the president through Timothy Pickering, the secretary of war.

The conversation reported by Fauchet revealed Randolph to be an ardent partisan of France. It contained references to the Whiskey Rebellion, an insurrection that had occurred a year earlier among farmers of western Pennsylvania who refused to pay an excise tax on the whiskey they produced and that had been suppressed when Hamilton led a force of fifteen thousand militiamen from Pennsylvania and adjacent states to the region. Coming as it had at the height of the war crisis with Britain, this threat to American internal security was welcomed by the British, and Randolph apparently claimed to Fauchet that it had actually been instigated by them. He suggested that proof of British involvement could be obtained if the French were prepared to pay for it, an assertion the minister seems to have interpreted as evidence of American venality ("Thus the consciences of the pretended patriots of America already have their prices") and perhaps as solicitation of a bribe.

Fauchet's meaning was not completely clear, since it depended upon references to "the overtures of which I gave you an account in my number six," but Dispatch No. 6 had not been among the papers furnished by the British minister (and had probably not been captured by the British). Nonetheless, Fauchet's wording and a less-than-accurate translation of the dispatch into English seem to have convinced Washington that Randolph had indeed solicited a bribe from Fauchet, a conclusion some present-day historians find erroneous.[14] Compounding the appearance of guilt was the fact that Randolph had been urging Washington most emphatically against signing Jay's Treaty, action that coincided perfectly with French interests.

In the presence of Wolcott and Pickering, Washington confronted Randolph with the dispatch and asked him to explain it. Randolph denied having solicited a bribe or having done anything else improper, but he immediately resigned, stating that his indignation at being thus confronted would not permit him to remain in the cabinet.

In an apologia he published sometime later (which included a bitter attack on Washington), Randolph explained that proof of British instigation of the Whiskey Rebellion had been in the hands of four New York flour merchants but that these gentlemen were afraid to disclose it lest their debts be used by the British to ruin them in retaliation. He said his proposal to Fauchet was that the French government procure this proof by paying the New Yorkers' debts for them.

While Lord Dorchester and his Secret Service were not above fomenting rebellion in the United States (as John Connolly's mission to Kentucky in 1788 demonstrated), it is difficult to see what role they could have played in bringing about the Whiskey Rebellion. Nonetheless, this may have been what Randolph believed and what he discussed with Fauchet. But even if the secretary of state was not soliciting a French bribe, he seems to have made himself a French asset in Washington's cabinet similar to the extent that Hamilton had been a British asset.

Not to be outdone by the British and French in the matter of intrigue in the new Republic, Spain got an early start in her own machinations to separate the western territories from the United States and join them to her Louisiana possession. Beginning in 1786 and continuing for more than twenty years, Spain conducted a series of unsuccessful intrigues aimed at promoting the secession and annexation of these lands. These conspiracies were managed by Spanish colonial officials in New Orleans and diplomatic ministers in Philadelphia, but they were executed by American agents of Spain, chief among whom was a man some now regard as the most consummate rascal of his time.

He was James Wilkinson, a native of Benedict, Maryland, who had attained the rank of brigadier general in the Continental army through an unabashed campaign of lying, cheating, double-crossing, and backstabbing, had been the architect of an unsuccessful plot to manipulate the Continental Congress into replacing Washington as commander in chief, and had finally been forced to resign his commission when he was caught embezzling army funds.[15]

After a brief turn at politics in Pennsylvania in 1783, he moved on to Kentucky, where he quickly became a local leader of the separatist movement. The movement had previously been devoted to establishing Kentucky—then a part of Virginia—as a separate state, but Wilkinson began scheming to split it off from the Union. Failing in this, he went to New Orleans in 1787 and set a new plan before Esteban Miró, the Spanish governor of Louisiana. He proposed to work as a secret agent of Spain in Kentucky, dangling the prospect of free navigation of the Mississippi before his fellow Kentuckians to induce them, first, to secede from the Union and, second, to accept annexation to Spain. Miró accepted, and after Wilkinson swore an oath of allegiance to the king of Spain, the governor granted him an annual salary of two thousand dollars and the right to ship goods through New Orleans in remuneration for his secret service.[16]

Although Wilkinson's Mississippi trade was enormously successful, it failed to persuade his fellow Kentuckians to join in the secession-annexation movement. His scheme was dealt a fatal blow in 1792 when Kentucky was granted statehood. Miró continued to pay his agent the annual stipend, however, on the grounds that he was still providing valuable intelligence of Kentucky affairs. But to be sure he was not being double-crossed, the Spaniard hired one of Wilkinson's co-conspirators, the Kentucky judge Benjamin Sebastian, to spy on Wilkinson.[17]

The situation continued to be profitable for Wilkinson, but it failed to satisfy his taste for treachery. He secured a commission in the United

States Army in 1791. While serving under Anthony Wayne, the commanding general of the army from 1792 to 1796, he conducted both open and covert campaigns to discredit him. On the death of Wayne in 1796, Wilkinson succeeded him. Meanwhile, he still continued to collect his annual stipend from Miró, a payment that had now become a spectacular espionage bargain, as it paid for a Spanish agent who had managed to become the highest-ranking officer and the commanding general of the United States Army. This situation, although remarkable in the annals of international intrigue, was actually of little use to Spain, which had signed a treaty with the United States in 1795 (Pinckney's Treaty) granting the use of the Mississippi and New Orleans for American trade, thereby removing any immediate cause for war between the two countries.[18]

The Spanish territories of Louisiana and the Floridas continued to inspire intrigue, both domestic and foreign. In 1796–97 Robert Liston, the British minister to the United States, became involved in a conspiracy hatched by Senator William Blount of Tennessee to raise an army of frontiersmen and attack Louisiana and the Floridas with the support of the British fleet. Blount expected that British possession of Louisiana would enhance the value of western lands, in which he had heavily speculated. Don Carlos Martínez de Casa Yrujo, the Spanish minister, learned of the plan and called it to the attention of Secretary of State Timothy Pickering in July 1797. Pickering confronted Liston with the allegation. The British minister denied any British involvement, although he admitted to Pickering a few days later that "some persons" had come to him during the previous winter and proposed such a scheme, but he denied having given them any encouragement.[19] He had, in fact, sent one of these persons to London for further consultation,[20] but he had proceeded with such caution and discretion that he retained "plausible deniability" in the matter and thereby avoided a diplomatic incident.

The British employed at least one American-born agent in the affair in order to keep the matter at arm's length from His Majesty's government. Dr. Nicholas Romayne of New York was a prominent member of the American medical profession, a trustee of Columbia College, where he taught medicine, and an original member of the New York Board of Regents. He was also a fellow of the Royal College of Physicians, and it may have been through his British medical connections that he was recruited to the British Secret Service. Romayne's Secret Service assignment was to collect intelligence regarding American military strength and fortifications in the border areas adjacent to Louisiana and the Floridas.

Secretary Pickering, having somehow learned of Romayne's role, hired a secret agent to investigate him further. The agent was William Eaton, an army officer who had recently resigned from the service in a dispute with his commanding officer. Eaton had been found guilty of insubordination and other charges by a court-martial, and although he persuaded the War Department to reverse the decision, he saw his military career as ended and left the army. In the role of a disgruntled officer who had been cashiered by the army, he worked his way into the confidence of Dr. Romayne.

Romayne was cautious when Eaton called upon him and offered to sell him detailed information on army fortifications in Georgia. The British chargé d'affaires in New York checked out and confirmed the ex-officer's story that he had been court-martialed but failed also to discover the other facts in the case and therefore advised Romayne that Eaton was what he claimed to be. The physician proceeded to deal with Eaton, who immediately arrested him and confiscated papers incriminating him and others involved in the plot.[21]

Pickering turned over the evidence to Congress. The Senate immediately expelled Blount, who fled to Tennessee one jump ahead of federal officers sent to arrest him. There he enjoyed the protection of his fellow frontiersmen and spent the few remaining years of his life (he died in 1800) as president of the state senate. Impeachment proceedings against him were begun in the United States Senate but were eventually dismissed. Liston, of course, reaped the benefits of his caution, remaining in his post as ambassador to the United States until 1801. Romayne abruptly left the country but returned after a short period abroad, perhaps having realized that there was little the United States government could do to him; there were no laws on the books prohibiting espionage or sedition.

Amidst so much British spying and scheming, it is ironic that the first federal laws aimed at foreign espionage and subversion were passed during a spy scare inspired by France. In 1798 there were an estimated twenty-five thousand Frenchmen in the United States, most of whom were Jacobin refugees who had fled France after the fall of Robespierre but were sympathetic toward the French Directory, which had come to power since their exodus.[22] The Directory had suspended diplomatic relations with the United States in 1796 and had begun seizing or sinking American merchant ships, thereby precipitating an undeclared naval war that was to last until 1800. The presence of so many "enemy" aliens in the country, together with the extreme pro-French sentiment of the Democratic Republicans, triggered widespread xenophobia and Francophobia, especially among the Federalists. In the House of Representatives, the Speaker warned of an impending French invasion of American shores. It was in this climate of fear that the Alien and Sedition Acts were passed in 1798.

The sedition law provided the legal mechanism to prosecute persons suspected of committing espionage and other acts against the government, but the law defined sedition so broadly that it included within the term to "write, print, utter or publish . . . any false scandalous and malicious writing or writings against the government, . . . either house of Congress, . . . or the President, or to bring either of them into contempt or disrepute; or to excite against them . . . the hatred of the good people of the United States." The Federalists had defined it thus to provide themselves with the legal means to silence political criticism, but the move backfired and helped bring an end to the Federalist party in the elections of 1800. The law was permitted to expire the following year, leaving the United States government once again without the means to prosecute foreign spying and political sabotage.

Throughout these first decades of the nation's life, Britain, France, and Spain—each with territorial interests in North America or the Caribbean and all engaged in mutual warfare—had powerful motives to collect intelligence in the new Republic and try to influence its foreign and domestic policies. The United States government had nothing resembling a counterespionage or internal security service, and there were no federal laws against espionage or subversion. Most Americans had yet to develop a strong sense of nationality and were therefore susceptible to foreign allegiance. For some this meant a weakness for the appeal of common

English blood and sentimental ties to the mother country; for others it was a predilection for the ideology of the French Revolution. The Spanish, having neither basis upon which to make their appeal, resorted to gold. The results speak for themselves: both the British and the French managed to penetrate Washington's cabinet through their assets, while a paid Spanish agent became the commanding general of the United States Army.

Despite the remarkable position of their agent, the Spaniards failed to advance their policy through espionage or covert action, perhaps a consequence of their purely mercenary approach. The French did little better, but their failure was probably due to their own domestic turmoil: the elaborate internal and foreign intelligence apparatus that had been established under Louis XIV, XV, and XVI was destroyed by the revolution, and the succession of revolutionary regimes did not provide the secure and stable base needed to build a new secret service. Genet, for example, might have turned over his American assets for development by other French intelligence officers had he not been too afraid of losing his head to return to France.

The British were by far in the best situation to conduct clandestine operations in the new republic. Common language and customs, a large population of Loyalist refugees in Canada, a fifth column of closet Tories remaining in the United States, and the proximity of Canada as a staging area and listening post—all combined to give them the opportunity to establish a first-rate intelligence apparatus within the United States. Dorchester, Beckwith, and their successors never failed to take advantage of this opportunity, and they proceeded with the skill and professionalism that have been the hallmark of British intelligence from the time of Elizabeth I.

The Anglo-American treaty of 1794 (Jay's Treaty) did not mark the beginning of an era of warmth and friendship between the two countries, and as the nineteenth century dawned, there yet remained many irritants that pointed to further conflict. For this reason the British Secret Service continued to cultivate its American assets and carefully watched events south of the border from the vantage of its Canadian station.

Chapter Seven

Espionage and Subversion in the Second British War

By 1803 Btitain was again at war with France, a situation that was to continue for the next dozen years. Napoleon's armies prevailed throughout much of Europe, but Britain ruled the seas. As in 1794, American trade with France aggravated Anglo-American tensions. The British exacerbated matters by kidnapping American seamen on the high seas and forcing them to serve in the Royal Navy.

Lacking a navy with which to resist these warlike acts, President Jefferson resorted to an embargo, forbidding both American and foreign vessels to depart American ports except in coastal trade. The object of this action was to inflict economic retribution on Britain by denying her the raw materials and finished products she normally imported from the United States; the actual effect was to do worse damage to the American economy, especially in New England, which depended more heavily upon trade (and where British depredations were seen through the tolerant eyes of a traditionally Anglophilic Federalist population).

Perhaps unable to believe that the United States could continue to submit to such humiliation, Britain ordered her Secret Service to update its political and military dossiers regarding American readiness for war, especially in areas along the Canadian-American border. As before, the British intelligence stations in Canada were to be the staging areas for the espionage operations within the United States.[1]

Both Dorchester and Beckwith were gone from Quebec by 1807, and the Secret Service duties there devolved upon Herman W. Ryland, a relative of the royal family who had served under Dorchester (i.e., Carleton) in New York City during 1781–82, when he was about twenty-one years of age, and had come to Quebec with Dorchester four years later. He was secretary to Dorchester and two of his successors, Sir Robert Prescott and Sir James Craig, and thereby became something of a power in the administration of Canadian affairs. Ryland was no Beckwith, however: the British *Dictionary of National Biography* says he was "a somewhat prejudiced Englishman," a characteristic not at all desirable in an intelligence officer.[2]

One of Ryland's American agents was John (or James) Henry, a walk-in. Henry's origins and background are obscure, but by one account he was an Irishman who became an American citizen, served as an artillery officer in the United States Army, resigned his commission, and went to Montreal to study law.[3] Sometime around 1808 he offered his services as a spy to Sir James Craig, who turned him over to Ryland. Henry proposed to travel through New England to assess local public opinion regarding Anglo-American issues and identify those Federalists of such strongly pro-British sympathies that they might be cultivated as assets in the event of war. His proposal accepted by Ryland and Craig, Henry set out on his mission.

Henry dutifully sent his reports to Craig through Ryland as he journeyed throughout New England. The task he set himself was not a difficult one and can hardly even be called espionage, since the local Federalists made no secret of their British sympathies. Although he did meet with and interview several Federalist leaders, much of what he sent back to Craig was nothing more than warmed-over editorials from local newspapers. While this material was certainly of some intelligence value to the British Secret Service, it hardly required the services of a secret agent to collect it, and Craig was shocked to discover, upon Henry's return to Canada, that the man actually expected to be paid for his work, and to the munificent tune of $160,000.[4] Unable to obtain satisfaction of the claim from the governor general, Henry set out for England to set his case before the Foreign Office.

Meanwhile, a more effective intelligence-gathering operation was mounted out of Halifax by Sir John Wentworth, the lieutenant governor of Nova Scotia.[5] In November 1807 Wentworth sent Lieutenant William Girod of the British 101st Regiment to collect "accurate information of the military movements, occurrences and intentions" in the United States.[6] In the guise of a Swiss, Girod visited Castine, Maine, on Penobscot Bay, and found "not the smallest appearance of any hostile preparations" at the military post there. He continued on to Portland, Boston, Newport, New York, and Philadelphia and found no evidence of either offensive or defensive preparations.

In all, Girod spent more than six months traveling through the United States. Upon his return to Halifax in May 1808, he reported that neither the United States Army nor Navy had made any preparations for war, and in fact each was in a very poor state of readiness. He found little popular support for a war and reported: "With respect to the general sentiments of the people, I am disposed to think them favorable to Great Britain. . . ." But he cautioned, "Yet are we not to suppose that all those who from various motives have been induc'd to favour the Executive, are hostile to Great Britain, neither are we to imagine all those to be favorable to her interests who oppose the views of the President."

Yet, Girod felt that "a declaration of war against Britain, unless some new cause of dissatisfaction be given wou'd be odious and unpopular, and at this time would prove highly injurious to the interest of Mr. Maddison whose election to the presidential seat . . . he has very much at heart."[7] (James Madison was at this time secretary of state and President Jefferson's heir apparent.)

Reports of the popular pro-British and antiwar sentiment had already reached London, probably from David M. Erskine, the British minister in Washington, now the nation's capital. Perhaps a new height of Federalist Anglophilia was achieved by Senator Timothy Pickering of Massachusetts, who had been secretary of state under Washington and Adams (and, ironically, the architect of the Sedition Act), when he offered to serve as a "confidential correspondent" (i.e., a spy) for Great Britain.[8] The British government hoped to make the most of such sympathies. On February 13 the colonial secretary wrote to Wentworth's successor, Sir George Prevost:

> It is believed that the Leaders and Inhabitants in general of the North Eastern States entirely disapprove of hostile measures against this Country. . . . If this spirit be as sincere and as general as we are led to suppose, no means should be unemployed to take advantage of it.
>
> With this view, I am to desire you will use your utmost endeavours to gain Intelligence with regard to the projects of

the American Government in General, and particularly those of the States bordering upon His Majesty's Territories. . . .

If, upon the breaking out of Hostilities, you shall find the adjacent States indisposed to active Warfare, and willing to enter into any private arrangement for mutual convenience in point of Trade; you may possibly turn this Disposition into a Means of facilitating the Introduction of British commodities and manufactures. The Power you will have of giving the Americans Indulgence in Fishing, in obtaining Gypsum from New Brunswick, or coals from Cape Breton, will enable you to make Arrangements of this kind and such measures will show that as the Eastern States of America seem to disapprove the violence of the Southern States of the Union, Great Britain is disposed to make a just distinction in the Conduct of the War, towards them.[9]

Once again London dreamed of exploiting internal American differences to recover part of her lost territory. But this time British hopes were not limited to Vermont; they included all of New England.

In obedience to the colonial secretary's instructions, Prevost selected a secret agent to send to the United States. The individual was John Howe of Halifax, the king's printer of Nova Scotia and publisher of the *Halifax Journal*. Howe, then fifty-four, had been born in Boston and had come to Halifax in the first exodus of Massachusetts Tories in 1776. The ostensible purpose of his visit to the United States—to see old friends—was therefore plausible.

Prevost gave his agent a specific list of intelligence-collection requirements. He was to ascertain American attitudes toward Britain "and whether any and what measures could be adopted to re-establish and preserve a future good understanding between the two Nations." He was to learn the relative strengths of the Federalist and Democratic Republican parties in each state. He was to assess the chances of a Democratic Republican victory in the upcoming national elections and the likelihood of war in the event the Democratic Republicans prevailed. He was to learn the state of readiness of the armed forces. And in the event war suddenly threatened, he was to give warning by the swiftest means available.[10]

Howe arrived in Boston on April 22, 1808, remained there through the first week in May, making side trips to Salem and Marblehead, and then traveled to New York City by way of western Massachusetts and Connecticut. In June he continued on to Philadelphia and Washington, returning to Halifax in mid-summer. In November Prevost sent him on a second mission over the same route, this time under official cover—that is, as a government courier bearing official dispatches for the British minister in Washington. Howe was back in Halifax in early January.

Howe's voluminous reports to Prevost during his two spy missions provide a fascinating picture of America in 1808–9, drawn by an expatriate who had lived abroad for more than thirty years. They also contain a great deal of hard military and naval intelligence, including a detailed breakdown of the organization, strength, and equipment of the state militias; a complete list of American naval ships, giving the numbers of guns and state of readiness of each vessel; detailed reports on the locations of military and naval arsenals; and so on.

On his first visit Howe confirmed and amplified the picture Lieutenant Girod had drawn. Jefferson's embargo had produced an economic depression in New England and New York. In Boston some five hundred stores and houses were vacant because the former occupants had been driven from urban commerce to rural agriculture. In New York bankruptcies were "innumerable, and to immense amount." The supply of British goods having ended, those wares that had been imported before the embargo had risen in price as much as 20 percent.

"Every one feels that he suffers," Howe reported, "and he is daily led to enquire, Why he thus suffers, and who are the authors of his sufferings."[11] Most blamed the government in Washington, not Great Britain, Howe learned, and the feeling was not limited to the Federalists.

"A large proportion of the Democrats [i.e., Democratic Republicans], with whom I have freely conversed, appear as much opposed to the present measures of the Government as their opponents. . . ."

And, "The present suffering of the Country, though a temporary inconvenience, will, I am convinced, be ultimately very beneficial to Great Britain. [Americans] feel how necessary her friendship is to their prosperity."[12]

Turning from political to military intelligence, Howe reported: "As far as respects military preparations in this Country, there are none whatever. . . . There is . . . as far as respects hostile preparations, nothing taking place in this Country, at present, to excite the smallest alarm in His Majesty's Government."[13]

Notwithstanding the widespread dissatisfaction with Jefferson's embargo, even among Democratic Republicans, the Federalists failed to take power in the 1808 elections, and James Madison became president. Returning to New England in November, Howe found that differences over British relations had actually been exacerbated. If Washington persisted in the embargo, he reported, "not a doubt can be entertained but that a separation of the Eastern States will ensue." In that case, he warned, the Madison administration would "endeavour to preserve the Union by plunging the Country into a War with Great Britain, in hopes that a sense of common danger, will excite a unanimity, they will have no other means of offering."[14]

High treason was briefly relieved by low comedy as Britain and the United States moved steadily toward war. John Henry, the British agent who had tried unsuccessfully to collect $160,000 for his services from Sir James Craig, had fared no better when he presented his bill to the Foreign Office in London. Henry lingered in London until the autumn of 1811, when, abandoning any remaining hope of coaxing some payment from the Crown, he embarked for Boston. During the Atlantic crossing he met a fellow passenger who introduced himself as Count Edouard de Crillon, the black sheep of a French noble family and an intimate of Napoléon. Henry confided his troubles to Crillon and showed him the file of his correspondence with the Canadian governor general, which documented his secret reconnaissance mission. The charming young Frenchman immediately saw a way by which the documents might be turned into ready cash and of diverting it into his own pockets.[15]

It so happened that he owned a piece of choice real estate in the south of France, Crillon told Henry. It was Saint Martial, his country estate at Le Beur on the Spanish border, and it would be just the spot for a former secret agent to find peace and quiet. Crillon just happened to have the title to the place with him, and he proposed to deed it to Henry in exchange for whatever price he could obtain from the United States government for the Craig-Henry correspondence. Henry accepted the Frenchman's proposition with enthusiasm.

Upon landing in Boston, Crillon continued immediately to Washington, while Henry stayed behind to await word of his associate's negotiations with the government. Crillon introduced himself to a startled M. Serrurier, the French minister, who had never heard of his visitor but was so impressed by the documents he carried that he quickly introduced him to Secretary of State James Monroe, who in turn presented the young Frenchman to President Madison.

Few things could have been more welcome to the two Virginia Democratic Republicans at that moment than a package of evidence incriminating the New England Federalists in treason with Great Britain. While Crillon passed January and February in Washington at a succession of teas, receptions, balls, and dinners at the White House in his honor, Monroe and Madison gave the papers a close and enthusiastic—but apparently uncritical—examination. Finally, convinced that the Craig-Henry papers were just the stick he needed to beat the Federalists, Monroe asked the Frenchman's price. Crillon named the startling sum of $120,000, to which Monroe responded that the amount was out of the question, but that he could manage $50,000.

Crillon summoned Henry from Boston for consultation, and the spy accepted Monroe's offer with the stipulation that the papers not be published until he had left the country and was safe from the retribution of angry Federalists. The exchange was consummated, and Henry departed on the next ship for France, the title to his country estate in hand.

On March 9, with Henry on the high seas, President Madison forwarded the Craig-Henry papers to Congress with a statement that the British government had conspired with the New England Federalists to foment resistance to American foreign policy and, ultimately, the secession of the New England states. But after the initial panic had subsided, the Federalist senators and congressmen gave the documents a closer examination than Monroe seems to have done and found, to their relief, that there was nothing in Henry's reports that could not have been read in the editorial pages of New England newspapers. More to the point, Henry's letters did not name even one of the Federalists allegedly in treasonable conspiracy with the British (Senator Pickering of Massachusetts was certainly not the only Federalist who must have whispered a devout prayer of thanksgiving that the president could not prove what they all knew to be true). The Federalists turned from retreat to attack and demanded of Madison that he disclose the names of the purported traitors.

The president, who now realized that he had been misled by his own enthusiasm into reading more than there truly was in the correspondence, could only answer that he knew nothing beyond what was in the Henry letters. Summoned to testify before Congress, Crillon could add nothing more. At this juncture the young Frenchman announced that he must heed the call of duty and return to France in order to join his friend Napoléon in the upcoming campaign in Russia. As a favor, he agreed to carry with him a packet of diplomatic correspondence from Secretary of State Monroe to Joel Barlow, the American minister in Paris, and dispatches from M. Serrurier to the foreign minister.

Crillon was well gone from American waters when Secretary Monroe received a dispatch from Minister Barlow in Paris, whom he had sometime earlier asked to make inquiries regarding Crillon. To the chagrin of the secretary of state and the president, Barlow reported that there was no town of Le Beur in the south of France, no country estate of Saint Martial, and most of all, no Count Edouard de Crillon. The president had paid fifty thousand dollars out of the federal Treasury to a clever young con man, a fact the Federalists did not fully fail to exploit. With Crillon proved a fraud, the authenticity of the Craig-Henry papers seemed also to have been impugned.

By this time John Henry had undoubtedly discovered the same melancholy truths that Barlow had reported to Washington. His later career is as obscure as his origins, but by one account he returned to the espionage game in 1820, when he was sent to Italy to dig up derogatory information about Caroline, queen of George IV.[16] Crillon, whoever he may have been, disappeared from history with Henry's fifty thousand dollars, perhaps justifying his fraud to himself with the maxim that it is impossible to cheat an honest man.[17]

The farcical character of the Crillon affair did not completely eclipse the underlying fact that the British government had sent a secret agent into the United States on a mission of espionage and subversion. But whatever public indignation this disclosure inspired may be assumed to have been centered on those already antagonistic toward Britain and is unlikely to have converted many Federalists to the ranks of the Anglophobes. When war finally came, it was after a succession of much more serious abrasions— for example, a shooting incident between a British and an American warship in American waters—and evidence that the British were again inciting the Indians in the Northwest to attack American settlers. Underlying these events was pressure from the "war hawks," Democratic Republican congressmen from the western states whose agenda included the territorial conquest of Canada and Spanish Florida. Nonetheless, when Congress declared war on June 18, 1812, the measure was passed by only nineteen to thirteen in the Senate and seventy-nine to forty-nine in the House, a less than overwhelming mandate of the American people to make war on Great Britain.

It may be confidently assumed that British intelligence failed to forecast the outbreak of hostilities, for whatever agents the Secret Service sent in 1811–12 to retrace the routes of Lieutenant Girod and John Howe could only have made the same reports of American military preparations as did their predecessors—that there were none and that the United States Army was undermanned, ill equipped, poorly trained, and poorly led. And a British mole in the War Department would also have discovered that no war plan worthy of the name existed and that American military intelligence had virtually gone out of existence in 1783 when Washington paid off his spies and bade farewell to his troops.

Basic intelligence is the relatively static information about a region—the terrain, climate, roads, seaports, indigenous culture, and so forth. Since the end of the Revolutionary War, the army had undertaken a few missions to gather basic intelligence regarding the vast continent beyond the country's western frontier. In 1804 Captain Meriwether Lewis and Second Lieutenant William Clark led a two-year expedition up the Missouri River, eventually reaching the mouth of the Columbia. They carried secret orders to make accurate terrain studies and maps of the West. In 1805 and 1806 Commanding General James Wilkinson (in one of his few good works) sent First Lieutenant Zebulon M. Pike on expeditions to explore, respectively, the headwaters of the Mississippi and the Spanish territory that is now the states of Colorado and New Mexico (the latter mission was undertaken under the cover of having gotten lost while en route to Natchitoches in the Louisiana Territory). But no such expedition had ever been sent into Canada, and the army was completely ignorant not only of the strength and disposition of British forces north of the border, but even of the geography and terrain of the Canadian areas President Madison and the Congress now ordered invaded.

On the eve of the war, the United States Army consisted of 6,744 men stationed at twenty-three forts and posts in detachments of usually fewer than 200 men each.[18] Madison's strategy, such as it was, called for an invasion of the Canadian province of Quebec and the capture of Montreal in order to cut British communications on the Saint Lawrence River and prevent a British invasion of the Northwest. Since the invasion of Canada was impossible with a force of fewer than 7,000 seasoned troops, this strategy depended completely upon the use of New England militias—that is, a large volunteer force from the very center of pro-British sympathy. Some months before the declaration of war, however, the Federalist governors of Massachusetts, Connecticut, and Rhode Island had refused to call out their militias, thereby depriving the army of some 14,500 men.

Frustrated in his initial plan, Madison devised another: a two-pronged invasion of Canada from Detroit on the west and the Niagara River on the east. To lead the western assault, Madison selected William Hull, the governor of the Michigan Territory, who happened to be in Washington on official business (by one account, to urge Madison to abandon any plans for an invasion of Canada because of the tremendous logistical problems involved).[19]

Hull, who was nearly fifty-nine in the spring of 1812 when Madison chose him, had a distinguished Revolutionary War record, having seen action at Boston, White Plains, Trenton, Princeton, Saratoga, Monmouth, and Stony Point, rising to the rank of lieutenant colonel. He was enough of a strategist to know that the president's invitation to take command at Detroit—the western end of a two-hundred-mile-long line of communication that ran through a wilderness full of hostile Indians and along the shores of Lake Erie, then controlled by the British fleet—was an honor a prudent man might choose to decline, and that is just what he did at first. But Madison refused to take no for an answer, and the newly commissioned Brigadier General Hull reluctantly set out for Detroit in April, resolved to do his best in the coming war.

At Dayton, Ohio, on May 25, Hull took charge of a force consisting of twelve hundred militiamen and three hundred regulars of the Fourth Infantry Regiment. A week later he set out through two hundred miles of uncharted wilderness for Detroit. It is typical of the opéra bouffe character of the war that word of the declaration of war, passed by Congress on June 18, did not reach him until July 2, two days after the British had been notified by Washington. This delay proved to be an intelligence windfall for the British, for on June 24 Hull had entrusted his army's baggage to an American schooner on the Maumee River, confident that the vessel would be permitted to pass beneath the British guns of Fort Malden on the Canadian shore of Lake Erie and deliver her cargo to Detroit, where it would await Hull and his column. But, alas, the ship was stopped and the baggage seized, including the general's trunk, which the gleeful British found to contain, inter alia, the muster rolls of Hull's column, with complete data on the number and character of the force, and his official orders.[20]

These documents were most welcome to Major General Sir Isaac Brock, the governor of Upper Canada. Brock had a force of only three hundred British regulars, four hundred militiamen, and six hundred Indians with which to defend the province.[21] This was roughly comparable to the size and strength of Hull's column, but the American commander was at the disadvantage of not knowing this fact. Brock immediately saw the opportunity to mislead Hull into believing he was facing a much superior force.

Hull had not completely ignored the question of military intelligence and in fact had displayed some foresight in sending an agent, one John Howe, into Ontario months earlier to learn the British strength in the province. Not to be confused with John Howe of Halifax, the agent Sir George Prevost sent into the United States in 1808–9, Hull's John Howe was a former British soldier who had served under General Gage in Boston in 1775 and had operated as a spy for Gage before the Battles of Lexington and Concord. He had defected during the siege of Boston, joined the Continental army, and served in the Light Dragoons. After the war he went to the Northwest, worked in the fur trade, and eventually settled in the Michigan Territory, where he became acquainted with Governor Hull. Hull probably selected him for the mission because his background as an old British soldier would have given him entrée to the garrisons of Ontario. Howe returned to Hull with, as the spy later recalled, "the necessary information, the number of men and pieces of artillery." [22]

This information was several months old on July 12, however, when Hull led his force into Canada, and Hull knew that the British might have reinforced Ontario, as tensions had heightened during the intervening period. The general, who was a pessimist in such matters, was therefore ready to fall for such deception devices as Brock's trick of dressing his local militiamen in red uniforms so that Hull's scouts would count them as British regulars. Faced with a continuous flow of such deception and disinformation, Hull quickly discounted Howe's intelligence, concluded he was outnumbered, and fled back to Detroit.

Brock seized the initiative and followed, arriving on the Canadian side of the river, opposite Detroit, on August 15. He had in the meantime contrived to have a fabricated dispatch fall into Hull's hands; the document indicated that Brock's command now included a force of five thousand Indians. Faced with what he believed to be an overwhelming force and fearing the depredations of the Indians upon the women and children of Detroit (who included his daughter and grandchildren) if he continued to resist, Hull surrendered Detroit on August 16 after Brock's initial artillery barrage. For this he was later court-martialed, convicted of cowardice and neglect of duty, and sentenced to death. President Madison pardoned him, however, in consideration of his service in the Revolution (and perhaps in recognition of his own responsibility for the debacle in forcing the command upon the reluctant and uncertain Hull).[23]

The loss of Detroit was only the beginning of the most fumbling and incompetent war effort in the history of American arms. Too much should not be made of the nearly total lack of military intelligence in the United States Army in the War of 1812, however, since intelligence, no matter how good, could not have compensated for the other deficiencies of the army and the government. But the failure to have made even the most fundamental intelligence preparations is a reliable index of the official malfeasance that permitted a foreign army to march through the streets of Washington and burn the Capitol and the White House.

That shameful event occurred two years after the fall of Detroit and a succession of military disasters that included the defeat of a second expeditionary force in Canada, the result of the New York militia's refusal to cross the Niagara River and come to the aid of its countrymen. And a third invasion of Canada, this time near Lake Champlain, was also stymied for the same reason. Pro-British sympathy was so intense in the Northeast that some residents of New London, Connecticut, signaled to British warships offshore when Commodore Stephen Decatur attempted to slip his squadron through their blockade on the night of December 12, 1813. Because the traitors used blue lights to signal, the term Blue-Light Federalist came into currency in reference to all those who tried to undermine the war effort—for example, the New England bankers who refused to lend money to the government to pay for the war and the New England merchants who continued to supply the British forces in Canada.

The abdication of Napoléon in April 1814 left the British free to concentrate their military attention on the United States. There should have been no doubt in Washington as to their intention to send a large force to American shores in the near future. Americans in England on official business—to try to negotiate an end to the war—reported it to Madison in a letter he received on June 26, a full month before a British troop convoy arrived at Bermuda, which was to be the staging area for a landing in the Chesapeake Bay.[24] Indeed, the British did not try to make a secret of their intentions, and English and Canadian newspapers had for some weeks been carrying stories of a coming British move to "chastise the savages." A file of these papers reached Washington in mid-July; they reported the embarkation of thousands of British troops in France bound for America and included such details as the regiments involved.[25] But nowhere in the United States government was there an official or an agency specifically responsible for collecting, collating, and analyzing such easily available intelligence.

To John Armstrong, Madison's secretary of war, the prospect of a British attack on Washington was unthinkable; he couldn't conceive of anyone wanting the tiny, undeveloped city, which he disparaged as "the sheep walk." It fell to the president, then, to make whatever preparations were to be made to defend the nation's capital. Early in July Madison established a new military district to include Washington and the surrounding area and put it under the command of Brigadier General William H. Winder. Winder was a Baltimore lawyer with little military background, but he had one outstanding qualification: he was the nephew of Levin Winder, the governor of Maryland and a staunch Federalist. Madison hoped that putting the governor's nephew in charge of defending Washington might forestall the formation of a Blue-Light Federalist fifth column to his rear as he faced the British invaders.

Winder had virtually no troops to command, however, Secretary of War Armstrong having decided to call out the militia only if the British appeared. Thus, a British force under Major General Robert Ross landed at Benedict, Maryland, on August 19 completely unopposed. Neither Winder nor anyone else in the government could make an educated guess as to its objective. Secretary Armstrong persisted in his belief that Baltimore, not Washington, was its target. Secretary of State Monroe believed the invaders were bound for Washington; he put aside his duties as a cabinet officer and assumed those of a scout, riding about the countryside in search of the British vanguard. General Winder, who had no staff at all and would not have known what to with one if he'd had, wore out three horses riding around the Washington area, substituting activity for action. In a fabulous stroke of good luck, Allan McLane suddenly appeared before him. McLane, who had left his post as customs officer at Wilmington, Delaware, to volunteer his service in the defense of the capital, happened to have been one of General Washington's most experienced intelligence officers during the Revolutionary War (it was he who received the Royal Navy's signal code from James Rivington before the Battle of the Chesapeake Capes). But Winder could think of no better use for this officer than to set him the task of rounding up three hundred axes to be used in felling trees across the path of the British advance, should that route ever be divined![26]

Winder was utterly without order-of-battle intelligence—information regarding the numbers and organization of the opposing force. Because he had no experienced scouts to send out on reconnaissance missions, he was forced to rely on the estimates of frightened civilians who had seen the redcoats advancing and thereby concluded he was facing a British force of ten thousand, which was in fact more than double the actual strength of Ross's column.[27] He therefore abandoned the opportunity to attack when Ross was marching from Nottingham, Maryland, to Upper Marlboro, a location that would have given him the tactical advantage.

The question of whether Washington or Baltimore was to be the British objective was an idle one: General Ross had decided to capture *both* after first disposing of a United States Navy fresh-water flotilla on the Patuxent River. When the navy obliged him by blowing up the flotilla and retreating inland, Ross was free to turn his column westward toward Washington. His plan was to hold the capital for ransom before moving on to Baltimore, a more important strategic prize. But when he arrived in Washington after having beaten Winder's numerically larger force at the Battle of Bladensburg, he found no one to whom he could address his demands, the president, the cabinet and the government having fled the city along with its other residents. He therefore settled for burning the Capitol, the White House, and other public buildings before withdrawing and re-embarking his force in preparation for an assault on Baltimore.

The defenders of Washington actually had fielded two thousand more men and nineteen more cannons than the invaders. The causes of their failure to turn back the British are so numerous as almost to defy sorting out. Nonetheless, the utter lack of defensive preparations that must be counted as the underlying cause was the result of a major strategic intelligence failure, that of anticipating a heavy British assault in the Washington area. And although Winder's inability to deploy his numerically superior force effectively may be characterized in general as the result of his incompetence as a commander, it often was the direct and specific consequence of an absence of tactical intelligence. So, while it would be difficult to defend the premise that the fall of Washington could have been prevented by competent intelligence alone, the disaster must nonetheless be counted among the half dozen or so worst intelligence failures in American history.

The burning of Washington and the (unsuccessful) attack on Baltimore were part of a British strategic plan to harass the eastern seaboard, thereby forestalling another American invasion of Canada. The British raided the coasts of Connecticut, Massachusetts, and Maine and remained in Maine for some months after an end to the war was negotiated, in the expectation of annexing a portion of that state to provide a direct overland route between Quebec and Halifax.[28] It is credibly reported that many of the local residents welcomed the prospect and were unhappy when it did not come to pass.

The war was not an unmitigated military disaster for the United States, however. American privateers did serious damage to British maritime commerce, especially in the West Indies. An invading British force was soundly defeated and turned back by American defenders at Plattsburgh, New York. And a last-minute British bid to capture New Orleans and thereby control the vital Mississippi River resulted in an overwhelming victory by American forces under General Andrew Jackson.

The Treaty of Ghent, which officially ended the war when it was ratified by the Senate on February 16, 1815, made no mention of the impressment of American seamen, the major American casus belli. But neither did it grant any American territory to Britain; and recovering part of Maine and moving the American border southward to accommodate an Indian buffer state between the United States and Canada had been major British war objectives. The treaty, therefore, was in the nature of an armistice that neither side could claim as evidence of its victory over the other.

Yet the United States was fortunate to have survived the war intact, and it owed its survival as much to British war-weariness after two decades of almost continuous fighting with France as to any feats of American arms. Beyond America's total lack of preparedness for the war, including an absence of any strategic or tactical intelligence, the problem of massive resistance and outright subversion by a large segment of the population opposed to the war was probably greater even than those posed by anti-war dissent in the Civil War, the First World War, or the Vietnam War. The sense of nationality by which an American distinguished himself from an Englishman was not yet completely developed, and it was indeed fortunate that no major military campaign was conducted in New England and that the British Secret Service did not undertake a massive covert-action operation to foment open rebellion in the region. Unprepared for the most elementary requirements of positive military intelligence, the United States totally lacked the counterintelligence capacity to deal with even minor episodes of espionage and subversion.

Chapter Eight

The President's Men

Secrecy in government, an idea that has become anathema to many Americans in the last decade or so, is generally supposed by antagonists to be a recent development in our history—perhaps a creature of the cold war—and very much against the traditions established by the Founding Fathers. This supposition, a kind of corollary to the belief that a capacity for espionage and deception goes against the American grain, might seem to be supported by the record of incompetence of the United States government in intelligence and counterintelligence in the early years of the new Republic as recounted in the two previous chapters. But in fact, government secrecy and foreign intelligence operations are almost as old as the Constitution, under which they were properly sanctioned soon after that document was ratified.

American secret foreign intelligence activities received official sanction on July 1, 1790, when Congress appropriated funds to pay "persons to serve the United States in foreign parts." Although the president was required to account for most such disbursements, Congress exempted him from this duty in the cases of "such expenditures as he may think inadvisable to specify." When the payment was for services of a sensitive nature, he needed only to sign a certificate to the effect that the amount had been spent, without disclosing the recipient or the purpose. Thus was born the president's Contingent Fund for Foreign Intercourse, known informally as the Secret Service fund, which not only provided the wherewithal for foreign covert operations, but also represented Congress's tacit recognition that some of the business of the executive branch must be done in secret.[1]

This self-imposed limitation by Congress of its own power to review and approve the president's actions in the field of foreign affairs reflected the political philosophy underlying the Constitution itself. In the *Federalist* No. 64, John Jay observed:

> It seldom happens in the negotiation of treaties of whatever nature, but that perfect *secrecy* and immediate *despatch* are sometimes requisite. There are cases where the most useful intelligence may be obtained, if the persons possessing it can be relieved from apprehensions of discovery. Those apprehensions will operate on those persons whether they are actuated by mercenary or friendly motives, and there doubtless are many of both descriptions, who would rely on the secrecy of the president, but who would not confide in that of the senate, and still less in that of a large popular assembly. The convention have done well therefore in so disposing of the power of making treaties, that although the president must in forming them act by the advice and consent of the senate, yet he will be able to manage the business of intelligence in such manner as prudence may suggest.[2]

Jay's words were based on his experience in foreign affairs, including his service on the Committee of Secret Correspondence. The committee had withheld from the Continental Congress many of the details of its sensitive negotiations with France, explaining, "We find by fatal experience, the Congress consists of too many members to keep secrets."[3]

As to the constitutional role of the Senate in foreign affairs, the Framers seem to have had it specifically in mind that this be limited to the business of treaty making as it is explicitly stated in the Constitution. Thomas Jefferson wrote, "The transaction of business with foreign nations is executive altogether; it belongs, then, to the head of that department [i.e., to the president], except as to such portions of it as are specially submitted to the Senate. Exceptions are to be construed strictly."[4]

Thus, all foreign-affairs matters beyond treaty making, including foreign intelligence activities, were deemed literally to be none of the Senate's business and could properly be conducted under a cloak of secrecy when the president felt it necessary to do so.

The Contingent Fund made it possible for the president or the secretary of state to employ executive agents in a wide variety of overseas tasks, including intelligence gathering and other covert operations. The executive agent was a private person sent abroad on public business. He did not have the powers of a minister or an ambassador, but he could be appointed without the consent of the Senate and therefore could safely be assigned the most secret or sensitive missions. Many executive agents were sent abroad for purposes other than covert intelligence collection, however, and often their role as representatives of the executive branch of the United States government was not hidden from the governments of the countries they visited. For example, the first executive agent was Gouverneur Morris, whom Washington sent to London in 1790 to discuss the problem of the northwestern forts and other outstanding matters of Anglo-American relations, and his purpose was, of course, made known to the British government beforehand.

The first use of executive agents in a covert operation was made by President Washington in a curious prefigurement of events of the 1980s: the secret attempt to ransom Americans held hostage by Arab terrorists. For centuries the Arab states of the Barbary Coast—Morocco, Algiers, Tunis, and Tripoli—had preyed upon European shipping in the Mediterranean, seizing ships and holding crews and passengers as slaves or hostages. Although large maritime powers such as Britain and France had the wherewithal power to end these depredations, they chose instead to pay "protection money" to the Barbary States for the cynical reason that the Arab terrorists kept smaller nations, unable to afford such blackmail, from competing in the transportation of goods through these waters. With the establishment of independence, the United States lost the protection of the British flag and joined the ranks of such smaller or weaker nations. It was not long before the Arab terrorists began to prey upon American shipping.

Between 1785 and 1794 Algiers seized more than a dozen American ships and 119 American seamen. The hostages were forced to work as slaves at hard labor. The conditions of their captivity were barbarous; for example, minor infractions were punished by severe beatings, while major offenders might be beheaded, impaled, or burned alive. Since the object of the Algerians was ransom, however, the hostages were encouraged to petition the United States government to purchase their release.

From his post as American minister to France from 1785 through 1789, Thomas Jefferson tried to rescue the hostages. He advised the government to establish a navy to deal with the Barbary terrorists rather than pay them blackmail or ransom, but when the Continental Congress chose the latter course as the cheaper one, he did his best to facilitate matters. He worked in absolute secrecy through the Mathurians, a French religious order dedicated for centuries to the recovery of Christians held by Islamic kidnappers. In today's covert operational parlance Jefferson hoped to use the Mathurians as a cutout to conceal official United States involvement in the ransoming, thereby reducing the monetary demands of the Algerians. The ruse failed, however, and the Algerians actually increased the size of their demands beyond the price the government could pay.

Washington inherited the problem of the hostages when he and the federal government were inaugurated in 1789. The Congress followed in the steps of the Continental Congress and again chose to pay blackmail rather than use force. The Senate earmarked forty thousand dollars for the purchase of a "peace treaty" with Algiers and agreed to a twenty-five-thousand-dollar annual payment to Algiers for the continuing non-molestation of Americans. It also agreed to ransom the Americans already held hostage in Algiers.

President Washington proceeded to carry out the policy with as much secrecy as remained possible in view of Congress's involvement in the affair. The money to be paid in the ransom operation was allocated to the Contingent Fund, thereby placing the matter under the official cloak of executive secrecy.[5] Washington selected Admiral John Paul Jones, who was then living in Europe, as a secret executive agent to conduct the negotiations with Algeria, and Secretary of State Jefferson personally drafted Jones's commission to ensure that knowledge of the officer's role would be limited to himself, the president, and Thomas Pinckney, who carried the commission to Europe.

Jones died before Pinckney could deliver his secret commission, however. Jones's successor also passed away before he could act, and the assignment devolved upon David Humphreys, the American minister to Portugal. Matters dragged on, and it was not until 1795 that the hostages were ransomed and a "peace treaty" signed with Algiers. By then the total cost to the United States government had escalated to $642,000, plus an annual tribute of $21,000. Similar arrangements were purchased from Tripoli and Tunis during the next two years, but at somewhat smaller sums.

The six-figure sum covered not only the demands of the ruler of Algiers, but the other costs of the covert operation that brought about the release of the hostages; things were done in the Mediterranean then just as they are done there today, and it was necessary to pay "commissions" to several intermediaries to facilitate matters. Since these persons cooperated with the United States under the promise of confidentiality, President Washington refused to identify them to Congress.[6]

Payments of ransom and blackmail did not purchase an end to the depredations by the Arab terrorists, of course. The first Barbary State to repudiate its "peace treaty" was Tripoli, which declared war on the United States in 1801. By then the United States had established a navy, and the government sent a frigate, the *Philadelphia,* to blockade the port of Tripoli. Unfortunately, the ship struck a reef a few miles offshore in November 1803 and was captured, along with her complement of 307 officers and men, by the Tripolitan terrorists. The captives were eventually released, however, as the direct result of an American paramilitary operation, the first such operation aimed at the overthrow of a foreign government. It is notable that this operation was a purely executive action, mounted without a declaration of war or any other form of congressional sanction.

The leader of the operation was William Eaton, the same former army officer who had worked as an undercover agent for the State Department in the Blount conspiracy. Eaton had been appointed United States consul in Tunis in recognition of his service in that matter, and he held that post in 1801 when Yusuf Karamanli, the pasha of Tripoli, resumed his terrorism against the United States.

Eaton advocated a plan conceived by one of his fellow consuls to overthrow Karamanli. The pasha had gained his throne by murdering his eldest brother, who had previously ruled, and exiling his surviving older brother, Hamet. Eaton's plan involved obtaining the recognition of Hamet as rightful ruler by the sultan of Turkey, who held nominal suzerainty over

Tripoli and the other Barbary States, and then providing military support to Hamet. The hoped-for result of these moves would be the rallying of Hamet's supporters in Tripoli and the overthrow of Yusuf. Eaton believed that Hamet would prove a far easier pasha for the United States to deal with than his younger brother was.

Eaton proposed the plan to the secretary of state, James Madison. After conferring with President Jefferson, Madison replied:

> Although it does not accord with the general sentiments or views of the United States, to intermeddle in the domestic contests of other countries, it cannot be unfair, in the prosecution of a just war, or the accomplishment of a reasonable peace, to turn to their advantage, the enmity and pretensions of others against a common foe. How far success in the plan ought to be relied on cannot be decided at this distance, and with so imperfect a knowledge of many circumstances. The event, it is hoped, will correspond with your zeal and with your calculations.[7]

But Madison's philosophical ruminations were not authorization for Eaton to execute his plan. It was necessary for the consul to return to Washington in 1803 and make a personal appeal to President Jefferson before he was given that approval. Even at that, the president and the secretary of state preferred to distance themselves from the project: in case it should fail or otherwise become an embarrassment, it was to appear as something done on Eaton's own initiative. Thus, the State Department memorandum authorizing the advancement of forty thousand dollars to Eaton noted only that the sum was "for use in restoring peaceful relations between the United States and Tripoli."[8] A War Department memorandum recorded the fact that one thousand rifles had been delivered to Eaton but didn't note the purpose. And the State Department quietly transferred Eaton to the navy, which service gave him the sui generis title United States Naval Agent on the Barbary Coast. Thus was "plausible deniability" achieved in 1804.[9]

Robert Smith, the secretary of the navy, had been the only advocate of Eaton's operation in the cabinet, and he was rewarded for his brashness by receiving overall responsibility for it. Wise in the ways of Washington, however, he adroitly fobbed off both the operation and Eaton on Commodore Samuel Barron, the commander of the Mediterranean Fleet:

> With respect to the ex-pasha [sic] of Tripoli, we have no objection to your availing yourself of his cooperation with you against Tripoli, if you shall, upon a full view of the subject, after your arrival upon the station, consider his cooperation expedient. The subject is committed entirely to your discretion. In such an event you will, it is believed, find Mr. Eaton extremely useful to you.[10]

This general disinclination of the chain of command to be very specific about what was to be done and who was to do it worked to Eaton's benefit: since no one had ever heard of a navy agent before, none was certain just where he stood within the naval command structure. This left him free to carry on as he wished, limited only by Commodore Barron's willingness to provide the support of his ships and personnel.

Because Hamet Karamanli was passing his exile in Egypt, Eaton elected to mount his operation from that country. He arrived in Alexandria aboard the U.S.S. *Argus* in November 1804. There he assembled a motley army of mercenaries—Arabs, Greeks, and men of various other nationalities—augmented by a contingent of seven United States Marines and a midshipman from the *Argus* under the command of Lieutenant Presley N. O'Bannon. Together with Hamet's retinue—some 80 Bedouin cavalry and 150 infantry—the force totaled some 400 troops. Eaton assembled a baggage train of 107 camels and a few other animals, and the column set out across the Libyan desert on March 6, 1805. Their destination was Derna, a seaport on the Tripolitan coast some five hundred miles to the west, where Hamet had strong support.

Eaton's march to Derna was hampered by repeated mutinies of the Arab mercenaries and the irresolution of Hamet. Sometimes the American met these crises with gold, and when the gold ran out, cold steel and audacity, and finally with the display of so fearsome a wrath as to put the fear of Allah into the refractory Arab troops. On April 18 he rendezvoused with the *Argus* at the Gulf of Bomba, about twenty miles east of Derna, and on the twenty-seventh he led the attack on the city under cover of a naval artillery bombardment by three American warships standing offshore. That afternoon Lieutenant O'Bannon raised the American flag over Derna, the first time in history that the Stars and Stripes was raised over foreign soil.

Derna was to have been only the intermediate objective of Eaton's operation; he planned to lead his little army another five hundred miles westward to capture the city of Tripoli, the seat of Pasha Yusuf Karamanli. The fall of Derna, however, and the failure of his troops to recover it a few weeks later, caused Yusuf to reconsider his policy toward the United States. He reduced his ransom demands for the crew of the *Philadelphia* from two hundred thousand dollars to sixty thousand dollars and agreed to sign a new peace treaty with the United States if Eaton would evacuate Derna and persuade Hamet to return to exile. The American negotiators timidly agreed to all this, and Commodore Barron ordered Eaton to terminate the operation; evacuate Hamet, his retinue, and the European mercenaries from Derna; and abandon the rest of his little army to Yusuf's tender mercies.

"Six hours ago the enemy were seeking safety from them by flight," Eaton bitterly wrote of his Arab troops in his report to Barron as he prepared to obey his orders. "This moment we drop them from ours into the hands of this enemy for no other crime than too much confidence in us!"[11] It was, unfortunately, not the last time an American foreign legion was to be abandoned by the United States government at the end of a secret war.

Infuriated by the sellout, Eaton resigned and returned to the United States. Hamet returned to Egypt, where he died in poverty and obscurity. The ignominious "peace treaty" did not end Tripolitan treachery, of course, and probably encouraged Algiers and the other Barbary States to resume their attacks on American shipping. The depredations continued until 1815, when the United States ended them by sending a large naval force under Commodore Stephen Decatur to the Mediterranean, sinking or capturing several Algerian warships, killing the Algerian admiral, and convincing the Arab terrorists of the Barbary Coast that the United States government intended thereafter to pay no more blackmail and to answer all further insults with American naval and military might.

The next American venture in covert action began six years later, in January 1811, with the passage of a secret resolution by Congress regarding

East and West Florida, then still Spanish territories as a consequence of the treaty that ended the American War of Independence. Congress secretly resolved

> that the United States, under the peculiar circumstances of the existing crisis, cannot, without serious inquietude, see any part of the said territory pass into the hands of any foreign power; and that a due regard for their own safety compels them to provide under certain contingencies, for the temporary occupation of said territory....[12]

The "existing crisis" had been brought about by a chain of events beginning with Napoléon's conquest of Spain three years earlier, a shock that loosened Spain's grip on her American colonies. The Spanish colonial authorities in the Floridas held no allegiance to Napoléon's brother Joseph, who now sat on the Spanish throne. This left the two colonies dangling like ripe fruit, ready to be plucked by Britain, then in the eighth year of her war with Napoléon and on the verge of war with the United States.

Congress's secret resolution authorized President Madison to take temporary custody of the Floridas to forestall the British from seizing them. If possible, this was to be done through a peaceful arrangement with the local authorities; otherwise it was to be done forcibly. The term *local authorities* was left deliberately ambiguous: it could mean the Spanish colonial authorities, but in the event they were unwilling to cooperate, it could mean a provisional revolutionary government of American-supported insurgents.[13]

Apparently with the view that the latter route would be the most expeditious, Madison and Secretary of State Monroe dispatched a pair of secret executive agents to Florida: General George Mathews[14] and Colonel John McKee. The seventy-one-year-old Mathews had distinguished himself in the Revolutionary War, had served two terms as governor of Georgia, and had represented the state in Congress. McKee, thirty-nine, had represented the federal government in its dealings with the Cherokees and other Indian tribes.

Madison ordered the navy to send five gunboats and two sloops to the Saint Marys River, which separates Florida and Georgia, and to deliver twenty barrels of gunpowder and five hundred pounds of lead to Saint Marys, Georgia, across the river from Fernandina, East Florida. He also directed the War Department to move a regular army force to Point Petre, near Saint Marys.[15] These extensive naval and military preparations were ostensibly made to deal with the Florida smugglers who were circumventing the American embargo on foreign trade, a cover designed to protect the administration from domestic political enemies rather than in any serious hope of deceiving the Spanish or the British. Secretary of State Monroe further insulated the administration from possible embarrassment by committing to paper only the vaguest of instructions for Mathews and McKee: "The conduct you are to pursue in regard to East Florida, must be regulated by the dictates of your own judgements, on a close view and accurate knowledge of the precise state of things there, and of the real disposition of the Spanish Government."[16]

Thus, even though the operation had been sanctioned by a secret resolution of Congress, Madison and Monroe sent forth their agents only after having made provision for "plausible denial" in the event things should go wrong. These same measures obscure just how explicit an idea the president and secretary of state may have had regarding Mathews's plans, but none who knew the Georgian would have been surprised by the direct manner in which he approached his task.

Mathews simply went into East Florida and recruited a band of 250 "insurgents"—mostly American settlers—with promises of land. On March 16, 1812, he led his band to the gates of the Spanish fort at Fernandina and demanded the surrender of the town. The Spanish commander hesitated long enough to make an inquiry of the officer in charge of the American naval flotilla at the mouth of the Saint Marys River: if he refused the insurgents' demands, did the United States Navy intend to open fire? After receiving a suitably ambiguous reply, the Spanish commander surrendered to Mathews.

Mathews had accomplished his mission perfectly, but he had chosen the wrong moment. Word of his coup reached Washington at the very moment Madison was sending the Henry-Craig correspondence to Congress with a message excoriating the Federalists for conspiring with the British to promote the secession of New England. But if the British Secret Service had indeed sent John Henry into New England with the intention of splitting that region from the United States, how did that action differ, the Federalists demanded, from Madison's sending Mathews into Florida on his expansionist mission?[17]

Madison and Monroe, too fond of what they still believed was a stick with which to beat the Federalists, now retreated to the position that Mathews, "in a mistaken view of his powers," had on his own misguided initiative led some inhabitants of East Florida "to engage in certain revolutionary measures there."[18] Monroe revoked the executive agencies of Mathews and McKee and commissioned D. B. Mitchell, the governor of Georgia, to restore the status quo ante.[19]

Mathews, a simple man unschooled in intrigue, was outraged to be rebuked instead of rewarded for accomplishing the task given him, and he set out forthwith for Washington to have a showdown with his principals. Unfortunately, the elderly gentleman died en route, thereby saving the Madison administration further embarrassment, but denying history a complete account of the affair. The *Dictionary of American Biography* notes that he "carried to his grave much evidence that might explain his debatable conduct."

The Eaton and Mathews undertakings were not representative of early American covert operations, most of which were modest ventures in the collection of intelligence in foreign parts where there was no formal diplomatic representative of the United States. For example, in 1793 Secretary of State Thomas Jefferson asked James Madison to nominate someone "who will go to reside in N. Orleans [then part of Spanish Louisiana] as a secret correspondent for 1,000 dollars a year. He might do a little business, merely to cover his real office."[20]

Such missions were relatively rare until the 1820s, which brought the threat of new European territorial conquests in the Americas. France, after suppressing a revolution in Spain and restoring Ferdinand VII to the throne, proposed in 1823 to lead a European campaign to recover Spain's former American colonies, most of which had achieved independence by this time. The prospect of any European power establishing new colonies in the Western Hemisphere was viewed as a grave threat to American interests by John Quincy Adams, President Monroe's secretary of state.

Adams dispatched Alexander McRae, a close friend of Monroe, to Europe as a secret executive agent with the task of learning whatever he could of the French plan.[21]

Adams sent other secret agents abroad to collect intelligence in Latin America. In 1822 he secretly dispatched Joel R. Poinsett to Mexico to report on the situation in the newly independent republic as a preliminary to official American recognition.[22] (Poinsett's successful mission also yielded the bonus of the introduction in the United States of the dark red plant named after the agent that has become a part of American Yuletide festivities.) The following year the Philadelphia lawyer Condy Raguet, who was already serving as the American consul at Rio de Janeiro, was given an additional, clandestine assignment as "agent for commercial affairs"—that is, a collector of economic intelligence.[23]

In 1825 Adams, by then president, became concerned about reports that the Spanish colony of Cuba was in danger of internal revolt or foreign acquisition. He asked Thomas Bolling Roberts, federal judge and former governor of Louisiana, to visit the island as a secret executive agent and investigate the situation. Roberts was in poor health but declined the mission on other grounds: "I cannot, though sinking under a long and protracted disease, and standing probably on the verge of existence, consent to place myself in a place of doubtful respectability."[24]

That a direct request of the president of the United States could be refused on this ground is vivid evidence of the deep-rooted American distaste for espionage. But the ambiguity of this attitude is also evident: it is notable that at this very moment James Fenimore Cooper's novel *The Spy* was enjoying great popularity among the American reading public. And Enoch Crosby, a Revolutionary War veteran who was the real-life inspiration for Cooper's hero Harvey Birch, was about to step forward with his "as-told-to" memoirs and become a national celebrity.[25]

Other Americans were eager to undertake such tasks, however, and sometimes even volunteered. In 1823 George B. English, for example, approached Adams, then secretary of state, and offered to go to Turkey as a secret agent. Adams, who was long acquainted with this native of Massachusetts and fellow Harvard alumnus, knew English to be well qualified for the mission, although he regarded him as possessing "eccentricities, to the point of insanity."[26]

Several years earlier English had obtained a commission as lieutenant in the United States Marines with Adams's help. He served in the Mediterranean but resigned there to enter the Turkish army as an artillery officer. A student of theology who had written a tract against Christianity, English now converted to Islam, adopting not only the religion but the clothing and customs of a Turk. He distinguished himself in the Sudan in 1820–21 but then resigned from Turkish service and returned to the United States.

Despite the misgivings he must have felt, Adams was inclined to accept English's offer. He had earlier sent the Massachusetts lawyer Luther Bradish as a secret executive agent to Constantinople to investigate the feasibility and potential benefits of a commercial treaty with Turkey. Bradish's cover had been penetrated by Lord Strangford, the British ambassador to Turkey, who reported to his own government the American's official connection. Adams, who apparently did not think it ungentlemanly to read other people's mail, somehow came into possession of Strangford's reports and realized that Bradish's mission had been compromised.[27] He therefore accepted English's proposal, instructing him to return to Constantinople and "communicate, as often as you shall have convenient and safe opportunities, any information, commercial or political."[28]

The Yankee Muhammadan did so, managing to acquire a copy of the Franco-Turkish commercial treaty "quietly and without observation" while stopping in Marseilles en route to Turkey.[29] Upon reaching Constantinople, he resumed his Turkish persona, including turban and robes. "Under favor of this garb," he reported to Adams, "I penetrate almost everywhere, and have opportunities of learning the mode of transacting business at the Ottoman Porte which the European dress would infallibly exclude me from."[30]

English succeeded in collecting the required intelligence, and his mission laid the groundwork for an eventual Turkish-American treaty.

The confidentiality of the Contingent Fund and the secret executive agents was challenged by Congress in 1846, when it transpired that four years earlier President John Tyler's first secretary of state, Daniel Webster, had used the fund to pay secret executive agents to propagandize *within* the United States to win support for the Webster-Ashburton Treaty. The treaty, between Britain and the United States, settled some outstanding Canadian-American border questions, including the northern boundary of Maine. Tyler and Webster had employed secret propaganda agents to sell the unpopular agreement in Maine.[31] When a House investigating committee later learned of the matter, the House requested Tyler's successor, President James K. Polk, to supply a complete record of the Contingent Fund for Webster's tenure as secretary of state, including "copies of all entries, receipts, letters, vouchers, memorandums, or other evidence of such payments; to whom paid, for what, and particularly all concerning the northeastern boundary dispute with Great Britain."[32]

Polk refused and recalled the original intention of the Contingent Fund: "The expenditures of this confidential character, it is believed, were never before sought to be made public, and I should greatly apprehend the consequences of establishing a precedent that would render such disclosures hereafter inevitable."[33] He added,

> In time of war or impending danger the situation of the country will make it necessary to employ individuals for the purpose of obtaining information or rendering other important services who could never be prevailed upon to act if they entertained the least apprehension that their names or their agency would in any contingency be revealed.[34]

In extending the range of officially sanctioned covert activities to include "other important services," Polk was the first president to make the explicit claim that the Contingent Fund could legitimately be used for covert action—that is, covert propaganda, political operations, or paramilitary operations—as well as for intelligence gathering. This was no abstract, philosophical point; Polk was a firm believer that such covert action was preferable to all-out war, and when he wrote those lines, he had already dispatched covert operators to Texas and California to facilitate, by secret means, the acquisition of those territories by the United States.

But for the most part, secret executive agents were sent abroad as the pathfinders of American foreign policy, the eyes and ears of the president of the United States in places or situations in which a formally accredited diplomat could not function. There was, for instance, the Baltimore journalist Benjamin E. Green, whom President Zachary Taylor sent in 1849 to the Dominican Republic, a nation not yet recognized by the United States, to investigate secretly reports that the British were trying to establish a naval base there.[35] That same year Taylor sent the diplomat A. Dudley Mann on a secret mission to Hungary, then trying to gain its independence from Austria. He was authorized to extend recognition to the new republic if events seemed to warrant it (they didn't; the revolution was suppressed by Austria).[36] And in 1858 President James Buchanan sent the Austrian-born journalist Francis J. Grund to Europe as a secret agent with a roving commission to investigate a wide range of issues bearing on American foreign policy.[37] These are but three more names from the long roster of secret executive agents that extends into the twentieth century, although the growth of the American intelligence establishment in our own times has made their use relatively rare.

Foreign intelligence collection remained an ad hoc task in the federal government from its inception until the First World War. Gathering and analyzing intelligence was one of the miscellaneous duties of both diplomats abroad and the State Department's tiny staff in Washington. But whenever intelligence requirements arose that could not be satisfied this way, the president or the secretary of state resorted to the institution of the secret executive agent.

Secret executive agents were for the most part amateurs, untrained in the techniques of covert operations, who made up their tradecraft as they went along, often with surprising success. They were the president's men, but they understood that they were subject to disavowal if and when plausible denial of their missions served the best interests of their country. They usually worked alone and never with the support of any far-flung intelligence organization. They risked arrest, assassination, and a host of misadventures that could befall a traveler to the remote parts of the world in the nineteenth century. For all this they received modest wages, paid out of the Contingent Fund, but they were motivated by other things: sometimes by patriotism, adventure, or even eccentricity and often by sheer fascination with what has been called the Great Game.

Chapter Nine

Secret Service in the War with Mexico

Four years after Texas won its independence from Mexico in 1836, Britain recognized the Lone Star Republic and shortly thereafter signed several treaties with it: a commercial treaty, a treaty for the suppression of the slave trade, and an agreement by which Britain would mediate a treaty of peace between Texas and Mexico. All this was done in the hope of establishing both a hospitable market for British products and a convenient source of cotton for British mills. These moves came amidst a national debate over Texas in the United States: slaveholding interests favored accepting Texan overtures for annexation by the United States, while Northern abolitionists, fearful of a new slaveholding state, opposed the plan.

In an effort to discover just what Britain intended regarding Texas, President John Tyler sent a secret executive agent to London. The agent was Duff Green, a Baltimore newspaper publisher and a close friend of the president. Green soon learned that Britain had offered a large, interest-free loan to Texas on the condition that the Lone Star Republic abolish slavery.[1]

Upon receiving Green's report on the matter, President Tyler pressed for annexation, citing Green's information, which he attributed to "a private letter from a citizen of Maryland . . . in London."[2] Tyler expected that the specter of British intervention in Texas, with the inevitable benefit to British commercial interests at the expense of New England merchants, would cause Northern politicians to forget the slavery issue and support annexation. In the event, such Northern support failed to materialize in the numbers needed to provide the required two thirds Senate ratification of an annexation treaty. Green's role in the affair raised questions that soon went to the very essence of the presidential use of secret executive agents, however. Like the question of the domestic use of agents to sell the Webster-Ashburton Treaty, the Green affair challenged the secrecy of the Contingent Fund.

In May 1844, during the annexation debate in the Senate, opponents of the treaty sought to demonstrate that the Tyler administration had given a "cry of wolf where there was no wolf" and that the report of the British loan offer had originated with the notoriously pro-slavery Duff Green. Senator Thomas Hart Benton of Missouri, the leader of opposition to annexation, introduced a resolution to have the "citizen of Maryland," whoever he might be, summoned to the bar of the Senate. The secretary of state, Abel P. Upshur, had recently died, however,[3] a circumstance that enabled his successor, John C. Calhoun, to feign ignorance of the matter and reply that he was "unable to ascertain the name of the writer in question from any documents in the possession of the [State] Department."

The Senate tried again a few weeks later, on June 7, inquiring of Calhoun "whether Mr. Duff Green was employed by the executive government in Europe during the year 1843." Calhoun replied that there was "no communication whatever, either to or from Mr. Green, in relation to the annexation of Texas, to be found on the files of the Department," an assertion that may have been rendered truthful by actions taken personally by the secretary of state before his fireplace.

Not to be thwarted by such dissembling by the secretary of state, the Senate took the matter directly to President Tyler on June 12, inquiring whether Duff Green had received any money "out of the Treasury of the United States, or out of the contingent fund for foreign intercourse, for services rendered since the 4th day of March 1841."

By this time the annexation treaty had been rejected by the Senate. Tyler therefore had no trouble replying:

> Although the contingent fund for foreign intercourse has for all time been placed at the disposal of the President, to be expended for the purposes contemplated by the fund without any requisition upon him for a disclosure of the names of persons employed by him, the objects of their employment, or the amount paid to any particular person, and although such

disclosures might in many cases disappoint the objects contem-
plated by the appropriation of that fund, yet in this particular
instance I feel no desire to withhold the fact that Mr. Duff
Green was employed by the Executive to collect such information, from private or other sources, as was deemed important to
assist the Executive in undertaking a negotiation then contem-
plated, but afterwards abandoned.[4]

   Tyler knew he had lost the annexation battle for the moment, but he
did not intend also to surrender the presidential power to send abroad
secret executive agents.

Tyler achieved annexation of Texas during the final days of his presidency
through the expedient of a joint resolution of Congress, which, unlike a
treaty ratification by two thirds of the Senate, required only a simple majority in both houses of Congress. While waiting for the Texas legislature to
convene and approve the annexation, Tyler's successor, President James
Polk, launched another covert-action campaign aimed at thwarting what
he believed were British designs on the Mexican territory of California.
He commissioned Thomas O. Larkin, the American consul at Monterey,
California, as a secret executive agent. Larkin was instructed to disseminate secretly to local California leaders (most of whom were American
emigrants) the sum of the United States policy regarding the territory:
if California declared her independence from Mexico, the United States
would "render her all the kind offices in our power, as a sister Republic."
If California achieved independence, the United States had no plans for
acquisition "unless by the free and spontaneous wish" of the Californians.[5]
Polk hoped thus to counter any British propaganda aimed at persuading
an independent California to join the British Empire.
   Polk expected the Californians to declare their independence in the
event of hostilities between the United States and Mexico, a development
made likely by the fact that the Mexican government had declared that
it regarded Congress's joint resolution to annex Texas as an act of war
and had broken off diplomatic relations immediately thereafter. Hoping
to avert hostilities, Polk again resorted to a secret executive agent, Dr.

William Parrott, a dentist who had lived in Mexico for some time. Parrott's mission was to pave the way to a reopening of relations; he went in secret so that Polk could exercise plausible denial in case he failed. Secretary of State James Buchanan instructed him to approach the Mexican president and other officials and persuade them "by every honorable means . . . to restore friendly relations between the two republics." He was to do this in the guise of a private citizen; if they assented, "then and not till then you are at liberty to communicate to them your official character. . . ."[6]

Parrott was successful and paved the way for Polk to send Senator John Slidell to Mexico as the American minister in November 1845. When Slidell arrived, however, the Mexican government refused to receive him, notwithstanding what it had told Parrott. The Mexican domestic political situation had become precarious: the acting president, José Joaquín Herrera, a moderate, feared that the more hawkish opposition, led by General Mariano Paredes y Arrillaga, would overthrow his government if he appeared to have implicitly accepted Texas annexation by treating with Slidell.[7] Herrera's caution did not forestall General Paredes from accusing him of just that, however, and the general toppled the Herrera government in December 1845. A few months later Paredes ordered his army to attack an American force under General Zachary Taylor that was occupying a disputed zone in southern Texas. Because the engagement resulted in American casualties on what he regarded as American soil, President Polk asked Congress for a declaration of war and received it on May 13.

In terms of military intelligence, the United States Army was hardly any better prepared for the Mexican War than it had been in 1812. Despite Zachary Taylor's presence near the southern border of Texas since the previous July, he had not acquired basic intelligence regarding the roads and terrain immediately to the south.[8] In fact, one of the few reliable compendiums of basic intelligence the army possessed regarding Mexico was that collected by Lieutenant Zebulon Pike during his expedition to the region some thirty years earlier.[9]

Taylor's disadvantage in the matter of basic intelligence was more than outweighed, however, by his superior artillery in the first major battle of the war at Palo Alto, a few miles northeast of today's Brownsville, Texas, where he drove a numerically superior (almost three to one) Mexican force from the field. Superior training, discipline, and generalship won Taylor several more victories, and by the end of 1846 almost all of northeastern Mexico was in American hands. At about the same time, American ground and naval forces overcame all Mexican resistance in California.

At this juncture Taylor nearly suffered a serious reverse as a result of a major lapse of American communications security. General Winfield Scott was planning a massive amphibious landing at Veracruz to begin an advance across the mountains to Mexico City, a stroke that would bring the war to an end. He sent a dispatch to Taylor in January 1847 revealing his plan and directing Taylor to detach the bulk of his regular force for use in the operation. The dispatch was intercepted by Mexican forces, and with the benefit of foreknowledge of the American plan, General Antonio López de Santa Ana, the Mexican commander in chief, decided to counterattack Taylor's army in northern Mexico while it was in this weakened condition. In the event, Santa Ana failed to accomplish his aim and was defeated at the Battle of Buena Vista, but the battle was closely contested and might easily have had a different outcome.[10]

Having achieved by arms all he had tried to do through diplomacy, Polk now hoped to end hostilities without the necessity of attacking Veracruz and Mexico City; he resorted once again to the use of a secret executive agent. The individual he selected for the job was Moses Y. Beach, the owner and publisher of the New York *Sun*. According to Polk, Beach had proposed the mission himself in November 1846 while visiting Washington. He met several times with Secretary of State Buchanan and once with Polk, advising the latter that he was shortly to visit Mexico on private business, that he was well acquainted with General Juan N. Almonte, a former Mexican foreign minister, and with other prominent Mexicans, and that he believed he could influence them in the direction of the restoration of peace.[11]

According to his son, Beach's mission actually originated with a group of influential Mexican dissidents who feared that a protracted war would result in the "entire absorption of Mexico" by the United States. The group reportedly was allied with the Roman Catholic church, which sought to "save its property from the inevitable confiscations of war."[12] The younger Beach asserts that the group hoped for a negotiated peace in which the United States would be granted California and the other Mexican territory west of Texas in exchange for the assumption of the outstanding Mexican debts owed to private American citizens (next to the Texas question, the major issue of pre-war Mexican-American relations) and the restoration of Mexican property seized in the war by the United States Army.

The dissidents reportedly conveyed their peace plan to General Mirabeau B. Lamar, a former president of the Republic of Texas who was then serving with the United States Army in Mexico. Lamar passed along the initiative to Beach, while an associate conveyed it to the American Catholic prelate Bishop John Hughes. The younger Beach says it was Hughes who brought the matter to the attention of the Polk administration and implies that Hughes proposed the use of the senior Beach, a prominent Catholic layman, for the confidential mission.[13]

Secretary Buchanan's letter of instruction to Beach sheds no light on any of this and contains only the vague implication that the publisher might somehow advance Polk's desire "to make peace on just and honorable terms."[14] It is explicit only in constraining him to keep his official connection absolutely secret, to be on guard against the Mexicans' "wily diplomacy," and to "communicate to this Department, as often as perfectly safe opportunities may offer, all the useful information which you shall acquire."

Late in November Beach set out on his mission. He was accompanied by his twenty-six-year-old daughter and a translator, Mrs. Jane McManus Storms.[15] The trio traveled first to Havana, where Beach obtained British passports through the friendly offices of the British consul. Together with his companions he proceeded to Mexico, ostensibly carrying official diplomatic dispatches from the British consul.[16]

Beach and his party arrived in Veracruz in mid-January and proceeded to Mexico City via Perote and Puebla, receiving close official scrutiny at each stop along the way. He was contacted by the dissidents at Puebla and again in Mexico City and was advised of an impending church-sponsored uprising against the government of President Valentín Gómez Farías. Gómez Farías had come to power in December after the fall of the Paredes government, which toppled in the wake of a series of American victories in the north. He was attempting to finance the war by confiscating church funds, and the dissidents, influenced by the church, were therefore planning his overthrow.

Beach's activities in Mexico City are obscure. His son says that "he held many conferences with men of leading position in the government, as also with leading members of the Mexican Congress, and with high officials of the Church," and thereby paved the way for an eventual negotiated peace.[17] Other accounts (including his own) have him taking a role in the church-instigated uprising against Gómez Farías, which took place late in February and was crushed when Santa Ana returned to Mexico City and took power shortly thereafter.[18] There seems general agreement, however, that he and his party abruptly fled Mexico City in fear of their lives early in April and found sanctuary at Veracruz, which by then was in the hands of General Winfield Scott.

Scott had landed a force of some fourteen thousand men on the coast two miles south of Veracruz on March 9. The landing was unopposed; General Juan Morales, the Mexican commander at Veracruz, had only about forty-three hundred troops and chose to keep them within the city's walls. When no significant Mexican force arrived to lift the siege after three weeks, the defenders surrendered the city on March 29. In his report to Secretary Buchanan, Beach claimed that the insurrection in Mexico City had held Santa Ana there long enough for Scott to achieve an easy victory at Veracruz, which seems plausible. But his related claim to have fomented the uprising may have been something of an overstatement.[19]

Polk's secret diplomacy to end the war having failed, it was now necessary that Scott press his campaign against Mexico City. Once again, the United States Army was at a loss for basic intelligence, a deficiency likely to present major problems in the advance through the 230 miles of rugged mountainous terrain between Veracruz and the capital. At Cerro Gordo, some thirty miles inland, he encountered Santa Ana's forces holding a strongly fortified position, but mounted reconnaissance by a young engineer officer, Captain Robert E. Lee, uncovered the fortress's vulnerabilities, bringing about a decisive victory. Santa Ana fled back into the mountains with the remainder of his army. Scott's use of engineer officers for such technical reconnaissance missions when important terrain obstacles or fortifications were encountered proved most effective[20] but fell far short of fulfilling all of his intelligence requirements.

Having no such position as intelligence officer on his staff, Scott turned over the intelligence function to his able inspector general, Lieutenant Colonel Ethan Allen Hitchcock. Hitchcock was an unusual man to be found in the profession of arms. A member of the West Point class of 1817, he had proved himself an able staff officer in the Seminole War. He taught at West Point and was the commandant of cadets there for four years. He was also a bookish man and something of a mystic; he read widely in philosophy, including such arcane schools as Eastern mysticism and ancient alchemy.[21] In later life he published works on Swedenborg, Christ, and Dante and edited Shakespeare's sonnets. It was perhaps this hidden dimension of his mind that suited him so well to the craft of intelligence.

In mid-May Scott occupied Puebla, a city some seventy miles southeast of the capital. Aware of the conflict between Santa Ana and the church, Hitchcock advised the general to exploit the situation by promising protection to all who would remain neutral. Scott did so, and as a result, Hitchcock received from the Puebla clergy the valuable intelligence regarding Santa Ana's weaknesses.[22]

One of Scott's own weaknesses was becoming critical, however: his supply lines, stretching some 150 miles from Veracruz, had become vulnerable to attack by the guerrilla remnants of Santa Ana's army. To protect the supply lines and also gather needed intelligence, Hitchcock recruited a notorious Mexican bandit, Manuel Dominguez, and his band to serve as a scouting unit, officially known as the Mexican Spy Company.[23] By one account,[24] Dominguez had been a law-abiding weaver but turned to banditry after he was robbed by a Mexican officer. Whatever his motivation, he and his band gave Hitchcock yeoman service during Scott's subsequent advance on Mexico City.

The Mexican Spy Company provided Hitchcock with vital basic intelligence regarding the terrain, roads, and fortifications along the route of Scott's advance. By scouting the movements of Santa Ana's guerrillas, it helped Scott protect his vital line of communication with the coast. And when Scott arrived before Mexico City in mid-August and laid siege to the capital, Dominguez's men passed through the Mexican lines to gather intelligence of Santa Ana's defenses.[25]

Dominguez remained faithful to the Americans despite several inducements by Santa Ana to change sides, but his fidelity and that of his men was not rewarded in kind. Although they were evacuated to New Orleans after the war, the War Department did little more than offer them a meager subsistence there in return for their wartime service.[26]

Mexico City fell on September 14. Santa Ana had fled the previous night, and his army was scattered, no longer an effective fighting force. The remaining Mexicans organized a new government and negotiated a peace treaty by which they recognized the Rio Grande as the boundary of Texas and ceded to the United States New Mexico (including the present states of Arizona, New Mexico, Utah, and Nevada, a small corner of present-day Wyoming, and the western and southern portions of Colorado) and Upper California (today's state of California). In return, the United States government paid Mexico fifteen million dollars and assumed the outstanding Mexican debts to American interests. The treaty was ratified in March 1848, and the United States Army departed Mexico the following August.

It had been America's first truly foreign war (the expeditions into Canada and Louisiana in 1812–15 hardly count as such), and the army learned much about fighting at the end of a long international line of communications. Viewed strictly in terms of intelligence, the American performance deserves only the faint praise of having been much better than in the second British war. Whatever lessons were learned were learned by Hitchcock, Scott, Buchanan, and Polk; there was no way to incorporate them into the institutional memory of the army or the State Department so long as those agencies had no distinct intelligence organs.

In all, it was a most meager rehearsal for the great conflict that was soon to come.

Part Three

ADVENT OF THE PROFESSIONALS:

The Civil War

Chapter Ten

Allan Pinkerton and the Civil War

The Civil War did not burst upon the nation suddenly and without warning. Keen observers had seen the shadows of coming events years earlier, and none could have misread the signs during that secession winter of 1860–61. Washington, in the interregnum between election day and inauguration day, had become a place of rumor and dark apprehensions. South Carolina had seceded from the Union on December 20; Mississippi, Florida, Alabama, Georgia, Louisiana, and Texas followed suit during the next few weeks. The seceded states had begun taking possession of Federal property within their borders, including forts, arsenals, and navy yards. During the first week in February, representatives of the seceded states met in Montgomery, Alabama, and proclaimed the Confederate States of America. By March, when the new president-elect arrived in Washington for his inauguration, there was no longer any question of whether there would be war, only when, where, and how it would begin. It is difficult to understand, therefore, that when the Confederate artillery shells began to fall on Fort Sumter on April 12, neither the Confederates nor the Federals had made the least preparations in the matter of military intelligence.

Although the Confederacy had fired the first shot, its strategic stance was passive; it had already achieved its principal war objective: secession from the Union. The ball was in the North's court. Southern optimists found reasons to hope the North would prefer to accept the new status quo rather than fight a major war to recover the seceded states.

For its part, the North found reasons to hope for recovery of the seceded states without bloodshed. Within a week of the fall of Fort Sumter, the United States Navy began a blockade of the South that soon extended from Virginia to Texas. This, and a federal prohibition against trade with the seceded states, was aimed at the economic strangulation of the South and the interdiction of military supplies from abroad. General Scott formulated the Anaconda Plan (as it was somewhat derisively called by his detractors), which called for continuing the blockade, achieving the physical and economic division of the Confederacy by controlling the Mississippi River, and ensuring the national government at Washington through military control of northern Virginia. With the South thus isolated and cut in two, Scott hoped that Unionist sentiment in the Confederacy would eventually prevail and that the rebellious states would return to the Union peacefully.

This bilateral wishful thinking resulted in a three-month "phony war" in which no significant military engagements took place. Both sides took advantage of the lull to prepare for a real war, however, including establishing intelligence apparatuses.

The Union's most serious immediate problem lay in the field of counterespionage and countersubversion. There was widespread secessionist sentiment in the border states of Missouri, Kentucky, Delaware, and Maryland. The nation's capital lay some sixty miles south of the Mason-Dixon Line, deep within an area of divided loyalties. Indeed, secessionist feeling was so strong in Maryland that Lincoln was forced to travel to Washington for his inauguration in disguise, to thwart a plot to assassinate him as he changed trains in Baltimore. If the president needed a further reminder that Baltimore, lying athwart the major railroad route to the Northeast, was a hotbed of secession, it came on April 19, when a mob attacked units of the Pennsylvania and Massachusetts militias passing through the city en route to Washington.

The Baltimore Plot to assassinate Lincoln had been discovered and frustrated by Allan Pinkerton, a forty-one-year-old Scottish-born private detective. Lincoln was acquainted with the man: Pinkerton's detective agency held a contract to provide security for the Illinois Central Railroad, and Lincoln had been an attorney for the line. In a time when there were no federal or state police organizations and the responsibilities of local constabularies stopped at the city limits, Pinkerton's private agency was the closest thing to a national investigative bureau.

On April 21, nine days after Fort Sumter fell, Allan Pinkerton offered his services and those of his detective staff to Lincoln "in the way of obtaining information of the movements of the Traitors, or Safely conveying your letters or dispatches."[1] Although the Federal government lacked any kind of internal security agency other than the army, nothing came of Pinkerton's proposal at that moment.[2]

When he returned from Washington to his Chicago headquarters, Pinkerton heard from Major General George B. McClellan, who had recently taken command of the army's Department of the Ohio. McClellan had been second in the West Point class of 1846, had served in the Mexican War, and was one of the engineer officers who carried out technical reconnaissance missions for General Scott in the advance from Veracruz. In 1857 he resigned his commission to become chief engineer of the Illinois Central Railroad. Later he became vice president of the line and in 1860, president of the Ohio and Mississippi Railroad. During his railroad service he became well acquainted with Lincoln and formed a close personal friendship with Allan Pinkerton, whose agency did detective work for both lines. Now returned to active duty, he asked the private detective to establish and run an intelligence service for him. Pinkerton agreed and moved his staff to Cincinnati, where McClellan had his headquarters. In July McClellan went to Washington to take command of the Army of the Potomac, which was demoralized and disorganized in the wake of the Union defeat at Bull Run. In August Pinkerton and his detectives followed the general to Washington and became the Secret Service of the Army of the Potomac.

Pinkerton's name was well-known and virtually synonymous with private investigation, so he adopted the pseudonym Major E. J. Allen while serving as McClellan's chief of intelligence. He had both an intelligence and a counterintelligence responsibility; in the latter capacity he was responsible for catching Confederate spies in the North, an activity that was quite similar to his peacetime detective work and one in which he and his staff acquitted themselves well.

One of Pinkerton's first counterespionage cases was that of Rose O'Neal Greenhow, a forty-four-year-old widow and lady of fashion. A native of Port Tobacco, Maryland, a lifelong resident of Washington, and a prominent figure in the city's social life, Greenhow was a passionate partisan of the Southern cause. She was well situated to collect intelligence for the Confederacy; such Washington notables as William Seward, now the new secretary of state, and, Charles Francis Adams, soon to be the American minister to Britain, were frequent guests at her salons and dinners, as were powerful senators and congressmen. Soon after Fort Sumter she was recruited as a spy by Thomas Jordan, ex–United States Army officer, currently a lieutenant colonel in the Confederate army and adjutant general to Brigadier General P. G. T. Beauregard. Jordan made her his principal agent and head of the espionage ring he had established in Washington.

According to General Beauregard, intelligence supplied him by Greenhow was crucial to his victory over Federal forces at Bull Run in July 1861. There is no doubt that Beauregard had the advantage of Greenhow's reports at Bull Run, but exactly what role this intelligence played in the Confederate victory remains somewhat uncertain and is questioned by many present-day students of the war. In his memoirs Beauregard claimed that a ciphered dispatch from Greenhow was the reason he asked to be reinforced by General Joseph L. Johnston, a move that seems to have been crucial to the Confederate victory. But some historians have pointed out that he did not make the request until after his outposts had been driven back by the advancing Federals.[3] Beauregard may have unwisely discounted Greenhow's report yet later attributed his moves to it, thereby striking a blow for gallantry while at the same time covering up a mistake that could have had serious consequences.

Greenhow's espionage did not fail to attract the attention of the Federal authorities. Soon after Pinkerton moved his operation to Washington, he was asked by Assistant Secretary of War Thomas A. Scott to place Greenhow's Sixteenth Street home under surveillance. Pinkerton handled the matter personally, proceeding much in the manner of a divorce-case investigator, and managed to observe an army officer visit the spy to exchange military information for her favors. The detective reported the results of his surveillance to Scott, who immediately ordered the arrest of the officer involved and of Greenhow shortly thereafter.[4] Other members of her network were rounded up during the next day or so as they appeared on her doorstep. She and several female members of her ring were held at her home under house arrest until the following January, when she, having been discovered attempting to send further intelligence to Jordan, was moved to the Old Capitol Prison.[5]

Greenhow was released and exiled to the Confederacy in June 1862. She was warmly received by the Confederate government and rewarded for her secret services. In August 1863 she traveled to Europe, where she was presented to Napoléon III and to Queen Victoria, both sympathetic to the Southern cause. While in England she wrote and published an account of her experiences,[6] which was both a financial success and an effective piece of Confederate propaganda. In August 1864 she returned to the Confederacy carrying dispatches from Confederate agents in Europe. The ship on which she was traveling ran aground in a storm while attempting to run the Federal blockade outside Wilmington, North Carolina. Greenhow was drowned while attempting to land in a small boat. She was buried with Confederate military honors.

In the field of positive military intelligence, Pinkerton failed to match his effectiveness as a chief of counterintelligence. His failures did not arise from an inability to operate behind Confederate lines, however. He sent many of his detectives deep into Confederate territory "for the purpose of obtaining information concerning the numbers, equipments, movements, and intentions of the enemy, as well as to ascertain the general feeling of the Southern people in regard to the war."[7] In the guise of "a gentle-man from Georgia," Pinkerton himself made two undercover reconnais-sance missions into western Virginia (today's West Virginia), reporting to McClellan on such basic intelligence as roads, rivers, and bridges, as well as Confederate military strength and disposition and even the names and residences of local Union sympathizers.[8]

Pinkerton's most valuable undercover agent in these behind-the-lines operations was Timothy Webster, a former New York City policeman whom Pinkerton had hired several years before the war. Webster not only pene-trated the Confederate capital of Richmond, Virginia; he also managed to persuade the Confederate secretary of war Judah P. Benjamin to accept his services as a secret courier between Richmond and the secessionist underground in Baltimore, a role with a double bonus: he not only was able to read the secret Confederate communications before delivering them, but he also was able to report regularly in person to Pinkerton all the intelligence he collected in the Confederate capital.

Webster made two round trips between Richmond and Baltimore during the winter of 1861–62, collecting some of the most valuable intelligence that Pinkerton's staff was to acquire at any time during the war. Unfortunately, two other Pinkerton agents, sent to Richmond to support Webster during his second mission, were apprehended and, to save their own lives, turned Webster in. The two were eventually released, but Webster was arrested, tried, convicted of espionage, and hanged.

Pinkerton's positive intelligence failures were in the matter of order of battle: the identification, the organization, and, especially, the strength of the enemy forces. Pinkerton consistently overestimated Confederate strength, thereby encouraging the unfortunate tendency of General McClellan to drag his feet in prosecuting the war.

After taking charge of the Army of the Potomac in July 1861, McClellan discovered excuse after excuse to postpone offensive operations against the Confederate army. Late the following January a finally exasperated president issued General War Order No. 1, which decreed a general Union advance. Nonetheless, McClellan managed further to drag his feet for more than another month. At last, in March, he moved eighty-five thousand troops—most of the Army of the Potomac—by water from Washington to Fort Monroe, Virginia, at the tip of the peninsula formed by the York and James rivers. He planned to advance up the peninsula and capture the Confederate capital of Richmond, bringing the war to an end. Pinkerton went along on the expedition, of course.

McClellan halted his advance up the peninsula after one day's march when he encountered Confederate resistance at Yorktown. Although there were in fact no more than 17,000 Confederates holding an eight-mile line across the peninsula, McClellan believed he was facing a far larger force. Instead of attacking, he settled down for a protracted siege that lasted nearly a month. The delay gave the Confederates time to move in reinforcements, building their strength along the Yorktown line to 60,000. At the same time, however, McClellan's peninsula force grew to 112,000.[9] But although he outnumbered the enemy almost two to one, he believed there were twice as many Confederates facing him as there actually were. The source of this grossly erroneous intelligence estimate was Pinkerton.[10]

Pinkerton had been seriously overestimating Confederate strength almost from the beginning of his service as McClellan's chief of intelligence. In August, shortly after he moved his detective staff to Washington, he advised McClellan that there were at least 100,000 Confederate troops across the Potomac River in Virginia, a figure more than double the real number.[11] In November he estimated that there were 126,000 Confederate troops in Virginia, a wildly inflated figure. He estimated that their strength at Manassas alone was between 80,000 and 90,000[12]; in fact, only 35,000 Confederate troops were positioned at the strategic railroad junction. McClellan reported Pinkerton's figures to Lincoln and used them to justify his temporizing to the impatient commander in chief.

Even after the Confederates withdrew from Yorktown and began to retreat up the peninsula, Pinkerton continued to overestimate their strength; and in June, when an infusion of troops under General Thomas J. "Stonewall" Jackson brought the strength of the Confederate forces defending Richmond to 80,000, Pinkerton reported to his chief that he was facing a force of 200,000.[13] Having been thus advised that he was outnumbered almost two to one, McClellan yielded the strategic initiative to General Robert E. Lee, who was now in command of the Confederate defenders, and took his actually superior force back down the peninsula to Harrison's Landing, where he entrenched and awaited orders to abandon the campaign against the Confederate capital.[14]

Some historians have attributed Pinkerton's inflated estimates to the lack of military experience of his detectives, which supposedly rendered them incapable of accurate observation of Confederate forces during their behind-the-lines secret reconnaissance missions. Those who have closely examined the way Pinkerton arrived at his estimates, however, fault not his raw data but the analytical process by which he converted them into aggregate figures.[15] It seems unlikely that McClellan received these enormous estimates without once reviewing Pinkerton's arithmetic, and a commander less prone to hesitancy in the field would probably have discounted the figures or directed the private detective to use a

more realistic method of computing them. But Pinkerton's inflated estimates fitted perfectly with his chief's propensity always to want more time
and more troops before acting, a characteristic of McClellan that Lincoln
dubbed the slows. Historian T. Harry Williams wrote, "Either Pinkerton
was completely incompetent, or he sensed that McClellan wanted the
enemy army magnified as an excuse for inaction. . . . McClellan believed,
or made himself believe, Pinkerton's calculations."[16]

Pinkerton was fiercely loyal to McClellan and seems to have regarded
his service as a personal one to his friend and former business associate rather than as a professional one to the United States government.
Thus the Confederates were not the only targets of his espionage; he also
spied on other army officers and even on Lincoln and his cabinet when he
believed McClellan's best interests were at stake. After the Army of the
Potomac evacuated the peninsula in mid-August and McClellan's personal
stock was declining rapidly in Washington, Pinkerton reported to his friend
frequently on the machinations of his "enemies" in the capital. Late in
August he wrote the general that one source had advised him that Lincoln,
Secretary of War Edwin Stanton, and General Henry W. Halleck, the general in chief of the army, planned to replace McClellan as commander of
the Army of the Potomac and leave him in command of the Federal outpost at Fort Monroe. "This will keep you and your friends quiet and thus
enable them to get rid of you and your dangerous influence," he reported.[17]

"Today I thought after I had seen Lincoln leave the White House that
I would call on Nicolay (Prest's. Private Secy.) and did so," he reported
several days later. "The conversation soon turned to you. . . ." He gave
McClellan a detailed summary of what "your enemies" were saying to
the president.[18]

And a few days later:

> The Prest. is several times every day at Halleck's house or
> headquarters and from all I can learn Halleck lays all his plans
> before him for approval. This is understood to be very agreeable
> to Lincoln who desires to know all and will probably then tell
> it to the first M.C. [member of Congress] who calls—and whom

he wishes to conciliate, who in turn retails it to the newspaper reporters and the [illegible] and excitable crowd at Willard's [Hotel].

I learn that the rulers more than ever dread doing anything with you since the Army of the Potomac began to arrive at Alexandria. I find that many of the general officers are expressing themselves very strongly in favor of your having moved on Richmond. . . .[19]

McClellan never admonished the private detective to cease his political espionage. Indeed, even before the Peninsula Campaign the general himself believed he was the victim of a conspiracy. Recalling in his memoirs that he had been ordered to leave a small part of his force in northern Virginia to protect Washington at the outset of that campaign, he wrote, "I had now only too good reasons to feel assured that the administration, and especially the Secretary of War, were inimical to me and did not desire my success."[20] McClellan believed that he had failed because he had been stabbed in the back by Lincoln and Stanton, and everything Pinkerton reported seemed to confirm that to him.

One incidental outcome of the Peninsula Campaign was the ascent of General Robert E. Lee, who succeeded General Joseph Johnston in the overall command of the Confederate forces in Virginia after the latter was seriously wounded in the defense of Richmond. Lee believed that the South would eventually lose if it persisted in its defensive strategy and yielded to the Union the initiative to choose the times and places of the major battles. As McClellan withdrew from the peninsula, Lee persuaded the Confederate president Jefferson Davis to approve a plan for a bold offensive strike through Maryland and into Pennsylvania. Lee's plan called for the capture of Harrisburg, Pennsylvania, a move that would cut the Union's major east-west railroad link. The Confederate commander's venture was to fail as the result of an intelligence coup by McClellan, perhaps the most important of the war. It was not the result of careful, professional intelligence work, however, nor was it achieved by Pinkerton. It was plain dumb luck.

As soon as McClellan began to remove his army from the peninsula, Lee moved his army north, engaging and defeating a Union force under General John Pope at the Second Battle of Bull Run on August 29 and 30. Lee pushed on across the Potomac River into Maryland. To safeguard his line of supply through northern Virginia, he planned to reduce the Federal garrison at Harpers Ferry. On September 9 he issued Special Orders No. 191, which divided his army into four parts; three of the elements were to converge on Harpers Ferry, while the fourth advanced to the vicinity of Hagerstown, Maryland. Four days later a copy of the orders was found by a Union soldier, wrapped around three cigars in a field at Frederick, Maryland, where the Confederates had been bivouacked when Lee issued it. The document was delivered to McClellan, who recognized its authenticity and importance.[21]

McClellan sent his cavalry to monitor Confederate progress in executing Lee's order while at the same time cautiously moving his army toward the divided Confederate force.[22] Lee's own reconnaissance discovered McClellan's advance, and he hastily reunited his force at a defensive position behind Antietam Creek, near Sharpsburg, Maryland. The ensuing battle on September 17 was the bloodiest day of the war. It ended in a Federal victory in the sense that McClellan held the field while Lee turned back to Virginia.

McClellan's failure to follow up his temporary advantage and pursue Lee into Virginia only confirmed a decision already tentatively reached by Lincoln: he replaced him as commander of the Army of the Potomac on November 5. Believing his friend had been dealt with unjustly, Pinkerton resigned shortly thereafter and took his detective force back to Chicago. For the moment the Army of the Potomac had no intelligence service whatever.

Chapter Eleven

Civil War Intelligence: Sources and Methods

When he wrote his Civil War memoirs a quarter century later, Pinkerton so inflated his exploits as to give the impression that he had been chief of intelligence for the Federal government, not simply General McClellan's intelligence officer. In fact, the functions of intelligence and counterespionage were never centralized in a single, national Federal agency. Military intelligence was left to individual field commanders, both Union and Confederate, to deal with (and sometimes to ignore) as they saw fit. There were no standard procedures on either side. Intelligence was the responsibility of the command's provost marshal in many cases, but sometimes it was assigned to the adjutant, the signal officer, or the chief of staff, and sometimes the commander himself took a major hand in the matter.

One of the more enduring espionage myths that obscure the facts of Civil War intelligence is the belief that the United States Secret Service existed during the war and was the major Federal intelligence and counter-intelligence agency. The United States Treasury Department agency of that name was not established until shortly after the war, however, and it had no intelligence function until several decades later. The popular error is partly the fault of Pinkerton, who in his war memoirs styled himself "Chief of the United States Secret Service."[1] But most of the blame should probably be allocated to Lafayette C. Baker, who outdid even Pinkerton in overstating his wartime role when he entitled his Civil War memoirs *The History of the United States Secret Service*.

Baker was a former member of the San Francisco Vigilance Committee, as the notorious local vigilante society was called. Thirty-four years of age at the outbreak of the Civil War, he went to Washington and offered his services as a spy to General Scott. Scott sent him on an espionage mission into Virginia in July 1861 to learn the strength and disposition of Confederate forces at Manassas and elsewhere in the state. Baker returned safely after having been arrested and imprisoned in Richmond for a time on suspicion of espionage. Scott then recommended him to Secretary of War Simon Cameron, who hired him to catch blockade runners smuggling arms and ammunition to the Confederates. Shortly thereafter, he was hired by Secretary of State Seward to establish and run a counterespionage service for the Department of State. In February 1862 Baker and the staff of detectives he had hired were transferred back to the War Department, and he began reporting to the new secretary of war, Edwin M. Stanton.[2]

Headquartered in a building at 217 Pennsylvania Avenue, Baker and his detectives arrested some Confederate spies, most notably the legendary Belle Boyd, but rounded up a far greater number of suspected Southern sympathizers, army deserters, bounty jumpers, war profiteers, prostitutes, and corrupt government employees.

The appellation *United States Secret Service* was a postwar innovation of Baker or his publisher. During the war Baker styled his unit the National Detective Bureau, and sometimes the National Detective Police Department, titles that connote a much larger area of responsibility than he ever actually held.[3] Officially the unit had no name, and Baker's title was provost marshal of the War Department. Lines of responsibility were loosely drawn at the time (e.g., Pinkerton's charter overlapped Baker's from August 1861 until January 1863). Baker's activities seem to have been concentrated in counterespionage and miscellaneous law enforcement within the greater Washington area, although he had a small field office in New York City for a time, and his agents sometimes ranged as far afield as Canada.[4] Notwithstanding the several grandiose names Baker gave his little unit, it was not a government-wide intelligence or counterespionage agency.

The mistaken notion that the Confederacy had a government-wide central intelligence agency has been encouraged by the fact that there *was* a national-level agency in Richmond known as the Signal and Secret Service Bureau. A full account of the charter and history of this agency does not exist because its official records were lost (by some accounts, destroyed) when the Confederate government fled Richmond in early April 1865. What is known of it has been assembled by historians from such fragmentary sources as dispatches, personal correspondence, and memoirs.

The Signal Bureau was established within the Confederate War Department in May 1862 and occupied a suite of offices among other bureaus of the department on Bank Street in Richmond. "The great majority of people in Richmond thought that it was only a sort of headquarters for the officers and men of the Signal Corps," one veteran of the agency recalled many years later.

> A few others knew enough to stimulate the imagination with some sense of mystery. Only a small number, even of the well informed, knew that from those rooms was conducted a correspondence, usually in cipher, with numerous agents beyond the limits of the Confederacy, that in them, with occasional interruptions mail was received from Washington almost as regularly as from Charleston, and that through them cipher dispatches between generals in the field and the Departments were constantly passing.[5]

The Signal Bureau was headed by Major (later Colonel) William Norris, a native of Baltimore and a member of the Yale class of 1840. Norris was a Baltimore lawyer and businessman before the war. He was an ardent secessionist, and soon after hostilities began, he went to Richmond to volunteer his services. He was accepted as a civilian aide on the staff of General John Magruder, the commander of Confederate forces on the Yorktown peninsula, and subsequently commissioned as a captain. Norris set up a semaphore signaling system on the peninsula and across the James River for Magruder. When the Signal Bureau was established the following May, he was released from Magruder's staff and put in charge of it.

The bureau supervised the Confederate army's Signal Corps—that is, the signal officers and men attached to the various Confederate field commands for which they provided secure communications (by semaphore, courier, and other methods). It was responsible for the manufacture and procurement of signal and cipher apparatus and the training and assignment of signal personnel to the field commands, and it performed other tasks associated with communications. All this was done openly, of course, and under the rubric of the Signal Bureau. But the bureau had a covert side known only to those authorized to read the correspondence Norris and his staff sent beneath letterheads reading SIGNAL AND SECRET SERVICE BUREAU or sometimes simply SECRET SERVICE BUREAU.[6]

The principal covert function of the bureau seems to have been to provide secure communication between Richmond and Confederate agents in the North, Canada, and Europe. The bureau operated the Secret Line, a network of couriers, agents, safe houses, and Southern sympathizers linking Richmond with secret Confederate assets in enemy territory. The Secret Line transported agents, scouts, and others on official business to and from the North; carried letters and dispatches to and from the Confederate capital; procured books, newspapers, and other items from the North for the Confederate leaders; and observed and reported on Federal military movements on the Potomac River.

The Potomac, which separated secessionist Virginia from "loyal" (or at least acquiescent) Maryland, was heavily patrolled by Federal gunboats and pickets and was therefore the most serious obstacle to the Secret Line. Secure crossings were achieved at several points along the river, however, where Confederate safe houses occupied by resident agents were situated. Most of these crossing points seem to have been between King George or Westmoreland counties on the Virginia shore and Charles or Saint Marys counties on the Maryland side. These safe houses also provided convenient observation posts for monitoring Federal maritime activity on the river.

Although the Secret Service Bureau collected military intelligence when its communication activities provided the opportunity to do so, this seems to have been an incidental function. There certainly was no office within the bureau or anywhere else in Richmond charged with compiling and correlating such intelligence; instead, the bureau passed along the raw information to those government officials and commanders in the field who seemed likely to be interested in it.[7]

There is an assortment of tantalizing scraps of evidence suggesting that the Secret Service Bureau may also have had a covert paramilitary role. Some bureau personnel were peripherally involved in the Northwest Conspiracy, a Confederate plot to foment uprisings against the United

States government in the Northern states. John H. Surratt, whose mother was hanged for conspiracy in the assassination of President Lincoln and who himself was accused of involvement in the crime, was a courier for the bureau.[8] And Thomas A. Jones, who sheltered John Wilkes Booth after the assassination, operated one of the Potomac River safe houses on the Secret Line.[9] But most of the extant record suggests only that the Secret Service Bureau was principally a clandestine courier service the besieged Confederacy used to keep in contact with its friends and agents beyond the seceded states.

William Norris never published his memoirs; his personal papers were lost when his home was destroyed by fire in 1890.[10] Charles B. Taylor, an enlisted man who served as acting adjutant of the Secret Service Bureau during the last year of the war, published a very brief and sketchy account of the agency in 1903 in which he noted that a full narrative would "demand a volume."[11] None of the other veterans of the bureau ever set their memoirs before the public, and indeed even the names of most of them are unknown. Unless some forgotten manuscript or cache of documents turns up, the story of the Confederate Secret Service Bureau is fated to remain untold, like so much of the true secret history of the Civil War.

The Civil War was fought at a pace much swifter than that of any past conflict. Military railroads and telegraphs were having their first extensive use. An army could be moved in hours across distances that generals customarily measured in days of marching. This was especially relevant to the Confederacy, which was employing its interior lines of communication—especially its railroads—to concentrate its numerically inferior forces in response to the strategic initiatives of the North. And although the Confederates desperately needed to know where and when the Union's blows were to fall, a Federal general invading Southern territory needed to know not only what lay ahead, but what was on his flanks and to his rear if he was not to be caught in a Confederate trap. And he needed to know these things with a speed commensurate with that of his enemy's transport and communications.

Although the secret agent is the focus of almost all the popular literature of Civil War intelligence, spies were only one of many sources of military information. For example, much military intelligence was simply gleaned from the other side's newspapers. One task the Confederate Secret Service Bureau is known to have performed was the prompt procurement of complete files of Northern newspapers. The bureau delivered Washington and Baltimore dailies to the desk of Jefferson Davis within twenty-four hours of publication, while New York and Philadelphia papers required an extra day to reach the Confederate president.[12] Northern newspapers were an important, if uncertain, source of military and political intelligence for the Confederacy.

The Northern press gave extensive coverage to the war, of course; such New York papers as the *Times*, the *Tribune*, and the *World* typically devoted fully a third of their daily column space to war news.[13] Smaller papers got their war news from their Washington bureaus, from the Associated Press wire service, or from other papers, but many of the big-city papers sent special correspondents into the field to travel with the army and make eyewitness reports of operations. There were more than 150 such "specials," as they were called, reporting the war news for Northern newspapers during the war. *Harper's Weekly* and *Frank Leslie's Illustrated Weekly* often had as many as a dozen artists in the field sketching the action for reproduction by woodcuts.[14] The papers carried reports of battles, battlefield maps, lists of casualties, and sometimes word of military plans, troop movements, troop strengths, and other information of value to the Confederates.

War correspondents and the speed with which news could be reported by telegraph and printed were security problems beyond the experience of the military establishment in 1861, and it took some time for the potential danger to sink in at the War Department. In October Secretary of War Simon Cameron released to the press a report, including complete order-of-battle information, on Federal forces in Missouri and Kentucky; the report was published verbatim by the New York *Tribune* on October 30.[15] In releasing the report, Cameron had violated his own department's general order, issued two months earlier, forbidding the publication of anything having reference to army movements—past, present, or future—except with the express permission of the general in command. Under the department's Article 57 violators were liable to the death penalty. But Secretary Cameron was not the only person to ignore the order, and the flood of military information continued in the press. In another effort to plug the leaks, the War Department imposed strict telegraph censorship in February 1862, but inconsistencies in enforcement led to an investigation by the House Judiciary Committee, which charged that the Lincoln administration was using military security as an excuse to stifle legitimate discussion and criticism of the war effort.[16]

General William T. Sherman, whose press relations were often poor, regarded newspaper correspondents simply as Confederate spies. "I *know* that the principal northern papers reach the enemy regularly & promptly," he fumed to a friend.

> I say in giving intelligence to the enemy, in sowing discord and discontent in an army, these men fulfill all the conditions of spies. . . . I am satisfied they have cost the country hundreds of millions of dollars & brought our country to the brink of ruin & that unless the nuisance is abated we are lost.[17]

Sherman was here voicing the feelings of many Federal commanders, as he probably was when having been informed that three journalists had been killed by an exploding shell, he exclaimed, "Good! Now we shall have news from hell before breakfast."[18]

The War Department and the army continued to struggle with the newspaper problem throughout the war, never really solving it. The ambiguity of the department's censorship rules confused both censors and reporters, and though a few reporters were briefly jailed and a few papers were temporarily suspended from publishing, censorship remained generally ineffective. The Confederates quickly discovered that they could not rely completely upon the Northern papers as intelligence sources, however. Much of the reportage was inaccurate, some of it invention, and the headings IMPORTANT—IF TRUE or RUMORS AND SPECULATIONS, while common, were not always placed over reports of dubious authenticity. Wise Confederate commanders must have taken what they read in the Northern press with a judicious grain of salt.

The Confederacy's own press-censorship problems were much simpler. There were fewer papers in the South, with fewer pages of column space to censor, because of a wartime shortage of newsprint; only about 5 percent of American paper mills were in the Confederacy, and even in peacetime they did not produce half enough newsprint to fill the demand of Southern newspapers. Many papers suffered from the general Confederate labor shortage and were forced to shut down when their printers or editors were drafted into the army.[19] Those papers that continued to publish carried little current war news because the army commanders simply excluded reporters from the battlefronts, and the Richmond government encountered no domestic dissent when it enforced tight censorship. The Press Association of the Confederate States of America, a cooperative wire service established in 1863, succeeded in having the rules loosened somewhat, but censorship continued to be more stringent than that enforced in the North.[20] Notwithstanding all these factors, potentially damaging disclosures of military information sometimes occurred, but the actual damage done was probably small; it is unlikely that Federal intelligence officers paid close attention to what was generally a poor source of intelligence.

Newspapers are just one intelligence source rarely or never mentioned in the popular literature of Civil War spying. Prisoners of war, deserters, refugees, and in the case of Federal intelligence, runaway slaves all carried potentially valuable intelligence through the lines, although it took a special talent for an interrogator to distinguish between solid data and deliberate disinformation or to achieve an accurate interpretation of a civilian's version of a military situation. Reconnaissance by cavalry was an even more important source of combat intelligence. General Robert E. Lee, who never established a formal military intelligence function within the staff of the Army of Northern Virginia, relied on his cavalry under Major General J. E. B. Stuart to serve as "the eyes of the army." And perhaps surprisingly, aerial reconnaissance played an important role in Civil War intelligence.

Manned balloons were used in Europe for military reconnaissance as early as 1794, but they were not used extensively or systematically for that purpose until the Civil War. By 1861 the art of ballooning was well advanced in the United States; passenger-carrying balloons easily achieved altitudes of one thousand feet, and ascents of as much as twenty thousand feet had been accomplished as early as 1850. With the outbreak of the war, several leading American balloonists—the popular contemporary term was *aeronaut*—proposed the military use of the craft to the Federal government.

Thaddeus S. C. Lowe, a twenty-eight-year-old self-styled professor from New Hampshire, demonstrated the military potential of balloons to President Lincoln during an ascent over Washington in a tethered balloon on June 18, 1861. He carried with him a telegraph set connected to the War Department's telegraph system by a cable linking the craft to the ground, and two telegraphers. Floating five hundred feet above the Columbia Armory near the foot of Capitol Hill, Lowe sent the following message to President Lincoln in the White House:

> To the President of the United States:
> This point of observation commands an area near fifty miles in diameter. The city, with its girdle of encampments, presents a superb scene. I have pleasure in sending you this first dispatch ever telegraphed from an aerial station, and in acknowledging indebtedness to your encouragement, for the opportunity of demonstrating the availability of the science of aeronautics in the military service of the country. T.S.C. Lowe.[21]

Favorably impressed, Lincoln sent Lowe to General Winfield Scott, the general in chief of the army, with the suggestion that Lowe and his aircraft might prove useful, but Scott, perhaps distrustful of the newfangled reconnaissance technique, put off meeting with the aeronaut. It was not until August that Lowe overcame the general's resistance and succeeded in being hired by the Army of the Potomac's Bureau of Topographical Engineers.

Lowe made a very practical demonstration of the effectiveness of the aircraft a month later, when the Confederates attacked Federal positions near Fort Corcoran on the Potomac, south of Washington. He directed artillery fire from his airborne vantage point, telegraphing range and azimuth corrections to the gunners on the ground.[22] By the end of the year, he had built a fleet of seven balloons and hired a staff of nine aeronauts to operate them.

Lowe's balloons represented the contemporary state of the art. The gas envelopes were made of gored sections of pongee, a type of silk, sewn together in double thicknesses. The envelope was filled with hydrogen gas, which was produced by the action of sulfuric acid on iron filings in a wagon-borne gas generator. The hot gas produced by the reaction was passed through water-cooled copper pipes to lower its temperature and through lime filters for purification. The generator wagons were part of the balloon train, the convoy of wagons that carried the balloon, ropes, telegraph equipment, gas filters, and so forth to the place from which the craft made its ascent. When inflated, the balloons towered several stories above the ground, and the larger models could carry several passengers, often the aeronaut and a commander who wanted to see things for himself instead of relying upon the airborne telegraph reports.

When General McClellan led the Army of the Potomac to the Yorktown peninsula in March 1862, he brought along Lowe and his balloon corps.[23] During April, while McClellan laid siege to Yorktown and moved his heavy artillery into place for an all-out assault on the Confederate stronghold, Lowe could survey enemy defenses along the eight-mile Yorktown line running across the peninsula. The assault had not yet begun on May 3 when Lowe made a midnight ascent accompanied by Brigadier General Samuel P. Heint-zelman, one of McClellan's corps commanders. Lowe recalled:

> The entire great fortress was ablaze with bonfires, and the great-est activity prevailed, which was not visible except from the balloon. At first the general was puzzled on seeing more wagons entering the forts than were going out, but when I called his attention to the fact that the ingoing wagons were light and moved rapidly (the wheels being visible as they passed each camp-fire), while the outgoing wagons were heavily loaded and moved slowly, there was no longer any doubt as to the object of the Confederates.[24]

General Joseph Johnston, having halted McClellan at Yorktown for a month while he moved tens of thousands of reinforcements to the penin-sula to stand between Richmond and the invaders, was now falling back toward the Confederate capital. Lowe's early warning of the move enabled McClellan to rouse his own sleeping army in the early hours of the morn-ing and overtake the Confederates at Williamsburg.

The Confederates did not fail to see the advantage of reconnais-sance balloons, but they lacked the materials and expertise available to the North. One rebel officer, Captain Bryan,[25] made several ascents over Yorktown to observe McClellan's forces early in May, just before General Johnston evacuated the stronghold. Unlike Lowe's craft, Bryan's makeshift balloon was lifted by hot air, not hydrogen, and he communicated with the ground by signal flags. During the Seven Days' Battles of June and July at Fair Oaks, Virginia, the Confederates used a hydrogen balloon to observe the Federal forces to the east of Richmond. The craft was inflated with illuminating gas in Richmond, then tied to an engine of the York River Railroad, and moved to the front, where the reconnaissance ascents were made.[26]

According to legend, the balloon's envelope had been made from "the last silk dresses in the Confederacy," volunteered to the Southern cause by the ladies of Richmond. Its capture by Federal troops was characterized by Lieutenant General James Longstreet many years later as "the meanest trick of the war and one I have never yet forgiven."[27]

In the Army of the Potomac, opinions varied as to the military value of Lowe's balloon corps. General McClellan believed the craft to be quite useful, and Brigadier General Fitz-John Porter, one of McClellan's division commanders, rated them highly. Porter himself made more than one hundred flights with Lowe.

Other officers were not as fully convinced of the balloons' usefulness, however. The inability of the sluggish balloon trains to move rapidly when necessary to keep up with the army was generally recognized as a serious drawback.[28] Opinion as to the military worth of the balloons probably depended upon whether or not an officer had been willing to go along on flights with Lowe or the other aeronauts. A telegraph report from a civilian aeronaut could not have been nearly as effective to a commander as direct visual observation of the battlefield from the craft's vantage. Photography was not employed by the balloon corps, perhaps because of the difficulty of lugging bulky cameras and darkroom equipment along in the already overburdened and unwieldy balloon trains.

A stepchild, the balloon corps was often neglected in the matter of logistics and even pay. Lowe was frequently forced to pay for supplies and services out of his own pocket and then had to try to obtain reimbursement from the army.[29] On occasion the army quartermaster withdrew the wagons, teams, and drivers that had been assigned to the balloon corps for assignments regarded as more important. Lowe might have fared better in such cases had he and his aeronauts been commissioned officers rather than civilian employees of the army.

In April 1863 the balloon corps was transferred to the Corps of Engineers. The chief engineer, perhaps reflecting the opinion of the chief of staff, Major General Daniel Butterfield, cut Lowe's pay from ten dollars per day to six dollars. Lowe resigned in protest, and the army disbanded the balloon corps the following month. This marked the end of aerial reconnaissance in the Civil War.

Communication intercepts are yet another intelligence source not generally associated with the Civil War, but they played a much greater part than in any earlier American conflict. In earlier wars military communications were only in the form of written dispatches, and communications intelligence necessarily involved gaining possession—temporary or permanent—of the actual piece of paper bearing the message. But the Civil War saw the extensive use of two new ways to transmit information: visual flag signaling and the magnetic telegraph.

Although signaling by flag had long been known in the navy, the Civil War saw its first systematic use by American armies. Dr. Albert J. Myer, an army surgeon, devised an efficient flag-signal code while serving in the Southwest in the late 1850s. In 1860 the army adopted the wigwag system, as it was called, and Myer was commissioned as a major and appointed chief signal officer—the army's first.

The United States Army's wigwag system involved the use of large flags with patterns and colors picked for easy visibility. Lanterns were used for signaling at night. Signal posts were established at the tops of tall buildings, hills, mountains, and specially constructed wooden towers, which often rose more than one hundred feet. Signalmen used telescopes and field glasses to observe distant wigwag stations, and as an incidental bonus to their communication work sometimes detected enemy military activity from their elevated vantage points. The Confederate Signal Corps used virtually the same system, which was taken south by Myer's assistant, Lieutenant E. P. Porter, when he resigned at the outbreak of the war and became General Beauregard's chief signal officer.

Flag and light signaling provided no inherent security whatsoever because anyone who could see the signalman could intercept the messages. This was obvious, and each side tried both to protect its communications through encipherment and to read the enemy's messages. Neither Myer nor Porter had a very sophisticated grasp of cryptology, however, and both sides relied heavily on monoalphabetic substitution ciphers—that is, cryptosystems in which a letter of the plaintext alphabet is always represented by the same ciphertext letter throughout any single message.[30]

Confidence in the security of the simple ciphers was so low that the commanders of both sides rarely entrusted vital communications to the wigwag system. When a truly important piece of communications intelligence was acquired by reading the enemy's flag signals, commanders tended to suspect that it was deliberate misinformation planted by the other side. Major General Joseph Hooker dismissed such an intercepted Confederate wigwag message revealing that General Lee had departed from Fredericksburg on his second invasion of the North in June 1863, for example; he realized the message had been genuine only after it was confirmed by a prisoner interrogation a week later.[31]

Notwithstanding the reluctance of commanders to use the wigwag system for especially sensitive messages, flag traffic was the main source of interceptions in the war, and a close study of even the enemy's routine administrative traffic could not fail to disclose useful military intelligence. General Grant recalled, "It would sometimes take too long to make translations of intercepted dispatches for us to receive any benefit from them. But sometimes they gave useful information."[32]

Like the observation balloon, the telegraph was given its first major military use in the war. An extensive civilian telegraph network, which had grown throughout the United States since 1844, was in place. The American Telegraph Company lines linked points on the eastern seaboard, while the Western Union's system ran westward through the Allegheny Mountains. Smaller telegraph companies served areas not covered by the giants. Most towns and cities served by the railroads were linked by telegraph lines.

The utility of the telegraph in war was obvious to the United States War Department. In October 1861 the Military Telegraph Service was established in the department as a civilian unit under the Quartermaster Corps. Headed by Anson Stager, the thirty-six-year-old former general superintendent of Western Union and now a captain of volunteers, the service was originally intended to provide only strategic communications between headquarters, while the Signal Corps—which had been in existence for a year—would continue to be responsible for tactical communications in the field: both wigwag flag signaling and portable field telegraph systems. Bureaucratic rivalry between Stager and Chief Signal Officer Myer led to the corps' loss of all telegraphic responsibilities in March 1864, however. Thereafter, the Military Telegraph Service was in charge of all military telegraphy.[33]

In the Confederacy some of the facilities and personnel of the civilian telegraph companies were pressed into military service for field communications by Confederate commanders. The Confederate Signal Corps, administratively under Major Norris's Signal (and Secret Service) Bureau, provided some limited field telegraph service but was primarily involved in wigwag flag communications. Generally, the Confederate army made less use than the North of military telegraphy.

Although inherently more secure than the wigwag flag system, the telegraph was still highly vulnerable to wiretapping. No new technology was needed to tap a line, since tapping had long been a routine maintenance technique used by linemen. To protect the security of military telegraphic communications, Anson Stager devised a simple yet reasonably effective word transposition system early in the war at the request of General McClellan, and the system became the standard telegraphic cryptosystem used by the Military Telegraph Service.

Also known as route transposition, Stager's system enciphered messages by rearranging the sequence of the words according to some pre-established pattern. This cipher proved surprisingly difficult, if not impossible, for the Confederates to break. Two former members of the Federal Military Telegraph Service, in their accounts of Civil War telegraphy and cryptology, state flatly that no Federal cipher message was ever solved by the Confederates,[34] a negative categorical assertion that ought to inspire some skepticism. The absence of positive information about any instance of Confederate success in breaking the Stager cipher lends credence to the claim, however.

*   *   *

The Confederates entrusted their important telegrams and other military communications to the Vigenère polyalphabetic substitution cipher, a system in which the relationship between the ciphertext and the plaintext alphabets constantly changes throughout the message according to some pre-established key. Thus the term *the enemy* might be enciphered VVQ TYIFC, the letter *e* taking on a different ciphertext equivalent with each occurrence in the plaintext message.

The Vigenère system will not yield to the simple cryptanalytic technique Poe described in "The Gold Bug." In fact, although the system had been known since the sixteenth century, the general method of solving it was not discovered until about the time of the Civil War, when it was published in German in a book unlikely to have come to the attention of Federal cryptanalysts until some years later.[35]

The Vigenère might have proved unbreakable by the Federals had the Confederate telegraphers known how to use it properly, but they did not. Their worst mistake was failing to encipher the entire message, believing that encipherment of only especially revealing words and phrases provided sufficient security. This classical error of the cryptology novice provided Federal cryptanalysts with vital contextual information that often enabled them to solve the enciphered portions. And the Confederates used too few keys for proper security.

The Federals happened to have a fair amount of cryptanalytic talent among the ranks of the Military Telegraph Service and the Signal Corps. David Homer Bates, Charles A. Tinker, and Albert B. Chandler—three young telegraphers who worked in the War Department's telegraph office, next door to the White House—were especially adept at breaking Confederate ciphers.[36]

There has as yet been no comprehensive study of wiretapping in the Civil War, but the fragmentary information encountered in accounts of telegraphy in the war suggests that it was done extensively by both sides, perhaps more frequently by the Confederates because the Federals possessed more lines to tap.

Despite the security of Stager's word transposition cipher, enough Federal telegraph traffic was sent in plaintext to make Confederate wiretapping worthwhile, however. In mid-July 1864 General Lee ordered telegrapher Charles A. Gaston to tap the Federal lines between the War Department in Washington and General Grant's headquarters outside the besieged Confederate capital. Guarded by a small detachment of Confederate troops in civilian disguise, Gaston remained at his tap through August, September, and part of October, copying the Federal traffic and sending the intercepts to Lee by courier. Although most of the intercepted telegrams were in cipher, the plaintext traffic provided some useful intelligence to the Confederate commander.[37]

Communications intelligence was only one benefit of telegraph wiretapping. Both sides also used taps to send false information or orders—disinformation, in modern intelligence parlance—to the other side. This was not easily done, however; an operator's personal touch on the telegraph key—his so-called fist—was as uniquely distinctive as his voice.

The master of telegraph deception seems to have been the Canadian-born George A. Ellsworth, the former assistant superintendent of the Texas Telegraph Company who served as a wiretapper for the legendary Confederate general and raider John Hunt Morgan. Morgan's specialty was making lightning raids deep into the North to disrupt communications, destroy railroad lines and equipment, and burn Federal supplies. Ellsworth went along on these raids, tapping wires to discover and evade Federal countermeasures and sending bogus orders and other dispatches to confuse and disrupt Federal forces.[38]

When an enemy wiretap was detected, it offered an excellent means of feeding disinformation to the enemy. General Sherman reportedly did exactly this in March 1864, when he learned that the Confederates had tapped the telegraph wires near Memphis, Tennessee. Sherman is said to have telegraphed orders dispatching one of his divisions to Savannah, Tennessee, thereby drawing the Confederate general Nathan B. Forrest to lead his cavalry to Savannah to cut off the isolated Federal force. At the same time Sherman secretly ordered a strong cavalry force to the town and nearly managed to trap Forrest.[39]

* * *

Newspapers, aerial reconnaissance, and communication intercepts are notable as Civil War military intelligence sources not because they ever proved crucial to the course of the conflict—although they were certainly important—but because they were entirely new dimensions in the age-old business of espionage. The human capability to collect and process information increased dramatically in the nineteenth century in terms of both speed and volume, and intelligence, an information-processing business, had to change to keep up with it. The spy still remained the main means of spying, but the craft of intelligence had begun the expansion that would lead to reconnaissance satellites, computers, and electronic surveillance a century later. The world's second oldest profession would never be quite the same.

Chapter Twelve

European Intrigue in the Civil War

"Ⅰf the Lord would only give the United States an excuse for a war with England, France or Spain," Secretary of State Seward remarked soon after Fort Sumter, "that would be the best means of re-establishing internal peace."[1] Seward believed the Confederacy would rejoin the United States to fight a common enemy. Three weeks after Lincoln's inauguration he proposed that the president "send agents into Canada, Mexico, and Central America, to rouse a vigorous continental spirit of independence on this continent against European intervention." He wanted to demand explanations from Spain and France for their interference in Mexico and Santo Domingo in violation of the Monroe Doctrine, and if satisfactory explanations were not forthcoming, "convene Congress and declare war against them." Convinced that Lincoln had no grasp of foreign affairs, Seward in effect proposed that the president appoint him prime minister to deal with the Confederacy and the great powers of Europe.[2]

Lincoln quietly pigeonholed the proposal and helped the secretary of state recover his senses, leading him to realize that the last thing the Union needed was more enemies and to comprehend what American diplomatic objectives in the war must be: to prevent Europe from aiding the Confederacy or even recognizing the secessionist government and to persuade European maritime nations to accept the United States blockade of Southern ports.

Confederate foreign policy was exactly the reverse, of course. In March, a full month before Sumter, the Confederate government sent three commissioners—William L. Yancey, A. Dudley Mann, and Pierre A. Rost—to Britain and France to seek recognition and treaties of friendship and commerce. They were to remind their European hosts that 95 percent of American cotton was grown in the South, and that England and France annually manufactured some six hundred million dollars' worth of goods from imported cotton. Thousands of mills and hundreds of thousands of mill workers would be idled if Europe accepted the Federal blockade of Southern ports. Cotton seemed so mighty an influence that local Committees of Public Safety in many Southern seaports had actually passed domestic embargoes on exporting the commodity, lest some Southern merchant manage to ship cotton to Europe despite the blockade and erode its power as an instrument of foreign policy. King Cotton, as the Confederate leaders called this inducement, and the decades-old European resentment of the Monroe Doctrine and American commercial competition were the cards the South held in the game of foreign affairs.

The view from London and Paris was a little different. Certainly, the prospect of the disintegration of the Union was welcome in both capitals, but it was not so alluring that either nation was ready for a war with the United States. The Confederates had miscalculated European demand for cotton, basing their estimates on the recent annual exports to Europe, not on the number of bales actually used; at the outbreak of the war, the warehouses of Southampton and Liverpool held enough cotton to supply English and French mills until the end of 1862. In fact, there was also a surplus of manufactured cotton products, forcing the factory owners to shut down temporarily or work part-time. It would be some time, therefore, before King Cotton could make his influence felt. As to the Monroe Doctrine, the war itself seemed to have put that policy on hold; Washington was too busy with the secession to police the Western Hemisphere, a fact France's Napoléon III seems to have appreciated. Finally, slavery, the institution that the South had seceded from the Union to preserve, was condemned by the British and French governments and unpopular in both countries. The Confederates soon realized they were obliged to fight a second war, one for the hearts and minds of Europe.

While the Confederate political strategists laid plans for the propaganda war in Europe, the secretary of the Confederate navy, Stephen R. Mallory, was devising a more direct means of dealing with the Federal blockade.

"The United States have a constructed Navy; we have a Navy to construct," he told Jefferson Davis.[3] The South could not hope to compete with the United States Navy in numbers of ships, he realized, but most of those vessels had been built before the latest advances in naval architecture had been achieved in Europe. In 1859 France had launched the *Gloire*, the first ironclad warship, and Britain was at work on one of her own, the *Warrior*. Given a small fleet of ironclads, superior in offensive and defensive capability to the ships of the United States Navy, the Confederacy could break the Federal blockade, and destroy Northern merchant shipping as well.[4]

Mallory proposed obtaining such vessels from the shipyards of Britain and France, the only places with the technical ability to build them. There was one big obstacle to this plan, however: both nations had proclaimed their neutrality soon after the Federal blockade was put in effect. The British and French proclamations forbade both the North and the South to recruit their citizens or equip or arm warships in their ports or territorial waters. (The proclamations did not prohibit the belligerents from purchasing munitions or other supplies in the neutral countries but served warning on British and French citizens that they would deliver such goods to the Union or Confederacy at their own risk and not under the protection of their respective flags.) Mallory realized, therefore, that the procurement of ironclad warships by the South would have to be done covertly. For this task he selected as his secret agent a sailor of considerable experience and discretion and a loyal Southerner, James Dunwody Bulloch.

A native of Georgia, Bulloch was the son of an old and distinguished Southern family (and his half sister, Martha, was the mother of Theodore Roosevelt). He had joined the United States Navy as a midshipman in 1839 but had risen only to the rank of lieutenant with no prospect of promotion after fourteen years' service. He resigned from the navy and took a job with a New York shipping line as master of a coastal mail and passenger steamer plying between New York and New Orleans. At the outbreak of the war, he immediately resigned and wrote to Secretary Mallory offering his services. Mallory asked him to come to Montgomery, then still the Confederate capital.

"I am glad to see you," Mallory said when Bulloch walked into his office. Then, without more ado, "I want you to go to Europe. When can you start?"

Startled, Bulloch replied that he could start as soon as he was told what he was to do.[5] Mallory explained his assignment, and Bulloch, having destroyed his notes of the conversation after committing them to memory, left on his mission the following night. He traveled to Canada by way of Detroit—it was early May 1861, and travel between the South and the Midwest was still generally unrestricted—then embarked from Montreal, arriving in Liverpool on June 4.

Bulloch quickly selected a Liverpool shipbuilder and an engineering firm to design and build the *Florida,* a cruiser. He evaded the British neutrality laws through the simple expedient of omitting to mention the real identity of the ship's purchasers:

> The contract was made with me as a private person, nothing whatever being said about the ultimate destination of the ship, or the object for which she was intended. . . . Before the completion of the ship, Messrs. Fawcett, Preston and Co. and Messrs Miller [the engineering firm and the shipbuilder] may both have had a tolerably clear notion that she would at some future time, and by some subsequent arrangement, pass into the possession of the Confederate Government; but they never mentioned their suspicions. . . .[6]

To discourage curiosity, Bulloch put out the story that the ship, known in the shipyard as the *Oreto,* was being built for "a mercantile firm doing business in Palermo."

As soon as the arrangements for the *Florida* were in place, Bulloch contracted with a second shipbuilder, John Laird and his sons, for the construction of a second cruiser, the *Alabama,* or as she was known in the shipyard, the *Henrica.* With work under way on the two cruisers, he next purchased a nearly new Scottish-built steamer, the *Fingal,* loaded her with arms and ammunition, and sailed to Bermuda. Under cover of darkness, he slipped through the Federal blockade and delivered ship and cargo to Savannah, Georgia. The United States Navy tightened the blockade at Savannah shortly thereafter, however, and Bulloch was unable to take the ship back to England with a cargo of cotton, as planned. He relinquished command of the *Fingal,* which the Confederates later converted into the ironclad monitor the *Atlanta.* He left again for England in February aboard a Confederate blockade-runner out of Wilmington, North Carolina, and returned to Liverpool in mid-March to resume his covert procurement program.

The United States government was well aware of Bulloch's activities and those of other Confederate secret agents in Europe. In fact, an elaborate Federal Secret Service was in place in England even before Bulloch first arrived in Liverpool. The chief of the network was Henry Shelton Sanford, a thirty-eight-year-old veteran diplomat who had served in Saint Petersburg, Frankfurt, and Paris and whom President Lincoln had appointed as minister to Belgium in March.[7]

Secretary Seward's instructions to the new minister advised that "the most important duty of the diplomatic representatives of the United States in Europe will be to counteract by all proper means the efforts of the agents of that projected Confederacy at their respective Courts." Sanford believed that "proper" did not exclude covert, for he soon was urging Seward to "provide sufficient secret service funds" to counter the Confederate agents in London and Paris.[8] The secretary of state did so, and by mid-June Sanford had hired several local private detectives and was organizing a network for the "systematic following up of the Secession agents." He planned to use the organization to do more than spy on the Confederates: he regarded it as an action agency, a covert arm of the United States military that would prevent the Confederates from shipping arms home.[9]

Because Britain was the principal zone of Confederate covert procurement, it was also the focus of Sanford's network. Although this presented a problem for the American minister to Belgium, whose presence and attention were required in Brussels, he was aided by Freeman H. Morse, the newly appointed American consul in London. Morse, a fifty-four-year-old former congressman from Maine and a prominent Republican, had been appointed to the post by President Lincoln purely as political patronage, but he proved adept at the craft of intelligence.[10]

Morse hired a former London police detective, Ignatius Pollaky, as principal agent in London to run the British part of Sanford's network. Pollaky enlarged the British network and established observation posts in London and Liverpool from which Bulloch and his cohorts could be observed. The detectives made daily reports on the Confederates' movements. They paid letter carriers one pound per week to furnish daily lists of the postmarks and dates of the letters they delivered to the Confederate agents; when several letters were received from one seaport, a detective went there to search for a ship that might be loading a cargo of arms destined for the South. Other detectives kept close watch on telegraph offices and sometimes managed to learn the contents of the Confederates' telegrams. Pollaky paid a clerk in the employ of Isaac Campbell and Company to report on the arms supplier's dealings with the Confederates. By mid-August Sanford reported to Seward that the network had been able to "fix upon every agent of the Rebellion" in Europe and some of their most important business associates.[11]

Several of Pollaky's agents had no other duties than to watch Bulloch. "He is the most dangerous man the South have here and fully up to his business," Sanford told Seward. "I am disbursing at the rate of 150 pounds a month on this one man which will give you an idea of the importance I attach to his movements."[12] Edward Brennan, one of Pollaky's detectives, discovered that Bulloch had purchased the *Fingal* and was loading a cargo of arms aboard it at Greenock, Scotland. From a room in the Old Sailors' Home, he made hourly reports of the activity to Pollaky, who passed on the information to Sanford. On October 9 he reported the ship had sailed.[13]

There was little to be done about such arms shipments through diplomatic channels. British neutrality laws did not prohibit them. Sanford's early warnings of the voyages of such ships as the *Fingal* were often used to alert the United States Navy, but the interception in international waters of a ship flying the British flag, ostensibly carrying a cargo to the British island of Bermuda, would have been an act of war. The navy had to do its best to stop the ships when they tried to run the blockade.[14] To Sanford that was just not good enough.

In July Sanford, having discovered yet another ship due to carry supplies to the Confederacy, urged Seward to station a warship off the British coast to intercept her. "Get her once outside [British waters] & and I will go for *taking* her no matter what her papers. We can discuss the matter with the English afterwards," he wrote. He renewed his request several times in the next few weeks and in August proposed that two or three American warships be stationed in British waters, "directed to touch in frequently at specific ports & times for information & to act upon indication which shall leave little doubt as to the character of the vessel."[15]

Seward, by this time having regained his senses and discarded his plan of preserving the Union through a foreign war, regarded British neutrality as too important to be violated in order to interdict the flow of Confederate arms. He refused Sanford's request for the warships. The minister was frustrated further when Consul Morse declined his request to arrange the sabotage of the British steamer *Thomas Watson*, which left Liverpool in September carrying war materials to the Confederacy. When Sanford complained about Morse's refusal to Seward, the secretary pointed out that the ship had been caught by the United States Navy while trying to run the blockade.

Sanford was not to be put off. In October he proposed to Seward the enlargement of the British network for the purpose of covert action against Bulloch's arms shipments. He wanted more Secret Service funds to buy the cooperation "in every port of importance . . . [of] subordinate officials who are in the employment of the Dock and Steamship Companies, men who in the discharge of their Daily duties necessarily obtain without effort the information desired, . . ." such information to be used by the navy in interdicting the ships in British waters. Without waiting for a reply, he hired Captain Edwin Eastman, an old acquaintance and a New York merchant marine captain, to organize the hijacking of British ships carrying Confederate arms by means of American agents signing on as crewmen and seizing the ships on the high seas.[16]

The initial target of the plan was the *Gladiator*, a British steamer Pollaky's men discovered to be loading a cargo of 22,240 Enfield rifles for the Confederacy. The operation hit a snag, however, when Captain Eastman discovered that the ship had already signed on a full crew. Sanford resorted to the alternative plan of trying to bribe a river pilot to ground the ship on a mud bank as she made her way down the Thames from London. He persuaded the captain of the U.S.S. *James Adgar*, an American warship in British waters on other business, to join in the plan and seize the *Gladiator* after she grounded. In the event, the operation came unglued at the last moment, the pilot went unbribed, and the *Gladiator* escaped to the ocean unmolested.[17]

Sanford's reckless disregard for Anglo-American relations was beginning to disturb the American minister to Great Britain, Charles Francis Adams.

Adams may also have been embarrassed to read in the London papers such stories as the one that appeared in the December 6 *Chronicle,* which stated that "a system of espionage of the most extensive and searching character has been for some time going on in England," and that "every move of a warlike character has been immediately reported to the Government of the United States." The story stated that Federal agents had been stationed in all British seaports to learn the destination and cargo of every vessel leaving port and that the information was sent to Washington by way of London. Other stories, reporting on the network's activities in Liverpool, had already appeared in the London press in October.[18]

Adams, of course, was fully informed of Sanford's network and its activities. Whatever he thought of Sanford's covert-action program, he chose to protest to Seward on the narrow grounds that the minister to Belgium was unable to be in England often enough to handle the network, and therefore, there had been a duplication of Secret Service expenditures by Consul Morse (who had separately purchased the same information regarding the *Fingal*). Adams proposed that the Federal Secret Service responsibility in Britain be transferred to Morse. Seward agreed and so instructed Sanford in November.[19]

Sanford had undertaken quite enough clandestine affairs on the Continent to continue to keep himself fully occupied, however. His intelligence network extended from Brussels to Liège and Verviers, Belgium; Paris and Toulon; Genoa; and as far south as Barcelona. Whenever he learned of a Confederate order for war supplies from a European firm, he tried to preempt the order, purchasing the material for the Union, and was often successful. He bought up all the saltpeter—an ingredient of gunpowder—available in Europe and shipped it to the United States.[20] But for the moment Britain remained the principal source of Confederate shipbuilding and supplies and had to be left to Morse. On the Continent Sanford found himself in the war for the hearts and minds of Europe.

"You have no friends in Europe," the former Confederate diplomatic commissioner Yancey told a throng of well-wishers who had gathered at his New Orleans hotel to greet him upon his return from Europe early in 1862.

The sentiment of Europe is anti-slavery, and that portion of public opinion which forms, and is represented by, the Government of Great Britain, is abolition. . . . Their opinion of the character of the people of the South and the cause in which we are engaged is derived from Northern sources. They never see the journals and periodicals of the South. . . . It is an error to say, "Cotton is King." It is not. . . . The nations of Europe will never raise the blockade until it suits their interests.[21]

In London and Paris the three Confederate commissioners had been given sympathetic hearings but nothing else. In Richmond early optimism gave way to a realistic reappraisal of Confederate diplomacy. When Yancey, frustrated and disgusted, tendered his resignation in September, Jefferson Davis and Confederate Secretary of State Robert M. T. Hunter decided to dissolve the cumbersome joint diplomatic commission and appoint permanent commissioners to each European capital. The two remaining members of the joint commission, Dudley Mann and Pierre Rost, were assigned to Brussels and Madrid, respectively. For the critical London post, the Confederate leaders selected James Murray Mason, a former senator and respected Virginia aristocrat who had been chairman of the Senate Foreign Relations Committee in the ten years before the war.

Davis and Hunter named former Louisiana senator John Slidell as the Confederacy's representative in Paris. Slidell, a transplanted New Yorker now more Southern than a native, owned a plantation near New Orleans and was married to Mathilde Deslonde, the aristocratic Creole sister-in-law of General Beauregard. He was the same John Slidell whom President Polk had sent on the abortive mission to Mexico, and he seems to have been destined to play the role of diplomat manqué twice.

Mason and Slidell did much to gain British sympathy for the Confederacy and nearly precipitated an Anglo-American war before even setting foot in Europe. Traveling together, the pair had sailed aboard a blockade-runner from Charleston to Nassau, thence to Havana, where they took passage for England aboard a British mail packet, the *Trent*. The ship departed on November 7 and was stopped the following day by a shot across her bows fired from the U.S.S. *San Jacinto*, whose commander, Captain Charles Wilkes, had read of the Confederates' itinerary in a Cuban newspaper some days earlier while stopping in Cienfuegos. He went immediately to the Bahama channel to await the *Trent*. Wilkes boarded the packet, arrested the Confederate diplomats and their secretaries, and took them to Boston, where they were put in prison.

Wilkes's action made him a hero in the North. Secretary of the Navy Gideon Welles commended him and promoted him to commodore, and the House of Representatives passed a resolution expressing its gratitude to him. The affair was not equally popular in Britain, however, where the stopping of foreign vessels in international waters to seize the passengers was apparently seen as a strictly British prerogative. The British government, unaware that Secretary Seward had discarded his well-known formula for saving the Union through a foreign war, prepared to fight. Eleven thousand British troops embarked for Canada as dockside military bands played "Dixie."

In Washington some believed London was bluffing, but Secretary Seward, having long since come round to Lincoln's view that one war at a time was enough, released the Confederates, explaining that Wilkes had exceeded his instructions. But he did not resist the temptation to add an expression of his pleasure that Britain had at last accepted the principles for which America had gone to war in 1812.

When a transport carrying part of the British military expedition found the Saint Lawrence River closed by ice, she was forced to put in to Portland, Maine. Seward graciously permitted the troops to continue overland to Canada. The sight of the redcoats marching through Maine must have irritated most of the Yankee abolitionists, but it may have warmed the hearts of whatever Blue-Light Federalists survived at that late date.

When Slidell arrived in France in July 1862, he found the government well-disposed toward the Confederacy and the loyal Opposition opposed to it. The liberals, the monarchists, and the republicans saw the war as a crusade to destroy slavery. Napoléon III, his ministers, and his supporters professed to see it as a struggle for Southern independence. In fact, the emperor saw it as an opportunity. In October 1861 he had joined with Britain and Spain in a joint military expedition to Mexico to collect debts after the Mexican congress had voted to suspend payments for two years. The

British and Spanish had withdrawn from the expedition, but the French remained in Mexico, ready to carry out the emperor's clandestine plans to acquire a new French foothold in the Western Hemisphere while the United States was preoccupied with the Confederacy.

Slidell soon discovered that his predecessors had done little to propagandize the Southern cause among the French; so strong was their belief in the power of King Cotton that they had disdained to court the press. Some Southerners living in France as private citizens had attempted to argue the Confederate case in letters to newspapers and in other public forums, but their efforts came to little. Slidell was dismayed to learn that most Frenchmen, including well-informed newspapermen, blamed the cotton shortage—now beginning to be felt in the local economy—on the Confederacy's embargo rather than on the Federal blockade. The ill-conceived embargo had been lifted, but it continued to be blamed for the shortage because of the skillful clandestine efforts of John Bigelow, former owner and editor of the New York *Evening Post* and now the United States consul general in France, who was responsible for American covert propaganda in that country.[22]

Edwin De Leon, a former Georgia newspaperman and former United States foreign-service officer, arrived in France at about this time, having been sent by the new Confederate secretary of state, Judah Benjamin, "for the special purpose of enlightening public opinion in Europe through the press."[23] De Leon brought along a Secret Service fund of twenty-five thousand dollars to be used to subsidize journals and journalists friendly to the Southern cause, and he used most of this money to buy the cooperation of *La patrie, Le pays,* and *Le constitutionnel.*[24] The first two were semiofficial newspapers that had already taken a hard pro-Southern line before De Leon appeared on the scene, but *Le constitutionnel* had been sitting on the fence, and it may have been the Confederate agent's money that caused it finally to come down in favor of the South.[25]

By the end of 1862, De Leon had gone through the entire Secret Service fund and asked Benjamin to send more money. The secretary replied, promising to send additional funds and asking the propaganda agent to "extend the field of your operations, and to embrace, if possible, the press of Central Europe in your campaign."[26] De Leon tried but was unable to turn back the tide of pro-Northern sentiment in Germany, Austria, and Prussia.

He returned to France, where he wrote and published a pamphlet, *The Truth About the Confederacy*, an ill-conceived project that tried to argue the merits of slavery and succeeded only in focusing French attention on that unpopular aspect of the Southern cause. His European mission was cut short in 1864, when Slidell, angry with the agent for meddling in purely diplomatic matters, complained to Benjamin and brought about his recall.

Far more cost-effective as a Confederate gray propagandist[27] was Swiss-born Henry Hotze, not yet thirty years of age but already a veteran of the United States foreign service—he was secretary of the legation in Belgium in 1858–59—and former editor of the Mobile, Alabama, *Register.* Hotze enlisted in the Confederate army in April 1861, but his talents and knowledge of Europe were soon recognized by the War Department, which sent him to Europe in August to purchase war material. He remained in London as a covert propagandist, operating under official cover as a Confederate commercial agent.[28] He was given an annual budget of two thousand pounds for his work, money he spent to much greater effect than De Leon's much larger Secret Service allowance.[29]

Although Hotze began by working as a correspondent and editorial writer for such British periodicals as the *London Post*, the *Herald*, the *Standard*, and the *Money Market Review*, he soon devised a much more ambitious method of disseminating the Confederate point of view. On May 1, 1862, he brought out the first issue of the *Index, A Weekly Journal of Politics, Literature, and News*. Ostensibly written by Englishmen for Englishmen, the *Index* was edited by Hotze and published the work of established London journalists Hotze hired to moonlight for him. Hotze paid them regular salaries to write to his specifications and encouraged them to recycle the same material for sale and publication elsewhere. Within two years material from the *Index* was appearing regularly in some twenty papers throughout England, the Continent, and even across the Atlantic in the American North.[30] The *Index* continued to publish pro-Southern material every week for the next three years, building such momentum that it did not come to a halt until August 12, 1865, more than five months after General Lee surrendered at Appomattox Court House.

The *Index* was not Hotze's only project. Through his thrift and energy he found money and time to print circulars giving a digest of the needs of the Southern markets, which he mailed to the leading British wholesale merchants; he placarded London with designs of the newly adopted Confederate flag; he subsidized the circulation of books and pamphlets dealing with the South in a friendly way; he helped other Confederate agents organize peace meetings in the north of England and the signing of a giant peace petition, which pro-Southern Englishmen presented to Parliament; and he organized and conducted campaigns against Federal recruiting in Europe.[31]

After De Leon was recalled from France in 1864, Hotze more than filled the void left in Confederate propaganda in Europe. Where his predecessor had achieved marginal results through the expenditure of huge sums, Hotze won huge propaganda victories without spending a penny. Rather than pay French journalists to write pro-Southern stories, he furnished hard news of the war in America to a press hungry for such information. He accomplished this by convincing Charles Havas of the Havas-Bullier Telegraphic and Correspondence Agency that he could furnish more accurate reports of military matters than anything available from Northern newspapers or press agencies. Havas agreed to take everything Hotze could give him and distribute it through his agency without editing it. Since Havas had a monopoly on supplying the French press with foreign news, this arrangement put Hotze in complete control of what every Frenchman read in his daily newspaper about events in America. Although all of Hotze's news was true, he made sure that truths not helpful to the Southern cause did not make it into the French prints.[32]

Hotze's chief opponent in the secret war of words was Henry S. Sanford, who had given much attention to propaganda in Europe after the British branch of his surveillance network was taken from him late in 1861. He had already begun on a small scale in England by sending complimentary subscriptions to the pro-Northern London *News* and *American* to some five hundred influential British opinion and policy makers and by trying to get the less friendly *Times* to balance its columns with some Federal views.[33]

He set about to recruit paid propaganda agents on a dozen or so of the leading European papers. In May 1862 he paid six thousand francs to the editor of the *Indépendant belge* and in August, one thousand francs to A. Malespine of the Paris *Opinion nationale*. Malespine not only planted pro-Northern material in his publication; he also acted as a psychological-warfare consultant to Sanford, persuading him to de-emphasize preservation of the Union as the Federal war aim and focus on slavery as the central issue of the war. Sanford spent lavishly to influence European opinion, often using his own money when the Secret Service fund ran out; in the first six months of 1863 alone, he paid fifteen thousand dollars from his own pocket to finance the secret war.[34]

Sanford's closest clandestine associates in France were John Bigelow, the American consul general, and Nelson M. Beckwith, a wealthy American who spent most of his time in Paris. Both men took part in the gray propaganda campaign, but they also participated in Sanford's intelligence-gathering operations. In July Beckwith reported to Sanford that he might soon have to match wits again with his old adversary James Bulloch. Beckwith had information that the Confederate naval agent planned to transfer his shipbuilding activity to France.[35]

The *Florida* and the *Alabama*, the two cruisers Bulloch had contracted to have built in England, were completed in March and July 1862, respectively, and put in service by the Confederate navy. Both ships were wooden, however, and when Bulloch arrived back in England in March, he set about to fulfill Secretary Mallory's basic plan, the procurement of ironclad warships. In June he contracted with the Lairds, builders of the *Alabama*, for two armored warships. The ships were intended for coastal warfare and so were to be of shallow draft. Each was to be equipped with two revolving armored turrets and a protuberance of the bow below the water line for the purpose of ramming enemy vessels.[36] While the *Florida* and the *Alabama* had been built for the ostensible purpose of commercial transportation, the obvious function of the Laird rams, as they were called, was war, and British neutrality laws immediately came into question.

Both Bulloch and the Lairds had independently consulted lawyers, however, and had been advised that so long as the ships were not fitted with guns or loaded with ammunition, building them and selling them to Bulloch could not be a violation of the neutrality laws. But Charles Francis Adams, aware of the ironclads, was putting increased pressure on the British government to stop them, citing the extensive damage already done to American merchant shipping by the *Florida* and the *Alabama*. By February 3 Bulloch was pessimistic in his cipher dispatch to Mallory:

"Think British Government will prevent iron ships leaving, and am much perplexed; object of armoured ships too evident for disguise."[37]

Mallory thought he saw a neat solution to the problem: he contacted Slidell in Paris and instructed him to find a French proxy to whom Bulloch could transfer ownership of the rams and from whom the Confederacy could then receive them. Slidell selected A. Bravay et Compagnie of Paris, who purchased the ships, ostensibly for the pasha of Egypt. This seemed to remove the pressure from the British government to intervene, but Adams was having none of it. To British Foreign Secretary Lord John Russell's explanation that his government could not interfere in a purchase by the French or by the Egyptian pasha, he replied that the rams, if permitted to leave British waters, would immediately depart "on a hostile errand to the United States." He closed his note to Russell with the chilling declaration, "It would be superfluous in me to point out to your Lordship that this is war."[38]

The British, comprehending the danger of the situation, ordered the rams detained while they tried to find a way out of the situation. "They even went to the expense of sending a commission to Egypt to examine the Viceroy and his Grand Vizier as to their business relations with Messrs. Bravay," Bulloch recalled. And

> finally, after coquetting for some time about the purchase of the ships, they sent down experts from the Admiralty, who carefully examined and valued them, and then, with the law-suit in one hand and the valuation in the other, they made a direct offer to Messrs. Bravay, which was accepted, and the preliminary terms upon which the two rams should pass into the Royal Navy were settled on about the 20th of May, 1864.[39]

The loss of the Laird rams was not a complete surprise to Bulloch, who had been skeptical about the final effectiveness of Mallory's proxy-buyer ploy. At about the same time he transferred the British-built ironclads to Bravay et Compagnie, he decided to build subsequent warships in France, and he selected the Bordeaux firm of M. L. Arman et Compagnie, France's leading shipbuilder. In July he contracted with Arman for four ironclads.[40]

In moving his operations to France, Bulloch was relying upon assurances received from Slidell, Arman, and others that the French emperor was well-disposed toward the Confederacy and would not prove troublesome, as had the British. Napoléon had become more deeply involved in his Mexican adventure by this time, however, and had no wish to antagonize the United States any further than necessary at the moment. He might therefore have wished that were Arman and Bulloch to do business at all, they do it in the utmost secrecy. He certainly would not have wished for Sanford and Bigelow to get wind of the matter, but as it happened, the ink on the Arman contract was hardly dry before Beckwith reported the matter to Bigelow and Sanford.

Beckwith had supplied the information but not the proof. The Americans were still debating how best to raise the matter with Napoléon's government when, on September 10, one of those strokes of luck intelligence officers sometimes enjoy appeared on Bigelow's doorstep in the person of M. Trémont, a clerk in the French firm of Voruz et Compagnie. Voruz was a shipbuilder to whom Arman, momentarily busy, had subcontracted two of the four Confederate ironclads.[41]

Bigelow's caller offered to sell him, for the sum of twenty thousand francs, documents showing that Confederate ironclads were being built in France. The consul general bargained the price down to fifteen thousand francs, paid the money, and received the evidence, proving beyond question that the French shipbuilders were building warships for the Confederacy.

William L. Dayton, the American minister to France, set the evidence before the French foreign minister. The action produced prompt results: the French government, threatening M. L. Arman with imprisonment, ordered that the ships be sold to "some foreign merchant and dispatched as ordinary trading vessels."[42] The ships were sold to Prussia, Peru, and Denmark. The Danish ship was eventually acquired secretly by the Confederacy and christened the *Stonewall*, but she had gotten no closer to the Confederacy than Havana by May 11, 1865, weeks after the war had ended.

The impact of the Federal and Confederate Secret Service operations in Europe is difficult to assess. The *Alabama* sank, burned, or captured more than sixty ships. The *Shenandoah*, a ship Bulloch purchased from British owners, captured nearly forty ships, valued at about $1.4 million in all. All together, the British-built Confederate cruisers did more than nineteen million dollars in damage to Northern shipping.[43] But Bulloch never realized Mallory's aim of acquiring armored warships to defeat the Federal blockade, and Sanford's intelligence networks played a major role in keeping him from doing so.

The blockade itself was only partially effective. It is estimated that in 1861 not more than one in ten blockade-runners was intercepted, and even after Federal forces had captured most of the seaports in 1865, only half of the interlopers were caught.[44] How important Sanford's surveillance networks were in making those captures is a matter that remains to be studied systematically.

The effect of the propaganda war on relations with Britain and France is imponderable, Many students of the subject believe that the actual course of military events in America—battles won or lost—far outweighed the covert manipulation of opinion but that propaganda may have enhanced the psychological effects of each side's victories. The failure of Lee's invasion of the North at Antietam may have ended all possibility of European intervention on the side of the South, and one historian believes that "after November, 1862, all wartime diplomacy receded into insignificance."[45] Yet one must wonder what the talented and energetic Henry Hotze might have accomplished had Richmond recognized his talents and furnished him with real resources a year earlier. And one can only speculate on the enormous damage Sanford might have unwittingly done to the Northern cause in Britain had not Seward been so wise as to rein him in at the end of 1861.

The fairest assessment of the secret war in Europe may be this: Confederate covert operations, in the end, came to very little. They might have come to very little in any case, but the activities of the Federal Secret Service made that outcome certain.

Chapter Thirteen

Civil War Subversion

The Civil War was a sectional conflict, but neither the North nor the South enjoyed anything like unanimous popular support for its war effort. Large segments of the population of both sides did not support their respective governments, and disloyalty posed a serious internal security problem for both the Union and the Confederacy. These two large disaffected groups presented favorable environments for enemy covert operations, and neither side neglected the opportunity to exploit them.

There were many in the South who supported the Southern viewpoints on such issues as slavery and states' rights but did not believe secession from the Union was the way to resolve the conflict with the North; Southerners of this view even included the vice president of the Confederacy, Alexander H. Stephens, who acceded to secession reluctantly and took a dissident position throughout the war. There were, further, a great many Southerners who did not own slaves or depend upon them for their livelihood and so held no great personal interest in a major issue of North-South contention. And there were more than a few Southerners who were as passionately abolitionist as any in the North. The Confederate government exacerbated the problem of internal political dissent posed by these elements and created active opposition to its policies by enacting tax and conscription measures that favored the wealthy planter at the expense of the poor farmer. As the latter complained, it seemed like "a rich man's war and a poor man's fight."[1]

Antiwar, antisecession, and abolitionist sentiments provided a favorable environment for the growth of three secret subversive organizations in the Confederacy. In the hill counties of northwestern Arkansas, a stronghold of Unionist sentiment, the Peace and Constitutional Society flourished.

Far more potent was the Peace Society, which existed in Alabama, East Tennessee, Georgia, Mississippi, and perhaps Florida. In North Carolina, southwestern Virginia, and East Tennessee the Order of the Heroes of America worked secretly to subvert the Confederacy. All three groups were replete with the paraphernalia of the secret society: passwords, countersigns, secret handshakes, and degrees of membership corresponding to levels of access to the organization's innermost secrets.[2]

The secret societies worked against conscription, encouraging men of military age to evade the draft and sheltering those who did so. They urged those already in the Confederate service to desert and assisted draft evaders and deserters who wished to do so to cross to Federal territory and enlist in the United States Army. They penetrated the rank and file of the Confederate army, spreading disaffection and encouraging desertion. Their members are believed to have penetrated local draft boards and the army's conscription department, where they tried to frustrate conscription. They supported anti-war candidates in state and local elections.[3]

The organizations maintained continual contact with Federal forces and supported them in every way possible, and in return they were protected from Federal foraging and other depredations. In Alabama members of the Peace Society carried out sabotage, destroying railroads, telegraph lines, and bridges, and served as guides for Federal cavalry detachments on raids throughout the state. In Florida they mounted an unsuccessful plot to kidnap the governor.[4] The most valuable service rendered by the Southern dissident groups, however, was intelligence.

In North Carolina the Reverend Marble Nash Taylor, a leader of the Heroes of America, was believed to have supplied the Federals with important military information.[5] In Mississippi a Presbyterian minister, the New York–born Rev. John H. Augey, a leader of the Peace Society, regularly collected military intelligence and passed it along to Federal commanders.[6] Mrs. Jeannette Laurimer Mabry, the wife of a loyal Confederate colonel of Knox County, Tennessee, was a secret and ardent Unionist who provided a steady stream of intelligence to the Federals. And Robert W. Boone, another East Tennessean and a great-grandson of Daniel Boone, ran an intelligence network out of Knoxville that extended into North Carolina, South Carolina, and Georgia. During his Federal secret service Boone penetrated eight different Confederate regiments, serving variously as a private and as a commissioned officer, and rescued hundreds of Federal prisoners of war.[7]

These were but a handful of Southern dissidents, those whose service as Federal spies became a matter of record; the number of those who did as much or more but remained anonymous to ensure their postwar safety must be legion. The secret societies of the South provided a dissident infrastructure within which Federal intelligence chiefs found ready-made networks for the collection and transmission of military intelligence.

While most of this chapter of the history of American intelligence and espionage has been lost, probably forever, some interesting fragments have been recovered through the painstaking efforts of a few researchers. One such fragment is the story of the Richmond Underground. Throughout the war an efficient network of Unionists operated in the Confederate capital, carrying out sabotage, aiding escaped Northern prisoners of war, and transmitting intelligence to the Federal forces. It reportedly extended into the Confederate War and Navy departments and, according to one account, even penetrated the household of President Jefferson Davis. The Richmond Underground was led by Elizabeth Van Lew, a prominent Richmond spinster, and Samuel Ruth, the superintendent of the Richmond, Fredericksburg and Potomac Railroad.[8]

Van Lew, born in Richmond in 1818, was the daughter of two transplanted Northerners: John Van Lew, originally of Long Island, New York, who became a prosperous hardware merchant in Virginia, and Elizabeth Louise Baker, the daughter of a mayor of Philadelphia.[9] Sent to Philadelphia for her education, Elizabeth Van Lew returned an ardent abolitionist. After her father's death she freed the family's nine slaves and purchased and freed several of their relatives.[10] By one account, she began sending confidential reports to Washington on conditions in Richmond soon after John Brown's raid at Harpers Ferry in 1859.[11]

The complete history of the Richmond Underground as told in official records of the War Department is lost forever; in December 1866 Elizabeth Van Lew asked for all the dispatches she had sent during the war and all other papers relating to her; she was given all but a few of the documents, and she is presumed to have destroyed them in order to protect the members of her wartime network.[12] Most of what is known of the underground's activities is based on statements filed after the war with the United States government by some of its members in application for financial compensation or other official consideration of their wartime service.

Van Lew's partner in leading the Richmond Underground, Samuel Ruth, was born in Pennsylvania, also in 1818. Ruth moved to Virginia in 1839, after receiving some training as a mechanic. He married, became a resident of Richmond, and went to work for the Richmond, Fredericksburg and Potomac Railroad. By 1853 he had risen to the rank of superintendent.[13] Just when he began working as a Federal secret agent is unknown, but during the Peninsula Campaign he was reporting intelligence regarding the situation in Richmond to General McClellan before June 1862.[14]

As earlier noted, railroads were vital to the Confederate war effort. They enabled the Confederacy to concentrate its numerically inferior forces quickly in response to strategic initiatives by the Union. The Virginia lines were of particular strategic importance, as General Beauregard demonstrated when he used them to rush reinforcements from distant points in the west to help turn back the Federal advance at the First Battle of Bull Run. The Richmond, Fredericksburg and Potomac Railroad was a crucial link in the Virginia rail network, linking Richmond with the Confederate stronghold at Fredericksburg, halfway between the Confederate and Federal capitals. And this vital link was under the stewardship of Samuel Ruth, a co-director of the Richmond Underground.

Ruth's use of his position to sabotage General Lee's army during the Fredericksburg and Chancellorsville campaigns of 1862–63 seems to be the earliest well-documented instance of the underground's subversive operations.[15] During this period trains of the RF&P moved supplies to the front with unwonted slowness, railroad bridges destroyed by Federal raiders were slow to be rebuilt, private freight was given priority over military shipments, and railroad equipment was damaged or destroyed in unaccountable accidents. General Lee was so dismayed by Ruth's apparent lack of "zeal and energy" that he tried unsuccessfully to have him replaced in January 1863. The Unionist's sabotage of Lee's line of supply played an important part in the Confederate defeat at Chancellorsville, and some historians have speculated that a Confederate victory in that battle might have led to a Confederate victory at Gettysburg and, ultimately, to a different outcome of the war.[16]

* * *

Although Elizabeth Van Lew seems to have been active throughout the war, one of the few operations of the Richmond Underground in which her participation is recorded in extant official documents began in early February 1864, when one of her couriers arrived at the Federal outpost of Fort Monroe with a dispatch from her to Major General Benjamin Butler, commander of the Eighteenth Army Corps, which was headquartered there. The message, which is the one Van Law report somehow overlooked by the War Department when it acceded to her 1866 request for all her wartime correspondence, informed Butler that all the Richmond prisoners of war were soon to be sent to Georgia and that a large part of the force defending Richmond had either been sent to North Carolina or been otherwise removed from the Confederate capital. In addition, the courier orally reported to Butler the assessment of Charles Palmer, a wealthy Richmond merchant in the underground, that no more than thirty thousand troops could be mustered on five days' notice to defend Richmond and the estimate of Quaker, yet another member of the Richmond Underground and one whose true name is lost to history, that the Confederate capital could be taken in a swift raid by some ten thousand Federal cavalry.[17]

Van Lew's dispatch set in motion two Federal military operations aimed at freeing the Richmond POWs before they were sent south. The first of these was ordered by General Butler on February 6, immediately after he received the dispatch, and consisted of a raid up the Yorktown peninsula. The element of surprise was lost, however, and the raiding party was turned back several miles east of Richmond. The second operation was more ambitious: it was intended to seize the Confederate capital.

On the night of February 28, a Federal force of thirty-five hundred cavalrymen led by Brigadier General Hugh Judson Kilpatrick and Colonel Ulric Dahlgren crossed the Rapidan River near Chancellsorsville and struck south. At the same time Brigadier General George Armstrong Custer led a smaller cavalry force on a diversionary raid into Albemarle County, a hundred miles to the west of Richmond. When Kilpatrick and Dahlgren arrived before Richmond—they had split their force and arrived separately—they found that the element of surprise had again been lost, and the Confederate defenses were too strong to assault. While withdrawing his force, Dahlgren rode into a Confederate ambush and was killed.

Papers found by the Confederates on the officer's body showed that the raiders had intended to burn Richmond and assassinate Jefferson Davis and his cabinet. Although the authenticity of these papers still remains a matter of dispute among historians, the defenders of Richmond believed them genuine at the time. Instead of returning Dahlgren's body to the Federal authorities as was customary, the outraged Confederates subjected it to public display and other indignities and then buried it in an unmarked grave.

Rear Admiral John A. Dahlgren, the dead officer's father, exerted his considerable influence on the Federal authorities to recover his son's body, and the Confederate officials soon acceded to General Butler's entreaties in the matter. Upon opening the unmarked grave, however, the Confederates discovered that the body had been removed. But before they could advise Butler of the development, the Federal commander had had word from the Richmond Underground that put him in a very difficult situation.

"The remains are . . . in the hands of devoted friends of the Union," he advised Admiral Dahlgren. He continued:

> I hardly dare suggest to [the Confederate official in charge of the matter], when he reports to me, as he will, that he cannot find them, that I can put them into his possession, because that will show such correspondence with Richmond as will alarm them, and will redouble their vigilance to detect my sources of information.[18]

The body had been removed from its supposedly secret grave at the direction of Elizabeth Van Lew, who also arranged to have it sealed in a special metal coffin, smuggled out of Richmond, and reburied for eventual postwar exhumation and return to the Dahlgren family. There could hardly have been a more impressive demonstration of the potency of the Richmond Underground, and one can easily understand General Butler's unwillingness to make the Confederate authorities aware of the situation.

*   *   *

The intelligence role of the Richmond Underground became increasingly important in the spring of 1864, when General Ulysses S. Grant began the campaign in Virginia that would culminate a year later in the fall of Richmond and the defeat of the Confederacy. In March the underground may have warned Dr. Orazio Lugo de Antonzini that the Confederate authorities were about to arrest him as a Federal spy. Dr. Lugo, who said he was of Italian birth, was a Federal espionage agent sent into the Confederacy by the United States Navy to collect detailed technical intelligence regarding torpedoes (i.e., submarine mines). The warning notwithstanding, Lugo was apprehended by the Confederate counterespionage authorities, but the evidence against him was insufficient to hang him, and he was instead expelled from the Confederate States.[19]

Samuel Ruth's intelligence activities in 1864–65 became a matter of official record after the war when he applied to Congress for monetary consideration of his service. Sometime in early autumn 1864 he sent Brigadier General George H. Sharpe, General Grant's chief intelligence officer, details of the strength of forces guarding the principal bridges of the Virginia Central and his own RF&P. Later that fall he reported that large quantities of bacon smuggled into the Confederacy from Maryland were being shipped to Richmond on his railroad. Just before Christmas he advised Sharpe of the exact number of reinforcements Lee had sent to Wilmington, North Carolina. In January he reported on the rapidly deteriorating condition of the Virginia railroads and the resulting shortages of quartermaster stores in Richmond and Petersburg. In February he reported details of General Jubal Early's forces in the Shenandoah Valley shortly before General Philip Sheridan dealt Early his final defeat. Also in February he reported a Confederate plan to ship four hundred thousand pounds of tobacco north to the vicinity of Fredericksburg on the RF&P, to be illegally traded for smuggled bacon from the North; warned of the deal, the Federals raided Fredericksburg, seized the tobacco—valued at $380,000—and thereby denied the Confederates the much-needed food. In March he warned of Lee's impending attack on Fort Stedman, a vulnerable point in the Federal lines around Petersburg; the attack failed and the Confederates sustained heavy losses.[20]

After the war General Sharpe advised Secretary of War Stanton that in appraising the value of the services rendered by Ruth and several of his underground associates, he was "unwilling to name a less sum than forty thousand dollars."[21]

Throughout these final months of the war, Elizabeth Van Lew was in daily contact with Generals Grant and Sharpe, but the flow of intelligence from her Richmond mansion to the commander's headquarters tent can only be guessed at. Some indication of the importance of her work was given by General Sharpe, however, who wrote after the war, "The greater portion [of our intelligence of 1864–65] in its collection and in good measure its transmission, we owed to the intelligence and devotion of Miss Van Lew."[22]

Van Lew, Ruth, and the members of their underground were defectors in place, indigenous volunteer agents acting on their own initiative. The presence of such intelligence assets at the nerve center of the Confederacy was a stroke of luck, not the result of Federal preparations. Still, such opportunities have often gone a-begging in the chronicles of espionage, and Generals Butler, Grant, and Sharpe must be given credit for making good use of the opportunity when it was presented to them.

Dissent in the North was not limited to the border states and such secessionist strongholds as Baltimore. The Copperheads, as the antiwar faction of the Democratic party was called, were strong in the Northwest (today's Midwest) and in New York. In Ohio, Indiana, and Illinois, where an estimated 40 percent of the population was of Southern birth or parentage, the Copperheads received heavy support in the elections of 1862, and major northwestern newspapers took a strong Copperhead editorial stand. In New York City thousands of recent immigrants were simply indifferent to the issues of secession and abolition and were therefore unwilling to submit to conscription or make other sacrifices for the war effort. Fernando Wood, New York's Copperhead mayor, advocated that the city do as the Confederate states had done and secede from the Union as an independent "free city."[23]

As in the South, the climate of political dissent fostered the growth of secret subversive societies, one of the first of which was the Knights of the Golden Circle. The KGC had actually been established before the war and was the creature of George Washington Leigh Bickley, a Virginia-born huckster with a keen sense of the allure such paraphernalia as secret oaths, passwords, countersigns, handshakes, and all the other regalia of the secret society holds for many people. In the Copperhead strongholds of Illinois, Indiana, and Ohio, the idea of a secret secessionist society was enormously popular. Bickley created the KGC to meet that demand. At a membership initiation fee of five dollars per head, the Knights proved most remunerative.

The KGC was far from being a harmless outlet for puerile fantasies, however. In the Northwest the draft was resisted, recruiters were ambushed and killed, enrollment papers were destroyed, and men of draft age were encouraged to resist or go South and join the Confederate army. Arms were stolen from Federal arsenals. Federal property was sabotaged, and the homes of men who had joined the state militia or the United States Army were burned.[24] How much of such mischief can be attributed to the KGC and similar Copperhead secret societies is disputed by historians, at least one of whom denies that the organization was ever a serious threat to internal security in the Northwest or elsewhere.[25] But at the very least, the KGC was an index of the widespread disloyalty in the North, and it provided a ready-made dissident infrastructure for Confederate covert operations there.

One of the first Confederate leaders to recognize the opportunity offered by the KGC was Brigadier General John Hunt Morgan. Morgan's Raiders had been making lightning cavalry raids deep into Federal territory in Kentucky and Tennessee, and the general saw the advantage in knowing who his friends were while so far from home. During the winter of 1862–63, Morgan sent one of his officers, Captain Thomas H. Hines, on several undercover missions into Kentucky to contact the local leaders of the Copperheads and the KGC and organize an underground to support his cavalry raids.[26] The following June, Hines undertook a mission through Indiana and Ohio for the same purpose.

In July 1863 Morgan led some twenty-four hundred troopers into Ohio and Indiana. He planned to release and arm a large number of Confederate prisoners of war held near Indianapolis and, with the help of the KGC, precipitate a Copperhead uprising that would achieve the secession of

Indiana and bring it into the Confederacy.[27] But the Copperhead support failed to materialize, and the local militia did not switch sides as Morgan expected, but joined Federal forces in repelling the invaders. Morgan's expedition was routed, and Morgan and 364 of his force, including Hines, were captured. Morgan, Hines, and several of the other captives later managed to escape and make their way back through Confederate lines.

In February 1864 Hines went to Richmond with a letter from General Morgan introducing him to President Davis. Davis, Secretary of War John Seddon, and Secretary of State Benjamin met repeatedly with Hines and listened to the plan he had come to propose. Essentially, Hines's scheme was an ambitious elaboration of what he and Morgan had attempted the previous July: the freeing and arming of Confederate prisoners of war, who with the help of Northern dissidents would overthrow the state governments. But Hines's plan was of a much grander scale: it was to be mounted from Canada with the help of the hundreds of escaped Confederate prisoners living there; it was to involve the release of as many as fifty thousand prisoners of war; and it was to dovetail with a Copperhead uprising reportedly planned for midsummer throughout Ohio, Indiana, Illinois, and Missouri. With these states split from the Union, Michigan, Wisconsin, Minnesota, Iowa, and Kansas would be geographically isolated and therefore forced to follow. The end result was to be a Northwest confederacy, which would ally itself with the South.[28]

The dream of a Northwest confederacy had been part of Confederate wishful thinking for a long time. Hines's plan was ambitious, perhaps unrealistic, but the Confederate leaders must have seen that it need not succeed completely to save the South; a large armed uprising in the Northwest would paralyze the Northern war effort. In any case, the Confederacy had little to lose in trying it.

The operation was put under the overall supervision of three Confederate commissioners stationed in Canada: Jacob Thompson, who had been President Buchanan's secretary of the interior before serving as a colonel on the staff of Confederate lieutenant general John C. Pemberton; J. P. Holcomb, a Virginia lawyer and Confederate congressman; and former United States senator Clement Clay of Alabama.

Soon after arriving in Canada, Hines established a liaison with the leaders of the Copperhead underground in the Northwest. The KGC had by this time virtually ceased to exist as an organization, following the arrest and imprisonment of Bickley.[29] Never more than a loosely organized network of dissidents lacking strong, central leadership, it lost its momentum and was supplanted by a new organization, initially called the Order of American Knights and later the Sons of Liberty (perhaps in memory of the eighteenth-century organization of that name).

The SL was headed by Clement L. Vallandigham, an Ohio lawyer and journalist who had represented his state in the House of Representatives from 1858 to 1862. Outspoken in his opposition to the war and Federal policies, he was arrested in May 1863 for violating a local military order against "declaring sympathy for the enemy." After a trial by court-martial (although he was a civilian), he was imprisoned, then banished to the Confederacy. The Confederate government helped him through the Federal blockade and on to Canada. He was staying in Windsor, Ontario, when Thompson and Hines visited him.

Vallandigham and several of the state leaders of the SL met with Thompson and Hines on June 11, 1864. They told the Confederates that there were three hundred thousand Sons of Liberty, including eighty-five thousand in Illinois, fifty thousand in Indiana, and forty thousand in Ohio. Many of the members were recently discharged veterans of the United States Army, they said, and therefore seasoned soldiers. Vallandigham reportedly said that all were ready to follow him in an armed uprising to establish a Northwest confederacy if money for arms and miscellaneous expenses related to such an undertaking could be provided.[30] Thompson, who commanded the large contingent fund the Confederate government had provided the Canada commissioners for covert-action operations, readily agreed to furnish the cash. The Confederate agents and the Copperhead underground leaders then laid plans for the operation.

There was to be a presidential election in the North in November. If the Copperheads could nominate a peace candidate on the Democratic ticket, the campaign could be counted on to exacerbate antiwar sentiment throughout the United States. The Democratic National Convention was scheduled for July 4, and it was to be held in Chicago, a center of Copperhead activity and the site of one of the largest POW camps targeted by Hines. The Confederate agents therefore decided to make Chicago the center of the revolt, and scheduled it for July 4. The plan was disrupted, however, when the Democrats decided to postpone the convention until August 29 in the hope that anticipated Federal battlefield reverses would heighten antiwar sentiment during the summer. Hines and the SL rescheduled the uprising for that date.

Hines arrived in Chicago on August 28 with sixty hand-picked Confederate commandos to discover that the SL leaders had been unable to assemble a promised two thousand Chicago followers, nor had they brought the downstate contingent to the city. Once again, the date of the planned uprising was rescheduled, this time for November 8, election day.[31]

While the leaders of the Sons of Liberty attempted to materialize their evanescent underground, the Confederate commissioners in Canada mounted several independent operations. On September 19 a team of twenty Confederate commandos hijacked a pair of steamers on Lake Erie in an operation aimed at capturing the U.S.S. *Michigan*, a Federal gunboat. The plan failed, however, when the Federal authorities learned of it from a Confederate defector.

One month later Confederate raiders struck again, this time in the Northeast. On November 19 a group of some twenty-five Confederate commandos took over Saint Albans, Vermont, a town close to the Canadian border, robbed the town's three banks, taking a total of two hundred thousand dollars, and set fire to the hotel and other public buildings.

In an ensuing gun battle one resident was killed and others were wounded. Taking their loot, the raiders mounted horses stolen from the local livery stables and fled back to the border with a posse of townspeople in hot pursuit. Thirteen of the raiders were captured in Canada and held there by the Canadian authorities pending extradition. They remained in Canadian custody until after the war, then were released.

The hijacking of the two Lake Erie steamers heightened Federal apprehension and watchfulness. In October Federal authorities rounded up some of the Indiana SL members and put them on trial. The planned election day raid on the POW camps was betrayed to the Federal authorities by yet another of the Canadian Confederates. On the fourth or fifth of November, Maurice Langhorne, a Confederate deserter who had insinuated himself into the confidence of Thompson and Hines, sold the details of the plan, including the date, the names of all involved, and the existence of an arms cache at an SL leader's house, to Colonel Benjamin Sweet, commandant of one of the POW camps.[32] On November 6, two days before election day, the authorities rounded up most of the ringleaders of the plot, bringing what came to be known as the Northwest Conspiracy to an end.

Confederate commissioner Clement Clay, who was residing in Saint Catharines, Ontario, just across from Niagara Falls, had authorized the Saint Albans raid and seems to have been in charge of all covert-action operations in the Northeast. He did not know that much or all of his correspondence with Secretary of State Benjamin and the other Confederate leaders in Richmond was being read at the War Department in Washington.

Sometime in 1863 or 1864 Richard Montgomery, a young government clerk in Washington, offered the War Department his services as a spy. His offer was accepted. Montgomery passed through the lines and, calling himself James Thompson, visited Richmond, where whatever story he told was accepted by the Confederate authorities. He was employed as a courier, probably by Colonel Norris's Secret Service Bureau. Montgomery was soon making regular runs between Richmond and Saint Catharines, carrying official dispatches to and from Clay.[33]

Montgomery routinely stopped at the War Department every time he traveled between the Confederacy and Canada and turned over the Confederate mail to Assistant Secretary of War Charles A. Dana, who had the dispatches opened, copied, and resealed. To prevent detection, Dana arranged for the Confederates' seals to be copied and even went to the length of obtaining English-made envelopes of the kind sold in Canada to replace those used by Clay, which had been destroyed in the process of opening them. Montgomery explained the delays caused by such procedures as the result of difficulties he encountered in crossing the Federal lines.

"At any rate," Dana recalled, "the confidence of the Confederates in our agent and in theirs never seemed to be shaken by any of these occurrences."[34]

Montgomery learned the general plan of the Saint Albans raid before the fact but wasn't able to find out which New England town was targeted.[35] One of Clay's dispatches to Secretary of State Benjamin disclosed plans for "a new and really formidable military expedition" against Burlington, Vermont. In order to retain possession of the document without blowing Montgomery's cover, Dana contrived to have the double agent arrested, searched, and sent off to the Old Capitol Prison, then arranged his "escape" a day or so later. The Confederates may have canceled the Vermont expedition when they realized that the element of surprise had been lost or because of American pressure on the British authorities to crack down on the Canadian operations, or for both reasons.[36] Montgomery's warnings of planned Confederate raids on Buffalo and Rochester were also, he said, instrumental in preventing them.[37]

Another Clay-to-Benjamin dispatch Montgomery delivered to Dana before carrying it on to Richmond disclosed Confederate plans to burn down a large part of New York City.[38] This assault was originally intended to take place on election day in coordination with Hines's long-delayed attempt to liberate the POWs. According to Lieutenant John W. Headley, one of the eight Confederate agents who took part in it, the operation was supposed to trigger an uprising of the New York Copperheads, the seizure of the United States Subtreasury Building on Wall Street, and the release of Confederate POWs held in Fort Lafayette in New York Harbor. The arrival in the city of a large force of Federal troops under Major General Benjamin Butler on November 4, however, and news of the arrest of the Chicago SL leaders a few days later caused the Copperhead leaders to lose heart, and the operation was scrubbed. Headley and seven other Confederates carried out the incendiary part of the plan on November 25, however, setting fire to several hotels, two theaters, and Barnum's Museum.[39]

The fires had the intended effect of causing a panic in the Broadway business district, but they failed to achieve much destruction.[40] They were, in fact, extinguished without undue difficulty. Headley and his comrades managed to escape back to Canada.

In December, John Yates Beall, the leader of the steamer hijackings on Lake Erie, undertook a final mission for Jacob Thompson. Near Buffalo, he tried to free some Confederate officers by derailing a train taking them from Johnson's Island in Sandusky, Ohio, to Fort Lafayette. He failed, was captured, and was hanged as a spy. This marked an end to the Confederate covert-action operations mounted from Canada.

The hope that a small paramilitary offensive will trigger a general uprising among local dissidents is seductive and not at all a notion unique to the Confederacy; the same idea was basic to the CIA's Bay of Pigs invasion a century later. To be successful, such a scheme must be grounded in the very best intelligence regarding the organization and capabilities of both the dissidents and the countersubversion machinery opposing them. Thompson and Hines were clearly ignorant of the actual potential of the Sons of Liberty, which was either a largely nonexistent organization created in the fantasies of men like Vallandigham or else a plaything of those who might enjoy dabbling with clandestine matters but had no real commitment to treason. If there was among the radical Copperheads a potential Elizabeth Van Lew or Samuel Ruth, the Confederate Secret Service seems never to have made contact with them.

In contrasting the success of the Richmond Underground with the failure of the Confederate covert-action schemes in the North, it appears that they resulted from a common factor: a nearly complete failure of Confederate counterespionage. With very little difficulty Federal agents or defectors in place penetrated the Sons of Liberty, the Confederate apparatus in Canada, and the Confederate nerve center at Richmond.

The Confederates, especially the leadership in Richmond, seem to have been trusting to a fault. Jefferson Davis and his associates were ready to accept at face value just about anyone who appeared in Richmond and professed dedication to the Confederate cause. Consequently, Confederate security was penetrated repeatedly by such bogus walk-ins as Lafayette Baker, Timothy Webster, Dr. Lugo, and Richard Montgomery. There is no obvious alternate to naïveté, for example, to explain why strangers like Webster and Montgomery were entrusted in such sensitive positions as secret courier between Richmond and Confederate assets north of the Federal lines.

A partisan of the Lost Cause might explain such credulousness as a reflection of the Southern aristocrat's lack of Yankee guile, but this hardly sheds any light on how seasoned intriguers like Thompson, Clay, and Benjamin could have been taken in so often. It is more likely that the Confederates fell victim to their own absolute faith in the righteousness of their cause and the iniquity of abolitionists, a faith that made it difficult to suspect there could be traitors in their midst and banished all doubt that there were tens or perhaps hundreds of thousands of Northerners ready to risk the gallows or the firing squad to defend secession, preserve slavery, or throw off the Yankee yoke by establishing a Northwest confederacy.

Chapter Fourteen

The Professionals

When Allan Pinkerton resigned from the Army of the Potomac in November 1862 in the wake of Lincoln's dismissal of McClellan, he took his entire detective staff with him. Major General Ambrose E. Burnside, who succeeded McClellan, did not organize a Secret Service to replace Pinkerton and his detectives, although he might eventually have done so had he served a longer term. Burnside was not entirely without intelligence resources, however. He had his cavalry, which was often used for reconnaissance in the Civil War, and he had Professor Lowe and his balloon corps. He also had John C. Babcock, one member of Pinkerton's Secret Service who had not been an employee of the private detective agency before the war and therefore stayed on after Pinkerton departed.

Babcock, a twenty-six-year-old native of Warwick, Rhode Island, had been a member of a large Chicago architectural firm and one of that city's best-paid architects until August 1861, when he enlisted in the Sturgis Rifles, McClellan's personal guard. Three months later he was transferred to Pinkerton's Secret Service, probably to answer a call for a draftsman-mapmaker. After his enlistment expired in 1862, he remained in his intelligence post and was carried on the army rolls as a civilian employee of the Topographical Department.[1] Babcock had been one of Pinkerton's best people, and it later transpired that he was a far better order-of-battle specialist than his boss. He was a civilian, however, and far too junior to take the initiative in filling the vacuum Pinkerton had left behind.

Had General Burnside availed himself fully of Babcock's talents, and had he made full use of balloon and cavalry reconnaissance—had he, in short, recognized his own critical need for intelligence—he might have been able to assemble some sort of an order-of-battle picture of the strength and, especially, the disposition of Lee's forces at Fredericksburg, the site he had selected to cross the Rappahannock on his first step to Richmond. And had he compiled such a picture, he would certainly not have launched the attack at that point on December 13, 1862. He would thereby have avoided the slaughter and defeat that a month later brought about his replacement by Major General Joseph Hooker.

Three days after Hooker succeeded Burnside and became the third commander of the Army of the Potomac, he appointed Colonel George H. Sharpe his deputy provost marshal and gave him the task of organizing a Secret Service.[2] Sharpe, a thirty-five-year-old native of Kingston, New York, had graduated from Rutgers and studied law at Yale before practicing in New York City. After a brief stint with the foreign service as secretary of the American legation in Vienna, he returned to Kingston in 1854 and opened a law office. As a prominent citizen of Ulster County, he raised a company of volunteers for the Ulster Guard—the Twentieth New York Regiment—and led it at the First Battle of Bull Run. After his enlistment expired, he returned to Kingston and in August 1862 raised the 120th New York Regiment, of which he was named colonel. The regiment became part of the Army of the Potomac under McClellan.[3]

Sharpe's intelligence service was called the Bureau of Military Information. Recognizing the intelligence experience Babcock had gained in the year he served under Pinkerton, as well as the topographical expertise he brought to the job, Sharpe appointed him his civilian deputy. He also brought into the bureau his fellow Kingstonian, Captain John C. McEntee, to serve as the third ranking member of the unit. Sharpe assembled some seventy scouts and agents, carried on the army rolls as "guides," to gather intelligence in the field and beyond Confederate lines.

The Bureau of Military information was soon functioning as a modern military intelligence service, collecting information from all possible sources—prisoners of war, Confederate deserters and refugees, Southern newspapers, Lowe's balloon corps, Signal Corps observation posts, cavalry, communication intercepts, liaisons with other Federal commands, and of course, from the bureau's own scouts and agents. Sharpe and his deputies collated, analyzed, and digested this flow of information and produced concise and accurate intelligence for Hooker.[4]

The bureau's first test came late in April 1863. The Army of the Potomac had spent the winter camped near Falmouth, across the Rappahannock from the scene of the Fredericksburg debacle. Lee, meanwhile, had detached part of his army and sent it to southern Virginia on a foraging expedition, reducing his strength at Fredericksburg to sixty thousand. The bureau kept track of the shift, and Babcock, now the order-of-battle expert, estimated the diminished Confederate strength to within one quarter of one percent of the true figure.[5] One of Sharpe's agents living behind Confederate lines pinpointed a gap in the lines at Chancellorsville, several miles west of Fredericksburg, enabling Hooker to move half of his army to Lee's rear on April 26.[6] Although the enveloping movement floundered at Chancellsorsville a week later, the failure is attributed primarily to Hooker's yielding the initiative and Lee's superiority as a commander. The Bureau of Military Information had performed impressively in its initial trial.

Early in June, Lee began shifting his army westward from the Fredericksburg area. The bureau was, of course, aware of the movement, but not of Lee's intentions. On May 27 Sharpe had reported to Hooker: "The Confederate Army is under marching orders, and an order from General Lee was very lately read to the troops, announcing a campaign of long marches and hard fighting, in a part of the country where they would have no railroad transportation."[7]

By mid-June, however, Sharpe's agents had learned that the Confederate force was en route to the Shenandoah Valley, and it became apparent that Lee was making a second attempt to take the war into the North. Sharpe sent Babcock to Frederick, Maryland, a major stop along Lee's route north the previous September, to organize local agents and locate the Confederate force after it crossed the Potomac.[8] Alerted by Sharpe that the Confederates had crossed into Maryland, Hooker moved northward along a parallel route, concentrating the Army of the Potomac at Frederick by June 28. At this moment General Lee was encamped near Chambersburg, Pennsylvania, and his army was in an extremely vulnerable situation, strung out in a line some sixty miles long stretching from McConnellsburg, near the Pennsylvania-Maryland line, to the Susquehanna River. Lee had just ordered advance elements of his force to cross the Susquehanna. He believed that Hooker and the Army of the Potomac was far to the south, somewhere in Virginia. He was completely unaware that it was, in fact, concentrated less than fifty miles away, on the east side of the Catoctin Mountains, ready to annihilate his Army of Northern Virginia piece by piece in a series of overwhelmingly unequal engagements.

Lee was not without his own intelligence service, although he never mounted anything as ambitious as the Bureau of Military Intelligence. Reconnaissance was one of the principal tasks of Major General J. E. B. Stuart's cavalry. In addition to overt reconnaissance from the saddle, Stuart employed some very capable scouts and spies who collected intelligence behind Federal lines. But when Lee was marching northward through Pennsylvania, serenely ignorant of the disaster that threatened, he had not heard from Stuart for three days. The cavalryman, humiliated by a Federal surprise attack three weeks earlier at Brandy Station, Virginia, and stung by the resulting criticism in the Southern press, had sought to re-establish his reputation with a bold raid concurrent with Lee's northward march. With Lee's permission he set out on June 25 on a route northward between Hooker (then still in northern Virginia) and Washington. Three days later, as the Army of the Potomac was gathering at Frederick, Stuart was preoccupied with a raid on Rockville, Maryland, and the northern suburbs of the nation's capital and was unaware of the movement of the Federal force. But at that same moment a Confederate agent was about to complete one of the most significant feats of espionage of the Civil War.

Lieutenant General James Longstreet commanded the First Corps of the Army of Northern Virginia. After the death of General Stonewall Jackson at Chancellorsville, he became Lee's senior lieutenant. Early in June he began to make preparations for the invasion of the North, including the dispatching of a spy—known to history only by his surname, Harrison—to Washington to collect any "information of importance" that might be available.

Three weeks later, on the night of June 28, Harrison reported to Longstreet in the latter's tent at Chambersburg. The general later recalled:

> He . . . brought information of the location of two corps of Federals at night of the 27th, and approximate positions of others.

General Hooker had crossed the Potomac on the 25th and 26th of June. On the 27th he had posted two army corps at Frederick, and the scout reported another near them, and two others near South Mountain, as he escaped their lines a little after dark of the 28th.[9]

Advised of the intelligence, Lee quickly pulled back his advance elements from the Susquehanna and ordered all of the Army of Northern Virginia to concentrate at a quiet little Pennsylvania crossroads called Gettysburg.

Sharpe's Bureau of Military Information and an otherwise unidentified Confederate spy named Harrison had set the stage for one of the great turnings of American history.[10] It was the eve of the pivotal Confederate defeat, and within five days the ultimate fate of the South would be determined. Federal intelligence had thwarted Lee's final effort to take the war into the North, but a Confederate agent had saved Lee from the total annihilation that would have brought the war to a swift conclusion. Espionage has seldom been so potent a master of events.

After Gettysburg, Sharpe's reputation and that of the Bureau of Military Information spread westward, and in October, Major General William S. Rosecrans, commander of the Army of the Cumberland, asked for Sharpe's help in keeping track of Confederate movements around Chattanooga, Tennessee. When General Ulysses S. Grant took overall command of the Union army in March 1864, he arranged for Sharpe to join his staff as his chief intelligence officer and promoted him to brevet brigadier general the following December. Babcock was put in charge of the bureau, although the new arrangement was largely theoretical, since Grant had taken the field and co-located his headquarters with those of the Army of the Potomac. Sharpe, Babcock, and the bureau served both Grant and Major General George G. Meade, who had succeeded Hooker. When Grant began his siege of Petersburg and Richmond in the final phase of the war, Sharpe and the bureau took over direction of the Richmond Underground.[11] With the war's end the bureau was dissolved. Sharpe and all the other Civil War spy masters soon returned to civilian life.

*   *   *

The Civil War saw the advent of the professional intelligence officer in both the military and the foreign service. Pinkerton and Baker were able to translate their peacetime police and investigative work into the area of counterespionage. Sharpe, Norris, Sanford, and Thompson discovered, as have many others since, that the practice of law seems to be excellent preparation for the craft of intelligence. Sharpe and Sanford also had some background in the diplomatic service, another field of experience readily transferable to intelligence and espionage work. Even the civil engineering background of John C. Babcock found uses in a business that deals so often with topography, fortifications, and lines of communications.

Like the farmer-surveyor-politician who commanded the Continental army eight decades earlier, the Civil War spy masters learned their craft on the job. But unlike General Washington they were, for the most part, full-time intelligence officers, permitted to practice what had suddenly been recognized as a distinct field of specialization within the military and diplomatic professions. Moreover, the personnel who carried out the tasks of intelligence began to be organized into specific units and agencies—the Confederate Secret Service Bureau, Lowe's balloon corps, and most of all, the Bureau of Military Information.

The Bureau of Military Information was the United States Army's first professional military intelligence agency. Earlier army units with an intelligence function never became complete intelligence services. Such units as Knowlton's Rangers, the Mexican Spy Company, and Lowe's balloon corps primarily carried out reconnaissance missions, while the many Secret Services of American commanders from General Washington to General McClellan were espionage networks. Like them the bureau collected information through scouts and spies, but it also systematically exploited every other possible source of information, from newspapers to prisoners of war. In short, it was the first all-source military intelligence service. Furthermore, it took responsibility not only for the collection of intelligence, but for its evaluation, its correlation with other evaluated information, and the production of finished intelligence, the end product of the intelligence process. In sum, it represented the realization by the men who ran the army that intelligence is a distinct military speciality, like communications or logistics, and ought to be done by specialized personnel and units.

Beyond this vital lesson in the organization and management of the intelligence function, a mass of experience in the methodology of intelligence had been accumulated during the war: cryptology and signal interception, aerial reconnaissance, order-of-battle estimation, prisoner interrogation, techniques of running covert operations in foreign countries, and other types of intelligence tradecraft.

All of this expensive education was lost, however, when the individual intelligence officers who had acquired it left government service. It had failed to become part of the institutional knowledge of the army or the diplomatic service because the War and State departments lacked general staffs, the organizational machinery necessary to absorb, retain, and practice it.

With the exception of Thomas Jordan, an 1840 graduate of the United States Military Academy, no important Civil War intelligence officer on either side came out of West Point. Every other significant figure in the intelligence history of the war was a civilian before it began, and all but one returned to civilian life soon after it was over. Had it been otherwise, some of the intelligence veterans of the war might eventually have joined the West Point faculty, and their acquired knowledge might have been integrated into the military academy's curriculum. But nothing of the sort was to happen until well into the next century.

The Civil War had marked the advent of intelligence professionalism in America, but within a year after Appomattox, the United States government was nearly as devoid of an intelligence service as it had been when the Confederates fired on Fort Sumter.

Part Four

THE BIRTH OF THE INTELLIGENCE COMMUNITY:

1865–1919

Chapter Fifteen

Intelligence and the Game of War

In 1882 the United States Navy established the Office of Intelligence within its Bureau of Navigation. Three years later the War Department created the Military Information Division as part of the army's Adjutant General's Office. Both actions were aimed more at rescuing the armed services from obsolescence than at filling the need for what today would be called intelligence.

For a brief moment in 1865, the United States was the strongest military power on earth. But such strength, marshaled to preserve the Union, was not to be sustained after it had accomplished that mission. The job of the postwar army was reduced to maintaining order within the United States: enforcing the policies of Reconstruction in a resentful and recalcitrant South, suppressing the more violent labor disturbances in the increasingly industrialized North, and protecting white settlers, now moving West in unprecedented numbers, from Indian uprisings. Over a million men strong at Appomattox, the army was cut to a mere twenty-five thousand by 1869. Except for some of the larger Indian campaigns, the army was involved more in police work than in military operations, and the art of war was largely neglected.

During this same period military technology made rapid strides in Europe, however, spurred on by perennial resentments among traditional adversaries. Many innovations that appeared in rudimentary form during the Civil War were developed and perfected in Europe during the 1870s: the breech-loading rifle, the machine gun, the modern shrapnel shell, the reconnaissance balloon, the military telegraph, and breech-loading, rifled artillery.

New weapons technology was not necessary for dealing with labor riots or Indian uprisings, however, and such things were known in the

United States Army only by those officers who kept up with European military publications. But if the United States Army marked time while military technology marched on, the United States Navy actually stepped backward.

The wartime blockade had given new life to the navy. During the war the service had experienced unprecedented growth, but after the war the fleet was drastically cut. Many of the ironclads were sold abroad, and the rest were left to rot and rust. As an economy measure the navy turned back from steam, which had proved its superiority in the war, and returned to sail.[1]

Meanwhile, naval technology surged ahead in Europe. Self-propelled torpedoes, improved armor plate, large rifled guns with unprecedented range and accuracy, and improved marine engines—all were developed by European nations in the post–Civil War decades. The muzzle velocities of naval guns were greatly increased through the development of improved gunpowders, and newly designed breech mechanisms increased the rate of fire. These developments were watched with interest and envy by dedicated officers of the United States Navy, but most other Americans were unaware of the vast disparity between their own navy and those of other nations.

There were some practical demonstrations of the naval gap. When a Spanish gunboat stopped the *Virginius*, a gunrunner flying the American flag, between Cuba and Jamaica, took it into the port of Santiago de Cuba, and executed the American captain and fifty-two others, the United States went to the brink of a war with Spain. As tensions deepened, the administration of President U. S. Grant assembled a naval flotilla at Key West. It was the largest display of American naval power mobilized in one place since the end of the war, but it was also pathetic. One officer later estimated that "two modern vessels of war would have done us up in thirty minutes."[2] But the crisis was resolved through diplomacy. Americans were spared the spectacle of their rusting fleet being sunk by a pair of Spanish warships and so continued blissfully indifferent to the navy's condition.

The 1879–84 War of the Pacific made a greater impression on American policy makers, however, even though the United States was not directly involved. Chile, on one side, and Bolivia and Peru, on the other, fought for possession of the nitrate-rich Atacama Desert, which was claimed by all three. The navies of both Peru and Chile possessed several European-built ironclads, and their use in actual combat attracted worldwide interest.

The warships had been in service for some years and did not represent the latest state of the art; in fact, they were obsolescent. But they were, nonetheless, superior to every ship in the United States Navy. The Chilean bombardment of the port of Callao, Peru, with accurate, long-range naval guns made a special impression in the United States; American coastal defenses employed the same smoothbore batteries that had failed to repulse the attack. The realization that a small South American nation could do the same to San Francisco or Seattle came as a distinct shock in Washington.[3] It had also become apparent that the much greater superiority of new European warships over those of the United States Navy made the Monroe Doctrine unenforceable. Finally, there was the basic bread-and-butter issue of maritime trade: the economic impact of the Federal blockade of the South was a matter of living memory, and every schoolchild knew of the hardships inflicted by the British blockade in the War of 1812. The example of the War of the Pacific demonstrated to Congress that a weak navy could prove to be a foolish economy.

The long task of rebuilding the navy was begun by the administration of President Chester A. Arthur in the early 1880s. Arthur's secretary of the navy, William H. Hunt, took one of the first steps in the new navy program on March 23, 1882, when he established the Office of Intelligence within the navy's Bureau of Navigation. Shortly thereafter, the unit became known as the Office of Naval Intelligence.

The word *intelligence* was not used in the nineteenth century to mean what General Washington meant by it or as it is used today in the national-security context—that is, information about an adversary useful in dealing with him; in the 1800s and even in the early 1900s, the word meant "information in general" and it often connoted news. Thus, the ONI was not initially envisioned as, for example, simply the naval equivalent of the Army of the Potomac's Bureau of Military Information. Commodore John G. Walker, chief of the Bureau of Navigation, explained the agency's purpose this way: "The Office of Naval Intelligence was established in order that the Navy Department might be supplied with the most accurate information as to the progress of naval science, and the condition and resources of foreign navies."[4]

Thus, the ONI had two functions: gathering intelligence (in the modern sense of the word) about foreign navies and what today would be called technology transfer, the acquisition of naval technology from abroad for use in building the new navy. And it is noteworthy that Commodore Walker stated the latter function first. As the navy embarked on its massive reconstruction program, American shipyards were incapable of building modern steel warships, American armaments makers were incapable of supplying the fast and accurate breech-loading naval guns used by the navies of Europe, and there was not even an American steel mill capable of rolling the armor plates the navy needed. All of this technology and more had to be imported from Europe. That was the reason for the ONI, and that was to be its primary task.

The first chief of the ONI was thirty-four-year-old Lieutenant Theodorus Bailey Myers Mason, an officer who had already spent much time abroad studying the navies of Europe. With his staff of more than a dozen young officers, he collected and compiled a massive data base from translations of foreign technical publications, consular reports on foreign maritime commerce supplied by the State Department, and reports of observations of foreign navies from designated intelligence officers aboard navy vessels in foreign waters.

Beginning in 1879, the ONI began sending naval attachés to serve at American embassies in Europe, where they collected books, journals, blueprints, reports, and every other form of information on European naval matters.[5] The attachés filled such requests as those of the chief of ordnance for the windage of European guns; the head of the Electrical Bureau for information regarding electric lighting on Italian warships; and the Bureau of Construction for the exact weights of machinery, engines, boilers, and condensers on European vessels.[6] Most of the information requested was for use in building the new American fleet, and not for intelligence against the possibility of war with a European power. It was, in other words, technology transfer, not naval intelligence.

The Franco-Prussian War of 1870–71 demonstrated in actual combat the military technology and tactics recently introduced into the armies of Europe. It also convinced General William T. Sherman, then and for the next dozen years or so the commanding general of the army, that the United States Army was indeed falling behind the rest of the world in the art of war. The stirring of such awareness within the American military establishment led four years later to the world tour of Major General Emory Upton, lately the West Point commandant, to study foreign armies. His report, published as *The Armies of Asia and Europe* in 1878, provided a detailed look at the armies of Japan, China, India, Persia, Italy, Austria, Germany, France, and Britain, together with his analysis of how some of what he had observed might be applied to the United States Army.

The information Upton and other officers collected abroad was deposited with the adjutant general, and in October 1885 the Military Information Division was established within the Miscellaneous Branch of the AG's office.[7] The stated function of the MID was to collect "military data on our own and foreign services which would be available for the use of the War Department and the Army at large."[8] Like the ONI the MID was a central repository for two types of information: progress in the military arts and foreign military intelligence. Additionally, the unit was made the repository of such domestic information as basic intelligence—for example, maps and topographical studies—about the United States, especially the western territories, and the strength, equipment, and availability of the National Guard for service in case of sudden demand.

The MID's main job, however, was to keep abreast of European progress in military organization, methods, and technology, a task that was accomplished with much greater effectiveness after 1889, when the army followed the navy's example and began sending military attachés abroad. The duties of the attachés were spelled out in a memorandum from the secretary of war:

> Examine into and report upon all matters of a military or technical character that may be of interest to any branch of the War Department and to the service at large. Keep informed . . . of the occurrence of all military exhibitions and trials of Ordnance. . . . Examine the military libraries, bookstores and publishers lists in order to give early notice of any new or important publications or inventions or improvements in arms, or in any branch of the service; also give notice of such drawings, plans, etc.; which may be of importance and within your power to procure.[9]

In short, the attachés were to be the technology transfer scouts of the army.

As the flow of information into the MID increased, the unit was made a separate division of the AG's office. The staff and files of the unit grew steadily. The role of the MID was re-examined in 1892; the War Department concluded that "the duties of the information division are as broad as the military service and the art of war itself," and hence it must be a "general intelligence division."[10] But *intelligence* still meant "information in general," and the role of intelligence in today's sense continued to be just one of many kinds of information to be collected and indexed. Like the ONI the MID remained a central reference facility, and technology transfer remained the principal job of the overseas attachés. The impetus that was to transform both organizations into true intelligence agencies was to come from yet a third institution.

The Naval War College was established in 1884, a product of the same naval-modernization program that had created the ONI two years earlier. It was the brainchild of Commodore Stephen B. Luce, who had spent much of his career in naval training, including a tour as commandant of midshipmen at Annapolis and another as commander of all apprentice training ships. The college was conceived as a place for the advanced training of officers who had already seen duty at sea. Naval strategy and tactics, international law, and foreign relations were to be among the subjects offered, but Luce cautioned that the college would not try to teach warfare, something he regarded as impossible. Instead, it would provide "a place of original research on all questions relating to war and to statesmanship connected with war, or the prevention of war."[11] In today's governmental parlance the Naval War College was conceived as part think tank, part mid-career development program.

The college was placed within the Bureau of Navigation, the same department that supervised the ONI. It was located on Coasters Harbor Island in Narragansett Bay, near other navy facilities at Newport, Rhode Island. The college opened in September 1885 with a student body of four lieutenant commanders and five lieutenants. The faculty consisted of Luce, the navy's librarian, and a lieutenant lent by the army to lecture on military affairs. The course lasted only four weeks, hardly enough time to undertake any of the serious studies Luce had prescribed. Luce was ordered back to sea to take command of the North Atlantic Squadron shortly thereafter. The librarian returned to his duties at the Office of Naval Records and Library in Washington. Curiously, this left the army lieutenant as the only member of the faculty of the navy's college. All in all, the college had made only a very modest beginning.

Luce's successor as president of the college was Captain Alfred T. Mahan, the son of Dennis H. Mahan, a civil engineer and the late dean of faculty at West Point, who had taught military science, especially engineering, to most of the great Union and Confederate generals of the Civil War. Despite his origins, Captain Mahan had shown no special interest in military or naval history until receiving the Naval War College assignment late in 1885. To prepare for the job, he took off a year for research and study; the result of his labors was *The Influence of Sea Power upon History, 1660–1783*, a seminal work of naval geopolitics that was to shape the thinking of Theodore Roosevelt and the navalists of Roosevelt's generation.

While Mahan's studies of the days of fighting sail offered principles still applicable to the geopolitics of sea power, they provided little useful insight into making war on the sea in the age of steel and steam. Yet there was little in the way of more recent naval history to study: although the navies of Europe and even those of Latin America had been equipped with the new technology, few shots had been fired in anger at sea since the first ironclads met in battle off Hampton Roads in 1862, and this was meager grist for the mills of naval theoreticians. Fortunately for the college and its studies of naval warfare, however, a medical board had just invalided out of the navy the young officer who held the solution to this dilemma.

William McCarty Little had graduated from Annapolis in 1866 after serving as a midshipman in the wartime Federal blockade. He had published a book on seamanship even before entering the Naval Academy and turned out a stream of technical articles thereafter. Although a scholar, he was first of all a sailor and went to sea with enthusiasm. A gun accident ashore cost him the sight of one eye, however, and eventually caused the medical board to put him on the beach. In 1884 he settled in Newport, his wife's home and the scene of fond memories of his days as a midshipman (the Naval Academy had been temporarily relocated there from Annapolis during the Civil War years). Little had served under Luce, and when the latter opened the Naval War College the following year, he asked the young ex-officer to help him deal with such details as establishing a library for the school and preparing teaching aids. When Mahan succeeded Luce, Little continued to lend a hand at the college.

One of Little's Newport neighbors was Major William K. Livermore, an army engineering officer stationed at Fort Adams, just across the bay from Coasters Harbor Island. Livermore was the author of the 1879 volume *The American Kriegspiel*, the first American work on the subject of war-gaming, and through him Little became interested in the subject.[12]

Although largely unknown in the American military establishment before Livermore, war-gaming is an activity that shares the same ancient origins as the game of chess. In the seventeenth and eighteenth centuries the Prussians and French invented variations of chess that corresponded more closely to the realities of warfare and used them to train military students in the basic principles of the art of war. In 1811 a Prussian war counselor invented *Kriegspiel* (literally, "war game"), in which he moved the play from the chessboard to the sand table, a scale model of an actual battlefield with porcelain pieces to represent men and equipment. Later elaboration by other Prussian instructors increased the realism of the play by making the rules less rigid and employing an umpire to judge the effects of fire and other eventualities, based on actual combat experience. It was the writings of these Prussian war-game pioneers, translated into English by a British army officer, that first interested Livermore in the subject. In his *American Kriegspiel*, the American officer elaborated on and improved the Prussian game, drawing on actual combat statistics compiled in the Civil War and introducing mathematical tables to govern the relationships between such variables as the size of forces and the speed at which they could move or between enemy firepower and losses sustained. In the game calculations took into account such minute details as the state of training of troops, their morale, and even variations in the terrain for which they fought. To free American *Kriegspiel* from the rigid rules of the Prussian versions and to represent the role chance plays in war, Livermore introduced the use of dice.

Through Livermore, Little comprehended the enormous value of war-gaming in studying the art of war. He realized that the point of the exercise is not simply to become proficient at playing. "It is a matter of small moment who is adjudged the winner," he wrote, "while on the other hand it is of great importance to ascertain as nearly as possible what conditions make for success or failure."[13]

Little devised a war game that could be used to study naval engagements. With Mahan's approval he introduced it into the Naval War College's curriculum when the third class was formed in 1887. He continued to develop naval gaming techniques, and by the following year lectures on war-gaming as well as play became a permanent part of the college program. He persuaded Livermore to take an active part in the college's war-gaming program, and by 1889 the army officer was lecturing on the subject at the college.

Mahan's successor as president of the college was Captain Henry C. Taylor, who proved to be an even more enthusiastic advocate of war-gaming than Mahan had been. Under Taylor the college course extended to four months and ran from June to September. Each year Taylor assigned a war problem as a class exercise to be done in addition to other, smaller war-game exercises. The problems were posed so as to represent realistic strategic and tactical situations based on actual current international conflicts and realistic representations of actual navies. For example, the 1894 problem supposed a British fleet off New York Harbor with six battleships and ten cruisers about to be joined by an invading force from Halifax with one hundred transports, ten battleships, twenty cruisers, and other vessels; the American fleet opposing the British consisted of only five battleships, fifteen cruisers, and some smaller vessels. The class was divided into committees representing the two adversaries. They worked out the problem with ship models on huge map tables and sometimes simulated particular formations and maneuvers with steam launches in the waters of Narragansett Bay.[14]

The hypothetical Anglo-American naval war the college considered in the summer of 1894 led to some surprisingly specific practical conclusions about American naval policy: The United States Navy could deal effectively with a superior naval force in such a situation only by avoiding battle on the open sea, fighting instead in bays, sounds, and interior waterways. Therefore, American warships ought to draw less water than those meant for fighting at sea but need not strive for extreme high speed, which would be of little use in coastal combat. Among the other detailed recommendations coming out of the exercise was a proposal for a ship canal across Cape Cod to improve American naval mobility in such a situation.[15]

The following year the college's class problem again involved an Anglo-American war, but this time it was inspired by events actually unfolding as the students assembled at Newport. The previous November a British fleet had blockaded the Nicaraguan port of Corinto and sent ashore a force of marines to seize the customs house and occupy the town, all to collect a debt of seventy-five thousand dollars claimed by Britain. This high-handed flouting of at least the spirit of the Monroe Doctrine exacerbated anti-British feeling in Congress and the American press and may have inspired the administration of President Grover Cleveland the following July—just as the college class of 1895 entered its second month—to send Britain a proposal, somewhat pugnacious in tone, to mediate a long-standing dispute with Venezuela over the boundary between that country and British Guiana. Britain rejected the note, Anglo-American relations deteriorated rapidly, and the two nations seemed on the brink of military action in December, when a sudden German war scare afflicted the British, and Her Majesty's government yielded to the United States in the Venezuelan boundary matter.

During the Venezuelan crisis both Britain and the United States had made military and naval preparations. At the Naval War College the unfolding crisis became the subject of the class problem.[16] After the students returned to duty in September, Captain Taylor, Little, and the other members of the college faculty continued to work on it and presented their conclusions to the ONI and the secretary of the navy that winter. The worked-out Venezuelan-crisis problem amounted to a contingency war plan, something previously unknown in the American military and naval establishments. In preparing such a plan, the college had, in effect, functioned as a naval general staff, something the ONI had aspired to be but had failed to become. Indeed, the ONI had virtually failed to take notice of the crisis and did not even report on the British military and naval preparations.[17]

The ONI's nonperformance in the Venezuelan crisis threatened to relegate it permanently to the functions of technology transfer and information storage and retrieval. Its salvation came the following April, however, when Lieutenant Commander Richard Wainwright became the new chief of the intelligence office. From the outset Wainwright pursued a policy of cooperation with the Naval War College. When the college posed as an exercise scenario a possible conflict with Japan over Hawaii (then not yet an American possession), he sent an officer to make a strategic reconnaissance of the islands and gather data for use in the problem.[18] He realized that the war-gaming activities at the college were creating something the ONI had never known before: intelligence requirements—that is, lists of specific elements of information needed by the navy in order to fight, or plan to fight, a potential adversary. Given such a sharpened focus for its collection activities, the ONI under Wainwright was to become a partner with the college in the navy's general-staff function and, for the first time, a true naval intelligence agency.

The college's class problem for 1896 postulated a war with Spain, another scenario rooted in the headlines of the day. A year before Cuban insurgents had renewed their long-running struggle to break their island free from Spanish rule. In the United States popular opinion sided with the rebels. Cuban émigrés and some of their American allies mounted filibuster expeditions from American territory in support of the revolt, and the failure of the United States government to enforce firmly its neutrality laws led to a deterioration in Spanish-American relations. In April 1896 Spain rejected an American offer to mediate her conflict with the insurgents. Meanwhile, the Spanish military authorities in Cuba tried to isolate the guerrillas from their peasant supporters by herding the entire population of the countryside into coastal concentration camps, a policy that was causing hundreds of thousands of deaths from famine and disease and creating enormous popular pressure in America for the Cleveland administration to intervene militarily.

Against this backdrop the college's 1896 class problem was clearly much more than an academic exercise. Wainwright assigned his best staff officer, Lieutenant William W. Kimball, to go to Newport and work with Captain Taylor, the faculty, and students on what was clearly to be a Spanish-war contingency plan. When work on the problem had been completed in November, two separate plans had been produced, because

Taylor disagreed with some of the details of the plan Kimball worked out. The plans had many common features, however: a naval blockade of Cuba and Puerto Rico (the other Spanish colony in the Caribbean), a land operation to capture Havana, and the capture of Manila in order to use the Philippines as a bargaining chip in negotiations to end the war and liberate Cuba.[19] Planning for a Spanish war continued through 1897 and was again the subject of the college's class problem. Tensions had increased so much by then, however, that an ad hoc panel was convened at the Navy Department in Washington to revise the Kimball and Taylor plans and produce additional variations. Theodore Roosevelt, who took over the job of assistant secretary of the navy in April, was in frequent consultation with both Wainwright and Kimball. The author of the definitive history of the naval side of the War of 1812, Roosevelt took a personal hand in the planning activity.

Spanish-war tensions were also felt in the army's MID, which acquired a new chief in April 1897. Major Arthur L. Wagner was more intelligence-oriented than any of his predecessors, although his attitude toward espionage embodied the classic American ambivalence toward the subject. In his *Service of Security and Information*, a book published in 1893 while he was on the faculty of the army's Infantry and Cavalry School at Fort Leavenworth, Kansas, he remarked that civilian agents "often deserve the obloquy so often cast upon spies in general" and warned against recruiting agents from the "superior classes." Practical experience as the army's intelligence chief may have altered his views, however, for by mid-1897 he was receiving reports from the military attaché in Madrid containing details of Spanish deployment of troops to Cuba and by December was asking the secretary of war for permission to send an officer on a secret reconnaissance of the island.[20]

The MID, which now consisted of eleven officers and received reports from sixteen attachés overseas, had been collecting basic intelligence on Cuba since 1892. One of its principal sources of such information was a systematic study of the island that had been made by Captain George P. Scriven of the Signal Corps in 1893 while on a visit to Cuba. Cuban émigrés in New York City had also begun furnishing the MID with information about the Caribbean area.[21] But as war tensions deepened during 1897 and the real possibility that the army might soon be operating in Cuba increased, collecting such intelligence no longer took a backseat to the demands of technology transfer. Wagner increasingly felt the need to dispatch one of his staff to Cuba to collect intelligence and perhaps serve as liaison with the Cuban guerrillas in the field.

Wagner was certainly aware of the activities of the ONI in support of the Naval War College's war-gaming and planning program; the ONI and the MID shared the same building, the State-War-Navy building next door to the White House. Although the army as yet had no formal planning unit, the commanding general and his staff had long since begun to consider the army's role in a Spanish war. Enlightened by the ONI example, Wagner was making over the MID, turning it for the first time into a true military intelligence agency.

In November Lieutenant Commander Wainwright left the post of ONI chief, having accomplished more in his brief tenure than any of his predecessors. In partnership with the Naval War College, the ONI had acquired a far more important role within the navy than it had had at any time in its fifteen-year history. And Wainwright himself was destined for greater things; his new billet was that of executive officer aboard one of the navy's newest vessels, the battleship *Maine*.

Chapter Sixteen

Espionage in the War with Spain

Spanish-American relations, especially regarding Cuba, had reached an extremely delicate state as the year 1898 began. A new and more liberal government had come to power in Madrid the previous August, and it had adopted a more moderate policy toward the Cuban insurrection. The harsh concentration-camp program aimed at separating the populace from the guerrillas had been ended. The new regime also offered Cuba a form of limited autonomy short of complete independence from Spain. These compromises failed to achieve their intended result, however; the insurgents refused to lay down their arms without full independence, while the *peninsulares*—the Spanish on the island who wanted to retain strong ties to the homeland—began demonstrating against what they perceived as a surrender to American pressure and the first step toward turning over Cuba to the United States.

In Washington the administration of President William McKinley watched these developments anxiously while resisting popular pressure to take a stronger stand. Early in December the American consul general in Havana, Fitzhugh Lee, reported that the militant *peninsulares* in Cuba were fomenting an anti-American plot. He urged the administration to send a warship to Havana. McKinley compromised by sending the *Maine* to Key West and giving Lee the authority to summon her to Havana if the situation warranted it.[1]

The *Maine*'s commander was Captain Charles D. Sigsbee, an officer with an extensive oceanographic background. He was quite familiar with Key West, having often visited the key twenty years earlier, when he was in command of the research vessel *Blake*, charting the floor of the Gulf of Mexico. Among the many locals who greeted Sigsbee upon his arrival at Key West was the manager of the local telegraph company, Martin L. Hellings.

Hellings was a transplanted Pennsylvanian who went to work for the Western Union Company after the Civil War and was sent to Key West to manage its subsidiary, the International Ocean Telegraph Company, which operated the submarine cables running between Havana, Key West, and the Florida mainland. Hellings owed Sigsbee a favor or two from their earlier acquaintance, and the captain now asked Hellings to assist him in his assignment at Key West. Consul General Lee had been assigned an open code to send in a telegram to Sigsbee in the event he wished the *Maine* to come to Havana. To prepare for all contingencies, however, Sigsbee asked Hellings to notify him immediately if the Havana–Key West cable should be shut down for any reason.

Hellings agreed and also offered to use his influence—he was the son-in-law of one of the richest men in Florida, as well as telegraph-company manager—to help Sigsbee in other ways. He arranged with the officers of the *Olivette*, a steamship that regularly plied between Havana, Key West, and Tampa, to serve as secret couriers between Sigsbee and Consul General Lee. But Hellings discharged his obligation to Sigsbee a hundredfold when he offered him the Western Union employees in Havana, who ran the cable office in the governor general's palace there, as secret intelligence agents for the navy. Hellings's telegraphers were able to send him instantaneous reports of events in Havana. Equally important, if not more so, they saw all the official telegrams between Havana and elsewhere in Cuba and those going over the Caribbean and Atlantic cables linking Havana with Madrid. Through Hellings the United States government suddenly had access to the highest-level communications intelligence regarding the Cuban crisis.[2]

Just why the McKinley administration sent the *Maine* to Havana on January 25, 1898, remains something of a mystery. The order that finally sent the battleship to Cuba did not come from Consul General Lee but from President McKinley through the secretary of the navy, and its true motivation is hidden beneath the official cover story that the *Maine* was to pay "a friendly naval visit" to the Cuban port "in a day or two." In any event, the ship arrived before American diplomats in either Havana or Madrid had been notified, and Sigsbee steamed into Havana Harbor in his heavily armed battleship blithely unaware that the Spanish authorities had not consented to the visit and did not even know it had been planned.[3]

Whatever impending crisis precipitated the dispatch of the *Maine* to Havana, it must have failed to materialize.[4] The Spanish authorities offered a cool but correct welcome to the warship and led her to a mooring in the harbor. The crew was not given shore liberty, but the few officers who visited the town experienced nothing more hostile than the sullen silence of the *peninsulares*. A week passed, then another, but Havana remained tranquil. Shortly before 10:00 P.M. on February 15, however, Hellings went to the United States naval station on Key West to advise that he had just received a telegram from one of his agents in Havana saying that the *Maine* had exploded and was sinking in the harbor.

Her hull ripped open, the *Maine* sank in some forty feet of water and came to rest on the muddy harbor bottom while parts of her twisted superstructure protruded above the surface. Of the 268 Americans killed or missing and presumed dead, all but two were enlisted men; the explosion had been centered in the forward part of the ship, where the crew's quarters were located. Sigsbee, Wainwright, and most of the other officers survived unharmed.

A United States Navy Court of Inquiry found that the battleship had been destroyed by a submerged mine (a conclusion contradicted by a recent reinvestigation of the matter by Admiral Hyman Rickover and a team of navy scientists.)[5] While the court was unable to fix responsibility for placing or detonating the mine, the obvious implication was that if the Spanish authorities were not directly responsible for the act, they were at the very least gravely negligent in not having prevented some radical *peninsulares* from sabotaging the *Maine*.

The navy court's report, released by the McKinley administration to Congress on March 28, unleashed a powerful wave of pro-war sentiment in the United States. On April 19 Congress passed a joint resolution directing the president to use armed force to end Spanish rule on the island. Three days later the United States Navy established a blockade of Cuban ports, an act of war.

* * *

The United States executed a revised version of the Spanish-war plan worked out by Kimball and Taylor at the Naval War College several months earlier. Assistant Secretary of the Navy Roosevelt, an assiduous student of the war plans and an ardent proponent of the war, had taken advantage of the temporary absence of his chief two months earlier to order the navy's Asiatic Squadron to Hong Kong in preparation for an attack on the Philippines in case of war. Now Commodore George Dewey, commander of the squadron, was ordered to Manila to capture or destroy the Spanish fleet there.

For more than two months Dewey had been preparing for the Philippine mission, and those preparations included collecting intelligence. The navy's war plans did not include the specific tactical intelligence Dewey needed to plan the attack, and the Asiatic Squadron's information regarding Manila and the Spanish squadron based there was spotty. Curiously, it included comprehensive order-of-battle intelligence: the ships of the Spanish fleet, their armaments, and even the names and ages of their officers and the decorations they held. But basic intelligence about the Philippines was deficient; Dewey had to resort to buying every chart of the islands he could find in Hong Kong to supplement the navy's maps and charts of the area.[6] His most critical intelligence requirement concerned the naval defenses at Manila Bay, however, especially in regard to mines.

Dewey filled the gap by having his aide, Ensign F. B. Upham, pose as a civilian traveler and interview the crews of steamers arriving at Hong Kong from Manila. In addition, an American businessman living in Hong Kong—his name is lost to history—made frequent visits to Manila and reported his observations to Dewey.[7]

From this makeshift intelligence service, Dewey was able to construct a fairly complete picture of the Manila defenses, including the size and location of coastal artillery batteries guarding the twin channels that open from the bay to the sea.[8] In general, Dewey concluded, the Manila defenses were weak, and the Spanish squadron was in a poor condition of readiness. In the event, his estimates proved correct. On May 1 the Asiatic Squadron steamed into Manila Bay and completely destroyed the Spanish squadron in a matter of hours without losing a ship or a man.

*   *   *

A major step of the navy's Spanish-war plan was now nearly complete: the capture of Manila for later use as a bargaining chip in negotiating the independence of Cuba and the end of the war. Dewey hadn't actually captured Manila, however; he did not have a sufficient force of marines to land and take the city. But he was in complete control of Manila Bay. He blockaded the port and settled down to a long wait for an army expeditionary force to cross the Pacific and complete the capture of the Philippines.

According to the navy's war plan, the main theater of operations was to be the Caribbean. The blockade of Cuba was already in place, but the plan also called for an expeditionary force to land in Cuba and capture Havana or some other major seaport. Thus, the navy had done its part, for the moment, and the ball was in the army's court. But the United States Army, still only twenty-five thousand strong, was dispersed at garrisons throughout the West and Alaska, and after thirty-three years of domestic peacekeeping work, it was going to require some considerable shifting of gears to mount two major overseas amphibious expeditionary forces. Throughout May army training camps tried to process the overwhelming flow of recruits who rushed to answer President McKinley's call for volunteers. At the same time the ports of Tampa and San Francisco became the scenes of barely controlled chaos as the army struggled with the unfamiliar task of assembling men, arms, supplies, and transports for the two overseas expeditions.

The Spanish did not sit by passively while all this was taking place, of course. In the Spanish naval center of Cádiz, Admiral Miguel de la Camara began to assemble a task force to go to the Philippines and lift Dewey's blockade. And a squadron of five cruisers and four destroyers under Admiral Pascual Cervera y Topete had left the Cape Verde Islands late in April and was last seen steaming west, presumably to the Caribbean. Camara's squadron was of special concern to Washington because its armor and guns were known to be superior to those of Dewey's force at Manila. Cervera's squadron posed a potential threat to the Cuban expedition: the prospect of its sinking the army transports in the Florida Strait inspired nightmares and indigestion in Washington. And the possibility that Cervera would steam up along the East Coast of the United States shelling coastal cities along the way set off a wave of panic from Florida to Maine. The tasks of tracking the progress of Camara's preparations at Cádiz and discovering Cervera's whereabouts fell to the Office of Naval Intelligence.

Throughout its sixteen-year history the intelligence office had collected only openly available information, but now it suddenly found itself with a job that could be done only by espionage. It is a well-established principle of the craft of intelligence that espionage networks are not built overnight; they take years to set up. Fortunately, the officers of the ONI and the naval attachés in Europe did not know this. Within a week or so after the declaration of war, they had established an impressive secret intelligence apparatus in Europe and the Mediterranean, and even extending into Madrid and Cádiz.

Late in April the Navy Department dispatched two young officers to Europe who had volunteered for secret service work. Ensigns Henry H. Ward and William H. Buck arrived in Liverpool on May 8. In the guise of wealthy Englishmen, they separately chartered yachts and sailed to the Spanish coast. Buck remained in Spanish waters, learning what he could of Admiral Camara's progress in readying his task force, while Ward went to Gibraltar, thence to the Madeira Islands and on to the Caribbean to see whether he could locate Admiral Cervera's squadron.

In Berlin Commander Francis M. Barber, the American naval attaché, recruited Edward Breck to go to Spain as a secret intelligence agent. Breck, an American fencing champion who had studied at Heidelberg, took to the role of spy with dramatic gusto and equipped himself with false mustaches, hidden pistols, and other paraphernalia straight out of an E. Phillips Oppenheim spy novel. Breck went to Spain in the guise of a German doctor on vacation, accomplished little important espionage, but, surprisingly, did not get caught.[9]

The naval attachés in Paris and London undertook far more extensive and professional intelligence operations. The Paris attaché, Lieutenant William S. Sims, spent lavishly from the navy's Secret Service funds to organize a network stretching from the Canary Islands, where an agent watched for the possible return of Cervera's squadron, to Spain, where an Italian citizen received three hundred dollars per month to report on naval movements, to Port Said, where a retired Swedish army officer watched for Camara's squadron to pass en route to the Philippines.[10] Sims's apparatus also included an impoverished French baron, a doctor practicing among the Spanish aristocracy in Madrid, and the mayor of a French town near Paris who moonlighted as a private detective.[11] None who had read his report of May 19 could doubt the thoroughness of Sims's methods. It described a letter sent by a French mechanic working on a Spanish cruiser at Cádiz, and received the day before by his family at Le Havre, mentioning that the vessel would be "ready for sea within a few days."[12]

Sims's counterpart in London, Lieutenant John C. Colwell, also spent freely to run his own networks. Three agents Colwell sent to Spain were each paid fifteen hundred dollars per month. Colwell paid an employee of Spain's London embassy two hundred dollars per month for espionage services. He paid his Port Said agent one thousand dollars per month. Late in May he closed one of his reports to the secretary of the navy with the observation, "This business is expensive; funds are needed." In all, Colwell spent twenty-seven thousand dollars on spies during the three-month war.[13] But in Washington the intelligence they bought with the money was considered a bargain, especially that regarding Admiral Camara's progress in readying his task force to lift Dewey's Manila blockade.

The Spanish attempted to run their own secret intelligence service in the war, but not on so grand a scale as that of the ONI. With the declaration of war, the naval attaché at the Spanish embassy in Washington, Lieutenant Ramón Carranza, went to Montreal, where he set up an intelligence station. Carranza hired a Canadian detective agency to help him set up a secret intelligence network south of the border. The agency provided him with Frank Mellor, a former Canadian artilleryman willing to recruit other veterans of the Canadian army to go to the United States, enlist in the armed forces, and serve as espionage agents. One of his first recruits, however, an Englishman, reported the scheme to the British consul at Kingston, Ontario, and the British immediately reported the matter through diplomatic channels to the United States government. As it happened, Washington was already quite familiar with Carranza's operation.[14]

*   *   *

As the federal law-enforcement agency at the time, the United States Secret Service was called upon to furnish plainclothes agents to the Justice Department and other federal agencies when the need arose. With the approach of the Spanish war, a mild spy scare swept the country, and the job of investigating the many suspicious persons and situations reported by the public fell to the service.

The Secret Service was headed by John E. Wilkie, a thirty-eight-year-old former Chicago crime reporter who had accepted the federal post in February.[15] When the Spanish minister and his retinue left Washington on April 21, Wilkie sent along two Spanish-speaking agents to accompany them as far as Canada, ostensibly to protect them from harm. At the same time the Secret Service chief dispatched two more auxiliary agents to Toronto to await the arrival of the Spanish party. One of the latter agents managed to get a hotel room adjacent to the one Lieutenant Carranza was staying in while in the city. On May 6 the agent, eavesdropping on Carranza through the connecting door, overheard the Spanish officer recruiting one of his first agents, an Englishman named George Downing who had served in the United States Navy as a petty officer aboard the U.S.S. *Brooklyn*.

Secret Service agents followed Downing to Washington and intercepted a letter he posted to Carranza via a Montreal mail drop, reporting on a visit he had made to the Navy Department, where he managed to pick up a surprising amount of militarily useful information. Downing was arrested and jailed. Two days later he was found hanging in his cell, apparently a suicide.[16] Meanwhile, Secret Service agents in Tampa arrested Frank Mellor and one of his recruits, both of whom had tried to enlist in the United States Army and join the Cuban expedition being assembled in the Florida port.[17]

In Montreal, Secret Service agents managed to steal a letter Lieutenant Carranza had written to his cousin, a senior naval officer in Madrid. Among the many indiscreet observations contained in the long missive was Carranza's casual remark,

> I have been left here to receive and send telegrams and to look
> after the spy service which I have established. . . . We have had

bad luck because they have captured our two best spies, one in Washington, who hanged himself—or else they did it for him— and the other day before yesterday in Tampa. The Americans are showing the most extraordinary vigilance.[18]

The State Department presented a photographic facsimile of the letter to the British minister in Washington and permitted him to examine the original and verify its authenticity. Armed with this conclusive evidence that Carranza had violated British neutrality by running his espionage operation from Canadian soil, the British government expelled him from the country, effectively ending Spanish intelligence operations in the United States.[19]

On December 28, 1897, nearly a month before the *Maine* was sent to Havana, army intelligence chief Major Arthur Wagner asked the secretary of war for authority to send one of his officers in the MID to Cuba "to examine into and report on the military situation." Apparently, his request was ignored, but he renewed it ten days after the *Maine* disaster. This time it was approved, and Wagner sent Lieutenant Andrew S. Rowan on the mission.[20]

The forty-one-year-old Rowan was the ideal officer for the job. He was experienced in this type of mission: in 1890 he had made a covert recon-naissance of the full length of the Canadian Pacific Railroad, collecting information of military interest for the War Department about the line and the region it traversed. He had also done similar work in Central America.[21]

Rowan left Washington in mid-April and traveled to Jamaica, where he was met by a party of Cuban insurgents. Rowan and the Cubans sailed to Cuba in an open boat and landed at Oriente Province on the southeast coast on April 24, two days after the war began. He journeyed inland to the town of Bayamo, where he met the Cuban insurgent general Calixto García Iñiguez. García furnished him with maps and other intelligence and sent a delegation of officers with him on his return to Washington for the purpose of coordinating the insurgents' operations with those of the American armed forces.[22]

Contrary to legend, Rowan incurred little personal risk in his famous mission in Bayamo. The more enterprising American journalists routinely visited García and General Máximo Gómez y Báez, another Cuban insurgent leader, at their strongholds in the countryside. Except for the city of Santiago and a few other enclaves, the Spanish by this time had lost control of eastern Cuba, and apart from the slim chance of being intercepted in Cuban waters by a Spanish patrol vessel, there was not much danger of being caught. The same was not true of the island of Puerto Rico, however, where there was no insurgency and the Spanish were still very much in control. Two other American officers were to discover this at about the same time Rowan was visiting García.

Early in May, Wagner sent Lieutenant H. Whitney on a covert reconnaissance of Puerto Rico. To reach the island, Whitney posed as an ordinary seaman aboard a British merchant vessel. Word of his mission somehow leaked to the press while he was en route, and the Spanish authorities were waiting for the ship when it arrived in Ponce, on the southern side of the island. His cover withstood official scrutiny, however, and he managed to continue with his reconnaissance of the island, switching his cover to newspaperman, then to British officer. Whitney must have been a talented actor and utterly audacious, for he managed to pull off his impostures and return to Washington with the valuable intelligence that there were relatively few Spanish regular troops on the island. Whitney learned the position of the troops, the topography of the island, and the condition of the harbors, all crucial intelligence the MID lacked.[23]

Not as skilled in the art of deception was Ensign Henry H. Ward, one of the two young officers who, posing as wealthy Englishmen, had chartered yachts for intelligence missions in Spanish waters. Ward's search for Admiral Cervera's squadron had taken him to the Madeira Islands and the Caribbean, where Cervera was presumed to be heading. In June his odyssey brought him to Puerto Rico, where the Spanish authorities on the island did not believe his cover story and arrested him. He was released only after being vouched for by the British consul.[24]

By the time Ensign Ward reached Puerto Rico, the United States Navy already knew the whereabouts of Cervera's squadron, but not until after the continuing mystery had escalated the panic along the eastern seaboard. Throughout May the McKinley administration had been bombarded with demands by chambers of commerce, boards of trade, and congressmen that battleships be stationed off the eastern coastal cities they represented to protect them from the Spanish squadron. The governor of one state declared that he would not permit the National Guard to be nationalized; he proposed to keep it home to defend the state's coastline against a Spanish invasion. Banks in Worcester, Massachusetts, were unable to provide all the safe-deposit-box space demanded by Boston businessmen who wanted to move their securities inland. High over Sandy Hook, at the entrance to New York Harbor, a Signal Corps officer stood in the basket of a tethered balloon and swept the horizon with his binoculars. The navy sent two cruisers to investigate a reported sighting of the Spanish squadron off the New England coast. Two more cruisers were sent to the Windward Islands and another to Puerto Rican waters to search for Cervera.[25] But the whereabouts of the Spanish squadron remained unknown.

The most important piece of intelligence about Cervera's squadron was not really its location but its condition. Over his protests and against his better judgment, Cervera had been forced to sail for the West Indies even though his ships lacked sufficient coal, ammunition, and other necessities and were in a very serious state of disrepair. They posed a negligible threat to the eastern seaboard and were utterly incapable of lifting the Cuban blockade. Their only value was as "a fleet in being," a concept Admiral Mahan defined as a squadron "the existence and maintenance of which, although inferior . . . is a perpetual menace to the various more or less exposed interests of the enemy, who cannot tell when a blow may fall, and who is therefore compelled to restrict his operations . . . until that fleet can be destroyed or neutralized."[26]

But to neutralize Cervera's "fleet in being" it was necessary first to know where it was. Surprisingly, the squadron's whereabouts were finally discovered by the United States Army Signal Corps.

Cervera arrived at Curaçao on May 14, perilously short of coal. One of his seven ships had broken down completely near the island of Martinique two days earlier, and he was forced to leave her there. He managed to obtain some coal at Curaçao, just enough to take the squadron on to Cuba. On May 19 he arrived at the southeastern Cuban seaport of Santiago. Since the American blockade was concentrated on the western end of the island—Havana and Cienfuegos, where the navy expected Cervera to land—there were no blockaders in sight, and he was able to slip into the harbor unseen. Once through the narrow entrance channel he was invisible from the sea.

One of Admiral Cervera's first acts upon going ashore was to telegraph the Spanish governor general in Havana, advising him of his arrival. In the cable office at Havana, an employee of the International Ocean Telegraph Company scribbled down the message and handed it to a messenger to take to the governor general. Then he turned back to his telegraph key and relayed the news to Martin L. Hellings, ninety miles to the north, at Key West.

The Havana–Key West cable had not been shut down when the war began; it was too valuable to commercial interests on both sides of the Florida Strait and was kept in service by mutual Spanish-American consent. The navy turned over Hellings and his intelligence apparatus to the army, and Hellings was commissioned as a captain in the United States Volunteer Signal Corps. He remained on duty at the Key West telegraph office, which was taken over by the Signal Corps for the duration of the war. Thus, whenever an important piece of intelligence was reported to Hellings by one of his agents in Havana, he immediately telegraphed the information to Signal Corps headquarters in Washington, and it was passed on to an improvised war room on the second floor of the White House.[27] While horse-drawn traffic passed by on Pennsylvania Avenue, the president of the United States could sit in his command center in the White House and read situation reports from the Cuban war zone, in some cases only minutes old:

> May 11th: "Report received from Havana. Cienfuegos being bombarded. . . . Can't get more as [telegraph] instrument is guarded. Do not give sources of information as my man will be shot if found out."
>
> May 18: "The Spanish in official quarters evidently have news of the coming of their fleet. . . ."

And finally,

> May 19th: "Five Spanish vessels arrived Santiago-de-Cuba. . . . The Spanish flagship arrived Santiago-de-Cuba. The Admiral hastily wired Madrid."[28]

Within hours of Cervera's arrival at Santiago-de-Cuba, the Navy Department sent orders to the North Atlantic Squadron to blockade the port. With Cervera's squadron bottled up in the Cuban harbor, the strategic situation was suddenly and drastically changed.

Several of the early versions of the Spanish-war plans worked out at the Naval War College called for naval attacks on the Spanish coasts in parallel to navy operations in the Caribbean and the Philippines. One of the reasons this element of the plan was abandoned was that the navy simply did not have enough ships. But if Cervera's fleet could be captured or destroyed, the Cuban blockade could be reduced, leaving most of the North Atlantic Squadron free to cross the Atlantic and threaten Spanish ports. Spain would then be forced to keep Camara's task force—all that was left of the Spanish navy—in home waters to defend her coasts. This would amount to surrendering the Philippines to the United States. The navy planners estimated that Spain would then sue for peace, yielding the troublesome island of Cuba in order to retain the valuable Philippine archipelago.

In reality, the United States Navy was already able to execute this strategy, but it failed to realize it. Unaware of the poor state of Cervera's ships, the naval commanders continued to count the Spanish squadron as a significant unit of sea power and to believe that the entire North Atlantic Squadron was needed to keep it inside Santiago Harbor. McKinley and his advisers therefore elected to land an army expeditionary force and capture Santiago and, with it, the Spanish squadron. The force that was being assembled at Tampa for an invasion of the western end of Cuba was redirected to prepare for the Santiago expedition. By the first week in June, it was ready to embark, but so powerful was the mirage projected by Admiral Cervera that there was a full week's delay.

There had been erroneous reports that some of Cervera's ships had been sighted in the Nicholas Channel off the northern Cuban coast and on the route the American task force was to traverse to Santiago. Therefore the army transports remained at Tampa until the matter could be investigated. Lieutenant Victor Blue, an officer from the blockade, was sent ashore to make a direct observation of the Spanish ships in Santiago

Harbor. Blue had some experience in this kind of mission: two weeks earlier he had gone ashore farther west along the Cuban coast to establish contact with the Cuban insurgent general Máximo Gómez. Now, guided by the insurgents, he slipped through the Spanish defense perimeter and reached a position from which he could see the harbor and verify that all of Cervera's ships were there.[29]

Reassured by Blue's reconnaissance, the army task force sailed from Tampa. On June 22–24 sixteen thousand troops landed unopposed at Siboney and Daiquirí, a few miles east of the entrance to Santiago Harbor, and began to advance northwest toward the city of Santiago. After the Battles of San Juan Heights and El Caney on July 1, the Spanish fell back and concentrated their forces near the city. The American forces settled down for a protracted siege.

Although the MID's publication "Military Notes on Cuba," a compendium of basic intelligence about the island, proved useful to the expeditionary force, the army had poor maps and little topographical detail regarding the countryside around Santiago. To fill this void, the expeditionary force made use of an observation balloon to reconnoiter the route of the advance. The balloon was also used to good effect to collect tactical intelligence during the early hours of the Battles of San Juan Heights and El Caney, but an overly eager staff officer ordered it too close to the Spanish lines, and it was shot down.[30]

Faced with the imminent probability that Santiago would fall to the American forces, the Spanish commander in Havana telegraphed Admiral Cervera, ordering him to try to run the blockade rather than permit his squadron to be captured. Cervera realized he had no chance of passing through the blockade, but he obeyed the order nonetheless. He led his squadron out of Santiago Harbor on July 3; after a two-hour running sea battle, the blockading fleet destroyed all six of the Spanish ships.

Although the war was to continue for another six weeks, during which Manila and Puerto Rico fell to American forces, the outcome was apparent to all after the destruction of Cervera's squadron. Admiral Camara's task force, which had reached Suez on its way to the Philippines, was called back as expected, to defend the Spanish coasts against an anticipated American naval attack. The Spanish government waited somewhat too long to ask for a cease-fire and was therefore in a poor bargaining position when the peace treaty was negotiated a few months later. Under the treaty Spain granted independence to Cuba but also ceded Puerto Rico and Guam to the United States and agreed to sell the Philippines to the United States for twenty million dollars.

As a practical and dramatic example of the value of contingency war planning, the war with Spain also demonstrated the value of peacetime intelligence collection. Through its participation in the war-planning process and its espionage operations in Europe, the ONI achieved prestige it had not previously enjoyed. Flushed with its wartime successes, the office was elevated by Congress to a permanent, formally organized office within the Bureau of Navigation (it had previously been only the creature of an executive order of the secretary of the navy) and was given an increase in its size and budget.

Nonetheless, the ONI failed to learn perhaps the most valuable piece of intelligence in the war: that Cervera's squadron was in such poor condition it presented a negligible naval threat. Had that intelligence been available to the war managers in Washington, they might well have decided against the ground assault on Santiago and instead have blockaded that port with a small squadron while sending the larger portion of the fleet to threaten the Spanish coast and frustrate Spanish plans to rescue Manila. Had this been the course of events, hundreds of Spanish, Cuban, and American lives might not have been lost in the land and sea battles of Santiago.[31] This is a classic example of the way in which inadequate intelligence in war is often paid for with unnecessary bloodshed; when in doubt regarding the level of violence necessary to achieve its war aims, a belligerent will usually follow the policy that it is better to be safe than sorry.

The whereabouts of Cervera's squadron, intelligence crucial to American operations, were not acquired through the efforts of the ONI or any other element of the armed forces with intelligence responsibility. Hellings's resourcefulness in establishing an apparatus to collect the most important communications intelligence must be regarded as the height of professionalism, although Hellings was an amateur and not employed by the government at the outset. But this fortunate situation grew out of a chance encounter between Hellings and Captain Sigsbee twenty years earlier; it was pure dumb luck. (Hellings's actions, which were endorsed by Western Union president Thomas T. Eckert, are an early example of the cooperation American business was to give American intelligence services throughout much of the twentieth century.)

The army's MID played a much smaller and less important role in the Spanish-American War, notwithstanding the dramatic exploits of Lieutenants Rowan and Whitney, but it did an adequate job in accomplishing what was expected of it. Unlike the ONI, however, the MID's role in the war did not earn it greatly increased status and prestige. For the MID those rewards were still twenty years in the future.

The work of the Secret Service in countering the minimal threat of Spanish espionage did not inspire the McKinley administration to provide for a permanent counterespionage or internal-security apparatus. With the end of the war, it was difficult for most Americans to imagine that the country might again be threatened by internal enemies, but this complacent attitude was shortly to change.

The Spanish-American War profoundly changed the role of the United States in world affairs. Almost overnight the staunchly isolationist republic had become a world power with a dominion stretching from the Caribbean to the Far East. Having stepped into the international arena, America soon found that she had made new friends and new enemies. This new American world role conferred an unprecedented importance upon the United States intelligence community.

Chapter Seventeen

Adversaries—Black, Green, and Orange

Captain Charles D. Sigsbee, who had commanded the *Maine* on her final and fateful voyage, became chief of the Office of Naval Intelligence in February 1900. The disaster in Havana Harbor exactly two years earlier had become the central event of his life, and the presumption that it had been foreign treachery was now the prism through which the new naval intelligence chief viewed world affairs. He saw that war could come suddenly and without warning, and although we now know his premise was probably in error—the explosion of the battleship seems to have been accidental—his new view of the world was a valid intimation of what lay ahead in the new century.

Sigsbee was understandably security-conscious; one of his first acts as ONI chief was to complain to the chief of the Bureau of Navigation about the offhand manner in which the intelligence office had handled classified information under his predecessors: file cabinets lacked locks, and the civilian clerks who handled highly sensitive material had not been indoctrinated in their responsibilities to safeguard it.[1] But his security concerns extended beyond the ONI to the fleet. On March 11, 1903, he proposed a navy-wide investigation of the loyalty of many of the service's enlisted men. Specifically, he recommended that those with German surnames should be examined to discover whether they were "native born or naturalized; how long in the service before naturalization; how long in this country; how long in the navy; whether their tattoo marks are emblematic of patriotism to Germany or to this country, etc."[2]

Sigsbee was, in fact, extremely worried about the loyalty of German-Americans in the navy. He suspected that many of them were German spies and that even more of them would prove unreliable shipmates in the event of war with Germany.

Such a mind-set seems unworthy of an officer of the United States Navy, especially when viewed retrospectively in the light of two world wars in which the United States and Germany were indeed adversaries and all but a tiny segment of German-Americans were not only loyal but valiant in the defense of their country. But Sigsbee did not have the benefit of such hindsight, and his fears were shared by many other Americans at the turn of the century.

The nation of immigrants was an experiment without historical precedent, and fear of an "enemy within" had been an element of the national consciousness since the undeclared war with France in 1798–1800. There had been no significant Mexican element of the population in 1846–48, nor a Spanish faction in 1898, but as the twentieth century dawned, one in five Americans had some German ancestry. Between 1851 and 1900 nearly four and a half million Germans had emigrated to the United States.[3] Thus, tens of millions of Americans were either German-born or the children of German immigrants. As the United States emerged as a world power in the wake of the Spanish-American War, the loyalty of such products of the "melting pot" remained untested.

That Sigsbee's concern focused on Americans of German extraction, and not on those whose roots were in Ireland, Italy, Poland, or the other major sources of post–Civil War immigration, was not the result of an obsessive anti-German prejudice. Rather, it reflected the opinion of most American strategic thinkers of the day that Germany was far more likely than any other nation to be the country's next adversary. There was impressive evidence to support this view.

With a burgeoning population that had already exceeded the capacity of her territory to support it, Germany coveted overseas territories; without them she could only continue her state-sponsored program of massive emigration, a solution unacceptable to one of Europe's most nationalistic nations. Kaiser Wilhelm II was an undisguised admirer of the navalist theories of Admiral Mahan, and he was determined to make Germany ruler of the seas and a major colonial power. His expansionist campaign came at a time when the United States was also moving onto the world stage, with overseas possessions in Puerto Rico, the Philippines, Hawaii, and Guam, and navalists in both countries agreed that they were in direct competition and apparently on a collision course. Advocating a strong United States Navy "to interfere promptly if Germany ventures to touch a foot of American [i.e., Latin American] soil," Theodore Roosevelt explained that he did so "without the least feeling that the Germans who advocated German colonial expansion were doing anything save what was right and proper from the standpoint of their people. . . . We are all treading the same path."[4]

German-American rivalry was not merely the stuff of abstract geopolitical theory. The two nations had nearly come to blows over Samoa in 1889; the arrival of a hurricane at the Samoan harbor of Apia is credited with having prevented German and American warships from opening fire on each other. As Spanish-American tensions over Cuba approached a peak late in 1897, a German fleet threatened to shell Port-au-Prince unless the Haitian government acceded to the kaiser's demand of reparations and an apology for an alleged insult to the German flag. The McKinley administration nervously watched the movements of the German squadron, and the visit of two of its warships to Havana late in January may have triggered the dispatch of the *Maine* to Cuba.[5] German violations of the American naval blockade of Manila Bay in July 1898 led Admiral Dewey to warn the local German naval commander in very blunt language that if he was trying to provoke a war, the United States Navy was ready to accommodate him. And German-American relations became dangerous again in 1902, when Germany (along with Britain and Italy) blockaded and bombarded Venezuela over the latter country's refusal to pay her international debts. The United States responded with a show of naval force, and the incident prompted Admiral Dewey to assert publicly that American naval officers regarded Germany as "their next enemy."

Dewey's assertion was certainly true of Captain Sigsbee, and the ONI chief's apprehensions were not limited to the vision of a German-American engagement somewhere in the Caribbean or the Pacific. Sigsbee believed Germany was planning to invade the United States mainland. In January 1903 he warned Secretary of the Navy William H. Moody that the nation's capital itself would be the target of any German attack. Recalling the route of the British invasion in 1814, he guessed that German war plans called for the landing of an amphibious force at Annapolis, then an advance on Washington.

While American strategists of the day feared that Germany might send a task force to the Caribbean to gain a foothold in the Western Hemisphere, few shared Sigsbee's estimate that the United States itself was the object of German invasion plans. From the viewpoint that has become fashionable among many recent historians, even the Caribbean scenario was a fantasy invented by American expansionists to promote a bigger navy and justify further overseas adventures by the United States.[6] Sigsbee's invasion fears—were they not now so obscure as to escape most historians' scrutiny—would surely be noted as an example of the sort of paranoid delusion now popularly attributed to "the military mind." But a recent exploration of German naval archives has disclosed that Sigsbee was right.[7] The ONI chief erred only in underestimating the ambitiousness of the German plans to invade the United States mainland.

Like their American counterparts at the Naval War College, young German naval officers were assigned annual war-planning problems—*Winterarbeiten* ("winter works," after the season in which the problems were assigned). While these strategic studies traditionally considered hypothetical wars with Britain, in 1897 the emerging naval power of the United States prompted the German naval staff officers to shift their focus to contingency planning for an American war.

The first American invasion plan called for a German fleet to engage and destroy the United States Navy's North Atlantic Squadron off the eastern seaboard. Having thus gained control of the coastal waters, a German amphibious force would land and capture Norfolk, Hampton Roads, and Newport News. These Virginia ports would then be the staging area for a thrust up the Chesapeake Bay aimed at Baltimore and, just as Sigsbee warned, Washington.

The 1897–98 *Winterarbeiten* plan was superseded the following year by a plan for an invasion of New York City. The plan called for the blockade of Long Island Sound, an amphibious landing on Long Island, and a naval artillery shelling of Manhattan. In 1900 and 1901 the German planners shifted their focus farther northward and considered capturing Cape Cod as a staging point for assaults on Boston and New York. In 1902 the plans were elaborated to include a preliminary invasion of Puerto Rico, from which a blockade of the American coastline from the Gulf of Mexico to New England would be established, followed by a landing on Long Island and a combined land-sea assault on Brooklyn and Manhattan.[8]

The *Winterarbeiten* were definitely not mere abstract intellectual exercises devised to occupy the minds of young German naval officers while ashore. The Admiralty levied specific intelligence-collection requirements on the German military and naval attachés in Washington in support of the plans. The earliest of the *Winterarbeiten* was based on data collected by Captain Count G. Adolf von Gotzen prior to 1897.[9] The later elaborations used intelligence gathered specifically for the purpose by Lieutenant Hubert von Rebeur-Paschwitz. In fact, Rebeur-Paschwitz took an active role in the planning process itself, and apparently the shift in targets from Washington to New York and Boston in 1899 was the result of his advice that "an occupation of [Washington] would make no impression whatsoever since neither trade nor industry are of any significance here." The attaché proposed instead "unsparing, merciless assaults against the northeastern trade and industrial centers."[10]

Reuber-Paschwitz had personally inspected Cape Cod late in 1899 to assess its feasibility as a German beachhead. Two years later, on the specific orders of Admiral Otto von Diederichs, chief of the Admiralty Staff, he inspected all possible landing sites in the Boston–New York area. Von Diederichs was in deadly earnest in directing the contingency planning for an invasion of the United States, and while he did not make German foreign policy, he was in frequent consultation with the man who did: Kaiser Wilhelm regularly met with the admiral to review the invasion plans.[11]

Captain Sigsbee was aware of Reuber-Paschwitz's frequent lengthy absences from Washington, but he could only speculate on his itinerary or purpose. "The Office begs to submit that it is unusual for a Naval Attaché to roam the country without the knowledge of the Navy Department as to his precise whereabouts and locations," he advised his superiors in the Bureau of Navigation. But the navy was unable or unwilling to persuade the State Department to place any restrictions on the travels of attachés. Sigsbee sent ONI agents to follow Reuber-Paschwitz and discover what he was up to, but the German attaché always gave them the slip.[12] Still, there were only a few likely explanations for the mysterious journeys, and coastal reconnaissance may have seemed the most probable to the ONI chief.

Sigsbee's conclusion that Germany was considering an assault on the American mainland was neither an exercise in clairvoyance nor simply luck. In 1901 Baron Franz von Edelsheim, an officer on the German General Staff, had published a book forecasting exactly the sort of invasion of the American East Coast then being worked out in the Admiralty Staff's *Winterarbeiten*.[13] Although the German Foreign Office, General Staff, and Admiralty all quickly disavowed any official connection with Edelsheim's theories, American strategists saw the book for what it was: an inadvertent disclosure of what, at the very least, the German military and naval planners were mulling over. Sigsbee did not underestimate the audacity of the kaiser and his advisers, and he saw that execution of such plans was a real possibility.

The German plans to invade the American eastern seaboard were not born of a wish to conquer the United States and subjugate the American people, nor did they even reflect a personal dislike of Americans by the German leaders. The operation was intended, in the words of one high-ranking German naval planner, "to confront the American people with an *unbearable* situation through the dissemination of terror and through damaging . . . trade and property." And the purpose of such confrontation? To force the United States to cede Puerto Rico—the strategic key to the Caribbean—to Germany and to revoke the Monroe Doctrine, thereby giving Germany a free hand to acquire colonies in South America.[14]

The kaiser and his planners recognized one serious obstacle to their plans, however: their exposure to traditional enemies in Europe. One planner stated, "Any uncertainty in Europe would preclude a successful war against the United States."[15]

But there was growing uncertainty in Europe, at least regarding the hegemony Germany had held on the Continent since her defeat of France in 1871, and by 1906 it was clear that the stable political situation the German planners deemed necessary to their invasion no longer existed. Added to that was the growth under President Theodore Roosevelt of the United States Navy, which by 1907 had reached a strength of sixteen battleships and six armored cruisers, favorably comparable to Germany's twenty-three battleships and eleven large cruisers. In the face of such a formidable navy and the threat of ancient enemies on the Continent, the kaiser pigeonholed his American invasion plans in 1906.

*   *   *

The German threat was the focus of the ONI's attention during Captain Sigsbee's tenure as chief of the intelligence office, from February 1900 to May 1903. The ONI encouraged the navy to send three engineering officers to study at the Berlin Technical School of Naval Architecture, and Sigsbee sent a clerk to help the naval attaché in Berlin. The attaché, Lieutenant William H. Beehler, was sending back reports of alarming German advances in naval technology—advanced torpedoes, torpedo-boat destroyers, and experiments with the newly invented wireless telegraph. Sigsbee reported to the secretary of the navy that "the Germans are considerably ahead of what the Office had any idea could be accomplished by this time."[16]

In raising the alarm over the German peril, Sigsbee was often preaching to the converted. Such leading American foreign-policy analysts as Brooks Adams, Henry Cabot Lodge, and John Hay had long held Germany to be America's major adversary. As President Theodore Roosevelt made plans for a ship canal across the Central American isthmus, Germany's Latin American designs became of even greater concern. The canal was strategically vital to the United States if she was to remain a naval power in both the Caribbean and the Pacific; therefore, the kaiser's presumed plans to secure a foothold in the Caribbean basin presented an immediate strategic threat, not simply an economic or political challenge.

In the summer of 1903, the Naval War College adopted the scenario of a German-American clash in the Far East as the basis for a war-gaming problem.[17] Nonetheless, the navy continued to anticipate the Caribbean as the most probable scene of a war with Germany.

In the wake of the Spanish-American War, naval war planning became one of the general staff activities of the newly created General Board of the United States Navy, an advisory panel consisting of the chief of the ONI, the chief of the Bureau of Navigation, and the president of the Naval War College and chaired by the highest-ranking officer in the service, Admiral George Dewey. Dewey, who had been eyeball-to-eyeball with Admiral von Diederichs at Manila in 1898, was more Germanophobic even than Sigsbee; and during his long chairmanship of the General Board (1900–17), planning for a German war was a major activity of the panel. In 1913 the board worked out a detailed contingency war plan for an American counterattack against an anticipated German thrust into the West Indies. In the color code the board assigned to potential adversaries, Germany was black. Thus the German contingency plan was War Plan Black.

While Sigsbee and Dewey focused their attention on Germany, the fears of other American war planners were centered on the Pacific. Japan's recent military and naval success had been impressive. In 1894–95 Japan had waged war on China and defeated her, had acquired Formosa and the Pescadores, and established suzerainty over Korea, formerly a Chinese protectorate. Ten years later Japan made war on Russia in the Far East, destroyed the Russian fleet, acquired part of the Siberian island of Sakhalin and Russian-controlled territory in China, demanded and received fishing rights off the Siberian coast, and secured her control over Korea. Only a half century after emerging from centuries of self-imposed seclusion, Japan had suddenly burst forth as a major imperial power.

Captain Seaton Schroeder, Sigsbee's successor as ONI chief, had taken notice of Japan's rising naval power even before the Russo-Japanese War. When the war began in 1904, he dispatched a number of assistant naval attachés to the war zone especially to observe the Japanese navy in action against the Russian fleet.[18]

President Roosevelt made frequent requests for detailed reports on the war from the ONI. Roosevelt had long kept a wary eye on Japan, which he regarded as "a power jealous, sensitive and warlike, and which if irritated could at once take the Philippines and Hawaii from us if she obtained the upper hand on the seas." To maintain the balance of power in eastern Asia, which would be destroyed by an overwhelming victory on either side, and also in the hope of obtaining some advantage for the United States, Roosevelt agreed to mediate the dispute. This proved a thankless task, however; when the peace treaty the president midwifed at Portsmouth, New Hampshire, in August 1905 failed to deliver all Japan had hoped for, Japanese public opinion turned bitterly against the United States. Roosevelt did manage to achieve some measure of security for the Philippines, however, through a dubious informal agreement with Japan in which the United States promised to recognize Japanese suzerainty over Korea in exchange for a Japanese disavowal of designs on the Philippines.

Postwar economic troubles in Japan drove record numbers of Japanese to emigrate to the United States; by 1906 about a thousand new immigrants per month were arriving in California, a situation that quickly created resentment and the white population's fear of competing with the cheap labor the newcomers offered employers. Racism soon raised its ugly (and familiar) head in San Francisco, when the Board of Education established a segregated school for Asians. The incident caused indignation and outrage in Japan, where American federalism was not understood, and the idea that the actions of petty municipal officials in San Francisco were without the sanction of the United States government and beyond its power to reverse seemed completely incredible. Amazingly, the situation rapidly developed into an international incident, giving rise in both countries to talk of war.

"The infernal fools in California," fumed President Roosevelt, "insult the Japanese recklessly and in the event of war it will be the nation as a whole which will pay the consequences." He did not underestimate the danger of the situation; to Senator Lodge he confided, "The Japanese seem to have about the same proportion of prize jingo fools that we have."[19] Frustrated by the failure of his fulminations to impress the San Franciscans, Roosevelt reluctantly resorted to conciliation, bringing the eight-member school board to Washington at government expense. There he and his secretary of state, Elihu Root, did a masterful job of mediating the crises, obtaining from the Californians a promise to rescind their segregation order in exchange for a guarantee that Japanese immigration to their state would end, and from Japan a promise to issue Japanese laborers no more visas for travel to the American mainland in exchange for an end to segregation in San Francisco. The arrangement with Japan, which was not a formal treaty, was made through an exchange of diplomatic notes now known to history as the Gentlemen's Agreement.

The Japanese-war scare of 1906–7 lasted only a few months, but it triggered intense intelligence- and war-planning activity of longer duration by the navy's General Board and the ONI. Lieutenant Irvin van Gorder Gillis, an officer fluent in Asian languages, went to China and tried to establish a secret intelligence network, apparently without much success. Attachés in Europe undertook similar projects in an attempt to verify rumors of huge Japanese orders for warships (which turned out to be unfounded). The

ONI hired a Japanese-speaking civilian as a full-time translator for the flow of Japanese materials now being acquired by the office.[20]

Although Japanese-American tensions eased considerably with the Gentlemen's Agreement and Japan warmly welcomed a visit by a fleet of sixteen American warships Roosevelt sent on a round-the-world cruise in 1907–9,[21] the ONI continued to focus on the Japanese threat. Lacking any counterespionage agents of its own, the office borrowed Secret Service agents to watch suspected Japanese spies in the United States. Three young officers—two navy men and a marine—were sent to Japan to learn the language. At the same time the ONI began a massive campaign to collect every sort of basic intelligence available on Japan and eastern Asia.[22] Yet the next perceived Japanese threat did not appear in the Pacific, but south of the border, in Mexico.

In 1910 the administration of the aging president Porfirio Díaz, which had ruled Mexico almost continuously since 1876, began to lose control of the country. By May 1911 insurgents led by Francisco Madero had driven Díaz from power. Shortly before Díaz's fall, Washington began to receive reports of a secret Japanese diplomatic initiative toward the old regime.

As early as 1908, the American minister in Guatemala had reported a rumor that Japan, by secret treaty, had leased land for a naval base on Magdalena Bay, an inlet on the Pacific Coast of Baja California.[23] The rumor was revived in February 1911, during the last days of the Díaz administration, when the Secret Service received reports that the Japanese had again proposed the Magdalena Bay project.[24] The story received some credence when the Mexican government informed Washington that it would not renew a three-year agreement under which the United States Navy was permitted to use the bay for target practice and coaling operations.[25] Further unease was engendered in April by the visit to Mexico City by Admiral Yashiro, grand admiral of the Japanese navy, and reports of his public exhortation of the Mexican government to unite with Japan against their common enemy, presumably the United States.[26] At about the same time, the New York *Evening Sun* carried a story claiming the Díaz government had signed a secret treaty with Japan and that the American ambassador to Mexico had seen a copy of the document, an assertion the ambassador denied.[27]

Just what was going on here remains something of a puzzle. Six years later Captain Horst von der Goltz, a defector from the German Secret

Service, claimed in his published memoirs that at the time of the affair he had been assigned by his government to steal a copy of the alleged secret treaty from the Mexican finance minister in Paris. Goltz claims to have accomplished his mission and sent the document back to Berlin, whence the Foreign Office forwarded it to the American ambassador in Mexico. According to the former German operator, the whole affair was a Machiavellian scheme cooked up in Berlin to provoke a war between Mexico and the United States; the German government somehow inspired and encouraged the purported Japanese-Mexican treaty, then contrived to use it to sabotage Mexican-American relations, all for the purpose of keeping the United States busy while Germany flouted the Monroe Doctrine and established colonies in South America.[28]

Like many other spy memoirs, Goltz's tale seems to be a skillful interweaving of what he had truly learned as a German espionage agent and clever guesswork or perhaps intentional falsehood, all in the interest of making a good story better.[29] Historians generally accept the American ambassador's denial of having seen the purported treaty and doubt that such a treaty ever existed. Nonetheless, Goltz's assertion that the whole affair was fabricated by Germany to exacerbate tensions between the United States, Japan, and Mexico seems to be true. The *Evening Sun* exposé of the secret treaty was planted by Major Herwarth von Bittenfeld, the German military attaché in Washington and Mexico City.[30] Major Bittenfeld was the author of other black propaganda in the American press calculated to incite white fears of "the yellow peril," a phrase (*Die gelbe Gefahr*) coined by the kaiser himself. Bittenfeld's activities were only a small part of a major secret German diplomatic and propaganda campaign aimed at exploiting Japanese-American tensions and the chaotic situation in Mexico.[31]

Like any effective lie, however, the Magdalena Bay story had at least a kernel of truth. A Japanese business consortium had indeed been negotiating for the purchase of a tract of land in the area; the prospective sellers were not Mexicans, however, but American businessmen. After the secret-treaty story was published and word of the proposed sale surfaced in the Senate, the Japanese government denied that the consortium was acting with official sanction and indeed stated that Tokyo had discouraged the project. The Japanese spokesmen pointedly added that the tract in question included no water frontage, implicitly noting that it would have been useless as a naval base.[32]

Notwithstanding Japanese denials, the Magdalena Bay affair, together with the continuing upheavals in Mexico, attracted ONI attention south of the border. In March 1911 two naval officers made a secret reconnaissance of Veracruz, Tampico, and other points on Mexico's Gulf Coast, giving special attention to the problems of amphibious landings. War Plan Green, covering the contingency of an American intervention in revolutionary Mexico, was completed in 1912. It called for a blockade of Baja California, seizure of Mexican shipping on the Pacific Coast, and the capture of Veracruz. At about the same time the Green Plan was worked out, the General Board put the finishing touches on War Plan Orange, an elaborate contingency plan for a war with Japan that the board had been developing for a year.[33]

In the fourteen years since the Spanish-American War, the Office of Naval Intelligence, the Naval War College, and the General Board had become almost exclusive custodians of United States intelligence and contingency-planning activities. In fact, the ONI was once again the only true intelligence agency in the federal government. The War Department had created a General Staff in 1903—a major step in modernizing army management—and placed within it the newly created Army War College. But the war college soon swallowed up the army's Military Information Division. Symbolic of the decline of intelligence within the War Department was the transfer of the MID files and personnel from the State-War-Navy building next to the White House to the war college's building on the outskirts of Washington. By 1908 the War Department's military intelligence function had almost ceased to exist.[34]

The decline of intelligence activity in the army created special problems for the navy's war planners; few of the contingency plans produced by the General Board covered wars fought entirely upon the sea. To provide some measure of coordination between the services in war-planning activity, the Joint Army and Navy Board was created. In 1913 the ONI was busy collecting fresh intelligence on the Caroline and Marshall islands, Guam, and the Philippines to assist the joint board in updating War Plan

Orange—new racial discrimination by California officials had touched off another Japanese-war scare—when word of the joint board's planning operations leaked to the press. Irritated by the disclosure in the sensitive atmosphere surrounding the new Japanese crisis and convinced that the members of the board had attempted to force him to take measures—strengthening of the naval forces at Hawaii—he and his cabinet had already rejected, the newly inaugurated President Woodrow Wilson temporarily suspended the joint board from further meetings.[35]

Although President Wilson's decree had little practical effect on the board—it did not usually meet in the summer in any case, and the president restored it to normal business the following October—the affair seemed to imply an antiwar-planning mood in the new administration. Adapting, perhaps mistakenly, to this perceived climate, the ONI rather quickly returned to its nineteenth-century role as a central reference service for technology transfer.[36]

It was a particularly unfortunate time for such a retrenchment. America, faced with powerful adversaries in Europe, Latin America, and eastern Asia, with trouble across the border in Mexico, and soon to be embroiled in the most terrible war in history to date, again lacked any real intelligence capability.

Chapter Eighteen

America Blindfolded

Some American presidents have had the bad luck to encounter a foreign-policy problem that monopolizes their attention and energy, largely eclipsing all other issues, foreign and domestic. For Lyndon Johnson it was Southeast Asia. For Jimmy Carter, in the final year of his presidency, it was Iran. Woodrow Wilson was in just this sort of situation as he took office in 1913. His devil was Mexico.

Wilson, altruist and reformer, had looked on approvingly when Francisco Madero overthrew the iron-handed regime of Porfirio Díaz in 1911. But he was dismayed in February 1913—the eve of his own inauguration—when one of Madero's generals, Victoriano Huerta, overthrew the Mexican leader and proclaimed himself president. And he was horrified a few days later when Huerta had Madero and his vice president murdered. One of Wilson's first acts as president, therefore, was to refuse to recognize the Huerta government on the grounds that it had come to power by unconstitutional means. This was a departure from the American practice, since the days of Thomas Jefferson, of recognizing established governments without regard to the way in which they had come to power.

Wilson declared a noninterventionist policy regarding Mexico, but at the same time he yearned to drive Huerta from power. This wish was shared by Venustiano Carranza and Francisco ("Pancho") Villa, two leaders of insurgencies against the Huerta regime, and after a year Wilson partially lifted an arms embargo that had been in force, permitting the insurgents (but not Huerta) to obtain weapons in the United States. The move drew bitter criticism from the many American and foreign interests heavily invested in Mexico, as indeed the nonrecognition policy already had; like Díaz, Huerta was far friendlier to foreign investors than to the Mexican masses, which was yet another reason Wilson detested him.

As pressure, both foreign and domestic, increased on Wilson to bring an end to the civil war raging in Mexico, and with the failure of the insurgents to topple Huerta even after the American arms embargo was lifted, Wilson resorted to military intervention. He used a minor incident involving crewmen from an American warship visiting Tampico as cause to demand a formal apology from Huerta, an apology he knew the dictator could not give without suffering severe domestic political injury. When it was not forthcoming, Wilson asked Congress for authority to use military force in Mexico to defend "the national honor."

Armed with the requested authority, Wilson sent an army-navy task force to capture Veracruz and occupy it until Huerta apologized. The true purpose of this move was to interdict Huerta's supply of European arms, which flowed to the dictator through the seaport. American occupation of Veracruz (and the subsequent fall of the port of Tampico to the insurgents) soon had the intended effect. Cut off from his European arms suppliers and in the face of military gains by Carranza and Villa, Huerta was forced to accept mediation of his war with the insurgents by Argentina, Brazil, and Chile. In July the Mexican leader stepped down and left the country, but he left behind a chaotic situation, with Carranza and Villa now fighting each other.[1]

Although Wilson managed to remove Huerta, his Veracruz operation failed to achieve his overall objective: ending the civil war in Mexico and bringing a democratic regime to power. He was blocked from taking further action to end the civil war and nurturing a democratic regime in Mexico when the insurgents themselves expressed their resentment of the occupation and demanded that the Americans withdraw from Veracruz. Carranza, chief of the Constitutionalist faction of the insurgents and the man Wilson wished to see in power, threatened to fight both Huerta and the American forces if the latter pressed their invasion of Mexico. Wilson had clearly failed to comprehend the depth of Mexican resentment toward the Colossus of the North; he had failed to realize that anti-American feeling was so powerful a political factor in Mexico no Mexican leader could afford the luxury of overt American intervention in his behalf. Forestalled by this reaction from further intervention, Wilson could do nothing but sit by and watch while Mexico continued to suffer civil war between the Carranzistas and the Villistas.

* * *

Throughout the summer of 1914, the unresolved Mexican crisis and a personal tragedy—his wife was gravely ill and near death—preoccupied President Wilson. It is unlikely, then, that the assassination of the Austrian archduke Franz Ferdinand by a Serbian terrorist in the Bosnian-Herzegovinian capital of Sarajevo on June 28 captured anything more than his momentary attention. That the event would set in motion a series of diplomatic moves leading inexorably to a world war a few weeks later was certainly beyond his ability to foresee. Forecasting political developments in Europe was also beyond both the charter and the capability of the Office of Naval Intelligence, of course. Unfortunately, that responsibility was not to be found elsewhere in the federal government in 1914.

The proper place for the making of foreign political-intelligence estimates would have been the Department of State. From the earliest days of its antecedent, the Continental Congress's Committee of Secret Correspondence, the State Department had been intimately concerned with foreign political intelligence, although there had never been a division or section specifically concerned with the intelligence function. While there had always been a copious flow of information into the department from American legations and executive agents abroad, the department never had an adequate system for storing and later retrieving these reports for the production of finished intelligence.

Without the capability to correlate what has just been reported with what is already known, an intelligence service can do no better than serve up isolated pieces of a jigsaw puzzle to its customers, one at a time. But in 1914 the heart of the state's information-retrieval system remained what it had always been: the memory of the oldest employee in the department.[2]

The State Department's human computer was Alvey Augustus Adee, who had joined the diplomatic service in 1869 and was now the second assistant secretary of state. Adee read nearly every incoming and outgoing dispatch and seemed to remember them all. Beyond his remarkable ability to recall information, Adee had a greater than average ability to make sense—that is, intelligence—of it.

Unfortunately, when events began to unfold in the summer of 1914, he was on his annual bicycle tour of Europe; before leaving in May, he had

requested and received permission to extend his usual two-month vacation to three. There were others in the department capable of interpreting
European events, of course, but many of them were also on vacation.

Only Frank Mallett, the vice-consul general in Budapest, seems to have
seen what was coming. On July 13 he wrote a dispatch to the department
forecasting war between Austria-Hungary and Serbia, but due to official
parsimony, he was forced to send it by mail rather than cable. It arrived on
July 27, but by then urgent telegrams saying the same thing were pouring
into the department from every American legation in Europe.[3] The following day the Austrian foreign ministry informed the Serbian government that
a state of war existed between the two countries. Within a week Germany
had joined Austria-Hungary in a war against Russia, France, and Britain.
The Great War, in which the United States was soon to be embroiled and
which was to change profoundly the nation's role in the world, had arrived.
The storm that had been gathering for decades had finally broken, but the
White House and State Department, lacking any true foreign-intelligence
capability, had been taken almost completely by surprise.

Two weeks after the war began in Europe, President Wilson issued a
proclamation that "the United States must be neutral in fact as well as
in name." Unwilling to restrict American foreign trade, the United States
claimed the right to use the sea-lanes unmolested, to trade with the belligerents of both sides, as well as with the neutral European nations, and
to protect the safety of American passengers traveling on ships of the belligerent nations. Freedom of the seas swiftly became the issue threatening
Wilson's neutrality policy most directly.

The British stopped, searched, and escorted American vessels into British ports to prevent trade with Germany or even with neutral nations
that might transship American goods to the enemy. Germany, unable to
blockade British or French ports, resorted to submarine warfare to interdict
transatlantic shipping.

On May 7, 1915, a German U-boat sank the British liner *Lusitania*; 128
of the 1,198 passengers lost were American citizens. Another liner was
sunk in August, with the loss of two Americans. A German submarine
attacked a French liner in the English Channel the following March; two

of the passengers injured in the attack were Americans. Secretary of State Robert Lansing threatened to break off relations with Germany unless Berlin ended attacks on passenger and cargo vessels once and for all. The German crisis could not have happened at a worse moment: the United States was on the brink of war with Mexico.

From almost the beginning of the Mexican revolution, Washington had been concerned that the troubles could spill over the two-thousand-mile unguarded border into the United States. In February 1911 President William Howard Taft had sent an army division to Texas to patrol the Mexican border. Refugees from the fighting along the border fled into the United States, and shots were sometimes fired northward across the Rio Grande. In February 1913 Taft sent more troops to the border, and soon a large portion of the United States Army had been deployed along the Mexican frontier.

The task of guarding the border was complicated by an almost total lack of current intelligence regarding the civil war in Mexico. In February 1914 the chief of the Army War College Division—that element of the War Department's General Staff that had swallowed up the MID six years earlier—proposed assigning an intelligence function to some of the officers of the units guarding the border. This was done, but with the stipulation that the officers not cross into Mexico; therefore, intelligence collection was limited to interrogating refugees who crossed into the United States.[4] No effort was made to use Veracruz as a base for intelligence collection in Mexico during the American occupation of that seaport (April–November 1914).

By the end of 1915, Carranza had all but defeated Villa. In a move apparently aimed at embarrassing Carranza politically and eroding his popular support, Villa began a campaign aimed at forcing another American incursion into Mexico. On January 10, 1916, Villistas stopped a train near Santa Ysabel, Mexico, and took off eighteen young American mining engineers who had returned to the country at Carranza's invitation and supposedly under his protection. The insurgents murdered all but one, who managed to escape. On March 9 Villa led a force of five hundred mounted men across the border into New Mexico and attacked the town of Columbus, killing fifteen Americans and wounding others.

In response to the Columbus raid, Wilson sent a punitive expedition under Brigadier General John ("Black Jack") Pershing into Mexico in pursuit of Villa. Carranza refused either to approve the incursion or join the American force in its operations. In order to avoid precipitating an all-out war with both Mexican factions, therefore, the president tried to offend Carranza's political sensibilities as little as possible; he had no choice but to handicap Pershing by qualifying his order to catch Villa with the stipulation that the expedition not occupy Mexican towns and avoid contact with the Carranzistas. The latter condition was not easily met, since the Carranzistas held the anti-American sentiments of most Mexicans and initiated action with Pershing's expedition on numerous bloody occasions. This sensitive and difficult situation was confounded further by Pershing's critical lack of military intelligence, an area in which Villa had the decided advantage.

"Our various forces have had to rely for their guidance upon the inaccurate knowledge of untried American employees," Pershing reported,

> or else upon the uncertain information of frightened or unwilling natives. Thus have well laid plans miscarried and the goal has moved further and further into the future. While this is all true as to ourselves, almost the exact contrary is true as to Villa and his men. Villa is entirely familiar with every foot of Chihuahua, and the Mexican people, through friendship or fear, have always kept him advised of our every movement.[5]

Pershing thus faced the classic problem of the search-and-destroy mission in hostile territory that for political reasons must be treated as friendly or neutral. Among the several elements crucial to success, Pershing continued, was "a very full and accurate knowledge of the country through which we may operate, to be obtained by careful study and reconnaissance."

Pershing quickly improvised his own intelligence service, headed by cavalry Major James A. Ryan, and including personnel with some background in intelligence work. Ryan was fluent in Spanish, but he seems to have been unable to perform this duty; he was succeeded by Captain W. O. Reed as the expedition's intelligence officer on April 30. Reed hired Mexican agents to report on both the Villistas and Carranzistas. The agents were augmented by approximately twenty Apache scouts employed by the army. Pilots and aircraft from the Signal Corps' Aviation Section were sent from San Antonio to provide aerial reconnaissance services, but the low-powered planes then in use by the army proved ineffective in the high altitude of the Mexican territory in which Pershing was operating. The scouts and agents working on the ground were very effective, however, and Pershing soon overcame much of the intelligence advantage Villa had enjoyed.[6] Nonetheless, Villa himself remained elusive, while the presence of the punitive expedition in Mexico over the protests of Carranza continued to exacerbate relations with Mexico.

Both the occupation of Veracruz and the punitive expedition resembled American military operations of the second half of the twentieth century far more closely than they did those of their time. Both involved the strictly limited use of military force in order to bring about political change in another country (the removal of Huerta and Villa, respectively). It is extraordinary that such sophisticated and sensitive politico-military operations were undertaken by an administration that lacked virtually any foreign-policy-making establishment, including any mechanism at all for collecting and analyzing political intelligence, and with an army almost totally lacking a military intelligence capability.

The year 1915 marked the nadir of American military intelligence. Intelligence work came to a complete halt in the General Staff's Army War College Division. Some war-planning activity took place, with a particular focus on contingencies that might arise from the war in Europe. Nonetheless, when Wilson read in a newspaper that "it is understood that the General Staff is preparing a plan in case of war with Germany," he demanded to know whether the statement was true; if so, every officer of the General Staff was to be relieved of his duties and transferred out of Washington. The president relented when the chief of staff informed him that contingency war planning was required by the same law that had created the General Staff. Still, the lingering atmosphere on the General Staff after the incident did not encourage much initiative in the areas of planning and intelligence.[7]

Faced with turmoil in Mexico, which presented a continuing threat to the southern border, with the threat of war with Germany over the

freedom-of-the-seas issue, and with the prospect of an increasingly belligerent Japan, it is remarkable that Wilson had no larger appetite for information. One would expect him to wonder, for example, whether Germany
or Japan might exploit the Mexican problem to achieve her own objective.
There were more than a few rumors of them doing just that, but precious
little reliable intelligence.

Late in 1915—before his raid on Columbus—Villa had met in Juárez
with Major General Hugh L. Scott, the army chief of staff, and told him
of being approached by "an envoy of Japan in Mexico who asked what
Mexico would do in case Japan made war on the United States" (Villa
claimed he had rebuffed the overture).[8] Earlier that year rumors of Japanese designs on Magdalena Bay were revived when the *Asama,* a Japanese
cruiser, went aground in San Bartolomé Bay (or, as it was known north of
the border, Turtle Bay) in the Gulf of California and remained there for
six months while other Japanese cruisers and several supply ships came
and went.[9] The Japanese accused Germany of using the incident to incite
the rumors, and there was probably a germ of truth in that; the kaiser
continued to promote his yellow-peril propaganda campaign, now with
the purpose of keeping the United States from joining the Allies in the
war in Europe. But a young officer in the Arizona National Guard (which
had been mobilized to help guard the border after Pershing advanced into
Mexico) made a secret reconnaissance of the Sonora desert to the north of
the Gulf of California and found evidence that large numbers of Japanese
troops had been on maneuvers there and may even have briefly crossed
into the United States.[10]

Similar reports had also reached the ONI. At the same time the office
was receiving unconfirmed reports of German activities in Latin America,
including one about a secret submarine base supposedly located on the
Yucatán Peninsula.[11] Captain James Harrison Oliver, who had taken over
as chief of ONI in January 1914, was unwilling simply to file and index
such reports without making some effort to investigate them. Despite the
anti-intelligence mood that seemed to prevail in the Wilson administration, he revived a practice that had not been used by the office since the
Spanish-American War: espionage. The ONI hired informants throughout
Latin America to report on German and Japanese activities in their localities. The fund for such secret service was limited, but Oliver augmented

the ONI's hired spies with the volunteer services of American businesses operating in Latin America—for example, Wells, Fargo; Standard Oil; American Tobacco; and United Fruit.[12]

This laudable program failed to discover the true extent of foreign activities in Mexico, however. American opposition to Japanese expansion in China tempted some leaders in Tokyo to encourage Mexican-American hostilities in order to forestall United States interference in Japanese moves in China. In 1916, after Villa's raid and Pershing's punitive expedition brought the United States and Mexico to the brink of war, Japanese naval officials met with a secret Mexican military mission to Japan and agreed to furnish Carranza with arms and munitions. The Japanese navy was indeed making preparations for an American war at this time, and the *Asama* incident and the reports of Japanese reconnaissance sorties in the Southwest probably related to actual Japanese military preparations in the area. Nonetheless, when Wilson withdrew the punitive expedition in the face of the deepening German-American crisis early in 1917, Mexican-American tensions eased, and apparently for this reason the Japanese abandoned their Mexican scheme.[13]

Little of all this was divined by the ONI, of course. Even had the office been fully supported by the Navy Department and the White House, the complex Japanese-Mexican situation transcended what may properly be called naval intelligence. An adequate assessment of the situation could have been made only through the coordination of naval, military, and political intelligence; and even had there been adequate reporting from diplomatic sources in Tokyo, Mexico City, and perhaps elsewhere, there was simply no national intelligence activity in the federal government capable of assembling the pieces of the puzzle and recognizing the picture that might have emerged.

Regarding reports of secret German submarine bases and wireless stations in Mexico, the ONI was unable to substantiate them because they were, in fact, untrue. There had been a conflict in Berlin between the military and Foreign Office factions. German naval agents had indeed sought to build a submarine base in Mexico and were on the point of doing so in November 1916 when the plan was overruled by the German foreign minister.[14]

German covert operations in Mexico in 1914–16 were almost completely limited to political activity. An ambitious gray propaganda campaign aimed at winning Mexican sympathy for Germany and against the Allies was undertaken in 1914 and by 1911 involved the coven subsidy of a half-dozen major Mexican newspapers.[15] No covert psychological campaign was needed to win Carranza, however; the Mexican leader had in fact been courting Germany to obtain leverage against the United States, and he redoubled his efforts while Pershing's punitive expedition was in Mexico. It had been a secret proposal from Carranza to Berlin in 1916 envisioning a close economic and military relationship between the two countries that had led to the submarine-base project, and it was in response to this same climate that the German foreign minister, Arthur Zimmermann, conceived his plan to obtain the alliance of Mexico against the United States in the event the latter entered the war on the Allied side.[16] But little of this emerged in the picture the ONI was trying to construct of events south of the border. The State Department, which was the proper place for such political-intelligence assessments, was of course entirely incapable of making them.

Although naval intelligence and contingency war planning had enjoyed a new importance in the years immediately following the Spanish-American War, the United States government failed to develop an adequate intelligence community to deal with the problems America encountered in her new role as a world power. Even the modest naval and military intelligence units and the war-planning boards were forced to take several steps backward during the Taft and Wilson administrations. But the most critical area of deficiency lay in foreign political intelligence, which had never existed as a formal, distinct function within the government organization. The vital importance of accurate information to foreign-policy making and defense planning seems never to have been obvious to those who served in the White House between 1898 and 1916.

Woodrow Wilson, a former president of Princeton University, was the best-educated man ever to serve in the White House, but his knowledge of foreign affairs was limited, a fact he readily admitted as he took office.[17] His first term as president was a period of international peril and complexity such as the United States had not faced since the Civil War. Yet in dealing with the Mexican crisis and the European war, he relied solely upon his own personal judgment and the advice of his close adviser, Edward M. ("Colonel") House, a man with little more knowledge of foreign affairs than himself.

A man of undoubted good intentions, Wilson acted as though his own personal sense of ethics and morality was all America needed to deal with the world. Both his suspension of the Joint Army and Navy Board in 1913 and his threat to dissolve the War Department's General Staff in 1915 seemed to reflect a refusal to see any distinction between making war plans and making war, a refusal to think about that which, by his lights, a Christian should regard as unthinkable.

It need hardly be said that secret intelligence collection—spying—was quite beyond the bounds of propriety in Wilson's view. The awakening was to come, of course, in February 1917, when the British turned over to Wilson the Zimmermann telegram, the intercepted dispatch from the German foreign minister to his ambassador in Mexico City disclosing the scheme to seek an alliance with Mexico in a war with the United States.

"I not only did not know it when we got into this war," Wilson would recall, "but did not believe it when I was told that it was true, that Germany was not the only country that maintained a secret service."[18] But soon he did believe it, and with that realization and the exigencies of American entry into the European war came a new attitude toward intelligence. Before he would leave office in 1921, Wilson would complete the process that had begun with the creation of the ONI in 1882: the establishment of a national intelligence community as a permanent element of the United States government.

Chapter Nineteen

The Enemy Within

Black Tom Island has long since been swallowed up by the landfill encroachment of Jersey City, but in 1916 it was a mile-long promontory jutting out into New York Harbor's Upper Bay just opposite the Statue of Liberty. The Lehigh Valley Railroad had a large freight terminal on Black Tom, with warehouses, piers, and a network of tracks, and it was through here that much of the war material sold by American firms to the Allies passed en route to Europe. Freight cars loaded with munitions arrived from inland factories and were placed on sidetracks, often standing there for a week or more before their contents were transferred to barges and carried out to ships in the harbor.

On the night of July 29–30, 1916, there were thirty-four cars on Black Tom filled with ammunition: eleven carried high explosives, and seventeen were filled with artillery shells; there were three carloads of nitrocellulose, one of TNT, and two of combination fuses—in all, a total of 2,132,000 pounds. There were additional explosives aboard the ten barges tied up at the pier on the north side of the promontory; one of them was loaded with one hundred thousand pounds of TNT and 417 cases of detonating fuses.

July 30 was a Sunday. Only a handful of night watchmen were on Black Tom, and they fled in panic at 12:45 A.M., when a fire was sighted in one of the loaded freight cars. At 2:08 the Upper Bay was rocked by a tremendous explosion, followed thirty-two minutes later by another. Nearly every window in Jersey City was broken by the force of the blasts; in Brooklyn and Manhattan thousands of plate-glass windows were blown from skyscrapers and fell into the street. Shrapnel from exploding shells fell on Governors Island on the Brooklyn side of the bay. Buildings on nearby Ellis Island were wrecked, and the immigrants awaiting processing had to be evacuated. The two initial blasts were heard as far away as Camden, New Jersey, and Philadelphia. A series of smaller explosions followed during the next three hours. The sky above the harbor was lighted by a fire that was visible for miles.

The Black Tom explosion took the lives of three men and a child. Damage was estimated at fourteen million dollars. It was neither the first nor the last act of sabotage by German agents in the United States during the First World War, but it was one of the most spectacular.[1]

From at least the eighteenth century, German leaders never had any difficulty in seeing the importance of intelligence nor any scruples about employing espionage to collect it. The German victory in the Franco-Prussian War was due in no small measure to the work of the Intelligence Bureau of the Prussian General Staff and, to a much greater degree, to the Central Intelligence Bureau of the Foreign Office.[2] In 1890 the Central Intelligence Bureau was dissolved, leaving the intelligence function entirely to Section IIIb, as the Intelligence Bureau of the General Staff had come to be known. Sometime later the specialized needs of the navy were recognized, and the Naval Intelligence Service was created.

When the war began in Europe in 1914, Section IIIb was headed by Lieutenant Colonel Walther Nicolai, a hardworking forty-one-year-old officer who had run the German intelligence apparatus in Russia for several years. He had set up extensive agent networks in France, Belgium, and Russia (Britain, the world's leading sea power, was the responsibility of the Naval Intelligence Service). Only one part-time agent reported to Nicolai from the United States, however. The General Staff's war plans envisioned a swift victory in Europe but no involvement at all with the United States. But as the war dragged on into 1915 and America became the Allies' principal arms supplier, both IIIb and the Naval Intelligence Service undertook a covert-action campaign—sabotage and subversion—within the United States.

The director of all German covert activities in America was Count Johann von Bernstorff, a career diplomat who had been the German ambassador in Washington since 1908. Bernstorff kept a discreet distance from the actual operations, of course. The projects were managed directly by Captain Franz von Papen, the German military attaché in Mexico and the United States; Captain Karl Boy-Ed, the naval attaché; and Dr. Heinrich Albert, the German commercial attaché. Operations on the West Coast were run by the German consul general in San Francisco, Franz von Bopp.[3]

Dr. Albert, who was a former German minister of the interior, was responsible for a large variety of economic and psychological operations, none of which was illegal but all of which had to be done covertly in order to succeed. Through an American intermediary Albert formed the Bridgeport Projectile Company, a proprietary company in modern intelligence parlance. Purportedly, the firm was an American munitions company ready to do business with the Allies. In reality, its function was to deny munitions to the Allies through the tactic of placing enormous preemptive orders with American manufacturers of machine tools, hydraulic presses, rolling mills, and other machinery essential to munitions production, thereby frustrating the efforts of firms actually dealing with the Allies. The company also succeeded in tying up the Aetna Powder Company's whole capacity for the production of gunpowder until the end of 1915 with an order of five million pounds.[4]

Bridgeport Projectile actually contracted with Allied governments to supply munitions but was careful to insert a provision in the contracts absolving the firm of any penalty in case of failure to deliver, which, of course, was just what the company intended to do. The company also fostered labor unrest in other munitions companies actually working for the Allies by paying its own employees inflated wages.[5] Albert compounded the munitions makers' labor problems by encouraging sympathetic German-Americans among the engineers and skilled workers in the munitions industry to leave their jobs; he established an employment service to place them in other industries not contributing to the Allied war effort.[6]

Albert's other economic sabotage schemes involved cornering the markets on chlorine, the poisonous gas being used on the European battlefields, and other strategic materials and attempting to buy the Wright Aeroplane Company and its patents.

In psychological-warfare operations Albert was assisted by Dr. Bernard Dernburg, a former German colonial secretary. Albert and Dernburg, together with several Americans of pro-German sentiment, formed a Propaganda Cabinet to direct the psychological operations. The most important of the American members of the cabinet was George Sylvester Viereck, a German-American writer who edited and published *The Fatherland*, a pro-German weekly.[7]

The Propaganda Cabinet ran a white (i.e., overt) propaganda agency, the German Information Service, which distributed a daily compilation of pro-German news stories and editorials to several hundred American newspapers free of charge. The cabinet distributed thousands of pamphlets, magazines, and books carrying a pro-German, anti-British, or pacifist line. Viereck advocated obtaining control of at least one major newspaper in each of thirty American cities, but the cabinet succeeded only in purchasing a controlling interest in the *New York Evening Mail*.

Since there was never a real prospect of bringing the United States into the war on the side of Germany and Austria-Hungary, selling a pro-German viewpoint and exploiting the sentiment of German-Americans were only a lesser part of the German psychological campaign. Perhaps more important was the exploitation of anti-British, isolationist, or pacifist elements of the American public to create political resistance to the prospect of the United States joining the Allies against Germany and to block American arms sales.

Irish-Americans were especially receptive to the anti-British line, and Sir Roger Casement, an Irish nationalist leader seeking German aid for an uprising against British rule in Ireland, gave the German Foreign Office the names of several Irish-Americans willing to work for the German Secret Service in the United States.[8] Among them was Jeremiah O'Leary, whose American Truth Society served as a gray propaganda agency for the cabinet. The cabinet even provided covert subsidies to the Friends of Freedom for India, a group dedicated to ending British rule on the subcontinent.

Hindu-Americans comprised a minuscule ethnic faction in the United States, but Irish nationalists had been making common cause with them against Britain long before the war. The membership of the Society for the Advancement of India included many altruistic Americans, including college professors, who provided education in the United States to selected Indian youths. And the lure of Eastern mysticism attracted many wealthy New York dilettantes to the Indian groups, thereby increasing their influence considerably.[9] Therefore the Propaganda Cabinet did not overlook this ethnic faction as a medium for covert political influence within some very influential strata of American society.

Isolationism and pacifism had an even broader appeal than anti-British sentiment. The cabinet subsidized or otherwise aided such groups as the League of American Women for Strict Neutrality, the American Humanity League, the American Independence Union, and the Arms Embargo Conference, all of which could be counted on to agitate against arms shipments to, or American support for, the Allies.[10] The cabinet established the University League, which recruited sympathetic professors on American campuses in order to use their academic prestige to promote covert German propaganda themes in pamphlets and articles.[11]

This elaborate German covert propaganda machine had its work cut out for it. Traditional American sympathies for France and a pro-British spirit that had been growing since the Anglo-American rapprochement of the Spanish-American War meant an uphill struggle for Dr. Albert and his cohorts in the Propaganda Cabinet.[12] Their task became nearly impossible after the sinking of the *Lusitania* in May 1915.

The loss of American lives, including those of women and children, in the sinking moved President Wilson to a step rather incongruous with his abhorrence of the clandestine: he instructed Secretary of the Treasury William G. McAdoo to put the German and Austro-Hungarian legations under surveillance by the Secret Service.

On July 24 Special Agents William H. Houghton and Frank Burke followed Viereck and Albert when they emerged from the latter's offices in the headquarters of the Hamburg-American Steamship Line at 45 Broadway and boarded a Sixth Avenue elevated train at Rector Street. Houghton followed Viereck when the latter got off at Twenty-third Street, and Burke stayed on the train, in the seat immediately behind Albert. The commercial attaché was carrying a briefcase, which he set on the seat beside him when he opened a newspaper and began to read. Albert was still engrossed in the paper when the train pulled into the Fiftieth Street station, but he looked up in time to see where he was. Jumping up, he dashed out of the car, leaving the briefcase on the seat. Once on the platform, however, he remembered it and rushed back. Meanwhile, Special Agent Burke had grabbed the case and, seeing Albert get back on the train, got off. The attaché rushed off the train again and pursued the agent down to the street, but Burke jumped aboard a streetcar and made away with the briefcase.

Secret Service Chief William J. Flynn turned over the purloined briefcase to Secretary McAdoo, who had the contents translated from German into English. The unhurried view that the documents provided McAdoo (and, apparently, President Wilson) of everything from the Bridgeport Projectile Company to covert German subsidy of Viereck's *The Fatherland* was certainly an eye-opener, but it disclosed nothing that violated any federal law. McAdoo saw a way to neutralize the entire secret campaign, however: publicity. After receiving a promise that the source would not be disclosed, the secretary handed over copies of the papers to Frank I. Cobb, editor of the *New York World*.

On Sunday, August 15, the World broke the story under a page-one headline: HOW GERMANY HAS WORKED IN U.S. TO SHAPE OPINION, BLOCK THE ALLIES AND GET MUNITIONS FOR HERSELF TOLD IN SECRET AGENTS' LETTERS. "The World to-day begins the publication of a series of articles raising for the first time the curtain that has hitherto concealed the activities and purposes of the official German propaganda in the United States" ran the lead of a story that crowded almost everything else off the front page, except for a sidebar on the documents, facsimiles of two letters between Albert and Viereck, and a somewhat wistful full-face photograph of the latter.

"The affair was merely a storm in a tea-cup," Count von Bernstorff later claimed. "The papers as published afforded no evidence of any action either illegal or dishonorable."[13] But the huge and expensive covert psychological campaign was not simply neutralized; it had been made to backfire, dealing a devastating propaganda blow to Germany. As to the economic operation, Papen admitted, "Our contracts were challenged, cancelled or replaced by other 'priority' orders, and our scheme came to an end."[14]

German physical sabotage operations were better hidden. Physical sabotage was the joint responsibility of Captains Papen and Boy-Ed, the military and naval attachés, respectively. Papen opened a suite of offices in New York City at 60 Wall Street; Boy-Ed established his own office around the corner, in the German consulate, at 11 Broadway; both lived at the Deutscher Verein (German Club) on Central Park South. While it may have seemed a bit unusual for a pair of foreign attachés to locate themselves outside of Washington, there was nothing covert about the arrangement; Papen hung out a shingle billing his establishment as the Bureau of the Military Attaché, and sometimes even referred to it as the War Intelligence Center. The two attachés based their covert-action campaign elsewhere, however, a bit farther up Broadway, at number 45, the offices of the Hamburg-American Steamship Line. Much of the program was run by Paul Koenig, chief of security for the Atlas Line, a Hamburg-American subsidiary.

Shrewd and tough, Koenig was called the bullheaded Westphalian by those who worked for him, but never to his face. He and his staff of private detectives knew the longshoremen, tugboat skippers, merchant seamen, bartenders, madams, flophouse owners, and all the other denizens of New York waterfront society. In Koenig and his men Papen saw the ideal instrument for sabotage and other covert strong-arm activities, and he wasted no time in employing them for those purposes. On August 22, 1914, within weeks of the outbreak of the war, he recruited the security man.[15]

Mysterious fires and explosions began to plague the munitions industry almost as soon as American arms companies started producing war material for the Allies. On August 30, 1914, a Du Pont Company powder mill at Pompton Lakes, New Jersey, blew up. There were several other munitions-plant explosions that fall and winter, and their frequency increased the following year. The pace continued throughout 1916.

Exactly how many of these explosions and fires were the work of the German Secret Service is impossible to determine. Certainly, the production of explosives is a dangerous business under any circumstances, and many of the incidents were probably caused by the manufacturers' haste to meet the surge of Allied orders. Others may have been the work of German sympathizers acting on their own, without the direction or even the knowledge of Papen and Boy-Ed. But the two attachés and their accomplices were directly implicated by postwar investigations in so many of the fires and explosions that it seems likely they were also responsible for many of the remaining incidents.[16]

The base for the incendiary operations was a German safe house at 123 West Fifteenth Street. The four-story brownstone, quietly luxurious, with a well-equipped kitchen, a basement wine cellar, and a sumptuous dining room, was rented by Martha Held, a handsome, middle-aged woman employed by Section IIIb and said by some to be married to a German baron. Neighbors who saw so many male visitors to the house at all hours of the day and night concluded it was a brothel, an impression Frau Held encouraged. Other observers may have thought the brownstone a place of secret assignation; Papen often visited with a striking young woman on his arm—Mena Edwards, a model whose photograph so often adorned the ads of the Eastman Kodak Company that she was known as the Eastman Girl.

J. Irving Walsh, owner of the brownstone, visited from time to time and later recalled that "there was a great deal of wine and liquor about, and that it always had quite a German atmosphere."[17] But hidden from the landlord's eyes was the large store of explosives and detonating mechanisms the German agents kept in the place; the safe house was their bomb factory.

Although the sabotage campaign of Papen and Boy-Ed was producing some spectacular results, they were not enough to satisfy the high command in Berlin. The fires and explosions had actually interfered little with the continuing flow of American munitions to the Allies. If the two attachés had proved less than effective, perhaps it was because they came to their task by accident, having been the only representatives of the army and navy who happened to be attached to the Washington legation when the war commenced. In March, Berlin decided to dispatch a specialist to the United States, someone with superior qualifications for fighting the secret war against the munitions shipments. He was Captain Lieutenant Franz von Rintelen, a naval reservist serving on the Admiralty's General Staff.

The thirty-eight-year-old Rintelen was the son of an aristocratic German family. He had served in the navy before embarking on a career in international banking. In 1906 he had come to the United States as a representative of the Disconto Gesellshaft, Germany's second largest bank. After three years in New York City, he had spent a year in Latin America before returning to Germany. At the outbreak of the war, he returned to active duty and served as a financial adviser to the Admiralty Staff. Early in 1915 he began to brief the Foreign Office, the War Ministry, and the Finance Ministry on his plan to go to the United States and stem the flow of munitions to the Allies, a presentation he invariably concluded with the line, "I'll buy up what I can, and blow up what I can't."[18]

On April 3 Rintelen arrived in New York, traveling as Emile V. Gauche, a Swiss businessman. He took a room in the Great Northern Hotel on Fifty-seventh Street and opened offices on Cedar Street, in the financial district, in the name of E. V. Gibbons, Inc. Armed with a credit of half a million dollars, he hoped to corner the American munitions market. He soon discovered, however, that this ambition was beyond even the capacity of the German Treasury to realize. Unable to buy up the munitions, therefore, he resorted to blowing them up.

A small fleet of German merchant ships lay idle in New York Harbor, where their captains had elected to keep them at the outbreak of hostilities the previous August rather than risk capture or sinking by the British navy in international waters. The stranded crews lived aboard the idle vessels but were free to go ashore. The members of this German community floating in New York Harbor were soon adopted by Karl von Kleist, a retired German sea captain living in Hoboken, New Jersey. Rintelen knew Kleist's family in Germany and now introduced himself to the old gentleman. Kleist readily agreed to help Rintelen in the latter's sabotage schemes.

Rintelen recognized that it would be far easier to organize sabotage in New York Harbor and other major American seaports than in the far-flung munitions plants. He therefore decided to ignore the plants and concentrate on the ships that carried their output to the Allies. He enlisted Dr. Walter T. Scheele, a German chemist who had emigrated to the United States in the 1890s and had been reporting on American chemical progress to Section IIIb for most of the ensuing years; Scheele agreed to construct small incendiary devices that could be planted in the cargo holds of the munitions ships.

Kleist introduced Rintelen to the officers and crew of the S.S. *Friedrich der Grosse*, one of the ships interned at New York. Karl Schmidt, the chief engineer, and several of the crew agreed to set up a factory aboard the liner for the production of incendiary-bomb casings. Schmidt and the others in the shipboard factory cut lead tubing into cigarlike sections and soldered a copper disk in the middle, thereby dividing each "cigar" into two water-tight compartments. The cigars were then taken to Dr. Scheele's laboratory in Hoboken, where the German chemist filled them with sulfuric acid and picric acid, placing each chemical in the adjacent compartments of the cigar and sealing the ends with wax. The disk blocking the middle of each cigar was of a thickness calculated to withstand the action of the acids for a predetermined interval, at the end of which time the chemicals would mix and ignite, causing an intense flame to burst through the two wax plugs.[19] Rintelen's assembly line was soon producing the cigars at the rate of fifty per day.

Herr Hossenfelder, the assistant German consul general in New York, had made contact with local Irish nationalists as part of Dr. Albert's propaganda campaign. Hossenfelder introduced Rintelen to one of the Irish leaders, who agreed to put the German officer in contact with Irish-American longshoremen willing to plant the incendiary devices in the holds of ammunition ships.[20]

The first target was the S.S. *Phoebus*, carrying a cargo of artillery shells from New York to the Russian port of Archangel. Rintelen's cigars started a fire aboard her at sea, and the captain flooded the hold, extinguishing the flames but rendering the shells unusable. She had to be towed into Liverpool by a British warship. After a few similar successes, Rintelen expanded his operation to the ports of Boston, Philadelphia, Baltimore, and New Orleans.

Throughout the spring and summer of 1915, there was a rash of mysterious fires aboard ships at sea. Sometimes the cigars were discovered before they ignited, but the longshoreman usually planted several of the devices in different locations aboard the vessel, in one case as many as thirty. About half of the sabotaged ships made it to their destination unscathed; Rintelen guessed that either the cigars had failed to ignite, or else the fire was noticed early and extinguished. Nonetheless, the incendiary campaign seemed to be having a serious impact on the munitions traffic, and Rintelen congratulated himself when he read that the Russian minister, Prince Miliukov, had told the Duma—the Russian parliament—that the delay in the transport of munitions was becoming increasingly serious.[21]

With his ship-bombing organization in place and functioning, Rintelen turned his attention to other projects. The prosperity in some American industries resulting from war contracts created a favorable climate for increased demands by labor and, therefore, the possibility of crippling strikes. Through David Lamar, a dubious character the newspapers had dubbed the Wolf of Wall Street, he organized Labor's National Peace Council. The council held a convention in June at a Washington hotel, where it elected Representative Frank Buchanan, former president of the ironworkers' union, as its head. Armed with a huge strike fund secretly furnished by the German Treasury by way of Rintelen, the council was able to paralyze the New York waterfront with a longshoreman's strike and tie up the Bethlehem Steel Works with another walkout. Rintelen's labor operations were soon frustrated, however, by Samuel Gompers, the British-born president of the American Federation of Labor.[22]

The bombings, the economic sabotage, and the propaganda comprised most of the activities of the German Secret Service in the United States during the period of American neutrality, but there was also a miscellaneous assortment of other projects. One of the first tasks assigned to Papen and Boy-Ed was the repatriation of German and Austrian males of military age for service in the war. Many men holding commissions or enlisted status in the reserve were eager to return and serve on active duty, but the British blockade of Europe prevented holders of German or Austrian passports from simply booking passage home. Papen recruited Hans von Wedell, a naturalized American citizen, to procure passports of neutral countries that the reservists could use to get home.

For payments of ten or fifteen dollars Wedell was able to purchase the passports of sailors from neutral countries or hire Americans to acquire United States passports and turn them over to him. He skillfully pasted a reservist's photograph over that of the legitimate holder and delivered the fraudulent document to its new owner. The technique was simple but not at all secure. Every passport seller was also a potential informer and blackmailer, and Wedell soon learned that the Department of Justice was making discreet inquiries about him. Using a piece of his own handiwork, Wedell became Rosato Sprio, a Mexican, and tried to return to Germany aboard a Danish liner. His passport deceived the American authorities but not the boarding officer from a British patrol boat that stopped the liner in international waters. Having evaded an American prison, Wedell did not live to see the inside of a British one; the patrol boat struck a German mine and went down with all aboard.[23]

The great majority of the German reservists succeeded in getting home using the counterfeit documents, however. When they arrived, Section IIIb thriftily collected the passports and issued them to secret agents bound for Britain and other European assignments. Only through sad experience did the service come to recognize that which should have been obvious: documents twice tampered with (at least once by an amateur) and bearing the name of a living person liable to turn up anywhere (if he could not readily be found in the New York telephone directory) were not likely to deceive a counterespionage officer. After numerous Allied firing squads had done their work, the service took the trouble to manufacture their own bogus passports, which proved to be as good as the real article.[24]

Section IIIb and the German Foreign Office undertook several covert political and paramilitary operations during the war aimed at diverting Allied military resources from the war in Europe. They worked, for example, with Sir Roger Casement to arm the Irish nationalists for an uprising against the hated British rule in Ireland. The Irish operation was largely run out of Berlin, although early in the war Casement was in New York, where he conferred with Papen. A parallel German operation was aimed at British rule in India, and this project involved Papen and the rest of the Section IIIb apparatus in the United States.

"We did not go so far as to suppose that there was any hope of India achieving her independence through our assistance," Papen recalled, "but if there was any chance of fomenting local disorders we felt it might limit the number of Indian troops who could be sent to France and other theaters of war."[25] Indeed, a sufficiently large uprising in India would have required British troops to be diverted from Europe to restore order in the British possession.

In addition to exploiting influential Americans' sympathy for the Indian subjects of British colonialism through covert subsidies to the Friends of Freedom for India and the Society for the Advancement of India, Papen worked directly with the Gadar[26] organization in the United States. Gadar had been founded in San Francisco in 1913 by Har Dyal, an Oxford-educated Hindu doing postgraduate study at the University of California at Berkeley. The organization, which advocated the violent overthrow of

British rule in India, drew its popular support from the seven thousand Indian laborers, mostly Sikhs from the Punjab, then living in California.[27] At the outbreak of the war, Har Dyal accepted an invitation from the German Foreign Office to come to Berlin, leaving his deputy, Ram Chandra, as head of the Gadar organization. In Berlin, Dyal became the protégé of Herr von Wesendonck, chief of the Foreign Office's Indian Section and chairman of the Indian Independence Committee, a German political front. The committee became the central coordinating body for all Indian revolutionary movements worldwide.[28]

Early in 1915 the committee sent Heramba Lal Gupta, an Indian who had graduated from Columbia University, to the United States to serve as its principal agent. The Foreign Office instructed Bernstorff to put 150,000 marks at his disposal and assist Gupta in organizing a sabotage network among the Indians living in the United States. Of course, the ambassador put a safe distance between himself and the Indians by delegating the guidance of Gupta and his associate, one Dr. Chauracanta Chakrabarty, to Papen. Since most of the Indian expatriates lived in California and the Gadar organization was being directed by Ram Chandra and other Indian intellectuals on the Berkeley campus, Papen worked through Franz von Bopp, the consul general in San Francisco.[29]

Bopp and his assistant consuls, Wilhelm von Brincken and E. H. von Schack, had been quite active in running the West Coast branch of the German sabotage operation in the United States, directing their attentions to transpacific munitions shipments from the United States to Russia (their most spectacular success was the May 30, 1915, explosion of a munitions barge in Seattle Harbor). One of their highest-priority tasks was to carry out orders received from Berlin in January 1915 "to destroy the Canadian Pacific in several places for the purpose of causing a lengthy interruption of traffic." The presence of a large community of Indian laborers in Vancouver suggested a means of accomplishing this task. Papen supplied one of Bopp's agents with four thousand dollars to purchase a ton of dynamite to be used by the Indians against the railway and fifty rifles fitted with Maxim silencers for the removal of railroad guards.

The Canadian Pacific operation was merely a sideshow to the principal German-Indian conspiracy, however, namely, fomenting an armed uprising in India. Section IIIb had already infiltrated a network of Har Dyal's Indian agents in the Punjab to organize the mutiny; all they lacked was arms. The task of supplying weapons and ammunition was assigned to Papen, who, working through the New York agent for Krupp, the German arms manufacturer, had procured eight thousand rifles and four million cartridges and shipped them to San Diego. There they were secretly loaded aboard the *Annie Larsen*, a small steamer chartered by Bopp using laundered funds and several cutouts to disguise German involvement.

On March 8, 1915, the *Annie Larsen* cleared port, ostensibly bound for a Mexican port but actually en route to Socorro, a Mexican island in the Pacific several hundred miles south of Baja California. According to Papen's plan, the steamer was to be met at Socorro by the *Maverick*, an oil tanker Bopp had purchased from Standard Oil. The cargo of arms and munitions was to be transferred from the *Annie Larsen* to the tanker and concealed in her empty tanks. The *Maverick* was then to proceed to the Indian coast near Karachi (then part of India), where the arms would be landed by fishing craft and put in the hands of Har Dyal's agents.

"The British Secret Service got wind of the affair," Papen recalled, "how, I shall never know. . . ."[30] The British may have been responsible for the delay in the *Maverick*'s reaching the appointed rendezvous, a delay that forced the *Annie Larsen* to depart after a month's wait in search of fresh water, which was not available on Socorro. In any case, a British warship was waiting when the *Maverick* finally arrived. A boarding party searched the ship but of course found no arms. The *Annie Larsen*, meanwhile, was wandering around the Pacific and eventually put in at Hoquiam, Washington, on July 1, four months after leaving San Diego. Customs inspectors, probably having been tipped off by the British, immediately seized the cargo.[31]

News of the seizure of the *Annie Larsen* reached Papen and Bopp before their plan to have Indian agents sabotage the Canadian Pacific could be executed. Unnerved, and probably wondering whether British intelligence had also penetrated this scheme, the Germans broke off contact with the Indians in Vancouver, and the Canadian operation withered on the vine.[32]

German covert-action operations in the United States during the period of American neutrality worked at cross-purposes. As Bernstorff realized (if one accepts the self-serving but basically plausible claim he makes in his often dubious memoirs), Germany's interests would have been best served by doing everything to keep America from entering the war on the Allied side.[33] But even had German propaganda been more effective and Dr. Albert more cautious with his briefcase, it would still have been obvious that there was a German hand behind the physical and economic sabotage operations. Whatever limited impact the bombings, strikes, and other mischief may have had on the Allied war effort, every incident eroded isolationist sentiment in the United States and increased the likelihood of American entry into the war.

There was, however, one area in which covert German intervention had quite the opposite effect: Mexico. A Mexican war would certainly have kept the United States from joining the Allies in Europe and would probably have siphoned off a large part of the output of American munitions production from the Allied market. President Wilson's Mexican problem was of his own making, and the United States moved pretty far down the road to war with Mexico without any foreign encouragement. It is therefore surprising that German covert efforts to bring about such a war were so limited and so late. One reason Berlin was slow to play the Mexican card was the perception of Heinrich von Eckardt, the German ambassador to Mexico, that the inevitable American victory in such a war would mean new American economic expansion in Mexico, a development that would have precluded Germany's own imperialist designs on the country.[34] Others in the Foreign Ministry saw things differently, but in their Mexican schemes they were constrained to work around Ambassador Eckardt.

There is no solid evidence that Germany was behind the so-called Plan of San Diego, an abortive scheme to foment an uprising of Mexican-Americans, native Americans, and African-Americans in the Southwest in 1915.[35] There is ample evidence, however, that a covert-action operation aimed at precipitating a Mexican-American war was mounted by the German apparatus in New York in 1915. The object of the plan was to restore Huerta to power in Mexico, a step likely to elicit new military intervention in the country by President Wilson.

Huerta had gone into exile in Barcelona after having been forced from power in July 1914. By some accounts, Rintelen visited him there while en route to New York in February 1915; Rintelen says otherwise.[36] In any case, Huerta turned up in New York City on April 13, ten days after the German officer arrived in the city.

Huerta's arrival could hardly escape notice by the New York press, but the former Mexican president declared that he had come to the United States to live out his retirement and planned to purchase an estate on Long Island.[37] During May he met quite discreetly with someone from the German embassy, possibly Boy-Ed, who seems to have been Huerta's case officer at this point. The Mexican project was handed over to Rintelen on orders from Berlin shortly thereafter, however.[38] Rintelen and the Mexican leader, together with several other Germans and Mexicans, met in Huerta's hotel, the Holland House on Fifth Avenue at Thirtieth Street, on June 1.[39]

Huerta presented Rintelen with his conditions for a new campaign for power in Mexico: money to buy arms, which were to be delivered to the Mexican coast in German U-boats, and moral support. In return, and if he regained power, Huerta would make war on the United States.[40] Rintelen reported Huerta's demands to Berlin, but apparently confident of receiving approval, he set in motion the machinery to meet them. Through Dr. Albert and his assistant, he arranged to have eight hundred thousand dollars deposited in Huerta's account at the Deutsche Bank in Havana and another ninety-five thousand dollars in a Mexican account. Eight million rounds of ammunition were purchased in Saint Louis and orders for three million more were placed with New York munitions representatives.

From the moment of his arrival in the United States two months earlier, Rintelen had been made to feel unwelcome by Papen and Boy-Ed, who regarded him as a fifth wheel and interpreted his very presence as an implied rebuke by Berlin. For Boy-Ed this impression must certainly have been heightened when Berlin took the important Mexican project away from him and handed it to Rintelen, an officer of lower rank in the German navy and a reservist, as well. For his part, Rintelen saw the two attachés as dull-witted drones and amateur meddlers in the serious business of subversion, and apparently he did little to conceal his feelings from them. He also managed to offend Bernstorff by refusing to tell him exactly what his official position and duties were in the United States, and the ambassador's resentment was heightened when the Foreign Office ignored his request for that information.[41] Thus, Bernstorff affixed his approval to the cipher cable Papen and Boy-Ed sent the German high command warning that

Rintelen was going about his sabotage schemes in a reckless and dangerous manner and ought to be recalled. The high command consented, and
on June 6, five days after his meeting with Huerta, Rintelen received his
recall from Berlin.[42]

Boy-Ed and Papen were again in charge of the Huerta project, which
by now was promising to become the main act in German covert action in
the Western Hemisphere. Boy-Ed took over the negotiations with Huerta,
while Papen went to the Mexican border to reconnoiter the terrain and
arrange safe houses and other assets for the use of Section IIIb in Texas.
On June 25 Huerta boarded a train, ostensibly on his way to visit the San
Francisco Exhibition. The following afternoon he left the train at Kansas
City and boarded another bound for El Paso and points west. At dawn the
train pulled into the little town of Newman, New Mexico, twenty miles
from the border, and the Mexican leader quietly got off. General Pascual
Orozco, an old ally who had helped Huerta overthrow Madero, was waiting in an automobile. But there was also a second welcoming committee
awaiting Huerta in Newman: Zachary N. Cobb, an agent of the United
States State Department; two United States deputy marshals; a United
States Army colonel; and a squad of twenty-five American troops. Cobb
arrested Huerta and Orozco and took them to El Paso, where they were
confined in the county jail.[43]

Rintelen booked passage for Rotterdam on the *Noordam* of the Holland-
American Line, traveling once again as the Swiss businessman Emile V.
Gauche. On August 13 the ship touched at Falmouth. British officials came
aboard and arrested him. He was interned as a prisoner of war and turned
over to British Naval Intelligence for interrogation.

On September 1 the British authorities at Falmouth boarded another
Dutch ship, the *Rotterdam*, and searched the luggage of an American
journalist, James J. Archibald. They discovered a hoard of official and
private correspondence from the German and Austrian legations in the
United States, which Archibald, in the role of secret courier, was carrying
to Europe. The documents included progress reports from Papen and
Boy-Ed on the sabotage campaign; canceled checks and other records of
payments to saboteurs and propagandists; reports on the Huerta project;

and a report from the Austrian ambassador, Count Dumba, on his work promoting strikes among Hungarian-American workers in munitions plants. The British cheerfully turned over the take to Walter Hines Page, the American ambassador to Britain, and also published some of the juicier items as a Parliamentary White Paper.[44]

On September 8 the State Department declared Ambassador Dumba persona non grata and demanded his recall. The Wilson administration waited another three months to drop the other shoe: on December 1 the State Department declared Papen and Boy-Ed persona non grata as well, demanding their recall. Bernstorff himself escaped the fate of the others by a hair's breadth: Archibald had also offered to carry the ambassador's secret papers to Berlin; Bernstorff smelled a rat, however, and declined the offer.[45]

Archibald, an adventurous war correspondent, had been the first American wounded in the Spanish-American War when he was grazed by a Spanish bullet while covering an early firefight in Cuba for the San Francisco *Post*. Bernstorff would have been convinced the man was a penetration agent had he known of Archibald's work as a secret agent for the Office of Naval Intelligence in eastern Asia during the Russo-Japanese War. But there is no evidence that in this incident he was anything but what he claimed to be: an American with pro-German sympathies during the period of American neutrality.

The organization that had tipped off the Falmouth authorities to Archibald's mission, that had alerted those same authorities to the true identity of Emile V. Gauche, that had learned of the German project to restore Huerta to power, that had scuttled the German plot to arm the Indian uprising in the Punjab, that had indeed penetrated all of the German covert-action operations in the United States was not the United States Navy's Office of Naval Intelligence.

It was the British Admiralty's Naval Intelligence Department.

Chapter Twenty

British Intelligence and American Countersubversion

The record of British intelligence operations in the United States in the decades following the War of 1812 is surprisingly sparse. For reasons not altogether clear, secret intelligence and covert action were very much in decline in the British government as the nineteenth century wore on.[1] Nonetheless, the threat to England and Canada posed by Irish-American nationalists immediately after the Civil War seems to have sparked some British secret intelligence activity in the United States. The Fenian Brotherhood, as the Irish-American group called itself, staged an abortive invasion of Canada in 1866 and launched terrorist attacks against Great Britain from American soil. British secret surveillance of Irish-American nationalists continued through the turn of the century, and the British apparatus in the United States may be presumed to have been enlarged in response to other Anglo-American crises of the period—for example, the 1895 Venezuelan boundary dispute. During this period, which also saw the Boer War and increased Anglo-German tensions, intelligence units were established in both the Admiralty and the War Office.[2]

In 1914, sometime during the first months of the World War, the Admiralty's Naval Intelligence Department was contacted by Wickham Steed of the London *Times*. Steed reported that he had just been visited by a representative of Tomáš Masaryk, the leader of the Czech and Slovak nationalists who sought independence from Austria-Hungary. The man was Emanuel Victor Voska, a native of the Austrian province of Bohemia (now part of Czechoslovakia) who had emigrated to the United States in 1894, when his political activities as a Social Democrat got him into trouble with the government of Austria-Hungary. Now a successful businessman in the marble-quarrying and stonecutting industry and a prominent figure in the Czech émigré communities in the United States, Voska had traveled ro Prague to meet with Masaryk on the eve of the war. On his way back to the United States, he had stopped in London to convey Masaryk's proposal for cooperation between the Czech-Slovak independence movement and the Allies.

In order to gain an audience with Lord Kitchener, the secretary of state for war, Voska contacted Steed, an influential journalist and friend of Masaryk. After meeting with Kitchener and the Russian ambassador to Britain, he returned home to establish a secret intelligence organization among the Czech and Slovak émigrés in America for the purpose of frustrating German and Austro-Hungarian covert operations in the United States. Apparently, he conveyed something of his plans to Steed, who reported it to Naval Intelligence. The department passed the information along to its representative in the United States, Captain Guy Gaunt, an Australian-born naval attaché at the British embassy in Washington.

Gaunt made contact with Voska and met with him in a British safe house in New York City.[3] After a subsequent meeting with Sir Cecil Spring-Rice, the British ambassador to Washington, Voska agreed to put his Czech-Slovak intelligence apparatus at the service of British intelligence.

The Bohemian National Alliance, an umbrella organization that eventually included 320,000 Czech and Slovak émigrés living throughout the United States, provided an almost unlimited supply of talent for Voska's organization. "If we wanted an expert in safe construction, telegraphy, telephone wiring, chemistry, handwriting, police work, a dozen other specialties," Voska recalled, "I had only to give the word and he bobbed up, sometimes within an hour."[4] But the émigrés' most valuable talent had been imposed upon them early in life by the cultural policies of Austria-Hungary: every Czech spoke flawless, unaccented German, and every Slovak was equally fluent in Hungarian. They were indistinguishable from Germans, Austrians, or Hungarians and were therefore easily able to penetrate the covert operations of the Central Powers in the United States.

Four of Voska's agents worked in the Austrian consulate in New York. Two of his men worked for Paul Koenig, the detective chief of the Atlas Line who ran sabotage and espionage errands for Papen and Boy-Ed. Voska had at least one agent aboard each of the interned German ships in New York Harbor, including the S.S. *Friedrich der Grosse*, site of Rintelen's bomb factory. He had agents in the Austro-Hungarian consulates at Cleveland, Saint Louis, Chicago, New Orleans, and San Francisco. An agent in the international wireless station at Sayville, Long Island, supplied Voska with copies of the German diplomatic traffic between Berlin and the Washington embassy. Another Voska agent worked in the embassy itself. Yet another was employed in the German consulate in Chicago. The Czech governess for a wealthy German family in New York made detailed reports on her employer's conversations with Ambassador von Bernstorff, a frequent guest in the house. The superintendent of the building in which the Indian nationalists had their New York offices worked for Voska. Yet another agent worked as a printer in the offices of George S. Viereck's *Fatherland*. And Voska's daughter, Villa, managed to get a job as a stenographer with Dr. Heinrich Albert, the German commercial attaché who ran the covert economic and psychological operations until he forgot his briefcase.[5]

Voska ran his far-flung intelligence organization from his crowded home on East Eighty-sixth Street and from the offices of the Pneumograph Company, a cover organization with offices in lower Manhattan. At the latter location a photostat machine was in constant use, copying in triplicate everything the Voska organization collected. One copy went to Captain Gaunt, a second into Voska's files, and a third to John R. Rathom, editor and general manager of the *Providence* (Rhode Island) *Journal*.

Australian-born and educated at the prestigious English public school Harrow, Rathom became an American citizen and worked on the Chicago *Record-Herald* for several years before joining the *Providence Journal*. He was on friendly terms with many influential Americans. Gaunt selected his fellow Australian as the man to entrust with the job of transforming Voska's intelligence into anti-German propaganda and disseminating it throughout the United States.

From the outset the British had the propaganda advantage in America. With the cutting of the transatlantic cables by the Royal Navy early in the war, Britain gained complete control of the war news sent to the United States. No American correspondents were permitted to visit the Allied side of the European front, so American papers were reduced to reprinting stories from the London press. Charles F. G. Masterman, chief of British propaganda, consolidated his American advantage by appointing the Canadian-born Sir Gilbert Parker as chief of a division responsible for winning American hearts and minds. With headquarters in Wellington House, near London's Victoria Station, the division was a white propaganda operation—that is, it was officially, if quietly, avowed by the British government. The amiable Sir Gilbert preferred the term *publicity* to *propaganda* and directed a stream of pamphlets, cartoons, articles, speeches, photographs, and sometimes even motion picture films to a carefully selected mailing list of some quarter million Americans who had some influence, however small, on public opinion or official policy. He also supplied the American press with articles presenting the British view of the war by such popular British writers as G. K. Chesterton, Sir Arthur Conan Doyle, H. G. Wells, and Rudyard Kipling.[6]

The role of Rathom and the *Providence Journal* was far different and was probably unknown to Sir Gilbert. Rathom's was a gray propaganda operation, not only for the usual reason (to enhance the impact of the material by making it appear to have come from an independent and objective source) but to protect Voska's secret intelligence operations. In composing exposés from the documents Voska provided him, Rathom deliberately introduced minor errors of detail so the Germans and Austro-Hungarians would not realize the information had come from the very heart of their covert-action operations and was not, for example, simply from some careless talk overheard by a hostile eavesdropper. The true sources of the stories were further obscured by the newspaperman's propensity for improving upon his material with his creative imagination, a practice probably motivated as much by the desire to increase circulation as by considerations of security. His postwar confessions of this practice led some to conclude incorrectly that most of his material had been invented. But his credibility was not often questioned during the war, and such respectable papers as the New York *World*, the Saint Louis *Globe-Democrat*, and the Chicago *Record-Herald* syndicated his stories, running them under the lead, "The *Providence Journal* will say this morning . . ."[7]

Rathom was not the only beneficiary of Voska's intelligence, of course. Captain Gaunt passed along choice tidbits to Colonel Edward M. House, President Wilson's close adviser and alter ego. House was much taken with the British naval attaché.

"Captain Guy Gaunt was my most interesting visitor," House wrote in his diary on one occasion.

He tells me the British Intelligence Service is marvellously good. They have reports of everything going on in Berlin, and oftentimes they get copies of letters and documents of great value. He says in one letter von Bernstorff gives his estimate of me and claims that he "has House in his pocket." Gaunt promised to show me a copy of this letter. I doubt whether Bernstorff said this.[8]

Of course, Gaunt could not disclose to House the officially embarrassing fact that the British government, through the Voska organization, was bending the American neutrality laws, and probably breaking them, by spying on the accredited representatives of two sovereign nations in the United States. House, however, and possibly Wilson, were unofficially aware of Voska's activities, at least to some extent. Voska believed the president had been fully briefed on his operation by Charles R. Crane, a prominent American philanthropist and a major contributor to Wilson's 1912 presidential campaign.

Crane was the son of a wealthy Chicago plumbing-supply magnate. He left the running of the family business to his brother while he roamed the world studying mankind and using his fortune in a wide variety of humanitarian projects. He was strongly influenced by Sir Richard Burton, the British explorer and adventurer, whom he met during an early visit to Damascus. Crane was especially interested in Russia and Eastern Europe. He became a friend of Tomáš Masaryk in the early 1900s and was sympathetic to Czech and Slovak aspirations for independence from Austria-Hungary. He was therefore also a natural ally of Emanuel Voska, and the Czech spy master turned to him at the outset of his operations in the United States and asked him to "use his good offices with the President." Just what Voska meant and what Crane understood is unclear. Crane apparently talked to the president, then told Voska Wilson that "if we kept within reasonable limits, the administration would put no obstacles in the way of our agitation for racial independence."[9]

Voska recalled that "Crane told [Wilson] what my organization was doing; and by keeping his hands off of us he gave us tacit approval." But if "agitation for racial independence" was the euphemism Crane and the president used in discussing Voska's organization, it is doubtful that the latter understood it to mean espionage, and it is very unlikely that Wilson, at this stage, would have considered penetration of the German and Austro-Hungarian legations as activity "within reasonable limits." But Crane also steered Voska to the more pragmatic Colonel House. Just what the Czech spy master discussed during his several visits to House in New York early in the war is unknown, but Voska recalled that "he was receptive at the beginning and friendly at the end."[10] It is unlikely, however, that Voska disclosed his arrangement with the British Naval Intelligence Department, and House probably continued to believe that the occasional items of intelligence Captain Gaunt passed along to him had all been collected by British agents in Berlin, not by Czech agents in Washington and New York.

After mid-1915, when Robert Lansing became secretary of state, Voska's regular channel to the Wilson administration was Crane's son, Richard, who was Lansing's private secretary.[11] The younger (thirty-three-year-old) Crane had resigned the presidency of the Crane Valve Company to accept this important but subordinate position, and it is not implausible that he did so at his father's request, in order to provide Voska with such a channel. (It is significant that four years later Richard Crane became the first American ambassador to the newly created republic of Czechoslovakia.)

Secretary Lansing himself was far better disposed than the president toward such things as espionage. He would not have been horrified had he known that one of Voska's agents had been listening through a microphone concealed in a New York hotel room's draperies when Rintelen met with the exiled Mexican leader Huerta to negotiate German support for his return to power.[12] While Lansing probably was not treated to such interesting details, Voska's organization was his source of information about the Rintelen-Huerta conspiracy.

Early in the war Voska did not report German sabotage plans directly to the federal authorities; instead, British intelligence, working through Allied purchasing agents, warned the owners of the targeted ships and plants, who in turn called in the local police, private security agencies, the Secret Service, or the Justice Department's Bureau of Investigation. But at some point he made contact with the director of the Bureau of Investigation and his two immediate subordinates at the insistence of the elder Crane. He filled them in on the general outlines of his organization, except his

British connection, and agreed to tip them off whenever he had evidence of past or planned violations of United States law.

The Bureau of Investigation (which became known as the Federal Bureau of Investigation in 1935) needed all the help it could get in dealing with German sabotage and subversion. Established only a few years earlier, in 1908, by Attorney General Charles J. Bonaparte on orders from President Theodore Roosevelt, the bureau had started with nine special agents transferred from the Secret Service and fourteen Justice Department investigators.[13] The agency grew rapidly to a force of three hundred agents, but its size and, especially, its institutional experience were inadequate in dealing with the sophisticated German covert-action apparatus in the United States. The bureau's thirty-two-year-old director, A. Bruce Bielaski, had seen nothing like it in the nine years since he joined the Department of Justice as a young George Washington University Law School graduate.

Bielaski and the bureau were further hampered by a lack of jurisdiction. The bureau was restricted to investigating violations or suspected violations of certain specific federal laws, but except for the acts of physical sabotage, few of Section IIIb's activities violated any American law. This problem was remedied to some extent on July 1, 1916, when Congress authorized the bureau to conduct investigations for the Department of State.

The Secret Service was also working closely with the State Department by then, having been ordered by President Wilson immediately after the sinking of the *Lusitania* a year earlier to watch the German and Austro-Hungarian legations. In addition to surveillance reports from his agents, Secret Service Chief Flynn received daily transcripts of the wiretaps the agency had installed on the telephones in the two embassies and the New York offices of the German attachés. The transcripts, which often included titillating conversations between Ambassador Bernstorff and one of his many lady friends in Washington, were typed with multiple copies, as were the surveillance reports. One copy of everything went to State. In turn, State passed to Chief Flynn copies of the information British Naval Intelligence occasionally gave to Edward Bell, the second secretary of the American embassy in London: items concerning German subversion in the United States, which usually came from Room 40, the department's code-breaking unit, in which case they were first "sanitized" by the British to conceal their source.[14] State probably also passed on to Flynn some or all of the information Richard Crane received from Voska.

Thus the State Department, not the Department of Justice, assumed the leadership role in dealing with German subversion and sabotage, an arrangement that reflected the Wilson administration's understanding that it was more a problem of foreign relations than one of domestic law enforcement. The hub of this counterespionage constellation of the Secret Service, the Bureau of Investigation, the Voska organization, and British Naval Intelligence was Frank L. Polk, the counselor of the State Department—that is, the second ranking officer in the department and its chief legal officer. Wilson appointed Polk to the post in mid-1915 after promoting Lansing, the incumbent, to secretary of state. Polk came to the job with little knowledge of foreign affairs (a deficiency he quickly remedied) and no experience in counterespionage. But as a former corporation counsel of New York City who fought the Tammany machine, he was no stranger to intrigue.

Secretary Lansing believed that victory by the Central Powers would lead to German domination of Europe and an eventual German threat to the United States in the Western Hemisphere. Therefore, unlike President Wilson, he advocated American entry into the war to ensure an Allied victory. He recognized that neither the president nor the American public was ready to take this step, however, so he resolved to expose German subversion in America in the meantime. Thus, the events of August and September 1915 could hardly have been more welcome to him.

When the British authorities arrested Rintelen aboard the *Noordam* at Falmouth, they discovered his files. British Naval Intelligence turned over copies of the documents to Edward Bell at the American embassy, and they were soon in Lansing's hands. The papers provided proof of that which the administration already knew: Germany had been behind Huerta's attempt to regain power in Mexico.[15]

A few weeks later Bell received another present from British Naval Intelligence: copies of the dispatches James Archibald had been carrying to Germany and Austria-Hungary, which had been seized by the British after Voska tipped off Gaunt. (Voska's agents in the Austro-Hungarian consulate in New York learned of the parcel Archibald was to carry and obtained a list of the documents therein; the Austrian courier who took the parcel aboard the *Rotterdam* and delivered it to Archibald was also a Voska agent.)[16]

The next haul of confidential Central Powers documents came a week or so later, when James W. Gerard, the American ambassador to Germany, "accidentally" opened a parcel of mail from the German embassy in Washington to the Foreign Office in Berlin, which the State Department carried by American diplomatic pouch as a courtesy to Ambassador von Bernstorff. The documents in the packet included vouchers of payments to a host of Americans serving as covert propagandists for Germany, as well as other evidence of German subversion throughout the United States and Latin America. Gerard shipped the package back to Washington, where its contents were photographed before it was resealed, apparently by so accomplished a hand that the German Foreign Ministry did not notice the tampering when the parcel was finally delivered in Berlin some days later.[17]

Even before this spate of discoveries, President Wilson had told Colonel House, "I am sure that the country is honeycombed with German intrigue and infested with German spies. The evidence of these things are multiplying every day."[18]

The expulsion of Papen and Boy-Ed from the United States in December 1915, a direct result of the documents seized by British intelligence, led to yet another haul of evidence of German subversion in the United States. The steamer carrying Papen back to the Continent put in at Falmouth on January 2, and although the attaché was traveling under a safe-conduct issued by the United States government, the British authorities chose not to interpret the guarantee as extending to Papen's luggage. The mass of documents and records seized by the Naval Intelligence Department included his checkbooks and canceled checks that Papen had made out to the small army of propagandists and saboteurs in the United States on the payroll of Section IIIb. One check, drawn on the Riggs National Bank in the sum of two hundred dollars on September 1, 1914, was made out to a Mr. Bridgman Taylor and proved of particular interest to Naval Intelligence.

Taylor was in fact Captain Horst von der Goltz of Section IIIb, who was at that moment occupying a cell in Reading Gaol, the British prison immortalized by Oscar Wilde. The authorities had nothing on Goltz except that he was a German who had entered Britain with a false American passport in the name of Bridgman Taylor and had failed to register as an enemy alien. Papen's check, however, was enough to hang him, a fact Goltz immediately perceived when Captain William R. ("Blinker") Hall, director of Naval Intelligence, personally presented it to him. Goltz saw the light and, in exchange for his life, gave Hall a detailed account of his adventures as a German secret agent. The story must have been fascinating: it covered Goltz's ten years in Section IIIb, during which time he had operated in Russia, Switzerland, France, Mexico, and the United States.[19]

Goltz had worked for Papen for less than two months; he had been sent to New York from Mexico at the outbreak of the war in August 1914 and was summoned to Berlin in October to brief the kaiser on Mexico and the United States. He was on his way back to New York when he was apprehended by the British. During his brief tour in New York, however, he was involved in Papen's abortive plan to blow up the Welland Ship Canal—linking Lakes Ontario and Erie—while Canadian troop transports en route to France were passing through it. When informed of this by British intelligence, the United States government requested his extradition. Goltz arrived in New York on March 29, 1916, and was turned over to the Justice Department.

With the State Department's expulsion of Count Dumba, Boy-Ed, and Papen in the wake of the earlier exposures, the German apparatus in the United States was left in the hands of Papen's assistant, Wolf von Igel. Igel took over Papen's offices at 60 Wall Street, where he received a sudden and unexpected visit by Secret Service agents on April 18, three weeks after Goltz's return to New York. Goltz had been as forthcoming with the Justice Department as he was with British Naval Intelligence, and the information he supplied about the Welland Canal conspiracy provided the government with probable cause to arrest Igel. The raid had been timed fortuitously, probably with the help of wiretaps: Igel had opened the office safe and was preparing to package his files for shipment to the German embassy for safekeeping. Over his vehement protest the Secret Service agents took the seventy pounds of documents into custody along with Igel.[20]

Igel was released after Ambassador von Bernstorff claimed diplomatic immunity for him, but when the State Department offered to return the seized papers if Bernstorff wished to declare them official documents of the German embassy, the ambassador declined.[21] He certainly had no wish to put the stamp of German officialdom on the complete files of the Papen sabotage apparatus, which included such details as the telephone numbers of his agents and exposed the German schemes to foment uprisings in Ireland and India.

The documents seized in the Igel raid, together with the earlier hauls by British intelligence and the contents of Dr. Albert's briefcase, completely exposed and neutralized the German covert-action apparatus that had been run out of New York. This did not bring an end to the sabotage, however. The massive Black Tom explosion was still months away, and the pace of fires and explosions at munitions plants and aboard munitions ships continued at about the usual level through the balance of 1916. And the following January a four-hour fire at the Canadian Car and Foundry Company near Kingsland, New Jersey, set off half a million three-inch explosive shells and produced the most spectacular munitions disaster since Black Tom.[22] The German agents who continued to carry out these sabotage and subversion operations did not report to Section IIIb or to German naval intelligence through Papen, Boy-Ed, or Igel; they either worked for Bopp, the German consul general in San Francisco, or else they reported to Berlin through some other channel—for example, the German legation in Mexico. German intelligence did not put all its American eggs in one basket. Neither did British intelligence.

The quiet, boyish-looking young man with the upper-class British accent and impeccable manners was known while in New York City as William Wisdom, director of W. Wisdom Films, Inc. Those who encountered him at the British embassy in Washington, however, were introduced to Sir William Wiseman, a purchasing official of the Ministry of Munitions. He was indeed Sir William Wiseman, tenth holder of a baronetcy dating from 1628 and a descendant of Sir John Wiseman, who had been knighted by Henry VIII. His only involvement with munitions, however, was to frustrate German efforts to keep them from the Allies through sabotage and subversion in the United States. Sir William was chief of the American station of MII(c), the recently created foreign-intelligence unit of the War Office.[23]

At the outbreak of hostilities in Europe, the War Office Intelligence Department was a poor relation of the longer-established and much more successful Naval Intelligence Department and had no representative in the United States. Late in 1915, however, in the face of the German covert-action campaign (and probably in response to the rival Naval Intelligence Department's successes in dealing with it), MI1(c) decided to send an officer to the United States and began to look about for a candidate. Sir William was ideal for the job.

The thirty-year-old Cambridge-educated baronet had spent five years in investment banking in Canada and Mexico after a two-year stint as a reporter for the London *Daily Express* (the title did not bestow independent means upon its holder). He was commissioned as a captain of artillery in the British army at the outbreak of the war and was gassed at Flanders in 1915. He was recuperating in England when he was recruited by MI1(c). Arriving in New York City early in 1916 he established the intelligence station, a two-thousand-dollar-per-month operation described by the contemporary British consul general in the city as "watching suspicious ships, shipments and persons; and . . . obtaining information asked for by the Foreign Office and . . . Embassy."[24] Just what, if anything, Sir William was able to add to the accomplishments of Captain Gaunt and the Voska organization is unknown, but the British nobleman was destined to make a far different contribution to his country's war effort.

Captain Gaunt, who spent most of his time in New York, where he based his countersubversion work, usually acted as messenger whenever the British ambassador, Sir Cecil Spring-Rice, wished to communicate discreetly with Colonel House, who also lived in New York. Such communications were frequent, for the ambassador found President Wilson to be aloof and unapproachable. In this he had plenty of company; it would not be putting it too strongly to say that the only living person with any influence on the president's thinking was Colonel House.

Edward Mandell House was born in 1858, the son of a Texas millionaire. He became a power in Texas politics, successfully managing the campaigns of Texas governors in 1894, 1898, and 1902 (thereby acquiring his honorary colonelcy). He preferred being the power behind the throne to occupying the throne himself—"the public is almost childish in its acceptance of the shadow for the substance," he once remarked.[25] A liberal Democrat, he hoped to find someone to carry his personal agenda to the White House. In 1911 he found his paladin in Woodrow Wilson, then governor of New Jersey. He introduced himself and met with Wilson several times during the winter of 1911–12.

"We found ourselves in such complete sympathy, in so many ways," he recalled, "that we soon learned to know what each was thinking without either having expressed himself."[26]

House mobilized the Texas delegation to the Democratic National Convention in support of Wilson and won over William Jennings Bryan, thrice the Democratic presidential nominee and a power in the party, to Wilson's cause. With the help of Theodore Roosevelt's split with Taft and the Republican party in 1912, Wilson won in a landslide.

With Wilson in the White House, House settled into the role of Silent Partner, as the press soon characterized him. He did not move to Washington, but he was a frequent guest at the White House, while the president almost invariably stayed with House while in New York. Wilson devised a code for them to use so they could converse freely on the telephone.

House's admiration for the president did not blind him to his shortcomings. Wilson put off dealing with difficult problems; his prejudices were "many and often unjust"; he had difficulty in conferring with people he disliked, of which there were many; and he had "a one-track mind," unable to "carry along more than one idea at a time." One fault proved useful, however: Wilson was fond of flattery. House saw this, and in his letters to Wilson, he often laid it on so thick as to risk inspiring doubts about his sincerity. No such suspicion crossed the president's mind, however, for he knew his friend was only speaking the truth. Indeed, such frequent proofs of House's perspicacity only increased Wilson's predilection to accept his Silent Partner's counsel and guidance. Years later House admitted that to get Wilson to adopt a particular course of action, all that was necessary was to suggest that it would help ensure for him an even more glorious place in history.[27]

The Washington diplomatic corps was not slow to recognize House's unofficial but very real importance in the Wilson administration. Bernstorff often slipped away from Washington and took the night train to New York, where he could confer with House without being noticed by the press.[28] Dumba and Jean-Jules Jusserand, the French ambassador, were also soon familiar visitors to the Colonel's New York apartment. And, of course, Captain Gaunt was a frequent caller on behalf of Ambassador Spring-Rice.

On December 17, 1916, Sir Cecil wished to make a confidential suggestion to House regarding the terms of a German peace feeler. Captain Gaunt was on leave, so he asked Wiseman to convey his message. It took only a few minutes for Sir William to pass along the communication, but House, who had not met the young baronet before, asked him to stay for a talk. House was favorably impressed by the young man and thought him "the most important caller I have had for some time," and at his request Sir William came back for three more conversations during the following month.[29] On January 26 House reported to the president:

> Wiseman came this afternoon. . . . He told me in the *gravest confidence*, a thing which I had already suspected and that is that he is in direct communication with the Foreign Office, and that the Ambassador and other members of the Embassy are not aware of it.
>
> I am happy beyond measure over this last conference with him, for I judge he reflects the views of his government.[30]

To House it was most welcome news, since there had been a change of government in Britain a few weeks earlier, and Sir Edward Grey, the former foreign secretary with whom House had established a close working relationship that short-circuited the two countries' formal diplomatic representatives in Washington and London, was not to be in the new British cabinet. Wilson was equally pleased by the development. He had long felt little confidence in either Spring-Rice or his own ambassador in London, Walter Hines Page.

Captain Gaunt returned from leave on January 30 and greeted Sir William's progress with something less than unalloyed enthusiasm. Undertaking a little intramural sabotage, he told House that London was complaining about Sir William's activities. When House brought up the matter, the baronet replied that Gaunt's knowledge of London matters was limited to what the Naval Intelligence Department told him. He then secured his new relationship with House by disclosing it to Spring-Rice, who swallowed whatever resentment he may have felt in recognition of its value to Britain and granted his approval.[31]

Thus did the Wilson White House suddenly find itself with a back channel to Whitehall that would circumvent the clumsy and inefficient machinery of conventional diplomatic representation. And thus did MI1(c), the British Secret Intelligence Service, suddenly acquire a potent agent of influence at the very heart of the Wilson administration.

Sir William's top-priority task was, of course, the same as that of every other member of the British legation: to bring America into the war on the side of the Allies. But his influence with House and, by extension, Wilson soon proved superfluous in this regard. To Ambassador von Bernstorff's dismay, Berlin seemed set on accomplishing this unaided. Over his protests the German government had decided to resume submarine attacks on neutral shipping. Ambassador Gerard had already read the signs in Berlin and reported them to Washington; the only question was when the sinkings would commence. On January 31 Bernstorff delivered a note to Secretary Lansing announcing the date: February 1. That same day Wiseman informed House that there was furious activity in the German and Austro-Hungarian consulates in New York. The Central Powers diplomats knew what was to follow and were making hurried preparations for their departure from the United States. They were not mistaken. The United States severed diplomatic relations with Germany on February 3.

Britain's most powerful instrumentality for bringing America into the war at this point was not the MI1(c) chief of station in New York, however, but a piece of paper reposing in the safe of Admiral Sir Reginald ("Blinker") Hall, the director of Naval Intelligence. It was the plaintext of a cipher telegram sent by German Foreign Minister Arthur Zimmermann to his ambassador to Mexico, Heinrich von Eckardt, on January 16:

> We intend to begin unrestricted submarine warfare on the
> first of February. We shall endeavor in spite of this to keep
> the United States neutral. In the event of this not succeeding,

Lacking any training in even the basics of intelligence tradecraft, volunteer spy Nathan Hale was quickly discovered by the British and hanged outside the Dove Tavern, which stood near today's intersection of Third Avenue and Sixty-sixth Street in Manhattan. (*Library of Congress*)

General George Washington often handled his agents personally, instructing them in such tradecraft details as the use of invisible inks and the establishment of cover. (*Author's collection*)

Before undertaking his ill-fated mission, Nathan Hale told a brother officer that he considered espionage in the service of one's country an honorable activity. He is memorialized by the statue outside CIA headquarters at Langley, Virginia. (*Central Intelligence Agency*)

General Benedict Arnold distinguished himself repeatedly as a hero of the Revolutionary War before, disgruntled, he became the highest ranking defector in place of the Continental Army. Unmasked through the discovery and capture of Major John André, he fled to British-occupied Manhattan. (*Library of Congress*)

As British General Henry Clinton's chief of intelligence, Major John André was deeply involved in negotiations with the American traitor Benedict Arnold for the surrender of West Point. Captured behind American lines in civilian clothes, André made this pen-and-ink self-portrait shortly before his execution. (*Yale University Art Gallery*)

Cipher letter of July 15, 1780, from Benedict Arnold to Sir Henry Clinton, offering to surrender West Point to the British for 20,000 pounds. (*William L. Clements Library*)

Arnold's letter of July 15, 1780, as deciphered by Jonathan Odell. (*William L. Clements Library*)

Major Benjamin Tallmadge organized and ran the Culper Spy Ring in New York for General Washington. He played a crucial role in apprehending Major John André and thereby uncovering Benedict Arnold's treason. (*Library of Congress*)

Sent to Paris by the Committee of Secret Correspondence, Silas Deane helped arrange the secret trade of American foodstuffs for French arms before serving as a diplomatic representative at Versailles. Later alienated from the American cause, he cooperated with British intelligence in a propaganda scheme, thereafter living in exile in Europe. (*Library of Congress*)

A master of intrigue, Benjamin Franklin conducted the secret diplomacy of the American Revolution while serving as minister plenipotentiary to the French court. Some historians suspect he also ran a high-level agent network in England. (*Library of Congress*)

A businessman, inventor, and playwright, Pierre Augustin Caron de Beaumarchais was also a French secret agent who, together with Silas Deane, arranged the secret supply of arms to the Continental Army. (*Library of Congress*)

As General George B. McClellan's chief intelligence officer, detective Allan Pinkerton (right) proved more effective at catching Rebel spies than in estimating the strength of the Confederate forces facing his chief. (*Library of Congress*)

Former San Francisco vigilante Lafayette C. Baker was provost marshal of the War Department, in which position he hunted spies and other miscreants in and around Washington. After the war he cultivated the myth that he had been chief of the U.S. Secret Service, an agency that did not exist at that time. (*Library of Congess*)

Pinkerton's successor as intelligence chief of the Army of the Potomac was George H. Sharpe (left), who organized the Bureau of Military Information, a modern, professional, and highly effective intelligence service. Sharpe's deputies were John C. Babcock, seated to his immediate left, and John McEntee at the far right. The identity of the fourth man in this photograph is unknown. (*Library of Congress*)

An architect in civilian life, Babcock proved to be a talented intelligence officer whose estimates of Confederate troop strength were far more accurate than Pinkerton's. (*Library of Congress*)

Probably the most valuable federal agent of the Civil War, Elizabeth Van Lew led an espionage network in Richmond, Virginia, the capital of the Confederacy. Of middle age during the Civil War, Van Lew is shown here in later life. (*The Valentine Museum*)

Although the Confederates employed such devices as this cipher disk to secure their communications, Federal codebreakers had little difficulty in penetrating their systems. (*The Museum of the Confederacy*)

Despite the complaints of U.S. Army commanders, Northern newspapers printed reports of battles, battlefield maps, and lists of the killed, wounded, and missing; they also sometimes published military plans, troop movements, and troop strengths, as well as other information useful to Confederate intelligence. The 1863 field headquarters of the *New York Herald* is shown here. (*Library of Congress*)

The Civil War saw the first use of manned balloons for military reconnaissance. Here the Army of the Potomac's balloon *Intrepid* is prepared to reconnoiter the area of Fair Oaks, Virginia, during the Peninsula campaign in 1862. The two crates in the center are gas generators. (*Library of Congress*)

Thaddeus S. C. Lowe began experimenting with balloons several years before the outbreak of the Civil War. After demonstrating the capabilities of the craft to President Lincoln, he was hired as "chief aeronaut" of the Army of the Potomac and put in charge of its balloon corps. (*Library of Congress*)

Scion of a distinguished Georgia family and the uncle of Theodore Roosevelt, James D. Bulloch had been an officer in the U.S. Navy and a merchant marine captain before the Civil War. As head of the Confederate naval secret service in Europe, he procured warships for the South, including the raiders *Florida* and *Alabama*. (*Author's collection*)

The State Department sent New York newspaper publisher John Bigelow to Paris to disseminate anti-Confederate propaganda. He also played a crucial role in thwarting James Bulloch's efforts to obtain French-built warships for the Confederacy. (*National Archives*)

Veteran American diplomat Henry S. Sanford ran the Federal secret service in Europe, countering Confederate propaganda and opposing James Bulloch's arms procurement operations. (*Library of Congress*)

During seapower theorist Alfred T. Mahan's term as its president in the late 1880s, the Naval War College introduced war-gaming into its curriculum, a step that ultimately transformed the Office of Naval Intelligence into a true intelligence agency. (*Library of Congress*)

The explosion and sinking of the battleship U.S.S. *Maine* in Havana Harbor in February 1898 set in motion events that led to the Spanish-American War, thrusting the United States into the role of world power. (*Author's collection*)

During the Spanish-American War, an American agent in the Spanish cable center in Havana kept the White House operations room (shown here) updated on events in and around Cuba, sometimes within minutes of when they occurred. (*Library of Congress*)

Communications intelligence disclosed that the Spanish fleet was trapped in the harbor of Santiago de Cuba, information that led to the American amphibious landings at nearby Siboney and Daiquiri, and the Battle of San Juan. Here troops of the Sixteenth Infantry crouch under Spanish fire from San Juan Hill. (*Library of Congress*)

Lieutenant Colonel Theodore Roosevelt and the Rough Riders atop a hill overlooking Santiago de Cuba. (*Library of Congress*)

The Battle of San Juan began with a barrage from American artillery. (*Library of Congress*)

Lacking accurate and detailed maps of the Santiago de Cuba area, U.S. Army officers relied on aerial reconnaissance to plan and monitor the battle. (*National Archives*)

The belief of Captain Charles D. Sigsbee, commander of the *Maine,* that his ship had been destroyed through foreign treachery colored his views of world events when he became director of the Office of Naval Intelligence two years later. (*Library of Congress*)

Prior to serving as executive officer aboard the *Maine* on its final voyage, Lieutenant Commander Richard Wainwright had been director of naval intelligence and had been instrumental in developing the plans that led to a swift American victory in the war with Spain. (*Author's collection*)

Navy Lieutenant Victor Blue made several trips behind Spanish lines at Santiago de Cuba, one of which confirmed that the entire Spanish fleet was bottled up in the harbor. (*Author's collection*)

Under the direction of former Chicago newspaperman John E. Wilkie, the U.S. Secret Service carried out its first foreign counterintelligence role by catching Spanish agents during the war with Spain. (*Author's collection*)

Major Arthur L. Wagner (shown here), chief of the U.S. Army's Military Information Division, sent Lieutenant Andrew S. Rowan to Cuba with the celebrated "message to Garcia." (*National Archives*)

Intelligence coordination and analysis were miscellaneous duties of the State
Department's chief clerk, whose office as it was in the 1880s is shown here. On
the eve of World War I, the State's intelligence-retrieval system remained what it
had always been: the memory of the oldest employee of the department. (*National
Archives*)

The sabotage and subversion campaign of the Central Powers in the United States
during 1914–17 were run from the German Embassy in Washington. (*Author's
collection*)

The official ultimately responsible for the Central Powers' campaign was Count Johann von Bernstorff, the German ambassador to Washington. (*Author's collection*)

Captain Franz von Papen, the German military attaché, was responsible for the execution of the campaign. Papen would later be Adolf Hitler's vice-chancellor, and during World War II would run the high-level penetration of the British embassy in Turkey known as "Cicero." (*Author's collection*)

Dr. Konstantin Dumba, the ambassador of Austria-Hungary in Washington, ran a network of agents fomenting labor unrest in American munitions plants during 1914–17. (*Author's collection*)

Captain Karl Boy-Ed, the German naval attaché in Washington, helped Papen run the campaign of sabotage and subversion. (*Author's collection*)

The May 7, 1915, sinking of the British liner *Lusitania* by a German submarine and the loss of 128 American lives created a wave of anti-German and pro-war sentiment in the United States. (*Author's collection*)

British codebreakers intercepted and solved the Zimmerman telegram, a German proposal for a Mexican alliance against the United States in which Mexico would recover the territories she lost to the U.S. in the Mexican war. Public disclosure of the telegram in the United States inspired indignation, as reflected in this *New York Evening World* cartoon, and strengthened popular support for the Wilson administration's decision, several weeks later, to enter the war. (*Author's collection*)

The July 30, 1916, explosion of more than two million pounds of munitions at the Black Tom Island railroad terminal in New York Harbor was one of the most spectacular incidents of sabotage by the Central Powers in the United States. (*National Archives*)

Brigadier General Marlborough Churchill became chief of the Army's Military Intelligence Division shortly before the end of the war. He led a contingent of twenty intelligence officers to the Paris Peace Conference and, together with Herbert O. Yardley, was instrumental in establishing the "American Black Chamber," the joint State and War departments' code-breaking unit. (*National Archives*)

While American naval attaché in Paris during the Spanish-American War, Lieutenant William S. Sims ran an agent network in Europe. During World War I Rear Admiral Sims commanded all U.S. naval forces in Europe and established an intelligence department in his London headquarters. (*Sims, The Victory at Sea*)

Veteran special agent William J. Flynn headed the U.S. Secret Service during most of World War I, while the agency was countering the Central Powers' campaign of sabotage and subversion. He later directed the Justice Department's Bureau of Investigation. (*Library of Congress*)

Self-taught cryptanalyst Herbert O. Yardley was chief of MI-8, the code-breaking unit of the Army's Military Intelligence Division in World War I. Later he headed the joint State-War Departments' Cipher Bureau, the "American Black Chamber." His tell-all book of that title was a sensational best-seller in 1931 and set back the U.S. Navy's attempts to break Japanese codes and ciphers in the 1930s. (*National Archives*)

The M-94 cipher device, adopted by the U.S. Army in 1923, was based on an invention of Thomas Jefferson's. The Army used the device until early in World War II. (*George Marshall Foundation*)

we make Mexico a proposal of alliance on the following basis: make war together, make peace together, generous financial support, and an understanding on our part that Mexico is to reconquer the lost territory in Texas, New Mexico, and Arizona. The settlement in detail is left to you.

You will inform the President [of Mexico] of the above most secretly as soon as the outbreak of war with the United States is certain. . . .

Please call the President's attention to the fact that the unrestricted employment of our submarines now offers the prospect of compelling England to make peace within a few months. Acknowledge receipt.

Zimmermann.[32]

Zimmermann had sent the message by several different routes, including via the Washington embassy, where Ambassador von Bernstorff was instructed to relay it to Eckardt in Mexico City. In a marvelous piece of chutzpah, the German minister dispatched the telegram to Bernstorff over American diplomatic cables between the United States embassy in Berlin and the State Department in Washington. At House's insistence Wilson had instructed the State Department a few weeks earlier to transmit ciphered German cables between the Foreign Ministry and Bernstorff to facilitate discussions of the recent German peace feeler. Room 40, British Naval Intelligence's code-breaking unit, was routinely reading American diplomatic traffic, and the British were "highly entertained" as they proceeded far enough in the painstaking task of deciphering the telegram to begin to understand the audacious German abuse of this American courtesy. But Captain Hall was more perplexed than amused when, by February 5, enough of the telegram had been deciphered for him to see both the tremendous value of what he had in hand and the dilemma he faced in trying to use it.

The Foreign Office quite naturally wished to turn over the telegram to the Wilson administration for its value in hastening American entry into the war. The problem was how to do this without the German Foreign Ministry realizing, after Washington had released the document to the press, that its high-level diplomatic cipher had been broken. His solution was nearly as ingenious as his code breakers' feat of deciphering the telegram.

Hall knew from his code breakers' experience that communications between the German embassies in Washington and Mexico City used a simpler, lower-level cipher than that employed to protect transatlantic diplomatic traffic. If he could convince Berlin that his agency had intercepted the copy of the Zimmermann telegram Bernstorff, as ordered, had relayed to Eckardt over the Western Union's wires, the German Foreign Ministry would not be alerted and would not change its high-level cipher. To this end, he had a British agent in Mexico City obtain a copy of the telegram as it had been received there. Small differences between it and the message as actually intercepted in Europe—for example, the new serial number Bernstorff had put on it when he sent it from Washington and the January 19 dateline, reflecting the three days that had elapsed between the transmittal from Berlin to Washington and the transmittal from Washington to Mexico—all supported the conclusion that the British must have intercepted it somewhere in North America and not in Europe.[33]

The sanitizing of the Zimmermann telegram complete, Hall, with the approval of the Foreign Office, showed it to Edward Bell, the American embassy's intelligence liaison officer, on February 22. After a day of conferences with Hall, Bell, and Irwin Laughlin, the first secretary of the embassy, Ambassador Page transmitted the message to Washington in the early hours of the twenty-fourth. Counselor Polk showed it to a thunderstruck and indignant Wilson that evening. A day or so later Polk telephoned House and told him of the development. House wrote to the president, telling him, "I hope you will publish the despatch to-morrow."[34]

On Wilson's instructions Secretary Lansing gave the story to E. M. Hood of the Associated Press at Lansing's home the following evening, without disclosing that the telegram had been intercepted and deciphered by the British. When it appeared in the morning papers March 1, the AP account stated only the substance of the telegram and the fact that it was in Wilson's possession. The popular inference in the United States was that British intelligence had been the source, but the British press, skillfully inspired by Captain Hall, cited the interception as an example of the superiority of the American Secret Service over their own. American pacifists in Congress believed the thing had come from the British and, furthermore, that it was a forgery. The authenticity debate raged for two days but ended on March 3, when to the amazement of all concerned, Zimmermann himself called a press conference and confirmed that he had sent the telegram.

The prospect of Mexican troops armed with German guns marching across the border to reconquer the Southwest did much to end isolationist opposition to American entry into the war. This national mood still prevailed on March 17, when the news arrived that German submarines had sunk three unarmed American ships in the Atlantic: the *Vigilancia*, the *City of Memphis*, and the *Illinois*. On the twenty-first German torpedoes sank the *Healdton*, with the loss of twenty-one American lives.

President Wilson dwelt at length upon the sinkings when he asked Congress for a declaration of war on April 2, but he raised the matter of German covert action near the end of his message, seemingly as a clincher:

> One of the things that has served to convince us that the Prussian autocracy was not and could never be our friend is that from the very outset of the present war it has filled our unsuspecting communities and even our offices of government with spies and set criminal intrigues everywhere afoot against our national unity of counsel, our peace within and without, our industries and our commerce. Indeed it is now evident that its spies were here even before the war began. . . . But they have played their part in serving to convince us at last that the Government entertains no real friendship for us and means to act against our peace and security at its convenience. That it means to stir up enemies against us at our very doors the intercepted note to the German Minister at Mexico City is eloquent evidence.

The United States was at last in the war. Now Captain Gaunt, Sir William Wiseman, and the other British intelligence operators in the United States had a new job: making sure America had the intelligence service she was going to need.

Chapter Twenty-one

Intelligence Redux

Sir William Wiseman did not wait for the American declaration of war to lay the groundwork for a wartime liaison between British intelligence and whatever its American counterparts were to be. He, of course, had long known that Frank L. Polk, the State Department's counselor, was the focal point of intelligence matters, such as they were, in the Wilson administration, and in mid-February he disclosed to Polk his role as MI1(c)'s man in the United States. He soon was passing along to Polk such information as possible German submarine positions and British measures to protect shipping from them.[1] But he continued also to operate at the highest level: several days before Wilson delivered his war message to Congress, House gave Sir William the text so that the Foreign Office could orchestrate in advance a suitably enthusiastic reception in the British press. By now the British intelligence operator had discovered the way to the president's heart, and Wilson was pleased to learn from House that the English baronet had asserted that Shakespeare himself could not have improved on the message's prose.[2]

With the United States now actually preparing to commit troops to the conflict in Europe, Sir William gave some attention to the matter of the United States Army's military intelligence capability. At this moment that capability consisted of one person, Major Ralph H. Van Deman, the only professional intelligence officer in an army that did not know there was such a thing.

Ralph Van Deman had studied law for a while after graduating from Harvard in 1888 but then went on to earn a medical degree from Miami

Medical School in Cincinnati. Immediately after graduation in 1893, he went on duty as a surgeon with the United States Army. He stayed in the army, but he soon put aside medicine for the profession of intelligence. He served in the Military Information Division during the Spanish-American War and in the Philippines during the insurrection against American rule after Spain ceded the islands to the United States. He was assigned to the Bureau of Insurgent Records of the Army's Philippines Department and helped transform it into the department's own Military Information Division, a true tactical intelligence and counterintelligence unit.[3]

In 1906, after graduating from the newly created Army War College, he was sent to China on a covert reconnaissance mission. Six years earlier the army had taken part in the international expedition to rescue the foreign nationals in Peking who were threatened by the Boxer insurgents, an undertaking that had suffered from a lack of basic intelligence on the routes between Peking and the sea. Van Deman and another officer went to China to fill this gap in case another rescue operation should ever be necessary.[4]

Van Deman returned to Washington in March 1907 and took over the Map Section of the MID, which by then was part of the recently created War Department General Staff. During the Japanese war scare of 1907–8, he produced weekly intelligence reports on Japanese activities for President Roosevelt, an experience that convinced him of the importance of intelligence to national policy making and made him a lifelong advocate of a centralized intelligence service in the War Department. In 1908, however, the MID was swallowed up by the General Staff's War College Division. Van Deman served in the merged unit until 1910, then spent the next two years back in Manila with the Philippines Department's MID.[5]

In 1915 Van Deman, by then probably the most experienced intelligence officer in the army, was again assigned to the War College Division in Washington. Intelligence activity in the division had all but ceased, a situation that distressed Brigadier General H. H. Macomb, chief of the division, but one that he had been unable to correct. Macomb's proposal to re-establish a military information unit within the division had been rejected by the chief of staff, Major General Hugh L. Scott, a member of the West Point class of 1876 who had spent most of his career fighting Indians on the western plains and had little understanding of military intelligence.[6]

In Van Deman, Macomb found just the determined and energetic ally he needed to help him overcome Scott's opposition and restore the intelligence function to the General Staff. The following March, Van Deman completed a staff study tracing the history of intelligence in the War Department, outlining the sort of military intelligence organization the army was going to need in the future, and warning of the dire consequences of not having such a unit. Macomb forwarded the paper to Scott with his strong endorsement, but the chief of staff simply filed it and forgot it.

Van Deman had not had the benefit of a West Point education and was therefore less impressed with the importance of doing things by the book or in accordance with the wishes of the army's chief of staff. Just exactly what he did do on his own in the way of intelligence work after Scott pocket vetoed his staff paper is unclear, since it was done without creating a trail of official memorandums. His intelligence activities between March 1916 and the American entry into the war might have remained completely unknown but for a passing reference made by Macomb's successor, Brigadier General Joseph E. Kuhn, in a memorandum to the chief of staff in April 1917. Kuhn revealed that Van Deman had been directing "secret intelligence work" for the past year in close cooperation with the State Department, the Department of Justice, and the Treasury Department and that despite a shortage of funds and personnel, "a vast amount of information has been collected and collated which will be of vital importance to whatever agency shall be charged with the duty of carrying on the work of military secret service."[7]

It is likely that Van Deman established an informal working arrangement with State Department counselor Polk, the focal point of United States government counterespionage activities, and arranged to receive copies of reports bearing directly on military security—for example, those describing suspected German agents in the army. He may also have made informal contacts for the same purpose with adjutants general and provost marshals throughout the army, officers he had come to know personally during his twenty-five years in the service. And it is quite possible that he was put in direct contact with Voska at this early date, for, as we will see, he took the Czech spy master and much of his organization into army intelligence after America entered the war. Whatever his method, Van Deman began to amass counterespionage and countersubversion files in the War

College Division more than a year before President Wilson delivered his war message to Congress.

With American entry into the war, Kuhn and Van Deman expected Scott to relent and permit the official establishment of an intelligence section within the War College Division. Such was not the case, however. When Kuhn submitted his proposal to Scott on April 11, a week after Congress declared war, the chief of staff flatly rejected it. Scott's position was that an American military intelligence unit would be superfluous, since he expected the Allies' intelligence agencies would furnish whatever intelligence the United States Army might need. When Van Deman came back two or three times to try to change his mind, the chief of staff told the major in the most emphatic way to drop the subject. But inexplicably Scott sent Kuhn a memorandum a few days later instructing him to form a military information section within his division.[8] Sometime between Scott's rejection and his change of mind, Van Deman had met Lieutenant Colonel Claude Dansey of MO5, the British Security Service.

The forty-one-year-old Dansey's background included a tour with the Field Intelligence Department of the British army during the Boer War and a 1911 mission to the United States for the Security Service to investigate Thomas Fortune Ryan, an American multimillionaire erroneously believed by the British to have ties to the Irish-American nationalists. Dansey, by now one of the most senior members of British intelligence, was in the United States as part of a British military liaison team arranged by Sir William Wiseman. When he saw for himself the paucity of the American military intelligence capability, and when Van Deman explained the reason for it, he asked Sir William to speak to Colonel House, who in turn made sure that General Scott saw the light.[9]

Van Deman was appointed to head the new unit, which was called the Military Intelligence Section. Although a highly experienced intelligence officer himself, he was glad to accept Dansey's tutelage. The British intelligence officer quickly composed a handbook on intelligence organization and methods, presenting it to Van Deman in the form of a memorandum covering everything from secret-intelligence-collection operations to techniques of disinformation.[10]

The MIS began modestly: Van Deman was given two officers and two clerks. But it soon was growing at an explosive rate: there were more than a hundred officers in the unit by the end of the year, and almost three times as many by November 1918. The number of civilian employees of the MIS grew at an even faster rate, reaching 1,159 persons by the end of the war.[11]

Dansey's influence was reflected in the internal organization of the MIS, which followed the British taxonomy of positive intelligence—information about the enemy—and negative intelligence—counterespionage and other activities aimed at denying the enemy information about oneself. Thus the Positive Branch of the MIS consisted of MI-2 (Foreign Intelligence), MI-5 (Military Attachés), MI-6 (Translation), and so forth, while the Negative Branch was composed of MI-3 (Counterespionage in the Military Service), MI-4 (Counterespionage Among Civilian Population), MI-10 (Censorship), and so on. The *MI* prefix was, of course, borrowed directly from the British.[12]

MI-8, part of the Positive Branch, was designated Cable and Telegraph, which was a cover designation for the communication-intercept and code-breaking section; insiders knew the unit as the Cipher Bureau. Crypt-analysis, the breaking of enemy codes and ciphers, had never been part of the repertoire of the Military Intelligence Section or its predecessors. Such knowledge of cryptanalysis as the army possessed upon entry into the world war reposed in the heads of a half-dozen officers of the Signal Corps, but since the primary cryptologic responsibility of the corps was in devising (the technical term is *compiling*) ciphers and codes to be used in securing the army's own communications, none of the six spent anything like full time in code breaking.[13] Van Deman tried to obtain their services for the MIS, but the Signal Corps needed them elsewhere.[14] He was therefore initially reduced to relying upon the volunteer services of a curious civilian establishment, the Riverbank Laboratories.

Located in Geneva, Illinois, a suburb of Chicago, Riverbank was the creation of George Fabyan, a slightly eccentric midwestern textile heir who established the institute to study a variety of things that either seemed potentially useful or simply piqued his curiosity. The laboratory's projects included such dubious undertakings as an anti-gravity device and a perpetual-motion machine but also did solid work in botany and genetics. Riverside had established a rather sizable Cipher Department because Fabyan had become a disciple and patron of Mrs. Elizabeth Wells Gallup, a former Michigan English teacher and high-school principal who believed there were ciphers hidden in the original texts of Shakespeare's plays, which when deciphered, would prove they had actually been written by Sir Francis Bacon.[15]

On March 17, 1917, Fabyan wrote to the War Department offering the services of his Cipher Department. About a month later Captain Joseph O. Mauborgne, one of the six Signal Corps officers with code-breaking knowledge, visited Riverbank. Upon his return to Washington, he recommended that the MIS take Fabyan up on his offer.[16] Van Deman did so, and the MIS began sending whatever intercepted cipher messages it acquired to Riverbank for solution.

The Shakespearean cipher project had consisted of trying to find a simple substitution cipher, devised by Bacon in the seventeenth century, supposedly hidden in the texts through the use of varied printing fonts; thus the staff of the Riverbank Cipher Department had acquired little experience applicable to the solution of the sophisticated military and diplomatic ciphers and codes used by the Central Powers. Fabyan's contribution to the MIS, therefore, was not a ready-made code-breaking outfit but a group of people who had displayed some talent at cryptanalysis and might eventually learn enough of the black art to be useful to the government. Among them was William F. Friedman, a young agricultural geneticist fresh out of Cornell University whom Fabyan had hired two years earlier to try to develop a strain of wheat that would grow in arid climates. Friedman had shown a talent for cryptography, however, so he also worked on the Shakespeare project. He was eventually to become America's greatest cryptologist, but at this point he was, like all the other Riverbank code breakers, no more than a talented amateur.

Dr. J. A. Powell, formerly director of the University of Chicago Press, was another of the Riverbank code breakers. Fabyan sent him to the Army Service Schools at Fort Leavenworth to take the cryptanalysis course then being given by Captain Mauborgne of the Signal Corps. Powell mastered Mauborgne's syllabus and returned to Riverbank to establish a cryptology school there for the War Department. But Riverbank was far from becoming the American equivalent of the British Naval intelligence Department's Room 40. Van Deman would have been forced to look elsewhere for a code-breaking genius to run MI-8 had not the ideal candidate stepped forward and volunteered at this moment.

Herbert Osborn Yardley, twenty-seven, had graduated from high school in Worthington, Indiana, before becoming a railroad telegrapher. In 1912 he joined the State Department as a telegrapher and code clerk. Although he had no formal training in mathematics, he had a great natural talent for cryptanalysis, and he passed the long night watches in the State Department's code room by breaking American diplomatic codes for his own amusement. When he called his nocturnal achievements to the attention of his superiors, they were sufficiently unsettled to change the department's codes—he also broke the new ones with little difficulty—but none seems to have been tempted by the thought that the young clerk's talents might be better employed in the national interest by solving the ciphered dispatches between foreign governments and their embassies in Washington.[17]

Soon after American entry into the war, Yardley presented himself to Van Deman and convinced the MIS chief of his cryptologic abilities. Van Deman arranged to have Yardley released from the State Department, commissioned as a first lieutenant in the United States Army, and assigned to the MIS, where he was put in charge of MI-8. Yardley was commissioned on June 10, 1917, and given two civilian assistants to form the nucleus of the section. He was faced immediately with the same problem Van Deman had confronted: where to find qualified code breakers or, at least, people possessed of the basic skills needed by cryptanalyst trainees. He found "a few scholars who seemed to have a superficial knowledge of ciphers" and ordered them commissioned.[18]

MI-8 eventually grew to a staff of 151 officers, civilian cryptographers, typists, and stenographers. In addition to its code-breaking staff, the unit had laboratories in New York and Washington, where intercepted mail was chemically tested for invisible-ink messages; a shorthand section, which could read fifty-four different American and foreign shorthand systems; a cryptographic subsection, which devised cryptosystems to protect the security of communications between the MIS and American military attachés overseas; and a communications subsection, which maintained secure cable and telegraphic communications with about forty military attachés and intelligence officers in foreign countries and with MID agents throughout the United States.[19]

The creation of MI-8 was a milestone in the history of American intelligence. It was the first formally established agency in American history for the collection of foreign communications intelligence, a late entry in a business the European "black chambers" had been engaged in for centuries. As we will see, it was destined to take on an independent postwar existence as the American Black Chamber and sharply define the line separating the two opposing American attitudes toward intelligence and espionage.

The war in Europe was at a stalemate when the United States entered it in April 1917. After rejecting Allied proposals that American troops be integrated into the British and French armies, Wilson selected Major General Pershing to command an American Expeditionary Force in Europe. Pershing arrived in France in June and began making preparations to assemble the AEF there. Most of the American troops sent to France in 1917 were new draftees; Pershing's general headquarters was given the monumental task of training, organizing, and equipping them. Pershing saw that he was going to need an able general staff to deal with the welter of planning and logistic problems. After studying the structures of the British and French general staffs, he organized that of the AEF into five sections, which he designated G-1 (Organization and Equipment) through G-5 (Education and Training). The Military Intelligence section was designated G-2, an appellation that was to become synonymous with military intelligence for half a century.

As chief of the G-2 section, Pershing selected Major Dennis Nolan, a member of the West Point class of 1896 who had served in the Spanish-American War, the Philippines, and on the War Department's General Staff. Nolan, a close personal friend of Van Deman, had an excellent grasp of military intelligence and proceeded to establish an effective unit to meet the intelligence needs of the AEF. Ideally, Nolan's G-2 would have concentrated on tactical intelligence and received strategic or basic intelligence bearing on the AEF's theater of operations from the MIS in Washington. The MIS, however, having just recently sprung into being, was not at all prepared to fulfill that function. Consequently, Nolan took the view that his G-2 should be concerned with watching the enemy not only on the western front, where the AEF was to fight, but on the eastern, Italian, and Macedonian fronts as well, on the theory that developments in these theaters directly affected the situation in France and Belgium.[20]

While the G-2 did not fully assume the ambitious role Nolan envisioned for it, he enlarged its scope well beyond battlefield intelligence on the western front. G-2 had a Secret Service Subsection headed initially by Lieutenant Colonel W. O. Reed, who had run Pershing's intelligence service in the punitive expedition in Mexico, and later by Colonel A. B. Coxe, the officer who had accompanied Van Deman on his secret mapping mission to China in 1906. G-2's Secret Service unit had a counterespionage staff run by Major Aristides Moreno. Moreno established several intelligence stations in neutral European countries for the purpose of collecting political and military information.[21]

Much of what G-2 could not obtain from the MIS in Washington it received from the Allied intelligence services in Europe. It exchanged liaison officers with the Second Bureau of the French War Ministry—that is, French Military Intelligence—and with British Military Intelligence. Major Stewart Menzies, the chief of British counterespionage and security in France, was on especially good terms with Nolan, whom he regarded as "precisely the man for the job, clear-headed, and very penetrating in his criticisms and questions."[22]

Coordination between G-2 and Van Deman's MIS was not as satisfactory. The problem may have had its roots in Pershing's feeling that the War Department's General Staff was ill prepared to meddle in AEF matters and that when it did, it was more hindrance than help.[23] Van Deman found that G-2 had interposed itself between the MIS and the French War Ministry, stemming the flow of valuable information the French had been providing Washington before the AEF arrived in Europe. An official protest to G-2 from the War Department failed to correct the situation, and when Van Deman proposed to send an MIS liaison officer to France to work with the Second Bureau, Nolan protested and claimed the G-2 should be the sole American contact with the French intelligence service.[24] Van Deman persevered, however, and with the approval of the new chief of staff, General Tasker H. Bliss, sent liaison officers to London and Paris to coordinate the work of the MIS with the British and French military intelligence services.[25]

Notwithstanding the mild friction that seems to have developed between Nolan and Van Deman, the MIS played a useful role in supporting the G-2. Nolan had adopted the British military intelligence organization in which every combat unit from battalion up had an intelligence section. It fell to the MIS to train the hundreds of officers and enlisted men to fill these positions. Van Deman also filled Nolan's order for fifty French-speaking sergeants with investigative experience; this group became known as the Corps of Intelligence Police.[26]

In spite of such support requirements and a heavy emphasis on counterespionage and countersubversion in North America, the MIS did not neglect its original function: collecting and processing military intelligence worldwide to be ready to answer questions from the General Staff on short notice about any part of the world. The MIS Positive Branch produced and updated "strategic indexes," detailed analyses of foreign countries based on attaché reports, communication intercepts from MI-8, and a variety of other sources.[27] Although the major focus of its strategic intelligence production was Germany, the Positive Branch did not neglect such regions as Russia, which was becoming a subject of much concern to the Allies as 1917 wore on.

Misgovernment, long a characteristic of czarist Russia, was exacerbated by the stresses and strains of war. In June 1915 the czar dismissed his incompetent minister of war, and in September he fired the commander in chief of the army and took the field himself. In his absence from the capital, conditions worsened on the home front: there were labor shortages, the country's railroad system was disrupted, and the cities suffered food and fuel shortages. Rumors of treason in high places shook the morale of the army and the general population, and by 1916 the long-suppressed forces of upheaval seemed on the verge of toppling the czarist government.

The German high command did not fail to recognize the opportunities presented by the situation: a revolutionary Russian regime might take the country out of the war, freeing two million German troops on the eastern front for use against the French and British in western Europe. Germany therefore mounted a massive covert propaganda campaign in Russia aimed at overthrowing the czar. Russian prisoners of war were indoctrinated in revolutionary ideology and sent home, and, of course, the German government facilitated the return to Russia of Vladimir Ilyich Lenin from exile in Switzerland.

In March 1917, when the provisional government of Aleksandr Kerensky was established following the abdication of the czar, the possibility
that Russia would soon leave the war became a grave concern in Allied
capitals. President Wilson appointed a commission, headed by former Secretary of State Elihu Root, to go to Russia and discover the new regime's
intentions. Root soon reported that the Russian army was being greatly
influenced by a massive German propaganda campaign and by agitation
by the Bolshevik faction, which urged an immediate withdrawal from the
war. He recommended a massive counterpropaganda campaign.[28]

In fact, the Wilson administration was already working with British
intelligence to mount a joint Anglo-American covert propaganda operation in Russia. The key to this was, of course, Sir William Wiseman. Early
in April Sir William received word from the Foreign Secretary, Lord Arthur
Balfour, that there was "real danger of revolutionary pacifists obtaining
the upper hand" in the Russian provisional government. Shortly thereafter, MI1(c) advised Sir William that the revolutionary pacifists were Jews
and directed Sir William to ask Richard Gottheil, professor of Semitic
languages at Columbia University and a prominent Zionist, to work with
him to secure the help of American Jewish leaders in countering the influence of the Russian pacifists. Although Gottheil persuaded Justice Louis
Brandeis, former ambassador Oscar Solomon Straus, and Rabbi Stephen
Wise to join with him in signing a statement for public release in Petrograd encouraging Russian Jews to continue the fight against Germany, the
project had little effect.[29]

In May Sir William advised Colonel House that

> the Germans are counting on their propaganda to bring about
> a separate peace with Russia; but the details of their intrigue
> are not so well known.
>
> We have reliable information that the Germans are orga-
> nizing from every neutral country panics of Russian refugees,
> largely Jewish socialists. These parties are sent to Petrograd
> where they are organized by German agents posing as advanced
> Socialists. . . .
>
> German agents have already been at work in the United
> States, and are sending Russian-Jewish Socialists back to

Petrograd who are either knowingly or unknowingly working in the German cause.[30]

Sir William proposed to House that the United States send to Russia Russian émigrés who had made good in America, as well as Czech, Slovak, and Polish leaders, all to carry the message that the German Secret Service had been conducting subversive operations in the United States and to warn the Russians against similar German activities in their country. Somehow, Sir William hoped to link the German government with the discredited czarist regime in the minds of the Russians.

House endorsed the plan and conveyed it to Wilson, believing that when Sir William assured him "we have reliable information," the "we" was British intelligence. This was a natural inference: Sir William's role as a back channel between Whitehall and the White House had been all but formalized by Foreign Secretary Balfour and President Wilson when the former visited Washington late in April. In a procedure that virtually cut Ambassador Spring-Rice out of the picture, House arranged, with the approval of Balfour and Wilson, that all urgent business between the two governments be conveyed in a special British government code between Sir William and the Foreign Office. Sir William soon moved to an apartment at 115 East 53rd Street, the building where House lived, to facilitate the exchange of the top-priority dispatches with House, who had private telephone lines linking him directly to the president and the secretary of state.[31]

When Sir William proposed to the Foreign Office that he direct the propaganda operation as a joint Anglo-American undertaking, he implied that the plan was based on intelligence acquired by the United States government. If Whitehall knew anything of American foreign political intelligence capabilities, it must have been somewhat skeptical, but Sir William also added a remarkable postscript that made Lord Balfour eager to approve the intelligence officer's involvement and also kick in seventy-five thousand dollars for the joint operation:

It is possible that by acting practically as a confidential agent for the United States Government I might strengthen the understanding with House so that in future he will keep us informed of steps taken by the United States Government in their foreign affairs, which would ordinarily not be a matter of common knowledge to the Governments of the two countries.[32]

Or in other words, Sir William hoped to become a kind of double agent. But where *did* Sir William learn that the Germans were using Russian émigrés as propaganda agents? He may not have been completely disingenuous when he implied to House that it was British intelligence and to Balfour that it was American intelligence, for his source may have been someone who also was working for both Washington and London.

"The outbreak of war in the United States found me without a regular job," Emanuel V. Voska recalled. Van Deman, who had taken the key members of the Voska organization into the MIS, offered him a commission and an intelligence assignment.

> I felt I could be most useful in that capacity. But meantime Charles R. Crane began urging me to go to Russia. . . .
>
> Crane, his son, Richard, and others in the State Department felt that, what between the Czech Legion [a unit of the Russian army made up of Czech émigrés], the local Czech and Slovak colonies and the war prisoners, we had in Russia enough people to counteract German influence. Charles R. Crane believed that we could organize them for this purpose just as we had organized our Czechs in the United States. . . .
>
> My instructions were simple: "Go to Petrograd. Establish there a branch of the Slav Press Bureau. Organize the Czechs and Slovaks of the Empire, to keep Russia in the war."[33]

The plan for the propaganda operation may have originated with Charles R. Crane, who was soon to be a member of the Root mission. Crane's son, Richard, was, of course, Secretary of State Lansing's private secretary and the State Department's case officer for the Voska organization. State Department counselor Frank L. Polk, the Wilson administration's intelligence coordinator, had acquired his own private secretary soon after Congress declared war: Gordon Auchincloss, former United States attorney for the Southern District of New York and Colonel House's son-in-law. The lines of communication and influence linking the Wilson administration with British intelligence and such "shadow government" figures as House and Charles Crane are almost too complex for the resolution of such questions as the origin of the propaganda campaign.

In any case, Wilson and House agreed to go along with the project, which was to be directed by Sir William. Voska might have seemed the logical choice for the principal agent on the ground in Petrograd, but Sir William had another candidate: the British writer W. Somerset Maugham.

Many readers of Maugham's *Ashenden* spy stories do not realize they were based on his experiences as a covert officer of MI1(c) in Switzerland in 1915–16. At the time Sir William mounted the Russian operation, Maugham was traveling in the United States, apparently not on active duty with the Secret Intelligence Service. The reasons Sir William selected him are obscure and probably unrelated to the fact that the two were related by marriage. Maugham recalled: "I was diffident of accepting the post, which seemed to demand capacities that I did not think I possessed; but there seemed to be no one more competent available at the moment and my being a writer was very good 'cover' for what I was asked to do."[34]

Maugham accepted in mid-June. He met with Voska and also consulted with Rabbi Wise and several other leaders of the Russian Jewish community in America. On July 28 he sailed from San Francisco for Vladivostok via Tokyo. He proceeded via the Trans-Siberian Railroad, arriving in Petrograd sometime in September. Voska, traveling by way of Vancouver with three prominent Czech-Americans, arrived in Petrograd shortly thereafter and joined Maugham at the Hotel Europa.[35]

With the help of Tomáš Masaryk, who was already in Petrograd serving as spokesman for the Czech Legion, Voska set up the Slav Press Bureau and began disseminating anti-German propaganda. He found that Russia presented an unusual problem for a psychological-warfare operation: "Only four per cent of the Russian people could read.... Speech was the only door to the popular mind."[36] German intelligence had already overcome that problem:

> On every street corner, in every public square and every hall, orators—some of them speaking Russian with a German accent—bawled out the same theme: ... Russia must make peace at once and begin to build a workingman's paradise....

The Bolsheviki were talking themselves into power, and no one was talking back. I prepared to flood the streets and squares with orators of Czech blood and Russian birth.[37]

There were seventy thousand Czechs in Russia ready to join the shouting match under Voska's orders, but the Allied propaganda campaign began too late. Maugham, who had met with Kerensky and other members of the provisional government, sent a series of dismal cipher cables to Sir William during September and October. On the night of November 7, 1917, the Bolsheviks rose, Kerensky's ministers were arrested, and the Winter Palace was sacked by the mob; the reins of power were seized by Lenin and Leon Trotsky. A day or so earlier a British destroyer had delivered Maugham to Scotland, and he was in London reporting to British and American officials on his final meeting with Kerensky, in which the provisional leader made an urgent plea for Allied assistance. Lord Balfour's secretary remarked that the message was "of only historical interest now."[38]

A day or so later Maugham briefed House, Wiseman, and Gordon Auchindoss; House and the others had arrived in London on November 7 as an American liaison mission. There was some talk of sending Maugham back to Russia to forge an alliance with the Cossacks against the Bolsheviks and the Germans, but the matter was dropped, partly because the strain of his Russian mission had aggravated Maugham's tuberculosis. The writer was forced to retire to a sanitarium in Scotland and remained an invalid for the next two years.

The Bolshevik regime immediately offered Germany an armistice and peace. On December 15 the armistice went into effect on the eastern front. The joint Anglo-American venture in covert action had failed to keep Russia in the war, although Maugham later reflected, "It seems to me at least possible that if I had been sent six months before I might quite well have succeeded."[39]

The Russian venture had been a signal success in advancing Sir William's personal agenda, however. While in England, House told the king that Wiseman was "one of the most efficient men of his age I had ever met." Sir William, whom House now described in his diary as his "liaison officer between me and the British Government," carried House's farewell note to the king when the American delegation departed for home. Soon after he returned to the United States, Sir William was invited to the White House for an hour of what the president called "a bully talk," and a few days later Wilson invited him back for a luncheon meeting with himself and Secretary of War Newton D. Baker to discuss the British army's manpower problems.[40]

Of course, Sir William did not have the same access to the president as House, but Wilson obviously now felt it sometimes more expedient to deal directly with the British intelligence officer than to work through his Silent Partner in New York. Measured against his ambition of parlaying his role as chief of a joint Anglo-American propaganda operation into the position of "practically . . . a confidential agent of the United States Government," the MI1(c) station chief had succeeded beyond his most hopeful expectations.

Chapter Twenty-two

The Secret War in Mexico

When the United States broke diplomatic relations with Germany early in February 1917, Section IIIb and German Naval Intelligence moved the base of their Western Hemisphere sabotage and espionage apparatus to Mexico City. The Section IIIb chief of station was Anton Dilger, also known as Delmar, a thirty-one-year-old American physician of German parentage who had studied medicine at both Johns Hopkins and Heidelberg. He had been in Germany when the war broke out and was recruited by Section IIIb, which sent him back to the United States in 1915. He set up a bacteriologic-warfare laboratory in Chevy Chase, Maryland, where he prepared glanders and anthrax cultures for other German agents to use to infect horses and mules scheduled to be shipped to the Allies.[1]

Dilger returned to Germany in 1916. After American entry into the war the following year, he was sent to Mexico City as chief of Section IIIb's Mexican station, arriving there in August 1917. His deputy was Frederick Hinsch, a former sea captain of the North German Lloyd steamship line who had run a branch of Rintelen's sabotage operation in Baltimore Harbor and had also worked with Dilger in his bacteriologic-warfare project. Hinsch was one of several German agents responsible for the Black Tom and Kingsland explosions.[2]

The head of German Naval Intelligence in North America was Kurt Jahnke, who was born in Germany in 1882 but had emigrated to the United States before the war.[3] When the war broke out, he was recruited by Captain Boy-Ed and went to work for Franz von Bopp, the German consul general in San Francisco and the head of the West Coast section of Papen's sabotage network. In May 1916 he became chief of all Bopp's sabotage operations. Although his principal area of activity was the western states, he also had a hand in the Black Tom explosion.[4]

From Mexico City, Jahnke ran agent networks in the United States and elsewhere in the Western Hemisphere.[5] His priority tasks were the construction of U-boat bases on the Mexican coast of the Gulf of Mexico and subversion and sabotage north of the border. The former project required the cooperation of the Mexican government, of course, as did the use of Mexican territory for bases of agent operations in the United States. Jahnke was therefore in conflict with Dilger, whose planned projects included sabotage of the Mexican oil fields at Tampico and the organization of raids by Mexican bandits into American territory, both of which operations would jeopardize relations with the Carranza regime.

Ambassador von Eckardt naturally opposed Dilger's proposed Mexican sabotage plans, and late in 1917 he persuaded Berlin to grant him veto power over the Mexican-based operations of both Section IIIb and Naval Intelligence.[6] Nonetheless, Dilger attempted to work around Eckardt. From May to July 1918, with the help of Mexican general Plutarco Calles, he prepared a force of several thousand Mexican and German troops in the border state of Sonora for an attack on the American Southwest, then applied directly to Berlin for the go-ahead, which, however, was flatly refused.[7]

Eckardt's intervention undoubtedly saved Mexican-German relations from Dilger's ill-advised schemes, but his newly acquired veto power probably subdued Jahnke's activities as well. In any case, the incidence of sabotage in the United States, which had dropped off markedly with the departure of the German legation in February 1917, never resumed its earlier level. Jahnke accomplished the construction of at least one U-boat base in Mexico by August 1918, but for some reason the German navy never made use of it for attacks on American shipping in the Gulf of Mexico.[8]

High on Eckardt's own covert agenda was the delicate balancing of Carranza and his domestic opposition. The German ambassador was committed to keeping the Mexican president in power so long as he maintained his government's neutrality and to toppling him if he did not. Probably both Dilger and Jahnke took part in setting up and running the extensive networks of German agents within the government and the opposition. Eckardt's highest-placed agent was Mario Mendez, the minister of communications, whom the German ambassador reputedly paid six hundred dollars per month.

Carranza learned he was the beneficiary of German spying when Eckardt warned him of a planned coup d'état. But Eckardt also kept in close touch with former Huerta ally Higinio Aguilar, whose anti-Carranza force was still based in Veracruz, and with the Catholic church, which had suffered from Carranza's anti-clerical policy.[9]

Eckardt's veto power over Dilger and Jahnke did not, of course, extend to projects ordered directly by Berlin. Early in 1918 the high command specifically ordered Jahnke to undertake several operations, including sabotage of the Panama Canal and the incitement of a revolt in the United States Army. Whatever Jahnke may have attempted on the canal is unknown, but he did try to mount an army mutiny, as well as a more general uprising in the United States. Jahnke's principal agent for the operation was a twenty-two-year-old German naval lieutenant, Lothar Witzke.

At the outbreak of the war, Witzke had been serving aboard the light cruiser *Dresden*, which was scuttled by her captain after being trapped in Chilean waters by three British warships. The Chilean government interned the officers and crew of the German ship, but Witzke managed to escape and made his way to San Francisco in May 1916.[10] There he reported to Consul General Bopp, who put him in touch with Jahnke. He became one of Jahnke's most effective saboteurs; among his accomplishments was the detonation of 250,000 pounds of gunpowder at the Mare Island naval base in San Francisco Bay, extensive arson in Oregon lumber camps, and a major hand in the Black Tom explosion.[11] When Jahnke moved his base of operations to Mexico City early in 1917, Witzke went along.

In his plan to foment a general uprising in the United States and a mutiny in the United States Army, Jahnke planned to employ the radical syndicalist labor organization, the Industrial Workers of the World. Organized in 1905 as a protest against skilled craft unionism and the conservative policies of Samuel Gompers's American Federation of Labor, the IWW spurned collective bargaining and favored strikes and sabotage; in fact, the word *sabotage* was introduced into the United States by the organization.[12] The IWW's ultimate objective was the destruction of capitalism through class struggle and revolution.

The IWW was violently opposed to American entry into the war, which it saw as largely a scheme for the enrichment of munitions makers. The organization resisted the wave of patriotism that followed the declaration of war. One IWW leader proclaimed, "It is better to be a traitor to your country than to your class."[13]

The IWW found relatively little support from newly arrived immigrants in the East, but it had considerable strength among native-born Americans in the western states in such strategically important industries as lumber, mining, and agriculture. Throughout 1917 the organization fomented strikes and labor unrest in these industries, creating a serious impact on the war effort.[14] Although the organization opposed the draft, it refrained from urging its members to refuse conscription. Ninety-five percent of the eligible IWW members registered with their draft boards and served when called, but their reliability and loyalty was a source of some concern to the army authorities. In fact, many IWW members entered the service with the intention of agitating against the war effort within the army.[15]

The IWW was, therefore, an obvious natural ally of German intelligence, a fact that Jahnke clearly recognized. In January 1918 he sent Lothar Witzke to Nogales, on the American border, to meet with five IWW officials from New Mexico, Arizona, and California to work out plans for the proposed general uprising. Two of the IWW delegates were black. With the intention of using them to foment rebellion in the black communities of the West, Jahnke sent along William Gleaves, a Canadian-born black who had been raised in Pennsylvania and had lived in Mexico for twenty-five years before being recruited by the German Naval Intelligence Service; on Jahnke's instructions, Gleaves had joined the IWW. Also accompanying Witzke was another German agent, Paul Bernardo Altendorf, an Austrian Pole who worked on the staff of General Plutarco Calles, the former Huerta ally who was now military governor of Sonora. Altendorf's task was to introduce Witzke to Calles and obtain communication and security support from the general for Witzke while he was in northern Mexico.[16]

Witzke, Gleaves, and Altendorf left Mexico City on January 16, traveling by train to the Pacific seaport of Manzanillo. The twenty-two-year-old Witzke sought to impress his companions, hinting at the planned uprising and, after a few drinks, boasting of his many sabotage exploits, including his role in the Black Tom explosion.[17]

The three took a steamer from Manzanillo to Mazatlán, then proceeded by rail to Hermosillo in the state of Sonora. There Altendorf took leave of his companions after introducing Witzke to General Calles. Calles agreed to forward Witzke's ciphered dispatches to Jahnke over his private telegraph line to Mexico City. As to providing the German agent security, the general simply gave him a revolver and a permit to carry it in Mexico. After his interview with Calles, Witzke set out for Nogales accompanied by Gleaves.

On the morning of February 1, Witzke crossed the border at Nogales en route to an American bank, probably with the intention of depositing some of the one thousand dollars he was carrying in a money belt and elsewhere on his person. He had hardly stepped onto American soil, however, when he was accosted by two men with drawn guns who disarmed him and put him in handcuffs. The pair identified themselves as United States Army agents. Specifically, they were members of Van Deman's Military Intelligence Section.

Astonished at being apprehended before his mission had even begun, Witzke soon learned the reason: Paul Altendorf, his fellow agent and the companion to whom he had boasted of his sabotage exploits and his current mission, was also working for the MIS. After leaving Witzke with General Calles in Hermosillo, Altendorf had rushed ahead to Nogales and alerted Byron S. Butcher, a local MIS officer in the border town, and Butcher prepared the reception.

After taking Witzke into custody, Butcher and his boss, Captain Joel A. Lipscomb, crossed to the Mexican side of Nogales and bribed the desk clerk at the Central Hotel to turn over Witzke's baggage to them. The most interesting item they found among the German agent's personal effects was a letter written in cipher, which they immediately sent off to Washington to be worked on by Yardley's code breakers in MI-8.

Butcher hoped to complete the sweep by rounding up Witzke's black accomplice, William Gleaves, about whom Altendorf had alerted him. He may have supposed that the agent, sensing trouble, had fled back to Mexico City. In any case, he was surprised to find the man waiting for him at the offices of E. M. Lawton, the United States consul in Mexican Nogales. Gleaves, it transpired, was a double agent working for the ubiquitous British Naval Intelligence Department. Although Gleaves and Altendorf had often met in Mexico City, neither was witting of the other's true role. They were doubtless relieved to know that Witzke at least was a genuine German spy, else the trio's stealthy mission to the American border would have been no more than a preposterous comedy of errors.

Gleaves's case officer was the British novelist and playwright A. E. W. Mason, whom Admiral Sir Reginald ("Blinker") Hall had had commissioned as a major in the Royal Marines in order to put him in the field for the Naval Intelligence Department. Mason had operated in Spain and North Africa before Hall sent him to Mexico City in 1917 in the guise of an eccentric British lepidopterist.[18]

Witzke had been carrying a Russian passport identifying him as Paul Waberski. In Washington Dr. John Matthews Manly of MI-8 worked on the cipher letter found in Witzke's luggage. Manly, former head of the University of Chicago's English Department, had been involved with the Riverbank Laboratory's Shakespearean project before offering his services to the MIS. By May 18 he had succeeded in deciphering the document and translating it from German into English:

> TO IMPERIAL CONSULAR OFFICIALS IN THE REPUBLIC OF MEXICO. STRICTLY SECRET! THE BEARER OF THIS IS A CITIZEN OF THE REICH WHO UNDER THE NAME OF PABLO WABERSKI IS TRAVELLING AS A RUSSIAN. HE IS A GERMAN SECRET AGENT. IT IS ASKED THAT YOU AFFORD HIM PROTECTION AND ASSISTANCE, ALSO ADVANCE HIM ON DEMAND, UP TO ONE THOUSAND PESOS OF MEXICAN GOLD, AND SEND HIS CODE TELEGRAMS TO THIS EMBASSY AS OFFICIAL CONSULAR DISPATCHES. VON ECKHARDT.[19]

Interned in the stockade of Fort Sam Houston, Witzke was confronted with the damning evidence by Butcher, who told him the only way to escape the gallows was to tell all he knew. The young German steadfastly refused, however, and was convicted of espionage by a United States Army military court and sentenced to death. After the war President Wilson commuted the sentence to life imprisonment, and Witzke was released from Leavenworth in 1923, partly in recognition of an act of heroism he performed during a boiler explosion in the prison.[20]

* * *

One of the many German agents both William Gleaves and Paul Alten-dorf knew in Mexico City was a Texas-born German-American named William Neunhoffer. Jahnke had recruited Neunhoffer when he turned up in the Mexican capital, apparently there to evade the draft and ready to defame his country at the top of his voice on the slightest provocation. The MIS undoubtedly had a thick dossier on Neunhoffer, compiled by Major R. R. Campbell, the American military attaché in Mexico City, but it did not include the fact that the German-American was an agent of the Justice Department's Bureau of Investigation, reporting to R. L. Barnes, the bureau's chief agent in Texas. Neunhoffer had been a San Antonio lawyer and a member of a Texas National Guard unit protecting the border when Barnes noticed that the twenty-eight-year old spoke both German and Spanish and immediately recruited him for the undercover assignment in Mexico.[21]

Neunhoffer's role became known after the war when he testified against many real draft dodgers who had fled to Mexico. It is unlikely that he was the bureau's only agent in Mexico City, and it is certain that Gleaves and Altendorf were not the only representatives of British Naval Intelligence and the MIS, respectively, in the Mexican capital during the war. In fact, the Allied (including the American) covert presence in Mexico probably surpassed that of Germany. At times Allied agents became so numerous as almost to trip over each other.

Zachary N. Cobb, the State Department's secret agent who had arrested Huerta and whose cover was that of a customs official on the border, had an agent in the confidence of the German consul in Juárez and another in the local telegraph office in that city. Nonetheless, he constantly complained to Washington about the activities of MIS agents who, he claimed, were interfering with his operations.[22] Even the Office of Naval Intelligence had a Mexican operation. New York stockbroker William Clarkson Van Antwerp, who directed the San Francisco office of ONI, ran agent networks in Mexico despite the jurisdictional protests of the commander of the navy's Pacific Fleet.[23]

A. E. W. Mason's Mexico City network was not the only British intelligence operation in the country, of course. Other British operators kept watch on the Indian nationalists living in Mexico, for example. And the French intelligence services were also quite active in the country and frequently passed along reports of German covert activities in Mexico to the United States State Department.[24]

Of course, the intercept and code-breaking activities of the British Naval Intelligence Department's Room 40 enabled both British and American intelligence operators to identify almost every important German agent in Mexico. State Department and MIS agents had both Jahnke and Hinsch under constant surveillance, and of course the MIS, the Bureau of Investigation, and British Naval Intelligence penetrated the German apparatus in Mexico with Allied double agents. Dilger was the only important German agent in Mexico who escaped observation, although an Allied agent was hot on his trail when he died of the flu in Spain in November 1918, one day after the war ended.[25]

Mexico, a not-always-so-friendly American neighbor lying just across a two-thousand-mile unguarded border, provides an excellent base for covert operations against the United States. This was understood by German intelligence in both world wars and by the Soviet Secret Services in the cold war. Political turmoil in Mexico from 1912 to 1920, with its consequent Mexican-American tensions, added the dimension of military and diplomatic diversion to the country's usefulness to America's adversaries. In retrospect, it seems clear that German hopes for postwar economic exploitation of the country inhibited Germany from making full use of Mexico in the war. It is also obvious that internal quarreling between Section IIIb and German Naval Intelligence hindered an effective Mexican-based covert campaign against the United States. Yet even had these handicaps been absent or overcome, the extensive penetration of the German covert apparatus in Mexico by the Allied intelligence services would have limited, if not entirely neutralized, the domestic threat to the United States.

The German plot to foment a general uprising in the United States through the use of the IWW seems to have been one of the most dangerous operations mounted by the German Secret Services against America during the war. The fact that it was thwarted by the Military Intelligence Section less than a year after Van Deman succeeded in bringing the agency into existence is clear evidence that intelligence was once again alive and well in America.

Chapter Twenty-three

Counterspies and Vigilantes

By infiltrating the Mexican base of the Central Powers' sabotage and subversion apparatus in the United States, the MIS had almost completely neutralized its remnants, but no one in the United States government knew that for certain, and it seemed too good to be true. And the possibility remained that Section IIIb or German Naval Intelligence might establish new networks in the country, using reserve assets—German-Americans and other sympathetic individuals who had not yet fallen under federal scrutiny. Viewed uneasily from Washington, the operational climate in the United States looked even more favorable for German subversion after American entry into the war than it had earlier.

Passage of the Selective Service Act by Congress after the declaration of war galvanized the anti-war element in America to new levels of action. In New York the well-known anarchist leaders Alexander Berkman and Emma Goldman formed the No-Conscription League to encourage resistance to the draft. An emergency convention of the Socialist party in Saint Louis on April 7, the day after Congress declared war, pronounced the declaration "a crime against the people of the United States and against the nations of the world" and called for "unyielding opposition" to the draft as well as other militant action.[1] In Oklahoma and Texas young men took up arms and fled into the countryside, promising to resist violently any attempts to draft them.

The radical Left—anarchists, Socialists, Communists, the IWW—a growing presence in America since the beginning of the post–Civil War industrial boom, had always seemed menacing to mainstream Americans. Now the American Left not only vowed to resist the war effort; it solidly identified itself with America's enemies by embracing the Bolshevik takeover, which had removed Russia from the war. The radical Left had cooperated with German intelligence in Russia; there was no reason to think it would not do the same in the United States. Indeed, the Lothar Witzke case showed that Germany believed the IWW was ready to do just that. It seemed the height of wishful thinking to suppose that other German agents would not follow in Witzke's footsteps and perhaps succeed where he had failed in fomenting an uprising in America through the IWW and other dissident elements.

As we know now, the specter of German subversion far surpassed the reality. Black Tom, Kingsland, and the hundreds of less spectacular fires and explosions of the past two years seemed to bespeak a ubiquity and potency well beyond what the German sabotage apparatus actually enjoyed. Indeed, Bernstorff, Papen, and the other German spy masters had made no preparations for a stay-behind network—that is, for a sabotage and subversion apparatus to operate in the United States after American entry into the war, a contingency they rather complacently failed to anticipate. But that comforting knowledge was denied to the Wilson administration. The long-held suspicion of German-Americans appeared to have been confirmed when more than a few of their number were found to have been involved in sabotage and other subversive acts. Was this merely the tip of a huge iceberg perhaps involving one in every five citizens?

Revelations of such vicious schemes as the San Diego Plan and the IWW uprising, viewed against the backdrop of actual bloodshed in the Villa raids in the Southwest, combined to form the impression that a real shooting war was being waged on American soil. If something had been needed to tie America's anxieties about Mexico to German subversion, the Zimmermann telegram filled the bill. For the first time since 1814, America stood in real fear of an invading army.

In a June 14, 1917 (Flag Day), speech in Washington, the liberal Democratic president warned that the leaders of Germany were "employing liberals in their enterprise" to deceive "all those who throughout the world stand for the rights of peoples and the self-government of nations." He spoke of German subversion in Russia and added:

> The sinister intrigue is being no less actively conducted in this
> country than in Russia and in every country in Europe to which

the agents and dupes of the imperial German Government can
get access. That government has many spokesmen here, in
places high and low. They have learned discretion. They keep
within the law. It is opinion they utter now, not sedition.

The following day Wilson signed into law the Espionage Act, which
had just been passed by Congress. Eleven months later he endorsed an
even stronger version of the law. The Espionage Acts not only made it a
federal offense to spy for an enemy nation or any other foreign country;
they also moved the line separating opinion from sedition a long way in
the direction of the former.

The laws prescribed penalties for urging resistance to the draft or insubordination in the armed forces; opposing the production of munitions and
other war material; speaking, printing, or otherwise expressing contempt
for the United States government or the Constitution, the flag, or the
uniform of the army or navy; using language calculated to aid the enemy;
using words favoring any country with which the United States was at
war; or saying or doing anything likely to hamper the sale of United States
government bonds. Furthermore, the acts gave the federal government
broad censorship powers over the press and even the authority to open and
inspect first-class mail. The sweeping, vaguely worded laws were the most
brutal attack on free speech in America since the Sedition Act of 1798.

This, then, was the anxious, if not paranoid, atmosphere that prevailed
in Washington during America's eighteen-month involvement in the war.

With the declaration of war, Wilson had invoked federal laws requiring
enemy aliens to register with the United States government and restricting
their movements and activities. Most of these individuals were immigrants
awaiting American citizenship, but some twenty-three hundred were considered potentially dangerous and were interned during the war. The task
of policing the activities of the more than one million alien males remaining free fell to the Justice Department's Bureau of investigation, which
was also responsible for enforcing the draft laws and protecting harbors
and war-industry zones, in addition to its regular federal law-enforcement
activities and, of course, enforcement of the Espionage Acts.

The size of the bureau's investigative staff was increased from three
hundred to four hundred agents in recognition of its growing work load,

but as a practical matter this enlargement did not begin to equip the bureau to deal with its new responsibilities.[2] The bureau could not even keep up with the avalanche of letters and telegrams from a newly spy-conscious public reporting instances of suspected German espionage and was forced to borrow clerks from other government agencies simply to sort the incoming mail.

Into this gap stepped Chicago businessman Albert M. Briggs, vice president of Outdoor Advertising, Inc., a billboard advertising company. Months before American entry into the war, Briggs had been among a group of businessmen who had been addressed by Hinton D. Clabaugh, the bureau's Chicago superintendent. Discussing the increasing flow of reports of suspected sabotage, Clabaugh complained that he simply did not have the resources to investigate them. His staff of fifteen agents was expected to cover a territory that included Illinois, Wisconsin, and Minnesota. Furthermore, Clabaugh pointed out, the investigators did not even have the use of automobiles in their work and were forced to waste time traveling by public transportation.

Briggs, a patriot and a citizen deeply concerned about the threat of subversion, organized a group of his fellow businessmen to provide a fleet of seventy-five automobiles for use by bureau agents in Chicago, Washington, and New York. A few weeks later he visited Clabaugh with another proposal of assistance to the bureau: an auxiliary force of unpaid volunteers to work with the bureau in investigating cases of subversion, sabotage, and other criminal acts inimical to the war effort. Clabaugh passed along the offer to the bureau's director, A. Bruce Bielaski. This was on March 14, three weeks before the United States entered the war. Events were then moving rapidly toward that consummation, however, and on March 20 Bielaski telegraphed Clabaugh and told him to accept Briggs's offer.

Bielaski cautioned Clabaugh to stress to Briggs that his volunteers should under no circumstances initiate arrests without prior consultation with the bureau. That he did so at the outset suggests he had some notion of the dangers involved in turning loose an army of amateur spy catchers upon the land. He may have believed that notwithstanding these dangers, the volunteers were better than nothing in dealing with the enormous gap between the bureau's work load and its resources. In retrospect, that judgment seems very questionable, however. To comprehend just how unwise it was to grant authority to a hoard of unqualified and untrained volunteers to investigate the loyalty of their fellow citizens, it is necessary to recall the atmosphere that pervaded the country at that moment. If official Washington was caught up in anxiety and paranoia, the rest of the country was in the grip of a xenophobic mania.

One of the sillier manifestations of the public madness was an attempt to purge the language of all things German. Hamburger became Salisbury steak, sauerkraut was liberty cabbage, and German fried potatoes disappeared altogether. In Brooklyn, Hamburg Avenue was renamed Wilson Avenue by local patriots; their midwestern cousins turned Germantown, Nebraska, into Garland, and Berlin, Iowa, into Lincoln. German shepherds became Alsatian shepherds, and dachshunds were transmogrified into liberty pups. Local symphony orchestras cleansed themselves of all things Germanic, including the works of Wagner, Beethoven, Schubert, and Schumann, and the mayor of East Orange, New Jersey, refused to permit the world-famous violinist Fritz Kreisler to perform in his city on the grounds that he had once served in the Austrian army. German-language schools were closed down. Boy Scouts burned German newspapers in Ohio, and the Wisconsin National Guard burned German books.

But there were even grimmer manifestations of the hysteria: people with accents that sounded German were fired from their jobs, as were some who simply "looked German" or were somehow associated with Germans. Those with solid German connections were sometimes treated more brutally: in Collinsville, Illinois, a mob lynched a German-American Socialist who had opposed the war.

The circle was soon enlarged to include other ethnic or political groups suspected of anti-war or pro–Central Powers sentiments. Those with roots anywhere in northern or Eastern Europe—Poles, Lithuanians, Scandinavians—came in for scrutiny and sometimes abuse; southern Europeans escaped attention because Italy was on the Allied side. Czechs and Slovaks, active in forming a legion of American émigrés to fight Austria-Hungary, were attacked by superpatriots who were unfamiliar with Central European history or politics and nonetheless did not permit their ignorance to inhibit their actions. Socialists, pacifists, and others opposed to the war were also victims of the wave of xenophobia; their ideas were foreign even when their surnames were Anglo-Saxon.

Positive thinkers strove to uplift the German-Americans and other foreign-born through Americanization campaigns calculated to transform the unfortunates into "real" Americans. When Emanuel Voska returned to New York, having barely managed to escape with his life at the completion of his secret mission to Russia on behalf of the State Department, he found "a smart, pleasant lady representing a patriotic society" on his doorstep waiting to Americanize him and his family.[3]

Millions of American men beyond military age but eager to participate somehow in the war effort were ready to join Briggs's American Protective League. Within three months of its establishment, it numbered one hundred thousand members; before the war ended, it had grown to a quarter of a million.[4] With national headquarters in Chicago, the APL had branches in every state and offices in every major city. National and local directors of the league were recruited from among successful businessmen, preferably those who had achieved some prominence in their communities. Briggs's second in command was Thomas B. Crockett, a descendant of the famous frontiersman. William C. Bobbs of the Bobbs-Merrill Publishing Company was director of the APL branch in Indiana. In Hollywood movie mogul Cecil B. DeMille organized an APL unit within the film industry.[5] The local Chicago APL branch (not the national headquarters) was headed by Charles D. Frey, like Briggs a successful advertising executive. Other managers of the large Chicago branch were also prominent local businessmen, usually not self-made men but with backgrounds in elite prep schools and Ivy League colleges.

The APL rank and file came from a different social stratum and were often employees of the businesses managed or owned by the APL directors. In fact, many of the APL operatives had the specific task of watching for sabotage or subversion among their fellow employees. For some this was an opportunity to get on good terms with the boss; others were drawn to the unpaid work by the puerile lure of the APL's tin badge (not to be displayed unless absolutely necessary to establish the agent's semiofficial status) and identification card. Undoubtedly, many others volunteered in order to obtain a measure of governmental authority over their neighbors.

In theory, an APL agent had none of the powers of a sworn law-enforcement officer; in practice, the members often stepped over the line and made arrests, tapped telephones, entered and searched private property, and otherwise exceeded their role as officially sanctioned private investigators. Managers of telephone and telegraph companies, banks, and office buildings who belonged to the APL facilitated such unauthorized snooping. Bielaski and other Justice Department officials frequently reprimanded the league for such acts, but short of criminal prosecution, there was little they could do to put teeth into their protests. The APL was doing 75 percent of the routine work of the Bureau of Investigation's Chicago office, 80 percent of the work load of the bureau's Cleveland office, and handling nearly the same percentage of the caseload of the bureau's office in New York City. Even though the bureau's investigative staff was increased to fifteen hundred agents during the war, the agency could not do its work without the help of the APL in handling the routine investigations. For the errant APL member there was little to fear but the unlikely prospect of losing his unpaid job.[6]

Although the APL was officially an auxiliary force of the Justice Department, it received no government funds to defray its overhead. The considerable expense of offices, clerical-staff salaries, stationery, postage, travel, telephone, and so forth—which ran into the millions by the end of the war—was covered by donations from businesses.[7] Many businessmen saw the contributions as a sound investment in preventing sabotage and discouraging agitation among their employees, and they did not particularly care whether or not the potential saboteurs and agitators caught by the APL were German agents. In other words, many businessmen who supported the APL valued its members' services less as counterspies than as strikebreakers.

The threat of IWW strikes and sabotage had caused a panic among businessmen and local government officials in the Northwest by mid-1917.[8] Fear of the radical organization was no less in other parts of the country. The governor of Montana wired President Wilson complaining that the IWW had so terrorized the miners in his state that the strategic copper industry had been shut down.

The IWW was the target of much APL attention not only because of its labor terrorism and suspected covert connection to German intelligence, but because of its overt anti-draft agitation, a violation of the 1917 Espionage Act and therefore a proper matter for the Bureau of Investigation and its volunteer auxiliary. APL members penetrated the radical organization to collect evidence against it and participated in the bureau's raids on twenty-one IWW offices nationwide on September 5, 1917. The raids and the subsequent prosecutions of the IWW leaders virtually broke the back of the organization and ended its influence on American labor.

Much of the APL's effort was directed against individuals rather than organizations. If the target had violated no federal law, Leaguers sometimes persuaded local law-enforcement agencies to prosecute him for disturbing the peace or inciting to riot; thus was a Long Beach, California, man sentenced to ninety days in jail for calling the president a "damned fool."[9] Intimidation was another APL weapon, sometimes used to remove offending pro-German books from the shelves of public libraries. But such subterfuge was usually unnecessary because the sweeping provisions of the Espionage Acts made almost any utterance critical of the war effort a federal offense.

The APL was further legitimized when the army's Military Intelligence Section also began to make use of its members as auxiliary staff. In his memoirs Major General Van Deman points out that the appearance of such unofficial spy-catching organizations as the League "was an extremely dangerous development" but that if one of them could be taught to obey orders, it could provide much-needed help.[10] He probably saw that it would be impossible to eliminate such vigilantism given the atmosphere of the times, and he wisely chose to throw MIS support to the APL in order to get some control over it.

In an effort to establish a measure of control over the APL, and perhaps get some useful work out of it, he commissioned Charles D. Frey as an army captain in November 1917 and put him in the MIS (by then Frey was one of the league's three national directors and chief of its headquarters, which had been moved from Chicago to Washington). This was the beginning of a regular APL liaison unit, which became an organic part of the MIS.

"In the beginning, there was a little trouble in getting some of the members to understand exactly what orders meant," Van Deman recalled, "and some of the smaller groups did make more or less trouble in questioning the loyalty of persons in their communities. However, that was dealt with [with] a pretty strong hand and within a short time such activities ceased."[11]

Van Deman seems to have gotten effective control over the APL members working for his MIS, for none of the League's more notorious abuses involved its work for army intelligence. But apparently he did not completely trust the League: he recruited his own volunteer Secret Service and kept its existence secret from the APL. This volunteer staff, which Van Deman placed under the command of Colonel Carl Reichmann of the MIS, was centered in the Midwest and consisted of retired army officers, AFL informants, private detectives, industrial security officers, and a handful of attorneys.[12] Reichmann saw the group as a "sort of competition" for the APL; Van Deman may have regarded it as a means of watching the watchers.

With the failure of German saboteurs to reappear in wartime America, draft resistance and draft dodging became the principal focus of both the bureau and the APL. By August 1918 draft evasion had become a particularly serious problem for the army; the War Department asserted that 308,489 men had failed to report for induction, while an unknown number of others had not even registered.

At the behest of the attorney general, the APL inaugurated a program of slacker raids—*slacker* being the contemporary term for draft dodger. In conducting the sweeps of hotels, restaurants, railroad terminals, theaters, and other public places, demanding that men of military age produce their draft cards and arresting those unable to comply, the APL was exceeding its authority, although this time it was doing so with the sanction of the Justice Department. Early in September 1918 the bureau and the APL conducted a three-day slacker raid in New York City, Jersey City, and Newark, New Jersey. The operation involved 35 bureau agents, 2,000 APL agents, 1,350 soldiers and National Guardsmen, 1,000 sailors, and several hundred local policemen. The raiders fanned out through the cities, indiscriminately arresting any male of military age unable to produce a draft card. During the three-day sweep, tens of thousands of unfortunates were dragged off and herded into armories and other public buildings (one account puts the number as high as fifty thousand). As it turned out, the great majority were not slackers but had simply forgotten to carry their draft cards on their persons.[13]

For once the APL had not been guilty of exceeding its brief; the League had done only what the Justice Department had told it to do and no more than the other participants in the slacker raids. Nonetheless, the auxiliary drew much of the outrage and indignation resulting from the New York–New Jersey raids. Newspaper editorialists were up in arms over the affair, and congressmen thundered. The elections of 1918 were only two months away, but, as it happened, so was the armistice. The shooting stopped and the xenophobic frenzy ended. Shortly thereafter, the APL went out of existence. During its brief life it carried out an estimated six million investigations.[14]

It failed to turn up one genuine German spy.

Chapter Twenty-four

A Gentleman's Profession

When General Pershing's intelligence chief, Colonel Dennis Nolan, seized both the tactical and the strategic intelligence roles in Europe for the AEF's intelligence service, he left Van Deman with little choice but to concentrate the resources of the MIS on domestic negative intelligence. But given the real and perceived dangers posed by German covert activity in the Western Hemisphere, Van Deman probably would have done things no differently even had Nolan's G-2 not taken the lead in positive military intelligence. Van Deman believed the enemy was much closer to home than the western front; he therefore saw the most important functions of the MIS as counterespionage and countersubversion. Before the war was over, he turned the MIS into the largest domestic security agency in the federal government.

The draft-resistance movement raised parallel concerns in Washington about the loyalty of some of the men who answered the draft calls or enlisted voluntarily. Secretary of War Baker was particularly worried about aliens born in Germany or Austria-Hungary who were serving in the army. His anxieties were heightened when the MIS discovered several German agents who not only had enlisted in the army but had managed to become officers.[1] Van Deman had responded to such cases by establishing MI-3, a section within the MIS's Negative Branch to investigate disloyalty and subversion within the army.[2]

The internal-security concerns of the MIS were not limited to disloyalty in the army ranks, however; in November 1917 Van Deman had established a parallel subsection, MI-4, to conduct "counterespionage among the civilian population." The army's legal jurisdiction in dealing with what amounted to a civilian law-enforcement problem was doubtful. In theory, the MIS worked closely with the Department of Justice, and the latter retained the sole power of arrest and prosecution, but in practice—for example, in the Lothar Witzke case—the MIS sometimes took over both functions. To steer the MIS clear of legal tangles, Van Deman commissioned the prominent New York attorney George S. Hornblower. Captain Hornblower and a small staff of assistants comprised MI-4G, which functioned as a general counsel's office for the Negative Branch of the MIS.

The principal section of MI-4 was MI-4B, which dealt with civilian subversion on a geographic basis. For example, its Southeastern Department concentrated on "Negro subversion and political demagoguery": Van Deman believed that agents of the Central Powers were agitating among the black population, and he sent two black undercover agents to travel through the black communities and disseminate counterpropaganda.[3] MI-4B's Eastern and Northeastern Department was concerned with foreign ethnic groups—especially Germans and other enemy aliens. The Central Department focused on pro-German ethnic organizations; the Southern Department, on border-control problems and subversion among the Mexican population. Since the IWW was most active in the West, it and other radical labor groups became the concern of the Western Department, as did the Japanese and East Indian populations.[4]

To support such far-flung investigative activities, the MIS established field offices in New York City, Philadelphia, Saint Louis, Seattle, Pittsburgh, and New Orleans. The largest of these was the New York office, which was run by Major Nicholas Biddle, a prominent New Yorker Van Deman had commissioned in the army for this purpose.[5]

Although the Allied intelligence services had penetrated and neutralized the German covert apparatus based in Mexico City, Section IIIb or the Naval Intelligence Service apparently succeeded in running a few agents in the United States during the period of American belligerency. For example, Milorad Raitchvitch, a Serbian stamp dealer, ran a letter drop for German agents from his offices in New York until the British intelligence officer Colonel Claude Dansey tipped off Van Deman, who passed along the information to Biddle in the MIS New York field office. Dansey also advised Van Deman that Frederick C. Moltke, a Danish aristocrat, was working for German intelligence in the United States. Dansey may also have advised that Moltke was a womanizer, for Van Deman used a female agent to collect enough evidence to justify the expulsion of the Dane.[6] But true German agents such as Raitchvitch and Moltke were rare. Therefore, most of MI-4's energies were directed against subversives who had no connection with foreign intelligence services.

Certain politically sensitive areas touching on sabotage and subversion required the most delicate handling. Chief among these were instances of disloyalty among Catholic priests—usually Irish-Americans—and within such moderate labor organizations as the AFL. To deal with these matters with the utmost discretion, Van Deman commissioned as an army major Eugene F. Kinkead, a prominent Irish-American active in labor matters.

A native of Ireland, Kinkead grew up in New Jersey, where he had been a Jersey City alderman before serving two terms in Congress. While sheriff of Hudson County, New Jersey, in 1915 he successfully mediated a strike at the Bayonne refinery of Standard Oil, obtaining highly favorable terms for the union. He was on close personal terms with AFL president Samuel Gompers, himself an enthusiastic supporter of the war effort. While serving as chief of the MI-4I unit (Labor and Sabotage), Kinkead was able to work through Gompers and other AFL officers to avert strikes in several strategically important industries. His influence with moderate labor leaders was also instrumental in the army's establishment of the Loyal Legion of Loggers and Lumbermen in the Northwest lumber industry as a rival to the IWW, which had been especially strong in the region.

Kinkead's status as a prominent Catholic layman enabled him to intervene quietly whenever an Irish-American priest's hatred of England overcame his patriotism and led him, for example, to fulminate against the war from the pulpit or engage in other subversive activities. In such cases the Justice Department was reluctant to prosecute the cleric for fear of the fallout among other American Catholics, so Kinkead would simply turn over the evidence in the case to James Cardinal Gibbons of Baltimore, the most influential Catholic churchman in America and another supporter of the war effort, and Gibbons would direct the local bishop to call in the errant priest, reprimand him, and read him a pamphlet entitled "A Lesson in Real Americanism."[7]

* * *

The Espionage Act of June 1917 and another emergency wartime law, the Trading-with-the-Enemy Act of October 1917, empowered the federal government to conduct wholesale censorship of mail, newspapers, telephone, telegraph, radio, and every other medium of communication in the United States.[8] In an executive order of October 12, 1917, Wilson established the National Censorship Board to administer this authority. The board was chaired by George Creel, the chairman of the Committee on Public information (the official wartime propaganda agency), and consisted of representatives of the Post Office and the War and Navy departments. Representation of the latter two departments eventually consisted of officers from the MIS and ONI.

Van Deman had created a special unit within the Negative Branch of the MIS to deal with censorship matters. MI-10, as it was designated, grew to be a very large unit, with a staff of three hundred officers and civilian employees (including postal workers and other government employees detailed to the unit), and consisted of fifteen different subsections created to deal with such specialized areas as prisoner-of-war mail, telegraph and telephone lines leaving the United States, radio communications, books, newspapers, and motion pictures. While most of MI-10's activity involved suppressing pro–Central Powers or anti-war propaganda (or anything deemed to be such), the unit also collected positive intelligence and counterintelligence information. MI-10E, Radio Interception, operated several mobile listening posts along the Mexican border to intercept radio messages originating in that country.

Wartime radio communications between Germany and Mexico were of particular interest to the United States government not only in light of the Zimmermann telegram affair but because Eckardt, Jahnke, Dilger, and the other German intelligence chiefs in Mexico City received their instructions from Berlin by radio and attempted to report back using the same medium.[9] To ensure maximum effectiveness in intercepting the German radio transmissions to and from Mexico, MI-10E set up a clandestine listening post in Mexico City itself. The intercepts gathered by the installation apparently included communications between Mexico and Japan, as well as communications with Berlin.[10]

MI-10E also established a clandestine receiving station in a farmhouse near Houlton, Maine, shortly before the end of the war. Maine was much closer to the German transmitting station outside Berlin, and a far more elaborate listening post could be built in a secluded American location than in Mexico City. The Houlton installation, which required the stringing up of thousands of feet of antenna wire, excited speculation among the local citizens that the mufti-clad army technicians were Secret Service agents bent upon some incomprehensible project. The listening post did not become operational until two weeks before the armistice, however, and probably collected little or no communications intelligence.[11]

MI-10B, Postal Censorship, also gathered important counterintelligence information. Censorship of the mail obviously involved opening letters and reading them, and letters arousing the censors' suspicions were forwarded to Yardley's MI-8 for expert examination.[12] If the letter had been deemed suspicious because it appeared to have been written in some obscure short-hand system, it was turned over to MI-8's Shorthand Subsection, which was located in New York City and managed by Franklin W. Allen, a partner in a prominent firm of law reporters. Allen's small staff of shorthand experts, which included two Spaniards and one German citizen (Miss Maria Nor-man, "a highly trusted employee, in spite of her German citizenship"),[13] was able to read fifty-four different shorthand systems, including foreign systems used to transcribe French, Spanish, Italian, Turkish, Greek, and several Slavic languages. While the translation of shorthand letters turned up many instances of pro-German or anti-American sentiments—many of which were punishable under the Espionage Acts—it failed to uncover any German spies.[14] What few German agents there were in wartime America used a different mode of cryptography—invisible writing. MI-8 operated two secret-ink laboratories, one in Washington and another in the Post Office's New York censorship office.

Given the spy mania sweeping the land, it is not surprising that a truly prodigious number of letters opened by the American postal censors were judged to be suspicious and forwarded to MI-8's secret-ink laboratories. Between July 1918 and the following February, for example, the laboratories examined an average of two thousand letters per week. In his memoirs of MI-8, Yardley mentions only three letters examined by the laboratories that were found to contain messages in invisible writing, and it is unlikely that there were many others.[15] The dearth of German spy letters was a consequence of the dearth of German spies.

By early 1918 the MIS's counterintelligence and security capabilities had become so well recognized in Washington that the State Department began requesting that the section conduct background checks on persons applying for passports or ocher documents in order to visit Europe. To meet this growing demand, Van Deman organized a unit of American Protective League volunteers under Captain Frey, the APL national director whom he had had commissioned in the army.[16] Presumably, the volunteers checked with the local APL office in the passport applicant's community to learn whether he was suspected of disloyalty, then passed along whatever gossip they received to State. Since such a procedure did not offer much opportunity for false arrests, Van Deman may have seen it as a reasonably safe way to keep his APL helpers busy and out of trouble. The volume of this passport-control activity by the MIS continued to grow and eventually included the screening of both arriving and departing transatlantic passengers, an important means of detecting foreign agents. In September 1918 a special subsection, MI-11, was created to handle the job.[17]

By this time the rapidly burgeoning MIS had also acquired such non-intelligence elements as MI-13, which investigated graft and fraud in the procurement of army supplies, and the Military Morale Section, which was supposed to foster the "psychological stimulation of American troops." These tasks diverted the resources of the MIS from true intelligence and counterintelligence activity, as Van Deman protested. But also by this time, Van Deman was no longer in charge of the unit. In August 1918 Major General Peyton C. March, the new chief of staff, ended the MIS's subordinate role as a section of the War College Division and re-established it as a separate division of the General Staff. This was, of course, just what Van Deman had been urging since he returned to Washington three years earlier, but ironically it spelled the end of his leadership of the unit. According to army administrative policy, the director of a General Staff division had to be a brigadier general, and Van Deman was not yet eligible for promotion to that grade. He was relieved and assigned to General Pershing's AEF staff in France, while a former member of that staff, Marlborough

Churchill, was hastily promoted to brigadier and put in charge of the newly elevated Military Intelligence Division.[18]

Van Deman arrived in Chaumont, site of AEF headquarters, late in June, and after interviews with Pershing and Nolan, he was given a sort of roving commission to travel about Europe consulting with American G-2 and Allied intelligence officers on sundry matters, apparently a make-work assignment in the absence of any suitable job for him on the AEF staff. In his peregrinations he encountered old acquaintances—Colonel Dansey, now with MI1(c), the British Secret Intelligence Service, running counterespionage operations in Holland and elsewhere on the Continent; and Emanuel Voska, whom Van Deman had commissioned as a captain in the United States Army and then sent to Europe to serve in Nolan's G-2. Voska was now constantly on the move, slipping in and out of neutral Switzerland, sometimes parachuting into Austria-Hungary, all to aid the secret intelligence networks he was running in Germany and his homeland.[19]

Van Deman managed to accomplish a great deal of useful work while in his uncertain status in Europe, especially in bringing about closer coordination between G-2 and the MID. He believed that he was eventually to return to Washington and take over the MID, presumably in the grade of brigadier general. But although he would achieve that grade and advance to major general before his retirement eleven years later, he never again commanded the intelligence unit of the General Staff. He had accomplished his major goal, however: the restoration of intelligence to an equal footing with other staff functions in the War Department.

Although a squadron of five American battleships was integrated into the British Grand Fleet, the principal tasks of the United States Navy in the war was the protection of the convoys that carried two million American troops and millions of tons of war material across the Atlantic and an offensive program to seek and destroy German U-boats in the North Atlantic and the Mediterranean. Eighty-five American destroyers operated from Queenstown in Ireland and from Brest, Gibraltar, and other ports; and several hundred small, wooden-hulled submarine chasers assisted in the war against the U-boats.

As in the case of the army, the navy created a new intelligence service in the war zone to support its combat operations, while leaving the Washington-based Office of Naval Intelligence to deal with counterespionage and countersubversion in the Western Hemisphere. The commander of all United States naval forces in Europe was Vice Admiral William S. Sims, the same officer who, as naval attaché in Paris during the Spanish-American War two decades earlier, had organized and run a highly effective secret intelligence network in Spain and throughout Europe. Sims, therefore, was no amateur at the intelligence business. He established an Intelligence Department in his London headquarters and put it under the command of his aide and personal friend, Commander John V. Babcock.[20]

Sims got along very well with the British first sea lord, Admiral John R. Jellicoe, whom he had known since the two officers met in China in 1901. Indeed, the Canadian-born Sims (his father was an American; the family moved to Pennsylvania from Ontario when Sims was fourteen) was criticized in Washington for being too sympathetic to British interests, a charge he indignantly denied.[21] The British regarded him as their best friend in the United States Navy, however, and were quite forthcoming with him in intelligence matters. British Naval Intelligence chief Blinker Hall briefed Sims daily on current intelligence matters, especially the movements of German U-boats in the Atlantic. This was considerably more intelligence than he needed, since the American destroyers and submarine chasers had been integrated into the Royal Navy and were not under Sims's operational control.[22] Hall did not withhold the fact that most of this intelligence came from communications intercepts deciphered by the code breakers of Room 40, but Sims reportedly sanitized the information when relaying it to Washington by attributing it to British secret agents.[23]

Sims was not content to let his own Intelligence Department simply be a repository for the information passed along by Admiral Hall. The department became the nucleus of Sims's Planning Section, a unit he described as "an idea that is advantageously used in many American industrial establishments, . . . the first, I think, which has ever been adopted by any navy." The section was made up of Naval War College graduates, and it conducted war-gaming exercises as a means of planning naval operations and improving existing organization and methods.[24]

"One of their favorite methods was to place themselves in the position of the Germans," Sims recalled, "and to decide how, if they were directing German naval operations, they would frustrate the tactics of the Allies."[25]

The Planning Staff studied the methods of using a submarine to sink a merchant ship, for example, and came up with techniques even better than those actually used by the Germans. The staff's studies addressed larger questions of strategy and tactics and defined doctrine in such matters as anti-submarine warfare, mine laying, cooperation with Allied naval services, and control of the North Sea. The studies were disseminated to both American and British naval officers and, wrote Sims, "had a considerable influence on operations."[26] As the American member of the Allied Naval Council, he was able to ensure that the work of the Planning Section was not merely filed and forgotten.

Like the Naval War College thirty years before, the Planning Staff discovered that the validity of its gaming exercises depended upon accurate intelligence, and the staff looked to the Intelligence Department to fill this need.

"If the desired information was not in [the Intelligence Department's] files," Sims later wrote, "or the files of the Allied admiralties, or was not up to date, it was [the Intelligence Department's] duty to obtain it at once."[27]

Sims's Intelligence Department probably got most of its information, and the best of it, from British Naval Intelligence. Sims also relied upon American naval attachés abroad, however. Unwilling to let their information first be filtered through the ONI in Washington, he wrested agreement from the chief of naval operations that the attachés' reports should be sent directly to him "so that I can collate them, compare them with the secret [i.e., British] information here, and send through what we consider to be the correct dope."[28] Thus did Sims make his Intelligence Department a fully autonomous positive naval intelligence service independent of the ONI with the same virtual monopoly on European war-zone intelligence as that enjoyed by Colonel Nolan's AEF G-2.

Captain Roger Welles, who had been made director of the Office of Naval Intelligence a few days before American entry into the war, liked to compare himself to his British counterpart, Admiral Blinker Hall. Whatever bases there may have been for such comparison, they did not include the respective intelligence services the two officers headed. While the British Naval Intelligence Department had been conducting large-scale communications intelligence and secret intelligence collection since 1914, Welles's predecessor, Captain James Harrison Oliver, had spent the intervening years struggling simply to overcome the anti-intelligence mood then prevailing in the Wilson administration and to rescue the office once again from relegation to the role of central reference service.

When Admiral Sims appropriated European naval intelligence jurisdiction for his own Intelligence Department, Captain Welles, like Van Deman, was left with the domestic countersubversion and counterespionage functions. This proved more than sufficient to keep the small ONI staff busy, however, for there were plenty of purely navy facilities—naval stations, shipyards, and factories with navy contracts—beyond the security responsibilities of the MIS or the Bureau of Investigation. To handle this new wartime work load, Welles turned to volunteers and reservists, and he did so with the enthusiastic assistance of Assistant Secretary of the Navy Franklin D. Roosevelt, who had organized the Naval Reserve Force a year earlier, and career diplomat Spencer Fayette Eddy.

Like Roosevelt, Eddy was a Harvard graduate and a New York socialite. The two selected other Ivy League graduates with similar social backgrounds, especially fellow members of their golf and tennis clubs. The ONI was soon filled with Wall Street lawyers, financiers, stockbrokers, and other members of the Philadelphia–New York–Boston establishment. Banker Reginald C. Vanderbilt, tobacco heir Griswold Lorillard, and Ralph Pulitzer—son of newspaper magnate Joseph Pulitzer—bore some of the more familiar aristocratic names to be found in the ONI. William Clarkson Van Antwerp, the New York stockbroker who ran an ONI network in Mexico, was another of the Roosevelt-Eddy recruits, as was New York lawyer Warren C. Van Slyke, who headed the ONI's legal section. Roosevelt's Harvard classmate Steuart Davis, who had helped the assistant secretary found the Naval Reserve, became aid for information in the Second Naval District, a crucial counterespionage post.

Captain Welles had no objection to staffing the ONI with newly minted officers whose experience of things nautical usually was limited to yachting. Indeed, he recruited one of the young aristocrats himself. Lieutenant (j.g.) Clifford N. Carver, son of a Long Island shipping tycoon, became the ONI director's personal aide, a position for which he was impressively qualified. The young Princeton graduate had been Colonel House's private secretary during one of the president's Silent Partner's European trips, and just before joining the ONI, he had served as assistant to Bernard Baruch, the influential Wall Street financier now chairing the War Industries Board, a panel responsible for the wartime mobilization of American industry.

Carver's value to Welles went beyond his skills as a man Friday. The ONI director was a frequent guest at the Carver estate on Long Island, where he came to be on familiar terms with Colonel House and other influential members of the northeastern establishment. Welles thereby obtained access to levels of national power far higher than those normally available to the director of a unit within the staff of the chief of naval operations.

The *Social Register* alone could not fill all of the ONI's wartime personnel needs, of course. Welles presided over a far-flung domestic security apparatus that covered the East and West coasts, the Gulf Coast, and the Great Lakes. Each of the thirteen naval districts in the continental United States had an aide for information, an ONI officer in charge of local security matters. With a staff of civilian employees and naval personnel, each aide was responsible for a variety of security functions, from running informant networks to inspecting ships in port. The largest such staff was in New York, where four hundred ONI personnel searched every ship entering the harbor and kept watch for a recurrence of the kind of ship-sabotage operation Rintelen had run so successfully in 1915–16. Most of the foot soldiers in this huge countersubversion force were not Ivy Leaguers but the same sort of ordinary folk who filled the rank and file of the MIS and the American Protective League.

The ONI spy catchers sometimes exhibited the same excessive zeal that characterized their APL counterparts. A naval officer was investigated because his housekeeper was "German-looking," and a Lutheran clergyman was removed from his post as navy chaplain when ONI investigators discovered that he had once argued the legal basis of Germany's action in sinking the *Lusitania*. Things Teutonic were not the only taboo of the ONI: when a woman stenographer employed by the navy organized her coworkers to press for pay equal to that of men doing the same work, the ONI's close scrutiny of her private life led to her dismissal.[29]

The nastiest and most irrational manifestation of the xenophobic mania was the ONI's reported distrust of Jews: a Jewish dentist was dishonorably discharged from the navy simply because he came from a section of New York inhabited by "German and Hungarian Jews," while non-Jewish officers fell under suspicion because they had married "Jewesses." For many of the socially prominent Anglo-Saxon Protestants now in the upper echelons of the ONI, such bias in an armed service of the United States seemed no more inappropriate than the anti-Jewish exclusionary policies of their country clubs and yachting clubs.[30]

Although Admiral Sims had preempted naval intelligence in the war zone and even subordinated to himself attaché reporting from elsewhere in Europe, Welles managed to mount an impressive ONI positive-intelligence program in Latin America and the Far East. Mexico, of course, remained a high-priority intelligence target. William Van Antwerp, the erstwhile New York stockbroker now running the ONI branch office in San Francisco, had an extensive secret intelligence network south of the border, and Welles himself dispatched agents to Mexico to search for German U-boat bases and wireless stations. Other ONI agents traveling in guises ranging from agricultural researcher to mining engineer made covert reconnaissances of suspected German activity in the Caribbean and Central and South America. Commander Edward Breck, the Heidelberg-educated fencing champion who had gone into Spain for the ONI in the guise of a German doctor during the Spanish-American War, again posed successfully as a German, this time in Brazil and Argentina, where he penetrated local German émigré communities and diplomatic legations, The naval attaché in Havana, Carlos V. Cusachs, broke up a German espionage network headed by Herman and Albert Upmann, prominent German-born businessmen in Cuba.[31]

As secret intelligence agents in the Far East, Welles recruited Americans with legitimate professional reasons to visit the region. A buyer for Bonwit Teller and Company collected intelligence for the ONI while she toured Asia on a clothes-buying trip, the curator of mammals at the American Museum of Natural History reported to Welles from China, and a salesman for a Rhode Island manufacturer reported to the ONI from the Orient through his home office.[32] The object of most of this covert attention was Japan, of course; the fact that Japan was on the Allied side did not allay American fears of a postwar confrontation with her in East Asia or even Mexico.

Lieutenant Commander Frederick J. Horne, the attaché in Tokyo, hoped to establish a secret intelligence network in Japan but was thwarted by Japanese suspicions and the closed character of Japanese society. Nonetheless, Horne's efforts marked the beginning of an ONI program that was to continue for twenty years, as we will see, and pay rich dividends in the Second World War.

Although Welles's elaborate foreign-intelligence apparatus was destined to be dismantled with the cessation of hostilities, he had put the ONI permanently in a business it had known only sporadically in the past: overseas secret intelligence operations. Perhaps even more significant in the long term, however, was the contribution of the spy buff and naval enthusiast Assistant Secretary Franklin D. Roosevelt: the transformation of secret intelligence work from the status of a necessary evil about which the less said the better into a profession properly pursued by gentlemen.

From the very beginning some of America's most important spies and spy masters had been Ivy Leaguers, of course. Nathan Hale and Benjamin Tallmadge graduated from Yale, as did Civil War spy masters George H. Sharpe and William Norris. George B. English, the eccentric ex-marine who turned Muslim and spied for John Quincy Adams in the Turkish court, was a Harvard graduate. Harvard was also the alma mater of James Lovell, the Revolutionary War code breaker. And both Ralph Van Deman and his successor, Marlborough Churchill, were Harvard men.

Each of these people found his own individual way into intelligence work, led there by wartime exigency or, in Van Deman's case, a vision of the critical importance of intelligence in military affairs. Whatever stigma may have attached in their minds to a job that demanded complete secrecy and often involved ruthlessness, deception, the solicitation of trust and then its betrayal, or the violation of personal privacy was overbalanced by the vital needs of the nation they served—a "peculiar service" in the words of Nathan Hale, made honorable only by "the exigencies of my country."

The clubbable young aristocrats who flocked to the ONI in answer to Roosevelt's call had a different view of the secret world of intelligence, however. Perhaps finding in themselves reflections of the aristocratic heroes who populated the then-popular spy novels of E. Phillips Oppenheim, they saw glamour in things their Victorian fathers and grandfathers would have deemed dishonorable. If there were any lingering doubts of the propriety and respectability of the cloak-and-dagger trade, they were dispelled by the call of the assistant secretary of the navy, himself a quintessential specimen of the northeastern establishment.

It would be overstating matters to attribute this sudden elevation of the world's second oldest profession entirely to the intervention of Franklin Roosevelt, of course. Frank Polk, Richard Crane, Gordon Auchincloss—the well-bred young men who ran intelligence operations for the State Department—had left their lofty posts in business and law for government service long before the assistant secretary issued his call. It is likely that they—and Roosevelt as well—had lately come to a new view of the world, a view shaped by the terrible advent of total warfare. No holds were barred in a conflict in which civilian populations were bombed by airships and the death of women and children was a "regrettable" but unavoidable consequence of submarine warfare.

There were no longer any rules. Pragmatism displaced chivalry. If it was permitted to gas an enemy, to crush him with tanks, to bury him alive in a trench with an artillery round, it would be fatuous indeed to stickle at the honorable treachery of espionage.

The transformation of intelligence into a gentleman's profession, fully as acceptable to polite company as banking, finance, or law, was an important turning. While most of Roosevelt's young patricians returned to civilian life after the war, their experience of the secret life had become an integral element of their understanding of the ways of the world. Intelligence would no longer be an underworld alien to the ethic of their class.

For those who were henceforth to run the American intelligence establishment, this new legitimacy meant an end to the isolation that had separated men like Van Deman from the highest levels of national power. The epitome of the new spy master was Captain Welles, rubbing shoulders with Colonel House and other American oligarchs on weekends at the Carver family estate.

It would take time for all of this to be fully realized. Social change does not take place overnight, but it is accelerated by war. Two decades would elapse before the intelligence establishment would complete its ascendancy, through another world war. When national exigency again legitimized ruthlessness, the secret services of the United States would once more call upon some of the best and the brightest to fight in the shadows.

Chapter Twenty-five
The Russian Muddle

The cruiser U.S.S. *Olympia* is best known as the flagship of Admiral George Dewey in the Battle of Manila Bay on May 1, 1898. Much more obscure, however, is the fact that she steamed into the Russian port of Murmansk almost exactly twenty years later or that a detachment of fifty men from her crew went ashore at Archangel on August 3, 1918, and engaged the Red Army in combat. Thus began a strange two-year escapade of American arms in Russia, an episode all but forgotten by Americans yet remembered and cherished as an anti-American grievance by the authors of Soviet history books.

American amnesia regarding our participation in the Allied intervention in Russia in 1918–19 is not born of shame, however, but of incomprehension. Major General William S. Graves, an American officer who was a principal in the affair, declared shortly thereafter, "I was in command of the United States troops sent to Siberia and I must admit, I do not know what the United States was trying to accomplish by military intervention." [1] Indeed, the immensely complex sequence of events that led to the adventure still nearly defies comprehension even in the light of historical investigation. [2] One thing emerges clearly, however: the entire episode was the result of a monumental intelligence failure by the Wilson administration.

Soon after the Bolsheviks took over in Russia in November 1917, the British and French began pressing for Allied intervention. The chief purpose of such a move was to return Russia to the war, or at least re-open the eastern front. The British had an additional objective: the suppression of bolshevism.

Neither the British nor French could spare forces for such an undertaking, but they knew that Japan, which already controlled southern Manchuria, was eager to extend her control to northern Manchuria and Siberia. The Japanese were unwilling to send troops into Siberia, however, without the approval and even the financial aid of the United States. Thus, President Wilson was the key to the matter, and the British were not long in attempting to obtain his assent through their agent of influence within the Wilson administration, Sir William Wiseman.

Initially confident of his ability to bring Colonel House, and thereby the president, around to the idea of endorsing the proposed intervention, Sir William soon discovered that both men were adamantly opposed to it. *Intervention* was a dirty word in the White House; the president and his adviser had not failed to learn the bitter lesson of their Mexican adventure. Furthermore, Wilson was, at first, not at all opposed to the Bolsheviks, and he cherished the hope that they would eventually turn away from their early revolutionary excesses and establish a democratic government. Indeed, Sir William was dismayed to learn from House that he and Wilson were seriously entertaining the idea of recognizing the Bolshevik regime, hoping thereby to undermine German influence over Russia.[3]

The situation in Russia was confused and chaotic following the Bolshevik coup in Petrograd. Lenin, Trotsky, Stalin, and the leaders of other Bolshevik factions jockeyed among themselves for control of the new regime. Lacking popular support, the Bolsheviks found it necessary to create the Cheka (All-Russian Extraordinary Commission to Combat Counterrevolution and Sabotage), a ruthless secret police, to suppress dissent. Anti-Bolshevik forces—the White Russians and the Cossacks—rallied in the peripheral reaches of the old Russian empire during the winter of 1917–18 and prepared to attack the Red Army in central Russia, touching off a civil war that was to last two years.

Although the Bolsheviks had concluded an armistice with Germany, the danger that Germany would intervene in Russia remained a concern until the two countries signed a peace treaty (Brest-Litovsk) in March 1918. Even afterward the presence in Russia of some 1.6 million German and Austrian former prisoners of war inspired fears among the Allies of a potential German military presence in the country.

The POWs were not the only alien military presence in Russia. The Czech Legion—originally seventy thousand troops from the Czech colonies of the old Russian empire and Czech defectors from the Austro-Hungarian army—had been an integral unit of the Russian army before the revolution. Afterward, as the czarist army collapsed amidst the revolutionary chaos, the legion remained intact and was thereafter recognized by the Allies as an Allied army, formally subordinated to the French supreme command. Unable to support single-handedly an eastern front, the Czechs wished to join the French on the western front. In March the legion began to move over the only route out of Russia left open to them—across Siberia to the Pacific port of Vladivostok and thence by sea to France. Two months later, when fifteen thousand of the Czechs had arrived in Vladivostok and the remaining forty thousand were strung out along the Trans-Siberian Railroad, relations between the Czechs and the Soviets broke down and fighting erupted. Joined by the White Russian Army, the Czechs soon took control of the three thousand miles of railroad between the Volga River and the Siberian city of Irkutsk. The two thousand miles between Irkutsk and Vladivostok remained under Bolshevik control, however; the Czech Legionnaires to the west of Irkutsk were thus blocked from proceeding to the Pacific.

There was one more aspect of the Russian situation that was of particular concern to Wilson and the other Allied leaders. In the months before the Bolshevik coup, the Allies had delivered great quantities of war material to Vladivostok and the northern Russian ports of Murmansk and Archangel. The inefficient Russian railway system had been inadequate in delivering these goods to the czarist army, so they remained where they had been stacked when off-loaded. In Archangel alone, some 160,000 tons awaited transportation. The material included metals and other commodities already in short supply on the western front; moreover, the goods had been bought on credit by the czarist government, but the Bolsheviks renounced any responsibility for their payment. But the most critical aspect of the situation was the danger that the material would fall into German and Austro-Hungarian hands to be used against the Allies. Given that interdiction of the Central Powers' supply lines seemed one of the few strategic factors likely to bring an end to the war, the Allies were understandably anxious about the ultimate disposition of the material.

Regarding this chaotic and constantly changing situation, Colonel House and the president received frequent reports, some of them accurate, some of them inaccurate or misleading, and some of them completely untrue. In the absence of any organization responsible for analyzing and correlating national intelligence—that is, the intelligence upon which the president must base national policy decisions—Wilson composed his view of events by selecting among the available data pretty much according to his own momentary disposition. Thus, for example, he abandoned his early inclination to recognize the Bolshevik regime, not because of its demonstrated brutality (about which he was probably incompletely informed), but because documents obtained from clandestine sources by Edgar Sisson, an official of the Committee on Public Information sent to Russia to disseminate white (i.e., overt) American propaganda, "proved conclusively" that Trotsky and Lenin were paid agents of the German government. Neither Sisson nor Wilson had the technical competence to determine whether these documents were forgeries, which, of course, they were.[4]

British intelligence, that mainstay of national intelligence in the Wilson White House, could not be viewed as an entirely reliable and objective source in the Russian matter, since the British so strongly advocated intervention. Colonel House, normally among the most Anglophilic of Americans, worried when Wilson invited Sir William to visit the White House, presumably to discuss intervention, and sent the president a letter strongly urging against the step. House no longer enjoyed his earlier degree of influence with the president; the second Mrs. Wilson, whom the president had married in December 1915, was hostile toward the Silent Partner and was increasingly undermining his position in the White House. The Colonel therefore resorted to trying to co-opt Sir William by dangling before him the prospect of the British ambassadorship in Washington, a thing that House's support could very well help realize.[5] The British intelligence officer resisted this temptation but nonetheless made little progress in changing the president's mind on the Russian question.

Wilson was as strongly opposed as House to intervention in Russia, and Secretary of State Lansing (whose opinions would probably have been ignored by the president in any case) agreed with both of them. Of the three, Lansing's opposition was the best informed. His knowledge of the situation in Russia was by far the best, for he had at least one secret intelligence agent who had been reporting to him from that country for the past four years.

While still counselor of the State Department in 1914, Lansing had recruited, through an intermediary, Xenophon Dmitrevich de Blumenthal Kalamatiano, a Greek-American with strong connections in czarist Russia. A native of Vienna, Kalamatiano was raised in Russia, Switzerland, and the United States. After graduating from the University of Chicago in 1903, he taught Russian there for several years before returning to Russia as a representative of the Case Company, a Wisconsin farm-machinery manufacturer. He later broke away from Case and became the independent agent in Russia for some thirty American and European firms.

Kalamatiano, whose mother's family had close ties to the Romanovs, married a Russian woman who was a member of the czarina's court. A year later, in 1914, while in the United States on a family matter, he was informally approached by Lansing's representative and asked to report to the counselor whatever court gossip he chanced to overhear. Kalamatiano agreed and began reporting to Lansing through a New York office he set up, ostensibly to service his American clients but actually as a mail drop. With American entry into the war in 1917, his intelligence role was expanded and formalized, and he was given an annual State Department salary of twenty-four hundred dollars. Lansing provided him with additional funds to hire subagents and open safe houses. Since wartime conditions made it impractical for him to continue to report through his New York mail drop, he was assigned a case officer: DeWitt Clinton Poole, a foreign-service officer attached to the American legation.[6] (Poole, who became chargé d'affaires after the Bolshevik takeover, served as an intelligence officer with the Office of Strategic Services in the Second World War and worked for the Central Intelligence Agency afterward.)

With the benefit of Kalamatiano's intelligence reports (and other intelligence assets in the country), Lansing acquired an early insight into the nature of the Bolshevik regime. He knew, for example, that the Sisson documents linking the Bolshevik leaders to the German government were bogus; Lenin and Trotsky were, in his view, "honest in purpose and utterly dishonest in methods." He did not share in the illusion of Wilson and House that recognition of the new regime might eventually lead Russia back into the alliance; to deal with the Bolsheviks, he maintained, would only spread the anti-democratic Communist virus. He foresaw the Bolshevik reign of terror, correctly predicting that the Russian Revolution would follow the course of the French Revolution, and he urged the president—unsuccessfully—to issue a policy statement condemning the Bolsheviks. But he opposed intervention on the grounds that an invasion of the Russian motherland, especially by a Japanese army, would tend to rally otherwise anti-Bolshevik Russians to the new regime.[7]

There were actually two separate Allied proposals for intervention in Russia. One concerned the use of Japanese troops in eastern Siberia, and the second envisioned landings by British, French, and American forces in northern Russia to safeguard the military stores at Archangel and Murmansk. Allied concern over the stores at Archangel heightened in February when the Bolsheviks, on the verge of completing their peace treaty with the Central Powers, began transporting the material inland from the port. There was nothing to be done immediately, since the port was frozen and therefore inaccessible, but in June the British went ahead, without waiting for American approval, and landed six hundred troops in Murmansk and occupied the port.

President Wilson meanwhile continued to entertain British appeals that the United States contribute troops to help occupy the two northern Russian ports. His intelligence of the situation in Archangel and Murmansk was poor. He was unaware of the British landing and occupation of the latter port and, therefore, of the fact that it had brought Allied relations with the Bolsheviks to a crisis. He believed the war material in question was at Murmansk, when in fact the largest quantity of stores had been delivered to Archangel and most of it had now been transported inland.[8] Perhaps most important, he did not know that the British envisioned something considerably more than the occupation of the two ports: they planned a move inland to link up with the Czech Legion and other anti-Bolshevik forces, all coordinated with the proposed Japanese invasion of eastern Siberia.[9] Apparently, Lansing was equally ignorant of most or all of these salient facts.

The one American agent best able to inform the Wilson administration of the actual situation was the United States consul in Archangel, Felix

Cole, and near the end of May he set about to do just that. "Intervention," he predicted, "will begin on a small scale but with each step forward will grow in scope and in its demands for ships, men, money and materials."[10]

To hold Archangel, he explained, it would be necessary also to hold part of the rail line leading southward from the port and part of the Dvina River, the two major routes to the seaport. But since the military stores had been moved inland, it would be necessary to occupy the railroad to Vologda and beyond, a distance of several hundred miles, and to control the river as far south as Kotlas, three hundred miles upstream.

"This means," Cole pointed out, "not the mere occupation of Archangel, but an expedition into the interior of Russia. . . . Every foreign invasion that has gone deep into Russia has been swallowed up. . . . If we intervene, going farther into Russia as we succeed, we shall be swallowed up."[11]

Cole mailed his report to Lansing from Archangel on June 1 and sent a copy of it to David R. Francis, the American ambassador to the czar's court, now in Vologda with the embassy staff waiting for the situation in Russia to stabilize. Francis, who despised the Bolsheviks, was an avid proponent of intervention, and he therefore did not trouble to hasten Cole's report on to Washington by cable. As a result, the dispatch did not reach Lansing until July 19, and by then it was too late to do any good. Wilson had decided in favor of intervention two days earlier.

The plight of the Czech Legion, as perceived by Wilson, had proved decisive. At about the time Consul Cole was drafting his report, the first clashes began between the Czechs and the Soviets in central Siberia. By early June Wilson had learned that most of the Czech Legion was stranded west of Irkutsk. Late in June the Czechs who had reached Vladivostok seized the city and appealed to the Allies for support in opening up the rail route to Irkutsk and rescuing their comrades. At a White House meeting held on July 5, Wilson decided on a joint Japanese-American expedition to join in getting immediate supplies of arms and ammunition to the Czechs at Vladivostok and in making available a military force to guard their line of communication as they moved westward.

Wilson's decision was rooted in misinformation. He believed, first of all, that the force standing between the Czechs in central Siberia and their comrades in Vladivostok was composed of the German and Austrian former prisoners of war, or, in other words, troops of the Central Powers. In the light of that misapprehension and the fact that the Czechs were officially part of the Allied armies, the situation seemed a clear-cut extension of the war America was already fighting. In addition, he believed the Czech Legion still intended to join the Allies on the western front; in fact, the Czechs, with British and French approval, planned to remain in Russia to fight alongside the White Russians against the Bolsheviks.

Although Wilson, in his dealings with the other Allied leaders over the Russian question, had always made a point of distinguishing between the question of the northern ports and that of eastern Siberia as two separate matters, he now decided also to acquiesce to British appeals for American help in occupying Murmansk and Archangel, agreeing to release three battalions from the western front for this purpose, providing Marshal Ferdinand Foch, the supreme commander in Europe, agreed that they could be spared. On July 17 he composed an aide-mémoire detailing his aims in the two Russian interventions.

This curious document denied that the United States was intervening in Russia and went so far as to recite the reasons the government opposed such intervention. It specifically limited American military action to the guarding of the military stores and "to help[ing] the Czecho-Slovaks consolidate their forces and get into successful cooperation with their Slavic kinsmen," as well as to assisting the Russians in defending themselves, presumably from the Central Powers.[12]

Secretary of War Baker carried a copy of the document to Kansas City, where he met briefly in the railroad station with Major General William S. Graves, the officer appointed to command the Siberian Expeditionary Force. As Graves climbed aboard a train departing on the first westward leg of his journey to Vladivostok, Baker pressed the paper into his hand and called out, "This contains the policy of the United States in Russia which you are to follow. Watch your step; you will be walking on eggs loaded with dynamite."[13] Like the occupation of Veracruz and the punitive expedition against Villa in Mexico, the Siberian military expedition had been dispatched on a highly sensitive politico-military mission, and in this case the underlying intelligence was even more deficient than in the earlier undertakings.

* * *

When General Graves arrived in Vladivostok with the major part of the American force on September 1, he discovered that the Czechs, supported by a large Japanese expedition, had already broken through to their compatriots west of Irkutsk. The principal objective of the American expedition was therefore already achieved. As to the planned evacuation of the Czechs through Vladivostok to France, that had, of course, been canceled, or at least postponed indefinitely, while the Czechs joined the Russian civil war on the side of the White Army. As to the military stores at Vladivostok, the commander of the large British contingent of the Allied expedition crisply informed Graves that they had been purchased with British money, were therefore British property, and he required no assistance (or interference) from the Americans in seeing to their disposition, thank you very much. Realizing that his brief, as detailed in Wilson's aide-mémoire of July 17, had been fully discharged, Graves saw that he had virtually nothing to do but help guard the Trans-Siberian Railroad against the German and Austrian former prisoners of war, who now seemed most conspicuous by their absence. He therefore settled down to await orders from Washington recalling the American force from Siberia, an abeyance destined to endure through all of the following year and part of 1920.

In the meantime, the tide of civil war turned in central Siberia. The White Army, together with its Czech allies, was pushed back and eventually collapsed. The Czechs appealed to Graves for help, which of course he could not give under the terms of Wilson's aide-mémoire. The Czechs, who understood only that the Americans claimed to have come to Siberia to help them, found this impossible to comprehend; thus did Wilson's gesture of friendship and loyalty ironically boomerang, creating only bitterness among the people he had believed he was rescuing. The Czech Legion did eventually complete its withdrawal from Siberia, but obviously it would have succeeded in doing so even without the presence of the American force in Vladivostok.

As to the fate of the Allied force in northern Russia, including three American battalions, it fulfilled nearly to the letter Consul Cole's prophesy. Under the overall command of a British general, the expedition struck southward along the railway and the Dvina River, not only because this was necessary to hold Archangel and attempt to recover the military stores, but because the British master strategy called for a thrust to the Trans-Siberian Railroad and a linking up with the Czech and White armies. It failed to accomplish this, of course, and after an autumn of bitter fighting and an equally bitter Russian winter, the American battalions were withdrawn in June 1919, although the British and other Allied troops remained until September. Of some 500 Allied troops killed in this generally futile effort, 139 were Americans.

Forewarned of the impending landing in Archangel, the Allied ambassadors fled the country a few days earlier. The junior military and consular staffs in Petrograd and Moscow did not receive the same consideration, however, and hundreds of them were rounded up and thrown in prison by the Cheka. Captain Francis N. A. Cromie, the British naval attaché in Petrograd who had been running a secret intelligence network inside the Russian navy, was murdered, ostensibly by an enraged Bolshevik mob; in fact, his network had been penetrated by Chekist agents.[14]

On September 18 DeWitt C. Poole, the American consul and chargé d'affaires in Moscow who was also Xenophon Kalamatiano's case officer, slipped past the Chekist guards surrounding the American consulate and escaped from the city. On the twentieth he crossed the Finnish frontier ten minutes ahead of his arrest warrant.[15]

Unaware of Poole's departure from Moscow, Kalamatiano visited the consulate no more than a few hours later with some letters and other information for him. He was immediately arrested by the Cheka. Feliks Edmundovich Dzerzhinsky, the cunning head of the Cheka, had an agent within the consulate, a former spy of the czarist secret police whom Dzerzhinsky had coerced into working for him a year earlier; from about October 1917 onward Dzerzhinsky had read all of Kalamatiano's intelligence reports.

The Cheka rolled up Kalamatiano's network and put him and his subagents on trial. Kalamatiano and his principal subagent, Lieutenant Colonel Alexandr Friede, a Russian officer, were sentenced to death. Friede was shot, but Kalamatiano was confined in Lubianka, the infamous Chekist prison, apparently on the orders of Lenin, who saw him as a potential pawn in dealing with the United States. The Wilson administration was unwilling to acknowledge Kalamatiano's role, however, and when Wilson fired Secretary of State Lansing in February 1920, the agent's fate appeared to be sealed. The famine already afflicting Russia was greatly worsened by a drought in the Ukraine that year, however, and when Lenin turned to the American Relief Commission for help, its director, Herbert Hoover, stipulated that Kalamatiano and other Americans held in Soviet prisons must first be released.

Kalamatiano was freed in August 1921 and returned to the United States. To the administration of President Warren Harding he was nothing but a curious relic of another presidency. After being debriefed by an indifferent State Department, Kalamatiano was paid off and given a railroad ticket to Chicago, where he resumed his work at the university and faded into obscurity.[16]

While Secretary Lansing's current intelligence of Russian events was considerably less than perfect, one must admire his foresight and enterprise in recruiting a principal agent and establishing an intelligence network in Russia in the easygoing atmosphere that prevailed in the State Department before the war. It is to be regretted, however, that he apparently did not have a comprehensive view of the management of the intelligence process—the collection, analysis, and integration of information upon which policy should be based. The case of Consul Felix Cole in Archangel is reminiscent of Frank Mallett, the vice-consul general in Budapest whose prescient forecast of a European war in July 1914 went to waste because the State Department scrimped on cable costs. And one might fault the security measures within the American legation in Russia, which permitted the Kalamatiano network to be penetrated by Soviet intelligence. But such criticism can be made only after acknowledging that these painful lessons, since repeated countless times, apparently still remain to be learned by the American foreign service more than seventy years later.

Notwithstanding such hindsight, it seems doubtful that Secretary Lansing's intelligence apparatus would have prevented Wilson's Russian blunders even had it been far more efficient and effective. It seems that in any case, Wilson was unalterably disposed to ignore his formal foreign-policy apparatus and to rely in such matters entirely upon his own views and those of his adviser, Colonel House. His extensive consultation with Lansing regarding Russian policy undoubtedly proceeded from the fact that the secretary of state happened to share, first, his opposition to Allied intervention schemes and, finally, his rationale for intervention. Had Lansing's intelligence been better regarding the situations in Siberia and northern Russia, it seems likely that Wilson would have chosen to ignore it.

It may not be completely unfair to blame Wilson's Russian blunder on British foreign policy in general and British intelligence in particular. After all, the Wilson administration had good reason to respect the judgment of its British ally in such matters, even though it initially resisted British invitations to intervene. One may only lament British failure to devise a more effective scheme for realizing their objectives in Russia. As Winston Churchill reflected many years later: "The day will come when it will be recognized without doubt throughout the civilized world that the strangling of Bolshevism at birth would have been an untold blessing to the human race."[17]

Chapter Twenty-six

The Inquiry—
Intelligence for
the President

One day in late September 1917 Secretary of War Newton D. Baker called his special assistant, Walter Lippmann, into his office and told him that Colonel House wanted to see him to discuss a secret matter. Lippmann, twenty-eight years old, had been associate editor of the *New Republic* until he joined the War Department three months earlier. He was well acquainted with both House and the president, both of whom held the young journalist in high regard. He met House in front of the State-War-Navy building, which stands on the west side of the White House, and as the two strolled down Pennsylvania Avenue, House proceeded to offer him a job in an entirely new executive agency few people even knew existed.[1]

In mid-July Felix Frankfurter, another of Secretary Baker's bright young assistants, had suggested to Wilson the creation of a planning organization to prepare American policy for the peace conference that would inevitably follow the cessation of hostilities. Wilson picked up on the idea and, in early September, told House he wanted a systematic study of the terms each of the Allies would be likely to insist on when the time came to negotiate a peace treaty with the Central Powers.[2] He asked House to gather together a group of specialists to address the problem. This was the genesis of a curious and little-known executive agency, known only by the somewhat cryptic name the Inquiry.

The mission Wilson gave to the new agency was no small or simple task. Most of the great nineteenth-century territorial settlements among the European powers had been disrupted by the war. Both the Allies and the Central Powers had entered into a crazy quilt of secret treaties among themselves to establish wartime alliances. Italy, for example, had been induced to abrogate her treaty commitments to Germany and Austria-Hungary and join the war on the Allied side through a secret treaty promising her territory at the expense of Austria-Hungary, a "just share" of the Ottoman Empire in Asia, and other blandishments. Romania joined the Allies on the basis of a similar secret agreement. And the Central Powers recruited Bulgaria to their side with the promise of Serbian Macedonia and a substantial sum of money.

The web of secret wartime treaties was so extensive that no one nation had a complete picture of the secret deals that had been cut, even on its own side. It was clear, however, that many of the secret treaties were mutually inconsistent and that reconciliation of the situation would be an extremely difficult diplomatic task of any conference aimed at securing a lasting peace.[3]

While it would obviously be impossible for the Inquiry to learn the full details of all the secret treaties in force, it could hope to establish just what were the war aims and expectations of the belligerents; to document the geographic, ethnic, economic, or legal bases for those objectives; and to identify possible arrangements that might be proposed to settle conflicting claims. Since the anticipated territorial disputes involved not only boundaries between European nations but the colonial territories of the belligerents in Africa, the Middle East, Asia, and even Latin America, the major work of the Inquiry was to be the collection and compilation of a truly enormous body of information about the world—basic intelligence in today's parlance.

To organize and direct this ambitious undertaking, House selected Sidney E. Mezes, the president of the City College of New York. Although Mezes's scholarly specialty had little applicability to the task—he was a philosopher of religion—his considerable administrative background—he had been dean and president of the University of Texas before joining CCNY—recommended him to lead and direct the work of the Inquiry. Mezes possessed an additional qualification that gave him preference over all other deans and college presidents: he was Colonel House's brother-in-law. House's predilection for placing relatives such as Gordon Auchincloss and Mezes in key foreign-policy positions in the Wilson administration was not crass nepotism—people in House's social circle did not need government employment—but a means of ensuring that the jobs were held by people he could trust and, perhaps, control.

Wilson approved Mezes's selection but also urged House to recruit Walter Lippmann as secretary of the new agency. A former university president himself, the president may have feared that the fifty-four-year-old Mezes might tend toward the stodgy and conservative and thought that Lippmann, whose reputation was somewhat that of a young progressive radical, would provide a counterweight.[4] For his part, Lippmann viewed the job as ideal and vastly preferable to his post in the War Department, so he accepted House's offer immediately.

House cautioned Mezes, Lippmann, and others he invited into the agency to keep its existence a profound secret. He and the president wanted to avoid public speculation and false hopes that creation of the agency reflected an imminent end to hostilities when, in fact, the foreseeable future held only the prospect of more bitter combat. To maintain as low a profile as possible, Wilson paid for the Inquiry out of his Contingent Fund (known in 1917 as the president's Fund for National Safety and Defense)[5] and directed that it not be housed in Washington. Headquarters of the Inquiry was initially established in a remote corner of the New York Public Library, where its presence was known only to the head librarian and one associate. A month or so later the growing agency moved uptown to the offices of the American Geographical Society at Broadway and West 155th Street; the society's director, Isaiah Bowman, kept its presence secret even from the society's board of directors. Columbia University historian James T. Shotwell, one of House's early recruits, struck upon the idea of naming the agency the Inquiry, which, he said, would be a "blind to the general public, but would serve to identify it among the initiated."[6]

Shotwell, who became the Inquiry's director of research, typified the staff. He was not only an academic but had been recruited from the faculty of an Ivy League university. Geography, economics, modern languages, and, especially, history were the disciplines best represented on the Inquiry staff. The study of recent history was not fashionable in academic circles of the time, nor was specialization in the history and languages of the non-Western world. Thus, some of the Inquiry's recruits were, for example, medievalists or students of ancient history; their general scholarly training was the only asset they could offer.

Charles H. Haskins had been a professor of medieval history at Harvard before supervising the work of the Inquiry's Northwest Europe Division.

Wallace Notestein taught English history at the University of Minnesota and had published a *History of English Witchcraft* four years before he became the Inquiry's expert on that Franco-German bone of contention, Alsace-Lorraine. Samuel Eliot Morison, destined to become a famous chronicler of American naval history in later life, had been an instructor in American history at Harvard before becoming an Inquiry specialist in Finland and the Baltic States.

Not all of the staffers were so lacking in a specific background applicable to the work of the Inquiry, however. Archibald Cary Coolidge, who had taught eastern European and Middle Eastern history at Harvard, had also published a diplomatic history of the United States before joining the Inquiry as chief of its Eastern European Division. Charles Seymour, an assistant professor of history at Yale, had published *The Diplomatic Background of the War* the year before he joined the Inquiry and became its specialist on nationalist problems within the Austro-Hungarian Empire. Columbia geologist Douglas W. Johnson had published *Topography and Strategy in the War* earlier in 1917; he worked as a cartographer for the Inquiry and served as liaison officer with the British and French governments.

The notion that scholars could be put to use solving practical problems of government had been introduced in Washington by President Wilson and, of course, came naturally to the former president of Princeton University. The United States Tariff Commission, the Interstate Commerce Commission, the Federal Trade Commission, and the Federal Reserve Board had been thickly populated with former academics long before the Inquiry was established. Army and navy officers of a scholarly bent seemed attracted to intelligence work long before Wilson took office, of course (one thinks especially of the navy captain French E. Chadwick, a sailor-scholar who headed the ONI in 1892–93 and later wrote a definitive two-volume history of the Spanish-American War). But the idea of drafting scholars directly from the campus and putting them to work in the analysis and production of finished foreign political intelligence was a departure from past practice, in which such work was usually done (when it was done at all) by diplomats whose academic training was frequently in law.

The Inquiry staff did include several lawyers, however. One, David Hunter Miller, was in charge of the agency's financial accounts, but he also was a major contributor to the Inquiry's studies of international law.

He actually had had no background in international law prior to joining the Department of State earlier in 1917, but he brought to that job and the one he held in the Inquiry another sort of qualification: he had been the law partner of Gordon Auchincloss, Colonel House's son-in-law.

The background of prospective recruits was investigated by the Bureau of Investigation. Several excellent candidates were rejected on the basis of derogatory or questionable information turned up in these checks, some of it rather flimsy. Chandler P. Anderson, a former counselor of the State Department, was turned down after a background check despite the fact that he had been recommended to the Inquiry by Secretary of State Lansing.

Relations between the Inquiry and the Department of State remained cordial, even though Secretary Lansing had quite reasonably expected President Wilson to establish the Inquiry as an agency of the State Department. The State Department forwarded copies of consular reports to the Inquiry and furnished whatever else was requested and was within the department's power to obtain. This fell far short of providing all the required intelligence, however; the State Department had no systematic intelligence-collection apparatus, so the Inquiry was constrained to turn to other sources.

The Inquiry received information from the Military Intelligence Division and eleven other units of the United States government (with the curious exception of the Office of Naval Intelligence). The agency's sources in the private sector included the National Geographic Society, the Carnegie Institution, and the Carnegie Endowment for International Peace. The General Rubber Company, the Standard Oil Company of New York, and the American Tobacco Company furnished information to the Inquiry, as did the American Board of Foreign Missions and an assortment of Zionist groups and European ethnic and nationalist associations.[7]

In a few instances, the Inquiry exceeded its charter as an intelligence research and analysis agency and actually sent agents into the field to collect intelligence. The agency borrowed James F. Abbott, a Washington University zoologist working for the MIS, and sent him to Japan to collect intelligence on Japanese business and its influence on Japanese government and foreign policy.[8] This intelligence requirement itself is evidence of how far-ranging and deep were the Inquiry's investigations.

The Inquiry's Eastern European Division chief, Archibald Coolidge, undertook a clandestine mission to Scandinavia to collect German publications. Later he joined Carl W. Blegen, an American archaeologist who was collecting intelligence for the Inquiry in Greece disguised as a Red Cross official. Harvard anthropologist Roland Dixon was preparing to lead a caravan expedition into Central Asia to collect information in November 1918 when the armistice cut short his plans.[9]

The *Comité d'études* was the French counterpart of the Inquiry, while the Political Intelligence Department of the Foreign Office did peace-conference planning for the British government. The Inquiry established liaisons with both agencies by sending geologist Douglas Johnson to Europe. Probably for the purpose of establishing his status rather than for any covert purpose, he went decked out with the rank of major in the United States Army and credentials as an officer of the Military Intelligence Section. Johnson reported back to the MIS and the State Department, as well as to the Inquiry. He found both the French and the British reasonably forthcoming but steeped in mutual suspicion and resolutely uncooperative with each other.[10]

The British were, of course, fully informed of the work of the Inquiry through Sir William Wiseman, who reported to Lord Robert Cecil of the Foreign Office, "It is, as you know, my chief duty here to keep in the closest touch with House and this organization of his."[11] Sir William urged the British foreign secretary, Lord Balfour, to permit him to convey more of the intelligence collected by the Foreign Office peace planners to House in order to obtain greater access to the work of the Inquiry. "It must be clear to you," he told Balfour's secretary, "that when in New York I occupy practically the position of political secretary to House. I think he shows me everything he gets, and together we discuss every question that arises."[12] With Balfour's consent Sir William placed his own personal representative within the Foreign Office's Political Intelligence Department, to keep him fully informed of the work of the British peace planners.

Wiseman had more in mind than a copious exchange of information between the Inquiry and the Political Intelligence Department. He hoped also to influence the work of the Inquiry, bringing its findings into line with British policy and postwar hopes. This he tried to accomplish not simply through House but by direct contact with some of the more influential

Inquiry staffers. George L. Beer, for example, the Inquiry's specialist on African colonial problems, was the recipient of Sir William's presentation of the British case for retaining Germany's African colonies after the war.[13] How successful he may have been in such undertakings remains undetermined; it is always difficult to gauge precisely the effectiveness of an agent of influence.

Neither Sir William nor any other Allied representative seems to have had much influence on what was probably the Inquiry's most important undertaking: the formulation of a policy proposal that led directly to President Wilson's Fourteen Points. Shortly after they took power in November 1917, the Bolsheviks published the secret treaties the czar had signed with the Allies. The purpose of the disclosure was to embarrass the Allied governments, and it certainly had that effect on the Wilson administration. The war, which the president had represented as a noble crusade for the preservation of democracy, was now exposed as a crass land grab by the European powers. Domestic opponents of the war in the United States made much of the Bolshevik disclosure, and public support for the war effort seemed in jeopardy. In order to distance himself from the Allies' territorial designs and put American involvement in the war on a more noble footing, Wilson needed to make an immediate statement of American policy regarding an end to the war. In the second week of December, House told Lippmann to get the Inquiry busy on preparing a policy proposal for the president.

The Inquiry had been in existence for little more than two months at this time and had hardly even become organized to begin its task. House's orders, however, amounted to a requirement that the agency complete its ultimate mission—formulation of an American peace policy—immediately. Obviously, if such an undertaking was to be completed in no more than the few weeks available before the president must make his proposals, the full staff of the Inquiry could not be employed, and the job would have to be done by Lippmann and one or two others. Lippmann organized a team consisting of himself, Inquiry director Mezes, lawyer David H. Miller, and Isaiah Bowman, the director of the American Geographical Society, to carry out the crash project.

Using maps, demographic and economic statistics, and studies of European national political movements, the team attempted to redraw the frontiers of Europe in ways that might grant self-determination to the various ethnic groups without creating new rivalries. In carrying out the task, the team was guided as much as possible by the formerly secret treaties in the hope of making the whole scheme as palatable as possible to the European powers.

Working almost round the clock for three weeks, the team finally produced their report on December 22. House went over the document with the president on Christmas Day and then gave it back to Lippmann with some of Wilson's comments. A revised report was in the president's hands by January 4. To the eight specific recommendations it contained, Wilson added six general recommendations of his own. On the eighth he assembled Congress in a joint session and presented the result, his Fourteen Points designed to appeal directly to the peoples of Europe over the heads of their governments.

The first five points, which had been added by Wilson, addressed such general matters as the need for "open covenants openly arrived at" (a reference to the secret treaties), freedom of the seas, removal of trade barriers, reduction of armaments, and adjustment of colonial claims with equal consideration to both the colonized and the colonizers. Points 6 through 13 were taken almost verbatim from the Inquiry report and treated territorial questions ranging from Russia's right of self-determination through the thorny problem of Alsace Lorraine to the independence of Poland. Point 14, added by the president, called for the establishment of the League of Nations.

The Lippmann team's work went a long way to completing the work of the Inquiry as initially envisioned by the president, but it had been much more a matter of inspiration than the systematic analysis of a vast body of intelligence. The latter task remained if the American delegation to the peace conference was to be adequately equipped with the intelligence needed to support American negotiations and achieve European acceptance of the Fourteen Points. Thus, the work of the Inquiry continued, although it soon became apparent that Lippmann had made his contribution to it.

Neither Sidney Mezes nor Lippmann seems to have been able to deal with the peculiar problems encountered in managing and directing the work of 126 academics (the maximum strength of the Inquiry staff). Mezes stood aside and let Lippmann pretty much run the agency through the winter of 1917–18 and the following spring, but the latter's management style apparently disrupted and disorganized the agency's progress. By June, when the situation was reaching a crisis, Lippmann was fortuitously approached by Captain Heber Blankenhorn, chief of the Psychological Subsection of MI-2, the Foreign Intelligence Section of the MIS.

The Psychological Subsection had been created in February to study enemy propaganda and create counterpropaganda, one of the many additional functions the MIS acquired during 1918. Colonel Van Deman had commissioned Blankenhorn, a former city editor of the New York *Evening Sun*, and put him in charge of the new unit.[14] Blankenhorn recruited six other communicators to help him, including Charles Merz, the *New Republic*'s Washington correspondent, and Yale Drama School instructor Edgar Montillion Woolley, better known later as Monty Woolley, the comedy character actor in dozens of Hollywood films. He proposed adding Lippmann to the group.

Blankenhorn explained to Lippmann that he needed someone who understood the politics of Germany and Austria-Hungary to explain Wilson's Fourteen Points to the peoples of those and other European countries. Specifically, he wanted Lippmann to accept a commission in MIS's MI-2, then go to London to serve as the American representative on an Inter-Allied Propaganda Board. Furthermore, he wanted him to act as liaison between MI-2 and the Inquiry in order that the propaganda unit could make use of the intelligence produced by the latter agency for psychological-warfare purposes.[15]

Lippmann accepted almost immediately, and the move was warmly endorsed by Colonel House, who was of course well aware that the young man was proving less than ideal as the Inquiry's de facto director. The Inquiry staff was at first pleased to be rid of Lippmann, but after a few weeks of working under Mezes's direction, most of the staff threatened to quit. After a few weeks of impending mutiny, House intervened and put Isaiah Bowman in charge of the Inquiry while returning Mezes to his role of figurehead.[16] The agency then achieved a degree of orderliness and tranquillity it had not previously enjoyed.

*   *   *

On November 29, eighteen days after the armistice brought an end to the
fighting, President Wilson announced the names of the peace commissioners who would accompany him to Paris for the peace conference: Colonel
House, Secretary of State Lansing, General Tasker H. Bliss, and Henry
White, a career diplomat and the sole Republican on the peace commission. Some members of the Inquiry were selected to join the small army
of staffers accompanying the peace commission to Paris, a process which
inevitably led to ruffled feathers and bruised egos among those left behind.

In Paris the Inquiry delegation became the Division of Political and
Territorial Intelligence of the American Peace Commission. The division
was only one element of the Peace Commission's intelligence support.
MID director Brigadier General Marlborough Churchill and twenty officers
from the division came along as the Peace Commission's General Military
Liaison Coordinating Staff.[17] Colonel Van Deman, already in France as an
officer of the AEF's G-2, was appointed the commission's chief of counterespionage, responsible for all security aspects of the commission except the
safety of the president, which was the job of a Secret Service contingent
headed by the service's chief, William H. Moran (several sergeants from
G-2's Corps of Intelligence Police were detailed to the Secret Service to
assist in ensuring the president's safety).[18] Captain Herbert O. Yardley,
chief of MI-8, the MID's cryptologic unit, was in Europe on a liaison
mission at the time of the armistice and was assigned to the Peace Commission and put in charge of establishing secure communications between
the commissioners and Washington.

Yet another element was added to the peace commission's intelligence
apparatus in February. The Division of Current Diplomatic and Political
Correspondence was a current-intelligence-collection agency with agents
and observers throughout Europe and, especially, in Germany. Headed by
foreign-service officer Ellis L. Dresel, the division consisted of eight civilians, four army officers, and one navy officer, plus clerical staff. One of the
civilians, the person in charge of Austria-Hungary and the Balkans, was a
young (twenty-six-year-old) foreign-service officer named Allen W. Dulles,
destined to become a major figure in American intelligence decades later.
Dulles, together with his brother, John Foster (also in the foreign service),

Van Deman, Lieutenant Adolf A. Berle of MID's MI-2 (also to become an important figure in intelligence and foreign affairs), and an assortment of other staffers served on a committee that met daily and debriefed the division's agents and couriers returning from the field.[19]

Some of the observers reporting to the division from the field were staffers on loan from the Political and Territorial Intelligence Division (i.e., the Inquiry). Archibald Coolidge and Robert J. Kerner (the latter an Austrian specialist) were sent to Central Europe. Other Inquiry veterans were appointed to represent the United States on the various international commissions and subcommittees established to deal with the many specialized subsidiary matters of the peace conference.[20]

The primary effort of the Inquiry veterans, however, was to try to ensure that the two thousand studies and the eleven hundred maps they had brought along to Paris—the cumulative result of fifteen painstaking months—did not go to waste. Although the State Department bureaucracy had never taken a hostile stance toward the Inquiry while it was tucked away inconspicuously in the American Geographical Society headquarters in New York, the climate became markedly colder when the scene shifted to Paris.

Apart from the "not invented here" attitude that some foreign-service officers may have adopted toward the voluminous output of the Inquiry, there was also an ivory-tower stigma attached to the agency's work: the Inquiry's professors and PhDs may have mastered the theory, but the practical matter of negotiations must be left to the diplomats. And the academics were indeed dismayed when they saw how many of their carefully researched and reasoned recommendations were thrown away by the diplomats at the bargaining table. Time put the matter in a different perspective for some of the participants, however. Years later Samuel Eliot Morison reflected:

> It is true that former members of the Inquiry who attended the peace conference left Paris in a somewhat baffled state of mind because they felt that their expert knowledge had not been used. I was one of such people. Looking back, however, I realize that there were considerations of international politics, strategy and common courtesy to our allies which in many,

perhaps the majority of cases, prevented President Wilson from following his experts' advice.[21]

David Hunter Miller found the degree of real influence the Inquiry had on the work of the peace commission to be imponderable, a thing that could be measured only if it could be compared with a peace treaty formulated without the assistance of the agency. The historian Lawrence E. Gelfand, who wrote the history of the Inquiry four decades after the fact, concluded:

> Lacking the Inquiry, the Wilsonian cause at Paris might easily have suffered to a greater extent than was actually the case. At least the American plenipotentiaries were able to compete successfully with the weapons of facts, figures, and previously assembled recommendations of ocher national delegations when the peace negotiations began in earnest.[22]

Viewed in the context of the development of American intelligence, however, the Inquiry's significance is much more clear-cut. It was the first American government agency charged with the production of national—as opposed to departmental—intelligence. Departmental intelligence is that used by a government department—for example, the army or the navy—in carrying out its mission; national intelligence is that required by the president and his advisers in order to formulate national policy. This distinction has been explicit and familiar within the United States intelligence community since the Second World War, but the idea that the president of the United States required a special level and type of intelligence for policy making was a novel insight in 1917 and remarkable in a president who so often had made up foreign policy out of his hat. Dilatory in planning for war, Wilson had grasped the necessity of planning for peace. Slowly and painfully, to be sure, he had learned the role of intelligence in government, and before he left office, he had acquired a better understanding of it than had almost any of his predecessors in the White House.

The Inquiry went out of existence at the end of the peace conference. The professors went back to their campuses, and none was again to play a significant role in American intelligence. But many of the other young American alumni of the peace conference—among them A. A. Berle, Allen and John Foster Dulles, William C. Bullitt, Joseph C. Grew, Christian Herter, Sherman Miles, and Whitney H. Shepardson—were to run the machinery of American foreign policy in the next half century, both within the government and through such influential private institutions as the Council on Foreign Relations. And through the work of the Inquiry and the other intelligence apparatuses of the peace commission, they had come to realize that intelligence is something more than the information base needed to win battles or plan wars.

Henceforth, it would also be a vital instrument of American foreign policy.

PART FIVE

The Road to Central
Intelligence:
1920–1962

Chapter Twenty-seven
The Red Menace

The end of the war in Europe brought with it the end to the wartime truce between American capital and labor. War-driven inflation had doubled the cost of living; now organized labor sought to recover what it had lost. There was a major steel-industry strike and another in the coal industry. A Seattle shipyard strike precipitated a general strike in that city, which was put down by federal troops. Thirty thousand textile workers walked out in Lawrence, Massachusetts, shutting down every mill in the city for sixteen weeks. Even the Boston police went on strike. In all, there were some thirty-six hundred strikes in 1919 involving four million workers. Many of the strikes were marked by violence on both sides.

Some of the strikers seemed to have taken inspiration from the Bolsheviks, or at least borrowed some of their revolutionary jargon. The word *council* (in Russian, *soviet*) was suddenly fashionable. In Butte, Montana, where miners walked out to protest a wage cut, the strike was controlled by the Soldiers, Sailors and Workers Council, a name that sounded like an echo from the Russian revolution. The Council of Workers, Soldiers and Sailors of Portland, Oregon, was formed "to strike the final blow against the Capitalist class." In Philadelphia the publication *Soviet World* foretold the coming of the Socialist Soviet Republic of the United States of America in two years.[1]

Such invocations of Russian-style communism by some elements of organized labor was not lost on the general public. A Seattle newspaper headlined its editorial condemnation of the general strike in that city with the line THIS IS AMERICA—NOT RUSSIA. And a political cartoon showing the Soviet banner flying above the Stars and Stripes was captioned NOT IN A THOUSAND YEARS.

At the time of the Seattle general strike—January 1919—an American Communist party was still no more than a gleam in the eyes of an assortment of Socialists, IWW members, Russian émigrés, anarchists, and other radicals who would meet in June and September of that year to found not one but two rival parties. It was therefore not possible for either party to have been responsible for the wave of terrorist bombings that began late in April.

The first target of the bomb campaign was Mayor Ole Hansen of Seattle, who had led the column of fifteen hundred federal troops and an equal number of policemen that entered the city and put down the general strike. On April 28 a package sent to him by mail was found to contain one third of a stick of dynamite, blasting caps, and a sulfuric-acid trigger that had failed to set off the device. The package was postmarked NEW YORK CITY and bore a return-address sticker from Gimbel Brothers department store and the designation NOVELTY.

The following day a bomb received in the mail at the Atlanta home of former United States senator Thomas W. Hardwick proved more effective: it exploded, tearing off both hands of the maid who opened it and burning the senator's wife, who was standing nearby. Hardwick had sponsored legislation aimed at excluding alien agitators from the country. The Atlanta package bore the same Gimbel Brothers label as on that sent to Mayor Hansen.

In New York City sixteen more of the Gimbel bombs reposed in the parcel-post division of the General Post Office, where they had been put aside because they bore insufficient postage. Alerted by descriptions of the Hansen and Hardwick packages, the postal authorities turned over the packages to the police. The parcels had been addressed to such prominent people as financiers John D. Rockefeller and J. P. Morgan, Jr.; Supreme Court justice Oliver Wendell Holmes, Jr.; Attorney General A. Mitchell Palmer; Secretary of Labor William B. Wilson; and Senator Lee S. Overman, chairman of the Senate Bolshevik Investigating Committee.

Discovery of the Gimbel bombs was followed by a one-month lull in the terrorist campaign, but on June 2 the bombers struck again. Attorney General Palmer was again the target, and this time the bombers chose to deliver the parcel in person rather than risk discovery in the mails. At 11:15 P.M. Palmer's Georgetown house was rocked by a blast that wrecked the front of the building but did not injure anyone in the household. The bomb had detonated prematurely, however, and parts of the bomber's body were found by Assistant Secretary of the Navy Roosevelt, who lived across the street, and other neighbors who opened their front doors after the explosion. At about the same moment, other bombs exploded at the homes of public officials and other prominent persons in seven other cities. The one fatality was a night watchman killed by a bomb left at the New York City home of General Sessions judge Charles C. Nott, Jr.[2]

A printed manifesto found at all the bombing sites declared war on "the powers that be" and "the capitalist class" and was signed THE ANARCHIST FIGHTERS.

Two days after the bombings Attorney General Palmer announced his plans for a full-scale crackdown on political radicals. He appointed Francis P. Garvan, a senior Justice Department investigator, as an assistant attorney general to deal with the radical problem. He filled the post of chief of the Bureau of Investigation, vacant since A. Bruce Bielaski resigned earlier in the year, with former Secret Service chief William J. Flynn. The attorney general also announced the creation of a special unit in the department to compile intelligence on political radicals. To head this new Radical Division, Palmer appointed J. Edgar Hoover, a twenty-four-year-old attorney who had become the Justice Department's expert on dangerous aliens during his wartime service in its Alien Enemy Bureau.

Although most members of the IWW and other radical labor organizations were American citizens, Palmer chose to focus the department's anti-radical campaign on foreign-born radicals because the law made it much easier to deal with them. Under the wartime Immigration Act, passed in October 1918 and still in force after the war, the government could deport "aliens who believe in or advocate the overthrow by force or violence of the Government of the United States or all forms of law; aliens who advocate or teach the assassination of public officials; aliens who advocate the unlawful destruction of property, . . . [and] aliens who are members of or affiliated with" any organization that believes in, advocates, or teaches such views and actions. It was a much easier matter to establish that an alien was a member of, say, the IWW and deport him through an administrative proceeding than to prove in court that a person had violated federal law.

Consistent with this procedure, Hoover's Radical Division did not investigate crimes; it compiled dossiers on persons and political organizations. Soon rechristened the General Intelligence Division, the unit employed forty translators, assistants, and readers to read and index hundreds of radical publications, domestic and foreign. Publications were not the GID's only source of information; the division also recruited and paid informers to penetrate and report on radical organizations. Within a year the GID had a card catalog of two hundred thousand entries and dossiers on sixty thousand "radically inclined" individuals.[3]

The first radical group targeted by Attorney General Palmer as a result of the work of Hoover's GID was the Union of Russian Workers, a national organization that was headquartered in New York and proclaimed itself composed of "atheists, Communists, and anarchists." In simultaneous raids in twelve cities on November 7, 1919, agents of the Bureau of Investigation arrested several hundred members of the organization. While many of those rounded up turned out to be naturalized American citizens and hence ineligible for deportation, a sizable number were Russian aliens.

The Immigration Bureau, then part of the Department of Labor, worked closely with Hoover and the GID to facilitate the administrative machinery for deporting the alien radicals. The War Department provided a troop transport, the U.S.S. *Buford*, to carry the deportees back to Russia. The ship sailed from New York on December 21 with 249 aliens aboard, including the well-known anarchists Emma Goldman and Alexander Berkman.

The November roundup of the Russian anarchists was merely a rehearsal for a much larger sweep of Communists. The Communist party and the Communist Labor party were only months old, but their membership ran to the tens of thousands, most of whom had previously belonged to the left wing of the Socialist party. Only a small percentage of Communists were native-born Americans; most were natives of eastern Europe or Russia, and a large percentage were aliens.[4]

Hoover was intensely interested in the Communist movement in both the United States and Russia. His requests to the State Department for obscure Russian publications—for example, specific back numbers of *Bednota*, the organ of the Russian party's Central Committee, and *Novaya Zhisn*, the Menshevik party paper—reflect a sophisticated knowledge and understanding of the subject.[5] Exploitation and analysis of open source material gave him the background to make the best use of such Justice Department informers as Francis A. Morrow (Special Agent K-97), a Camden, New Jersey, shipyard worker who penetrated the American Communist party and rose to its highest ranks in the early 1920s.[6]

Through his study of communism, Hoover was aware of the formation of the Communist International, or Comintern, by Lenin in March 1919. Predicated on the doctrine that the Bolshevik revolution could not survive in Russia without parallel Communist revolutions in Europe and the United States, the Comintern was organized to export revolution to the West. When the left wing of the American Socialist party seceded to form the Communist party and the Communist Labor party later in 1919, they adopted the Comintern's call for the forceful overthrow of the United States government. Hoover realized that this made alien members of the parties subject to deportation under the Immigration Act. Armed with these facts, Hoover, Attorney General Palmer, and Bureau of Investigation chief Flynn began planning a massive roundup of Communists.

Through a search of the GID's files, Hoover was able to identify more than three thousand aliens who belonged either to the Communist or the Communist Labor party. He forwarded this list to the Immigration Bureau, which issued an arrest warrant for each name. Hoover envisioned a nationwide dragnet consisting of hundreds of simultaneous raids in thirty-three cities to arrest the Communist aliens and seize the party-membership records needed as evidence for the deportation procedures. Since the Bureau of Investigation had only 579 agents, Chief Flynn asked for the assistance of local police forces and former members of the now-defunct American Protective League.[7] To avoid the question of authority to arrest that had arisen in the slacker raids, the bureau deputized the former APL members as temporary special agents.[8] In order to facilitate the dragnet further, Flynn and Hoover instructed the Justice Department's informers and penetration agents to call for local party meetings on the date selected for the raids, January 2, 1920.

More than four thousand Communists were rounded up that night, and more were arrested during the ensuing weeks; the total was later estimated to be ten thousand.[9] The suspects were herded into cramped detention centers, which often were unheated, unsanitary, and generally inhumane. More than half of those arrested were found to be American citizens and were released. The situation evoked memories of the bureau's slacker raids two years earlier, and the tide of public opinion began to turn against Palmer and the Justice Department.

The anti-Communist campaign received a serious blow in March, when Assistant Secretary of Labor Louis Post was given responsibility for the Labor Department's role in the deportation proceedings. Post, who had edited the liberal publication *Public* before joining the Wilson administration and was a personal friend of Emma Goldman, was vigorously opposed to the Palmer-Hoover-Flynn campaign against the Communists. Contrary to the intent of the Immigration Act, which specified that membership in a violent revolutionary organization was sufficient grounds for deportation, Post insisted on evidence that each prospective deportee was individually guilty of revolutionary activity. Post decreed that the simple fact of membership in one of the Communist parties was no longer enough to deport an alien. In June a federal judge, in a case growing out of the January raids, lent judicial force to Post's position when he ruled that membership in the Communist party or the Communist Labor party did not of itself subject an alien to deportation. This brought the Justice Department's anti-Communist campaign to a virtual halt.

Hoover's GID continued to gather intelligence on the Communists, however. Although deportation under the Immigration Act was no longer available as a weapon against subversives, thirty-three states had laws against sedition, anarchy, and similar offenses, and the Justice Department cooperated with these states in the prosecution of party members. Twenty Communists were convicted in Illinois and drew sentences ranging from one to five years. In California 264 party members were convicted, and an even greater number were prosecuted under the New York State sedition law. Evidence supplied by the GID was instrumental in 115 of these convictions.[10]

The Palmer raids and the state sedition prosecutions drove most of the membership from the Communist party, reducing its size from about twenty-five thousand members in 1919 to about five thousand the following year. Those remaining in the party were, of course, its hard core. Effectively outlawed by the sedition laws, the party went underground, resuming its activities under a veil of secrecy. The GID continued to monitor its activities, however, through informers and penetration agents.

One of the GID's principal agents within the party was Francis Morrow, the Camden shipyard worker. Morrow's reports to the GID led to the joint federal-state raid on a secret convention of the Communist party held in rural Bridgeman, Michigan, in August 1922. Although the raiders struck after the convention was over and most of the delegates had left, they rounded up seventeen party officials, including Charles Ruthenberg, party secretary, and future party general secretary Earl Browder. The GID seized a hidden cache of documents, including the registration of all the delegates attending the conference, checks, instructions from the Comintern in Moscow, and an assortment of other highly sensitive papers.[11]

Although Michigan's prosecution of the party leaders arrested at Bridgeman was unsuccessful (Ruthenberg alone was convicted, and he died while his case was under appeal), the raid convinced the party to abandon its underground existence. A few months later it re-emerged as the Workers Party of America, an organization constituted to evade the state sedition laws.

The GID was not the only federal intelligence agency interested in the Communists and other radical groups. Since the United States Army could be called upon to restore order in domestic disturbances, as it had recently done in the Seattle general strike, the MID continued to maintain domestic countersubversion files after the war. Furthermore, the experience of German subversion during the war and the fact that American troops remained in potential confrontation with the Red Army in Russia seemed to confirm the wisdom of monitoring American-based organizations of Bolshevik affinity. This activity raised some highly sensitive questions, however, since military meddling in the political process runs counter to American tradition and skirts the constitutional limits placed on the armed services. The sensitivity of the issue was heightened when the tide of public opinion began to run against the Justice Department in the wake of the excesses of the Palmer raids.

While Brigadier General Dennis Nolan, Pershing's wartime intelligence chief who had become director of the MID in September 1920, was acutely aware that the matter was a potential bombshell, other army personnel beyond his direct control did not share this sensitivity. Some wartime intelligence officers who had later become members of the army's

Military Intelligence Reserve were conducting unofficial surveillance of the radicals; their reserve status (which they sometimes invoked in aid of their investigations) obscured the fact that these activiries did not have the army's official sanction.

The inevitable explosion was not touched off by a reservist, however, but by a regular army officer, Lieutenant W. D. Long, post intelligence officer at Vancouver Barracks, Washington. On October 16, 1922, Long sent a circular to all county sheriffs in the state of Oregon. Claiming to speak on behalf of "the Intelligence Service of the Army," he requested the local law-enforcement officers to pass along to his office any information they might acquire regarding "organizations or elements hostile to the Government of this country, or who seek to overthrow the Government by violence." As examples of such organizations, Lieutenant Long listed the American Federation of Labor, along with the IWW, the Communist party, the Communist Labor party, the Union of Russian Workers, and other indisputably anarchist or revolutionary organizations.[12]

Copies of Lieutenant Long's missive found their way into the pages of the *Nation*, the *Labor Herald*, and other publications, where they ignited a nationwide firestorm of indignation. Samuel Gompers and other officials of the AFL were undoubtedly outraged, after their loyal support of the government during the war, to see themselves lumped together with such subversive organizations and enemies of trade unionism as the IWW and the Communists. In the wake of the deluge of protests received by President Harding over the affair, Secretary of War John W. Weeks ordered Lieutenant Long immediately relieved of military duty, and he put the army on notice that there was to be no repetition of the affair. Thereafter, the intelligence officers of the various army commands were explicitly prohibited from collecting any domestic intelligence, and the MID was limited to whatever it received from the GID under a formal exchange agreement worked out in 1920 between MI-4, the domestic counterespionage section of the MID, and J. Edgar Hoover.[13]

The GID was an excellent source of intelligence on domestic radical activities, of course, and it is doubtful that the MID could have added much significant information through its own efforts to the material Hoover was collecting so assiduously. This effective alliance was destined to end in 1924, however, when the GID went out of existence, lost in one of the political storms that regularly strike Washington.

The scandals that had plagued the Harding administration became public after the president's death in August 1923. Harding's attorney general, Harry M. Daugherty, came under intense criticism for his failure to have detected and prosecuted this wrongdoing and as a result of charges of corruption within the Justice Department itself. Harding's successor, President Calvin Coolidge, fired Daugherty in April 1924 and replaced him with Columbia Law School dean Harlan Fiske Stone. On the advice of Secretary of Commerce Herbert Hoover, Stone appointed J. Edgar Hoover (no relation) director of the Bureau of Investigation.

Under J. Edgar Hoover's predecessor, noted private detective William J. Burns, the bureau, in the words of one historian, "had become a private secret service for corrupt forces within the government."[14] Hoover had watched such conduct helplessly in the role of assistant director under Burns, and he was delighted to receive a mandate from Stone to clean up the bureau. But he probably was not equally enthusiastic to receive the new attorney general's orders to limit the bureau's activities "strictly to investigations of violations of law, under my direction or under the direction of an Assistant Attorney General regularly conducting the work of the Department of Justice."[15] In other words, abolish the GID, and stop collecting intelligence on political radicals.

Hoover may have been loath to abandon countersubversion, but he was willing to do so as the price for a very considerable step up the bureaucratic ladder.[16] The Justice Department was out of the countersubversion business. And, therefore, so was army intelligence.

When the Bolsheviks seized power they recognized the immediate need for their own version of the Okhrana, as the czar's secret police force was called. On December 20, 1917, Lenin established the All-Russian Extraordinary Commission to Combat Counterrevolution and Sabotage—the Cheka. To head this organization, he chose Feliks Edmundovich Dzerzhinsky, a Polish Lithuanian and the son of a wealthy landowner and professor of physics and mathematics. A one-time Catholic seminarian, Dzerzhinsky had abandoned his religious vocation for Marxist politics and served many years in czarist prisons between 1897 and 1917. Lenin first met Dzerzhinsky in 1906 during one of the latter's few periods of freedom.

The state of siege prevailing in Russia during the famine and civil war that followed the Bolshevik coup consolidated the power of Dzerzhinsky and the Cheka. After a Socialist revolutionary attempted the assassination of Lenin in August 1918, seriously wounding him, Dzerzhinsky unleashed a campaign of arrests, mass shootings, torture, and imprisonment. The Cheka swelled from an initial strength of twenty-three members in December 1917 to thirty-seven thousand by January 1919.[17] The functions of the organization multiplied beyond the role of secret police force and became the Communist party's instrument for controlling the economy, the transportation system, the armed forces, and every other sphere of Russian life. Terror, the Cheka's specialty, proved a powerful motivating force and a highly effective means of getting things done.

The Cheka and its successors, the GPU (State Political Administration) and the OGPU (United State Political Administration), established in 1922 and 1923, respectively, engaged in relatively few foreign operations during the first few years of Communist rule in Russia. Consistent with their internal-security function, the agencies limited their foreign activities to the surveillance of White Russian émigrés and the disruption of their activities. One of these operations, known as the Trust, was devised and carried out by Dzerzhinsky. It was a masterpiece of cunning and duplicity.

The essence of the Trust operation was the creation of an ostensible clandestine monarchist underground in Russia, which the Cheka used to control, neutralize, and eventually liquidate the more dangerous counterrevolutionaries, both in Russia and abroad. This devised facility was known as the Monarchist Association of Central Russia. To make its existence plausible, it was ostensibly shielded by a cover organization, the Moscow Municipal Credit Association (hence the Trust).[18]

Cheka agents disseminated news of the Trust throughout Russia and carried it abroad. Their disinformation theme was that communism was fading in Russia and that the Soviet system was riddled with the sort of people Lenin called radishes—Red outside and White inside. According to Trust disinformation, even the Cheka had been thoroughly penetrated by cryptomonarchists.

The Cheka pulled off the deception with consummate skill, convincing White Russian émigré groups, and even some Western intelligence services, of the Trust's authenticity. So effective was the deception that the Trust was able to solicit contributions from anti-Bolshevik elements abroad, money that went into the coffers of the Cheka. The Polish intelligence service was so thoroughly impressed with the Trust that it presented a gold watch to its Trust contact.[19]

Within Russia those who might have created a genuine anti-Communist underground instead joined the Trust. Many of the White Russian émigrés, including the most dangerous figures in the leadership, answered the Trust's siren call to return to Russia and participate in the counterrevolution. Even the legendary British agent Sidney Reilly was duped: he accompanied a Trust agent into Russia in order to establish a liaison with the leaders of the organization and was arrested and executed.

The Trust proved highly effective in forestalling counterrevolution inside Russia and disrupting or liquidating foreign-based anti-Bolshevik elements. It also provided a powerful medium for influencing Western opinion and manipulating the foreign policy of several Western nations with respect to the Soviet Union.

After the Allied failure to topple the Bolsheviks by aiding the White Russians in the civil war, the Western democracies sought to quarantine the Soviet Union by withholding trade, commercial, and diplomatic relations. To reverse this policy, the Cheka-GPU-OGPU sought to relieve Western fears that the Communists intended to export revolution worldwide, and they found that the Trust could be as effective in deceiving the Western governments as it had been in duping the White Russians. Ostensible White Russian émigrés who had returned to Russia and claimed to have found it gradually changing into a bourgeois state without ambitions beyond its borders promoted this version of the country in books published in both Russia and the West. The existence of a powerful monarchist movement in Russia was, of course, exhibit A in their case. Through this and other propaganda techniques the Soviet Secret Service succeeded in influencing a large segment of Western public opinion. In 1924 both Britain and France extended diplomatic recognition to the Soviet Union and began trade and commercial relations.[20]

So effective was the Trust in deceiving Western public opinion that many remained duped even after a senior official of the organization defected to Finland in 1927 and announced to the world that the Trust was actually a deception operation of the OGPU. (Even this defection is suspected by some as yet a more Byzantine elaboration of Soviet deception.)[21] Dzerzhinsky was dead by this time (in 1926, reportedly of natural causes), and his successor, Vyacheslav Rudolfovich Menzhinsky, may have felt that the Trust had outlived its usefulness. In any case, the Trust then went out of existence.

First through his terror campaign and then through the Trust, Dzerzhinsky had succeeded in securing the Bolshevik regime by 1924. As the threat of domestic and foreign-based opposition diminished, the Cheka turned its attention to foreign-intelligence operations beyond those aimed exclusively at the White Russian émigrés. One of its prime targets was the United States.

Although Attorney General Stone directed Hoover to abolish the GID and cease intelligence operations against the Communists and other radical groups in 1924, the membership of the American Communist party and its successor, the Workers Party of America, did not offer an attractive infrastructure for the development of a Soviet secret intelligence apparatus in the United States. The membership had been thoroughly identified and extensively penetrated by the GID when that agency was in existence. The division had gone out of business, but Moscow knew that its dossiers reposed somewhere in the archives of the Justice Department. The Comintern still valued the American Communists as potentially useful political agitators, but the Cheka and other organs of Soviet intelligence kept them at arm's length.

The United States still refused to recognize the Soviet Union (and would continue to do so until 1933). Therefore, Moscow was denied a diplomatic presence, which could have been used for a base of secret intelligence operations in the United States. This left one possible vehicle to be used in American espionage operations: commercial cover.

The GRU (Chief Intelligence Directorate), the intelligence department of the Red Army's General Staff, had pioneered the Soviets' use of commercial cover in 1921 when it set up the Eastern Trading Company in Berlin, ostensibly for the purpose of selling Soviet goods in Germany but actually to collect military and industrial intelligence in that country. The task of doing the same thing in the United States was greatly facilitated by the arrival of Dr. Armand Hammer in Moscow in 1921.

Hammer, then twenty-three, had just graduated from the Columbia University College of Physicians and Surgeons when he traveled to Moscow as the representative of his father, Dr. Julius Hammer. The senior Hammer, son of a Russian immigrant, had been a ranking member of the left wing of the Socialist party before it became the American Communist party in 1919 and had been a friend of Lenin's since the two met at a Socialist congress in Germany in 1907.[22] Apparently, Julius Hammer's Socialist beliefs did not preclude him from entrepreneurial ventures: in addition to his large gynecological and general practice, he owned a wholesale pharmaceutical business and part of a chain of New York City drugstores.[23]

Armand Hammer carried a letter of introduction from his father to Lenin outlining the purpose of the visit: the establishment of a trading venture to represent American firms in the USSR. Lenin warmly welcomed the Hammers' initiative and set up a Concessions Committee to cut through any red tape that might obstruct the younger Hammer's efforts. The chairman of the committee was Feliks Dzerzhinsky. The result was a joint venture of the Hammers and the Soviet government, the American Trading Organization, or Amtorg.[24]

With headquarters in Moscow, Amtorg was registered in New York State as an American company and opened offices in New York City. As the exclusive licensee of all goods imported or exported between the USSR and North and South America, the company began doing a large volume of legitimate business with American companies. At the same time the OGPU, GRU, and Comintern agents working under Amtorg cover began collecting intelligence and establishing secret intelligence networks in the United States.[25]

The first chairman of Amtorg was Isaya Hoorgin, who was also chief of the company's New York office. Consistent with Soviet intelligence practice then and since, however, the OGPU resident (i.e., the chief of station) was not a senior officer of the corporation but a member of its staff, one

Mikhail Chatsky.[26] Officers of the GRU and the Comintern under Amtorg cover reported to Chatsky regarding their clandestine undertakings and to Hoorgin in their legitimate commercial activities. Hoorgin may have lost sight of Amtorg's priorities in such matters, however; his body was found in Lake George in 1925, a death two of his associates later claimed was a political murder.

The work of the GRU officers was facilitated by Amtorg's policy of requiring plant inspections prior to contracting with an American firm. The OGPU operators had a much broader task than simply collecting industrial or military intelligence, however, and their legitimate duties as Amtorg employees gave them a plausible pretext for making contact virtually anywhere in the American business or government establishment. Such access enabled them to identify potential recruits—Americans prepared to work for the Soviet Union for ideological or other reasons.

In parallel with the commercial-cover operations of Amtorg, the Soviets infiltrated a large number of deep-cover illegal agents into the United States using the now-familiar techniques of fraudulent documentation. A Soviet agent would review the death notices in decades-old newspapers to compile lists of infant deaths. These lists were used to obtain copies of the dead infants' birth certificates. Further research would identify defunct schools and businesses for which the records were no longer available, and these institutions would be used to construct a cover legend of schooling and former employers that could not readily be checked out. By presenting these birth certificates and unverifiable legends to the appropriate agencies, the Soviet agents were able to obtain passports, driver's licenses, and other authentic documentation to support their notional identities.

One of the many OGPU intelligence operators who used this technique was Joszef Peter, a Hungarian, whose brother was an Amtorg employee. Using the pseudonym J. Peters, Peter entered the United States in 1924 and during the 1930s ran a network of American-born agents within the United States government, including Harry Dexter White, the assistant secretary of the treasury and, reportedly, Alger Hiss, a senior State Department official.[27] Peter was an expert organizer of both overt Communist political activities and secret intelligence operations, and he seems to have had the task of identifying American Communists whose background did not preclude them from espionage work for Soviet intelligence. He was the case officer of Whittaker Chambers, the American-born Communist agent who broke with Soviet intelligence and denounced White and Hiss.

Of the many OGPU and GRU officers who operated under Amtorg cover in the 1920s and 1930s, the most important was Gaik Badalovich Ovakimian, a Russian-born Armenian engineer who became the OGPU resident in New York in 1934. Ovakimian's recruitment of Soviet agents ranged from Canada to Mexico. One of the networks he established within the United States included Julius and Ethel Rosenberg, the Soviet agents executed in 1953 for stealing nuclear-weapons information.[28]

The establishment of diplomatic relations with the Soviet Union by the administration of Franklin D. Roosevelt in 1933 further facilitated Soviet intelligence operations in the United States. The opening of a Soviet embassy in Washington and Soviet consulates throughout the country provided new bases for operations by the OGPU and the GRU, as well as pretexts for increased contacts with Americans in government, industry, and other sectors of public life. Furthermore, the Soviet intelligence officers operating under diplomatic cover could act with even greater impunity than their colleagues in Amtorg and other Soviet commercial institutions. Possession of a diplomatic passport ensured that the worst that could be done by the United States government to a Soviet operator caught in the act of espionage or subversion would be to declare him persona non grata and expel him from the country.

Diplomatic immunity was little more than a theoretical asset of Soviet intelligence in the United States, however. The actual risk of arrest and prosecution was virtually nil. The Justice Department was responsible for prosecuting violations of the Espionage Acts, of course, but so long as the Bureau of Investigation was prohibited from collecting general countersubversion and counterintelligence information, it was unlikely to encounter evidence of such violations.

There were a few exceptions to the government's prevailing mood of indifference and apathy toward the threat of Communist subversion. Although the MID officially restricted its investigation of radical political organizations to collecting information from the public press, it may actually have gone a bit further. Master Sergeant John J. Maurer of the Corps of Intelligence Police, also a captain in the Military Intelligence Reserve, was in charge of all MID domestic political intelligence sometime in the late 1920s. His activities, which continued until his retirement in 1943, were considered to be so sensitive that few people in the MID knew of them.[29] Just what he was doing remains obscure, but it is conceivable that he was working "unofficially" with some discreet members of the Military Intelligence Reserve in active countersubversion operations.

Major General Van Deman, who retired to San Diego in 1929, would have been willing and able to cooperate with Maurer or other elements of the government in countersubversion investigations and may actually have done so. He reportedly ran a private counterintelligence service consisting of former members of the American Protective League and other private citizens and compiled their reports into an enormous collection of dossiers on "individuals he believed to be communists, communist sympathizers, or neo-Nazis."[30] By one unsupported account, the army provided filing cabinets and materials and paid the salary of two civilian assistants for this project, and the navy, the FBI, and local police organizations furnished other support.[31] This same account claims that Van Deman's volunteer agents penetrated the Communist party, labor unions, church groups, and other organizations.

Whatever use the War Department and other government agencies may have made of Van Deman's files, however, it is doubtful that they helped them penetrate the sophisticated espionage and subversion activities of Soviet intelligence. There have been many successors to the APL, and such private-sector counterintelligence services are generally characterized by bias, amateurism, and an inability to distinguish between foreign agents and people who simply hold views they dislike.[32] If Van Deman's private counterintelligence files were based on reports from such individuals, they could have posed little threat to the highly trained professionals of the OGPU and its successor, the NKVD. It is a laudable thing to be an anti-Communist, but it is scarcely the whole of counterintelligence.

Curiously, the only organ of the United States government to undertake a professional domestic counterintelligence operation against Soviet intelligence in the 1920s and early 1930s was the State Department. Those zealous Red hunters in the Bureau of Investigation, the GID, and the MID who lumped anarchists, labor radicals, and other bomb throwers together with the Bolsheviks did so because they failed to understand the nature of Soviet communism and to see that it was a far more serious threat than any of the former groups. Those in the foreign service who had some direct experience of the Soviet Union knew better, however. One of them was Robert F. Kelley, a graduate of Harvard and the Sorbonne who had served in the MIS as a military attaché in Denmark, Finland, and the Baltic States before resigning from the army in 1922 to join the State Department.

Kelley became assistant chief of State's Division of East European Affairs in 1925 and moved up to the position of chief of the division the following year. Under Kelley the division focused on Soviet affairs and became known as the Russian Division within the department. One alumnus of the division, the diplomat and historian George F. Kennan, described Kelley as "a scholar by instinct and dedication." "I am sure," Kennan wrote, "there was no geographic division in the Department of State that had a better knowledge of the area with which it dealt."[33] During the negotiations leading to the opening of diplomatic relations between the United States and the USSR, the Soviet foreign minister, Maksim Litvinov, wryly observed that the division had better records of the history of Soviet diplomacy than did the Soviet Foreign Office itself.

Kelley, who spoke Russian, established a State Department training program in which foreign-service officers studied Russian language, culture, and history in Europe. He assembled the best library on the Soviet Union in the United States and compiled voluminous files of materials collected from every possible source on every aspect of Soviet life.[34]

Kelley's subordinate, Robert L. Murphy, was known as the State Department's gumshoe man. Murphy maintained meticulous files on Soviet propaganda and subversion within the United States. His activities offended some State bureaucrats, who regarded them as spying and therefore "ungentlemanly." Others condemned him and Kelley as "anti-Soviet."[35] Kennan recalled that Kelley and the division took "a sharply critical view of Soviet policies and methods, and believed in standing up firmly to the Kremlin."[36] Charles E. Bohlen, another veteran of the division, wrote that Kelley saw the Soviets' ideology and their commitment to spreading world revolution as fundamental obstacles to a constructive relationship between the United States and the USSR.[37] These were unpopular positions in the State Department of the Roosevelt administration, whose ambassador to

Moscow, Joseph E. Davies, declared that "it is bad Christianity, bad sports-manship, bad sense to challenge the integrity of the Soviet government."[38]

In 1937 the under secretary of state, Sumner Welles, abruptly abolished the Division of East European Affairs, packed Kelley off to Ankara, Turkey, shipped the division's library to the Library of Congress to be broken up and dispersed within the general collection, and ordered the department's special files destroyed.[39] Both Kennan and Bohlen believed the orders came from the Roosevelt White House. Bohlen says that the ultimate source of the abolition was a campaign mounted by Soviet officials in Moscow and Washington. Kennan, a sober scholar not given to sensational speculation, reflects, "Here, if ever, was a point at which there was indeed the smell of Soviet influence, or strongly pro-Soviet influence, somewhere in the higher reaches of the government."[40] Ambassador Elbridge Dubrow, then the American consul in Moscow, recently stated that it was rumored at the time that Mrs. Eleanor Roosevelt had asked Under Secretary Welles "to get rid of that Russian-speaking fellow" because she was "sick of hear-ing about him."[41]

The abolition of the Division of East European Affairs came at a par-ticularly unfortunate time for American counterintelligence efforts against Soviet intelligence operations in the United States. Only a few months earlier President Roosevelt had personally instructed J. Edgar Hoover to resume general intelligence investigations of Communists and other radi-cal political dissidents. He further ordered that the FBI should join forces with the MID, the Office of Naval Intelligence, and the State Department in this effort.[42] Of the latter three agencies, however, only State had any real contribution to offer the FBI's counterintelligence program against Soviet intelligence.

It takes years to mount an effective counterintelligence program, and the core of such an operation is its files. The FBI had been out of the counterintelligence business since Attorney General Stone's injunction to Hoover thirteen years earlier and so was ill prepared to mount an internal-security campaign against Soviet intelligence in the near future. The staff of the East European Division and, especially, the files Kelley and Murphy had painstakingly assembled since 1925 would have provided an invaluable head start for the General Intelligence Section, the FBI unit Hoover created in response to the president's instructions. Instead, the FBI was forced virtually to start from scratch. A decade was to pass before the bureau made any significant progress in its campaign against Soviet intelligence operations in the United States. In the meantime, the networks put in place in the United States by the OGPU, the NKVD, and the GRU continued to operate with impunity, burrowing into some of the most sensitive areas of the United States government.

The roots of the American failure to stop the secret Soviet advance ran back to the First World War and beyond. The German campaign of sabotage and subversion of 1914–16 had seemed to confirm the dread of German-Americans harbored by Captain Sigsbee and other members of the pre-war intelligence establishment. A generation of intelligence officers who began their careers in the war came to view the essence of counterintelligence as the surveillance of aliens. This tendency was nourished by the wave of xenophobia then sweeping the country.

The wartime intelligence establishment lumped together anarchists, the IWW, pacifists, and Socialists and regarded them as pawns of the secret services of the Central Powers. Some less enlightened intelligence officers added to this general category Jews, trade unionists, and anyone else of whom they disapproved. It is not altogether surprising, then, that when the Bolsheviks made their appearance in America in the immediate post-war years, the intelligence agencies treated them as just another bunch of dangerous troublemakers and therefore failed to see just how dangerous they were or how grave the trouble they would eventually make. While both official and self-appointed Red hunters compiled dossiers on relatively harmless parlor Bolsheviks who marched in demonstrations or sent letters to newspapers in the postwar years, the highly trained agents of Feliks Dzerzhinsky went about their secret business in the United States unmolested.

This blindness might have been of short duration. Hoover's GID was well on its way to achieving a profound understanding of Soviet communism and the threat it presented to the West. But then the intelligence establishment shot itself in the foot. The zealotry, excesses, and outright illegalities of the early anti-Communist campaigns accomplished very little other than to turn the tide of public opinion against federal security agencies. Public support for those agencies was further eroded by corruption in the federal government and the ensuing Washington scandals. As a result, the GID was abolished. The MID, which had become the most powerful internal-security agency in American history during the war, was already out of the domestic counterintelligence business because of a blunder by a junior intelligence officer. By 1924 the federal government had divested itself of any counterintelligence service.

The Red hunters had given anti-communism a bad name, and the road they built with their good intentions became an eight-lane freeway for the Soviet secret services in the United States. It was, unfortunately, a pattern destined to be repeated in the 1950s.

Chapter Twenty-eight
Other People's Mail

Germany was eliminated as a military power, temporarily at least, by the conditions the Allies imposed on her at the Paris Peace Conference. Washington's anxieties about further trouble south of the border eased in 1923 through a diplomatic modus vivendi with Carranza's successor. Of the three pre-war threats to American national security, only Japan remained. She came out of the war more powerful than before, an even greater menace to American strategic interests in the Pacific. For the two decades following the First World War, American military strategists would see Japan as the chief potential adversary.

The navy was the armed service most directly concerned with Japan and the Pacific. As Japanese-American tensions increased in the early 1920s, the Office of Naval Intelligence tried to step up its efforts to collect intelligence in the western Pacific and update War Plan Orange, the navy's plan for war with Japan, first drafted in 1912. The ONI had been considering secret intelligence operations in Japan since 1902, but its only actual attempt to establish networks in the country—by Lieutenant Commander Frederick J. Horne in 1917—had been thwarted by Japanese watchfulness.[1]

As an intelligence target, Japan was a particularly tough nut to crack. The Kempei tai, as the military counterintelligence police were called, had achieved an efficiency and ubiquity that approached the reputation they assiduously cultivated among the Japanese public. But even had there been no secret police, the vast linguistic, psychological, and cultural differences between the Japanese and Westerners presented almost insurmountable obstacles to secret intelligence operations. Thrust abruptly into the modern world in the last half of the nineteenth century, the Japanese retained the xenophobic and isolationist attitudes that marked their recent feudal history. There was only one possible method of gathering important Japanese intelligence: through communication intercepts and cryptanalysis.

When Captain Herbert O. Yardley returned from the Paris Peace Conference in April 1919, he and Brigadier General Churchill, then still chief of the MID, began lobbying for the preservation of MI-8, which like other wartime staff units stood in danger of termination. Yardley and Churchill were supported in this by Secretary of State Lansing, then still in Paris, who apparently found the political intelligence developed by the unit to be so valuable he considered having it transferred to the State Department.[2] An agreement was worked out between Churchill and Frank L. Polk, the acting secretary of state in Lansing's absence, to retain MI-8 within the MID with State paying 40 percent of the unit's budget.[3]

Now known simply as the Cipher Bureau, the unit was moved from Washington to New York City, apparently because a legal technicality prohibited State's contribution from being spent within the District of Columbia.[4] The bureau—some twenty code breakers, clerks, and typists— moved into a townhouse at 3 East Thirty-eighth Street, which was also the residence of Yardley and his family. Some months later the organization moved to a four-story brownstone at 141 East Thirty-seventh Street. As cover the bureau operated as the Code Compilation Company, Inc., a devised facility, ostensibly in the commercial code business, which actually produced and sold the Universal Trade Code.[5]

Through a continuation of wartime agreements with Western Union and other cable companies, a bureau messenger visited the cable offices each morning to pick up copies of cables of countries of interest and returned them before close of business the same day. That the practice was a violation of federal law was overlooked by the companies, probably on the grounds that it was done at the insistence of the federal government.[6]

In his memoirs Yardley lists twenty countries whose codes he claims were broken by the Cipher Bureau.[7] By far the most important one was Japan, whose codes became Yardley's top priority at the time of the bureau's move to New York. On December 15, 1919, Yardley reported to General Churchill the first breakthrough on one of the several codes in use by the Japanese to communicate between Tokyo and their Washington embassy. By May three more Japanese codes had been broken, and the bureau was well on its way to breaking the more than thirty Japanese codes then in use. The Japanese project took on an increased urgency after Senator William B. Borah of Idaho introduced a congressional resolution in December 1920 calling for the United States, Japan, and Britain to hold a disarmament conference.

Britain and the United States had come out of the war as the two greatest naval powers in the world. A wartime development in naval technology—the conversion of warships from coal power to oil—soon set them upon an adversarial course. The United States had dipped deeply into her oil reserve to fuel her own fleet and that of the British. After the war Britain made provisions for her own future naval oil needs by maneuvering at the Paris Peace Conference to secure mandates for the oil-rich former Turkish territory of Mesopotamia (today's Iraq) and by secretly negotiating an exclusive oil agreement with Persia (today's Iran). Added to what she already controlled, Britain had cornered more than half of the world's known oil reserves through these moves.[8] The action further exacerbated Anglo-American relations, which were already suffering in the immediate postwar era from other irritants—for example, Britain's temporizing in the matter of repayment of her war debts to the United States.

Against this backdrop of mutual suspicion and animosity, Britain, the United States, and Japan embarked on a postwar armaments race, primarily in the area of naval shipbuilding. Of the three only the United States could afford the race, but the American shipbuilding program was strongly opposed at home by isolationists and fiscal conservatives. Senator Borah's call for a disarmament conference found much popular support and forced the hand of the incoming Harding administration. In July 1921 Harding's secretary of state, Charles Evans Hughes, invited the governments of the world's principal naval powers—Britain, Japan, France, and Italy—to meet in Washington to discuss naval limitations. The conference opened on November 12.

The purpose of the conference was to set maximum limits on the respective size of the participants' navies. The United States was prepared to accept parity of naval strength with Britain on the theory that British territorial interests in Africa, the Middle East, and Asia required the protection of about as much sea power as the United States needed to safeguard her own interests in the Western Hemisphere and the Pacific. Japan, however, whose interests were concentrated in the western Pacific and eastern Asia, would have local naval superiority in those areas unless she was limited to a smaller navy than Britain or the United States. Secretary Hughes therefore opened the conference by proposing that the three countries scrap enough existing and planned warships to bring their navies into a ratio of strength (measured in terms of tonnage of battleships and big cruisers) of 5:5:3.

Although the British readily accepted the idea of parity with the United States, the Japanese were displeased with having been presented the small end of the bargain, which not only conflicted with their estimate of how much sea power they actually needed but also seemed an affront to their national dignity. On the other hand, they realized that they could not afford to compete with the United States in a naval arms race, and they were likely to end up at a much greater disadvantage if they tried to do so. Tokyo therefore instructed its delegates at the Washington Conference to try to hold out for a better deal—say, a 10:10:7 ratio—but to yield on the point if absolutely necessary. On November 13 Tokyo sent a coded message to the Japanese delegation outlining its bargaining position:

> ... It is necessary to avoid any clash with Great Britain and America, particularly America, in regard to the armament limitation question. You will do the utmost maintain a middle attitude and redouble your efforts to carry out our policy. In case of inevitable necessity you will work to establish your second proposal of 10 to 6.5.[9]

The Japanese delegates found the Americans to be hard bargainers, however, and on December 10 Tokyo threw in the towel in another coded telegram:

> ... We have claimed that the ratio of strength of 10 to 7 was absolutely necessary to guarantee the safety of the national

defense of Japan, but the United States has persisted to the utmost in support of the Hughes proposal. . . .

Now therefore in the interests of the general situation and in a spirit of harmony, there is nothing to do but accept the ratio proposed by the United States.[10]

The coded telegrams had been intercepted and decoded by the Cipher Bureau, of course, and the texts were put in the hands of the State Department negotiators. In fact, the bureau had been reading all of the Tokyo-Washington diplomatic traffic regarding the conference since July 13, five days after Secretary Hughes proposed the meeting. During the conference itself, which lasted from November 12, 1921, until February 6, 1922, the Cipher Bureau decoded, translated, and forwarded to Washington some sixteen hundred intercepted Japanese messages.[11] As inveterate poker player Yardley remarked in his memoirs, "Stud poker is not a very difficult game after you see your opponent's hole card."[12]

The Cipher Bureau's Japanese code-breaking program was not the only United States communications-intelligence operation aimed at Japan. A second was centered in the navy's Office of Naval Communications, and it apparently had its origins in a highly irregular cloak-and-dagger operation carried out by the ONI in 1920.

Sometime in the late summer or early autumn of 1920, ONI agents, perhaps accompanied by special agents of the Bureau of Investigation, conducted a series of break-ins at the Japanese consulate in New York City. By one account,[13] the break-ins were prompted by a bureau report that "a Japanese naval officer was masquerading there as the vice-consul" (hardly a violation of federal or state laws). Another version[14] has it that female agents of the ONI, while partying with the Japanese naval attaché in Washington, learned that a copy of the Japanese fleet code reposed in the New York consulate. The accounts agree that ONI agents broke into the consulate, opened a safe, and photographed the codebook, which was thereafter known in naval intelligence circles as the Red Book. The navy's desultory handling of the Red Book indicates that it did not know quite what to do with it and suggests that it may have been an unanticipated bonus of an operation mounted for other reasons.

Acquisition of the Red Book started a slow chain of events that gradually moved the navy into the communications-intelligence business, a field in which it had very little experience. With the utmost secrecy the ONI hired Dr. Emerson J. Haaworth and his wife, a pair of former missionaries who had lived in Japan for many years, to translate the codebook into English.[15] Many of the highly technical naval terms in the code were beyond the Haaworths' experience, however, and a complete translation of the book had to wait until 1926, when the ONI acquired the services of Lieutenant Commander Ellis M. Zacharias, an officer who had served several years as naval attaché at the United States embassy in Tokyo, had become fluent in Japanese, and now was the navy's leading Japanese-language expert.

One of the few people who knew of the Red Book and perhaps the only officer who eagerly awaited its translation was Lieutenant Laurence F. Safford, a member of the Annapolis class of 1916 and, since January 1924, occupant of the Research Desk within the Code and Signal Section of the Office of Naval Communications, The Code and Signal Section was responsible for the United States Navy's own codes and ciphers, and the Research Desk—that is, Lieutenant Safford—was charged with studying new developments in code making and new methods of communications intelligence. Safford, whose knowledge and experience of cryptology was nil, seems to have been the only officer in the navy with any responsibility at all in the field of code breaking. What he lacked in expertise he made up in enthusiasm, however, and he soon persuaded the Office of Naval Communications to set up a radio listening post on Guam to intercept Japanese naval communications and to assemble a small staff of cryptanalysts to work under his direction in breaking other Japanese naval codes and ciphers. Safford had an ingenious method of recruiting prospective cryptanalysts: he conducted cryptogram contests and other puzzle competitions throughout the navy in order to identify the best code-breaking talent available in the service.[16]

Safford's communications-intelligence operation made rapid progress, even after Safford himself left for a three-year tour of sea duty in February 1926. Two more listening posts were established in the Philippines that year, and yet another on the fourth floor of the American consulate at Shanghai. Back in Washington, Mrs. Agnes Driscoll, one of the crypt-analysts Safford had hired, broke the code used by the Japanese admirals, thereby providing the means to tap into the most important Japanese naval communications.[17]

Solving the Japanese traffic was an exceptionally difficult task, not only because of the unfamiliar language involved but because the Japanese enciphered their messages after encoding them.[18] Cryptanalysis of the Japanese intercepts was greatly augmented by the second-story activities of the ONI within the United States. ONI agents sought to repeat the intelligence coup they achieved in the 1920 break-in at the Japanese consulate in New York. In March 1923 they managed to photograph the contents of a steamer trunk belonging to Eike Takeuchi, a Japanese officer visiting New York City. That same year the ONI conducted a series of surreptitious entries into the New York consulate again, but this time the agents were unable to open the safe. Apparently ignorant of the activities of Yardley's Cipher Bureau, the ONI tried unsuccessfully to obtain copies of Japanese cables from the telegraph companies, but ONI listening posts on the West Coast did intercept some Japanese radio telegrams and passed them on to Safford's unit.[19]

In 1926 ONI agents again broke into the Japanese consulate in New York and this time apparently were able to open the safe and photograph the codebooks. They repeated the operation the following year.[20] On five consecutive nights in September 1929, ONI agents broke into the office of the Japanese inspector of naval machinery in New York, opened the safe, and photographed its contents, which included Japanese codebooks, as well as a wealth of other valuable intelligence.[21] Possession of the codebooks was an incalculable advantage to the Washington cryptanalysts attacking the Japanese naval ciphers. "If we had been faced at the beginning with the task of solving the cipher plus an unknown code," Safford later reflected, "it might have been too much for us and, at least, it would have slowed our early efforts."[22]

At about the same time Agnes Driscoll broke the Japanese admirals' code, the navy began experimenting with floating listening posts. In October 1926 the destroyer U.S.S. *McCormick*, bristling with antennae and carrying a battery of powerful radio receivers, cruised the Yellow Sea, the East

China Sea, and the South China Sea, all the while monitoring the radio traffic of the Japanese fleet.[23]

The commander of the *McCormick* on this intelligence cruise was Ellis Zacharias, fresh from a tour with the code breakers in Washington and by now as ardent a promoter of electronic intelligence as Safford himself. Zacharias was an early alumnus of the navy's Japanese-language program, which was begun in 1910, interrupted by the war, and then resumed in 1920, when it was enlarged to include the study of Japanese military and naval affairs, in addition to the language. Two officers were selected to enter the program every year, spending a three-year tour in Japan, after which they were assigned to the ONI or the Office of Naval Communications. The program was to pay handsome dividends, especially in the Second World War.

The successful spy cruise of the *McCormick* prompted Zacharias to propose an "ambush by radio" when the Japanese announced their plans for grand maneuvers of their Combined Fleet in October 1927. The maneuvers consisted of a full-scale naval war game, in which the fleet would be divided into a Red Fleet assigned to defend Tokyo, and a Blue Fleet which would carry out a mock attack on the Japanese capital. Obviously, the command and control of the two fleets in such a realistic exercise would depend largely upon radio communications and thus offer the radio eavesdropper a uniquely valuable insight into Japanese naval operations. Washington gave its consent, and Zacharias fitted out the cruiser U.S.S. *Marblehead* for the intelligence mission.

One hundred and seventy Japanese warships took part in the exercise, which was held in the Pacific several hundred miles off the Japanese coast. The Red and Blue fleets met and fought their mock battle on October 24. Just over the horizon, out of sight of the Japanese fleets, the *Marblehead*, which had been waiting in the area since the twentieth, turned her antennae toward the scene. Zacharias's team of radiomen transcribed the flood of radio messages passing to and from the flagships, while Zacharias decrypted them using the codebooks provided by the Washington cryptanalysts. The operation yielded a rich harvest of intelligence, including details of Japanese aircraft-carrier operations, which were at the time an entirely new aspect of war at sea.[24]

Three years later the ONC mounted an even larger communications-intelligence operation when the Japanese fleet again conducted maneuvers in the western Pacific. "The rich intelligence haul made from the intercepts of Japan's 1930 naval maneuvers was officially compared to 'exploring virgin territory,'" Admiral Edwin T. Layton recently recalled,

> Since no one in our navy at the time had any idea of the professional concepts, communications routines, or even the battle tactics of the Japanese fleet. By assembling the decrypts, we were able to learn a great deal about how Japan intended to conduct any naval war against us.[25]

The war game was clearly intended to simulate a battle with the American fleet, and analysis of the communications intelligence gathered by the ONC led to the unsettling conclusion that Japanese Naval Intelligence had apparently obtained an accurate picture of the latest version of War Plan Orange, the navy's contingency plan for a Japanese war. If such was the case, however, the Japanese must have obtained the plan through human agents. In the matter of communications intelligence, the ONC claimed a "complete ascendency over the Japanese navy."[26]

Although communications-intelligence activity flourished in the Office of Naval Communications during the 1920s, the State-War Cipher Bureau, under the direction of Herbert O. Yardley, underwent a corresponding decline during the same period. One major reason for the decline was a scarcity of intercepted telegrams to work on. The cable companies were becoming increasingly reluctant to cooperate with the government, and their resistance probably increased in 1927, when Congress passed a tougher law against the unauthorized interception or disclosure of the contents of electrical and electronic communications.[27] Perhaps a more powerful factor in the Cipher Bureau's decline, however, was lack of interest.

The military intelligence required by the army was not likely to be found in the diplomatic traffic the Cipher Bureau acquired from the cable companies. In order to collect useful data on foreign armies through radio and telegraph intercepts, it would have been necessary to mount an aggressive clandestine collection operation overseas, similar to what the ONC was doing in the western Pacific. But the MID, which suffered a continuous erosion of staff and budget in the 1920s, was in no position even to consider such a proposition. Thus the Cipher Bureau, now housed in offices at 52 Vanderbilt Avenue, became largely irrelevant to the MID.

The State Department would seem to have had a greater interest in the Cipher Bureau's product, but, in fact, it lacked the organizational apparatus to coordinate communications intelligence with its other sources of information. Foreign intelligence had flourished briefly under Frank L. Polk, who became the first incumbent of the newly created post of under secretary of state in 1919. Polk, it will be recalled, had served as State's chief intelligence coordinator when he was counselor during the war. He sought to institutionalize intelligence as a major responsibility of the under secretary by creating a special unit—designated U-1—to carry on the intelligence coordination and liaison function. Polk returned to private legal practice in 1920, and the role of U-1 thereafter is somewhat obscure.

Harding's pragmatic secretary of state, Charles Evans Hughes, made good use of the Cipher Bureau during the Washington Conference, but it is not clear that this ad hoc venture led to the regular exploitation of the bureau's product by U-1. By one account, the unit suffered from the perennial malady of State Department intelligence lack of an adequate central-reference capability and the consequent inability to coordinate and integrate the flow of raw intelligence from American embassies worldwide.[28] In any event, President Coolidge's secretary of state, Frank B. Kellogg, abolished U-1 in 1927 and divided up the intelligence responsibilities, assigning them to the individual geographic area divisions (an arrangement that was already working out quite well for the Division of East European Affairs under Robert F. Kelley).

The decentralization of State Department intelligence took place at the same time the new Radio Act was passed, making the acquisition of foreign diplomatic telegraphic traffic more difficult and dangerous. Secretary Kellogg was not likely to urge Yardley to wink at the law, and it is remarkable that he even tolerated the continued existence of the Cipher Bureau. The fact that it was not under the secretary's nose in Washington, but out of sight in New York and administratively under the army, may have encouraged Kellogg simply to ignore it. This was precisely the wrong way, however, to manage Yardley, who was content to be let alone to pursue his several private enterprises (he had become a licensed real estate broker).

Although a talented code breaker who enjoyed that work, Yardley lacked the sort of initiative needed to manage an activity such as the Cipher Bureau without close supervision. He failed to institute any programs to conduct research in the methods and technology of cryptology or communications, nor did he establish a program to train new cryptanalysts to compensate for the inevitable attrition of his staff. By 1929 the size of the Cipher Bureau had shrunk to six people, including Yardley himself. By the summer of that year the War Department General Staff had just about decided to close the bureau and combine its code-breaking activity with the code making of the Signal Corps and related functions in the Office of the Adjutant General.[29] This move was overtaken by events, however.

The administration of President Herbert Hoover had come into office in March 1929, and the following May Under Secretary of State Joseph P. Cotton informed the new secretary of state, Henry L. Stimson, of the existence and activities of the Cipher Bureau. Stimson's reaction, reportedly "immediate and violent," was to condemn the bureau on grounds of both legality and propriety.

"Gentlemen do not read each other's mail," he remarked when recounting the incident to his biographer and amanuensis eighteen years later.[30]

He ordered that the State Department end its financial support of the Cipher Bureau, an act that put the organization out of business as of June. Yardley and the other five members of the bureau, none of whom had Civil Service status, were given three months' severance pay.[31]

The forty-year-old Yardley, whose dozen years of code-breaking experience was hardly marketable in the private sector, could not find a job, certainly nothing that would pay the then-handsome annual salary of seventy-five hundred dollars he had received as chief of the Cipher Bureau. In November the stock market underwent the great crash, ushering in the Depression. Yardley had to liquidate his real estate holdings "for next to nothing" and move back to Worthington, Indiana. Things were no better there, and in January 1931 he was forced to appeal to his former MI-8 colleague, Dr. John M. Manly, for a twenty-five-hundred-dollar loan.

Manly was unable to comply. Yardley then decided to sell the story of the
Cipher Bureau for some ready cash.

When Yardley left government employment, he took along with him
two boxes of classified documents, including many of the decoded Japanese cables that had enabled American negotiators to drive a hard bargain at the Washington Conference. By some accounts, he approached
the Japanese ambassador in Washington sometime in 1930 and sold him
the documents, together with an explanation of how he had broken the
codes, for the sum of seven thousand dollars.[32] Whatever the truth of that
allegation, there is no question that he next incorporated the material into
an account of the Cipher Bureau written for publication and entitled *The
American Black Chamber*.

The book was published by the Indianapolis house of Bobbs-Merrill
in June 1931 after three excerpts had appeared in the *Saturday Evening
Post* in April and May. Nearly 18,000 copies of the book were sold in the
United States, and another 5,480 were sold in Britain; it was translated into
French, Swedish, Chinese, and Japanese. For obvious reasons, the book
was an even greater success in Japan, where an outraged public bought
33,119 copies.[33]

In reply to public accusations that he had betrayed his country's secrets,
Yardley first offered the self-serving and hypocritical argument that he had
published the work in the same spirit that the State Department had shut
down the Cipher Bureau: to provide "an airing, publicly," of code breaking so that "such practices . . . be eliminated from the considerations of
diplomacy." Later he revised this, characterizing his book as "an exposé
of America's defenseless position in the field of cryptography."[34]

The army and the State Department responded to press inquiries simply by denying that any such entity as the Cipher Bureau had existed, a
course that minimized official embarrassment but precluded taking legal
steps against Yardley. The government did forestall publication of Yardley's sequel, *Japanese Diplomatic Secrets*, an elaboration of the secrets of
the Washington Conference, by causing Congress to pass a law to prevent
publication of any material that had once been prepared in an official
diplomatic code.[35]

Undoubtedly, official reluctance to pursue the matter of Yardley's disclosures vigorously was due in large part to the fact that the government

was still reading other people's mail. In addition to the elaborate and very successful operation against Japanese naval communications mounted by the ONC, the army had created a new communications-intelligence unit in May 1929, the very moment Secretary of State Stimson was signing the death warrant of the joint State-War Cipher Bureau. The Signal Intelligence Service was not part of the MID; it was a unit of the Army's Signal Corps. Its chief was William F. Friedman—agricultural geneticist, code breaker, and former director of Riverbank Laboratories' Cipher Department.

Friedman had done some code breaking for MI-8 while at Riverbank during the war. His principal contribution while at Riverbank during 1917 and early 1918, however, was in training army officers in cryptology for the MIS. Friedman wrote a series of monographs on cryptanalytic theory as instructional aids for the program. One of them, *The Index of Coincidence and Its Applications in Cryptography*, is regarded by the intelligence historian David Kahn (a writer not given to exaggeration) as "the most important single publication in cryptology."[36]

In May 1918 Friedman was commissioned as a first lieutenant in the army and assigned to G-2, the intelligence staff of the Allied Expeditionary Force in France. He worked in the Radio Intelligence Section, where he helped solve field codes used by the German forces. He served there until April 1919, when he returned to civilian life and Riverbank.[37] Toward the end of 1920, he quit Riverbank, however, and he and his wife, Elizabeth, another Riverbank cryptanalyst, moved to Washington to work for the Signal Corps.

Despite his title as chief cryptanalyst of the Signal Corps, Friedman did little official code breaking and was more concerned with securing the army's own codes and ciphers, teaching cryptology to Signal Corps personnel, and doing basic research in cryptologic theory. He testified as a cryptologic expert before a Senate committee investigating the Teapot Dome scandal in 1924 and occasionally helped out other government agencies—for example, the Coast Guard—in solving encrypted messages. (Mrs. Friedman worked for the Coast Guard during Prohibition, decoding intercepted radio messages between rum-running boats and their associates ashore.)[38]

When the army decided to transfer its code-breaking activities to the Signal Corps and combine them with its code-making functions in 1929 (coincident with Stimson's closing of the Cipher Bureau), the chief signal officer selected Friedman to head the new unit, which was formally established the following April. Initially, the new unit, dubbed the Signal Intelligence Service, consisted only of Friedman, but he soon hired several junior cryptanalysts—actually, cryptanalyst trainees. (Yardley reportedly was offered employment with the SIS but declined, probably because the salary offered was a mere fraction of what he had received as chief of the Cipher Bureau.)[39]

Frank B. Rowlett was a Virginian, just graduated from Emory and Henry College. Solomon Kullback, a New Yorker, had just earned a master's degree in mathematics from Columbia University, as had Philadelphian Abraham Sinkov. Friedman selected the three from among eight candidates sent him by the Civil Service Commission. Rowlett had a good knowledge of German; Kullback, of Spanish; and Sinkov, of French. Finding an American-born candidate able to read Japanese was not as easy, however, but Virginia congressman Joseph C. Shaffer proposed his nephew, John B. Hurt, who surprisingly turned out to have a superb mastery of the language. To complete the code-breaking staff, Friedman hired a young man, Harry Lawrence Clark, as an assistant cryptographic clerk. These five, plus a secretary and Friedman himself, comprised the Signal Intelligence Service, as they would for the next seven years.[40]

Japanese-American tensions increased during the 1920s, largely because of a recurrence of the old problem of Japanese immigration to the United States. The 1907 Gentlemen's Agreement had not completely stemmed the influx of Japanese laborers to the Pacific Coast, and political pressure from that region led to passage of the Immigration Act of 1924, which specifically barred Japanese immigration. Naturally, the law provoked widespread anti-Americanism in Japan, where the date it became effective was proclaimed National Humiliation Day.

Relations between the two nations worsened as a result of Japan's aggression and expansionism in the Far East in the 1930s. Japan seized Manchuria in 1931 in violation of its treaty commitments to the Allies, and the following January Japanese forces attacked Shanghai, ironically introducing the wholesale slaughter of civilians by aerial bombing into the catalog of the horrors of war. The brutality of the Shanghai attack triggered a worldwide wave of revulsion.

In 1934 Japan denounced the Washington naval treaty of 1922 and began unlimited naval construction two years later. In 1937 she launched an undeclared war on China. In an orgy of rape, mutilation, and murder lasting several days, the Japanese army systematically slaughtered 140,000 Chinese men, women, and children in the city of Nanking and the surrounding countryside in December 1937.

Before the slaughter began, the staffs of the American and other foreign embassies in the Chinese capital fled, many seeking refuge aboard the U.S.S. *Panay*, an American gunboat that was fitted out for communications interception and photographic intelligence and had been monitoring the Japanese advance on the city from the vantage of the Yangtze River. On December 12 Japanese planes attacked and sank the *Panay*, with the loss of two American lives and forty-eight casualties. Japan, claiming the attack had been carried out in error, apologized and paid an indemnity to the United States.

Within a few months after the rape of Nanking, Japanese forces occupied all the coastal ports and controlled the railroad lines and the major cities of China. in 1940 Japan joined the Axis, the German-Italian alliance in the war that had begun in Europe the previous year with Hitler's invasion of Poland and the declaration of war by Britain and France on Germany. Japan coerced the French government—now dominated by Germany—into granting her strategic bases in Indochina. In reaction to these developments, the United States embargoed the sale of iron and steel scrap to Japan, material of vital strategic importance to the Japanese war machine. In July 1941 the government followed up on this by freezing all Japanese assets in the United States. Britain and the Netherlands followed suit, with the result of a complete embargo on war materials to Japan, including oil. Japanese-American relations were approaching a crisis.

While these events were unfolding on the international scene, army and navy code breakers did their best with limited resources to collect communications intelligence on the Japanese target. Their task had been made considerably more difficult by Yardley's disclosures.

"Had the Japanese been allowed to believe that their systems in use between 1917 and 1929 were indecipherable," comments the official historian of the Signal Intelligence Service, "they might have continued to use the same principles, with the consequent possibility that their newer systems might have been solved with much less difficulty than was actually experienced."[41]

The basic change in Japanese cryptographic practice that came about at the time of Yardley's disclosures was a shift of emphasis from code to cipher. Although it had previously been Japanese practice to translate a message using a codebook and then further protect it by enciphering its individual characters, the ciphers used had been relatively simple ones; the Japanese entrusted the burden of their communications security to their codes. In the wake of Yardley's revelations, however, they decided to put their principal trust in highly complex—and, they hoped, impenetrable—ciphers.[42] The problem with this course, however, was that enciphering and deciphering a message is a considerably more tedious and time-consuming process than looking up words or code symbols in a codebook; and, in general, the more secure a cipher, the more tedious and time-consuming it is to use. The Japanese hoped to find a twentieth-century solution to this age-old cryptographic dilemma: a machine.

Although simple movable disks and cylinders had been used for enciphering and deciphering messages since the fifteenth century (one, invented by Thomas Jefferson, was at the time still in use by the army), complex electromechanical devices designed to reduce the drudgery of cryptography had been around for little more than a decade. The earliest may have been the 1915 invention of California inventor Edward Hugh Hebern, in which two electric typewriters were connected by a random bundle of twenty-six wires, so that when a key was struck on the keyboard of one machine, a substitute letter would be printed by the other machine. Hebern elaborated this very basic—and completely insecure—monoalphabetic cipher system through the use of electromechanical rotors, which permitted the use of more complex polyalphabetic ciphers. Although Hebern sold several of his machines to the navy, Friedman demonstrated that they were far less than foolproof, and the United States government eventually lost interest in the devices.[43]

Similar electromechanical cipher machines were being developed in Europe about the same time, however, and in Japan an inventor named

Ichiro Hamada proposed such a device to the navy and Foreign Ministry at the very moment the Japanese had elected to shift their communications-security emphasis from codes to ciphers. Hamada's first machine was dubbed the Type No. 91 after the year 2591, the Japanese calendar's equivalent of the West's 1931.[44] The Japanese navy put the new machine into use that year, while the Foreign Ministry adopted a slightly modified version at about the same time.

The ONC code breakers on the Research Desk recognized the new Japanese cryptosystem as a machine cipher, but this realization fell far short of the capability to solve the intercepted naval and diplomatic traffic. They understood some of the basic principles that, they reasoned, must underlie the cipher, because they were aware of the state of the cipher-machine art as exemplified by the Hebern apparatus and its European counterparts. But to divine the secrets of the Red machine, as they dubbed the new Japanese device, they hoped to get a look at one. After a fruitless covert intrusion into the Washington apartment of the Japanese naval attaché, however, the ONC Research Desk fell back on the considerable brainpower of Agnes Driscoll and another cryptographer, who succeeded in solving the Japanese machine cipher in 1935 and even in reproducing one of the Red machines in a navy workshop.[45]

The duplicated Red machine enabled the ONC code breakers to read Japanese diplomatic traffic on a regular basis from 1936 through 1938. In February 1939 the Japanese switched to a new cipher machine, however. While they continued to use the Red machine to communicate with their less important embassies around the world, communications with their legations in Berlin, London, and Washington were entrusted only to the new device, which the American code breakers called the Purple machine.[46] The Purple system proved to be much more difficult to penetrate than the Red. In fact, the navy code breakers were stumped.

Limited by its meager budget, the army's Signal Intelligence Service could do little more than train Signal Corps personnel in code breaking—the Signal Intelligence School was officially formed in 1934—and stay abreast of advances in such related technology as automated data-processing equipment and cipher machines during the first several years of its existence.

The SIS also suffered from another shortage, the same one that had plagued the Cipher Bureau—a shortage of intercepted traffic to work on. Although the Signal Corps had intercept stations scattered throughout the United States and in the Canal Zone, Hawaii, and the Philippines, the flow of foreign intercepts from these stations to the SIS was inadequate for a sustained code-breaking effort. More to the point, such electronic eavesdropping remained illegal, even after the 1927 Radio Act was replaced by the Communications Act of 1934.

With Japan's new aggression in China in 1937 and other increasing world tensions, however, the SIS was given an enlarged budget and permitted to expand its staff of civilian employees to eleven. The Signal Corps was now intercepting foreign diplomatic traffic and delivering it to Friedman and his code breakers on a weekly basis, and in January 1938 the listening post in Panama went on round-the-clock duty with orders to give top priority to Japanese communications with Rome and Berlin. The new Communications Act notwithstanding, the army chief of staff gave the Signal Corps secret authorization to "maintain and operate in time of peace . . . such radio intercept and cryptanalytical services as are necessary for training and national defense purposes."[47]

So rigid was the security compartmentation of the United States communications-intelligence effort that the SIS and the navy code-breaking unit—now bearing the inscrutable bureaucratic designation OP-20-G[48]—worked in complete isolation from one another. This security restriction was imposed at a great price in duplication of effort and perhaps sometimes the fragmentation of what might otherwise have been a coherent intelligence picture.[49] Faced with the prospect of the Purple problem consuming the entire cryptanalysis staff of OP-20-G, however, Commander Safford broached the idea of his unit's pooling its efforts with the SIS. An agreement was worked out between Rear Admiral C. E. Courtney, director of naval communications, and Major General Joseph O. Mauborgne, the army's chief signal officer, whereby the SIS would devote its entire code-breaking staff to Purple, while OP-20-G would take over all other cryptanalytic work of both the army and the navy.[50]

In 1935 an army major had been designated as officer in charge of the SIS, a move partly intended to free Friedman of the burden of administrative duties so that he could devote all his time to cryptologic work.

Apparently, the Parkinsonian expansion of government paperwork continued to encroach on the master code breaker, however, so that by early 1939 he was again completely mired in administrative work. But after the SIS code-breaking staff had struggled with Purple for some time, General Mauborgne told Friedman to drop everything else and take personal charge of the assault on the new Japanese cryptosystem.

The solution of Purple was not to be achieved quickly, however, even under Friedman's leadership. Nineteen thirty-nine passed into 1940, and the new cryptosystem continued to baffle the SIS code breakers. The availability of the Red machine, which the navy had turned over to Friedman, gave some clues to the Purple system, but in one way it also contributed to a hidden obstacle: the assumption that the Purple machine, like the Red and virtually all known cipher machines, used a set of rotors to vary the electrical connections the machine used to convert between the plaintext and the cipher message. In the end this false assumption was challenged by Harry L. Clark, the young cryptographic clerk Friedman had hired when the SIS was created in 1929 and who was now a member of the cryptanalysis staff.[51]

Clark speculated that the Purple machine might employ telephone stepping switches to perform the function of the rotors in the earlier machines. This suggestion proved to be correct, and while it was far from the complete solution to the problem, it removed a major hidden mental obstacle that had frustrated Friedman and his team for eighteen months. By August 1940 Friedman was able to read the Purple messages, and within a month the navy's technicians had succeeded in constructing a working copy of the Purple machine.[52]

The machine began deciphering intercepted Japanese traffic on September 25. It could hardly have been more welcome than it was at that critical moment. Two days later Japan signed the Tripartite Pact with Germany and Italy, creating the Tokyo-Berlin-Rome Axis.

The making and breaking of codes is probably as old as the other arts of espionage, warfare, and diplomacy, and Americans have been reading other people's mail since before the birth of the Republic. But the amateur cryptanalysts who solved Dr. Benjamin Church's incriminating spy letter for General Washington and puzzled out Cornwallis's desperate dispatches to General Clinton knew less of the mysteries of codes and ciphers than did the intrigants of Florence, Naples, and Venice two centuries earlier. Edgar Allan Poe popularized secret writing and found a niche for it in the body of American literature, but his grasp of cryptology did not approach that of his contemporaries in the armies of Europe. The telegraphers of the Union's Military Telegraph Service had little trouble solving Confederate cryptograms, but their own method of enciphering telegrams would not have withstood the attack of a French or German code breaker of the 1860s. Cryptology is one science in which the successful innovator does not rush into print to establish a claim for his accomplishments, and until the twentieth century knowledge of this arcane discipline was slow to move westward across the Atlantic.

The advent of radio telegraphy early in this century put a new premium on both the security of communications and the ability to penetrate it. The Austrians may have been the first to recognize the intelligence value of radio interception when they began eavesdropping on Italian transmissions in 1908, and the French were probably the first to intercept systematically the radio transmissions to and from foreign legations in their capital.[53] But it was the widespread use of radio in the First World War that made electronic interception a major instrument of intelligence collection. That same war made the American intelligence establishment a permanent peacetime institution.

It may be thought quintessentially American that the first American Black Chamber was created by a self-taught telegraph operator and part-time real estate broker and that the greatest American cryptologist (some would say simply the greatest) was a Russian-born Jewish immigrant who had been steered into code breaking by an eccentric American millionaire who hoped to prove a crank literary theory.

The ambivalence and polarity of American attitudes toward espionage can be found in microcosm in the history of United States communications-intelligence activity between the wars. While a secretary of state was closing down the Cipher Bureau on the grounds that reading other people's mail was ungentlemanly, gentlemen of the navy's officer corps were burglarizing foreign consulates in search of codebooks, and both the army and the navy were eavesdropping on foreign radio messages in violation of federal law.

It may be counted as one of the most remarkable stories of intelligence history that American code breaking went, in the space of only two decades, from the first feeble efforts of MI-8 and the Riverbank amateurs to a capability to reconstruct, sight unseen, the most sophisticated electro-mechanical cipher machine then to be devised. Even more remarkable is that this feat was the prelude to the most devastating intelligence failure in American history.

American intelligence gained seven-league boots in the time between the wars, but it had yet to learn that collecting all the pieces is but the first step in solving a jigsaw puzzle.

Chapter Twenty-nine

The Secret War
with the Axis

The fact that his father went down on the *Titanic* did nothing to diminish Vincent Astor's enthusiasm for seafaring. He served at sea in the United States Navy during the First World War, and afterward he spent two or three months every year cruising the Caribbean or the Pacific aboard his yacht, the *Nourmahal*. The 264-foot vessel was virtually a luxury liner herself, with eleven staterooms on three decks, a walnut-paneled dining room that seated eighteen, a pine-paneled library, and even a completely equipped operating room, ready should the ship's surgeon ever need it. With a crew of forty-two, the diesel-driven *Nourmahal* could cruise at sixteen knots and had a range of twenty thousand miles. Astor loved to take his friends on long voyages aboard her, and one of his most frequent guests was the president of the United States.

Franklin Delano Roosevelt had known Astor well since the war, when the two yachtsmen organized the United States Naval Reserve, and as scions of two wealthy old New York families with neighboring Dutchess County estates, their acquaintance went back even further. Their close friendship developed in 1921, when Astor invited Roosevelt, recently crippled by polio, to ease his paralyzed limbs in the heated indoor swimming pool on his Rhinebeck estate. Their fellowship continued through the 1920s, and when FDR became president in 1933, Astor conceived a new service to perform for his old friend and for his country: he became chief of President Roosevelt's personal intelligence service.

Despite the isolationist mood prevalent in the United States in the 1920s, many leaders of business, finance, and the academic community took the sort of interest in foreign affairs that had been rare in America before the war. In 1921 former Inquiry officers Isaiah Bowman and Archibald Cary Coolidge, former State Department under secretary and intelligence chief Frank L. Polk, and an assortment of other veterans of the Inquiry and the Paris Peace Conference formed the Council on Foreign Relations in New York City. (Anglophiles all, they had to abandon an earlier joint Anglo-American organization, the Institute of International Affairs, when they realized the depth of anti-British feeling in postwar America.) Membership in the council was by invitation only, and most new members were selected from the same American elites from which the founders had come. The well-born council members met regularly to study and discuss international questions and often to hear an address by a visiting head of state or the American secretary of state. In 1922 the council began publication of a quarterly journal, *Foreign Affairs*, edited by former journalist and MID veteran Hamilton Fish Armstrong. In time the council took on a quasi-official status as a sort of unofficial general staff to the American foreign service. Washington administrations came and went, and with them secretaries of state, but the Council on Foreign Relations remained constant as the American foreign-policy establishment.

Although he was keenly interested in international affairs (and deeply concerned with many other public-policy issues), Vincent Astor was not a member of the council. He pursued such interests through yet another organization, which he founded himself in 1927 with Kermit and Theodore Roosevelt, Jr., two of the late president's sons. Known simply as the ROOM, the organization was in fact a secret society of influential men who met monthly in an obscure apartment at 34 East Sixty-second Street to discuss politics, finance, and international affairs.[1] Some of the members, such as banker Winthrop W. Aldrich, foreign-service officer and businessman David K. E. Bruce, and publisher Marshall Field III, were also members of the Council on Foreign Relations, but the ROOM was a different sort of organization, apparently intended as a way of pooling the inside information personally acquired by its members and not, as in the case of the council, to pursue more general studies of world affairs.

Several of the ROOM's members had a background in intelligence. The naturalist C. Suydam Cutting had served in the AEF's G-2 in France during the war; the philanthropist William Rhinelander Stewart had been in the ONI. Mining expert Oliver Dwight Filley and archaeologist Clarence L. Hay also had intelligence backgrounds. And a few others had probably done some intelligence work.[2] One member of the ROOM had a truly extensive background in intelligence: Sir William Wiseman.[3]

Sir William's role as intermediary between the British government and the Wilson administration ended with President Wilson's stroke and physical collapse following the Paris Peace Conference. He settled in New York and returned to his pre-war career in investment banking, joining the Wall Street firm of Kuhn, Loeb and Company in 1921. Presumably his work as an officer in the Secret Intelligence Service ended at this time, but it is likely that he remained in regular contact with his successor as New York chief of station, Maurice Jeffes, and with the other British intelligence officers who held that post in the years between the wars.[4] If Sir William did indeed report to the British the intelligence he acquired from the other influential members of the ROOM, he did so more as a liaison officer than as a penetration agent; the members of the secret society were all ardent Anglophiles, and, as we shall see, Astor and several of the others were eventually in direct contact with British intelligence.

Although Franklin Roosevelt was not a member of the ROOM, he was a beneficiary of the information exchanged within the group through Astor, Kermit Roosevelt, Stewart, and Judge Frederic Kernochan, four ROOM members on the closest personal terms with FDR. Roosevelt's ascent to the presidency in 1933 seems to have marked the beginning of Astor's systematic reporting of intelligence to his old friend. Initially, Astor reported on general conditions in the Caribbean and the Panama Canal Zone, which he visited on his regular cruises to the region, but soon he enlarged the scope of his reporting when he began to observe Japanese activity during the *Nourmahal*'s visits to the Pacific. In 1938 Astor and Kermit Roosevelt cruised to the Gilbert and Ellice islands, where they met with local British intelligence officers, who conveyed important information to them regarding Japanese naval and military activities in the Marshall Islands.[5]

Astor's intelligence work for President Roosevelt took on a more systematic basis with the outbreak of the Second World War in Europe in 1939. The ROOM was now known as the CLUB, and its membership became a powerful intelligence asset, supplementing the limited capabilities of the State Department, the MID, and the ONI. ROOM/CLUB member Winthrop Aldrich, chairman of the board of the Chase National Bank, reported on Japanese financial dealings and transactions on the account of Amtorg, the Soviet intelligence's commercial-cover organization in the United States. The intelligence supplied by Aldrich and the other bankers of the ROOM/CLUB was priceless; as Astor explained to the president, "Espionage and Sabotage need money, and that has to pass through banks at one stage or another."[6]

The membership of the private intelligence service included directors of several telegraph and cable companies; Astor himself was a Western Union director. Federal law was therefore no longer a practical obstacle to interception of foreign diplomatic traffic. Astor passed along the choicest intercepts to the president and routed the routine traffic to the ONI.[7]

The great value of the ROOM/CLUB was that it was a private agency and its connection with the United States government was informal and unofficial. Powerful isolationists in Congress and elsewhere were utterly opposed to American intervention in another European war, and President Roosevelt had already come close to violations of the federal neutrality laws in his advocacy of the Allied cause. The official intelligence services of the army, the navy, and the State Department were therefore strictly circumscribed in dealing with the intelligence services of the belligerents. Astor had considerably more latitude, however, and although he and his associates in the ROOM/CLUB were also covered by the laws, they did not have to worry about the potential political fallout from dealing with the British SIS.

The SIS station in New York, like most SIS stations, had been run under cover of the British Passport Control Department since 1921. The New York station chief from 1935 to 1940 was Captain Sir James Paget of the Royal Navy, and while Astor had probably been in contact with him before, he established a regular liaison between the ROOM/CLUB and Paget and his deputy, Walter Bell, early in 1940 to "obtain leads useful to us."[8] The SIS furnished Astor with more than "leads," however. "In regard to the opening of diplomatic pouches in Bermuda and Trinidad," Astor told the president, "I have given my word never to tell anyone— with always you excepted."[9] Bermuda and Trinidad, both British possessions, were refueling and layover stops on international flights to and from the United States.

FBI director J. Edgar Hoover, and probably the ONI as well, were also recipients of intelligence the British sent by way of the Astor channel in early 1940, but word of the arrangement somehow reached the State Department, which complained to the British government about this violation of neutrality laws. London apparently then ordered Paget and Bell to break off the liaison with Astor. Astor's protests to FDR went unheeded, perhaps because the president felt that the intelligence the British provided, no matter how valuable, was not worth the potential political liability of the arrangement, particularly in the election year of 1940.[10]

This incident, as well as the increasingly desperate war situation, may have inspired a wave of nostalgia in British circles for the good old days of 1916–19, when the SIS station chief in the United States was also a powerful agent of influence with entrée to the White House. Sir William Wiseman was undoubtedly ready and willing to resume his former role but unable to do so effectively because that role had become well-known in the interwar years through the publication of Colonel House's papers and Sir William's candid replies to the inquiries of House's editor, former Inquiry staffer Charles Seymour. British prime minister Winston Churchill cast about for a new actor to play the Wiseman role in America and found him in a Canadian named William Stephenson.

A native of Manitoba, Stephenson had already led a fabulous life when Churchill tapped him for the assignment. He dropped out of high school in 1914 to fight with the Royal Canadian Engineers in France. Recovering from a gassing, he transferred to the Royal Flying Corps, became a combat pilot, and shot down several German planes before being downed and captured himself. He escaped from a German POW camp and made his way back to his squadron. After the war he settled in England and made a business out of his boyhood interest in radio and electronics. Royalties from his inventions made him a millionaire by the time he was thirty, and he branched out into such other ventures as aircraft manufacture, film production, and the steel industry. Along the way he also found time to win the world amateur lightweight boxing championship and set a world air-speed record.[11]

Stephenson's involvement in the Swedish steel industry led to his recruitment by the SIS in the late 1930s, his work as a part-time agent, and his involvement in an abortive British attempt to sabotage the Third

Reich's steel supply. But he was not actively involved in SIS operations in April 1940, when at Churchill's insistence, he was asked to undertake a mission to America by the director of the SIS, Colonel Stewart Menzies.[12]

The purpose of Stephenson's visit to the United States was quite specific and limited: to attempt to establish a liaison "at the highest possible level" between the SIS and the FBI to counter Axis sabotage and subversion in the United States. Through the boxer Gene Tunney, a mutual friend, he managed an interview with J. Edgar Hoover, who welcomed the British initiative but told Stephenson that it would be possible only if the State Department's injunction were lifted by President Roosevelt. Stephenson had the question set before the president through the good offices of Ernest Cuneo, a Democratic party official, who surprisingly was able to accomplish what Astor had not. With Roosevelt's blessing Stephenson became the SIS's channel to Hoover.[13]

Roosevelt's change of heart in the matter of a British liaison, from his refusal of Astor's request several months earlier to his action on Stephenson's proposal in May, may have been prompted by his newly acquired awareness of the extent of German covert activities in the United States. During this interval Hoover's FBI had penetrated an extensive network of Nazi subversion and espionage in the United States through the efforts of one loyal German-American known as William Sebold.

A native of Mühlheim, Germany, Sebold was born Wilhelm Georg Debowski in 1899. After serving in the German army in the First World War, he worked as a merchant seaman. In 1922 he jumped ship at Galveston, Texas, and remained in the United States. After changing his name to William Sebold, he became an American citizen and settled in San Diego, where he got a job as a mechanic with the Consolidated Aircraft Corporation. In February 1939 Sebold returned to Germany for an extended visit with his mother, his two brothers, and his sister. Because he had listed his occupation as aircraft mechanic in his travel documents, he attracted the attention of the Gestapo (the Nazi secret police), who threatened to turn over a twenty-year-old criminal record (he had done time for smuggling and other felonies) to the American authorities, thus jeopardizing his American citizenship, if he did not agree to work for the Abwehr (German military intelligence).

Sebold consented, and he was sent to Hamburg for three months of training, including courses in the operation of clandestine radio transmitters. He also managed to visit the American consulate in Cologne, however, where he disclosed his predicament to Vice-Consul Dale W. Maher. Maher proposed that Sebold go along with the Abwehr but also work for the United States government as a double agent. The German-American agreed, and in February 1940 he arrived in New York City, where he was met by agents of the FBI.[14]

Sebold was carrying microfilmed messages from Abwehr headquarters to agents and officers in New York. The bureau men copied them, then returned them to Sebold for delivery. The messages identified the members of an Abwehr Ring headed by Frederick Joubert Duquesne, a sixty-three-year-old South African who had fought against the British in the Boer War and worked as a saboteur in South America for Section IIIb during the First World War.[15] Working under FBI control, Sebold contacted Duquesne and was soon accepted as a member of the ring.

Sebold established a safe house for the ring in the Times Square offices of the fictitious Diesel Research Company he had incorporated. There the FBI recorded his meetings with the Abwehr agents and filmed them from an adjacent room through a two-way mirror. Sebold's principal function in the spy ring was communications, and he set up a clandestine radio transmitter in a house in a secluded section of Centerport, Long Island. His radio work was so effective that the Abwehr began using him to relay messages between Berlin and other networks in the United States and Latin America. The FBI, of course, saw all of the traffic sent and received, thereby acquiring a tap into most German covert operations in North America.

Thus, at the precise moment Stephenson made his appeal to FDR, the president was presumably beginning to learn from Hoover of the widespread Abwehr activities in the United States and south of the border. FDR was already concerned over other reports of Axis activities in Latin America. As Europe moved toward a second world war, it seemed likely that Germany would again use Mexico and other Latin American countries both as a staging ground for covert operations against the United States and for diplomatic troublemaking to divert America's energy and attention from the European front.

* * *

German emigration to Latin America had increased in the 1920s and 1930s, driven by the severe economic conditions in postwar Germany. When the Nazi party took power in Germany in the early 1930s, it recruited members from among the German émigrés through its Auslandorganisation (Foreign Organization), or AO. The AO was founded in 1931 by Ernst-William Bohle, a native of England who had been raised in South Africa.[16] The Nazi version of the old doctrine of Pan-Germanism, the AO had a worldwide membership of more than fifty-two thousand German émigrés or their descendants by 1939, and a large segment of them lived in Latin America.

In the two decades since the war, the number of German-controlled industries, businesses, and banks had steadily increased in Latin America. German émigrés held controlling positions in most of the Latin American airlines. In all, German interests controlled some twenty-two thousand miles of South American air routes.[17] On a continent where there were few roads or rail lines, and rugged mountains and trackless jungles separated centers of commerce and civilization, the economies of the Latin American republics had become completely dependent upon the German-owned or -controlled airlines. The principal posts in most of the German airlines were held by AO members, giving Berlin an additional stranglehold on much of the South American economy.[18]

AO members were even to be found within many Latin American governments, which had hired German émigrés for their expertise, especially in the field of military science: former German officers trained many of their armies. And Germans were on the editorial staff of Latin American newspapers, many of which had been purchased by Hitler's propaganda chief, Joseph Goebbels. Goebbels also established the Transocean News Service, which supplied inexpensive copy with a pro-German slant to the Latin American press.

Beginning in 1935 the AO began collecting foreign intelligence through its membership by requiring the local AO branch in each country to supply Berlin with political, economic, or military information. This intelligence-by-decree procedure produced little useful material, of course, since most of the local AO officers lacked espionage skills or training. The organization was invaluable to other organs of German intelligence, however, in providing a ready-made infrastructure of overseas Nazis available for recruitment. Of the several rival intelligence agencies of the Third Reich, the Abwehr was the first to place resident officers in Latin America and the first to begin recruiting agents from among the local AO members.[19]

The most important Latin American outpost was, of course, Mexico, where Abwehr station chief Werner Georg Nicolaus, a forty-one-year-old German war veteran who had worked for a German bank in Colombia, ran a network of agents recruited from the AO. Chief among them was Werner Barke, who had been living in Mexico since 1925 and, as an employee of a German shipping firm in Tampico, was well situated to run a network in that port and in Veracruz, collecting information on the cargoes of British and American ships. Carlos Retelsdorf, a wealthy Mexican-born planter of German parentage, ran a clandestine radio station that kept Nicolaus and other Latin American Abwehr officers in touch with Berlin. Paul Max Weber, a journalist who spoke perfect English and had lived in the United States, was responsible for establishing Mexican-based networks within that country. Kurt Franz Joachim Ruege, general manager of a Mexico City automobile dealership, had gone to Germany for eight months of training in Abwehr schools and returned to serve as Nicolaus's microdot technician.[20]

The Abwehr had similar covert apparatuses in Brazil, Argentina, and Chile, and from bases in these countries, the German intelligence networks penetrated virtually every other country south of the Rio Grande, using the readily available assets of the AO.

FDR had long feared that the Nazi strategy in the Western Hemisphere called for a coup in one or more Latin American countries by the AO working with local Fascist elements, followed by an overt German military incursion. An abortive uprising by the Fascist Greenshirts in Brazil in May 1938 followed by an attempted coup by the Blueshirts in Chile in September inspired suspicions in Washington that Germany was about to take such a first step in the Western Hemisphere. In the wake of these events, the White House became concerned at how dangerously close the Panama Canal was to the Colombian airfields of SCADTA (Sociedad Colombiano-Alemana de Transportes Aéreos), an airline founded in 1919 by German World War flying veteran Felix Hammer. All of the twenty-eight flying officers of SCADTA were German, and all were reserve officers in the Luftwaffe, the German air force.[21]

The neutralization of SCADTA was the first covert-action operation of the Roosevelt administration in Latin America. Point man for the operation was Spruille Braden, a forty-six-year-old mining engineer who had spent most of his life in Latin America before joining the United States diplomatic service in 1933.[22] President Roosevelt appointed Braden ambassador to Colombia in 1938, and it was Braden who alerted the White House to the dangers posed by SCADTA. On FDR's instructions Braden made secret overtures to Eduardo Santos, the middle-of-the-road president of Colombia, and arranged to have the Colombian government cancel SCADTA's charter to provide air-transport service in the country. Juan Trippe, president of Pan American World Airways and an old friend of FDR, worked with Braden to establish SCADTA's successor, Avianca, an airline owned jointly by Colombia and Pan American.[23]

Although the ad hoc operation against SCADTA was successful, FDR undoubtedly realized that more systematic methods would be needed to deal with Axis subversion throughout Latin America. Handling that problem required great delicacy because of the perennial and ubiquitous undercurrent of anti-American hostility south of the border, a force ready to surface at any moment in response to either American blundering or Axis incitement. FDR took one step toward winning Latin American hearts and minds in August 1940, when he established an executive agency, the Office of the Coordinator of Inter-American Affairs, a white propaganda agency headed by Nelson A. Rockefeller that worked in the open to sell the American viewpoint to Latin American audiences.[24] The responsibility for covert operations in the region was placed elsewhere, however.

In June 1940, at about the same time double agent Sebold's reports to his FBI handlers began to reveal the extent of Nazi subversion in the Western Hemisphere and FDR approved William Stephenson's proposal for an SIS-FBI liaison, the president created a sharply defined division of intelligence responsibilities among the MID, the ONI, and the FBI. On

June 24 FDR advised his intelligence chiefs that the FBI, working at the request of the State Department, would handle foreign intelligence in the Western Hemisphere. The MID and the OWI were to cover the rest of the world.[25]

In response to the president's decision, Hoover set up the FBI's Special Intelligence Service under his assistant director, Percy E. ("Sam") Foxworth. Anticipating events somewhat, Hoover had already dispatched a special agent to Mexico in May, perhaps as a result of Sebold's revelations of the German apparatus there. This was Gus T. Jones, who had worked with Mexican security services prior to September 1939 and would run the FBI's SIS operation in Mexico from 1940 to 1943.[26]

In his work against the Abwehr in Mexico, Jones received unofficial help from his friend Miguel Martínez, the chief of the Federal District Police. Through Martínez he received copies of cable and commercial radio communications between Mexico and Germany, and the Mexican postal service permitted him to open and read the mail addressed to Abwehr station chief Nicolaus and his associates before it was delivered. This generous cooperation received the official blessing of the Mexican government after November 1941, when the United States settled—on Mexico's terms—claims growing out of the Mexican government's expropriation of most of the Standard Oil Company of New Jersey's petroleum holdings three years earlier.[27]

The FBI's access to the Abwehr's communications became total in January 1941, when atmospheric problems prevented Carlos Retelsdorf, the Abwehr's Mexico City clandestine radio operator, from reaching Berlin directly, or indirectly through an Abwehr radio relay in Spain. Abwehr headquarters directed Retelsdorf thereafter to send and receive through Tramp, the operator of a powerful clandestine transmitter in the United States. Tramp was the code name for none other than William Sebold, the bureau's double agent and radio operator for the Duquesne Ring in New York.

Sebold not only provided copies of all the Abwehr's Berlin-Mexico traffic to his bureau handlers; on the FBI's instructions he censored and otherwise tampered with the messages, thereby frustrating German intelligence reporting and disrupting the activities of the Mexican apparatus. The game came to an end the following June, when the Mexican authorities—perhaps at Gus Jones's instigation—shut down Retelsdorf's clandestine transmitter. Hoover decided that it was also the moment to call Sebold in from the cold and roll up the Duquesne Ring and the other Abwehr networks in the United States. Thirty-three Abwehr agents were arrested and convicted of espionage, virtually shutting down German covert operations in America. The Abwehr's Mexican network, having been rendered useless through exposure, gradually disintegrated under the pressure of local press and government harassment.[28]

When William Stephenson returned from his successful mission to the United States in May 1940, Prime Minister Churchill invited him to dinner and proposed that he turn around and go back to take over the British SIS station in New York. Churchill had something more in mind for Stephenson than simply running British secret intelligence operations in the United States: he wished him to organize a British intelligence and covert-action unit to operate throughout the entire Western Hemisphere. But even this was the lesser part of what the prime minister wished the Canadian adventurer to do. Stephenson's assignment was to repeat what Sir William Wiseman had done a generation earlier: to act as an agent of influence in the highest levels of the United States government and bring the United States into the war. Stephenson accepted, and thus was born the agency known as the British Security Coordination.[29]

Stephenson and his wife arrived in New York on June 21, and he soon had installed his staff, a large part of which he brought down from Canada, on two floors of Rockefeller Center. He opened bases throughout the country, in such cities as Washington, Los Angeles, San Francisco, and Seattle, and quickly established a liaison with the Royal Canadian Mounted Police, which was responsible for counterespionage in Canada; with the British Imperial Censorship, which ran a mail-opening operation at the transatlantic air refueling stop of Bermuda; with the British SIS stations throughout Latin America; and, of course, with J. Edgar Hoover.

The BSC was more than the Western Hemisphere branch of the British SIS. It was the joint agency of the SIS and the Special Operations Executive, the newly created British agency for sabotage, subversion, and paramilitary warfare. Additionally, the BSC coordinated the Western Hemisphere operations of seven other British intelligence and security agencies, including Censorship, Codes and Ciphers, Security, and Communications.

Stephenson established Camp X in Oshawa, Canada, on the north shore of Lake Ontario. The clandestine installation was used for training SOE commandos and planning paramilitary operations.[30] He also set up Station M in Canada, where BSC technicians forged and fabricated a wide range of black propaganda and other documents in support of British covert operations. Station M produced bogus Nazi propaganda materials that the BSC fed to an unwitting Walter Winchell, the American radio commentator, who used them to attack Germany in his broadcasts. A letter forged by Station M was reportedly instrumental in Brazil's cancellation of the landing rights of the Italian airline LATI, although some students of the affair attribute that development to secret American diplomacy in the style of Spruille Braden's sandbagging of SCADTA in Colombia.[31]

Stephenson had the benefit of Sir William Wiseman's advice in establishing the BSC, and in at least one instance the English baronet took part in a BSC clandestine operation involving the German consul general in San Francisco, a disaffected member of the German foreign service reportedly toying with the idea of defecting to Britain. In the event, the official did not defect, but he gave Sir William some very valuable strategic intelligence he had acquired a little earlier, when he had been Adolf Hitler's aide-de-camp.[32]

Stephenson's role as chief of British intelligence in the Western Hemisphere was, of course, of secondary importance to his assignment to act as an agent of influence and bring the United States into the war. In furtherance of that, he turned over to the Roosevelt administration in October 1941 a map captioned in German and showing Central and South America divided into new political units. President Roosevelt was so impressed with the document that six days after he received it, he disclosed its existence and dwelt at some length on it in his Navy Day speech, noting that the Nazi planners proposed to divide the region into five German "vassal states." He further noted that one of the new states included the Panama Canal, demonstrating "the Nazi design not only against South America but against the United States as well."[33]

The map, a potent piece of anti-German propaganda both north and south of the border, had ostensibly been stolen by Stephenson's agents from a German diplomatic courier in Brazil. In 1984, however, a former BSC officer asserted that he had dreamed up the map, his draft was turned into a convincing forgery by Station M, and it was this that Stephenson passed on to Roosevelt. (Stephenson spoke out from his Bermuda retirement to deny the assertion.)[34]

Roosevelt was well acquainted with the Canadian-born chief of the BSC. Through Vincent Astor, Stephenson had arranged an interview with FDR soon after he returned to New York in June 1940 to establish the BSC. Presumably, Stephenson sought the meeting to brief the president on his plans for the organization and to lay the groundwork for further cooperation with the highest levels of the Roosevelt administration. At that moment FDR was preparing to send an unofficial observer to London to assess Britain's will and capability to withstand the German onslaught that was expected in the wake of the fall of France and the Low Countries to the advancing Wehrmacht. The president had selected a prominent Republican, William J. Donovan, for this mission. It is possible that FDR discussed Donovan's upcoming trip with Stephenson when he met the BSC chief. Stephenson later recalled that he had proposed both the mission and Donovan to the president. Donovan, who had not previously known Stephenson, believed otherwise.[35] The answer to the riddle may be that Stephenson knew *of* Donovan, possibly through the ROOM, of which one British historian believes Donovan was a member.[36] In any case, Stephenson began working closely with Donovan immediately after his interview with FDR.

Before he became a Wall Street lawyer in 1929, William Joseph Donovan had been, among other things, a war hero (a colonel in New York's famous Fighting Sixty-ninth, he had been awarded the Medal of Honor and numerous other decorations in the First World War), a federal district attorney, a United States assistant attorney general, and an unsuccessful candidate for the governorship of New York. He was a man of enormous energy and wide-ranging interests, which included foreign affairs. While honeymooning in Japan in 1919, he made an unscheduled trip to Siberia for President Wilson to report on the White Russian forces then battling the

Bolsheviks. Later he became a member of the by-invitation-only Council on Foreign Relations. He made frequent trips to Europe, and in 1935 he went to Rome, Egypt, and Ethiopia on an unofficial mission for the War Department to observe the Italian campaign against the latter country. In 1937 he attended maneuvers of the German army and inspected their new tanks and artillery. The following year he made an extended tour of Czechoslovakia, the Balkans, and Italy and visited the battlefields of the Spanish Civil War. By 1939 he knew as much about European military affairs as anyone in America.

Donovan's friendship with the president dated back more than thirty years, to when the pair had attended Columbia Law School together. He was an even closer friend of FDR's secretary of the navy, Frank Knox, a fellow Republican and veteran of Theodore Roosevelt's Rough Riders. Knox, who had first suggested to FDR the advantages of a bipartisan coalition cabinet, had nearly persuaded the president to appoint Donovan secretary of war. Given these connections and Donovan's familiarity with the situation in Europe, it is not surprising that FDR selected him to go to London in July 1940 to study British preparedness and morale.

Whether or not Stephenson had a hand in Donovan's selection, he must have been pleased with the choice. The United States ambassador in London, Joseph P. Kennedy, was regarded by Churchill as a defeatist and had indeed advised the president against American involvement in the war.[37] Donovan, on the other hand, had recently told the American Legion, "In an age of bullies, we cannot afford to be a sissy."[38] Stephenson cabled SIS chief Menzies suggesting Donovan be given full cooperation.

In London, Donovan met with Churchill, the king and queen, and an assortment of British government ministers, armed forces officers, and other leaders, and of course with Menzies and Rear Admiral John H. Godfrey, the chief of the British Naval Intelligence Department. With their cooperation he compiled a detailed picture of Britain at war, covering subjects ranging from food production and public morale to the British need for destroyers and other arms. Back in the United States in August, he delivered his findings to the president: Britain had the will to survive, but she needed American aid.

Donovan made no secret of this with Stephenson, who seems to have known exactly what he was advising the president. On August 21 the BSC chief informed London that "Donovan believes you will have within a few days very favorable news." The following day he reported that Roosevelt had agreed to send fifty-four destroyers to Britain.[39] So important did Stephenson regard Donovan's influence on FDR that when he learned that the president intended to send him on another transatlantic mission, he decided to go along.

The purpose of the second trip was, as Donovan recalled, to "make a strategic appreciation from an economic, political, and military standpoint of the Mediterranean area."[40] When Donovan left on the first leg of his journey from Baltimore on December 6, Stephenson was at his side. After they arrived later that day in Bermuda, the first refueling stop, they learned that weather conditions in the Azores made it temporarily impossible to proceed; the conditions prevailed for the next eight days. Stephenson took advantage of their enforced idleness to urge upon Donovan a proposition he had been preparing for some time: the establishment of an American foreign-intelligence service modeled on British intelligence, a completely secret intelligence agency working directly for the highest level of government.[41]

Stephenson recognized serious limitations in the American intelligence establishment as a result of its organizational and legal structure. In their intelligence collection and analysis, the MID and the ONI reflected the parochial interests of the Departments of War and the Navy, respectively. The FBI was first and foremost a domestic law-enforcement agency, a role Hoover had readily extended to counterespionage both north and south of the border, but the bureau could not reasonably be expected to perform a positive foreign-intelligence role as well (although Hoover claimed otherwise). The State Department collected and produced foreign political intelligence, but the demands of diplomacy and espionage are often in conflict, and State proceeded hesitantly in the latter field for fear of jeopardizing the former. All in all, the fragmented American intelligence establishment fell far short of being a well-oiled, smoothly functioning machine.

In addition to the principal intelligence agencies, a bewildering array of other New Deal agencies had representatives overseas collecting intelligence of one sort or another. These ranged from the Department of the Treasury through the Department of Agriculture to the Post Office and even, amazingly, the Department of the Interior. Altogether, it was estimated, federal agents overseas sent information to Washington at the incomprehensible rate of between two million to ten million words *every day*. This flood of information flowed into the multifold receptacles of the federal bureaucracy, where it was indexed and filed separately as *departmental* intelligence—that is, information required to support the aims and functions of the respective federal departments collecting it.[42] But there was no central agency charged with correlating and integrating this vast information resource to produce the national intelligence the White House needed to make foreign policy—nothing equivalent to what the Inquiry had done in the Wilson administration a generation earlier.

Stephenson also recognized that the American system of checks and balances severely limited the ability of the armed services and other executive-branch departments to conduct covert operations, especially in the sort of international circumstances then prevailing—that is, a period in which peace was in jeopardy, but war had not yet been declared. He saw the need for an agency that could operate beyond the blinding searchlight of congressional scrutiny to carry out black propaganda and other forms of subversion overseas against de facto adversaries in "peacetime."

These were the sort of problems Stephenson pointed out to Donovan during their enforced Bermuda layover, and the solution he proposed was the establishment of a single agency reporting directly to the president, a central intelligence agency.

Stephenson accompanied Donovan to London, where he helped arrange the latter's fact-finding tour of the Mediterranean. Donovan was gone for three months, returning to Washington on March 18 to brief the president, cabinet members, and department heads on his observations. Stephenson lost no time in picking up where he had left off in December, pressing his views on Donovan regarding the establishment of a national-level secret service. Now the BSC chief was often joined in making his sales pitch to Donovan by Sir William Wiseman, who endorsed his successor's proposal for an American central intelligence agency.

Donovan was receptive to the idea, although he resisted the suggestion that he should head such an agency. Just when he began broaching the matter to Frank Knox or the president is unclear, but at this time the matter of coordinating the work of the several federal intelligence agencies was already on FDR's mind. In the face of the worsening international situation, Brigadier General Sherman Miles, the chief of the MID, had opened an MID office in New York City in July 1940 for the same reasons Van Deman had done so during the First World War. But Miles's action brought him into conflict with Hoover, with whom he was already in disagreement over the FBI/SIS exclusive charter in Latin America. To further complicate matters, the ONI resented the freewheeling intelligence activities of Vincent Astor, which were also centered in New York. Astor, a reserve naval officer, had of course been going over the navy's head in dealing directly with the president. FDR resolved the matter by ordering the navy to make Astor controller for the New York area—coordinator of all intelligence and investigative activities undertaken in New York by the ONI, the MID, the FBI, or State. Other interagency jurisdictional squabbles continued, however, and by early April 1941—a few weeks after Donovan's return from the Mediterranean—the president was seriously considering creating a national coordinator of intelligence to resolve the problem.[43]

The president discussed the subject in a cabinet meeting on April 4. Sometime in the next three weeks Donovan discussed Stephenson's proposal with Secretary of the Navy Knox, and at Knox's suggestion Donovan sent him a letter on April 26 containing a brief description of "the instrumentality through which the British Government gathers its information in foreign countries."[44] The letter was actually a brief proposal for an American executive agency to have sole charge of intelligence work abroad, to coordinate the activities of military and naval attachés and others in the collection of information abroad, and to classify and interpret all information from whatever source for the president and for whichever of the services he would designate.

Donovan noted that he was discussing intelligence work in the narrow sense but added that modern warfare includes such things as communications intercepts, psychological warfare, and subversion, and he implied that such activities should also be handled by the proposed agency.[45]

Meanwhile, rumors that Donovan was campaigning to become FDR's intelligence czar somehow reached the ONI, which passed them along to

MID chief Miles. Miles advised Army Chief of Staff George C. Marshall that Donovan was trying to establish a "super agency controlling *all* intelligence," adding that such a move would be "calamitous."[46]

While the MID and the ONI desperately searched for some alternative to Donovan and the "super agency," Stephenson did what he could to advance the Donovan proposal. At the beginning of May, he cabled Menzies that he had been "attempting to persuade Donovan into accepting the job of coordinating all U.S. intelligence." He also persuaded the playwright Robert Sherwood, an FDR intimate and one of the president's speechwriters, to suggest to Roosevelt that Donovan was the man for the job. Also at Stephenson's insisting, John Winant, who had succeeded Joseph Kennedy as American ambassador to Britain, recommended Donovan for the job. Even Vincent Astor, who advocated J. Edgar Hoover for the coordinator's job, answered Stephenson's call to keep the subject of the new agency alive at the White House.[47]

Perhaps recalling FDR's naval background, Stephenson drafted the British director of naval intelligence, Rear Admiral Godfrey, into his campaign. On May 25 Godfrey arrived in New York with his thirty-three-year-old aide, Commander Ian Fleming, later famous for his creation of James Bond. Sir William Wiseman arranged through his friend Arthur H. Sulzberger of the *New York Times* for Godfrey to have a personal interview with the president and present his case both for an American central intelligence agency and for Donovan as its chief.[48]

Secretary Knox or the president apparently asked Donovan for an elaboration of his April 26 outline of the proposed agency. With his Georgetown houseguests Godfrey and Fleming looking over his shoulder and making suggestions, Donovan drafted a document entitled "Memorandum of Establishment of Service of Strategic Information." Although he did not use the terms, Donovan's paper stressed the distinction between departmental and national intelligence. Referring to the latter as "strategic intelligence," he pointed out that it was vital to the decisions of the president as commander in chief. The army and navy, he noted, had intelligence services to collect the technical and operational information those services needed to carry out their missions. But they did not provide an "effective service for analyzing, comprehending, and appraising such information as we might obtain . . . relative to the intention of potential enemies and the limit of the economic and military resources of those enemies." Much of that information, he asserted, was already in government hands, but lay scattered throughout its various departments, needing only to be pulled together "and studied in detail by carefully selected trained minds."

Donovan stressed the importance of national economies in total war and implied that the United States ought to prepare to wage economic warfare against the Axis before a shooting war developed. He stated that such a campaign required accurate and extensive economic intelligence. Likewise, he pointed to the use of radio for psychological warfare as already practiced by Germany and noted that an effective counterattack in kind would require intelligence for the formulation of propaganda.

To accomplish all this, Donovan proposed a "central enemy intelligence organization" that would collect the needed intelligence "either directly or through existing departments of government, at home and abroad," an agency directed by a "Coordinator of Strategic Information" who would report directly to the president and would be assisted by an advisory panel made up of the directors of the FBI, the MID, and the ONI.[49]

Donovan's paper was dated June 10. The document and its author circulated through the administration for some time thereafter. Donovan met with Secretary of War Stimson to resolve objections raised by the army and agreed to add language to his memorandum making it clear the proposed agency would "neither displace nor encroach upon" the MID or any other federal intelligence service. Meanwhile, Stephenson continued to lobby the White House through his friends and sympathizers. After several weeks of behind-the-scenes fence mending, back scratching, and arm twisting, Donovan's advocates had cleared the path, enabling the president to issue an order dated July 11 establishing the position of coordinator of information "with authority to collect and analyze all information and data, which may bear upon national security; to correlate such information and data, . . . and to carry out, when requested by the President, such supplementary activities as may facilitate the securing of information important for national security. . . ."[50]

Somehow Donovan's reluctance to take the job was overcome; FDR had probably insisted that he accept it. The presidential order named Donovan the coordinator of information.

In establishing the post, the president had not formally created an intelligence agency, but his order authorized the coordinator of information to "employ necessary personnel and make provision for necessary supplies, facilities, and services," which in effect gave Donovan the power to set up his organization, funded by the secret presidential Contingent Fund. In adding that provision to his order, FDR created the organization that would shortly be transformed into the Office of Strategic Services and would eventually become the Central Intelligence Agency.

The Office of the Coordinator of Information, or COI, as the organization was soon called, started from modest beginnings on July 11 in three rooms of the State-War-Navy building next to the White House, but Donovan soon needed more space for his rapidly expanding agency. Commander Fleming, whom Admiral Godfrey had left behind to lend a hand, thought a suite of offices in "the FBI building" would be suitable. Donovan wisely decided to stay a safe distance from J. Edgar Hoover, however, and in any case was planning an organization far more prodigious than might be accommodated on Justice Department real estate. Within two weeks the agency occupied thirty-two rooms in a government building at the foot of Capitol Hill; a month later it had moved to a complex of buildings in Foggy Bottom. Donovan opened a New York office and made plans for facilities on the West Coast and in London. Having been given an initial budget of nearly $1.5 million, the coordinator of information would go back to the well within two months asking for $10 million.[51]

Young Commander Fleming was brimming over with advice for the new intelligence chief, and he began regaling Donovan with a stream of memorandums on the general subject of "how to create an American Secret Service." When he realized his counsel was being courteously ignored, however, he grew discouraged and went back to London, leaving Donovan in Stephenson's capable hands. So close was the collaboration between William Stephenson and William Donovan that associates began speaking to each other of Little Bill and Big Bill to distinguish between the former and the latter.

But notwithstanding Stephenson's desire that the COI become a partner with his BSC in covert operations against the Axis in the Western

Hemisphere, such matters fell several rungs down on Donovan's agenda. FDR's order had provided the coordinator of information with authority to conduct "such supplementary activities as may facilitate the securing of information important for national security," a euphemistic reference to foreign espionage, but Donovan did not view secret intelligence as a priority function. He did, however, place great importance on psychological warfare, both overt and covert, and one of his earliest acts was to appoint Robert Sherwood chief of what soon became formalized as the Foreign Information Service of the COI, a unit that monitored and analyzed Axis propaganda and formulated overt American counterpropaganda.[52]

Recognizing the persuasive power of motion pictures, Donovan hired Merian C. Cooper, a First World War combat pilot who had become a Hollywood producer-director, best known for the 1933 *King Kong*. In turn, Cooper hired filmmaker John Ford, who, as a lieutenant commander in the Naval Reserve, had assembled a reserve unit of some two hundred other film professionals. Ford brought thirty members of the unit along to the COI, where they became the Field Photographic Division, an outfit destined to film the Normandy landings in June 1944.

Donovan's top priority, however, was, as he had originally told Knox and FDR, the coordination of intelligence—that is, the integration of the flood of information pouring into Washington—and the production of national intelligence for the president. He saw this as an intellectual process best performed by scholars, and so he turned to the poet and librarian of Congress Archibald MacLeish to help him assemble a staff of academic brainpower to cope with the problem. MacLeish, who had already set up a Division of Special Information within the library to supply COI with maps and other basic intelligence, guided Donovan to the best heads in academia.

Donovan recruited the historian Dr. James Phinney Baxter III to head the COI's Research and Analysis Branch, the section central to the intelligence-coordination function.[53] Baxter, who had been president of Williams College before answering Donovan's call, was, like Donovan, a member of the Council on Foreign Relations, and many of the scholars he recruited for the R&A Branch were fellow members of the council. Among those who soon joined were council members Conyers Read, professor of English history at the University of Pennsylvania, and the economist Calvin

Hoover, an expert on both Nazi Germany and Soviet Russia. One of the most prestigious additions to the R&A Branch was the Harvard history professor William L. Langer, also a council member. Thus, through the council there was a measure of continuity between America's first national intelligence agency, the Inquiry, and her second.

Council membership was, of course, not a prerequisite for serving in the branch. Sherman Kent, an assistant professor of history at Yale before he became head of the African Section of R&A, was not a member, nor was the Howard University political scientist Ralph J. Bunche, nor the German-born political philosopher Herbert Marcuse, three of the earliest recruits.[54]

In early September a Central Information Division was established within the R&A Branch to handle central filing, registry, and editing of intelligence reports. From his legal experience Donovan understood the value of a central reference service, and he had resolved that the COI should have the best possible central filing system possible. He set up a Board of Analysts to oversee the work of the R&A Branch and to serve as his personal panel of experts. To balance the academics on the board, Major General Frank McCoy and Commander F. C. Denebrink were added. Veteran diplomat John C. Wiley was also appointed to the panel, to represent the intelligence needs of the State Department. Sometime in the fall of 1941, a small staff was created and attached to the board to provide the administration with the latest political, military, or economic intelligence available through a secret weekly publication, *The War This Week*.[55]

By September there were forty people working for the COI. By December the figure had almost reached six hundred.[56] Donovan had every reason to believe he was well on his way to dealing with the Niagara of intelligence flowing daily into Washington. He was unaware, however, of one category of intelligence that only the president and a small handful of cabinet officers and department heads saw. Code-named Magic, it was the communications intelligence produced by the army's Signal Intelligence Service and the navy's Code and Cipher Section through the decipherment of Japanese diplomatic traffic with the Purple cipher machine. None of this intelligence was passed along to the COI, even though that agency had been specifically created to integrate *all* foreign intelligence. Neither Donovan nor the R&A staff even knew it existed.

* * *

On the first weekend in December, Donovan was in New York City. On Sunday he went to the Polo Grounds to watch a professional football game between the New York Giants and the Brooklyn Dodgers. Sometime in the second quarter he heard his name called on the public-address system. Rushing to the stadium box office, he was handed a telephone. The president's son, James, was on the line from Washington. Donovan was to report to the White House immediately. Mid-afternoon on the East Coast, it was still early morning in Hawaii, where Japanese aircraft had just attacked the army air bases at Hickam and Wheeler fields and the naval base at Pearl Harbor.

Chapter Thirty

Anatomy of Infamy

Port Arthur, at the tip of a finger of Manchuria pointing into the Yellow Sea, became an important Russian naval base in the latter part of the nineteenth century. On the night of February 8, 1904, seven Russian battleships and six cruisers lay at anchor in the Port Arthur roadstead. Russia was not at war, and therefore the warships were not in a state of alert. Thus, the sudden appearance out of the ocean darkness of the Japanese Combined Fleet came as a total and fatal surprise.

The Japanese surprise attack on Port Arthur and a coordinated attack the same night on another Russian force at Inchon, Korea, neutralized Russian sea power in eastern Asia and gave Japan naval superiority in the region. Not until two days later did Japan declare war on Russia.

As at Port Arthur, the objective of the Japanese surprise attack on Pearl Harbor was to destroy in one swift and unexpected blow the enemy's sea power in the Pacific. In those terms the attack was nearly a complete success. Some ninety-four American naval vessels—most of the United States Pacific Fleet—were in Pearl Harbor at 7:55 A.M. on December 7 when the carrier-based Japanese bombers and torpedo aircraft struck; only the fleet's three aircraft carriers happened to be at sea. Eighteen American warships, including seven of the fleet's eight battleships, were either sunk or damaged so severely as to be inoperable. Two thousand four hundred and three Americans were killed; 1,178 were wounded.

It was the worst single military defeat in American history, and it was also the most monumental intelligence failure. The blow had been struck without a declaration of war and while a Japanese delegation was still in

Washington negotiating outstanding differences with the United States government.

The Japanese preference for strategic surprise over the niceties of formal declarations of war was of course well known by 1941; repeating the Port Arthur scenario, Japan had attacked China without warning in 1937. "History shows that Japan strikes without warning," the ONI planners wrote in their 1937 update of War Plan Orange.[1] As Japanese-American relations approached a crisis in the late fall of 1941, the United States government had good reason to anticipate an unannounced Japanese attack on American forces somewhere in the Pacific. And, as eight separate official investigations would later show, American intelligence had considerable evidence in its possession indicating that the blow would fall at Pearl Harbor. One of the earliest indications was received more than ten months before the attack.

On January 27, 1941, Joseph C. Grew, the United States ambassador in Tokyo, reported to the State Department that the Peruvian minister to Japan, Ricardo Rivera-Schreiber, had advised an American diplomat he had heard credible rumors that the Japanese planned a massive surprise attack on Pearl Harbor in the event of trouble with the United States.[2] Grew did not press Rivera-Schreiber to name his Japanese source, who, it has since transpired, was a Japanese employee of the Peruvian ministry who in turn heard it from her boyfriend, a Japanese chauffeur.[3] The State Department passed Grew's report along to the ONI, which sent it to Admiral Husband E. Kimmel, the commander of the Pacific Fleet, with the comment, "Naval Intelligence places no credence in these rumors."[4] Kimmel's chief intelligence officer, Commander Edwin T. Layton, remembered the report two months later, however, while reading a book by a Japanese naval writer. The book referred to an American naval exercise that involved a mock carrier attack on Pearl Harbor, and it speculated on the possibility of Japan's carrying out such an operation in earnest.[5]

There had indeed been such an exercise as the one to which the Japanese author referred. It had taken place in February 1932 and involved the carriers *Lexington* and *Saratoga* under the command of Rear Admiral Harry E. Yarnell, an officer who had long warned of the Japanese threat. The mock attack was carried out at dawn on February 7, a Sunday, when Yarnell correctly estimated that the naval base would be least prepared to resist.

Just as in the real attack nearly ten years later, the planes approached from the northeast, taking advantage of the cover provided by the rain clouds that the trade winds produce during the winter when they blow against the mountains of the Koolau Range, which parallels the northeastern coast of Oahu. No aircraft rose to meet the sham invaders of this no-notice exercise, and the carrier-based planes were judged by the war-game umpires to have sunk all the naval vessels in the harbor.[6]

The results of Fleet Problem 13, as the Pearl Harbor exercise was designated, made little impression on the navy brass in Washington, but Japanese intelligence paid close attention to the demonstration. One Japanese officer who mastered the lessons Admiral Yarnell had taught was Isoroku Yamamoto, commander of the Japanese Combined Fleet.

Yamamoto, born in 1884, had graduated first in his class at the Japanese Naval Staff College and then studied for two years at Harvard, spending one summer hitchhiking to Mexico to work in the Mexican oil fields. A naval pilot, he had helped develop Japanese torpedo-bombing techniques, generally regarded as superior to those of the West. After sea duty and a tour as naval attaché in Washington, he joined the Japanese navy's General Staff as a war planner in 1928. During the 1930s he rose rapidly and in 1939 was made commander in chief of the Combined Fleet, the main Japanese naval force (consisting of the First Fleet, a battleship force; and the Second Fleet: aircraft carriers, cruisers, destroyers, and submarines).[7]

Although he enjoyed games of chance, he was not tempted to long shots in warfare. He was not optimistic about Japan's prospects in a war with the United States; in August 1940 he accurately predicted to the prime minister, Prince Konoye, "In the first six to twelve months of a war with the United States and Great Britain I will run wild and win victory upon victory. But then, if the war continues after that, I have no expectation of success."[8]

Because he knew that a short war was the only kind of war with the United States that Japan could hope to win, Yamamoto saw that it was essential to destroy American sea power in the Pacific at the very outset, in one swift surprise attack. The United States Navy had obligingly concentrated its entire Pacific Fleet in one place, but that place was the fortified naval base at Pearl Harbor, lying more than three thousand miles away. Was it possible for a carrier task force to cross that vast expanse of ocean undetected? Yamamoto thought so. Was it possible for the planes from the task force to destroy the American warships at their moorings? Yamamoto began giving that question very close consideration toward the end of 1940.

He remembered the lesson taught by Admiral Yarnell's Fleet Problem 13 in 1932. More recently, in April and May 1940, the Japanese navy had experimented with torpedoes launched by aircraft against warships at anchor in a harbor and concluded they were highly effective in such a situation. In November the results of the Japanese exercises were confirmed in actual combat, when twenty-one British carrier-based planes sank three Italian warships at Taranto in southern Italy. Yamamoto ordered the Japanese naval attachés in London and Rome to make detailed studies of the Taranto raid.[9]

Yamamoto's staff planners turned up one problem almost immediately: the waters of Pearl Harbor were much shallower than those in the Japanese exercise or the Taranto attack. Torpedoes launched from aircraft would bury themselves in the mud on the bottom of Pearl Harbor. But to Yamamoto this seemed a mere technical problem that could be overcome through the development of shallow-running torpedoes. Early in 1941 his staff completed a first draft of a Pearl Harbor attack plan. Discussion of this report in imperial naval circles may have resulted in the rumors heard by the Peruvian minister and passed along by Ambassador Grew to Washington late in January. Ironically, one of the several reasons the United States Navy "placed no credence" in the Peruvian's report was the belief that torpedoes could not be dropped effectively in less than seventy feet of water, nearly twice the depth of Pearl Harbor.[10]

The depth of Pearl Harbor and every other available fact about the naval base were in the files of the Third Bureau, as the intelligence department of the Japanese navy's General Staff was known. Since May 1940, when the United States Pacific Fleet made Pearl Harbor its home base, Japanese agents working under official cover as consular officials had been collecting intelligence in Hawaii for the Third Bureau. Consul General Kiichi Gunji and his successor, Otojiro Okuda, had only to read the Honolulu *Star-Bulletin*, which reported the fleet's movements accurately and in detail. To confirm what appeared in the press, the consulate assigned its treasurer,

Kohichi Seki, to take regular taxi rides around the harbor. The information thus collected was encrypted and sent to Tokyo by commercial cable.

Gunji, Okuda, and Seki were amateur spies, however, foreign-service officers who had been drafted into intelligence work. In March 1941 the Third Bureau put Pearl Harbor in more professional hands, those of twenty-eight-year-old Takeo Yoshikawa, a former naval officer who had been invalided out of the service and then became a highly trained intelligence agent specializing in American operations. The Third Bureau's dispatch of Yoshikawa to Honolulu to work under consular cover reflected the increasing seriousness with which the Japanese government was taking Yamamoto's plan for an attack on Pearl Harbor. Japanese-American relations were rapidly going from bad to worse.[11]

In a move to defuse the crisis in Japanese-American relations that had developed in mid-1941, Japan's prime minister, Prince Konoye, proposed face-to-face negotiations with FDR to resolve the impasse, but the president insisted on specific Japanese concessions in advance of such a meeting, and the proposal was dropped. This humiliation brought about the fall of the Konoye government in October 1941, and Konoye was succeeded by the far more hawkish Lieutenant General Hideki Tōjō, the former war minister.

Early in November, Tōjō sent a special envoy, Saburo Kurusu, to Washington to assist the Japanese ambassador in negotiating a way out of the deadlock. Kurusu presented Japan's final offer on November 20, 1941: Japan would withdraw from southern Indochina if the United States would release her assets, supply her with oil and other strategic materials, and refrain from aiding Chinese resistance to Japan. Six days later Secretary of State Cordell Hull made the American counterproposal: the United States would unfreeze Japanese assets and resume trade if Japan would withdraw from all of Indochina, and from China as well, and join in a multilateral nonaggression pact covering eastern Asia.

Hull had no illusions that the Japanese would accept; the following day he told Secretary of War Henry Stimson that the problem now lay in the hands of the army and navy. Stimson knew just what he meant because, ironically, the man who had shut down the Cipher Bureau some twelve years earlier had recently, along with Hull and other senior officials of the Roosevelt administration, been reading other people's mail.

After Friedman's team successfully reconstructed a Purple machine in September 1940, navy technicians built several additional machines. Two were for use in Washington by army and navy cryptanalysts, and a third machine was sent to a navy intercept station in the Philippines. A fourth was taken to Britain and presented to the Government Code and Cypher School, as the British code-breaking center was called, at Bletchley Park, a country estate some fifty miles north of London. The British had learned of Friedman's breakthrough less than a month after the event, reportedly from Brigadier General George V. Strong, chief of the War Plans Division of the United States Army's General Staff, who happened to be in London on a liaison mission.[12]

The foundation for Anglo-American code-breaking cooperation was reportedly laid by BSC chief William Stephenson during his meeting with FDR in 1940 and made into a formal arrangement by the British ambassador, Lord Lothian, when he met with the president the following July. In return for the Purple machine and its underlying theory, the British gave the United States an assortment of advanced electronic and cryptologic equipment, including, by some accounts, British know-how in breaking the Enigma machine cipher in use by Germany. Anglo-American cooperation at this time also included an exchange of Japanese intercepts made at the British listening post in Singapore and the United States Navy's station in the Philippines.[13]

By November both the army's Signal Intelligence Service and OP-20-G (the ONC's Communications Security Section) were reading the Japanese traffic; the work load was split so that the army's SIS processed the intercepts on even days of the month; OP-20-G, on odd days.

The Tokyo-Washington route of the Japanese diplomatic traffic was by commercial radio telegram and cable. The traffic went between Tokyo and San Francisco by radio and between San Francisco and Washington by land lines. The SIS had an intercept station at the Presidio in San Francisco, but most of the interception of the Tokyo-Washington traffic was done by the navy's Station S on Bainbridge Island, across Puget Sound from

Seattle. The Bainbridge intercepts were relayed to OP-20-G in Washington by teletype; those received at the Presidio went to the SIS by mail. Navy intercept stations in Hawaii and the Philippines picked up Japanese diplomatic communications with Berlin and Moscow and sent the traffic to the West Coast by weekly Pan American Clipper, to be forwarded to Washington.[14] The Japanese intercepts furnished by the British from their Singapore listening post were probably sent the same way.

The decrypts made with the Purple and Red machines, as well as other encrypted Japanese diplomatic traffic solved by the SIS and OP-20-G, were the intelligence collectively designated Magic.[15] The Magic material was the most sensitive national-security information held by the United States government; obviously, disclosure of the fact that American code breakers were reading the intercepts would cause Japan to abandon the Purple machine for a more secure cryptosystem. Initially, Army Chief of Staff general George C. Marshall, with the consent of Admiral Harold R. Stark, the chief of naval operations, restricted the dissemination of Magic to a small handful of senior army and navy officers, and Secretaries Stimson and Knox. Under an army-navy agreement of January 23, 1941, this group was enlarged to include the president, the secretary of state, the directors of the MID and the ONI, and the chief of the navy's War Plans Division.

After the Magic intercepts had been decrypted and translated into English, copies were made and hand-delivered in locked pouches to the recipients, each of whom held a key to his respective pouch. The number of people authorized to view the Magic material was somewhat larger than the distribution list. Presidential adviser Harry Hopkins saw it, as did the president's military and naval aides. Under Secretary of State Sumner Welles and three other senior State Department officials read the intercepts. Commander Arthur H. McCollum, chief of the ONI's Far Eastern Section, and his MID counterpart, Colonel Rufus S. Bratton, were of course cleared for Magic.[16]

The one Purple machine outside Washington (excepting the one given to the British) was at the navy's intercept station at Cavite in the Philippines. Since some of the Magic material was decrypted there, and because the Philippines were regarded as being at highest risk of a Japanese attack, the decrypted intercepts were also shown to Admiral Thomas C. Hart, commander of the United States Asiatic Fleet, based in the Philippines.

After FDR sent Lieutenant General Douglas MacArthur to the Philippines to merge the Philippine army with local United States Army units in July 1941, he, too, was shown some of the Magic material.[17]

Of greater retrospective significance are some of those who were not given access to Magic. The field commanders of major military and naval units were excluded, including Lieutenant General Walter C. Short, the army commander in Hawaii, and Rear Admiral Kimmel, commander of the Pacific Fleet. Both officers were sent intelligence derived from the Magic intercepts from time to time, but neither was a regular recipient of Magic nor even aware of the communications-intelligence operation. Washington's decision to hold Magic so closely was underscored in May when the Japanese Foreign Office warned Kichisaburo Nomura, its ambassador in Washington, in a Purple telegram, "According to a fairly reliable source of information it appears almost certain that the United States Government is reading your code messages," to which Nomura replied, also in Purple, after investigating the matter, "Though I do not know which ones[,] I have discovered the United States is reading some of our codes."[18] Obviously, the Foreign Office and Nomura did not suspect the Purple cipher had been broken, but they might have reached that conclusion if they had continued to worry about the matter. This flap may have been the reason Washington sent Admiral Kimmel no more Magic intelligence until early December, when it was almost too late.

Another name conspicuous by its absence on the Magic distribution list was J. Edgar Hoover. Robert L. Shivers, special agent in charge of the FBI's Honolulu office, along with local officers of the ONI and army intelligence and the Honolulu Police Department, had the Japanese consulate under surveillance and were convinced it was a center of espionage. Tokyo's instructions to the naval intelligence agent Yoshikawa were part of the Magic material and, together with Shivers's reports and other data in the bureau's files, might have given FBI headquarters a clearer picture of the objectives of Japanese espionage in Hawaii.[19]

But the most serious omission from the Magic distribution list was the name of William J. Donovan, who, as coordinator of information, had been given the presidential authority "to collect and analyze all information and data which may bear upon national security" and was charged with the task of correlating such intelligence. The president's chief intelligence officer, the one person in the government responsible for national intelligence, had not even been told of the existence of Magic.

Admiral Yamamoto's plan for the Pearl Harbor attack proceeded in parallel with the diplomatic crisis precipitated by the Anglo-American oil embargo in June. The First Carrier Division of the Combined Fleet had begun training for the operation early that month and had continued to do so throughout the summer and into the autumn. Kagoshima Bay on the southern end of Kyūshū, the southernmost of Japan's main islands, was selected as the training site because of its general similarity to Pearl Harbor. Throughout the summer and into the fall, bombers and torpedo planes of the First Carrier Division roared over the rooftops of the city of Kagoshima and out into the bay in simulated attacks on a mock Pacific Fleet.[20]

In September research on a shallow-running torpedo culminated in the testing of the Model II at the Yokosuka Naval Air Station. The Model II was found effective when dropped into twelve meters of water, roughly the depth of Pearl Harbor. Now the Japanese planners turned their attention to another problem: the possibility that the American warships at Pearl Harbor were protected by torpedo nets.[21]

During the first two weeks in September, the fleet commanders met at the Imperial Naval Staff College, where they tested the Pearl Harbor plan—now officially designated Plan Z—using tabletop war-gaming. The games turned up no serious problems in the plan, but they did generate a host of detailed intelligence requirements regarding the current situation at Pearl Harbor.[22]

On September 24 the Third Bureau sent a cable through the Foreign Office to the Japanese consulate in Honolulu. It was the first of a series of intelligence requests aimed at keeping a detailed and up-to-date picture of the Pacific Fleet at Pearl Harbor. The cable divided the harbor into five areas, designated A through E, for the purpose of reporting the locations of the American warships, and it concluded with this highly suggestive request:

With regard to warships and aircraft carriers, we would like to have you report on those at anchor (these are not so important), tied up at wharves, buoys and in docks. (Designate types and classes briefly. If possible, we would like to have you make mention of the fact when there are two or more vessels along side the same wharf.)[23]

The message, which had been sent in cipher, was intercepted by a Signal Intelligence Service listening post in Hawaii. The station, which had recently been set up, had no facilities for code breaking, and so the message was bundled with all the other Magic intercepts and mailed to SIS headquarters in Washington. The weekly Pan American Clipper flight to the West Coast was scrubbed because of bad weather, however, so this batch of intercepts went by sea to San Francisco and did not reach Washington until October 6. On October 9 the overworked code-breaking staff of SIS got around to decrypting and translating the message, and it was sent to Colonel Bratton, chief of the MID's Far Eastern Section.

Bratton was struck and somewhat alarmed by the "unusual interest" the Japanese were showing in Pearl Harbor. He showed the intercept to MID chief Brigadier General Sherman Miles. Miles dismissed it as routine Japanese naval espionage without any special significance. Bratton routed the message to Secretary Stimson, General Marshall, and the chief of the army's War Plans Division; none of them found it particularly interesting. The ONI speculated that the new grid system established in the message might merely be intended to improve communications efficiency, although someone in the office allowed that it might indicate a Japanese plot to sabotage American warships at Pearl Harbor. But the intercept made no impression, except on Bratton. Most of those who were shown the message did not even recall having seen it after its real significance was understood.[24]

Meanwhile, Takeo Yoshikawa, the Third Bureau's man in Honolulu, responded to the cable by making a survey of the harbor and noting the exact location and class of each warship. On September 29 he sent off a cipher cablegram to Tokyo containing this information and his own improvement on the grid system the Third Bureau had proposed. Throughout October and November, Yoshikawa made frequent tours of Oahu by bus, taxicab, and even sightseeing flights over the island. The sightseeing planes were forbidden to fly directly over the harbor, but they passed close enough to give the Japanese agent an excellent view of the fleet. Yoshikawa was also able to note the number and direction of the runways on Wheeler and Hickam fields from the vantage of the aircraft.

On the fifteenth of November the Third Bureau sent the following cipher telegram to Yoshikawa: "As relations between Japan and the United States are most critical, make your 'ships in harbor report' irregular, but at a rate of twice a week. Although you are no doubt aware, please take extra care to maintain secrecy."[25]

This intercept was mailed from Hawaii to Washington, where it was not decrypted and translated until December 3. The linkage of Japanese espionage at Pearl Harbor with the progress of Japanese-American diplomatic relations and the demand for semiweekly updating of the positions of American warships in the harbor seem extremely suggestive in retrospect. Nonetheless, the message did not attract any particular notice among the readers of Magic when they saw it less than a week before the attack.

During November the flow of Magic intercepts had turned into a flood. An average of twenty-six intercepts were received every day.[26] Most of them concerned the diplomatic negotiations in Washington, and it was Tokyo's instructions to the Washington negotiators, not its spying in Hawaii, that captured the attention of the Magic readers during this period.

On November 5 Tokyo informed Ambassador Nomura that it was "absolutely necessary" to obtain American agreement to its final offer by November 25. On the eleventh another cable to Nomura emphasized that the November 25 date was "absolutely immovable."[27] Both messages were decrypted, translated, and sent to the Magic recipients within twenty-four hours.

Special Envoy Kurusu arrived in Washington to join in the negotiations, carrying Tokyo's final offer to Washington, on November 15, the same day the Third Bureau emphasized to Yoshikawa the relationship between the negotiations and his espionage mission. Also on that date the Foreign Ministry again told Ambassador Nomura that November 25 was the deadline for the negotiations to achieve the results Tokyo desired.[28] The navy's cryptanalysts decrypted, translated, and distributed this message as soon as it arrived in Washington—that is, on November 15.

Kurusu and Nomura pleaded with Tokyo for more time. On November 22 the Foreign Ministry extended the deadline four days, to the twenty-ninth. "This time we mean it," Tokyo emphasized in its ciphered cablegram; "the deadline absolutely cannot be changed. After that things are automatically going to happen."[29] The navy's cryptanalysts decrypted, translated, and distributed this message the same day.

On November 26 Secretary of State Hull made the American counterproposal. As he expected, it failed to satisfy Tokyo. That same day the Magic cryptanalysts deciphered and translated a Tokyo-Washington message that had been intercepted on the nineteenth. Providing for the possibility that in a crisis the Tokyo-Washington cable channels might be cut off, the message established an open code, the words *East wind rain*, which would be included in Japanese shortwave newscasts, ostensibly as a weather report, in the event of an imminent rupture in Japanese-American relations. Upon hearing these words, the Japanese embassy was to destroy all its codes and secret documents.[30]

On November 28 the Foreign Ministry advised Kurusu and Nomura that "the negotiations will be de facto ruptured. . . . However, I do not wish you to give the impression that the negotiations are broken off. Merely say to them that you are awaiting instructions. . . ."[31] The following day Tokyo re-emphasized that the negotiators should not give the Americans the impression the negotiations had been broken off. Both messages were decrypted, translated, and sent to the Magic recipients the same day they were received by the Japanese embassy. On December 1 Tokyo returned to the same theme in another cable to its Washington negotiators: ". . . To Prevent the United States from becoming unduly suspicious we have been advising the press and others that though there are some wide differences between Japan and the United States, the negotiations are continuing. (The above is for only your information.)"[32] This was in the hands of the Magic recipients the same day it was received by the Japanese embassy.

It was obvious to readers of Magic that Japan was planning to make some grave aggressive move against the United States in the event she could not secure her diplomatic objectives and that this step would be taken around the end of November or shortly thereafter. It seemed most probable that this step involved further aggression in Southeast Asia and possibly also an attack on the Philippines. Collateral to the Magic intercepts of Japanese diplomatic communications, the MID and the ONI had learned that Japanese ground forces were moving south from China, and

Japanese naval forces were concentrating in the South China Sea, apparently preparing to strike Thailand or the Dutch East Indies.[33] This, however, was only part of the picture and, in terms of American interests, the less important part.

On November 5 the Japanese government had decided to execute Yamamoto's Plan Z—the Pearl Harbor attack—in the event the United States did not accede to its demands by November 25. As we have seen, Yamamoto had been moving ahead with his preparations since June and had put the operation into high gear after the war-gaming exercises at the Imperial Naval Staff College in September proved the plan to be feasible. In mid-October the Third Bureau sent several naval officers to Hawaii aboard the liner *Tatuta Maru* to double-check what agent Yoshikawa had been reporting. On October 22 a second Japanese liner, the *Taiyo Maru*, had departed Yokohama and headed for Honolulu by a northern route that passed between Midway and the Aleutian Islands, then turned southeast and finally approached Oahu from the north. It was the route Yamamoto had selected for the carrier task force, and the mission of the *Taiyo Maru* was to confirm the admiral's belief that his warships could make the trip undetected and to collect weather data en route. The liner arrived at Honolulu on November 1, having sighted no other ship or plane until she was within two hundred miles of the target.[34]

Between November 15 and 21 the Pearl Harbor task force assembled in Tankan Bay, a desolate outpost in the Kurile Islands north of Japan. It consisted of the six newest and largest aircraft carriers, with a total of 423 combat aircraft; a screen of nine destroyers and a light cruiser; a support force of two battleships and two heavy cruisers; three submarines; and a supply train of seven or eight tankers. The task force left the Kuriles and headed east on November 26 (November 25 in Washington), as the negotiations in Washington rapidly approached a climax.

As the Japanese fleet plowed through the stormy winter seas of the North Pacific, the Third Bureau worked to pin down the situation at Pearl Harbor with even greater precision. On the twenty-eighth it cabled Agent Yoshikawa, "Report upon the entrance or departure of capital ships and the length of time they remain at anchor, from the time of entry into port until the departure."[35] The bureau followed up the next day with yet another requirement: "We have been receiving reports from you on ship movements, but in the future will you also report even when there are no movements."[36] The Japanese intelligence chiefs were not taking the chance of missing one of Yoshikawa's messages; they wanted a regular report from him even if it was only that there was nothing new to report. The two messages were decrypted by the Magic code breakers in Washington on December 5. Once again, the Magic readers failed to recognize that the messages pinpointed Pearl Harbor as a Japanese target.

In Honolulu the ONI's district intelligence officer, Captain Irving Mayfield, had been watching the Japanese consulate carefully for months and had even tapped half a dozen of the consulate's telephone lines but had failed to turn up evidence of espionage or to identify Yoshikawa as the principal agent. Mayfield had tried to obtain copies of the consulate's ciphered telegrams in the hope that the navy's local cryptographic unit at Pearl Harbor might be able to read them, but the cable companies cited the law and resolutely refused to turn them over. In mid-November RCA president David Sarnoff was vacationing in Hawaii, and Mayfield appealed to him personally in the matter. Sarnoff agreed to have the RCA's Honolulu cable office cooperate discreetly with the ONI officer, but the consulate had a policy of rotating among three cable companies on a monthly basis. The MacKay Radio Company was handling the consulate's cables in November; RCA's turn would not come round again until December 1.[37]

On December 2 the Third Bureau cabled Yoshikawa:

In view of the present situation, the presence in port of warships, airplane carriers, and cruisers is of utmost importance. Hereafter, to the utmost of your ability, let me know day by day. Wire me in each case whether or not there are any observation balloons above Pearl Harbor or if there are any indications that they will be sent up. Also advice me whether or not the warships are provided with antimine [i.e., anti-torpedo] nets.[38]

Mayfield received a copy of the message from the RCA office and took it to Station Hypo, OP-20-G's local unit at Pearl Harbor, hidden away in the basement of an administration building on the naval base. The consular traffic was not sent in the Purple cipher but in one of the older and simpler Japanese cryptosystems. Therefore, the Hypo code breakers had already decrypted the consular messages the RCA office had given Mayfield on December 1 and had found the contents to be of "absolutely no value." They therefore put aside the extremely revealing December 2 message until they would have time to work on it.[39] Station Hypo was at this point in the midst of another crisis: it had lost track of the whereabouts of Japan's largest aircraft carriers.

Through radio direction-finding techniques and the monitoring of the routine, unencrypted Japanese naval communications, Hypo had been tracking virtually all the large warships of the Imperial Navy. During the third week of November, however, the six large carriers of the Pearl Harbor task force disappeared from the airwaves; in fact, they had been proceeding under strict and complete radio silence to the task-force rendezvous at Tankan Bay. The entire task force was now moving through the North Pacific in radio silence, the ships signaling each other when necessary by flag or blinker. (Intelligence updates and commands were radioed to the task force in a Japanese naval code that, unfortunately, had not yet been broken by any American cryptanalytic unit.) At Hypo the navy analysts concluded that the carriers had switched to the short-range radio frequencies they always used while in home waters, but by the end of November the continued silence was beginning to appear suspicious. To confuse matters further, the entire Imperial Navy switched call signs on December 1.[40] Thus, on December 2 the Hypo staff was completely occupied by the problem of sorting out the situation when the Tokyo-Honolulu intercepts were delivered. Had they chosen to decipher the December 2 message to Yoshikawa, the Third Bureau's questions about torpedo nets and aerial obstructions at Pearl Harbor might have suggested a possible answer to the mystery of the missing aircraft carriers.

Captain Mayfield could do no more than wait patiently for the decryption of the consulate's cables. He of course was unaware of the Magic operation or that a Magic intercept station on Oahu had also intercepted the telling December 2 message. In any event, the Magic intercept was not even mailed to Washington until December 11. It was decrypted, translated, and distributed on the thirtieth, at which time its significance was perfectly obvious and completely useless.[41]

* * *

Aerial photoreconnaissance, a major intelligence collection method during World War II and thereafter, had its roots in World War I. Here a pilot and observer plan a mission over France while a ground crewman installs the aerial camera in the Sopwith biplane. (*National Archives*)

Radio direction finding was yet another source of intelligence perfected between the world wars. Here a U.S. army direction-finding van is in use near Verdun, France, in 1918. (*National Archives*)

At the Paris Peace Conference of 1919, the American Commission to Negotiate Peace included an extensive current intelligence apparatus to support United States strategy at the Conference. In this photograph of some staff members, Colonel Ralph Van Deman is seated second from the left. The man standing directly behind him may be future Director of Central Intelligence Allen W. Dulles. (*National Archives*)

As General John J. Pershing's chief of intelligence in France in World War I, Major Dennis E. Nolan operated independently of Colonel Van Deman's Military Intelligence Division in Washington. After the war Brigadier General Nolan became director of the MID. (*Library of Congress*)

An alumnus of a U.S. Navy program to train officers in Japanese language and military affairs, Ellis M. Zacharias led the Navy's fledgling communications intelligence campaigns against Japan. (*U.S. Navy*)

In 1926 Zacharias fitted out the destroyer U.S.S. *McCormick* (top) as an electronic spy ship to intercept Japanese naval communications in the western Pacific. The following year he commanded the cruiser U.S.S. *Marblehead* (bottom) on a mission to observe electronically the war games of the Japanese Combined Fleet. (*U.S. Naval Institute*)

Brigadier General Sherman Miles
(shown here as a young officer) was
chief of Army Intelligence at the
time of the Japanese attack on Pearl
Harbor. Like other senior American
intelligence officers, Miles was aware of
the increasing likelihood of a Japanese
attack on U.S. forces in December 1941,
but was unable to foresee that the blow
would fall on Hawaii. (*National Archives*)

Architect of the Pearl Harbor attack and
commander in chief of the Japanese
Combined Fleet, Admiral Isoroku
Yamamoto had no illusions of his
country's prospects: "In the first six to
twelve months of a war with the United
States and Great Britain I will run wild
and win victory upon victory. But then,
if the war continues after that, I have no
expecttion of success." (*U.S. Navy*)

Although President Franklin D. Roosevelt
had appointed him Coordinator of
Information, i.e., chief national intelligence
officer, Colonel William J. Donovan was not
aware that U.S. code breakers were reading
all the Japanese diplomatic traffic in the
months before Pearl Harbor. (*U.S. Army*)

Lieutenant Commander Edwin T.
Layton was chief of intelligence for the
Pacific Fleet at the time of the Pearl
Harbor attack, but he too was unaware of
the crucial communications intelligence
held by the Army and Navy intelligence
chiefs in Washington. (*U.S. Navy*)

Despite the incredible achievements of American code breakers that enabled national military, naval, and political leaders to read all the Japanese diplomatic traffic in the months before the event, Pearl Harbor became the worst intelligence failure in American history. Shown here are a photograph of "battleship row" taken from a Japanese aircraft during the attack (top), and the explosion of ammunition magazines aboard the destroyer U.S.S. *Shaw* after it was hit by a Japanese bomb (bottom). (*Top: Naval Historical Center; bottom: National Archives*)

In the wake of Pearl Harbor, Admiral Yamamoto hoped to secure control of the western Pacific by capturing the strategically located island of Midway, but American code breakers gave the U.S. Navy the intelligence it needed to turn this battle into a major Japanese defeat and the turning point of the war in the Pacific. Here is a crippled Japanese cruiser after the battle. (*National Archives*)

Veteran Army intelligence officer and Japanese linguist Colonel Sidney Mashbir was chief of General MacArthur's Allied Translator and Interpreter Section, an intelligence unit responsible for the translation of captured Japanese documents and the interrogation of Japanese prisoners of war. (*Department of Defense*)

During World War II legendary Hollywood filmmaker John Ford led the Field Photographic Unit of the Office of Strategic Services. (*National Archives*)

Jedburgh was the code name of a joint operation of the Office of Strategic Services and the British Special Operations Executive aimed at sending agent teams into France to organize the Resistance in support of the D-day landings. Here a Jedburgh team prepares to depart. (*National Archives*)

An OSS agent practices wireless telegraphy at a training base at Jedburgh, Scotland. (*National Archives*)

Concealing a radio transmitter in a suitcase was a standard method of agent communications used by both sides in World War II. Here captured German agents and their suitcase radios are shown at a U.S. interrogation center at Épinal, France. (*Department of Defense*)

The Central Intelligence Agency grew in size and influence in the Korean War. Here the director of central intelligence, General Walter Bedell Smith, confers with MacArthur's intelligence chief, Major General Charles Willoughby (left), and Lieutenant General Matthew Ridgway in January 1951. (*Department of Defense*)

When the eccentric Iranian prime minister Dr. Mohammad Mosaddeq demanded the power to rule the country by decree in July 1952, he set in motion a series of events leading to the CIA-backed coup one year later. (*Wide World*)

Although psychological warfare was the principal means employed by the CIA to overthrow the Guatemalan regime of Jacobo Árbenz Guzmán, the bombing of selected targets in the country lent credence to the belief that Guatemala was under major military attack. (*Wide World*)

Although Jacobo Árbenz Guzmán (shown here with his wife) was not a Communist, his appointment of Communists to important government posts and a shipment of arms from Czechoslovakia alarmed the Eisenhower administration and led to the CIA-backed coup. (*Wide World*)

The U-2, a larger and more advanced version of the reconnaissance plane. (*Lockheed Aircraft*)

The high-flying U-2 reconnaissance plane collected vital intelligence of Soviet nuclear and missile development during the late 1950s. This U-2 photograph shows a Soviet space-vehicle launch site in south central USSR. The triangular pit diverts hot rocket exhaust away from the launch pad. (*Central Intelligence Agency*)

CIA Director John A. McCone was at first alone in his belief that the Soviets were installing offensive missiles in Cuba. (*Central Intelligence Agency*)

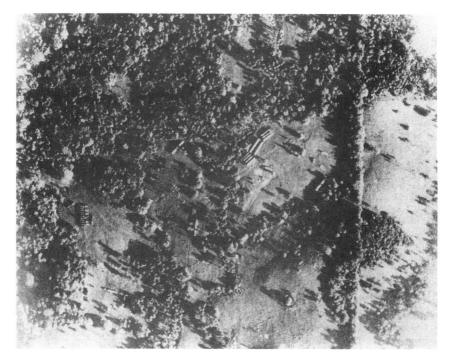

Aerial reconnaissance played a key intelligence role in the Cuban Missile Crisis of
October 1962. Here a U-2 photograph shows a medium-range ballistic-missile site
at San Cristóbal, Cuba. Missile trailers and erectors can be seen in the cleared area
near the center of the picture. (*Central Intelligence Agency*)

Soviet ship *Volgoles* leaving Cuba with Soviet missiles, November 9, 1962. (*U.S. Navy*)

Inadequate air support proved fatal to the CIA-backed invasion of Cuba. Here the *Rio Escondido*, a transport used by the anti-Castro Cubans, burns, off the Bay of Pigs on the morning of April 17, 1961. (*official Cuban photograph*)

After twenty months in Castro's prisons, surviving members of the Bay of Pigs invasion were ransomed by Attorney General Robert Kennedy through the payment of $53 million worth of food and drugs. Here some of the Cubans disembark at Homestead Air Force Base in Florida on December 23, 1962. (*Wide World*)

The personal prestige of Lieutenant General Hoyt S. Vandenberg, and the fact that his uncle was an influential senator, enabled him to enlarge the powers and charter of the Central Intelligence Group and set in motion the process that established the Central Intelligence Agency. (*Central Intelligence Agency; oil portrait by C. L. MacNelly*)

Rear Admiral Sidney W. Souers was named director of central intelligence by President Truman in January 1946. He took the job on the condition that he would be free to resign and return to civilian life after six months, an option he later exercised. (*Central Intelligence Agency; oil portrait by C. L. MacNelly*)

Rear Admiral Roscoe H. Hillenkoetter succeeded Vandenberg as director of central intelligence and was the first chief of the newly established Central Intelligence Agency. (*Central Intelligence Agency; oil portrait by Comis*)

Eisenhower called his Chief of Staff, General Walter Bedell Smith, "the general manager of the war." As director of central intelligence he transformed the CIA from an information-coordination unit with a modest overseas secret-intelligence apparatus into the important player in American foreign affairs that we know today. (*Library of Congress*)

During his tenure as Director of Central Intelligence, veteran spy master Allen W. Dulles was known in the CIA as "the great white case officer" because of his penchant for involving himself in running covert operations while leaving the day-to-day administration of the Agency to his deputy. (*Central Intelligence Agency; oil portrait by Garner Cox*)

A veteran of OSS secret intelligence operations in Europe, Richard M. Helms served as chief of the CIA Clandestine Service for several years before succeeding John A. McCone as director of central intelligence. Reportedly because of Helms's refusal to involve the CIA in the Watergate affair, President Nixon declined to reappoint Helms as DCI in 1973. (*Central Intelligence Agency; oil portrait by William F. Draper*)

After a well-publicized trial in Moscow and twenty months in a Soviet prison, U-2 pilot Francis Gary Powers was exchanged for a convicted Soviet spy. (*Wide World*)

Although U-2 flights over the USSR ended with the May 1, 1960, downing of Francis Gary Powers, overhead reconnaissance of Soviet territory resumed the following August with the launching of the first successful reconnaissance satellite. The *Discoverer* satellite was put into orbit by the Lockheed Agena spacecraft, shown here. (*U.S. Air Force*)

In Washington Special Envoy Kurusu and Ambassador Nomura kept talking with Secretary of State Hull beyond the November 29 deadline and through the first week in December, as they had been ordered to do by Tokyo. On Saturday, December 6, the Foreign Office advised Nomura that it was about to transmit a fourteen-part message containing Tokyo's response to Secretary of State Hull's November 26 counterproposal. The message was transmitted piece by piece throughout the night of the sixth and the early hours of the seventh. OP-20-G's listening post on Bainbridge Island in Puget Sound intercepted the radio telegram and relayed it to Washington by teletype. There the Magic code breakers were pleased to find that although the message was in the Purple cipher, it was also in English and therefore required no translation after decryption. The pieces of the message were delivered to the Magic readers probably a bit sooner than Nomura and Kurusu saw them. The message was a recapitulation of Japan's position in the talks. It concluded that "in view of the attitude of the American Government, it is impossible to reach an agreement through further negotiations," or in other words, Japan was breaking off the talks.[42]

Colonel Bratton, chief of the MID's Far Eastern Section, was reading the final part of the message in his office at 8:30 A.M. Sunday when yet another Magic intercept was handed him. It was from the Japanese foreign minister to Ambassador Nomura, and it concerned the fourteen-part message Bratton had on his desk: "Will the Ambassador please submit to the United States Government (if possible the Secretary of State) our reply to the United States at 1:00 P.M. on the 7th, your time."[43]

Bratton did not fail to grasp the significance of this Japanese punctilio. It seemed obvious, in view of Japanese history, that the fourteen-part message breaking off the negotiations was intended by Tokyo as a substitute for the breaking of diplomatic relations and the declaration of war and that the specific hour of 1:00 P.M., Washington time, was to coincide with a Japanese military attack on some American ship or territory. Lacking the authority to act on his own, he attempted to rouse from their Sunday-morning routine those on the Magic distribution list who could take action. Nonetheless, the military and civilian leaders he alerted were still trying to comprehend the situation at 1:25 P.M.—7:55 A.M., Hawaii time—when the planes from the Japanese task force broke out of the rain clouds north of Oahu and descended upon an unsuspecting Pearl Harbor.

* * *

"But they knew, they knew, they knew," William Friedman kept repeating as he paced in front of his radio that Sunday afternoon.[44]

But, did they know? What did they know?

By the last week in November, the Washington Magic readers—the president, his national security advisers, and the armed services chiefs—knew that Japan would shortly break off diplomatic relations, advance against British and Dutch possessions in Southeast Asia, and probably make war on the United States. On November 24 the chief of naval operations advised the commander of the Pacific Fleet:

> Chances of favorable outcome of negotiations with Japan very doubtful. This situation coupled with statements of Japanese Government and movements their naval and military forces indicate in our opinion that a surprise aggressive movement in any direction including attack on Philippines or Guam is a possibility. . . .[45]

On the twenty-seventh the CNO advised the commanders of the Pacific and Atlantic fleets:

> This dispatch is to be considered a war warning. Negotiations with Japan looking toward stabilization of conditions in the Pacific have ceased and an aggressive move by Japan is expected within the next few days. The number and equipment of Japanese troops and the organization of naval task forces indicates an amphibious expedition against either the Philippines, Thai or Kra Peninsula or possibly Borneo. . . .[46]

They knew, then, that the blow was about to fall. Why did they fail to see it was going to fall on Pearl Harbor?

There had been the rumor of Japanese contingency plans for a surprise attack on Pearl Harbor, passed on to the American embassy by the Peruvian minister in January. But this report was discounted by the ONI for substantially the same reasons that Yamamoto's staff officers were objecting to the plan at that time: the operation did not seem feasible.

Far more significant was the Magic intercept of September 24 in which the Third Bureau requested detailed information from its Honolulu agent regarding the positions of American warships within Pearl Harbor, including a notation when two or more vessels were alongside the same wharf. But so strongly did the ONI analysts hold the assumption that a Japanese surprise air attack was impossible, the most alarming interpretation any of them placed on this request was that it was evidence of planned sabotage.

The continuing stream of requests by Tokyo for specific information on the situation at Pearl Harbor throughout October and November and agent Yoshikawa's reports seem in retrospect unequivocal warnings of the impending attack. But these intercepts formed only a small fraction of the large number of intercepts of requests for similar information from Japanese agents on the East and West coasts of the United States, in the Panama Canal Zone, throughout the Western Hemisphere from Canada to Brazil, and in ports throughout the Far East, including the Philippines. A close study of all the Japanese espionage traffic intercepted by Magic throughout the fall of 1941 might have disclosed trends showing that Tokyo was showing a more frequent and more specific interest in Pearl Harbor, but such a study was not done.[47]

Why was it not done? As a congressional committee that investigated the event after the war asked:

> Why, with some of the finest intelligence available in our history, with the almost certain knowledge that war was at hand, with plans that contemplated the precise type of attack that was executed by Japan on the morning of December 7—Why was it possible for a Pearl Harbor to occur?

Many answers have been proposed. A perennial theory posits treachery in high places. The Japanese attack on Pearl Harbor not only thrust the United States into the war; it virtually eliminated overnight the isolationist and pacifist sentiment in the country that had tied the president's hands. Some historians and other writers have credited FDR with foreknowledge of the attack and have charged that he let it happen to bring about just such a transformation in American public opinion. The theory necessarily assumes a fairly large conspiracy, since all readers of Magic knew what the president knew, and many of them—for example, the Far Eastern analysts in the ONI and the MID—were able to spend much more time analyzing the information. The conspiracy theory continues to find advocates, but most scholars who have studied Pearl Harbor closely do not subscribe to it.

Perhaps one of the strongest appeals of the conspiracy theory is grounded in emotional reactions to the findings of the commission appointed by President Roosevelt to investigate the Pearl Harbor attack. Chaired by Associate Supreme Court Justice Owen J. Roberts and composed of senior army and navy officers, the commission fixed heavy blame for the lack of preparedness at Pearl Harbor on Pacific Fleet commander Admiral Husband E. Kimmel and Lieutenant General Walter C. Short, commander of the army's Hawaiian Department, while finding the secretaries of state, war, and navy, Army Chief of Staff George Marshall, and Chief of Naval Operations Harold R. Stark completely blameless. In view of the fact that the latter group had had access to Magic and had chosen to deny the material to Kimmel and Short, the Roberts Commission's findings have deemed by many as evidence of arrant scapegoating and by some as proof of treachery and conspiracy.

The denial of Magic to Kimmel and Short and the fact that Station Hypo was not supplied with a Purple machine (although a machine was given the British) have been cited by some students of the event as major blunders (at the very least) by the Roosevelt administration. But would Kimmel or Short or their intelligence staffs have been able to see what the Magic readers in Washington had failed to see? No answer is possible. Neither is it possible to know whether a larger list of Magic readers in Washington would have been able to piece together an accurate picture of Japanese intentions from the intercepts, nor whether the college professors in the Coordinator of Information's Research and Analysis Branch might have succeeded where the colonels and lieutenant commanders of the MID and the ONI had failed.

It is clear that there was a shortage of cryptanalysts and translators, both in Washington and at Station Hypo. Decrypting the intercepts with the Purple machine was not a completely automated process; some time-consuming trial and error was always necessary to identify the key in use in arty particular message. And those Japanese intercepts sent in something other than the Purple cipher—for example, the Third Bureau's communications with its agents—required the old-fashioned pencil-and-paper code-breaking methods. Thus, the Washington code breakers and translators of the SIS and OP-20-G, working round-the-clock, could not always keep current with the flood of intercepts and were forced to put some aside—for example, the espionage messages—to be worked on later. And Station Hypo chose to put aside the most telling of all the espionage messages—the December 2 request to the consulate—to make a traffic analysis of the Imperial Navy's unencrypted radio messages in an effort to resolve the question of the missing carriers.

It is also obvious in retrospect that the method used to relay to Washington the Magic intercepts made in the Philippines and Hawaii—airmail—was far too slow, given the importance of such items as the December 2 espionage message. The navy chose not to re-encipher those intercepts and send them to OP-20-G headquarters by radio telegraph because of the possibility that Japanese code breakers might read them and discover the existence of Magic. Thus, like the decision to limit Magic distribution to a short list of readers, security considerations may have critically reduced the value of the intercepts to national decision making.

In the most general terms, the fundamental cause of the intelligence failure of Pearl Harbor may be stated this way: The American intelligence system had developed a capacity to collect information that far exceeded its capacity to process and analyze it.

Consider the Civil War intelligence officer. Each day he had to read and digest the information sent him from agents behind enemy lines; reconnaissance reports from scouts, cavalrymen, and, sometimes, aeronauts; interrogations of prisoners of war and refugees; newspaper stories; and, rarely, telegraph wiretaps. Yet the daily flow of these handwritten documents, delivered to his tent by courier on horseback, seldom threatened to overwhelm his ability to integrate the new information with what he already knew. Thus, for example, General Sharpe's deputy, John C. Babcock, was able to maintain single-handedly an accurate and up-to-date order-of-battle table of Lee's army.

In the seventy-six years between Appomattox and Pearl Harbor, however, the rate of intelligence intake increased manifold, not only because of technological advances in communications but also as a consequence of the growing sophistication of the intelligence organization. The analysts of the MID and the ONI had to deal with much more information about the Japanese than the Magic intercepts. There was the radio traffic analysis and radio direction-finding reports on the location of Japanese warships. There were the reports of American naval attachés from Far Eastern capitals. There was the political reporting of Ambassador Grew and his embassy staff in Tokyo, which as we have seen, sometimes included important nuggets picked up along the local diplomatic cocktail circuit. There was the intelligence passed along by the British from their many sources in the Far East. Valuable information not otherwise known was found in the pages of the *New York Times*, the *Herald Tribune*, the *Washington Post*, and other national newspapers with correspondents in Tokyo and Shanghai. And there was the Japanese press, which generally provided an accurate reflection of the Japanese government's attitudes.

This flood of information was just one tributary to the river of similar data flowing into Washington from Europe, where the war had been raging for two full years; from Latin America, where Axis subversion was rampant; and from other hot spots around the world. And quite conceivably, events in any of those other places might have shed significant light on what was about to happen in the Pacific.

In a sense, there was too much information. One of the clearest and most insightful studies of Pearl Harbor is that of Roberta Wohlstetter. In her summing up, she finds:

> It is much easier *after* the event to sort the relevant from the irrelevant signals. After the event, of course, a signal is always crystal clear; we can now see what disaster it was signaling, since the disaster has occurred. But before the event it is obscure and pregnant with conflicting meanings. It comes to the observer embedded in an atmosphere of "noise," i.e., in the company of all sorts of information that is useless and irrelevant for predicting the particular disaster. . . .

In short, we failed to anticipate Pearl Harbor not for want of the relevant materials, but because of a plethora of irrelevant ones.[48]

In the familiar test for color blindness, the subject is shown plates covered with thousands of colored dots. People who can distinguish red from green see a figure formed by the red or green dots against the background of other colors; the color-blind subject sees a different figure or none at all. He fails to distinguish correctly between the "signals" and the "noise." Analogously, the intelligence analyst confronted with a vast assortment of data is challenged to perceive the significant pattern from the surrounding background.

Another psychological test provides an apt analogue to one major difficulty in completing such a task: the Rorschach inkblot test, in which the figure the subject sees comes from within, not from the blot itself.

"For every signal that came into the information net in 1941," writes Wohlstetter,

> there were usually several plausible alternative explanations, and it is not surprising that our observers and analysts were inclined to select the explanations that fitted the popular hypotheses. . . . Apparently human beings have a stubborn attachment to old beliefs and an equally stubborn resistance to new material that will upset them. . . .
>
> There is a good deal of evidence . . . that in conditions of great uncertainty people tend to predict that events that they want to happen actually will happen. . . .[49]

Wishful thinking, then, and the tyranny of preconceptions firmly held may have been the most powerful forces behind the Pearl Harbor intelligence failure. When Secretary of the Navy Knox received the report of the attack on Pearl Harbor, he exclaimed, "My God, this can't be true! This must mean the Philippines."[50]

The absolute certainty that Japan simply could not threaten the impregnable fortress of Pearl Harbor may have blinded the Magic readers to the warnings hidden amidst the confusing background of irrelevant or contra-dictory data. No American intelligence officer was less inclined to underestimate the Japanese than Captain William D. Puleston, who had served as director of the ONI from 1934 until 1937. But in his book *The Armed Forces of the Pacific,* published only months before the attack, Puleston wrote:

> The greatest danger from Japan, a surprise attack on the unguarded Pacific Fleet, lying at anchor in San Pedro Harbor [California], under peacetime conditions, has already been averted. The Pacific Fleet is at one of the strongest bases in the world—Pearl Harbor—practically on a war footing and under a war regime. There will be no American Port Arthur.[51]

Chapter Thirty-one

The Eyes and Ears
of the Allies

The surprise attack on Pearl Harbor was but the first of a fusillade of Japanese blows on American, British, and allied forces in the Pacific and the Far East. During the following six months Japanese forces swept through Southeast Asia and the western Pacific. Most of the United States Far East Air Force was destroyed on the ground in the Philippines on December 7. Three days later Japanese torpedo planes sank the British warships *Prince of Wales* and *Repulse* in the South China Sea, effectively eliminating all remaining opposition to Japanese sea power in the Far East. The British colony of Hong Kong, the strategically important American islands of Guam and Wake, and parts of the Philippines fell to the Japanese advance before the month was up. Throughout January and February, Japanese forces overran the Dutch East Indies, Malaya Singapore, and parts of Burma. At the end of February, Japanese naval forces inflicted severe losses on the United States Asiatic Fleet in the Battle of the Java Sea. On May 6 Japan completed her conquest of the Philippines with the capture of Corregidor and 11,500 American troops.

In March Admiral Yamamoto began planning a major naval attack on Midway, an American island some fourteen hundred miles northwest of Hawaii. The objective of the operation was to seize the strategically important island and draw out and destroy the remnants of the United States Pacific Fleet—including the three aircraft carriers that had not been at Pearl Harbor on December 7—thereby consolidating Japan's hold on the western Pacific. In Yamamoto's grand strategy the Midway attack was to be a preliminary to the invasion and capture of Hawaii, a move the Japanese commander believed would force the United States to sue for peace.

* * *

From the time of their initial success in breaking Japanese naval codes in the 1920s, the United States Navy's code breakers designated each successive new code the Imperial Navy adopted with the prefix JN followed by a number; thus the first code was JN1; the second, JN2; and so forth. By 1941 the Imperial Navy had progressed to JN25, a cryptosystem OP-20-G could recognize but scarcely read.

The JN25 code consisted of a list of some forty-five thousand words and phrases from the sailor's lexicon—*battleship, aircraft carrier, sink,* and so forth. Each word or phrase had a corresponding five-digit number, or group, and a message was encoded simply by looking up the words and writing down the corresponding groups. To confound further the unauthorized radio eavesdropper, the coded message was enciphered by adding randomly selected five-digit numbers to the code groups.[1] To the layman such a cryptosystem seemed absolutely impossible to break; to the professional cryptanalysts of OP-20-G, it seemed nearly so.

Just one year before the Pearl Harbor attack, the Japanese introduced a new version of JN25, which the OP-20-G code breakers promptly designated JN25b as they set to work on it. By the following November they were able to read parts of messages sent in the new code, but three days before the Pearl Harbor attack the Japanese confounded them again by switching to a different table of random numbers for the encipherment step.[2]

With the Japanese striking in every direction in the weeks after Pearl Harbor, foreknowledge of where and when the blows were to fall became crucial as American forces in the Pacific sought simply to survive while they regrouped and tried to mount a counteroffensive. About half of the encrypted traffic of the Japanese naval war machine was being sent in JN25b, and so breaking this cryptosystem became a matter of the utmost urgency. OP-20-G gave the job to Station Hypo, the COMINT (Communications Intelligence) Unit buried in the basement of the administration building at Pearl Harbor.

Alternatively known as the Combat Intelligence Unit and later designated FRUPAC (Fleet Radio Unit, Pacific Fleet), Hypo was the command of Lieutenant Commander Joseph J. Rochefort, a somewhat unusual—some would say eccentric; all would say brilliant—naval officer who had worked his way up from the enlisted ranks. He was an accomplished code breaker, having learned the black art from naval COMINT pioneer Lieutenant Commander Laurence Safford, whom he succeeded as chief of the ONC's Code and Signal Section in 1926. In 1929 he was sent to Tokyo as part of the ONI-ONC Japanese-language program.[3]

Rochefort took charge of Hypo in June 1941. The unit was then primarily concerned with tracking the Japanese Imperial Navy through radio traffic analysis and direction finding; its principal cryptanalytic activity consisted of attempting to break the Japanese flag officers' code. By October the situation in the Pacific had become so dangerous that Hypo went on a seven-day week and a round-the-clock watch. Rochefort would spend days at a time in the dank, subterranean chamber, wearing an old red smoking jacket and carpet slippers and living on a diet of sandwiches and coffee. Three days after the Pearl Harbor attack Rochefort was ordered to put aside the flag officers' code problem and concentrate all Hypo's code-breaking energy on the JN25b cryptosystem.

Of the thirty officers and men in the unit, Rochefort had only two seasoned code breakers; the rest were translators, clerks, and trainees. The latter group was soon augmented by the band of the U.S.S. *California*, redundant because the battleship had been badly damaged in the first few minutes of the Japanese attack. Someone theorized that cryptanalysis, like mathematics, was a talent closely allied to music, a hypothesis that was to be happily confirmed by subsequent events.

One of the pair of experienced code breakers working in the Hypo cavern was Lieutenant Commander Thomas H. Dyer. In 1932 Dyer had introduced an important innovation into American cryptanalysis: IBM electric punch-card equipment, the distant ancestor of the electronic computer. Sluggish and cumbersome by today's standards, the machines nonetheless relieved the tedious burden of repetitive pencil-and-paper operations involved in attacking Japanese cryptosystems. Now a battery of the machines whirred and clattered in one of Hypo's basement rooms, performing the repeated arithmetic operations on the five-digit code groups of intercepted JN25 messages in an effort to strip off the random-number encipherment.[4]

By March the men and machines of Station Hypo were able to decrypt fragments of intercepted JN25b messages of sufficient length to provide some useful intelligence. Toward April many of the partially decrypted messages were found to refer to a geographic location designated by the code MO, and some of the references seemed to imply that MO was to be the objective of a major Japanese naval operation. Some of the Hypo analysts guessed that MO stood for Port Moresby, a seaport on the south-eastern coast of the Australian territory of New Guinea.

Yamamoto was indeed planning an amphibious invasion of Port Moresby, in response to the Allied buildup in Australia. He also intended the capture of Tulagi in the Solomon Islands to protect the eastern flank of the Japanese in New Guinea, as well as the destruction of any American warships that might be sent to the area in response to the operation. By mid-April Hypo's traffic analysis showed that a large Japanese naval task force was assembling at Truk in the Carolines, evidence confirming the probability that New Guinea was to be the objective of the MO operation.[5]

On the basis of this intelligence, Admiral Chester W. Nimitz, the new commander of the Pacific Fleet, dispatched a pair of carriers—the *Lexington* and the *Yorktown*—to the Coral Sea, southeast of New Guinea and on the Japanese route from Truk. On May 7 planes from the *Yorktown* contacted part of the Japanese task force and sank the light carrier *Shoho*. The following day there was a general engagement, in which the Japanese carrier *Shokaku* was put out of action and the *Lexington* and *Yorktown* suffered damage, the former so severe she had to be scuttled. The Battle of the Coral Sea was not an American naval victory, but it ended the Japanese expedition against Port Moresby and was thus the first check encountered by the Japanese in their march into eastern Asia.

The Coral Sea setback did not discourage Yamamoto from his planned attack on Midway, however, preparations for which were proceeding apace at the time of the battle. Indeed, the Midway operation had now taken on greater importance. By Yamamoto's own pre-war estimate, Japan could not sustain more than twelve months of war with the United States and hope to win. The complete destruction of American sea power in the Pacific and the capture of Hawaii had therefore become crucial to his strategy.

Yamamoto's plan called for his carrier force to attack Midway on June 4 guarded by two fast battleships, two heavy cruisers, one light cruiser, and twelve destroyers. If this task force encountered American naval units before reaching Midway, it would engage and destroy them. A second prong of the task force was to steam to the south of the main attack force, ready either to intercept United States naval forces on their way from Pearl Harbor to relieve Midway or else to join in the Midway attack. Finally, a third Japanese force was simultaneously to attack Dutch Harbor, an American possession in the Aleutians, as a diversionary operation and occupy the Aleutian islands of Attu and Kiska. Throughout May two hundred warships of the Imperial Navy assembled in Japanese waters in preparation for the operation. The logistics of these preparations generated a huge volume of radio traffic.[6]

By early May, when Yamamoto began his Midway preparations, Rochefort's code breakers had progressed to the point where they typically were reading 90 percent of the text of intercepted JN25b messages.[7] The decrypts disclosed that the Japanese were preparing a major operation, and on May 14 they revealed that an invasion of a geographic location designated by the code AF was planned. By deduction Rochefort concluded that AF stood for Midway; however, OP-20-G headquarters in Washington believed that the Japanese objective might be Johnston Island, a tiny piece of land 760 miles southwest of Honolulu; or Oahu; or even the West Coast of the United States.[8]

Admiral Nimitz had only three aircraft carriers—the *Hornet*, the *Enterprise*, and the *Yorktown*—to use in repelling the Japanese attack. It was therefore crucial that Hypo confirm beyond any doubt that Yamamoto's objective was in fact Midway. A means of accomplishing that was suggested by Lieutenant Commander W. J. Holmes, an officer who had been invalided out of the service six years earlier, recalled to duty, and assigned to Hypo in mid-1941. Holmes knew that the Japanese had established a radio intercept station on Wake Island to monitor United States naval traffic and commercial radio broadcasts from Hawaii and the American West Coast. The station sent a daily message to Tokyo encrypted in JN25b summarizing the information it had collected. Holmes proposed that the American commander at Midway send a radio message to Hawaii reporting that the island's seawater distillation plant had broken down and requesting a bargeload of fresh water. This was done, and two days later Hypo intercepted a message from the Wake Island listening post to Tokyo advising that AF was short of fresh water due to a distillation-plant breakdown. There was no longer any doubt that AF was Midway.[9]

On May 20 Yamamoto transmitted an operation order containing most of the details of the Midway plan; Rochefort delivered the decrypted intercept to Admiral Nimitz on the twenty-fifth. A day or so later Hypo's code breakers solved the date-time groups in the message, revealing that the Midway attack was scheduled for June 4.[10] Nimitz immediately dispatched his carriers, accompanied by a force of cruisers and destroyers, to a point 350 miles northeast of Midway, there to wait in ambush for Yamamoto. He correctly anticipated that the Japanese force would first be detected by navy patrol aircraft operating from Midway itself.

While Nimitz's intelligence of the Japanese task force was complete down to the finest detail of the planned attack, Yamamoto was almost blind as he moved toward Midway. He believed the *Yorktown* had been sunk at the Battle of the Coral Sea, and he had no reliable information on the location of the other two American carriers. Had Takeo Yoshikawa, the Third Bureau's agent, still been operating at Pearl Harbor, he could have corrected this misapprehension and also reported the departure of all three carriers and their accompanying task forces in the last days of May. But Yoshikawa and the other members of the Honolulu consulate had been rounded up as enemy aliens immediately after December 7 (Yoshikawa's espionage role was still unknown to the FBI and the ONI) and repatriated.

In February the Japanese had dispatched three submarines to French Frigate Shoal, a point several hundred miles west of Honolulu, to stand by to refuel long-range Kawanishi seaplanes from the Marshall Islands. The planes were to continue from that point and fly reconnaissance missions over Pearl Harbor, thereby filling the intelligence gap left by Yoshikawa's departure. Unwisely, they also chose to use this scheme for a second bombing raid on Pearl on the night of March 3. A rainstorm obscured the target, and the bombs fell harmlessly on the slopes of some nearby mountains, but Pacific Fleet intelligence correctly guessed how the raid had been mounted. Admiral Nimitz deployed a tanker and two destroyers to French Frigate Shoal; the American ships were still there at the end of May, preventing the Japanese from making the vital aerial reconnaissance of Pearl Harbor.[11]

Resigned to his complete ignorance of what was happening at Pearl, Yamamoto hoped nonetheless to have timely reports of whatever force the Americans would send from that base in response to the Midway attack.

To this end his operation plan called for thirteen submarines to form a picket line across the route from Pearl to Midway to report on and attack the anticipated American relief force. The subs did not arrive until after the American carrier task force was already in place northeast of Midway, however.[12] Thus, the Japanese proceeded with the planned attack guided only by bad guesses and wishful thinking. It was to prove an intelligence failure as costly to them in the long run as Pearl Harbor had been to the United States Navy.

As Nimirz anticipated, first contact was made with the Japanese task force by navy PBY patrol planes from Midway on the morning of June 3 several hundred miles northwest of the island. The two naval forces engaged the following day, and the Battle of Midway continued until June 6. When it was over, the Japanese had lost their four heavy aircraft carriers, their entire complement of 253 planes, a heavy cruiser, thirty-five hundred crewmen, and one hundred of their most experienced carrier pilots. Yamamoto pulled back what remained of his forces toward Wake Island. On the American side the cost was the carrier *Yorktown*, the destroyer *Hammann*, 150 planes, and 307 crewmen.

Midway marked the turning point of the war in the Pacific. It was, as Fleet Admiral Ernest J. King, chief of naval operations, pointed out, "the first decisive defeat suffered by the Japanese Navy in 350 years. Furthermore, it put an end to the long period of Japanese offensive action, and restored the balance of naval power in the Pacific. The threat to Hawaii and the west coast was automatically removed...."[13]

Yamamoto had finally had his "decisive battle," and he had lost. It was a David-and-Goliath victory, and the element that had overcome the vast superiority of Japanese sea power was intelligence. More particularly, the crucial element was communications intelligence. That which could have forestalled the Pearl Harbor disaster, had it been properly used, prevented its sequel, and turned the tide of the war with Japan.

The role of communications intelligence in the Allied victory in the Second World War remained one of the best-kept secrets for decades thereafter, and its gradual disclosure in recent years has not yet been fully absorbed by the military history of that great conflict. There is now no question, however, that it was by far the Allies' most important source of intelligence throughout the war. The record of American COMINT between 1940 and 1945 fills volumes, and it is therefore impossible to do more than trace some of the more significant threads of the story here. The most important of these concerns a little-known War Department unit called the Special Branch.

In the wake of the Pearl Harbor intelligence failure, Secretary of War Stimson commissioned a complete review of the War Department's system for handling COMINT. Stimson, himself a senior member of the New York bar, selected the prominent New York attorney Alfred McCormack to carry out this study. After two months of reviewing and analyzing the operations of the Signal Intelligence Service and related War Department units, McCormack advised that the entire process of collecting communications intelligence, analyzing it, fitting it together with intelligence from other sources, and producing and disseminating finished intelligence reports should be viewed as an integral undertaking to be carried out by a single agency.

Guided by the McCormack report, Stimson placed the army's Signal Intelligence Service under the direction of the Military Intelligence Division (although it continued to be part of the Signal Corps for administrative purposes) and established the Special Branch, a unit within the MID, to be exclusively responsible for the processing and dissemination of COMINT.[14] He appointed Colonel Carter W. Clarke, a Signal Corps officer who had assisted McCormack in his study, as chief of the new unit. McCormack was given a direct commission as an army colonel and assigned as Clarke's deputy. The arrangement met the demands of army personnel administration; in reality, McCormack actually ran the unit.

The main job of the Special Branch was to do just what had not been done by the assortment of agencies participating in Magic before Pearl Harbor: take charge of the flood of Magic and other COMINT, squeeze every possible useful fact out of it, put it together with everything else that was known, and place the resulting finished intelligence in the hands of those who needed it. But the Special Branch's most important function was to serve as liaison with the British COMINT service; OP-20-G was doing very well with Japanese COMINT in the Pacific, but the British were the most important source of COMINT in the European theaters of the war. Just how the latter came to be is a story that began a decade and a half before the war.

In 1926 the German navy adopted a cipher machine for its secure communications. The machine selected was called the Enigma. It had been invented by Arthur Scherbius, a German engineer who had been offering it commercially since 1923. In 1929 the German army also adopted the Enigma, and the air force followed suit in 1935.[15] The Germans modified the Enigma to increase its security, making its cipher far more difficult to break than that of the commercial model of the machine. Apparently, they believed that the modified Enigma was virtually unbreakable.

Poland's intelligence service, which had been reading the older German ciphers prior to 1926, mounted a major cryptanalytic effort to break the German armed services' Enigma ciphers. They obtained one of the commercial models of the Enigma machine but were unable to reconstruct the German military modifications of it until 1931, when they were joined in their efforts by the French intelligence service. The French had obtained some important technical information regarding the modified Enigma, reportedly from a German walk-in agent who happened to work in the German army's cipher bureau.[16] By December 1932 the Polish cryptanalysts, with the help of the information provided by the French, had reconstructed the modified Enigma and were able to read the German armed forces' ciphers.[17]

Throughout the 1930s the Germans continued to elaborate their modified Enigma machines, making them increasingly more secure with each new wrinkle, while the Polish cryptanalysts responded to each such challenge by devising a means to defeat it. By 1938 the Poles had automated their cryptanalysis by constructing a machine known as the Bombe (sometimes called Bomba; literally, "a bomb," because of its loud ticking), a primitive electromechanical computer that drove a half dozen of the reconstructed modified Enigma machines, to solve intercepted German messages through high-volume trial-and-error methods. Unfortunately for the Poles, the Germans chose almost the same moment to add to the Enigma a new elaboration that so greatly enlarged the number of possible combinations in its cipher that only a Bombe ten times the size and complexity of the existing device could decrypt the intercepts. Such a machine was beyond the technical resources of the Poles.[18]

While the Polish code breakers continued their secret attacks on the German cryptosystem, Germany was placing increasing pressure on Poland to accede to her demands for the return of territory lost at the Paris Peace Conference. In March 1939, however, Britain and France promised to come to Poland's aid in the event of foreign aggression against that country. As part of the Polish contribution to that pact, the Polish code breakers turned over all their knowledge of the modified Enigma to the British and the French, including copies of the reconstructed Enigma machine. Within weeks of this transfer, German forces invaded Poland, and in November 1942 they subjugated France. Thereafter, Britain alone was the sole surviving repository of the Polish code breakers' knowledge of the Enigma.

The Enigma project was taken over by the Government Code and Cypher School at Bletchley Park, the head of which was Commander Alastair Denniston, a veteran of Room 40, the Naval Intelligence Department's First World War code-breaking unit. With the outbreak of the war, Denniston augmented GCCS's staff of about fifty with scholars from Cambridge, perhaps most notably the brilliant mathematicians Gordon Welchman and Alan Turing. Welchman and Turing devised a Bombe of greatly increased capacity to deal with the latest German Enigma modification, and by April 1940 the GCCS code breakers were able to read Wehrmacht and Luftwaffe communications traffic.[19] The Kriegsmarine (German navy) version of the Enigma proved more resistant to the cryptanalysts' efforts, but the Royal Navy's capture of the German submarine U-110 south of Greenland on May 8, 1941, yielded not only the boat's Enigma machine but key settings, user documents, and a quantity of deciphered messages. With the aid of this windfall, GCCS was able to read the Kriegsmarine traffic.[20]

Thus, throughout the war most of Germany's most sensitive military and naval communications, which the Germans believed to be completely secure, were actually an open book to the British, and they of course shared the intelligence with their American allies.

As we have seen, Anglo-American code-breaking cooperation was established in 1940 by William Stephenson and Lord Lothian in meetings with

President Roosevelt and bore its first tangible results in January and February 1941, when four American code breakers visited GCCS at Bletchley Park. Because William Friedman had just been hospitalized with a nervous breakdown, the price of his long and recently successful campaign to break Purple, the delegation was headed by Abraham Sinkov, one of the four cryptanalyst trainees Friedman had hired soon after the Signal Intelligence Service began operations in 1929. Recently commissioned as a major in the army, Sinkov was now one of the most senior officers in the SIS. The delegation included another SIS officer and two officers from OP-20-G.[21] This was the occasion on which one of the reconstructed Purple machines was delivered to Bletchley Park. The Sinkov delegation came home with an assortment of British COMINT technology, including a new high-frequency direction finder and, by one account,[22] the secrets of the Enigma breakthrough.

Within a few months of the Sinkov delegation's visit to Bletchley Park, the British and American COMINT services were cooperating on a worldwide basis. The GCCS intercept station at Singapore and an OP-20-G listening post on Corregidor were exchanging all their intercepts of Japanese communications. The British had similar arrangements with Canada and Australia, so that intercepts made at listening posts in Halifax, Melbourne, Canberra, and Darwin were made available to the other members of the COMINT consortium.[23]

With the creation of the Special Branch of the MID early in 1942, Anglo-American COMINT coordination became complete. In April 1943 Special Branch deputy chief McCormack visited Bletchley Park accompanied by Friedman (now fully recovered) and Lieutenant Telford Taylor (later famous as chief prosecutor at the Nuremburg war-crimes trials). The most important result of the McCormack delegation's visit to the British code-breaking center was the completion of a pact, the BRUSA Agreement, formally specifying the details of Anglo-American (as well as Canadian and Australian) COMINT cooperation.

The BRUSA Agreement provided for the exchange of personnel as well as technology and intelligence and established standardized security procedures and regulations for the protection of COMINT material. One minor consequence of the pact was the American adoption of the British code word Ultra to designate high-level communications intelligence.[24]

Telford Taylor stayed on in London as the chief American liaison officer at Bletchley Park. Other Special Branch officers were attached to individual commands and were responsible for keeping their respective commanders fully briefed on the latest Ultra intelligence. These coordinators, like Taylor, were selected by Special Branch deputy chief McCormack from a pool of bright young Ivy League university graduates. They included men like William Bundy, who was to become an important Far Eastern adviser in the Johnson administration; Alfred Friendly, future managing editor of the *Washington Post*; and future Supreme Court Justice Lewis F. Powell, Jr.

Ultra intelligence played a vital role in every major Allied operation in the European, North African, and Mediterranean theaters of the war, constantly guiding the hand of General Dwight D. Eisenhower, commander of American forces in Europe and later supreme Allied commander. Ultra intercepts revealed that the Germans were not prepared for the American landings in North Africa in November 1942 and also disclosed the movement of German forces immediately after the landings.[25] In April 1943, three months in advance of the Allied invasion of Sicily, the British Secret Intelligence Service forged documents stating that the actual objectives of the coming operation were Sardinia and Greece, planted them on the body of a putative British courier, and arranged for the cadaver to be washed ashore on the coast of Spain, where the forgeries would likely fall into the hands of German intelligence. Ultra intercepts showed that the elaborate deception operation had worked and that the Germans were reinforcing their units in Sardinia and Greece. Ultra also provided Eisenhower with the strength and order of battle of the German forces occupying Sicily. Ultra played the same role in the deception operation that convinced the German high command that the cross-Channel invasion of France in June 1944 was targeted on the Pas de Calais, not Normandy.[26] As British intelligence historian Ronald Lewin wrote,

> Ultra was fundamental for strategic deception—fundamental
> for knowing in advance which of the enemy's forces were sta-
> tioned where (the order of battle): fundamental for observing
> immediately his secret reactions to any attempt to deceive: and

fundamental for monitoring any redeployment of his troops which might confirm that he had been taken in.[27]

One of the most important uses of Ultra was in support of Allied anti-submarine warfare in the Battle of the Atlantic, as the fight to keep open the transatlantic shipping lanes was called. COMINT played an important role on both sides. The Kriegsmarine's cryptanalysts read much of the Allied merchant marine traffic and thereby guided the U-boats directly to their prey. But the German submarine commander, Admiral Karl Dönitz, insisted on maintaining tactical control of his submarine "wolf packs," a practice that generated a high volume of radio traffic between the U-boats and the command posts ashore and provided Allied cryptanalysts with a priceless opportunity. After the capture of the naval Enigma machine and materials from U-11 in May 1941, intelligence produced by the Bletchley Park code breakers enabled convoys to avoid the German submarine wolf packs and guided Allied anti-submarine forces to the U-boats and their support vessels. The crucial value of the Ultra intelligence to the convoy lifeline was dramatically and tragically demonstrated in 1942, when the Kriegsmarine suddenly introduced a modification to the Enigma that Bletchley Park was unable to counter for a period of ten months, during which time the loss of Allied shipping, measured in tons, nearly doubled that of the preceding year.[28] When the cryptanalysts finally solved the new cipher, the rate of losses dropped back approximately to their earlier level.

Code breaking was not the only high-tech intelligence weapon the Allies employed against the German submarines; radio direction finding proved to be of comparable value. HF-DF (high-frequency direction finding), or huffduff, disclosed the precise location of a U-boat when it transmitted one of the frequent radio reports that Dönitz demanded. OP-20-G operated an arc of huffduff stations along the East Coast and in the Caribbean, all of which flashed intercept-bearing data to a control center in Maryland, where it was transformed into map coordinates and relayed to anti-submarine vessels and aircraft. The huffduff network operated so rapidly the German U-boats were unable to evade it even when they resorted to burst transmissions—that is, the high-speed transmission of a previously tape-recorded message.[29]

Radio direction finding was a technique well understood and widely employed in the United States armed forces long before the war, but British scientists and engineers had made important advances in its technology in the late 1930s. Radar, another new weapon in the electronic arsenal, was yet another British innovation. These and other ELINT (electronic intelligence) instruments became available to American intelligence services through the Anglo-American intelligence liaison arrangements that were in place even before the United States entered the war.

COMINT continued to play an indispensable role in the Pacific after Midway. Early in 1943 the cryptanalysts of FRUPAC, as Station Hypo was then officially known, broke the Maru code. *Maru* was the Japanese term for their transports, tankers, and all other noncombat ships that supplied the far-flung naval and military presence in the Pacific and eastern Asia. The four-digit code that the Japanese used in communicating to or about their merchant marine was therefore dubbed by the FRUPAC code breakers as the Maru code. Its penetration proved to be an enormous asset to the United States submarine force in the Pacific.

Solutions of Japanese naval messages in the JN25 code had often disclosed to the FRUPAC code breakers the precise courses of enemy merchant marine vessels, but this information was only infrequently passed along to the navy's submarine command; the potential gain in sinking Japanese shipping seemed far outweighed by the possibility that a sharp increase in ship losses might provoke Japanese suspicion that JN25 had indeed been broken. FRUPAC was not equally cautious about the Maru breakthrough, however, since a change or abandonment of this code by the Japanese would not shut off the flow of priceless information contained in JN25. Thus from early 1943 onward, FRUPAC furnished the submarine command with the most detailed information about the courses and schedules of the Japanese merchant fleet. Given the vast reaches of the Pacific and the variety of islands and channels that may determine the route of a convoy in that ocean, this intelligence was of particular value. By mid-1943 American subs had doubled their 1942 rate of sinking Japanese transports.

"The sea, which had been a freeway for the [Imperial Navy's] aggressive operations, was becoming a barrier separating the parts of Japan's island empire from each other," FRUPAC's Captain Holmes later recalled. "The submarine attack on the marus was a direct attack on Japan's life-support systems."[30]

The success of the submarine war against Japan is measurable: in 1941 Japan had some 6 million tons of merchant marine vessels. The United States submarine force is credited with having sunk 5.3 million tons of Japanese shipping by war's end.[31]

Although the Japanese used the Purple cipher exclusively for their diplomatic communications, American access to it continued to yield highly valuable wartime Magic COMINT, sometimes even including military and naval intelligence. Some of the most interesting intercepts were those of Baron Hiroshi Oshima, the Japanese ambassador to Germany, who reported in copious detail to Tokyo on his conversations with the Nazi leaders in Berlin. These reports, transmitted in Purple between the Axis capitals by radio telegraph, were read in Washington and London at about the same time they were received in Tokyo.

". . . Our main basis of information regarding Hitler's intentions in Europe is obtained from Baron Oshima's messages from Berlin reporting his interviews with Hitler and other officials to the Japanese Government," General Marshall warned Governor Thomas E. Dewey of New York during the height of the 1944 presidential campaign, when Marshall feared the Republican candidate might be preparing to make Pearl Harbor and American code breaking a political issue.[32] But Oshima's reports not only yielded such important political intelligence; they sometimes also provided priceless military intelligence.

Not the least of the military nuggets that turned up in Oshima's dispatches was his December 1943 report of his inspection tour of the Atlantic Wall, the German defenses in Western Europe against the anticipated Allied cross-Channel invasion. The report contained an analysis of the German command structure, a description of the defensive systems, and the order of battle of German forces in the zone. A week later this dispatch was followed by one from a Japanese naval attaché in Berlin providing such additional details as the numbers and types of artillery, the positioning of machine guns and anti-tank guns, and the water depths at coastal points the Germans judged likely Allied landing points.[33] All of this intelligence was most welcome to Eisenhower and his staff—D day was less than six months away.

The most ironic chapter in the story of American COMINT in the Second World War is the record of an event that took place in mid-April 1943 in the Solomon Islands. On April 13 the code breakers at FRUPAC deciphered a Japanese naval message in the JN25 code announcing that five days thence Admiral Yamamoto would leave his headquarters on Rabaul to conduct an inspection tour of Japanese air bases on the southern end of Bougainville. The message stated that Yamamoto and his entourage would travel by medium bomber with a fighter escort, and it gave his scheduled departure and arrival times at each of the several stops on his itinerary.

Yamamoto's route brought him just within range of the United States Army Air Force's fighters based at Henderson Field on Guadalcanal. Knowing that the admiral made a fetish of punctuality, Nimitz realized that it would be possible to intercept Yamamoto's plane at some point along its route and shoot it down. The death of the commander of the Combined Fleet would be a serious blow to Japanese morale and, since there was no other officer of comparable stature, leave a gap in the Imperial Navy's chain of command. Nimitz decided that these gains outweighed the risk that the action might reveal the success of American code breaking, and he therefore ordered the interception.

Early on the morning of the eighteenth, eighteen P-38 fighters equipped with auxiliary fuel tanks took off from Henderson Field. Flying over the ocean at wave-top height to evade Japanese radar, the planes flew a semicircular route to the west and north, avoiding the Japanese-held Solomon Islands of Munda, Rendova, and Shortland. The route and speed of the P-38s had been worked out to bring them to a point on the Bougainville coast at the precise moment the two bombers carrying Yamamoto's party were due to arrive.

The precision paid off: the American fliers sighted the bombers and their fighter escort just as the Bougainville coast came into view. While fourteen of the P-38s engaged the escort, the remaining four attacked the two bombers, shooting them down and killing Yamamoto and his staff.[34]

"The shooting down of Yamamoto was a trauma for most Japanese," Nimitz's chief intelligence officer, Edwin T. Layton, recalled. "His death also struck at the fighting morale of their navy, not the least because Admiral Mineichi Koga, his chosen successor, was a conservative strategist who lacked flair and charisma."[35]

Although he never suspected it, American communications intelligence had been the most powerful influence on Yamamoto during the final fifteen months of his life: first, by failing to thwart the Pearl Harbor attack he masterminded; next, by dealing him a decisive defeat at Midway; and finally, by sealing his death warrant. Perhaps the final irony is that the Japanese continued in the belief that their naval codes and ciphers were secure. Apparently, they accepted the cover story promulgated by Nimitz that the interception had been made in response to reports by Australian coast watchers stationed along the Yamamoto party's route.[36]

Electronics was not the only technology fully exploited by American intelligence services for the first time in the Second World War; the older craft of photography also took on a new importance in intelligence collection. The camera had been used as an intelligence instrument since at least 1887, when the Office of Naval Intelligence began equipping ships of the United States Navy with cameras and darkroom equipment to make pictures of coastal defenses and other objects of foreign-intelligence interest.[37] By the 1890s the engineering of cameras and the chemistry of film had progressed to the point where it was practical to collect photographic intelligence from the air. The United States Army experimented with the use of remote-controlled cameras suspended from kites in the 1890s, but aerial photoreconnaissance came into its own only after the adoption of the airplane for military purposes more than a decade later.[38]

The Army's First Aero Squadron, which had flown visual aerial reconnaissance for General Pershing during the punitive expedition against Villa in 1916, adopted photography shortly thereafter. The squadron was sent to France in September 1917, where it benefited from the aerial photographic experience of the British and, especially, the French. Meanwhile, aerial photography was included in the training of student pilots at ground schools run for the army at several American colleges and universities.[39]

In December 1917 the Officers' School in Aerial Photography was established for the Signal Corps by Cornell University. One of its first graduates was George W. Goddard, a twenty-nine-year-old native of Tunbridge Wells, England, who had enlisted as a private in the Aviation Section of the Signal Corps several months earlier. Goddard graduated the following March, served for a time as an instructor at the school, and was commissioned as a second lieutenant but missed going to France when the war ended in November. In 1919, after completing pilot training, he was assigned to McCook Field at Dayton, Ohio, where he was put in charge of the army's research program in aerial photography. It was the beginning of a lifelong career in the field.

In the years between the wars, Goddard pioneered the development of a wide range of equipment and techniques, including night photography, infrared films, long-distance cameras, aerial photographic mapping, panoramic photography, and shutterless stereoscopic cameras, which matched the relative motion of the ground directly below the aircraft with the movement of the film in the camera, thereby creating long, continuous stereo strip photographs of the earth's surface.[40] Meanwhile, Eastman Kodak devised high-speed, low-grain film that permitted high-resolution photographs to be made from extreme altitudes, while Fairchild and other camera manufacturers engineered cameras especially for aerial photography.

In 1938 the British resumed their interest in aerial photoreconnaissance, a field in which they had had extensive experience in the First World War. In the pre-war months of 1939, an aerial photographic unit of the Secret Intelligence Service secretly photographed a large number of targets of intelligence interest in Germany, the Mediterranean, and the Near East. At the same time, the SIS developed sophisticated methods of retrieving useful intelligence from aerial photographs, employing the equipment and techniques of photogrammetry, the art of measuring objects using photographs of them, with impressive success.

After the outbreak of hostilities, the photoreconnaissance unit was transferred from the SIS to the Royal Air Force, where it became the Photographic Development Unit (later renamed the Photo Reconnaissance Unit). Spitfire fighter planes, specially modified for the purpose, were used for photoreconnaissance missions because their high altitude and speed made them relatively invulnerable to interception. After the fall of France in 1940, aerial photography became one of the most important sources of intelligence on German intentions. It was by far the most important means of identifying targets for bombing by the RAF and of making poststrike assessments of bombing missions. By the time of American entry into the war, British aerial photoreconnaissance was comparable to code breaking in its importance as an intelligence source.[41]

In the months before Pearl Harbor, Goddard and other United States Army Air Force officers working in aerial photoreconnaissance visited Britain and were briefed on the RAF's operation. The Americans were impressed by many of the discoveries the British had made in their actual wartime experience, especially their discovery that small, swift planes were better suited to photographic work than the converted heavy bombers both countries had previously been using. The most impressive British advances were not in the methods of aerial photography, however, but in the gleaning of intelligence from the pictures after they had been developed and printed at the Central Interpretation Unit, located in Dansfield House, a mansion at Medmenham, northwest of London.

Beyond the obvious business of looking for objects of military or naval importance in the photographs, the British photo interpreters (PIs) had devised an assortment of Sherlockian methods for drawing important inferences from what they saw (or found absent) in the pictures. In the summer of 1940, while Hitler prepared for the cross-Channel invasion that never took place, British PIs were reading such signs as this:

> Round St. Omer, for example, new telephone lines—betrayed by the shadow of each post and the pale circle of newly turned earth at its foot—indicated where local headquarters were installed. And five miles inland from Calais the myriad tracks of heavy lorries converging on the Forêt de Guînes left no doubt as to where the ammunition and stores for the invasion were being hidden.[42]

"You must know at a glance what is normal," a British master PI explained, "and then you can recognize the abnormal when you see it."[43]

The British had developed an efficient three-phase assembly-line process for handling the photographs. Prints fresh from the darkroom were scanned for "news items"—movements of ships, aircraft, railroad trains, canal barges, or new bomb damage. Within twenty-four hours the prints had been examined for less obvious details, and the information was fitted together with photos of adjacent areas to provide a summary of what appeared to be happening within the overall area. Finally, the photos were subjected to minute analysis, so that new information on such things as airfields, factories, and military installations could be integrated with previous intelligence.[44]

All of this was very much of a revelation to the American visitors. Although between the wars Goddard's team had made much greater progress than the British in the development of new equipment, films, and photographic techniques, the principal application of aerial photography by the United States Army Air Corps had been in mapping, and little attention had been paid to the matter of finding the intelligence hidden in aerial photographs. The British, however, driven by desperate necessity, had quickly invented this new intelligence speciality during the first two years of the war.

One of the Americans visiting the British PI operation at Medmenham in the summer of 1941 was Lieutenant Commander Robert S. Quackenbush, Jr., chief of the photography section of the United States Navy's Bureau of Aeronautics. Quackenbush was so thoroughly impressed with the British PIs that upon his return to the United States in August, he campaigned for the creation of a photo-interpretation school. The school was established at the naval air station at Anacostia, Maryland, and began operations in January 1942.[45] Captain Harvey C. Brown, Jr., of the United States Army Air Force, another Medmenham convert, came home to lobby for the same sort of institution in his own service. In March 1942 the Army Air Forces Intelligence School at Harrisburg, Pennsylvania, admitted its first class.[46]

The graduates of the American PI schools were soon working overseas, studying aerial photographs made by army and navy reconnaissance aircraft. By November 1942 the United States Army Air Force's Third Reconnaissance Group was photographing General Erwin Rommel's forces in North Africa. The group was commanded by Lieutenant Colonel Elliott Roosevelt, the president's son, who already had two years of aerial mapping experience with the air force. The group was later merged with British and South African photoreconnaissance units as the Allied Photographic Reconnaissance Wing, also commanded by Roosevelt. Throughout 1943 the Wing gathered intelligence for the assault on the German forces at Tunis and in preparation for the Allied invasion of Sicily.[47] The following year, under the command of the legendary photoreconnaissance pilot Colonel Karl Polifka, the Wing flew reconnaissance missions over the German lines in Italy as the Allied forces fought their way up the Italian peninsula.

Meanwhile, Commander Quackenbush had established the navy's South Pacific Photographic Interpretation Unit on Espíritu Santo in the New Hebrides, later moving it to Guadalcanal. The unit provided vital basic intelligence on the often unmapped islands of the South Pacific that were to be the central combat zone in America's amphibious war with Japan. Another navy PI unit at Adak, Alaska, covered the Northern Pacific area.

Aerial reconnaissance and photo interpretation provided the first evidence of the German V-1 and V-2 missiles, the Me-163 rocket-powered interceptor, and other German "secret weapons." The spectacular quality of these discoveries made them famous when they were disclosed after the war, but of far greater value to the Allied war effort was the routine, day-to-day photo reconnaissance.

The strategic bombing of German industry, which was a major factor in the Allied victory, was absolutely dependent upon photoreconnaissance for the identification of targets and the postattack assessment of the damage inflicted on them. Aerial photographs targeted German aircraft factories, synthetic-petroleum plants, machine-tool plants, and other vital industrial centers. Post-attack photos showed Allied air forces that the airborne radar then in use was inaccurate in guiding raids on targets hidden by darkness or clouds.[48]

Preparations for the D-day cross-Channel invasion of France involved the largest photoreconnaissance effort in history. More than seventeen hundred PIs studied a daily take of eighty-five thousand aerial photographs to locate German defenses along the beaches, troop dispositions, radar installations, and lines of communication and transportation between the beaches and inland points.[49] During the Allied eastward advance across Europe in the months following the landings, photoreconnaissance was one of the most important sources of tactical intelligence.

The Luftwaffe had its own aerial reconnaissance operations, of course. After the war was over in Europe, Allied PIs had a look at German photo intelligence and found it to be good, but not of the same quality as that of the Americans and British. Someone then recalled the prophesy of General Werner von Fritsch, commander in chief of the Wehrmacht until he fell out of favor with the Nazi leaders. Fritsch had foretold that the side with the better photographic reconnaissance would win the next war.[50] While the general may have slightly exaggerated the importance of aerial photography, his prophesy was nonetheless fulfilled.

"This was a secret war," wrote Winston Churchill of the electronic intercepts, the code breaking, the radio direction finding, the photoreconnaissance, and all the other weapons of what he called "the Wizard War,"

> whose battles were lost or won unknown to the public, and only with difficulty comprehended, even now, to those outside the small high scientific circles concerned. No such warfare had ever been waged by mortal men. The terms in which it could be recorded or talked about were unintelligible to ordinary folk.[51]

The high-technology intelligence campaign against the Axis was indeed unprecedented in the history of warfare. Communications intelligence and aerial reconnaissance, both of which had been introduced to the American intelligence arsenal in the Civil War, now had fully come of age. The war that saw the development of nuclear weapons and the long-range ballistic missile also marked the introduction of code breaking by computer and spying from the very edge of space. Photography and electronics—the information technologies—had become the most important sources of intelligence. Thereafter, the American intelligence establishment would become as much the province of scientists and engineers as it had formerly been that of soldiers and diplomats.

Still, the spy and secret agent had not been rendered completely obsolete.

Chapter Thirty-two

Cloak-and-Dagger: The OSS

M ore than four decades after the Office of Strategic Services was terminated, most of its records remain classified.[1] This fact notwithstanding, the general history of the agency and a considerable amount of specific information have been published in histories (both official and unofficial), biographies, and memoirs.[2] It would serve no purpose and, as a practical matter, would be impossible to recount here all that is now publicly known about the OSS. In its short existence, however, the OSS marked milestones in the evolution of American intelligence fully as important as the extensive use of communications intelligence and aerial photoreconnaissance in the war. These must be examined so their impact on subsequent developments may be understood.

One of the most familiar facts about the OSS is that it was the successor to the Office of the Coordinator of Information, the agency established in mid-1941 by presidential order and headed by William J. Donovan. Although the order was broad enough to cover cloak-and-dagger operations, Donovan emphasized intelligence analysis and overt propaganda programs during the first few months of his organization's existence. He abruptly revised his agenda a few weeks after Pearl Harbor, however, as a result of the first wartime meeting between Roosevelt and Churchill, the Arcadia Conference. The conference, which was held in Washington between December 22 and January 14, brought together the top American and British leaders, both civilian and military, to map the grand strategy for the war against the Axis. Although there was little discussion of the subject, one result of the conference was American acceptance of the point proposed by the British that an essential element in the grand strategy was to be the employment of subversion.[3]

In the context of covert operations, subversion, or as it is sometimes euphemistically called, special operations, encompasses a spectrum of adversative activities ranging from propaganda and other forms of psychological warfare through covert political and economic activities to physical sabotage and guerrilla, or paramilitary, warfare. In the framework of Clausewitz's dictum that war is the continuation of politics by other means, special operations fill the spectrum lying between normal adversative diplomatic relations and conventional warfare. Where a state of war already exists, special operations can be an effective supplement to conventional warfare. Given the state of military preparedness of Britain and the United States in December 1941, special operations and strategic bombing were the only modes of warfare available to attack the Axis in Europe.

Special operations were not unknown in earlier American history. The Sons of Liberty waged subversive warfare against the British before the Revolution, and both sides employed propaganda during that war. President Jefferson's attempt to overthrow the pasha of Tripoli with William Eaton's mercenary army was a special operation of both the political and paramilitary varieties. President Madison's efforts to foment an uprising in Spanish Florida was the same thing. President Polk made extensive use of subversion in promoting the annexation of Texas, countering British subversion in California, and sending Moses Y. Beach to Mexico during the war with that country in an attempt to undermine the government. Both sides waged psychological warfare for the hearts and minds of Europe during the Civil War, and the Confederate's Northwest Conspiracy was a classic example of a special operation gone wrong. President Theodore Roosevelt's encouragement of the Panamanian revolt against Colombia, which led to the independence of Panama and construction of the canal, falls within the category of special operations, as do American propaganda activities during the First World War.

Notwithstanding this rather extensive background in subversive warfare, the United States military establishment at the beginning of the Second World War seemed to have been afflicted with the traditional American ambivalence toward the honorable treachery of subversion and espionage.

Taken together, special operations and secret intelligence (i.e., espionage) are professionally known as covert operations. Such activities were not taught at West Point or Annapolis and were not within the conceptual schema of the armed forces establishment. Thus, neither the army nor the navy was particularly enthusiastic about mounting such operations, and both the MID and the ONI had been pleased to cede what little they had in the way of covert operations to Donovan and the COI late in 1941 and early the following year.

For his part, the energetic and enterprising Donovan was not at all reluctant to accept the responsibility for both types of covert operations. His post-Arcadia focus on special operations and secret intelligence quickly led to the growth of the importance of his agency to the American war effort. By March he had received approval to use the COI to aid anti-Nazi partisan forces in Yugoslavia, and he was authorized to recruit a force of two thousand Americans of Greek or Yugoslav origin as a commando force to operate in the Balkans.[4]

The armed services chiefs viewed all this with conflicting emotions. While they were pleased to be relieved of the burden of covert operations, they were alarmed at the growing importance of a civilian agency in the business of making war. Donovan was a personal friend of the president, had recruited FDR's eldest son, James, to the COI staff, and had the backing of the British prime minister, Roosevelt's partner in the newly forged Anglo-American alliance. Given all this influence and the COI's rate of accretion of additional functions, it seemed to some in the MID and the ONI only a matter of time before their organizations were swallowed up by Donovan's agency.

Army and naval intelligence were not the only agencies feeling threatened by Donovan and the COI. J. Edgar Hoover, ever jealous of the FBI's prerogatives, suspected Donovan of having designs on the bureau's Latin American unit, the Special Intelligence Service, and repeatedly accused the COI of trespassing on the bureau's exclusive intelligence jurisdiction south of the border.[5] Donovan also ran afoul of Nelson Rockefeller, whose Office of the Coordinator of Inter-American Affairs was in jurisdictional conflict with the COI over propaganda operations in Latin America. Others in the Roosevelt administration looked upon Donovan and the COI with a jaundiced eye for a variety of reasons—for example, Donovan's unbridled activism or his personal management style. By late spring of 1942, opposition to the COI was coalescing, and Donovan's Washington enemies were sharpening their knives. It was obvious that if events continued on their course, the COI would be carved up and its parts devoured by several rival agencies. No matter how distasteful it might be to the army and navy to absorb COI's covert-operations apparatus, the prospect of it continuing to grow beyond their control was even more so.

Donovan read the handwriting on the wall and took preemptive action in the bureaucratic struggle over the fate of the COI. Resigning himself to the loss of the prestigious position of the COI as an agency of the executive office of the president, he proposed that it be placed under the Joint Chiefs of Staff. This served to quell the military's fears of a rival war-making agency beyond the control of the armed services without necessitating their renewed direct involvement in covert operations. At the same time the new arrangement satisfied Donovan in that it kept most of the agency intact and did not subordinate it to the army or the navy. With the help of Brigadier General Walter Bedell Smith, secretary to the United States–British Combined Chiefs of Staff, Donovan obtained approval for the move. As part of the deal, Robert Sherwood's white propaganda unit was split off and established as a separate, independent agency, the Office of War Information. By a presidential order of June 13, 1942, the rest of the COI was placed under the JCS and renamed the Office of Strategic Services.[6]

During its three-year existence the OSS underwent several reorganizations, but the main body of the agency always consisted of two major directorates: Operations and Intelligence. The former was responsible for all subversive-warfare functions, while the latter encompassed the Research and Analysis Branch, along with secret intelligence, counterintelligence, and other cloak-and-dagger intelligence-collection activities.

As deputy director in charge of operations, Donovan selected Major M. Preston Goodfellow, a Brooklyn newspaperman who had served as an army officer in the First World War and had returned to active duty in 1941, serving for a time as liaison between the MID and the COI. Donovan had recruited Goodfellow in January 1942, before the transformation to OSS, and sent him to Camp X, the Special Operations Executive training school William Stephenson had established in Ontario.

Pleased that Donovan's organization was finally emphasizing covert operations as he had urged from the start, Stephenson put British training resources at the Americans' disposal. The principal British subversive-warfare agency, the Special Operations Executive, had been spun off from the Secret intelligence Service in 1940, put under the minister of economic warfare, and given Churchill's personal mandate to "set Europe ablaze." The SOE had a psychological-warfare unit, but the agency's central mission was to support sabotage and guerrilla operations by the anti-Axis underground in Europe. SOE specialists in irregular warfare trained OSS recruits at Camp X and later at OSS training sites in the Maryland and Virginia countryside.

Dirty fighting, the sine qua non of special operations, conflicted with the national self-image cherished by many Americans and was adopted with reluctance by some of the OSS trainees who had been raised to believe that only a coward or a sneak fights with his feet or hits below the belt. One OSS veteran recalled, many years later, the training in hand-to-hand combat he and other recruits received at Camp X from Major William Ewart Fairbairn, former assistant commissioner of the Shanghai police and the SOE's leading expert on silent killing. Fairbairn taught the OSS recruits there were no rules in staying alive. He taught them to enter a fight with one idea: to kill an opponent quickly and efficiently.[7]

Even in the gentler subversive art of psychological warfare, some OSS novices were shocked by the British methods. Edmond Taylor, an American journalist recruited by Donovan during the COI period, was sent to England to study the methods of the Political Warfare Executive, the principal British black propaganda agency. At the PWE's country head-quarters in Woburn Abbey, in Bedfordshire, Taylor was introduced to *sibs* (supposedly from the Latin word for whisper), "rumors dreamed up by the planners at the Abbey and intended for unattributable launching by 'black' radio, by secret agents, or by the resistance networks in occupied countries, and in other ways."

Sibs, Taylor learned, had to be devised with the utmost caution: "To launch, for example, the rumor that Hitler and Mussolini were united by bonds of homosexual lust might merely serve to enhance the prestige or glamour of the two enemy dictators in certain parts of the world."

To prevent such blunders, the PWE had established the Sib Committee, "a rather high-level interministerial and interservice committee that met every fortnight to winnow the latest crop of 'sibs' grown in the closes of Woburn Abbey." Taylor was impressed to watch "the eminent, and eminently respectable, bowler or brass hatted servants of His Majesty" gathering to rehearse calumnies that were often "more ruthless than any Nazi psychological warfare I had studied."

"From what secret peacetime drawers," Taylor wondered, "had the British taken out all these recipes for exploiting human weakness, all these mental philters, all these scoundrel skills accumulated through centuries of power struggle in every quarter of the globe which they were now so generously making available to an upstart ally and potential successor?" The answer was obvious: Britain had long ago recognized the difference between war (or, for that matter, peace) and cricket.

Taylor returned to the United States a confirmed believer in British-style well poisoning, but he found many of his COI colleagues horrified by the bag of dirty tricks he had brought back with him. Most of those who took this view departed with the COI's white propaganda staff and became the Office of War Information in June 1942. Taylor and other advocates of no-holds-barred psychological warfare stayed with the OSS Operations Directorate.[8]

OSS black propaganda was the province of the Operations Directorate's Morale Operations Branch. The MO Branch proved fully as skillful as its PWE mentors in creating and disseminating sibs. One rumor, sent forth in April 1943 and aimed at splitting Italy from the Axis alliance, had Mussolini applying to the Swiss for asylum in case of an Allied invasion of Italy. This sib proved so persuasive that it was reported to the State Department as fact by the United States minister in Bern, who requested that "the information be given careful protection."[9]

Physical sabotage and guerrilla warfare came under the directorate's Special Operations Branch. The SO Branch's first venture in the field began in mid-1942, when twenty-five British-trained operatives were dropped into the Burmese jungles to organize and lead the Kachin, a mountain people of northern Burma, against the Japanese occupation forces. Detachment 101, as the force was known, was one of the OSS's more notable successes.

The OSS men and their Kachin allies cut railroad lines, blew up bridges, and carried out hit-and-run raids and ambushes against the enemy. They spotted Japanese targets for Allied air strikes and protected Allied road-building projects. The original contingent of 25 OSS personnel expanded to 566 by the end of the war. By 1945 Detachment 101 and the Kachin guerrillas had accounted for 5,447 Japanese known dead and twice that number estimated killed or wounded, at a cost of 18 OSS men and 184 Kachins.[10]

The SO Branch's Maritime Unit had four functions: infiltration of agents into enemy territory by sea, supply of resistance groups and agents by sea, maritime sabotage, and the development of special equipment to be used in the other three functions. The movie actor Sterling Hayden commanded an MU fleet of fourteen schooners that ran arms and supplies through a German blockade to Yugoslav partisans. The unit was also effective in infiltrating agents into Italy, France, Greece, and Albania. In June 1943 it was spun off as a separate branch.[11]

SO Branch agents operated under cover in enemy territory and usually in teams of no more than a half dozen. The Operations Directorate also fielded larger units, however: the Operational Groups—platoons of thirty to forty highly trained foreign-language-speaking troops who fought in uniform behind enemy lines. The OGs, which were approximately the American counterpart of the British commandos and the prototype of the United States Special Forces (Green Berets), were especially useful in disrupting enemy transport and logistics in Italy and France during the last year of the war.

Secret intelligence—the other part of covert operations—was also put on a more professional footing after the Arcadia Conference. Prior to that meeting Donovan's sole venture into the realm of espionage consisted of a curious secret service run by Wallace Banta Phillips. Phillips, an American industrialist who served in General Nolan's G-2 in the First World War, had since lived in England, where he ran a petrochemical and rubber firm. Apparently as a sideline, the Sorbonne-educated Phillips, who had extensive personal and business ties to Sir William Wiseman, had established and run a private industrial-intelligence service, which, he claimed, "had on its payroll no less than seven ex-Prime Ministers."[12]

Late in 1939 Phillips offered his service and his services to the Office of Naval Intelligence, which accepted them. Known as the K Organization, Phillips's secret service was a motley collection of foreign agents and Americans living abroad in the Baltic republics of the USSR, France, the Balkans, North Africa, the Middle East, and Mexico. Just what it had accomplished for the ONI by August 1941 remains obscure, but at that time Phillips offered the entire organization, as a package, to Donovan with the blessing of Captain Alan G. Kirk, the director of naval intelligence. Like the army, the navy was eager to divest itself of covert operations, and the newly established COI was a convenient place to dump them.[13] Donovan could not of course accept Phillips's Mexican network on a permanent basis without trespassing on J. Edgar Hoover's Latin American jurisdiction. He therefore arranged to transfer control of the apparatus back to the ONI but did not act quickly enough to forestall a contretemps with Hoover and Assistant Secretary of State Adolf Berle early in 1942. The teapot tempest was a factor in forcing the COI-OSS transformation.[14]

Notwithstanding his close association with Sir William Wiseman, the British reportedly distrusted Phillips, and it was probably for this reason, as well as differences with Donovan in management style, that the COI director soon eased him out of his position as secret intelligence chief.[15] He was succeeded by David K. E. Bruce, former foreign-service officer, former businessman, son-in-law of millionaire financier Andrew Mellon, member of the Council on Foreign Relations, and an alumnus of Vincent Astor's ROOM/CLUB.[16]

Bruce immediately began building a professional secret intelligence service, which by October 1942 was formally constituted as the Secret Intelligence Branch of the Intelligence Directorate in what by then had become the OSS. In its formative months the branch benefited much from the tutelage of Stephenson's British Security Coordination office in New York and the British Secret Intelligence Service in London. As his London representative Bruce appointed Whitney H. Shepardson, a Rhodes scholar and Harvard Law School graduate who had served as Colonel House's special assistant at the Paris Peace Conference. While vice president of the International Railways of Central America from 1931 to 1942, Shepardson had maintained his interest in foreign affairs through membership in the Council on Foreign Relations, of which he had been a founder, a director, and, since 1933, its treasurer. It may have been through that organization that Bruce knew him.

The chief of the SI Branch's New York City office was another Paris Peace Conference veteran, Wall Street lawyer Allen W. Dulles. When he joined the COI early in 1942, Dulles, a former foreign-service officer and, since 1933, secretary of the Council on Foreign Relations, had just returned from Bolivia, where he had successfully de-Nazified the national airline in a State Department covert operation modeled on the one executed by Spruille Braden in Colombia two years earlier.[17] Dulles established the SI Branch office in Rockefeller Center on the floor above Stephenson's BSC headquarters.[18] In November Dulles left the New York post to establish the OSS SI Branch station at Bern, Switzerland.

The terms of cooperation between the OSS and the British clandestine services—the SIS and the SOE—were spelled out in a series of agreements Donovan negotiated with the British in mid-1942. The agreement with the SIS called for a complete exchange of information with the OSS. The SOE pact, known as the London Agreement, divided the world into British zones, American zones, and British-American zones. In the first, all special operations, whether SOE or OSS, would be under SOE command; in the second, OSS called the shots; and both agencies were to operate independently in British-American zones but would cooperate as closely as possible. As the senior partner in the war against Hitler, the British retained primacy in the matter of special operations in Europe.[19] (The OSS received much less cooperation from some American commanders; General Douglas MacArthur completely excluded the agency from his southwestern Pacific command.)

One immediate result of the OSS-SIS agreement was the visit of an SI Branch officer to England, where he was let into some of the British service's most closely held counterintelligence secrets—for example, the Controlled Enemy Agent Operation, which involved the use of double agents, many of them captured German agents who had been turned—to feed strategic disinformation to German intelligence. The heart of British counterintelligence was a vast collection of files, based on Ultra communications intelligence and other sources, concerning persons and organizations of every nationality and description that had been collected by British intelligence since the turn of the century.[20]

Stephenson had urged the necessity of an OSS counterintelligence service on Donovan, and after the SI representative returned and reported, the OSS director saw the significance of the British activity. Here was another black art to be learned at the knees of British spy masters.

As his counterespionage chief Donovan selected a member of his headquarters staff, the Washington lawyer James R. Murphy. In turn, Murphy nominated the first of the OSS students to go to England and learn counterintelligence. It was a curious choice: Norman Holmes Pearson, a thirty-three-year-old Yale English instructor and a man confined to a wheelchair much of the time as a result of a childhood illness.[21] Early in 1943 Pearson left for London together with Hubert Will, a young University of Chicago Law School graduate who had lately served in several federal government agencies (the Justice Department, the Office of Price Administration, and Alien Property Custodian); Robert I. Blum, who had been recruited from the Yale International Relations Department, where he was an instructor; and Dana Durand, another young recruit from the Yale faculty. They were the first of a procession of trainees that included James Jesus Angleton, who was to become chief of OSS counterintelligence in Italy and would spend most of the next three decades as the legendary and enigmatic chief of the CIA's Counterintelligence Staff.

The Americans received their training from SIS's Section V, the Counterintelligence Department, which was headed by Major Felix Cowgill. One of Cowgill's subordinates, the noted journalist Malcolm Muggeridge, recalled the American trainees:

> Ah, those first OSS arrivals in London! How well I remember them arriving like *jeune filles en fleur* straight from a finishing school, all fresh and innocent, to start work in our frowsty old intelligence brothel. All too soon they were ravished and corrupted, becoming indistinguishable from seasoned pros who had been in the game for a quarter century or more.[22]

Another of the Section V officers who showed the OSS men the ropes turned out to be somewhat more of a seasoned whore than Muggeridge and his associates then knew. He was Harold A. R. ("Kim") Philby, trusted SIS counterintelligence officer, deputy chief of Section V, and Soviet mole.

Pearson stayed on in London to serve as chief of OSS counterintelligence there, and as liaison officer with its tutors in Section V and MI-5, the British Security Service. By June 1943 OSS counterintelligence activities had expanded to such a degree that they were spun off as a separate branch of the Intelligence Directorate, the Counter-Espionage Branch, also known as X-2.[23]

While the OSS Counter-Espionage Branch necessarily worked closely with the SIS, the SI Branch became increasingly independent of British tutelage. One area in which the Americans took the lead was in the use of labor unions as a weapon in the fight against the Axis.

Heber Blankenhorn, the newspaperman who had headed the MIS's Psychological Subsection in the First World War, had been active in championing the cause of organized labor between the wars and in 1942 was again on active duty with the army and serving in the OSS. Blankenhorn convinced Donovan that European trade unions could be useful in the anti-Nazi resistance. Donovan recruited George Bowden, a former IWW organizer and labor lawyer who had been a legal associate of James Murphy, chief of the Counter-Espionage Branch.[24]

When he joined the OSS, Bowden brought along a young Chicago attorney with a labor practice, Arthur J. Goldberg, who was later to become secretary of labor, an associate justice of the Supreme Court, and ambassador to the United Nations. Bowden and Goldberg created the Labor Section of the SI Branch; Goldberg headed the unit.

The Labor Section established a devised facility, the Office of European Labor Research, in offices on Forty-second Street. Ostensibly a private organization without government ties, the OELR was staffed by German and Austrian émigré labor leaders under contract to the OSS. Working through the OELR and other former European labor leaders in Britain and the United States, the Labor Section was able to contact clandestine cells of suppressed unions in Axis and occupied countries and form them into secret intelligence networks. The networks proved invaluable in identifying industrial targets for strategic bombing and reporting on the flow of war material over European railroads, a reliable indicator of Axis military movements.[25]

The Labor Section also subsumed the Ship Observer Unit. Working through international maritime unions, the SOU recruited observers (i.e., informants) from among the crew of ships of neutral nations. Since such vessels routinely visited Axis or occupied ports, the observers were able to report on a wide variety of matters of intelligence interest—for example, harbor and beach defenses, enemy vessels under repair, content of cargoes and their destination, bomb damage, and civilian morale. SOU observers also procured maps and newspapers, photographed objects of intelligence interest, helped infiltrate agents into occupied countries, and carried out other clandestine errands.[26]

The main job of the SI Branch was to run agents into the occupied countries and Germany itself. First-generation Americans fluent in German, Italian, or French were of particular interest to OSS recruiters. Candidates for undercover missions in the SI or SO branches were examined by the OSS's psychological-assessment staff, which was headed by the distinguished Harvard psychologist Henry A. Murray and included John W. Gardner, later secretary of Health, Education, and Welfare in the Johnson administration and founder and president of Common Cause.

"The whole nature of the functions of the OSS were particularly inviting to psychopathic characters," Murray later remarked. "It involved sensation, intrigue, the idea of being a mysterious man with secret knowledge."[27] Murray and his staff devised tests and screening procedures to weed out the mentally unstable. SI candidates who passed were sent to the Farm, a one-hundred-acre estate in the Maryland countryside some twenty miles north of Washington.[28] There, and at other OSS training facilities in Maryland and Virginia, agent candidates were taught intelligence tradecraft, the skills the covert operator must master in order to operate in the field. These included the use of ciphers and clandestine radio transmitters; the employment of cover—that is, fabricated affiliations and identity documents; the methods of recruiting and running subagents; the use of small arms; silent killing; lock picking; and so forth. Trainees also learned to parachute and operate inflatable rubber boats, the two principal methods of infiltrating enemy territory.

The agent training course climaxed in a realistic field problem, in which the candidate was required to infiltrate a defense plant or other facility and steal classified documents; arrangements were worked out in advance with the FBI and local police in case the student was caught in the act.[29]

An OSS agent operating in enemy territory carried nothing that might give him away, even under the closest inspection. The SI Branch ran the so-called I Cash Clothes Project, in which a representative acting under cover and using a pretext traded new clothing, handkerchiefs, wrist-watches, eyeglasses, key rings, luggage, and other items for their used counterparts brought to the United States by European immigrants and refugees.[30] These items were used either to outfit the agent or to guide the fabrication of authentic copies by the Research and Development Branch.

The R&D Branch was headed by the industrial chemist Stanley P. Lovell. Agent authentication, as the fabrication of personal items was called, was but one task of the branch, which specialized in the invention and production of weapons for special operations—for example, a silent and flashless .22-caliber pistol; a high explosive called Aunt Jemima that looked exactly like wheat flour and could be mixed with milk or water, kneaded into dough, baked into bread, and then used to blow up a bridge; a barometric bomb that could be set to destroy an aircraft when it reached some pre-set altitude; a high explosive that looked exactly like coal, to be used in sabotaging steam locomotives; and similar products.[31]

The most important element of agent authentication was the fabrica-tion of passports, identification cards, and other documentation. While the R&D Branch was responsible for the physical authenticity of the documents—authentic paper, ink, glue, and binding—it relied upon the Censorship and Documents Branch for the information they contained. The C&D Branch, headed by Commander Henry S. Morgan of the United States Naval Reserve, a son of financier J. P. Morgan, Jr., collected and compiled intelligence from mail, cables, and telephone conversations inter-cepted by the War Department under the government's wartime censor-ship powers. This intelligence was disseminated to other branches of the Intelligence Directorate and also proved useful in fabricating agent cover.[32]

Another important item of agent equipment was cash. Every dollar, pound, franc, reichsmark, guilder, or other unit of the eighty currencies the OSS spent around the world had to be laundered so that it could not be traced back to the agency or the United States government. This was the task of the Special Funds Branch.[33]

Espionage behind enemy lines was not the sole method of intelligence collection practiced by the OSS, of course. The Foreign Nationalities

Branch of the Intelligence Directorate was founded by veteran diplomats John C. Wiley and DeWitt C. Poole. Poole had been director of Princeton's School of Public Affairs and a member of the nearby Institute for Advanced Study since his days as Moscow chargé d'affaires and case officer of the hapless American agent Xenophon Kalamatiano.

On the assumption, a correct one, that foreign émigré groups in the United States were well-informed about the situations in their native land, the FN Branch was created to make use of such groups as intelligence sources. The foreign-language press in the United States—some seventeen hundred newspapers in fifty-one languages—was an obvious source of information. One hundred scholars—all unpaid volunteers—at Harvard, Princeton, the Universities of Minnesota and Wisconsin, and more than a dozen other American colleges and universities translated and digested foreign-language publications for the branch.

FN Branch officers were in frequent contact with such politically important exiles living in the United States and Britain as the former Italian foreign minister Count Carlo Sforza, the former Czechoslovakian president Edvard Beneš, the former Czechoslovakian prime minister Milan Hodža, the French philosopher Jacques Maritain, and the Italian anti-Fascist leader Father Luigi Sturzo. FN Branch field offices kept in touch with émigré groups in a dozen American cities. And through Stephenson's BSC the branch maintained liaison with émigrés in Canada, while Nelson Rockefeller's Office of the Coordinator of Inter-American Affairs provided access to émigré groups in Latin America.[34]

The FN Branch consisted of some fifty regular OSS employees in addition to the hundred unpaid academics, a modest enterprise by OSS standards but one that apparently turned up a surprising amount of useful intelligence. Even the MID was favorably impressed when the branch unexpectedly came up with a survey of military, naval, and air installations in Greece. The branch obtained the first official information on a secret treaty concluded in July 1941 between the Czechoslovakian government-in-exile and the USSR, something about which the State Department had heard only rumors. State, in particular, found the branch's intelligence reports to be of value.[35]

Although they sometimes operated under cover, FN Branch officers generally were candid with the émigrés with whom they worked regarding their government service and, if pressed, would reveal that they were with the OSS. Since many of the émigrés had fled countries where the use of informers by the secret police was routine, this openness helped to dispel suspicion and encouraged cooperation. FN's credibility and goodwill were so well established, in fact, that Assistant Secretary of State Berle called upon the branch's good offices in making peace between the Czechs and the Slovaks in the United States when enmity between the two émigré groups reached crisis proportions in September 1942.[36]

The FN Branch also provided a convenient means of scouting the émigré communities for agent candidates for the SI and SO branches.

The original raison d'être of the COI had been neither special operations nor secret intelligence but the integration of all United States government raw intelligence and its conversion into finished national strategic intelligence. The premier OSS unit was therefore the Research and Analysis Branch, which became part of the intelligence Directorate in the reorganization that followed the transformation of the COI into the OSS. At about the same time, R&A chief James P. Baxter III was succeeded by the Harvard historian William L. Langer.

Like Colonel House's Inquiry in the First World War, the R&A Branch drew upon academia—especially the Ivy League colleges and universities—to assemble a staff of scholars, organize them by geographic area, and set them to the tasks of analyzing the available data pertaining to their respective areas and producing finished intelligence. While the Inquiry had worked toward the single goal of advising the American peace negotiators at Paris, however, the R&A Branch produced intelligence for both strategic and tactical use in wartime.

With Langer, Harvard's Coolidge Professor of History, at its helm, the R&A Branch had no difficulty in recruiting the cream of American academia. The complete list of Harvard scholars who served in R&A is too long to be recited here, and it is matched by the names of Yale academics who served in the branch. Princeton, Columbia, Cornell, and other Ivy League institutions contributed smaller numbers of scholars to R&A. Less elite campuses were also well represented.

The R&A Branch produced three general categories of finished intelligence studies: the comprehensive regional study, which included a detailed analysis of terrain, climate, transport, resources, and the social, governmental, and economic aspects of the region (in other words, basic intelligence); specialized studies focusing on one or more features of a region; and foreign-policy studies. A current-intelligence staff headed by Amherst College historian Sarell E. Gleason published daily and weekly summaries of political intelligence. All of this output was produced by teams of researchers working together on a single project, an approach that differed both from academia and from earlier American intelligence analysis (e.g., the Inquiry), where work was usually done on an individual basis. This method not only enhanced the comprehensiveness and objectivity of the R&A's product, thereby increasing its acceptance by customers in other agencies, but it was also the prototype of the method used by postwar American intelligence agencies (it should be noted that two deputy directors of intelligence for the CIA—R. Jack Smith and Ray S. Cline—were R&A veterans).

R&A intelligence production usually involved the painstaking examination of a large mass of data, much of which came from openly available sources, and the application of scientific disciplines—often economics—and logical deduction. For example, an early R&A study correctly challenged the prevailing opinion in other intelligence agencies that Germany's supplies of food and strategic materials would prove critical to her war effort. R&A economists found that the accepted forecasts of these supplies underestimated them. At the same time other R&A analysts, studying the publication of officers' obituaries in German newspapers and extrapolating these figures into the number of enlisted deaths using First World War German-officer-to-enlisted-man casualty figures, correctly forecast that permanent battle losses would cause a military manpower bottleneck far more critical to the German war effort than food and material shortages.[37]

The R&A Branch never quite became the ideal central-intelligence clearinghouse envisioned by Donovan in his April 1941 proposal to President Roosevelt. The principal reason it fell short of this goal was that it did not control the most important source of strategic intelligence, the Magic and Ultra intercepts, which the MID's Special Branch held very closely and only occasionally distributed to the OSS, and then only in paraphrased form. Even such sources as prisoner-of-war interrogations were sanitized by army intelligence to remove technical and combat data before being transmitted to the OSS. Curiously, the British intelligence services—SIS, SOE, and especially Stephenson's British Security Coordination—were far more forthcoming in furnishing intelligence to the OSS than was the MID.[38]

Notwithstanding this handicap, the output of the R&A Branch was widely distributed and apparently highly regarded throughout the United States government. In the year 1944 alone the branch's Map Division received a million requests for its products. The State, War, Navy, and Treasury departments, the FBI, every theater commander, and most overseas diplomatic missions were among R&A's (apparently) satisfied customers. Indeed, the demand for the branch's product was so large that the nearly one thousand researchers and analysts employed directly by R&A could not keep up with it, and it was necessary to subcontract some work to Stanford, the University of California, and other institutions.[39]

Just what specific influences the finished intelligence produced by the R&A Branch may have had on American conduct of the war or on the formulation of foreign policy cannot be assessed. But the wide distribution of the R&A product, the general lack of adverse criticism of it by its customers, and the "almost unanimous" response of those customers to a 1944 Bureau of the Budget survey that "the work which the Branch had done had been excellent and valuable" suggests that it was highly useful to national leaders.[40]

OSS headquarters in Washington was housed in the former Public Health Department buildings at Twenty-fifth and E streets, NW, in the Foggy Bottom section of the capital. The headquarters staff made up for Donovan's shortcomings as an administrator. Donovan's second in command was sixty-two-year-old G. Edward Buxton, the assistant director. Buxton, a Harvard Law School graduate and textile manufacturer, was a First World War army buddy of Donovan. The chief of the OSS Secretariat, which functioned as Donovan's personal staff, was Otto C. Doering, Jr., a partner in Donovan's Wall Street law firm. Donovan's executive assistant was James R. Murphy. Murphy, who later headed the Counter-Intelligence Branch, had been Donovan's assistant in the 1920s, when the OSS chief was a Justice Department official.

OSS headquarters included a large number of specialized support units, such as the Office of the General Counsel. As legal adviser to the OSS, the general counsel dealt with questions unprecedented in United States government practice. He established the proprietary corporations and other devised facilities, such as the Office of European Labor Research, and then dealt with the legal relationships—contracts, leases, or other obligations— into which they entered. He dealt with similar security considerations in matters of claims for casualties, losses, and death benefits. The general counsel also compiled all information collected by the OSS on war crimes, and the War Crimes Branch of his office became part of the American prosecutor's office during the postwar Nuremburg war-crimes trials. From 1943 to 1945, the OSS general counsel was James B. Donovan (no relation to the director), a Harvard Law School graduate who had practiced in New York City before the war.[41]

Because they had shared his pre-war professional habitat and he there-fore found it easy to understand and evaluate them, Donovan recruited heavily among members of the New York bar. When Drew Pearson charged that the OSS was made up of "Wall Street bankers," Donovan quipped, "These bankers and corporation lawyers make wonderful second-story men."[42] In fact, the fifteen thousand men and women who served in the OSS represented every American class and political persuasion. The first-generation Americans recruited for their fluency in their parents' native languages were largely from working-class backgrounds. And while the OSS included such staunch anti-Bolsheviks as Soviet expert DeWitt C. Poole, Communist veterans of the Spanish Civil War also served in the agency's ranks.

Notwithstanding this heterogeneous makeup, there was some founda-tion for the waggish claim that the agency's initials really stood for Oh, So Social. A great many names from the *Social Register* could be found in the roster of OSS officers. Andrew Mellon's son, Major Paul Mellon, served in the Special Operations and Morale Operations branches. Other Mellons and Mellon in-laws served in the Secret Intelligence Branch (including SI Branch chief Bruce). William Vanderbilt, a former governor of Rhode Island, was executive officer of the SO Branch in Washington. Lieutenant Alfred du Pont of the United States Naval Reserve, of the Delaware du

Ponts, served in the SI Branch. Theodore Ryan, son of multimillionaire Thomas Fortune Ryan, served in the SI Branch, as did Kermit Roosevelt, a grandson of Theodore Roosevelt. The scions of many less famous blue-blood American families also served in the OSS; typically their curricula vitae included such exclusive prep schools as Groton, St. Mark's, or Phillips (Exeter or Andover); undergraduate studies at Harvard, Yale, or Princeton; and a law degree from one of the Ivy League universities followed by a few years' experience with a prestigious Wall Street law firm.

"Donovan turned first to men whom he knew and trusted," his English biographer Cave Brown wrote, "bankers, lawyers, industrialists, conservative academics. In their turn, these men recruited among those they knew and trusted; and this gave the Donovan agency its tinge of well-to-do, Ivy League, often Republican, socially prominent men and women."[43]

The wellborn did not necessarily remain in comfortable and secure desk jobs far from the combat zones. Among those who did not were John A. Bross, a Chicagoan of the Groton–Harvard–Harvard Law mold, who parachuted into occupied France to coordinate French resistance units with the Allied landings at Normandy; John and Stewart Alsop, Connecticut Yankees with Groton-Yale profiles who did the same, as did Groton–Yale–Harvard Law product C. Tracy Barnes; and Princetonian Allen Dulles, related by blood or marriage to two secretaries of state and one ambassador to the Court of Saint James's and perhaps at fifty-one a bit too old to be jumping out of planes or over fences in the line of duty but whose job as OSS station chief in Switzerland, a political island completely surrounded by Axis territory, was hardly devoid of physical danger.

The significance of the service of such people in the OSS is not that the agency was a socially elite institution—it was not—but that the business of intelligence, espionage, and subversive war was on its way to acceptance in America as a gentleman's profession. This was the culmination of a process that had begun in 1917, when clubbable young aristocrats flocked to serve in the ONI under Captain Roger Welles, steered there by the blue-blooded assistant secretary of the navy, Franklin Roosevelt. Now another generation of wellborn young men was serving under Donovan, President Roosevelt's hand-picked spy master, going off to war in civilian disguise, equipped with concealed radios and invisible ink, armed with

silenced machine guns and explosive flour, and remembering Major Fairbairn's advice that the most effective knife stroke was upward, from the
testicles to the chin.

No systematic assessment of the contribution of the OSS to the Allied victory has been published. Such an evaluation would be difficult to make in
any case, since many Special Operations, Operational Groups, and Secret
intelligence detachments were integrated into local theater commands, and
their achievements are not easily distinguished from those of, say, army
counterintelligence agents operating in the same commands. In Europe,
which was a British zone of special operations, the SO Branch cooperated
so closely with the SOE that it is equally difficult to distinguish between
British and American contributions. And, of course, a comprehensive
appreciation of the OSS contribution in any instance cannot be undertaken until all of its records have been declassified. (It should be noted that
comprehensive accounts of all other United States intelligence services in
the war also remain to be written.) Until such a study is made, one must
be content with anecdotal accounts of OSS achievements. Enough such
data is now available, however, to demonstrate that the agency achieved
a very respectable record of accomplishment.

The first OSS triumph was in French North Africa, where an Anglo-
American invasion force landed in November 1942. "Rarely had intelligence and diplomacy meshed as smoothly," wrote OSS veteran William
Casey of the preparations for the landings.[44] Torch, as the invasion was
code-named, was a particularly difficult operation, involving a large-scale
military move in the midst of a highly sensitive political situation: the
French forces in Morocco and Algeria were nominally under the command
of the German-dominated Vichy regime, but a large element of the French
officers and troops was secretly loyal to General Charles de Gaulle's Free
French movement. The object of Torch was to return French North Africa
to Allied control, but it was to be done with the minimum of military
engagement of the Vichy defenders and, it was hoped, a maximum of
cooperation from the Gaullists.

The OSS supported this extremely delicate maneuver with both intelligence and special operations. A propaganda campaign mounted by the

OSS, together with the British Political Warfare Executive and Sherwood's Office of War information, succeeded in maintaining and intensifying pro-Allied sentiment among the native population and the French. OSS secret intelligence collection provided information crucial to the actual landings and subsequent military operations. Instead of the expected ten thousand Allied casualties, the operation cost two hundred men.[45]

OSS stations in neutral European capitals—Stockholm, Madrid, and Bern—produced significant intelligence. A large amount of intelligence on German scientific and technological progress was collected by the SI station in Stockholm, which ran agent networks into German-occupied Norway and Denmark and also into Finland and Germany itself.[46] The station, which was headed by the Harvard government professor Bruce C. Hopper in 1942–43, collected evidence proving that Sweden began supplying vital ball bearings to the Nazi war machine after the Allied air raids of August 1943 destroyed Germany's ball-bearing industry; the intelligence was instrumental in American diplomatic moves halting the Swedish sales.[47] The Madrid station chief, the multilingual perfume executive H. Gregory Thomas, established agent networks in south-western France that proved highly valuable during the Allied invasion of southern France.[48]

Allen Dulles's station in Bern, Switzerland, chalked up an impressive record of accomplishments. Dulles ran secret networks all over Europe, including Germany. The station reported extensive order-of-battle intelligence in 1943–44; technical intelligence on German air defenses, submarine production, and developmental work on the V-1 and V-2 missiles; and German chemical- and biological-warfare preparations.[49] Fritz Kolbe, an official of the German Foreign Office, switched sides and visited Dulles several times between August 1943 and mid-1944, bringing along thousands of documents containing intelligence of great political and military value. Through Kolbe, Dulles learned of a German penetration agent within the British embassy at Ankara, Turkey. Code-named Cicero, the agent was Elyesa Bazna, the ambassador's valet. The penetration had been masterminded by none other than Franz von Papen, who was serving as German ambassador to Turkey.[50] Through Hans Bernard Gisevius, another defector in place, Dulles penetrated the Abwehr and learned of the abortive German plot to assassinate Hitler in July 1944.

The Bern station provided monetary support to resistance fighters in France and Italy and received from them important military intelligence.[51] The station also learned that the Germans had broken the cryptosystem in use by the American legation in Switzerland and notified the ambassador in time to prevent the compromise of important diplomatic communications.[52]

Dulles climaxed his tour as Bern station chief by arranging American negotiations with General Karl Wolf for the surrender of German forces in northern Italy in April 1945, shortly before V-E Day.

The success of Detachment 101 in Burma has already been noted. Most OSS behind-the-lines operations were carried out in Europe, however. OSS secret intelligence agents identified European targets for Allied air raids. After American forces established a beachhead at Anzio on the Italian coast in January 1944, an OSS detachment located the first German reinforcements and correctly determined the direction of the main German counterattack. Other OSS detachments pinpointed a huge German supply depot at Belluno for destruction by the air force. And OSS agents obtained detailed drawings of the Gothic Line and other German defenses in Italy.[53]

The joint SOE–OSS–Free French operation code-named Jedburgh involved parachuting three-person special-operations teams into German-occupied France to coordinate resistance activities with the Normandy landings in June 1944. OSS Operational Groups led resistance fighters harassing German communications and transport behind the lines. At the same time British–OSS–Free French secret intelligence networks in France provided intelligence to the invasion force that General Eisenhower's intelligence staff found to be "very helpful" and of "gratifyingly high" accuracy.[54] Continuing OSS SI reports of the movement of a Panzer division from Hungary to France just before D day were singled out by the deputy chief of Eisenhower's intelligence staff as having saved perhaps ten thousand or twelve thousand American lives; he concluded that "the OSS has already paid for its budget in this theater."[55]

OSS support of the Allied landings in southern France in August 1944 received equally lavish praise from army intelligence. SI intelligence networks provided "phenomenally accurate" information on German military activity, according to a senior intelligence officer at Allied Force

Headquarters, while another AFHQ appraisal found that the joint SOE–OSS–Free French special operations in support of the landings "led the Germans to a state of utter confusion."[56] Lieutenant General Alexander M. Patch, who commanded the invasion, stated that the calculated risk of the operation could not have been assumed without the intelligence supplied by the OSS SI networks.[57]

After the landings Patch's Seventh Army dashed 150 miles around the German defenders' left flank, from Lyons to Besançon and on to Vesoul; the move was made possible by OSS intelligence agents, who located the hole in the German defenses. OSS agents also pinpointed the location of a Panzer division at Vosges and guided the Allied air attacks that destroyed it.[58]

The fund of such anecdotes of OSS successes seems limitless. While they do not provide the basis for a comprehensive assessment of the agency's contribution to the Allied victory, they demonstrate the reason the OSS was a significant influence in the subsequent development of American intelligence.

The most important single consequence of the OSS experience was the recognition of intelligence as a distinct professional specialty. Except for the arcane field of code breaking, intelligence had never been regarded as a career specialty in the army, the navy, or the State Department. Service in the MID or the ONI was regarded for the most part as just another tour of duty, and one not especially helpful to an officer's career. Intelligence was merely one more aspect of general staff work, not a military specialty comparable to infantry or artillery. Such attitudes would continue to prevail in the military establishment for two decades beyond the end of the war, but the OSS alumni preached a different creed.

In 1948 Sherman Kent, a Yale historian who had served in the R&A Branch, published *Strategic Intelligence for American World Policy*, a distillation of the experience of the author and other R&A analysts in the process of transforming raw data into finished intelligence. Central to Kent's study is the theme that "the intelligence of grand strategy and national security is not produced spontaneously as a result of the normal processes of government; it is produced through complicated machinery and intense purposeful effort."[59] Such machinery is necessarily large, Kent wrote, because of the sheer mass of information that must be processed.

> This means that the intelligence process becomes one of group—as opposed to individual—effort; that there must be a complicated and careful division of labor; and that there consequently emerge problems of personnel, organization, administration, and human relations which are peculiar to the nature of the enterprise, and by no means characteristic of all familiar and homely searches for truth.[60]

Kent argued that intelligence work was a specialty of the very highest order, and a profession quite distinct from those of the diplomat or the military officer: "My point is that not just anyone can hold a professional job in an intelligence organization. My point is that an intelligence organization is a strange and wonderful collection of devoted specialists molded into a vigorous production unit."[61]

If the most important legacy of the OSS was the concept of the career intelligence professional, almost of equal importance was the vast body of alumni who would pursue such careers in the next four decades. Four directors of the Central Intelligence Agency—Allen Dulles, Richard Helms, William E. Colby, and William J. Casey—served in the OSS; their combined tenure as heads of the CIA covered more than half of the first forty years of that agency's history. A multitude of other OSS veterans served in the CIA; Kent himself held the immensely influential post of director of the CIA's Board of National Estimates for eighteen years. Thus, in a very tangible sense, the CIA is the reincarnation of the OSS.

The second most important consequence of the OSS experience was the explicit adoption of subversion as an instrument of United States national-security policy. Nazi employment of propaganda and sabotage early in the war paved the way for the special-operations activities of the SOE and the OSS. As the unwelcome occupiers of Europe, the Nazis themselves proved the most vulnerable of the war's combatants to subversive warfare. "In no previous war, and in no other theater during this war," General Eisenhower wrote, "have resistance forces been so closely harnessed to the main military effort."[62] The demonstrated successes of Allied special operations meant that such modes of warfare could no longer be ignored, even by those holding the traditional American mainstream military attitude toward them.

Subversive warfare was soon to take on an increased importance: first, in countering Soviet efforts to undermine democracies in Europe and elsewhere through subversion and, second, after Soviet acquisition of nuclear weapons made total war impractical. Soon to acquire a new euphemism, *covert action*, subversive warfare was to become an important function of the CIA, where some of its leading practitioners were veterans of the OSS SO Branch.

American public acceptance of espionage and subversive warfare as legitimate and necessary weapons in the defense of freedom was less a consequence of the OSS than of Axis cruelty and ruthlessness. The postwar public image of the OSS was emblematic of that acceptance, however. Soon after V-J Day there was a flood of magazine articles and a few books celebrating the exploits of the OSS. Sinister Axis spies had been a staple of American wartime motion pictures, but immediately after the war Hollywood produced several "now-it-can-be-told" docudramas about the OSS. Alan Ladd starred in the 1946 *O.S.S.*, a motion picture that carried the endorsement of General Donovan immediately after its opening credits. Nineteen forty-six also saw Fritz Lang's *Cloak and Dagger* with Gary Cooper, Lilli Palmer, and Robert Alda. The film was loosely based on a book of the same name by Corey Ford and Alistair MacBain that recounted an OSS mission into occupied Italy; OSS agent Michael Burke, the real-life model for the Cooper character, was the film's technical adviser. The following year American moviegoers watched James Cagney play an OSS agent in the highly authentic Henry Hathaway film *13 Rue Madeleine*. Early in the film Cagney addresses a group of recruits at an OSS training base and, in his famous staccato style, sounds the keynote of the new American view of the realities of the secret war:

> Now, you're going to have a lot to remember, and a couple of things to forget. The average American is a good sport, plays by the rules. But this war is no game, and no secret agent is a good sport—no living agent. You're going to be taught to kill, to

cheat, to rob, to lie, and everything you learn is moving you to one objective—just one, that's all—the success of your mission.

Fair play? That's out. Years of decent and honest living? Forget all about them . . . because the enemy can forget. And has.

Hathaway eschewed the traditional Hollywood ending to underscore the point of the speech. In the final scene Cagney is desperately resisting Gestapo torture and hoping for death. In the last seconds of the film, he dies in an American air strike on the Nazi prison aimed at killing him before he can be made to talk.

The portrayal of OSS agents by such typically American film idols as Cagney, Cooper, and Ladd was not a falsification of reality. OSS personnel came from every walk of national life. Some of the famous who served in the agency have already been mentioned, and many others could be added to the list: the pollster Elmo Roper, who served as Donovan's deputy director throughout the life of the OSS; French chef Julia Child, who worked in the agency's Chungking office; the bridge expert Alfred Sheinwold, who was chief of the Cryptographic Security Section of the OSS Message Center; and *New Yorker* cartoonist Saul Steinberg, who taught Chinese guerrillas how to blow up bridges and later drew propaganda cartoons for the Morale Operations Branch.

Public fascination with the exploits of the OSS was short-lived, of course; it waned as attention turned away from the war and focused on postwar matters. But American acceptance of the imperatives of secret warfare was, if not permanently established, at least securely fixed in the mind of the generation that had fought the war. To those who had witnessed the evil of nazism and fascism, anything used to achieve their destruction was totally acceptable.

The OSS was the culmination of a process that had been begun a quarter century earlier, when Sir William Wiseman first visited Colonel Edward House at the latter's Manhattan apartment: the development of a permanent working partnership between British intelligence and its American counterparts. This partnership came about partly through the diligent efforts of the SIS, working through its Canadian-born instrument, William Stephenson, and partly as a result of circumstances.

Notwithstanding the distaste for British imperialism felt by many of the liberal and leftist elements within the agency, the OSS was possessed by a powerful spirit of Anglophilia. The eastern establishment caste that held so many important OSS posts was partial toward all things English. Many of the most important OSS intelligence officers—for example, Allen Dulles, Whitney Shepardson, and David Bruce—had been pre-war members of the Anglophilic ROOM/CLUB or the equally pro-British Council on Foreign Relations (recall that the latter organization had been originally conceived as the Anglo-American Institute of International Affairs). OSS Anglophilia was not simply a reflection of class prejudices, however; after all, Donovan, one of Britain's best friends within the agency, was the son of an Irish-American railroad worker and the grandson of a member of the Fenian Brotherhood.[63]

To conclude that the Anglo-American intelligence partnership, which became a permanent institution with the creation of the OSS, was the work of a conspiracy between British intelligence and some American Anglophiles would be to confuse cause and effect. The OSS was drawn to the British by necessity. Despite its praise of certain OSS accomplishments, the American military establishment viewed the agency with suspicion and hostility throughout the war and kept it at arm's length. The British secret services, however, which had taken a major hand in the creation of the OSS, clasped it to their bosom and played the parts of both mentor and comrade. Donovan exaggerated only slightly when he told a postwar interviewer, "Bill Stephenson taught us everything we ever knew about foreign intelligence operations."[64]

A wartime exigency, the partnership between the British and the American intelligence services (which, as we have seen, also encompassed code breaking and other technical intelligence functions) was to survive both the war and the OSS and would remain a permanent factor in the career of American intelligence.

To complete the list of major postwar consequences of the OSS, one must include the agency itself, which by V-J Day had become a prototypical central intelligence agency. The CIA, founded two years later, was established from the surviving apparatus of the OSS. This evolution nearly failed to take place, however. That it did was very much a result of the cold war.

Chapter Thirty-three

From OSS to Central Intelligence

The mood at the Riverside Skating Rink on the evening of September 28, 1945, was something like that of a college commencement exercise. Located near OSS headquarters in the Foggy Bottom section of Washington, the rink had been used as office space by the agency throughout the war; now its polished floor was lined with rows of banquet tables. More than a thousand men and women of the OSS had gathered to pay tribute to General Donovan and bid each other farewell. Henceforth, they would sort their memories into those things that happened after this night and those from the time before. Eight days earlier President Harry S. Truman had signed an executive order abolishing the OSS, effective October 1. It was done despite Donovan's best efforts to establish his organization as a permanent peacetime central-intelligence agency.

Donovan had begun lobbying for the postwar preservation of the OSS as early as September 1943, when at the request of General Walter Bedell Smith, he outlined a plan to integrate the OSS as a "fourth arm" of the American military establishment, with a status equivalent to that of the army, navy, or air force.[1] Nothing came of the proposal, but about a year later President Roosevelt asked Donovan for his thoughts on the postwar disposition of the agency. Donovan replied with a lengthy elaboration of his earlier proposal, outlining a central-intelligence service reporting directly to the president, which would have the same government-wide intelligence coordination envisioned in the original concept of the COI and would also collect intelligence and conduct "subversive functions abroad."[2]

Of course, Donovan's plan met with the same hostile attitudes at State, the Joint Chiefs of Staff, the MID, the ONI, and the FBI that those agencies had directed toward the COI early in 1942. The JCS responded with a proposal of their own for a central-intelligence agency, one that would be under the control of the War and Navy departments. Several months of bureaucratic maneuvering and negotiations among the interested agencies followed, but the process came to an abrupt halt on February 9, 1945, when newspapers in Washington, New York, and Chicago carried a syndicated story by Walter Trohan of the *Chicago Tribune* containing the verbatim text of Donovan's proposal.

NEW DEAL PLANS SUPER SPY SYSTEM, read the *Tribune* headline; SLEUTHS WOULD SNOOP ON U.S. AND THE WORLD; ORDER CREATING IT ALREADY DRAFTED. Trohan wrote that the proposed "all-powerful intelligence service" would "pry into the lives of citizens at home," as well as "on good neighbors throughout the world." He charged that the aim of the proposed agency was to give its director (implicitly Donovan) the power to "determine American foreign policy by weeding out, withholding or coloring information gathered at his direction." Furthermore, the newsman claimed, the agency would undermine FBI director J. Edgar Hoover. Trohan accused Supreme Court Justice Felix Frankfurter of being the éminence grise behind the scheme and dubbed the proposed agency Frankfurter's Gestapo. (Frankfurter was presumed to control Donovan through the justice's sister, Estelle Frankfurter, whom Trohan said held "a confidential personnel post in the OSS.")[3]

Trohan's story ignited a firestorm of outrage and denunciation in Congress and the editorial pages. Two days later the newsman followed up with the text of the JCS counterproposal in a story appearing under the headline ARMY, NAVY WANT CONTROL OF "SPY" SETUP; GENERALS, ADMIRALS DECLARE WAR ON OSS. The new disclosure added fuel to the fire.

Just who had leaked the proposals to Trohan was to remain a mystery. Donovan suspected J. Edgar Hoover. Decades later Trohan himself told the historian Thomas Troy that the documents had been sent to him by President Roosevelt.[4] Whatever its source, the story and its resultant tempest caused FDR to put on hold the entire question of a postwar intelligence service until the furor had abated. On April 5 the president instructed Donovan to negotiate a consensus among all the interested parties, a tall, if not impossible order, and certainly one that had the effect of postponing the question for some time. A week later Roosevelt was dead, and so was Donovan's plan.

The OSS director was not yet ready to admit defeat, however, and he continued to lobby for his agency's postwar existence. Meanwhile, the press campaign against the OSS, obviously inspired by Donovan's rivals, went into high gear, especially after May 8, when the end of the war in Europe made it possible to attack the agency on some matters without appearing unpatriotic. Walter Trohan, for example, published stories on May 18 and 19 charging that the OSS was "scarcely more than an arm of the British Intelligence Service."[5] Essentially false, the accusation possessed that supremely potent ingredient of the most damaging lies: a large measure of truth.

Donovan appreciated the splendid irony of the situation: the first American agency to wage wholesale psychological warfare was being destroyed through a campaign of calculated lies—sibs, as the British black propagandists would call them. Naturally, he responded with counterpropaganda, accentuating the positive view of the OSS through his own inspired press campaign. In August, shortly after V-J Day and the end of the war, he established the Reports Declassification Section to select the records of some of the more exciting and successful operations of the Special Operations Branch and the Operational Groups, sanitize them (that is, delete information that might jeopardize the security of continuing United States interests), and leak them to selected reporters and magazine writers.[6] The flood of newspaper and magazine stories about the OSS that appeared after V-J Day and the books and motion pictures about the agency's exploits were based on this declassified material.[7]

Neither Donovan's public relations campaign to preserve the OSS nor that of his rivals to abolish the agency had much effect on subsequent events, however, which were entirely in the hands of President Truman. Some writers assert that Truman held a grudge against the OSS director dating back to their mutual service in France in the First World War or to some subsequent incident of partisan politics, but the evidence supporting this claim seems pretty thin.[8] Even had the new president been one of Donovan's most ardent admirers, however, it is unlikely that the OSS would have had a different fate. The agency had little chance of surviving the budget-cutting mood of the Truman administration immediately after the war.

* * *

Truman's executive order did not completely liquidate the OSS; rather it dismembered it, annihilating some of its components while scattering the rest. The Research and Analysis Branch was transferred to the State Department, which Truman believed should have the central-intelligence role in the United States government. State also received the remnants of the two wartime white propaganda agencies, the Office of War Information and the Office of the Coordinator of Inter-American Affairs. In all, State acquired some four thousand additional employees. The former R&A Branch became known as the Office of Research and intelligence. Alfred McCormack, the New York lawyer who had created and guided the War Department's Special Branch, accepted the job of managing the unit.[9]

The OSS Special Operations Branch, the Morale Operations Branch, the Maritime Unit, and the Operational Groups—in other words, the entire OSS subversive-warfare apparatus—were abolished. The Secret Intelligence and Counter-Espionage branches were assigned to the Strategic Services Unit, a War Department caretaker unit reluctantly headed by Colonel John Magruder, the son of a distinguished old Virginia military family who had been Donovan's deputy director of intelligence. The role, and indeed the future, of the SSU was unclear, since the War Department already had an intelligence service, the MID. For the moment the principal function of the SSU was simply to preserve the OSS secret-intelligence assets—that is, agent networks, safe houses, and so forth—in Europe and the Far East.

The same day President Truman signed the executive order terminating the OSS he sent a letter to his secretary of state, James F. Byrnes, instructing him to "take the lead in developing a comprehensive and coordinated foreign intelligence program for all Federal agencies" and to create "an interdepartmental group, heading up under the State Department, which would formulate [intelligence] plans for my approval."[10]

Just why Secretary Byrnes failed to "take the lead" in reorganizing federal intelligence is unclear. It is likely that he gave the task a far lower priority than that of dealing with the country's growing postwar foreign-relations difficulties, especially the increasing hostility and aggressiveness of the Soviet Union. He was, in any case, out of Washington during much of the second half of 1945, participating in the Council of Foreign Ministers meeting in London in September, and on other diplomatic business. The secretary was away from his office so much of the time that one foreign-service wag quipped that "the State Department fiddles while Byrnes roams."[11]

Neglected, the intelligence situation deteriorated. Veteran diplomats and foreign-service officers distrusted the R&A veterans, regarding them as woolly-headed academics whose approach to foreign affairs was impractical. The situation also suffered from a strong element of bureaucratic rivalry: centralization of the intelligence function within the department—an arrangement that had been abandoned in 1927—was viewed by some senior State officials as a threat to their own power and prerogatives. And given the increasingly hostile character of East-West relations, the presence in State's intelligence office of such prominent leftists as OSS veteran Herbert Marcuse, chief of the Central European Section, inspired suspicions and accusations that the unit was filled with Communists or pro-Communists. Many of the best minds among the R&A veterans soon fled this uncongenial atmosphere and returned to academia.

The disarray of the intelligence establishment began to work a serious hardship on the chief executive. Truman recalled that "the needed intelligence information was not coordinated at any one place. Reports came across my desk on the same subject at different times from the various departments, and these reports often conflicted."[12]

Aware that the situation had become intolerable, the armed services stepped in to fill the vacuum left by Secretary Byrnes's inaction. In December the Joint Chiefs of Staff submitted a proposal to the president for a central organization to coordinate intelligence. The proposed organization would be under the joint control of the State, War, and Navy departments, each of which would retain its own intelligence service. Perhaps in desperation, Truman accepted the proposal and, on January 22, 1946, issued a presidential directive creating the Central Intelligence Group.

The CIG was not an agency or a commission or a board or any other recognizable bureaucratic entity. It was, in the words of the directive, "a cooperative interdepartmental activity," a thing with neither personnel nor budget; its staff and funds were to be contributed by State, Navy, and War. It had no director per se, but it was to function "under the direction" of an official to be known as "the Director of Central Intelligence." The DCI would sit as a nonvoting member of the National Intelligence Authority, a panel created by the same executive order to supervise the

CIG, and was to consist of the secretaries of State, War, and Navy and a personal representative of the president. The DCI would be "advised" by the Intelligence Advisory Board, a sort of steering committee made up of the heads of the MID, the ONI, and State's intelligence unit.[13]

Truman offered the DCI job to Rear Admiral Sidney Souers, the author of the JCS plan. Souers's muted enthusiasm for the invitation may be measured by the condition he imposed before accepting it: that he would be free to resign and return to civilian life after a few months in the job.[14]

Souers was not a career naval officer but a reservist who had left several lucrative businesses in Saint Louis to serve on active duty during the war. He made his mark as an intelligence officer by devising effective methods to find and sink enemy submarines, an achievement that led to his promotion to flag rank and the job of deputy director of the ONI. But five months after V-J Day, he was eager to return to civilian life, not to preside over the vaguely defined "activity" of the JCS proposal. One hundred and seven days after accepting the job, he exercised the option he had demanded.

During his brief tenure as DCI, Souers assembled a staff of 165 people from the three participating departments. The staff produced a "Daily Summary" for the president, a digest of the dispatches received by the army and the State and Navy departments during the past twenty-four hours, highlighting significant developments and summarizing the rest; it was, in effect, the president's personal daily newspaper. This was hardly the last word in interdepartmental intelligence coordination, but Truman seemed happy with it. Shortly before Souers returned to Saint Louis, the CIG staff began a second publication, the "Weekly Summary," which tried to put world events of the past seven days into some perspective and was delivered to the White House by noon on Saturdays so that Truman could peruse it while on his weekend cruises aboard the presidential yacht, *Mayflower*.[15]

Souers's successor was Lieutenant General Hoyt S. Vandenberg of the army air force. A West Pointer, war hero, and nephew of the powerful Republican senator Arthur H. Vandenberg, the new DCI had commanded the Ninth Air Force in Europe during the war. Since January he had been chief of the MID and therefore also a member of the CIG's steering committee, the Intelligence Advisory Board. He intended to be air force chief of staff, and he knew that whatever a "cooperative interdepartmental activity" might be, it was not a stepping stone. He resolved to fix that by enlarging the size and scope of the CIG and transforming it into a true independent agency. His personal prestige and the fact that his uncle was chairman of the Senate Foreign Relations Committee and president pro tempore of the Senate were going to make that possible.

Vandenberg saw that the sine qua non of a true government agency was a budget. The CIG did not have one, and the director had to go, hat in hand, to State, War, and Navy to ask for money whenever the CIG needed some. Vandenberg succeeded in pushing through a proposal under which the director of central intelligence would have the authority to pay personnel and purchase supplies. It was not exactly a budget, but it was a start.[16]

Next on Vandenberg's agenda was the enlargement of the CIG's intelligence role. The daily and weekly summaries published under Souers had scrupulously avoided any analysis or interpretation of the facts, an activity State continued to guard jealously as its exclusive province. Vandenberg persuaded the National Intelligence Authority to permit the CIG to get into this area, and in August he established the Office of Reports and Estimates to perform the analytic function. Next he acquired the Foreign Broadcast Intelligence Service. FBIS had been set up under the Federal Communications Commission to monitor Axis propaganda broadcasts during the war; now a part of the War Department, it listened to Soviet and Eastern European stations and gleaned political intelligence from the Communist world. But the greatest expansion of the CIG's role came with the transfer of the Strategic Services Unit from the War Department to the CIG. It put the CIG into the secret intelligence business.[17]

The CIG could become a truly independent agency only through legislation, however. At the time—mid-1946—the Truman administration was drafting legislation to unify the armed forces into a single government department, a project that would, of course, require the cooperation of Vandenberg's uncle. The younger Vandenberg saw the bill as the perfect vehicle upon which a proposal to establish the CIG as an independent agency could ride piggyback. He directed his general counsel to draft the necessary language, "A Bill for the Establishment of a Central Intelligence Agency," and send it to the White House. In response to the comments of Truman's special counsel, Clark Clifford, the proposed bill was redrafted and resubmitted in November 1946. After considerable negotiation and redrafting, the document was added to the National Security Act of 1947, which Truman submitted to Congress on February 26.[18]

The plan to create a Central Intelligence Agency was not without its opponents, of course. One of the bitterest enemies of the proposal was J. Edgar Hoover, who had already lost his Latin American jurisdiction to the CIG. With the death of FDR, Hoover had lost almost as much influence in Washington as had Donovan; Truman did not hold the FBI director in the same high regard as had his predecessor. Together with the responsibility for secret intelligence in Latin America, Vandenberg acquired the files of the FBI's Special Intelligence Service and many of its agents. He appointed his West Point classmate J. C. King to head the Western Hemisphere Division, the CIG component that would run secret intelligence operations in Latin America. Colonel King had served as military attaché in the toughest wartime post in Latin America, Argentina, and was therefore well acquainted not only with the FBI's SIS but with its assets—for example, informants, security officers of American companies, and sympathetic police chiefs—south of the border. Hoover was further outraged when King began to recruit from the ranks of the FBI agents who had served in the SIS.[19]

Vandenberg's CIA proposal was also resisted vigorously by a United States intelligence agency whose very existence has almost completely eluded historians. Even the official name of this unit cannot be found outside still-classified government archives, and it is therefore known only as the Grombach Organization. Without naming it, a senior CIA official recalled the Grombach Organization as "one of the most unusual organizations in the history of the federal government. It was developed completely outside the normal governmental structure, used all of the normal cover and communications facilities normally operated by intelligence organizations, and yet never was under any control from Washington."[20]

This shadow agency was the brainchild of Major General George V. Strong, who was chief of the MID when the OSS was created in 1942. One of the most rabid enemies of the OSS, Strong managed to establish his own secret foreign-intelligence unit even though such activity (except in Latin America) was supposed to be the exclusive domain of Donovan's agency. To head the unit he selected Colonel John V. ("Frenchy") Grombach, a member of the West Point class of 1923 who had left the army in 1928 to become a motion-picture and radio producer and writer and returned to active duty in 1941.

The Grombach Organization may have been jointly subsidized by several government departments with intelligence interests—perhaps State, the FBI, the FCC, and others in addition to the War Department. It conducted secret intelligence operations in Europe (and perhaps elsewhere) from 1942 to 1947 (and apparently afterward), but the only one of these yet to have come to light is that of James G. McCargar, who, writing under the pseudonym of Christopher Felix in 1963, recounted his work in running an agent network in Budapest in 1946–47.[21]

Vandenberg (coincidentally, a West Point classmate of Grombach) tried to move the Grombach Organization and its assets into the CIG. Grombach resisted this vigorously and lobbied Congress against establishing the proposed CIA, which he labeled "wrong and dangerous to our national security." He and several senior army and navy intelligence officers testified against the CIA legislation before a House committee in closed session on June 27.[22]

Testifying before the same committee, an MID officer expressed shock at having seen a reference to the War Department's secret intelligence service (i.e., the Grombach Organization) in a recent *New York Times* story. The existence of such an organization, he testified, had been known only to a few persons in the War and State departments and the White House at the time he retired from the service in 1944.[23] Grombach had lately been willing to disclose the existence of his supersecret unit to sympathetic journalists, however, if that would help to keep the CIG from swallowing it up. A week or so earlier the *Chicago Tribune's* Trohan had reported on "a furious behind-the-scenes battle" between the MID and the CIG to prevent the latter from absorbing the War Department's "worldwide secret intelligence work." A similar story with the same slant had appeared in the *New York Times* on May 21.[24]

Grombach and his organization had wielded considerable power during the war. The OSS, for example, had been well aware of his secret intelligence operations and knew that he had much influence in the War Department. Donovan regarded the organization as an infringement on the OSS's charter to conduct secret intelligence operations exclusively, but he was not inclined to make an issue of the matter.[25] Yet like Donovan and

Hoover, Grombach seems to have lost a great deal of clout after the end of the Roosevelt administration. He was unable to prevent the creation of the Central Intelligence Agency, but he did succeed in keeping his shadowy organization from being swallowed up by the new agency. It continued its strange existence into the 1950s.[26]

The National Security Act of 1947 created the Department of Defense, which unified the army, navy, and air force under a single cabinet-level officer, the secretary of defense. It also created the National Security Council, a coordination and policy-planning body consisting of the president, the vice president, and the secretaries of state and defense. And it created the Central Intelligence Agency as an independent agency reporting to the president through the National Security Council. The act did not abolish the MID, the ONI, or other departmental intelligence services; it stipulated that they would continue to perform their own intelligence functions. And perhaps to assuage President Truman's stated fears of creating "an American Gestapo," the act specifically denied the CIA any "police, subpena [sic], law-enforcement powers, or internal-security functions."[27]

The act was signed into law by Truman on July 26, 1947. The Central Intelligence Agency formally came into being on September 18. By then Vandenberg was gone from the CIG; he had achieved his personal goal several months earlier, in May, when he became air force chief of staff.

The act made the director of central intelligence the head of the agency. The first DCI to head the agency was Rear Admiral Roscoe H. Hillenkoetter, a veteran naval intelligence officer who had served as Admiral Nimitz's intelligence chief in the Pacific in 1942–43. Hillenkoetter had been a naval attaché in Paris when he was tapped to succeed Vandenberg as DCI in May. With the creation of the CIA, he became in effect the chief intelligence officer of the United States government.

At the outset the CIA was nothing more than the CIG without the awkward and unworkable management scheme that had made it the stepchild of three separate departments. Although the act did not explicitly authorize the agency to conduct covert operations, one paragraph enabled it "to perform such other functions and duties related to intelligence affecting the national security as the National Security Council may from time to time direct." These words provided the sanction for the agency's secret intelligence apparatus, which at this time still consisted of nothing more than the skeletal remains of the OSS SI Branch in Europe and the Far East, now known as the Office of Special Operations of the CIA. The agency's research and analysis activity was centered in the Office of Reports and Estimates, which consisted of specialists in geographic areas and an editorial staff that continued to produce the daily presidential summary begun in the CIG. The ORE's Global Survey Division also produced a monthly report for the National Security Council, the "Estimate of the World Situation."[28]

The world situation was tense as the CIA came into existence in the late summer of 1947; the tension was generated by the Soviet Union's expansionism in Europe and Asia.

The wartime alliance with the USSR had always been an uneasy one; the Western democracies could not easily forget that the Soviet Union had entered the war only after Hitler abrogated his mutual nonaggression pact with Stalin and invaded Russia or that the USSR had grabbed parts of Poland, Finland, and Lithuania through a secret protocol with the Nazis. As the end of the war came into sight, this marriage of convenience between the Allies and the Soviets began to show signs of stress.

Early in 1944 the Soviet Red Army opened a drive that carried it across the Ukraine, pushing the German forces back into Poland and behind the Carpathian Mountains to the south. Stalin intended that the Eastern European nations "liberated" by the Red Army would become Soviet vassal states, and he carried out his program with a campaign of intimidation, subversion, and naked force.

In Romania, for example, Red Army occupation forces seized control of the economy, the press, and radio stations. Railroad tracks throughout the country were changed to fit the gauge of Soviet rolling stock. No public meetings could be held without Soviet permission. The Soviets undertook a campaign of subversion aimed at establishing the Romanian Communist party as the principal political power in the country. Strong-arm thugs from the now-defunct Iron Guard—the Romanian Fascist organization— were recruited by the Communist party as political "enforcers." Food and medical supplies confiscated by the Red Army were doled out by the local Communists to buy political advantage. Soviet labor organizers staged mass meetings in Romanian factories.[29] Communist goon squads bullied printers and publishers into suppressing articles and books opposing the Communist campaign and pressured them to publish their own attacks on the provisional government. Special Romanian-language broadcasts from Radio Moscow encouraged the agitators and intimidated government officials.

Stalin's formula for subjugating the Eastern European nations became known in the West as the salami process—that is, taking over a country one slice at a time. Scenarios similar to that in Romania brought Bulgaria and Hungary into the Soviet orbit at about the same time. Czechoslovakia followed in 1948, triggering a war scare in Washington.

Early in March General Lucius Clay, commander of the American occupation forces in Germany, cabled MID director Lieutenant General Stephen J. Chamberlin, "For many months . . . I have felt and held that war [with the Soviet Union] was unlikely for at least ten years. Within the last few weeks, I have felt a subtle change in Soviet attitude which . . . gives me a feeling that it may come with dramatic suddenness. . . ."[30]

Clay's telegram and the Czech coup triggered an all-out effort by the CIA's intelligence analysts. On March 16 the agency delivered an estimate to President Truman stating that war was not probable within the next sixty days, hardly a warmly reassuring pronouncement.[31] But two weeks later the Soviets began putting pressure on Clay's command in Germany that seemed to confirm the general's apprehension.

Berlin, divided into American, British, French, and Soviet zones of occupation, was an island completely surrounded by Soviet-occupied territory and lying nearly a hundred miles east of the British and American parts of occupied Germany. On March 31 the Soviet occupation command declared that military passenger trains would not be permitted to travel to Berlin unless passengers and baggage were checked by Soviet authorities. This was the beginning of a series of harassing moves that culminated in June with the complete Soviet blockade of Berlin.

Yet the prospect of open warfare with the Red Army over Berlin remained less of a concern to Washington than the threat of further Soviet gains in Europe through subversion. Even in those parts of the Continent not occupied by Soviet forces, local Communist parties were exploiting the harsh postwar economic conditions to gain political advantage. In Greece Communist guerrillas had been fighting a civil war against the government of Georgios Papandreou, a centrist leader; the bordering Soviet satellites—Bulgaria, Albania, and Yugoslavia—furnished aid and safe haven to the guerrillas. Early in 1947 the United States had stepped in to fill the void left when the British could no longer afford to give economic and material support to the Greek government. In March the president announced the Truman Doctrine: "the policy of the United States to support free peoples who are resisting attempted subjection by armed minorities or by outside pressures." Three months later Secretary of State Marshall established the European Recovery Program. Popularly known as the Marshall Plan, it was aimed at frustrating further Soviet gains by creating political stability in Europe. Still, as the bitter winter of 1947–48 descended upon the Continent, there remained cause for concern over Soviet subversion.

"The Marshall Plan is vital," wrote Donovan, who was now watching events from the sidelines, in an *Atlantic Monthly* article entitled "Stop Russia's Subversive War."[32] "But in my view it is not the final solution." Among the measures he prescribed was to fight subversion with subversion.

> We must perfect our intelligence services, so that we may quickly unmask Soviet intention and develop those unorthodox tactics which World War II demonstrated to be essential.
>
> We must counter Soviet subversive attacks and help to build resistance in countries Russia attempts to subjugate.
>
> We must take the offensive on the psychological front and perfect our radio, the pamphlet and the press, and assist our allies in assembling facilities for getting the truth to the Russian people. . . .

Donovan went to the heart of the matter with an aphorism worthy of Clausewitz or Sun-tzu in its clarity and conciseness: "All war aims at the surrender of the mind—the conversion of the will to resist into a willingness to accept defeat."

Some members of the Truman administration were already thinking the same way. By mid-1947 the secretaries of state, war, and the navy had agreed that the United States must employ covert psychological warfare to counter worldwide Soviet subversion. The only open question was which department of the government would actually carry out such operations. In November the incumbent in the newly created post of secretary of defense, James Forrestal, together with the secretaries of the armed forces and the Joint Chiefs of Staff, recommended that the appropriate agency for all forms of propaganda—white, gray, and black—was the State Department, a proposal that was approved by President Truman later that same month. Three weeks later, however, the president reversed his decision after hearing vehement opposition to the plan by General George C. Marshall, the secretary of state. While Marshall favored covert action, he feared that possible exposure of such operations would damage American foreign policy if they were known to be carried out by State. In the face of the secretary's objection, the National Security Council directed that the operations be run by the CIA. On December 22 the Special Procedures Group was established within the agency's Office of Special Operations to conduct covert psychological activities.[33]

At that moment Italy was at the top of the list of American foreign-policy worries. The Christian Democrats controlled the coalition government, but nearly 20 percent of the seats in the Constituent Assembly were held by Communists. The Italian Communist party numbered more than two million members, many of whom held key positions in labor unions. Severe inflation had precipitated a general strike in December, and a CIA analysis forecast a Communist victory at the polls in the next election, scheduled for April 18.[34] Soviet expert George F. Kennan, chief of the State Department's Policy Planning Committee, grimly predicted, "If [the] Communists were to win [the] election there our whole position in [the] Mediterranean, and possibly in western Europe as well, would probably be undermined."[35]

The CIA's capacity to undertake a clandestine psychological operation calculated to influence the Italian elections was limited. Although one third of the agency's personnel at that time were OSS veterans,[36] relatively few had served in the special-operations side of the wartime agency. The agency's man in Rome was James Angleton, formerly of the OSS

Counter-Espionage Branch, an experienced covert operator but one whose background was not in psychological warfare. The agency's campaign of "inspired" stories in the Italian press and letters from Italian-Americans to their relatives in the old country seemed less than guaranteed to ensure a victory by the Christian Democrats.[37] One member of the National Security Council who was particularly worried that the program would prove inadequate was Secretary of Defense Forrestal.

Early in January, Forrestal had a talk with CIA Director Hillenkoetter and raised the question of whether the CIA might go beyond psychological warfare to help forestall a Communist victory in the elections. What he specifically had in mind was massive covert financial aid to the Christian Democrat candidates. He asked whether the CIA could do the job.

Hillenkoetter was cautious and diffident. He told Forrestal he didn't think he had the legal authority to do what the secretary proposed, but he promised to look into the matter. He turned the question over to Lawrence Houston, a young Wall Street lawyer who had been deputy chief of the OSS SI Branch in the Middle East and now was the CIA's general counsel.

Houston closely examined the part of the National Security Act of 1947 that had established the CIA. The only language he could find in it that could even be remotely construed as authority to do what Forrestal asked was the catchall clause authorizing the agency "to perform such other functions and duties related to intelligence affecting the national security as the National Security Council may from time to time direct." He thought it over, then gave Hillenkoetter his professional opinion: neither that clause nor anything else in the law authorized the CIA to pump money into an election campaign in a foreign country.

Hillenkoetter resisted the bureaucratic temptation to use Houston's finding as justification for a safe and negative response to Forrestal's request. Instead, he told the secretary of defense the CIA was ready to take on the job. Once again, in the space of a few weeks, the role of the agency had been enlarged. To secret intelligence and psychological warfare had been added covert political action.[38]

Forrestal and Hillenkoetter now had a new problem to solve. It was one thing to claim that the CIA had the legal authority to give money to the Christian Democrats, and it was quite another to come up with that money. The CIA's Rome station, in reply to an inquiry from Hillenkoetter, estimated the operation was going to cost at least ten million dollars. This went well beyond the amount of unvouchered funds in the CIA budget at that moment, and if the president's Contingent Fund was used, the Bureau of the Budget would find out about the operation. Everyone agreed that the fewer people in on the secret the better; thus, an alternative source of funds was found.

The Economic Stabilization Fund had been established during the war out of confiscated Axis assets. It was intended to dampen inflationary swings in the value of American and other currencies, and it was under the discretionary authority of John W. Snyder, the secretary of the treasury. Snyder, a rotund Rotarian and Missouri banker, was a close friend and confidant of President Truman, whom he had known since they met in the army in France during the First World War. Forrestal and Hillenkoetter approached Snyder and explained what they had in mind. Snyder agreed to the use of the fund for the operation, and even volunteered the support of the Internal Revenue Service in laundering the money and transferring it to CIA-controlled accounts in Italy.[39]

Any minor American ward heeler would immediately have recognized the techniques employed by the CIA in Italy. Funds were secretly handed to the Christian Democrats and other non-Communists, providing walking-around money to get out the vote. To be sure, some of the money was spent on pamphlets, posters, and the other paraphernalia of election campaigns, but by some accounts, money was also used to bribe voting officials and for other underhanded things.[40] One former CIA official recalls "efforts to split off Socialists from the united front group dominated by the Communists," without specifying the form those efforts took.[41] And of course, all of this covert political action took place in parallel with the CIA's earlier sanctioned propaganda program.

A few days before the election, the Rome newspaper *Tempo* published a summary of the so-called Zorin Plan, which reportedly outlined Soviet foreign minister Valerian A. Zorin's program for Italy after a Communist victory at the polls:

> The immediate conclusion of a military alliance with Russia
> and Yugoslavia; strict dependence of Italy on Yugoslavia, which
> would become a pattern for Italian social life, economy, and

foreign policy; strict control over the press, radio and movies; and elimination of all priests who do not swear devotion to the Communist state and Communist principles.[42]

Publication of the Zorin Plan was a serious blow to the Italian Communists. *Tempo* offered no details of the journalistic coup that had enabled it to obtain what was supposedly one of the Kremlin's most secret policy papers. While the plan was similar to the program enforced by the Communists in the Eastern European satellite countries, the *Tempo* story may well have been a clever piece of black propaganda created and planted by the CIA.

Forrestal may have been dismayed when he learned from the Italian ambassador to Washington just a bit more than two weeks before the election that the Soviets were spending between twenty-five and thirty million dollars—three times the American investment—for their own covert political operation in Italy and that this figure did not include a substantial amount of lire brought into the country from Yugoslavia.[43] But despite this imbalance in favor of the Communists, on April 18 the Christian Democrats won 307 of 574 parliamentary seats, thus excluding the Italian Communist party from any role in the government. The Truman administration attributed these results to the CIA's operation. The agency had undertaken its first covert-action operation, and it was deemed an outstanding success.

The CIA's Special Procedures Group, which had carried out the Italian operation, continued to do business in Central and Eastern Europe, but apart from its one venture into political action, it remained purely a clandestine propaganda organization. It acquired a radio transmitter for broadcasting behind the Iron Curtain, established a secret propaganda printing plant in West Germany, and was planning to send pamphlet-laden unmanned balloons across Eastern European borders.[44] The success of the Italian election operation suggested to some members of the administration, however, that the government ought to have a permanent agency to conduct all forms of subversive warfare. The leading advocate of the idea was the chief of State's Policy Planning Committee, George F. Kennan.

Fluent in the Russian language, a student of Russian history and literature, and as a career foreign-service officer, an eyewitness to much of the past three decades of Russian events, the forty-four-year-old Kennan was considered to be the State Department's leading expert on Soviet affairs. Having served several long tours at the American embassy in Moscow, he was well acquainted with Stalin and the other Soviet leaders, and he had formed a theory on the reasons for their postwar expansionism. In January 1947 he had given a talk on the subject to the Council on Foreign Relations in New York. He was requested to put his ideas in writing for publication in the council's journal, *Foreign Affairs*, and the July issue carried an article, "The Sources of Soviet Conduct," appearing under the mysterious pseudonym X, to avoid giving the impression that the ideas presented were official State Department policy.[45]

In his article Kennan took issue with the then-popular notion that Russian geography and history, more than Marxist philosophy, motivated Stalin, that the Soviet Union wished only to establish a *cordon sanitaire* to her west to forestall yet another of the invasions she had suffered from that direction over the centuries, the most recent of which had been that of Hitler's armies. On the contrary, he argued, the current antipathy between Russia and the West arose not from traditional Russian insecurity but because the Soviet leaders believed such antagonism must necessarily exist as part of an inexorable historical process of struggle between socialism and capitalism, that the Western industrial democracies were *necessarily* the enemy by virtue of their economic systems and regardless of whatever friendly overtures they might make. We should not be misled, he wrote, but should understand that East-West conflict was the fundamental axiom of Soviet foreign policy and would remain so "until the internal nature of Soviet power is changed."

The Soviets were content to play a waiting game, in Kennan's analysis, always keeping the pressure on the West but never ready to gamble all previous gains on a single roll of the dice, a full-scale war. But, he continued, time might well be working against the Soviet leaders. The growth of Soviet military and industrial might had been achieved through "the use of forced labor on a scale unprecedented in modern times under conditions of peace" and through the neglect of other phases of economic life. To that cost was added the enormous toll of death and destruction of the recent war.

"Soviet power," Kennan wrote, "like the capitalist world of its conception, bears within it the seeds of its own decay. . . ." His prescription for dealing with the Soviets, then, was to match both their pressure and their patience, with the result of:

> a long-term . . . containment of Russian expansive tendencies. . . .
>
> Soviet pressure against the free institutions of the western world is something that can be contained by the adroit and vigilant application of counter-force at a series of constantly shifting geographical and political points, corresponding to the shifts and maneuvers of Soviet policy, but which cannot be charmed or talked out of existence.

Although he submitted the paper in response to the request of the *Foreign Affairs* editor, he had originally written it while on the faculty of the National War College, at the instance of Secretary of Defense Forrestal. Forrestal had been so impressed by it that he had recommended it to the secretary of state, and it became a major influence on American policy making during the next several years.[46]

In his paper Kennan did not elaborate on what form the counterforce he prescribed should take. He later explained that he meant "not the containment by military means of a military threat, but the political containment of a political threat."[47] Apparently, this included covert political action, for shortly after the success of the Italian election operation in April 1948, he proposed to add to his own Policy Planning Committee a Special Studies Group, which would be a permanent directorate to wage political, economic, and psychological warfare. Kennan envisioned a director and a staff of eight people from State and Defense, a budget of unvouchered funds, and the authority to enlist other government personnel as needed who would operate under cover.[48]

The mood in the National Security Council was very receptive to Kennan's plan. The recent shocks of the Czech coup, the Clay telegram, and the growing crisis in Berlin had combined to create an atmosphere of high tension in the Truman administration. The president and his advisers faced an acute and frustrating dilemma: the Soviets had repeatedly turned a deaf ear to diplomatic reproaches, but the American domestic economic and political situation ruled out a military response to Soviet truculence. The organization Kennan proposed offered a third option: covert action against the USSR.

The National Security Council endorsed Kennan's plan and in June issued a directive authorizing a large, secret program of political, psychological, and economic warfare against the Soviet Union. The NSC directive established a unit called the Office of Policy Coordination to carry out this program. The council decided to put it in the CIA rather than make it a part of Kennan's Policy Planning Committee, probably to accommodate Secretary Marshall's resolve to keep covert-action operations at arm's length in the interest of appearances, should something go wrong. It was pure cosmetics, however; while the OPC would draw its budget from the CIA's unvouchered funds, it was not to be under the control of the director of central intelligence. The director of the OPC was to be designated by the secretary of state and would receive his orders from a joint State-Defense panel. The CIA was to be no more than the cloak covering this newly forged dagger.

On August 12, 1948, Kennan met with Hillenkoetter and Admiral Souers to work out the administrative details (Souers, whom Truman had persuaded to return to Washington, was now secretary of the National Security Council). In time of peace, State would take the preeminent position in guiding the new agency; in time of war, that role would devolve upon Defense. The Defense representative was to be General Joseph T. McNarney, a former commander of United States forces in Europe. Kennan himself would be the State Department's representative.[49]

The man designated to direct the OPC was Frank G. Wisner, the son of a wealthy Mississippi entrepreneur and a veteran of the OSS SI Branch who had gotten firsthand experience of Soviet subversion methods. A 1934 graduate of the University of Virginia Law School, Wisner had returned to his job with a Wall Street law firm after the war. His interest in foreign affairs, whetted by his service in the OSS, was not fully satisfied by his participation in the Council on Foreign Relations. In 1947 he joined the State Department as deputy assistant secretary for occupied countries, and he was in that post when Secretary Marshall tapped him for the OPC directorship.

Wisner proceeded cautiously at first. Although he met weekly with Kennan to receive State's policy guidance, he initiated few operations during the first year of OPC's existence, focusing his attention instead on building the organization. The OPC consisted of four functional staffs—political warfare, psychological warfare, economic warfare, and paramilitary operations—and six geographic divisions. With a 1949 budget of $4.7

million, the OPC had a staff of 302 within a year, a great many of whom were veterans of the SO Branch and other special-operations units of the OSS.[50] The size of the OPC was soon to increase twentyfold, however.

Late in August 1949 an American reconnaissance aircraft flying over the Pacific collected an air sample downwind of the Russian landmass. The sample contained radioactive fallout: the Soviets had the atom bomb. Those who understood the full implications of this development realized that total war would never again be a practical option in dealing with Soviet expansion. Suddenly, subversive warfare had become an immensely important alternative.

Six days before Japan surrendered in August 1945 and two days after an American plane dropped an atom bomb on Hiroshima, the Soviet Union declared war on Japan. The Red Army drove down the Korean peninsula, stopping only when they met American occupation forces at the thirty-eighth parallel. The line became the demarcation between the Soviet and American zones of trusteeship. The Soviets established their own puppet government in the north and resisted United Nations efforts to hold nationwide Korean elections aimed at unifying the country and establishing it as a single, sovereign nation. The UN then established the Republic of Korea in the south, and in 1949 the American occupation forces withdrew, leaving behind a small detachment of military advisers.

On Sunday, June 25, 1950, seventy-five thousand North Korean troops crossed the border, attacking at six main points, while two amphibious forces landed on South Korea's east coast. They were supported by more than 1,400 artillery pieces and 126 Russian-built tanks. The first elements of the force crossed the thirty-eighth parallel at 4:00 A.M. Korean time, almost eight hours before the news reached the president. UPI headquarters in New York had the story almost an hour and a half before an official report was deciphered at the State Department.

The CIA had yet to be heard from.

The CIA's failure to forecast the Communist invasion of South Korea would have been excusable had Director Hillenkoetter not exacerbated the situation by trying to place the blame elsewhere. In the hours following the North Korean invasion, while the Truman administration struggled with the problem of dealing with the crisis, the director of central intelligence strove to preserve his own image and that of the agency. In an interview with a *New York Times* reporter, he reportedly said that the CIA had been aware that "conditions existed in Korea which could have meant an invasion this week or next."[51] The next day, while the Truman administration continued to grapple with the crisis, Hillenkoetter testified in secret session before the Senate Appropriations Committee regarding the CIA's warnings. He reportedly stated that the CIA had indeed warned of the impending attack,[52] an assertion that immediately raised the question of why the Truman administration had been taken completely by surprise. Why, for example, had Under Secretary of State Dean Rusk told the House Foreign Relations Committee less than a week earlier, "We see no indication that [the North Koreans] have any intention of fighting a major war for that purpose [i.e., taking over South Korea]"?[53]

Hillenkoetter's claim apparently referred to an estimate the CIA had disseminated to State, Defense, and the White House on June 14 to the effect that the North Koreans had built up their military strength at the border to the level where they could invade South Korea at any time and capture Seoul within ten or twelve days.[54] But the buildup was not news within the government; it had been going on for more than a year. As CIA intelligence officer Lyman B. Kirkpatrick later explained,

> Like any military force anxious to achieve surprise, (the North Koreans] had drawn out their build-up over a long period of time in order not to arouse suspicion. If proper military security were observed, only a very few senior officers would know of the date and time of the attack. . . . Advance warning could have come only from an intelligence penetration—an agent—in the highest levels of the North Korean army, or from a communications slip, and there were neither of these.[55]

In other words, in its estimate the CIA had referred to the North Korean *capability*. It said nothing about intent, nor could it have without the help of a functioning crystal ball. Hillenkoetter would have been better advised to adopt that more reasonable defensive posture rather than making the untenable claim that the CIA had warned the administration about the impending disaster.

It is not hard to imagine Truman's anger and frustration. For whatever the CIA's estimate had been worth, it had been lost amidst the daily buzz of cables, reports, and estimates, and that was exactly what the president had been promised would not happen if he established a central-intelligence agency. Hillenkoetter had compounded the disaster by shifting an unwarranted share of the blame to the administration at the very moment when the president and his advisers were trying to rally national support for their response to the crisis.

The admiral's actions reflected the overall defensive mind-set he had developed during his tenure as DCI in response to the sharp criticism he received from the National Security Council and others in the intelligence community. He had never wanted to head the agency, and months earlier he had let it be known he wanted out, suggesting that the proper place for a sailor was at sea. The president, surely agreeing now that the sea was a far better place for this sailor than the CIA, accepted Hillenkoetter's resignation and gave him command of the navy's Seventh Task Force, which was assigned to protect Taiwan.[56]

In October the new director of central intelligence was sworn in: General Walter Bedell Smith. The CIA, which had been little more than an information-coordination unit with a modest overseas secret intelligence apparatus, was about to become the important player in American foreign affairs that we know today.

Chapter Thirty-four

The CIA Transformed

Walter Bedell Smith was not a West Point graduate. He had no more than a high-school education when he enlisted as a private in the Indiana National Guard in 1917. By 1939 he was a major in the regular army, assigned to the War Department General Staff in Washington. There his real strengths emerged: Smith was the perfect staff officer, a fact discovered by Army Chief of Staff George C. Marshall. Marshall recommended him to Eisenhower, who made him his chief of staff in September 1942.

Eisenhower found Smith to be "a master of detail," an officer who could keep at his fingertips the tens of thousands of complex details involved in planning the Normandy landings, anticipating his boss's questions before they were asked. To the supreme commander he was "a godsend," and "the general manager of the war." By war's end Smith wore the three stars of a lieutenant general. In February 1946 President Truman appointed him ambassador to the Soviet Union, a post he held during the first three years of cold-war tension.

Smith took over the CIA in October 1950. Truman would have preferred an earlier date, but the fifty-five-year-old general was recuperating from an operation in which two thirds of his ulcerated stomach had been removed, the price of his lifelong commitment to getting things done. The fact that he suffered from ulcers was well-known, and all who had worked for him knew him to be a victim of the condition. As director of central intelligence, he proved to be the perfect man for the job at that moment.

Smith was not a seasoned intelligence officer, however, and recognizing that fact, he cast about for an able deputy to handle the substantive business of the CIA while he dealt with the National Security Council, the State and Defense departments, and the White House. He chose William

Jackson, a Wall Street lawyer who had been General Omar Bradley's chief intelligence officer during the war. After the war Jackson had made a thorough study of British intelligence under OSS auspices. Thereafter, he was sometimes called in by General Vandenberg as a consultant to the CIA, and in 1948 the National Security Council commissioned him as part of a three-person team to make a management study of the CIA and the other intelligence services. Impressed by the report, Smith invited Jackson to serve as deputy director of central intelligence and help implement its recommendations. Jackson accepted and was sworn in the same day as Smith.[1]

High on Smith's agenda in reforming the CIA was the matter of national intelligence estimates. The national estimate is an attempt to forecast developments that will affect national foreign policy or security. It is an educated guess made in the hope of preventing unpleasant surprises. But in the three years since the CIA was created, the Truman administration had experienced a number of very unpleasant surprises—the Communist coup in Czechoslovakia, the Soviet atom bomb, and most recently, the Korean invasion.

No one expected the CIA to foretell the future. Its job was to solicit the best guesses of knowledgeable departments of the government and synthesize them into a single forecast for the president. The way the agency had been doing this was to produce a draft estimate, circulate it to State, the MID, the ONI, and other interested departments, collect the resultant comments, objections, and suggestions, and incorporate them into a second draft, then repeat the process as many times as necessary to obtain general agreement on a final draft. Unfortunately, the process was unacceptably slow, and often the end product was of little use to the president anyway. Some estimates were riddled with footnotes stating the dissent of individual departments to the estimate's overall conclusions and were therefore nothing but collections of individual guesses. Other estimates avoided dissenting footnotes by narrowing the scope of the matter under consideration or by substituting vague generalities for specific language.[2]

The estimate problem had been highlighted by the management study. Jackson, who had served briefly in the OSS, recommended former R&A Branch chief William Langer to deal with it. Smith persuaded Langer to take a year's leave of absence from Harvard to overhaul the CIA's national-estimate apparatus. Langer, in turn, recruited Yale historian and R&A

veteran Sherman Kent to serve as his deputy. Kent's recent book, *Strategic Intelligence for American World Policy,* was a blueprint for the production of national intelligence.[3]

Langer and Kent organized a two-tier structure within the CIA Intelligence Directorate: an Office of National Estimates, consisting of a support staff that assembled and summarized the data needed to prepare a draft of a national estimate, and a Board of National Estimates, which was a panel of highly respected senior specialists—former armed services officers, foreign-service officers, academics, and others—whose function was to oversee the estimating process and negotiate with the interested departments on the wording of the final draft of a national estimate.

Langer brought in a number of prestigious academics to serve on the board. To balance what he feared might be an overly theoretical approach to intelligence problems, Jackson arranged for a panel of outside consultants to review the draft intelligence estimates. The panel consisted of George Kennan—now out of the State Department and at the Institute for Advanced Studies; Hamilton Fish Armstrong, the editor of *Foreign Affairs*; and the atomic scientist Vannevar Bush. Since they met at the Gun Club at Princeton University, they were informally known in the agency as the Princeton Consultants.[4]

Although the board was located organizationally within the CIA Intelligence Directorate, it was conceived as a supercouncil transcending the parochial views and interests of a single member agency of the United States intelligence community. At the outset of the preparation of any national estimate, the board defined the initial "terms of reference" of the problem, partitioned the research and analysis to be done, and assigned the component staff studies to the appropriate agencies. Thus, political aspects of the estimate would go to State, military to the MID, and so forth. The job of the Office of National Estimates was to compile these staff studies and integrate them into a single, comprehensive draft for the board. After agreeing on the language of the final draft, the board forwarded the estimate to the Intelligence Advisory Committee, a panel chaired by the director of central intelligence and composed of the directors of the MID, the ONI, the intelligence units of State and the air force, and representatives of the Joint Chiefs of Staff, the FBI, and the Atomic Energy Commission (the latter two participating only in those estimates that their respective agencies had a hand in drafting). Estimates receiving final approval by the IAC were then submitted to the president through the National Security Council.[5]

The new arrangement worked well. The estimate apparatus in place, Langer returned to Harvard, leaving Sherman Kent as chairman of the board, a position he held until the late 1960s. The BNE-ONE system for producing national estimates was retained until the mid-1970s.

The NSC management study of the intelligence community had highlighted several problems. One was the national intelligence estimates. Another was the Office of Policy Coordination, the agency created late in 1948 to counter Soviet expansionism with subversive warfare. The OPC presented several problems, all of which arose from its anomalous position within the federal bureaucracy.

The OPC was physically co-located with the CIA in the Tempos, two rows of temporary wartime buildings along the Reflecting Pool on the Mall that had housed the OSS several years earlier. Although its budget and personnel were taken from CIA allocations, the director of central intelligence had no management authority over the OPC; Frank Wisner, the OPC director, reported to and received his instructions from the joint State-Defense panel set up for that purpose. Wisner was, in fact, even more autonomous than this arrangement suggests.

A former Wall Street lawyer, Wisner was well connected to the big New York and Washington law firms, which had become a major repository of power in the FDR and Truman administrations. The firms were filled with former senior government officials whose access to former colleagues in the federal bureaucracy gave them a powerful advantage in representing clients doing business with the United States government. Dean Acheson, for example, was a member of a major Washington law firm that represented many foreign governments, and he had shuttled between private law practice and several tours as an official of the Treasury and State departments before being appointed secretary of state in 1949.

Later known by the vague and imprecise term the Northeast Establishment, this network of Ivy League law-school graduates was the complex and invisible grid along which power flowed in Washington. It was a world completely alien to Admiral Hillenkoetter, but it was the natural milieu of Frank Wisner, whose family background, independent wealth, and Wall Street connections had given him entrée to such circles long before he went to Washington.

The Achesons and many of the other Washington movers and shakers were often to be found at the quiet dinner parties hosted by Polly Wisner in Georgetown or as weekend guests at the Wisners' country place in Galena, Maryland. They were charmed and amused by Wisner's skillful performance as raconteur, flattered by his attentions, and intrigued by his mysterious involvement in secret and dangerous things. Now and then the guest list was very short, so that some special business could be done over coffee, brandy, and cigars.

Between 1949 and 1950 the OPC's personnel strength blossomed from 302 to 584; the following year it nearly tripled.[6] Although brilliant and energetic, Frank Wisner was not a talented manager, and he found that the difficulties of administering a burgeoning government department were compounded by the very nature of covert-action operations. There was little experience with such things in American government. All of the lessons had been learned in the wartime OSS, and chief among them was the precept that covert operations could not be managed through bureaucratic routine and strict lines of authority. That had seemed an acceptable idea two years earlier, when OPC was still much the sort of thing George Kennan had had in mind when he proposed it—a small outfit that would be called upon infrequently when an unusual situation needed some covert troubleshooting. But in the heightened cold-war activity of 1950, that policy brought chaos.

In theory, the OPC was supposed to work this way: With guidance from the State and Defense departments, the four OPC functional staffs—political warfare, psychological warfare, economic warfare, and paramilitary operations—were supposed to initiate covert-action projects. These projects would be carried out by the geographic area divisions of the OPC and their subordinate overseas stations. The reality was quite different. Projects were initiated at every level in both the divisions and the stations. Virtually any proposal for some secret anti-Communist mischief received the stamp of approval without regard to its estimated cost, effectiveness, or place within the larger scheme of United States foreign policy. Because an OPC officer was judged by the number and the importance of the projects he started and ran, career ambition tended to spur his resourcefulness in dreaming up new ones. And in the atmosphere of heightened tension that followed Soviet acquisition of nuclear weapons, there was little tendency to say no.[7]

Wisner's internal management problems were aggravated by an ill-advised personnel policy that created deep resentment in the CIA. The OSS veterans, who comprised one third of the agency, saw an increasing number of familiar faces show up at the Tempos as Wisner built his staff by recruiting former members of the OSS SO Branch and other special-operations components of the wartime agency. The OSS veterans in the CIA's Office of Special Operations—the SI Branch veterans who had clung tenaciously to the profession of intelligence during the uncertain postwar years of the Strategic Services Unit and the Central Intelligence Group—did not warmly welcome the OPC newcomers.

There was, first of all, the professional mistrust, and perhaps jealousy, many secret intelligence professionals feel for covert-action operations. Secret intelligence is a slow, plodding business. Most of the Office of Special Operations people lived in a world of cables, dossiers, and index cards, and even those who ran agents overseas knew it was far less glamorous work than the readers of spy fiction supposed. Their work remained unheralded, even within the innermost circles of the government. Covert operations, on the other hand, were swift, swashbuckling, and spectacular, conducted in an atmosphere of urgency and closely followed from inception to completion by the White House and the National Security Council, albeit sometimes with much trepidation.

The OSO staff officers viewed their new OPC neighbors as Johnny-come-latelies to covert operations. Their resentment of the newcomers had an even more fundamental basis, however: pay. As an independent agency OPC was not constrained by the CIA's salary structure, and with a liberal budget Wisner was free to offer the newcomers handsomer wages than their OSO counterparts were receiving. And OPC was growing rapidly, offering far better advancement opportunities than the OSO.[8]

The result of the rivalry between the CIA's OSO and the OPC was most apparent in the field, where the two clandestine services maintained separate facilities and often competed to recruit the same foreign nationals as agents. The interagency squabbling reached crisis proportions in Bangkok, where the OSO attempted to recruit a senior Thai official who was already on the OPC payroll. The situation got so completely out of hand that the director of the OSO was forced to fly out from Washington to referee the situation.

These, then, were some of the problems the NSC study had identified when it examined the OPC.

Walter Bedell Smith's personal prestige in the Truman administration enabled him to take actions that were closed to Admiral Hillenkoetter. Immediately after taking office as director of central intelligence in October 1950, he cut the Gordian knot that had tied the hands of his predecessor and simply declared that henceforth the OPC would report to State and Defense only through himself. Having thereby made the OPC a true element of the CIA with a single stroke of the pen, he created the cryptically named Plans Directorate, which was to consist of the OPC and the OSO. To head the new directorate he recruited yet another of the authors of the NSC management study, Allen W. Dulles. Nonetheless, Smith stopped short of completely implementing one recommendation of the study: that the OPC and the OSO be merged into a single covert-operations unit.[9]

Wisner took the new arrangement with grace. In reality his autonomy was little diminished; Dulles, for whom he had worked briefly while in the OSS, was a full member of the Wall Street–Washington law establishment, president of the Council on Foreign Relations, of which Wisner was a member, and a personal friend. And Jackson, deputy director of central intelligence, had been Wisner's law partner on Wall Street.

Soon after transferring the OPC to the CIA, Smith also managed to bring about a change in the mechanism whereby covert-action operations received official approval. At his suggestion, the existing State-Defense panel was abolished; henceforth, operations would be subject to the approval of the Psychological Strategy Board, an arm of the NSC. While the new approval machinery made for a more systematic and rational program—the NSC was supposed to have the full picture in national-security matters—it did not promise a diminution in the number of covert-action projects mounted by the OPC. The NSC had only recently signed off on a document that virtually institutionalized the cold war.[10]

* * *

In January 1950, some four months after the Soviets tested their first atom bomb, President Truman ordered the Atomic Energy Commission to begin development of a weapon of almost inconceivable explosive power: the hydrogen bomb. At the same time Truman directed the National Security Council to undertake a complete re-appraisal of American policies in light of the recent fall of China to the Communists, the Soviet development of the atom bomb, and the prospect of an American hydrogen bomb. In April the National Security Council endorsed and released a position paper destined to shape American policy at home and abroad for the next generation. NSC-68, as it was designated, began with a review of the world situation: "Events since the end of World War II have created a new power relationship in the world which must be viewed not as a temporary distortion but as a long-range and fundamental realignment among nations. . . . The U.S. and the U.S.S.R. are the terminal poles of this new international axis."[11]

The Kremlin, the document said, had three main objectives: to strengthen its role as the center of international communism, to extend its power to new Soviet satellites, and to oppose any competing powers threatening its plans for world hegemony. The United States must try to oppose these plans by peaceful means, but "if peaceful means fail we must be willing and ready to fight."

The Soviets were foreseen as achieving nuclear parity with the United States by about 1954, or perhaps a few years later if the American hydrogen-bomb project was successful. In conventional warfare the Communists were already more powerful than the West. The prospects for reducing the threat of a nuclear holocaust through a negotiated arms reduction were poor.

NSC-68 called for "a bold and massive program of rebuilding the West's defensive potential to surpass that of the Soviet world, and of meeting each fresh challenge promptly and unequivocally." The paper was the official marching orders for the upper- and middle-level managers of the Truman administration. The cold war is here to stay, it said; we all better get used to it.

In adopting NSC-68 as its official policy, the Truman administration formally recognized the terrible postwar dilemma: peaceful negotiations with the Soviets wouldn't work. If a massive nuclear and conventional-force buildup failed to deter Soviet expansion, civilization might well be totally destroyed. In this grim atmosphere the third option of subversive warfare acquired an almost irresistible appeal. The NSC's Psychological Strategy Board was usually disposed to giving the green light to Wisner and the OPC. Covert-action projects were approved even more readily after Communist forces crossed the thirty-eighth parallel into South Korea in June 1950, two months after NSC-68 was adopted.

Intelligence and intelligence failures played a major role in the Korean War. The failure of American intelligence services to forecast the North Korean invasion in June 1950 found a sequel late in November, when the Chinese launched a massive invasion of North Korea, where the United States–United Nations forces were advancing toward the Manchurian border.

Throughout the war aerial reconnaissance by the United States Air Force provided nearly half of all the tactical intelligence of the U.S.-UN ground forces.[12] In Washington the war generated unprecedented demands on the CIA's Intelligence Directorate for economic and strategic intelligence,[13] but the CIA's principal role in the war zone was in the area of covert action.

The CIA's OPC established six CIA installations in Japan, the major one at Atsugi Naval Air Station, fifty miles south of Tokyo. Wisner's man in the Korean theater was Hans V. Tofte, a Danish-born veteran of the OSS SO Branch who was fluent in several languages, including Chinese and Russian. Tofte's first task after arrival in the war zone in 1950 was to establish an escape-and-evasion network in North Korea to assist American fliers brought down behind Communist lines.[14]

After the war became static in mid-1951, Tofte focused his efforts on guerrilla warfare, recruiting and training agents from among the thousands of North Koreans who had been evacuated to refugee camps in the south. The CIA guerrillas operated behind Communist lines, sabotaging railroad trains, ambushing truck convoys, and disrupting the flow of supplies from Manchuria and eastern Siberia to the Communist forces fighting in Korea. Reportedly, these operations were so effective that the Chinese commanders in Korea believed fifty thousand troops were operating north of the thirty-eighth parallel; in fact, the CIA force numbered only twelve hundred.[15]

Tofte also ran Operation Tropic, the support of third-force Chinese guerrillas (i.e., anti-Communist Chinese not affiliated with Chiang Kai-shek's Nationalist regime) on the Chinese mainland. According to a former CIA covert-operations officer, Tropic proved ineffective.[16]

Operation Paper was another CIA-OPC operation aimed at the Chinese. It involved the support of the scattered remnants of the Chinese Nationalist army that had fled into Burma after the Chinese Communist victory on the mainland in 1949. By using the refugee troops to threaten the Sino-Burmese border, the OPC hoped to force the Communists to divert some of their forces from Korea. Paper proved not only ineffective—the refugee forces failed to operate successfully against the Chinese Communists—but proved disastrous to Burmese-American relations when the armed refugees turned to banditry. The situation was eventually resolved in 1953, when William J. Donovan, whom President Eisenhower had appointed ambassador to neighboring Thailand, arranged the evacuation of the refugee troops to Taiwan.[17]

As a nonwar—it was officially designated a UN police action—the Korean War was the first conflict in which American military operations were constrained by the need to avoid escalation into a general nuclear conflict with the Soviet Union. Unlike most previous American wars, its object was not the capitulation of the enemy but a negotiated end to hostilities. This placed new and unprecedented demands on the intelligence services—for example, the requirement to conduct intelligence collection and covert action against Communist China while no formal state of war existed between that country and the United States. This blurring of the distinction between war and peace—a fundamental characteristic of the cold war—permanently enlarged the peacetime role of all American intelligence services, especially the CIA, and it again raised the premium put on covert action.

In August 1952 the OPC and the OSO were merged into a single clandestine service. Wisner was made deputy director for plans—that is, chief of the newly combined organization (Dulles had by this time assumed the number-two spot in the CIA, deputy director of central intelligence). Wisner's assistant deputy director was Richard Helms, a veteran of the OSS SI Branch who had stayed on at the Strategic Services Unit after the war and risen to the directorship of the OSO. With the former OPC chief in the top slot, the CIA Clandestine Service continued the agency's earlier emphasis on covert action over secret intelligence.[18]

The following January the Eisenhower administration took office. The president appointed John Foster Dulles—Allen's brother—as secretary of state. He moved Walter Bedell Smith from the CIA to the State Department to serve as under secretary of state. And he promoted Allen Dulles to director of central intelligence.

General Charles P. Cabell, former chief of air force intelligence, was the new deputy director of central intelligence. Allen Dulles preferred to leave the day-to-day running of the agency in Cabell's hands while he immersed himself in the world of Wisner's Clandestine Service (Dulles became known in the CIA as the Great White Case Officer).

The effect of the new arrangement was to raise covert operations in general, and covert action in particular, to the cabinet level. John Foster Dulles was an ardent and aggressive anti-Communist. He disdained the Kennan doctrine of containment of Soviet expansionism and favored an activist policy of liberation of the captive peoples of Soviet-dominated countries. In this he was in perfect agreement with Wisner. In the Dulles brothers Wisner now had an unofficial but highly effective direct channel to the Oval Office. The golden age of covert action had arrived.

Wisner had dreamed of liberating the captive nations since he first took charge of the OPC late in 1948. During his year at the State Department, he had been deputy assistant secretary of state for occupied countries, a post that involved him in the problems posed by the large number of refugees in Germany, Austria, and Trieste—Russians and Eastern Europeans who had fled to the West to escape Soviet domination. The refugees were strongly anti-Soviet and, of course, intimately familiar with the languages and society of their native lands. Wisner realized they would make ideal instruments of OPC operations. In 1949 he approached DeWitt C. Poole with a plan for making use of them.[19]

Poole had directed the OSS's Foreign Nationalities Branch, and his wartime experience and contacts with foreign émigré groups in the United States were directly applicable to what Wisner now had in mind. With OPC funds and direction, Poole formed the National Committee for a Free Europe in June 1949 to provide a cover for OPC's refugee operations. He enlisted the aid of *Fortune* publisher C. D. Jackson to round up a roster of prominent Americans ready to lend their names to the committee's letterhead. Jackson, who had been General Eisenhower's chief of psychological warfare during the preparations for the D-day landings, persuaded the general to take an active part in the committee. Eisenhower and General Lucius Clay organized the Crusade for Freedom, ostensibly a drive to raise funds for the committee from among businesses and private individuals and in reality a cover for the fact that the committee's money came from OPC's unvouchered funds.[20]

The committee worked to organize anti-Communist émigrés in both the United States and Europe. Its stated goals were "to keep alive the hope of freedom in the countries of Eastern Europe dominated by Russia, . . . to preserve such exiled leaders of those satellite countries as have found asylum in the United States for the day of liberation, [and] to help rededicate Americans to their heritage of freedom." To emphasize the putative unofficial nature of the committee, Secretary of State Dean Acheson publicly gave it his official blessing: "The State Department is very happy to see the formation of this group. It thinks that the purpose of the organization is excellent, and is glad to welcome its entrance into this field and give it its hearty endorsement."[21]

The committee's headquarters was a small office suite on Fifth Avenue in midtown Manhattan. The Intellectual Cooperation Division was set up in Washington with the cooperation of the Library of Congress as a center where refugee scholars studied economic and political developments in their homeland. The division also had a Mid-European Studies Center in New York, which received some support from New York University and the Carnegie Endowment for International Peace. The division established the Free University in Exile, in Strasbourg, France, to educate refugee youths for the day when, it was hoped, they could return to their native land and assume leadership.

The committee's American Contacts Division served as a lecture bureau for émigré leaders touring the United States. Under the National Councils

Division refugee groups were established for each of the Soviet satellite nations. The National Councils were to be virtual governments in exile, ready to be put in place whenever the satellite nation was liberated from the Soviets' grasp.[22]

These several activities of the National Committee for a Free Europe provided Wisner with long-term assets to be employed after the OPC's Eastern European operations got off the ground. The committee provided cover for a psychological-warfare operation to be undertaken immediately, however—radio propaganda directed against the Soviet-controlled governments of the Eastern European satellites. Plans were made for a battery of powerful radio transmitters to be established in West Germany operating under the name Radio Free Europe, a division of the committee. The first of these, a short-wave station with a signal that carried across Eastern Europe, was opened near Frankfurt in July 1950. The following May a broadcast-band station was put into operation in Munich, its signal beamed at Czechoslovakia.

The RFE stations broadcast talks by exiles, personal messages, replies to mail from listeners in the satellites, the names of Communist secret-police agents and informers working under cover in the target countries, news items embarrassing to or derogatory of the Communist government, and American jazz and other music popular in Eastern Europe but banned there. Uninhibited by an overt connection to the United States government, RFE was able to denounce the Soviet Union and communism in the harshest terms without causing diplomatic embarrassment to the United States. When a target government protested in Washington, the State Department simply shrugged and explained that it had no control over the RFE operation.

To Wisner the RFE and the committee were something much more than a clandestine propaganda operation; they were the first step in a program he intended would culminate in an anti-Soviet revolt from the Baltic to the Adriatic. That program remained on hold through the final years of the Truman administration, but with the inauguration of President Eisenhower, whose secretary of state advocated the liberation of the captive nations of Eastern Europe, it was ready to be activated.

Chapter Thirty-five

High Tech and Dirty Tricks

In its covert-action operations in Eastern Europe, Frank Wisner's OPC had two highly experienced partners. One was the British Secret Intelligence Service (the Special Operations Executive had been abolished after the war, making subversive warfare once again the province of the SIS). The other was the Gehlen Organization, the remnants of a German wartime military intelligence service commanded by Brigadier General Reinhard Gehlen, which still maintained agent networks in Eastern Europe.

Gehlen had been head of Foreign Armies East, the intelligence section of the German General Staff concerned with the Russian front. After the war the unit was not dissolved along with the rest of the German war machine but was made a wholly-owned subsidiary of the United States Army's Counter-Intelligence Corps. In 1949 it was transferred to the CIA.[1] Gehlen's agents recruited operatives for Wisner from the displaced-persons camps and among the Soviet and Eastern European émigré groups in West Germany, helped train them, and sent them back into Soviet-controlled areas on covert-action and secret intelligence operations.[2]

With the help of the Gehlen Organization, the OPC and the SIS mounted several joint paramilitary operations in Eastern Europe and the Soviet Union in the late 1940s and early 1950s. They were, for the most part, failures. The most spectacular OPC failure was in Albania, where the British SIS proposed a joint Anglo-American paramilitary operation to overthrow the Communist regime of Enver Hoxha, perhaps thereby precipitating a general anti-Soviet uprising in Eastern Europe.

The joint SIS-OPC operation began in April 1950, when the first of many Albanian émigrés who had been recruited in Egypt, Greece, and Italy and trained in Cyprus and Malta were sent back into Albania. Most of the agents were never heard from again; a few made their way back across the Greco-Albanian border to report that the Albanian militia had been waiting for them when they arrived in the country. By some accounts five hundred agents were captured and executed before the SIS and the OPC terminated the operation in 1952. The means by which the Albanian security forces learned of the time and place of the agents' landings became apparent several years later, when SIS officer Kim Philby was exposed as a Soviet penetration agent: Philby, the SIS's liaison officer with the CIA and FBI in Washington, had been one of the two British representatives on a four-member Anglo-American panel that managed the day-to-day running of the operation.[3]

Curiously, Wisner's first major success was not in Europe but in Southeast Asia. In 1946 the United States honored a long-standing commitment to the people of its Philippine Islands territory and granted them independence. Among the several problems that faced Manuel Roxas y Acuña, the president of the new nation, was the Hukbalahap (People's Liberation Army), a Communist guerrilla force that had fought the Japanese occupation during the Second World War and had begun an armed insurrection against the Philippine government. By 1950 the Huks, as they became known, controlled a large part of the principal Philippine island of Luzon and were threatening even the capital city, Manila.

Wisner sent Lieutenant Colonel Edward G. Lansdale to the Philippines to serve as the OPC chief of station. Lansdale had worked in advertising before joining the OSS in the Second World War. Later he was an army intelligence officer in the Philippines, where his interest in and understanding of Filipino society and culture enabled him to resolve postwar clashes between Filipinos and the United States Army. These traits together with mastery of the techniques of psychological warfare led Wisner to tap Lansdale for the Manila assignment in 1950.[4]

To Lansdale the Huk problem was not essentially a military one. The Huks were completely dependent upon the support of the rural population; the people supported them because the Philippine government was corrupt and repressive, a regime dedicated to the preservation of privilege for the few. Lansdale believed the best way of ending the Huk insurgency was by introducing democratic reforms in the Philippines. To do this he brought the resources of the CIA to bear in support of a Filipino leader he knew and admired, Ramón Magsaysay.[5]

A wartime guerrilla leader, Magsaysay was a popular congressman from Zambales, a province on the west-central coast of Luzon. As an outspoken critic of the government policies and social conditions that created popular support for the Huks, he seemed to Lansdale the ideal instrument of democratic reform. Lansdale resolved to make Magsaysay president of the Philippines.

One OPC officer who shared Lansdale's view of the Huk problem was Desmond FitzGerald, deputy chief of the OPC's Far East Division. A northeastern aristocrat with a St. Mark's–Harvard–Harvard Law background, OSS veteran FitzGerald had been active in reform politics in New York City after the war and before joining the CIA. He recruited fellow New York pol Gabriel L. Kaplan and sent him to Manila to assist Lansdale in his campaign in support of Magsaysay.[6]

In his days in New York politics, Kaplan had learned to work with veterans' groups, chambers of commerce, Rotary Clubs, and similar organizations. In the Philippines he recruited Filipinos with the talent for dealing with corresponding groups. Kaplan was behind the formation of the National Movement for Free Elections (NAMFREL), an organization secretly funded by the CIA that taught such practical matters as ballot thumb printing, voter identification, and other methods of ensuring an honest election. He and Lansdale secretly launched the Magsaysay for President Movement, which promoted the idea of Magsaysay as a national figure rather than simply a parochial politician representing Zambales. The movement sought to provide Magsaysay with a broad, multipartisan political base.

Magsaysay was appointed secretary of national defense in 1950. Lansdale and Kaplan worked closely with him in the campaign against the Huks and were responsible for introducing a variety of psychological and political measures, ranging from the exploitation of the Filipino peasants' superstitions to the establishment of community centers throughout the islands where modern methods of agriculture, health care, road building, and communications were taught.

Magsaysay reformed the Philippine army, firing corrupt officers and improving the food, quarters, and pay of the troops. Thus renewed, the army became more effective in conventional counterinsurgency tactics. Magsaysay offered amnesty to Huks who laid down their arms and instituted anti-Communist indoctrination of those who were captured. The effectiveness of these measures in eroding the Huks' popular support and destroying their morale gradually brought the insurgency to an end. Magsaysay's success in ending the Huk terror greatly enhanced his public image. In 1953 he was elected president in a landslide.

Nineteen fifty-three also saw another CIA covert-action success, one very different in method from Lansdale's in the Philippines. The scene was Iran, where the young shah Mohammad Reza Pahlavi sat uneasily upon the Peacock Throne while the elderly and eccentric prime minister, Dr. Mohammad Mosaddeq, steered the country into grave economic and political difficulties.

On the same day in May 1951 that the shah had bowed to political pressure from members of the Majlis, the Iranian legislature, and appointed Mosaddeq prime minister, Mosaddeq presented a bill to the Majlis calling for the nationalization of the British-owned Anglo-Iranian Oil Company. Although Iran earned half of its government revenues from royalties paid to it by the company, Anglo-Iranian was earning nearly five times that amount from the oil it took out of the Iranian ground and was paying more to the British government in taxes than it was to Iran in oil royalties. This obviously inequitable arrangement was unpopular with virtually all Iranians; Mosaddeq's bill was passed unanimously by the Majlis and signed into law by the shah.

In retaliation for the move, Anglo-Iranian withdrew all its personnel from the country, leaving Iran without the technical expertise and manpower to operate the wells, pipelines, and refineries. The company also declared its proprietaty rights to any oil that might be taken from the Iranian fields and threatened legal action against any foreign buyers of Iranian oil. The two moves were completely effective: Iranian oil ceased to flow, and the country was deprived of virtually all foreign revenue. A major economic crisis ensued.

In the face of the crisis, Mosaddeq demanded the authority to govern without recourse to the legislature and that he be given the powers of war minister. The shah refused and asked for the prime minister's resignation. Mosaddeq's party, the National Front, began rioting in protest. Moscow now decided to fish in the troubled Iranian waters: the Iranian Communist party, known as the Tudeh, aligned with Mosaddeq and joined in the riots. After five days the shah gave in and reappointed Mosaddeq. Three months later Mosaddeq broke off diplomatic relations with Britain.

Iranian discomfiture did little to assuage the outrage of the British public or government (the latter owned a large part of Anglo-Iranian). Britain mounted an international campaign aimed at the Mosaddeq regime. Prime Minister Churchill urged the United States to cut off its foreign aid to Iran ($23.4 million in fiscal year 1952), something the Truman administration—now in its final year—refused to do on the grounds that Iran had acted within her sovereign rights in nationalizing the oil facilities (the FDR administration had accepted an identical action by Mexico a dozen years earlier). At the same time Washington was concerned over the possibility that the British would carry out their threats of overt military action in the crisis, seeing it as likely to provoke a Soviet military move into Iran. The Soviets, along with the British and the United States, had jointly occupied Iran for strategic reasons during the Second World War, and the Soviets, covetous of the oil-rich northern province of Azerbaijan, adjacent to their own Azerbaijan Soviet Social Republic, had been slow to make good their promise to leave the country after the war. A British military incursion would give them an excuse to return, possibly precipitating a major East-West confrontation.

American fears of a Soviet takeover in Iran—already exacerbated by the Tudeh's support of Mosaddeq and the prime minister's diplomatic overtures to Moscow—provided the British with leverage. In November 1952 representatives of Anglo-Iranian approached CIA officer Kermit Roosevelt in London with a proposal for an Anglo-American covert-action operation to overthrow Mosaddeq.[7] Roosevelt, grandson of President Theodore Roosevelt and a northeastern aristocrat with a Groton-Harvard background, had served as assistant to the chief of the OSS SI Branch in the Near East during the war.

The Anglo-Iranian proposal was the latest in a series the company and the British Secret Intelligence Service had made to the United States government regarding action against Mosaddeq. The timing of this initiative no doubt reflected British hopes that Eisenhower, who had just won the presidential election of 1952, would be more favorably inclined to intervene in Iran than Truman had been. Their hopes were realized, and in June 1953 Roosevelt obtained approval from the Dulles brothers and Eisenhower's other national-security advisers for his revision of the operation plan proposed by the British. In essence, the operation, code-named Ajax, called for overthrowing Mosaddeq and strengthening the shah.[8]

The situation in Iran had worsened in the meantime, however. In February the shah had announced that he would abdicate. The announcement set off new rioting between his supporters and Mosaddeq's, the latter again including members of the Communist Tudeh party. Encouraged by the obvious extent of his support, the shah changed his mind and remained on the throne. Communist support for Mosaddeq increased, however, and the situation grew more unstable.

In mid-July Roosevelt entered Iran secretly and met with the shah, assuring him of Eisenhower's and Churchill's support if he should remove Mosaddeq. His resolve strengthened, the shah agreed to participate in the CIA-SIS operation.[9]

Essentially, the Ajax plan called for taking away from Mosaddeq control of the Iranian armed forces and police and putting them directly in the service of the shah, enabling the latter to remove the prime minister. The rank and file of the services were pro-shah, and the SIS had extensive assets in the officer corps. The fifty-thousand-man Imperial Iranian Gendarmerie had been commanded by former New Jersey State Police commander H. Norman Schwarzkopf during the wartime occupation; Schwarzkopf was brought into the operation, presumably to activate sympathetic former associates. While the police and armed forces were to enforce the shah's takeover, Roosevelt and a handful of CIA and SIS operators would organize and orchestrate the shah's considerable popular support to counter the anticipated protest demonstrations of the Tudeh and Mosaddeq's other supporters.

On August 9 the shah signed decrees removing Mosaddeq and appointing in his place General Fazollah Zahedi, a shah loyalist. Shortly thereafter, he left the country to await the outcome of the operation.

At midnight on August 14, the chief of the Palace Guard attempted to serve the decrees on Mosaddeq. He was arrested, and the following morning the prime minister announced in a radio message that because there had been an attempted coup inspired by foreign elements, he was taking complete control of the government. Mosaddeq also ordered Zahedi's arrest, but the general was out of sight, in a CIA safe house.

There followed several days of rioting by both the supporters of the shah and those of Mosaddeq. The *gendarmerie* was zealous in suppressing the Tudeh rioters but permitted the pro-shah demonstrators—led by CIA-paid agitators—to march through the streets of Tehran and other Iranian cities. At a critical moment General Zahedi appeared and led a column of tanks and a mob of anti-Mosaddeq rioters to the prime minister's residence. After a two-hour battle Mosaddeq fled into hiding, and Zahedi assumed the office of prime minister. The shah then returned to Iran and resumed his throne.

Mosaddeq was convicted of treason and sentenced to indefinite exile in his home village. Prime Minister Zahedi restored diplomatic relations with the British. An international consortium made up mostly of British and American oil companies signed a new agreement with terms more favorable to Iran than those of the old Anglo-Iranian contract. The United States granted Iran forty-five million dollars in immediate economic aid, and Iran remained a staunch American ally until the shah was deposed in 1979.

Sometime in the second half of 1953, during the cresting wave of enthusiasm that followed the success of Operation Ajax, the CIA and the State Department began making plans for yet another coup, this one aimed at the leftist president of Guatemala, Jacobo Arbenz Guzmán. Arbenz was a democratically elected head of state who enjoyed the mandate of 60 percent of his country's electorate. To that fact must be added, however, the observation that Jacobo Arbenz Guzmán's landslide was ensured by the assassination of his principal opponent several months before the November 1950 elections, a crime in which Arbenz was widely suspected of having taken a hand.

Arbenz's program emphasized social and economic reform aimed at bettering the lot of the poor and middle classes. This especially involved land reform and the reduction of the power of foreign interests in Guatemala. In 1952 Arbenz alienated American commercial interests when he signed a law expropriating much of the land held by the American-owned United Fruit Company.

The size, power, and American ownership of United Fruit made it a popular target of many, perhaps most, Guatemalans, despite the fact that the company had invested sixty million dollars in the country; constructed Guatemala's railroad, telegraph, and telephone systems; created nearly forty thousand jobs; and paid wages several times higher than other Guatemalan employers. United Fruit was not a philanthropic institution, however, and in exchange for such benevolences and its political support, it had extracted concessions from past Guatemalan governments that assured enormous profits and gave it a complete stranglehold on the country's economy. Not for nothing was it known in Guatemala as El Pulpo—the Octopus.[10]

In his confrontation with United Fruit, Arbenz received the enthusiastic support of the Guatemalan Labor party, as the Communist party of Guatemala called itself. Arbenz readily accepted the support of the Communists and regarded them as an integral part of his political coalition. Communists were best represented within the government's National Agrarian Department, the agency directly involved in the expropriation of United Fruit's landholdings.

It is a measure of the concern Arbenz's actions inspired in Washington that President Truman and Secretary of State Acheson, at the very time they were rebuffing British entreaties for a joint covert-action operation against Mosaddeq, agreed to support a Nicaraguan paramilitary operation against Arbenz. The plan apparently originated in the mind of the Nicaraguan dictator, Anastasio Somoza, who presented it to Truman and Acheson during a visit to Washington in the summer of 1952. Somoza proposed that if the United States would supply the arms, "I'll clean up Guatemala for you in no time."[11] The details of Somoza's plan remain obscure, but the proposed operation apparently involved joint military action by Nicaragua, Colombia, the Dominican Republic, and Venezuela. Reportedly, the operation had reached the point where the CIA, on Truman's instructions, had sent a shipload of arms to Nicaragua aboard a United Fruit freighter when it was canceled. The reason for the cancellation is also obscure, but it seems to have resulted when second-level officials in the State Department learned of the operation and argued emphatically against it. Their opposition seems to have been based on their assessment of the likelihood of the operation's success rather than on the desirability of its aims.[12]

Operation Success, the CIA's more elaborate plan for a Guatemalan coup, launched the following year, involved a psychological-warfare campaign to undermine the Guatemalan army's support for Arbenz; paramilitary support for a dissident group led by Juan Córdova Cerna, a prominent coffee grower and former Guatemalan minister of the interior; and economic and diplomatic pressure on Arbenz to step aside and permit Córdova Cerna to take power. When Córdova Cerna became seriously ill during preparations for the coup, his role was assumed by his associate, Colonel Carlos Castillo Armas, a former Guatemalan army officer.

State's principal officer for Operation Success was Raymond G. Leddy, a former FBI agent who had served in Spain and Latin America during the war and since 1952 had been a State Department specialist in Central American matters. Equally involved in planning the operation was the American ambassador to Guatemala, John E. Peurifoy, an anti-Communist activist who had recently served as ambassador to Greece. The CIA officer with overall responsibility was C. Tracy Barnes, a Groton–Yale–Harvard Law easterner who had parachuted behind German lines as an OSS SO Branch officer and later worked under Allen Dulles in Switzerland. Colonel Albert Haney, lately the CIA station chief in Korea, was field commander, and OSS veteran E. Howard Hunt was in charge of the political and psychological ends of the operation.[13]

Despite the provision for paramilitary support, the planners of Operation Success hoped that Arbenz might be displaced through psychological and political measures alone. A CIA attempt to bribe him to step down, and a gray propaganda campaign against him, begun in January 1954, had failed to remove the Guatemalan president by the following April, when CIA sources at the Polish port of Szczecin reported the sailing of the Swedish freighter *Alfhem* for Guatemala carrying two thousand tons of Czechoslovakian light arms and artillery. The nature of the cargo was confirmed when the *Alfhem* arrived at Puerto Barrios on Guatemala's Caribbean coast on May 17. The prospect of a Soviet-bloc country arming the leftist-leaning Arbenz government spread alarm in Washington and triggered execution of the paramilitary aspects of Operation Success.[14]

The CIA's clandestine radio-propaganda operation against Arbenz had already begun. Since May 1 short-wave transmitters in neighboring Nicaragua and Honduras had been broadcasting as the Voice of Liberation, a dissident station claiming to be based somewhere in the Guatemalan countryside. The station's broadcasts were calculated to intimidate Arbenz's supporters and encourage others to rally to Castillo Armas's insurgent movement.

On June 18 Castillo Armas led a force of some three hundred troops across the border from Honduras and stopped six miles inside Guatemala at the town of Esquipulas. But the Voice of Liberation announced that the insurgent leader was marching toward Guatemala City at the head of a column of several thousand troops. Meanwhile, the CIA's air force—some thirty Second World War aircraft—went into action throughout the country, bombing fuel depots, ammunition dumps, radio stations, and other targets and dropping clouds of propaganda leaflets over the capital. Like the leaflets, the air strikes had a psychological purpose, not a military one: they were calculated to convince the people and, especially, the army that the Arbenz government faced an enormously superior force. The success of the air strikes can be gauged by the nickname they were given by the Guatemalans—*sulfatos* (laxatives), for the effect they had on the Guatemalan armed forces. Indeed, the air raids were so exclusively psychological warfare that some planes dropped only smoke bombs, and during one nighttime raid on Guatemala City, the sounds of exploding bombs actually came from a tape played through a public-address system on the roof of the American embassy.

While Castillo Armas remained peacefully bivouacked at Esquipulas, the CIA charade gradually convinced Arbenz that he was losing a war, one that was not, in fact, actually being fought. By June 27 the psychological campaign had succeeded: Arbenz stepped down and sought asylum in the Mexican embassy. The military junta that replaced him accepted Castillo Armas as its leader, and on September 1 he assumed the presidency.

Except from the viewpoint of United Fruit, which regained its expropriated property through the new regime, the coup fell short of being a complete success. Whatever Communist threat had existed in Guatemala was removed, of course, but Castillo Armas did not have the qualities of statesmanship that the CIA believed it saw in Córdova Cerna, for whom the ex-colonel had been substituted at the eleventh hour. After thirty-five months of inept and unpopular rule, Castillo Armas was assassinated by one of his bodyguards, and Guatemala returned to the authoritarian oligarchic rule that had existed before 1944.

As an exercise in covert action, however, the Guatemalan coup seemed an unalloyed success: a Communist-leaning regime had been literally frightened out of power through psychological warfare spiced with a very modest amount of paramilitary activity. Following on the heels of the CIA's successes in Iran and the Philippines, the Guatemala operation strengthened the seductive idea that Soviet subversion could always be effectively countered by American subversion. This article of faith was held not only by Wisner and the Dulles brothers but by a committee President Eisenhower had commissioned to study the activities of the CIA Clandestine Service. The committee, chaired by wartime hero Lieutenant General James Doolittle, heartily endorsed the use of covert action in its report, submitted to the president a few weeks after the Guatemala operation.

"There are no rules in such a game," the report said of resistance to Soviet worldwide subversion (in words reminiscent of those spoken by the James Cagney character in *13 Rue Madeleine*).

> Hitherto acceptable norms of human conduct do not apply. If the United States is to survive, long standing American concepts of "fair play" must be reconsidered. We must develop effective espionage and counterespionage services and must learn to subvert, sabotage and destroy our enemies by more clever, more sophisticated and more effective methods than those used against us. It may become necessary that the American people be made acquainted with, understand and support this fundamentally repugnant philosophy.[15]

For Frank Wisner, the CIA's covert-action successes were confirmation that such operations could be used for something more than the containment of Soviet expansionism. At about this time, he put in motion the most daring and ambitious covert operation yet conceived in the CIA: Operation Red Sox–Red Cap, the training of a secret army of émigrés and refugees from Hungary, Poland, Romania, and Czechoslovakia to be used to liberate the Soviet captive nations of Eastern Europe.[16]

* * *

American fears of the Soviet atom bomb, the driving force behind the CIA's ventures in subversive warfare, also molded the agency's secret intelligence activities during the 1950s. At the top of the list of American intelligence-collection priorities was the demand for detailed and accurate information on the progress of Soviet nuclear-weapons development and the USSR's strategic-bomber and missile programs.

When the Soviets detonated their first nuclear weapon in 1949, they already had the capacity to deliver one to the continental United States. The Soviet TU-4 was a carbon copy of the American B-29, a bomber with a range of 5,830 miles. Polar projection maps began appearing at Washington briefings, a reminder that Soviet air bases and American targets were separated by no more than perhaps a dozen hours' flying time along great circle routes across the thinly defended expanses of Alaska and Canada. *Early warning* became the new buzzword in Washington.

Within weeks of the first Soviet bomb, the CIA Office of Special Operations began infiltrating agents into the USSR to report on military movements that might signal Soviet preparations for a nuclear assault on the West. Air dispatch—infiltration by overflights and parachute drops—was the preferred means of putting agents deep inside Soviet borders. The first flight took place on the night of September 5, 1949, when two young Ukrainian émigrés who had been recruited and trained by the CIA were parachuted into the Ukraine, there to report back to a CIA listening post in Germany by clandestine radio transmitter.[17]

The Ukrainian drop was the beginning of a series of agent dispatches—by land and sea, as well as by air—carried out by the OSO. Agent candidates were selected from émigré groups and displaced-persons camps in Europe and from recent defectors from the Red Army. After a ten-month training course they were sent into the USSR, singly or in two-agent teams. During the next five years agents were dispatched to observe and report on military intelligence targets ranging from the Baltic coast to installations on Sakhalin in the Sea of Japan. A few were rounded up by the authorities immediately after landing. Most were caught eventually; their transmissions contained the pre-established danger signal indicating they had come under Soviet counterintelligence control. In such cases, the OSO officers in Germany played along to keep the agent alive as long as possible. Others merely stopped reporting, perhaps having abandoned their radios and their espionage roles.[18]

The operation placed enough agents behind the Iron Curtain to ascertain that the Soviets were not preparing to wage an immediate war against the West. But the value of the reports on Soviet strategic military capabilities was minimal. Only a trained scientist or engineer would have been able to make sense of what might have been seen at the nuclear and missile test sites. The most obvious means of giving technically trained people a look at those sites was aerial photoreconnaissance.

Although it was possible to fly over Soviet territory with a good deal of impunity at night in the late 1940s and early 1950s, thereby making possible such missions as parachuting agents into the country, flying there in the daytime—a necessity for the kind of photoreconnaissance required—was another matter. Soviet ability to intercept and shoot down daytime intruders was good and getting better. Both the CIA and the United States Air Force wrestled with the problem. A 1946 study by the Rand Corporation—a think tank that worked for the air force—proposed the use of an artificial satellite for the mission, but the rocket and space technology needed to accomplish such a feat was a long way in the future.

Another Rand study looked into the use of unmanned balloons for the job. The CIA and the air force actually carried out a joint balloon reconnaissance project, but the craft were subject to the vagaries of the winds and sometimes failed to pass over the target areas. Others descended prematurely and fell into Soviet hands. Better than nothing, the program was no substitute for manned aircraft overflights.[19]

The RF-86, a reconnaissance version of the air force's Saberjet fighter plane, flew high and fast enough to make Soviet interception difficult, but its range was too short to permit reconnaissance flights deep into Soviet territory. Deeper penetrations were made possible by carrying the aircraft to the Soviet border slung under the belly of a four-engine B-50 bomber, but the increase in range achieved this way permitted penetrations of only several hundreds of miles, far less than what was needed to cover the vast expanses of the Soviet Union, and the risk of interception, although diminished, remained substantial. In general, air force photoreconnaissance of Soviet territory was limited to flights along the borders and long-range oblique photography. The results of these flights were far short of ideal, of course, and the reconnaissance aircraft—usually converted Second World

War bombers—were often attacked by Soviet interceptors even though they had not violated Soviet airspace.[20]

The British SIS worked closely with the CIA in piecing together fragmentary reports of the Soviet missile program. The 1948 defection to Britain of a colonel who had held a senior post in the Soviet missile program was an intelligence windfall for both services. Some German technicians who had been captured by the Red Army during the war and had subsequently worked for the Soviets modifying and testing captured German V-2 missiles made their way to the West in the early 1950s and were thoroughly debriefed by British and American officials.[21] Taken together, such items formed far less than the entire jigsaw puzzle, however, and offered far less than might be obtained from some good aerial photographs.

One area of particular interest was the Soviet missile test site at Kapustin Yar, a town some sixty-five miles east of Volgograd, on the western edge of the Kazakh Soviet Socialist Republic. Anglo-American intelligence services had known of the existence of the site since the spring of 1947, and in 1948 a team of Britons posing as archaeologists had gone to northern Iran to eavesdrop electronically on the test facility. By 1953 reports of Soviet missile progress had made an overflight of Kapustin Yar vital. An RB-57 of the Royal Air Force was used for the jointly sponsored CIA-SIS mission.

The RB-57 was the reconnaissance version of the British Canberra twin-jet tactical bomber, with an enlarged wingspan and other modifications that permitted it to fly at extremely high altitudes. The mission to Kapustin Yar was flown in July 1953. Departing from a base in West Germany, the aircraft crossed the Ukraine and the Russian republic, flew down the course of the Volga, made a photographic run over Kapustin Yar, and then flew south and landed in Iran. The photographs of the test sites proved useful, but the flight had come so near to interception—reportedly the RB-57 was riddled with bullet holes when it landed—that no subsequent missions were planned. The mission demonstrated that an aircraft capable of altitudes even greater than the high-flying RB-57 would be needed if further overflights of Soviet territory were to be made.[22]

The development of an ultra-high-altitude aircraft specifically for Soviet overflights was proposed the following year by a panel commissioned by President Eisenhower to study ways of reducing the chances of a Soviet surprise attack on the United States. The Surprise Attack Panel was chaired by James R. Killian, president of the Massachusetts Institute of Technology. Edward Land, president of the Polaroid Corporation and inventor of the Polaroid camera, chaired a subcommittee concerned with the intelligence aspect of the problem. The Land committee recommended the development of the reconnaissance satellite proposed by the 1946 Rand study. Recognizing that such a program could not be realized for several years, the committee also recommended a high-altitude reconnaissance aircraft as an interim solution. Such a plane had already been designed by C. L. ("Kelly") Johnson of Lockheed Aircraft Corporation, the aeronautical engineer who had designed the legendary P-38 Lightning fighter of the Second World War and the graceful four-engine Constellation airliner. Killian and Land recommended that Johnson and Lockheed be given the go-ahead for completion of the reconnaissance plane. Eisenhower did so in December 1954.[23]

The program to develop and fly the U-2, as the plane was designated, was given to the CIA, for several reasons. Eisenhower did not want to give the air force control of an intelligence source that would have such a great influence on that service's budget: Congress decided on the number of American bombers and missiles based on the size of the Soviet strategic threat. Also, the CIA was able to fund the program from its contingency reserve moneys, which could be spent without the risk to security presented by a detailed accounting to Congress or the Bureau of the Budget.[24]

The CIA program was managed by Richard M. Bissell, Jr. (Groton-Yale), an economist whom Allen Dulles had hired two years earlier as his special assistant. Bissell worked closely with Johnson and ensured that the usual red tape involved in the government's procurement of a new aircraft did not impede progress on the U-2. The project was completed in a phenomenally short time: the first U-2 was test-flown only eight months after the go-ahead, on August 1, 1955. The flight was made from Watertown Strip, a secret base in the Nevada desert, about a hundred miles northwest of Las Vegas.[25]

Essentially the U-2 was a light, single-seat sailplane powered by a jet engine. The first production model, the U-2b, had a maximum cruising speed of 460 miles per hour, a maximum range of three thousand miles, and an operational altitude ceiling of eighty-five thousand feet.[26] The plane was equipped with a specially designed aerial camera that was able to record a twenty-six-hundred-mile-long strip of land on a single piece of film, resolving details so accurately that golf balls could be identified on a green from an altitude of fifty-five thousand feet. The aircraft also carried instruments for intercepting and recording radio and radar signals emanating from the ground.[27]

In July 1955, as the first U-2 neared readiness for test-flying, President Eisenhower made his Open Skies proposal to the Soviet Union during an East-West summit conference in Geneva, Switzerland. According to the proposal, the United States and the USSR, as a step toward mutual disarmament, would permit unrestricted aerial photoreconnaissance of their respective countries and even provide the other side with the facilities (e.g., the use of air bases) for such flights. Eisenhower did not announce the U-2 program, of course, but it was at the root of his proposal: Soviet-authorized overflights of the USSR would rule out the risk of interception or other incident. The Soviets rejected the plan, however, and Eisenhower ordered the black overflight program to continue. One year later, on July 4, 1956, the first U-2 mission was flown into Soviet airspace.

The U-2 program was operated under cover of the National Advisory Committee for Aeronautics, a civilian agency that was the predecessor of the National Aeronautics and Space Administration. The ostensible purpose of the flights was meteorologic observation. The pilots were United States Air Force personnel who had been sheep-dipped for the program— that is, false Defense Department records were created to indicate that they had resigned or been discharged from the air force. The first U-2 detachment was stationed at Wiesbaden. The July 4 flight originated from the West German base and followed a route that took it over Moscow, Leningrad, and the Baltic coast before returning to Wiesbaden.[28]

More overflights followed during the first two weeks of July. The CIA had not expected the penetrations of Soviet airspace to go completely undetected, but it had not foreseen that Soviet radar would be able to track every flight from entry to exit. The Soviets used the precise routes and times to back up their diplomatic protests to the United States and their public denunciation of the overflights. Although the United States government did not admit to the charges, Eisenhower put the operation on an indefinite hold after the sixth flight and ordered that henceforth no overflights be made without his specific approval.[29] Thereafter, the penetrations were made quite sparingly. In 1957 the program became a joint Anglo-American operation when RAF pilots, sheep-dipped as their American counterparts had been, were assigned to the program. Under arrangements worked out between the CIA and the SIS, the British prime minister could also authorize an overflight, which was generally flown by an RAF pilot in such a case.[30]

Additional U-2 detachments were based at Adana, Turkey, and Atsugi, Japan. U-2s ranged over Eastern Europe, the western Soviet Union, the Ukraine, Siberia, and the Kamchatka Peninsula. Some flights originated in Peshawar, Pakistan, and passed over Soviet Central Asia, photographing the nuclear test site at Semipalatinsk and the new missile test facility at Tyuratam before landing in eastern Iran.[31] While only some twenty or thirty deep penetrations of Soviet airspace were made between 1956 and 1960, they produced a rich harvest of intelligence, not only on Soviet strategic-weapons progress but also on naval bases, industrial complexes, railroads, and the details of Soviet geography needed to produce detailed maps for the United States Air Force. Lacking the capability to shoot down the planes, the Soviets could do nothing more than protest the flights.[32]

The program came to an end, of course, on May 1, 1960, when a U-2 flown by Francis Gary Powers on an overflight originating in Peshawar and passing over the Tyuratam missile center was shot down over Sverdlovsk on the eastern slopes of the Ural Mountains. The Eisenhower administration's handling of the political fallout—first denying, then admitting that the overflight had been intentional and for intelligence gathering—exacerbated American embarrassment. The incident also led to Soviet cancellation of an impending Soviet-American summit meeting. These facts have caused the U-2 incident to be regarded as an unmitigated disaster, when in fact it was merely the price, long regarded as inevitable by the administration, of an intelligence program vital to national security. Without the knowledge the U-2 provided—that the Soviets were not yet capable of waging nuclear war on the West—East-West tensions of the late 1950s would have reached dangerous levels indeed.

U-2 overflights of Soviet territory ended with the Powers mission, but the flow of photographs of Soviet intelligence targets did not. Since 1958 the

CIA and the air force had jointly run a program to develop the reconnaissance satellite recommended by the Surprise Attack Panel.[33] On August 11, 1960, just three months after the U-2 incident, the satellite program bore its first fruit with the midair recovery of the film capsule from *Discoverer 13* over the Pacific Ocean near Hawaii. *Discoverer* was a modified Agena rocket that had been launched into a polar orbit (i.e., one passing over both the North and South poles of the earth) from Vandenberg Air Force Base on the California coast and had made high-resolution photographs of the earth's surface during repeated passes over the Soviet Union.

Camera, lens, and film technology had progressed to the point where reconnaissance photographs made more than a hundred miles above the earth could reveal almost the same amount of detail captured by the U-2 cameras at altitudes of only a dozen miles. Advances in the technologies of rocket propulsion and electronic guidance permitted cameras to be placed in orbit and later recovered. Space was not only beyond the range of Soviet interception, it was beyond the limits of Soviet claims of sovereignty. The Soviet Union had already implicitly renounced sovereign rights to the regions above the Soviet atmosphere: its own artificial satellites had been passing over the United States since 1957.

The advent of the reconnaissance satellite changed the intelligence business more than any other development since the Second World War. *Overhead reconnaissance*—a new term coined to encompass photography from both aircraft and spacecraft—rapidly became the principal source of American intelligence on Soviet strategic forces. Soon it was the major source of intelligence on a broad range of matters.

Space technology, driven by the concentration of scientific manpower and the expenditures of vast sums in the race to place an American on the moon in the 1960s, produced enormous technological advances that also benefited the collection of intelligence by satellite and other technical means. Advances in space communications led to parallel advances in the interception of foreign communications. Powerful new computers created to support the lunar program found yet another use in the processing of the new flood of data collected by technical means. A Science and Technology Directorate was created within the CIA in 1963, reflecting the new importance of the technical means of intelligence collection. By the 1970s verification through technical collection—especially the use of reconnaissance satellites—had become an essential ingredient in nuclear arms limitation agreements between East and West.

A culmination was at hand. Since early in the nineteenth century the human capability to collect and process information had been increasing exponentially in terms of both speed and volume, and this explosion of information technology had caused a revolution in American intelligence. The process that began with the balloons and telegraph wiretaps of the Civil War, that had been sustained in the aerial photoreconnaissance and computer code breaking of the first half of the twentieth century, had reached its climax. The spy had not been made extinct, but his—or her— relative importance had been displaced. Intelligence was no longer a craft; it had been made an industry.

In the spring of 1956 the CIA's Kremlinologists began to hear rumors of a momentous occurrence within the Soviet Communist party. In the power struggle that followed the death of Stalin three years earlier, Nikita S. Khrushchev, first secretary of the party's Central Committee, was emerging as the most powerful of the dictator's likely successors. Through adroit manipulation of the party apparatus, he controlled important appointments, packed the Central Committee with his allies, and eliminated all opposition in the Presidium, the committee's supreme policy council. Kremlin watchers anticipated that he would seize the occasion of the Twentieth Party Congress, scheduled for February 1956, to consolidate his power. The proceedings of the congress were not made public, but for weeks after the event, rumors were heard throughout Eastern Europe that he had given a speech making a dramatic break with the Soviet past. Allen Dulles told the CIA Clandestine Service to spare no expense in obtaining a copy of the Khrushchev speech. By April he had it in hand.[34]

The speech was a twenty-thousand-word indictment of Stalin, "his intolerance, his brutality and his abuse of power." It cataloged the dictator's crimes from his reign of terror in the 1930s to his paranoid and murderous campaign of anti-Semitism shortly before his death in 1953. It condemned his use of the secret police as an instrument of repression.[35]

To confirm the authenticity of the document, Dulles turned to Dr. Ray S. Cline, the agency's senior analyst for current intelligence on the USSR.

Cline pronounced the speech authentic and urged that it be made public as a source of "invaluable insights into the real workings of Stalinist Russia" and a "rare opportunity to have all the critical things we had said for years about the Soviet dictatorship confirmed by the principal leader of the Soviet Politburo [i.e., the Presidium]." He was amazed when his suggestion was opposed by Frank Wisner.[36]

Wisner fully realized how damaging the speech would be as a psychological and political weapon against the Soviet Union, and it was for just this reason he opposed publishing it at that moment. When released, the speech would undoubtedly add to the unrest in the Soviet Union's Eastern European vassal states, thereby aiding the Clandestine Service's Operation Red Sox–Red Cap—the planned anti-Soviet uprising in Hungary, Poland, Romania, and Czechoslovakia. But Red Sox–Red Cap was not yet ready to be launched; Wisner wanted to delay release of the Khrushchev speech until it was. Dulles overruled him, however, and the full text of the speech was published in the *New York Times* of June 4. The substance of the speech was broadcast to Eastern Europe by Radio Free Europe and to the Soviet Union by Radio Liberation, a Russian-language station secretly sponsored by the CIA.[37]

The influence of the publication and broadcast of the speech on subsequent events in Eastern Europe is imponderable. There was a violent strike and riots later that month in Poznán, Poland. In October anti-Soviet demonstrations in Hungary erupted into a nationwide popular uprising against the government and the Soviet occupation forces. Undoubtedly, the Khrushchev speech played a large part in triggering these events, but the substance of the speech had been widely rumored in Eastern Europe before the publication and broadcasts. What is clear is that Operation Red Cap–Red Sox had been overtaken by events. There was a full-scale revolt in Hungary, and the Soviets were preparing to respond with massive military force.

Wisner saw that for Red Sox–Red Cap it was now or never. Confronted by the revolt in Hungary, the Soviets would be hard-pressed to deal with simultaneous uprisings in Czechoslovakia and Romania. By one account Red Sox–Red Cap units were already in place in Budapest at the time of the uprising, assisting the Hungarian insurgents, while others had been infiltrated into Prague and Bucharest.[38] Wisner urged Allen Dulles to permit him to launch the operation. Robert Amory, the CIA's deputy direc-tor for intelligence, went even further, proposing that the United States demand that the Soviet Union cease reinforcing its forces in Hungary. If necessary, Amory proposed, the United States should launch a series of "surgical nuclear strikes" to cut the Red Army's supply lines between Russia and Eastern Europe.[39]

In his memoirs President Eisenhower implied that he might have resorted to major military force had Hungary been accessible to American sea power or if it had been possible to send American ground forces to her borders through the territory of an ally.[40] But as such was impossible, he decided against any action in Hungary, covert or otherwise. Dulles told Wisner to cancel Red Sox–Red Cap.

Five days after the uprising began, the Soviets launched a major assault on Hungary, sending two hundred thousand Red Army troops and four thousand tanks into Budapest. In the ensuing fighting, more than twenty-five thousand Hungarian insurgents were killed. Hungarians were fleeing across the border at the rate of three to four thousand a day. Wisner, who had gone to Vienna early in the crisis, spent a night on the Hungarian border helplessly watching the flash of the Communist border guards' automatic weapons as they hunted the refugees.[41]

Wisner flew back to Washington, stopping en route at the CIA's Rome station, where to Clandestine Service officer William Colby he seemed on the verge of a nervous breakdown.[42] It was not only the Hungarian debacle. Wisner now realized that the Dulles brothers' proud talk of lib-erating the captive nations of Europe was not supported by Eisenhower. Containment, yes; liberation, no.

Back in Washington he alternated between periods of black depression and frenetic enthusiasm. He was hospitalized but returned to work early in 1957. His judgment was now badly flawed.

"I think it's time we held Sukarno's feet to the fire," Wisner told the chief of his Far East Division.[43] Like other Third World leaders, the Indo-nesian president had been playing off the West against the Soviets. Wisner approved paramilitary support for a group of dissident Indonesian army officers planning a coup. In May 1958 this, too, ended in disaster, with a CIA pilot in jail awaiting execution (he had mistaken a church for a military target one Sunday morning, bombed it, and killed most of the congregation before being captured).[44]

Wisner was hospitalized again, this time for six months of shock treatments and other therapy at the Sheppard Pratt Hospital near Baltimore.[45] When he returned to duty, Dulles sent him to London as chief of station, a post deemed less stressful than others. His problems continued, however, and in 1961 he resigned from the agency. Four years later he turned a shotgun on himself at his country place in Galena, Maryland.

Chapter Thirty-six

Failure and Vindication

Whatever real prospects there had been for Red Sox–Red Cap to liberate the captive nations of Eastern Europe, the actual failure of the operation was the result of a major stroke of bad luck: the timing of the Khrushchev speech. The effectiveness of covert action had not been called into question, despite the occasional failure of an ill-conceived operation, such as the attempt to topple Sukarno. The CIA Clandestine Service drew its lessons not from its failures but from its successes. Quite reasonably, the service now sought to repeat the formulas that had worked before.

In 1954 the CIA sent Edward Lansdale to Vietnam to apply his proven methods of nation building to that former French colony.[1] The French were preparing to withdraw after an eight-year war with Communist insurgents that had recently climaxed in the decisive political and military defeat at Dien Bien Phu. The part of the country south of the seventeenth parallel—the demarcation line established at the cease-fire——remained in a state of political limbo while the Communists consolidated their control in the north. Lansdale hoped to do in South Vietnam what he had done in the Philippines: select and promote a strong national leader to rally the democratic forces in the country against the Communists and defeat the Vietminh—the Communist insurgents—through psychological warfare, civic action, community development, and standard counterinsurgency methods.

For the role of a Vietnamese Magsaysay, Lansdale picked Ngo Dinh Diem, a former French colonial official who was also nonetheless a Vietnamese nationalist and had previously refused to align himself with either the French or the Vietminh.[2] By the end of 1955, Ngo had been elected president of the Republic of Vietnam, but he had already begun to demonstrate that he was no Magsaysay, and Lansdale was beginning to realize that he had made a serious mistake. Lansdale had helped write the Vietnamese constitution, had trained Ngo's presidential guard, had organized political support for Ngo among Vietnamese veterans groups. But Ngo turned a deaf ear to the American adviser when he urged that the Vietnamese president permit the existence of a loyal opposition in South Vietnam.

Ngo was not interested in bringing democracy to Vietnam. He would tolerate no political opposition; he would institute no democratic reforms. His own political power derived less from popular support than from coercion. His bid for popularity was severely handicapped by the fact that he and his coterie were Frenchified and therefore reminiscent of colonialism; Roman Catholic and therefore alien to most Vietnamese; and corrupt. Perhaps for the first time Lansdale understood how much of his Philippine success he owed to the personality and character of Magsaysay.

Back in Washington Lansdale urged the Dulles brothers to pressure Ngo into making the democratic reforms he proposed. When they refused, Lansdale asked for and received a transfer from Vietnam.[3] The following year the Communist regime in North Vietnam launched a major campaign of terror and subversion in the south. Even before they struck, however, non-Communist South Vietnamese insurgents had risen against the Ngo regime. Ngo's political base rapidly eroded as a result of his abuses; by 1961 there were an estimated fifteen thousand Communist guerrillas in the south, and most of the countryside was under the influence of the Communist National Liberation Front. Lansdale's Philippine formula had failed in Indochina. The first act of America's Vietnam tragedy had begun.

Although the ultimate consequences of Lansdale's inability to repeat his Philippine wizardry in Vietnam took several years to materialize, another failed attempt by the CIA to apply an earlier successful covert-action formula in a different country was to have much more immediate results. In 1960 the agency made preparations to use the same method that had toppled Arbenz in Guatemala in an effort to overthrow the Soviet-sponsored regime of Fidel Castro in Cuba.

Relations between the United States and Cuba went into decline soon after Castro seized power in January 1959, when the new regime began the mass execution of officials of the overthrown Batista government. The situation began to move downhill more rapidly a few months later, when Castro began expropriating large amounts of American commercial property in Cuba; as in Guatemala, United Fruit was one of the biggest losers.

Evidence of Soviet influence in the Castro regime was far more alarming than it had been in the Guatemalan case. Castro appointed Communists to head his police and intelligence services. Major Ramiro Valdés became chief of the Cuban army's military intelligence service, and Major Manuel Piñeiro became his deputy in charge of counterintelligence; both men were longtime Communists. Another Communist, José Matar, became head of the Committee for the Defense of the Revolution, a nationwide network of informers. Under these officers the two organizations became highly effective secret police agencies on the Soviet and Eastern European model.[4]

Castro's involvement with the Soviet Union became overt in 1960 with the official visit to Cuba of Anastas Mikoyan, the first deputy Soviet premier. The visit resulted in an agreement covering trade and economic aid and provided for the sending of Soviet "technicians" to Cuba. In May, Khrushchev announced that the Soviet Union would defend Cuba against "American aggression." In July, Castro visited Czechoslovakia to purchase arms, stopping later in Moscow to enjoy a warm welcome from the Soviet leaders.

In March 1960 the CIA produced a planning paper proposing a covert-action campaign against Castro. The plan called for the creation of a unified anti-Castro Cuban exile organization, a clandestine propaganda campaign aimed at Cuba, the establishment of an underground to carry out secret intelligence and covert-action operations inside Cuba, and the development of a paramilitary force to be sent into Cuba to wage guerrilla warfare. The plan had been modeled on the Guatemala coup, with the participation of many CIA veterans of that operation. On March 17 President Eisenhower approved the plan and authorized its execution.[5]

The CIA established a task force—an ad hoc project organization—to carry out the operation. The Cuban Task Force came under Richard Bissell, who had succeeded Frank Wisner as chief of the Clandestine Service in 1958.[6] As in the Guatemala coup, overall responsibility was nominally in the hands of C. Tracy Barnes, who was now Bissell's assistant, although in practice Barnes appears to have played the ancillary role of liaison officer with the White House, the State Department, and the Joint Chiefs of Staff while Bissell was the true chief of the operation.

Reporting directly to Barnes was the task force director, Jacob D. Esterline. A veteran of Detachment 101, the OSS unit that fought behind Japanese lines in Burma, Esterline had managed a CIA paramilitary training base in Georgia and served as chief of station in Guatemala and Venezuela.[7] German-born Gerry Droller, who had organized French resistance groups while in the OSS, was political-action chief of the operation, a job that involved the creation of a Cuban-exile-front organization. E. Howard Hunt, who had run the political and psychological parts of the Guatemala coup, was assigned to work with Droller in the field, organizing Cuban exile groups. Propaganda operations for the Cuban project were the responsibility of David Atlee Phillips, a Spanish-speaking officer with extensive knowledge of Latin America who had worked for Hunt as a propaganda specialist in the Guatemala operation.[8]

A guerrilla-warfare training base was set up in the mountains of Guatemala near Retalhuleu, a town about thirty miles from the country's Pacific coast. The Frente Revolucionario Democrático, the Cuban-exile-front organization, recruited young Cuban émigrés in the Miami area and elsewhere in the United States. After screening by CIA doctors, psychologists, and security officers, the recruits were sent to Camp Trax, as the Guatemala training base was called. The first of the recruits arrived at the base in May 1960.[9]

The CIA constructed an airstrip near Camp Trax and obtained several C-46 and C-54 transports. All government markings were removed from the aircraft, which were to be used to air-drop guerrillas and supplies into Cuba and distribute propaganda leaflets. Experienced pilots were recruited among the Cuban émigrés in Miami and sent to Camp Trax for further training.[10]

While the paramilitary training operations got under way in Guatemala, David Phillips's propaganda campaign went into operation. Radio Swan, an ostensibly commercial fifty-kilowatt-broadcast-frequency station based on one of the Swan Islands in the Caribbean off the Honduran coast, began broadcasting in May. The station carried programs taped in the CIA radio studios in Miami, consisting of news analysis, entertainment, and anti-Castro speeches by Cuban exiles. Phillips also bought time on other stations throughout the Caribbean, arranging to broadcast relatively innocuous material at first, and prepared to broadcast strong anti-Castro material later.[11]

By summer 1960 the CIA had put in effect much of the operational plan. The Cuban Task Force had made contact with the underground in Cuba and had begun air-dropping supplies to guerrillas in the mountains. Agents were moving in and out of the country, often by Florida-based speedboats. But there were problems: the air-drop missions seldom found the agreed-upon light signals from the ground designating the drop zones. The CIA blamed the Cuban pilots; the pilots were resentful and whispered that the CIA-controlled guerrillas had been infiltrated by Castro's G-2, an army military intelligence service. Meanwhile, Castro's coast guard was becoming increasingly skilled at intercepting the insurgents' speedboats. Adding to the disarray, there was increasing dissension among the émigré factions.[12]

Concurrent with these setbacks in the CIA's covert-action operation, the flow of Soviet arms to Cuba increased, and Castro's secret police tightened its grip on the civilian population of the island. The CIA's planners began to doubt that Castro could be overthrown by guerrilla action and psychological warfare alone. In late summer or early autumn Bissell, Barnes, and Esterline began considering an enlargement in the scope of the operation: landing a small (two-hundred- to three-hundred-man) infantry strike force on the Cuban coast to establish an enclave that would attract anti-Castro dissidents in the area and perhaps inspire a general uprising throughout Cuba.[13]

According to a CIA estimate, there were between twenty-five hundred and three thousand Cubans active in the anti-Castro underground, and they were supported by some twenty thousand sympathizers. It was further estimated that about 25 percent of the Cuban population would actively support a well-organized and well-armed force after it had established a beachhead. The agency additionally estimated that an even larger number of Cubans would rally to the invaders' cause after it became apparent they would succeed in toppling Castro.[14]

Receiving tentative approval for the new plan from the Eisenhower administration, the CIA revised the training program at Camp Trax to emphasize conventional amphibious and airborne operations over guerrilla warfare. Having escalated from the hit-and-run tactics of the guerrilla to a conventional Second World War–style amphibious landing, the operation now required air support—the bombing and strafing of the enemy force sent to repel the invaders. Bissell brought in air force colonel Stanley W. Beerli to organize a combat air-support capability. Beerli, who had worked with Bissell before as commander of the U-2 detachment in Turkey, selected the Second World War–vintage B-26 light bomber as the operation's air-support weapon. He chose the 8-26 because so many of the bombers had been sold as surplus to nations around the world that its use would not necessarily imply United States involvement in the operation. Castro's air force possessed several B-26s, and the CIA planned a cover story that the invasion's air support consisted entirely of Cuban air force planes flown by pilots who had spontaneously defected to join the insurgents after the landing commenced. That cover story was to play a fatal role in disrupting the entire operation.[15]

Preparations for the invasion were nearing completion in November when Vice President Richard M. Nixon was defeated in the presidential elections by Senator John F. Kennedy. Unwilling to commit the incoming Democratic administration to the planned operation without consultation, Eisenhower put it on hold while Bissell and Allen Dulles briefed the president-elect. Kennedy gave his tentative approval to the plan late in November and told the CIA to continue its preparations.[16]

President Kennedy was lukewarm on the planned operation. Dean Rusk, the new secretary of state, advised against it, as did presidential assistant Arthur Schlesinger, Jr., on grounds of both feasibility and the adverse international reaction likely to result even if the operation was successful.[17] The prospect of success was uncertain; the Joint Chiefs of Staff had reviewed the plan and pronounced it as having a "fair chance" of success but qualified that assessment with several conditions, including the necessity of surprise.[18] It was unlikely that Castro was going to be surprised, however; since October Latin American newspapers had been carrying stories on the training activities at Camp Trax, and they were joined in early January by the *New York Times* and the *Nation*.[19] But Kennedy believed that if he canceled the operation, disgruntled anti-Castro Cubans would inevitably go public with the matter, and he would be accused of being soft on communism.

"If we have to get rid of these eight hundred men [the Cubans training at Camp Trax]," Kennedy said, "it is much better to dump them in Cuba than in the United States, especially if that is where they want to go."[20] On that less-than-wholehearted note, he continued his tentative approval of the operation. He did insist that the site of the landings be changed, however.

The planned landing site had been Trinidad, a city on the southern coast of Cuba about thirty miles east of Cienfuegos offering several advantages. It lies at the foot of the Escambray Mountains, where anti-Castro guerrillas were already operating; if the strike force was unable to hold a beachhead at Trinidad, it could join the guerrillas in the mountains. All of the land approaches to Trinidad crossed bridges that could be destroyed by the invaders, thereby blocking Castro's forces. And there were indications that the people of Trinidad were strongly anti-Castro.

The one drawback to the Trinidad site was the local airstrip, which was not long enough to accommodate the B-26s. The air-support missions were to be flown from the Nicaraguan base, but the fact that it was impossible for the bombers to operate from Trinidad would have demolished the planned cover story that they were Cuban planes flown by defecting Castro pilots. Placing a curious premium on deniability—all readers of the *New York Times* now knew that whatever was about to happen was sponsored by the United States government—Kennedy insisted that a different site must be chosen, one with an airstrip that would support the cover story and conceal American involvement.[21]

The CIA planners came up with the Zapata swamp, some twenty or thirty miles west of Cienfuegos and near the Bay of Pigs. The place was far less desirable than Trinidad: it was closer to the concentration of Castro's military forces around Havana, and the marshes would prevent the invaders from escaping in the event the landings failed. And the Escambray Mountains were fifty miles to the east, too far to offer safety in any case. But the new location had one feature that recommended it to the president: a forty-one-hundred-foot runway, near the mouth of the Bay of Pigs, which was adequate for a B-26 to land and take off.[22] If Kennedy and his White House advisers understood the grave problems with the Zapata location, apparently the airstrip and the deniability it supposedly afforded more than compensated in their view. Ironically, the invasion would soon no longer qualify as a covert operation; a series of articles by the journalist Tad Szulc in the *New York Times* during the second week of April disclosed the invasion preparations in detail.

The Zapata Plan called for seizing beaches along forty miles of the Cuban shore in and near the Bay of Pigs while an airborne force was dropped several miles inland to take control of the roads Castro's forces would have to use to cross the Zapata swamp and engage the invaders. The strike force was to hold the beachhead for three days, during which time it was supposed to be joined by some five hundred anti-Castro guerrillas said to be in the area. After that a general uprising presumably would begin.[23]

During the final weeks of preparations, several additional modifications to the operation plan were made at the insistence of the White House, pruning it further in the interest of deniability. Task force chief Esterline and his assistant began to feel that this whittling away of the original plan would result in failure. Both called on Bissell and threatened to resign, but the Clandestine Service chief prevailed upon them to accept the changes and stay in their posts.[24]

The decline in confidence within the CIA task force did not spread to Camp Trax, where the morale of the Cubans had never been higher. They were unaware of the doubts and debates within the Kennedy administration and were also ignorant of a ground rule Kennedy had insisted upon early on: no United States armed forces would be involved in the operation under any circumstances. Survivors of the operation later stated that the CIA personnel at Camp Trax had positively assured them that if necessary, United States air and ground forces would be brought in to assure its success. The agency personnel involved denied this, but the CIA inspector general later found that while no promises had been made to the Cubans, the Americans had probably been "as encouraging as possible."[25]

The invasion force, which had grown from the initial three hundred to more than fourteen hundred men, made its final preparations at Camp Trax early in April. The CIA had made confidential arrangements with the Garcia Line, a shipping company owned by an anti-Castro Cuban family, to transport the force from Puerto Cabezas, a seaport on Nicaragua's Caribbean coast, to Cuba. President Somoza gave the CIA permission to use the seaport for a staging area for the strike force and a nearby airfield as a base from which the B-26 air-support missions could be flown. On April

10 the first of the exiles arrived at Puerto Cabezas and began boarding the transports. By the morning of the fourteenth, the entire force was on its way to Cuba.[26]

Although the operation was already in motion, Kennedy had still gone no further than giving it his tentative approval; he continued to reserve the right to call it off up to twenty-four hours before its scheduled commencement. The task-force managers advised him that after midnight on the fourteenth it would be too late to cancel it.[27]

In addition to tactical bombers, Castro's air force had several T-33 jet fighters and British Sea Furies (propeller-driven fighters). The jet fighters posed a formidable threat to both the amphibious landings and the invaders' B-26 air support. The invasion plan called for catching Castro's small air force on the ground and destroying it at the very beginning of the operation, thereby guaranteeing air superiority to the invaders.

On the morning of April 15, nine B-26s took off from Puerto Cabezas and headed for Cuba. Eight of the planes attacked Castro's air bases, while the ninth went on to Miami, where the pilot, posing as a defector, announced the cover story that the air strikes had been carried out by other aircrews defecting from Castro's air force. The strikes had not destroyed all of the T-33s and Sea Furies, nor had they been expected to do so; a strike involving the number of B-26s necessary to accomplish the task completely would have strained the credibility of the all-important cover story. The critical task of finishing the job was scheduled for a second wave of attacks on the morning of the seventeenth, the day the landings were scheduled.[28]

Later on the fifteenth, at a meeting of the United Nations General Assembly's Political Committee, the United States UN ambassador, Adlai Stevenson, responded to Cuban charges of United States involvement in the air strikes by presenting a photograph of the B-26 that had landed at Miami International Airport and reading a wire-service report of the pilot's cover story. Stevenson, who had been incompletely briefed on the invasion, did not know of the deception flight and believed the representations he was making were true. When he learned otherwise after the UN meeting, he complained to Secretary of State Rusk of what he foresaw as a loss of credibility and personal prestige in the international body. By this time journalists had begun to call attention to the small but telling differences between the B-26 in Miami and those of Castro's air force and were raising questions about discrepancies in the pilot's cover story.[29]

Throughout the sixteenth the invasion force neared Cuba. At about 9:30 P.M. Kennedy canceled the second wave of air strikes against the Castro jet fighters, believing they would compound the problem of the unraveling cover story. Apparently unaware of the consequences of his act, the president ordered that no further strikes be flown until they could seem to have originated from the airstrip at the Bay of Pigs or, in other words, until the invaders had secured a beachhead. Bissell and the CIA deputy director, Charles Cabell, appealed to Kennedy to restore the air strikes, but to no avail.[30]

Three landing sites had been selected by the CIA planners. Playa Girón, a beach just to the east of the mouth of the Bay of Pigs, was designated Blue Beach. Red Beach lay at the northernmost end of the bay. Green Beach was on the coast some twenty miles east of Blue Beach.

The landings began at Blue Beach at 1:15 A.M. on April 17.[31] Resistance by a small group of Castro's militiamen was quickly overcome. Immediate but slight resistance was encountered at about the same time at Red Beach. Contrary to expectations, however, there were radio stations at both landing sites, and the defenders used them to alert higher command levels to the landings.

The landing at Blue Beach was still in progress at dawn when Castro's air force attacked. One of the transports, carrying ten days' supplies of ammunition and other material, was sunk. The ship also carried the expedition's communications center. Thereafter, communications between the expedition and the task-force commanders were limited and difficult. Also at dawn, Castro's aircraft attacked the transport unloading troops at Red Beach; 180 troops were still aboard the transport, which began sinking after the attack. After her skipper ran her aground, the Cubans managed to get ashore and made their way south, where they were later rescued by the United States Navy.

In the wake of Castro's air strikes against the landings at Blue and Red beaches, the CIA task-force commanders called off the Green Beach landing and ordered the remainder of the invasion flotilla to put out to sea. The troops who had managed to establish the two beachheads soon encountered heavy resistance from Castro's ground forces. By afternoon

Castro had brought into play both tanks and artillery. Over the beaches his T-33s were proving highly effective; four of the invaders' B-26s fell to the jet fighters that day.

The serious setbacks of the first day of the operation enabled the task-force managers to persuade President Kennedy that further air strikes against Castro's air force were crucial. Five sorties were flown against the Cuban air bases that night, but a combination of weather and darkness prevented the bombers from destroying any of the T-33s on the ground.

The force that landed at Red Beach, at the top of the Bay of Pigs, came under heavy attack during the night. By the following morning the Red Beach detachment had retreated down the bay and joined the invading force at Blue Beach. The airborne detachment that had controlled the roads some distance inland was also driven back toward Blue Beach. Castro's forces continued to assault this remaining beachhead throughout the day. In Washington the CIA task-force commanders had only a hazy idea of the situation because of the loss of the transport carrying the expedition's communication center. They were therefore unaware that the invaders were running critically short of ammunition. Efforts to resupply the beachhead by sea had been called off when it was apparent the transports would be sunk by Castro's bombers. A CIA plane made a small delivery of ammunition to Blue Beach before dawn, but three other transports turned back in the face of Castro's fighters.

Kennedy gave permission for United States Navy jets to fly over the beachhead to provide defensive air cover to the ammunition deliveries. He limited such cover to one hour, however. The task-force commanders set the hour for the deliveries between 6:30 and 7:30 A.M. Through a communications mix-up, however, the CIA and the navy were using different time standards, and the hour of air cover was flown by the navy before the invasion's transports arrived at the beachhead. No ammunition was delivered, and two of the invaders' B-26s, sent to provide air cover, were shot down by Castro's jets.

Hampered by the lack of ammunition and facing a far superior force, the invaders fell back and shortened their perimeter at Blue Beach until they were nearly driven into the surf. By nightfall of the third day, they ceased further resistance and attempted to slip through Castro's lines and disperse into the Cuban interior. A handful escaped by small boat to the safety of American warships offshore, but the rest were rounded up by Castro's forces within the next two weeks.

Repelling the invasion reportedly cost Castro dearly: 1,650 dead and 2,000 wounded, compared with the 114 invaders who were killed.[32] The 1,189 captured invaders were held for eighteen months, then released in exchange for sixty-two million dollars' worth of food and medicine provided by private American sources at the unofficial request of the Kennedy administration.

The inevitable postmortems were held to fix the blame for the disaster, but its causes are still debated. To those who blame Kennedy's cancellation of the air strikes, his supporters answer that some of Castro's air force would probably have survived to play havoc with the landings in any case and that the overwhelming strength of Castro's ground forces was actually the decisive factor.[33] One popular explanation of the debacle is the supposedly false CIA estimate that large numbers of Cubans would rise up to support the invasion; in fact, this argument reverses the facts. The CIA estimate of a popular uprising was predicated on the assumption that the invaders would have first successfully established an enclave on the island. This, of course, never happened.

It is worth noting, however, that even had the invaders established a secure foothold on the island, the expected uprising might not have materialized, owing to the operation's failure to surprise Castro. On April 15, in the wake of the opening air strikes, the Communist leader ordered between one hundred thousand and two hundred thousand Cubans rounded up and incarcerated.[34] The detainees were regarded as potentially disloyal to the Castro regime, and they probably included the backbone of any popular uprising.

It was generally agreed that the ultimate cause of the failure was the inadequacy of the organization managing the operation. As military writer Hanson Baldwin observed, "In effect, everybody had a hand in the Cuban venture and yet nobody was clearly in charge."[35]

"The Executive Branch of the government was not organizationally prepared to cope with this kind of paramilitary operation" was the conclusion of a commission appointed by the president to analyze the failure.[36]

The White House and the CIA task force certainly were working at cross-purposes, and the operation clearly suffered during the transition between the Eisenhower and Kennedy administrations.

CIA officer David Phillips lists the Eisenhower administration's decision to postpone the operation after Kennedy's election as one of the chief causes of the failure and the decision to change the landing site from Trinidad to the Zapata swamp as another.[37] Had Eisenhower gone ahead with the Trinidad Plan in the fall of 1960, the operation would certainly have had a far better chance of success, but it is of course impossible to say what the outcome would have been.

The failure of the Bay of Pigs invasion had dramatic consequences for the CIA and its future. Allen Dulles, Richard Bissell, and Deputy Director Cabell were forced into retirement. Bissell was succeeded as chief of the Clandestine Service by Richard Helms, an OSS SI Branch veteran who felt more comfortable with secret intelligence than covert action. The new director of central intelligence was John A. McCone, an industrialist, former under secretary of the air force, and former chairman of the Atomic Energy Commission. Unlike Dulles, the Great White Case Officer, McCone was content to let Helms run the Clandestine Service while he managed the intelligence community and gave increased emphasis to overhead reconnaissance and other technical methods of intelligence collection. Under McCone high tech matured as the wave of the future of the intelligence business.

Perhaps the most far-reaching consequence of the failed operation was the conclusion of many in the CIA and elsewhere in the national-security organs of government that covert action was not the panacea for dealing with Soviet expansion that it had seemed in the immediate wake of the Iran and Guatemala successes. The failure appeared to demonstrate, at the very least, that there was a limit to the size that a paramilitary operation could take and yet remain covert. Some, like Lyman B. Kirkpatrick, the CIA inspector general, saw an even more fundamental limitation: ". . . the most important lesson of all was that it is seldom possible to do something by irregular means that the United States is not prepared to do by diplomacy or direct military action."[38]

"Covert action," observed Roger Hilsman, a veteran of OSS Detachment 101 and chief of State Department intelligence under Kennedy, "was really nothing more than a gimmick. In very special circumstances, it was a useful supplement, but nothing more."[39]

But subversive warfare was not completely abandoned by the United States government. President Kennedy was shortly to order Operation Mongoose, a series of covert-action programs aimed at doing that which the Bay of Pigs had failed to do: overthrowing Castro. It, too, was to fail. In 1962 Kennedy would also order the CIA to wage a massive covert paramilitary campaign against Communist forces in Laos; although it, like the Bay of Pigs invasion, would eventually grow too large to remain clandestine, the operation would forestall a complete Communist takeover of the country until the United States pulled out of Southeast Asia in 1973. And covert action was to be a favorite instrument of the Reagan administration in the 1980s, most notably in Nicaragua and Afghanistan, despite congressional opposition. But the Bay of Pigs marked the end of the golden age of covert action, when men such as Allen Dulles and Frank Wisner could hope that subversive warfare was the complete answer to Soviet adventures around the globe.

Just why Premier Khrushchev put offensive nuclear missiles into Cuba in the fall of 1962 remains a matter of conjecture and debate nearly three decades later. There is no dispute, however, that the action moved the world closer to a nuclear holocaust than it has ever been, before or since the incident. United States armed forces went from DEFCON (i.e., defense condition) 5—peacetime alert—to DEFCON 2, just short of war. Five of eight divisions of the Army Strategic Reserve were placed on alert. The First Armored Division was sent from Texas to Georgia in anticipation of action in Cuba, and a command post for an invasion of the island was set up in Florida. American nuclear missile submarines left their base in Scotland and took up stations within range of the Soviet Union. Some of the nuclear-equipped bombers of the Strategic Air Command were dispersed to civilian airfields to make them less vulnerable to a Soviet first strike. SAC increased its airborne alert, that portion of the nuclear bomber force kept in the air at all times.[40] American intelligence played a crucial role in this crisis, and the event illustrated the function of intelligence in postwar national security in the most dramatic way.

The Soviet Union had been supplying Castro with conventional arms since 1960. The decision to export long-range nuclear missiles to Cuba seems to have been made in mid-1962. The new arms buildup was scheduled to take place in two phases. First, sophisticated defensive weapons were to be introduced, including twenty-four batteries of SA-2 SAM (surface-to-air) missiles and forty-two MIG-21 jet fighters. These defensive weapons were intended to protect the offensive missiles, which were to be introduced in the second phase: forty-eight MRBMs (medium-range ballistic missiles, i.e., having a range of eleven hundred nautical miles), twenty-four IRBMs (intermediate-range ballistic missiles, with a range of twenty-two hundred nautical miles), and forty-two IL-28 bombers, capable of delivering nuclear payloads over a round-trip range of six hundred nautical miles.[41]

The first phase began in mid-July with a procession of Soviet cargo vessels embarking from Black Sea ports and proceeding through the Mediterranean and across the Atlantic to Cuba. Reports of the convoys reached the CIA and other American intelligence agencies almost immediately. CIA agents in Cuba reported that the Castro government had evacuated all civilians from the port of Mariel on the northwest coast of the island to prevent observation of the cargoes being unloaded. Other extraordinary security precautions were taken at Mariel: trucks were lifted from the wharves by crane and lowered into the cargo holds of the Soviet ships, where they were loaded, covered with tarpaulins, then hoisted out again to begin the trip inland.[42]

On August 23 the CIA's Office of Current Intelligence issued a report on "Recent Soviet Military Aid to Cuba." It stated that twenty shiploads of Soviet arms had already reached Cuba, including transportation, electronic, and construction equipment, communications vans, radar vans, trucks, and mobile electric generators. Five more ships were en route from Black Sea ports.[43]

Aerial photographs of the ships at sea showed the presence of large crates on the decks. Photo interpreters and intelligence analysts in Washington guessed that the crates contained defensive SAM missiles, a conjecture that was supported by photos made during a U-2 flight over western Cuba on August 29 showing two SAM sites and six other locations that seemed under preparation as SAM missile sites.[44]

The introduction of essentially defensive missiles into Cuba did not seem particularly alarming to the intelligence analysts at the CIA. The possibility that offensive missiles would follow seemed remote. The Soviets had never placed such weapons beyond the borders of the USSR, not even in Eastern Europe. Placing them in Cuba would create serious command and control problems for the Soviets—that is, the technical difficulties involved in ensuring that orders from the highest levels of the Soviet government in Moscow regarding the use or nonuse of the missiles would be received and carried out by personnel half a world away. Offensive missiles would require the presence of a large number of Soviet technicians and military personnel in Cuba, and that would be a political liability for the Soviet Union in Latin America, or so the CIA analysts theorized.[45]

There was at least one dissenting voice at CIA headquarters, however, the new director of central intelligence, John McCone. Although he lacked any training or experience in the field, McCone had considerable native ability in intelligence analysis. He suspected that the purpose of the SAMs was to protect offensive missile sites from aerial photography or air strikes. His suspicions may have been inspired by P. L. Thyraud de Vosjoli, the liaison officer of French intelligence in Washington, who had recently visited Cuba and had reportedly advised McCone that the Soviet buildup on the island included offensive missiles.[46] Whatever the reasons for his suspicions, McCone conveyed them to President Kennedy on August 22. Apparently, he failed to persuade the president, however, and the administration continued to act on the assumption that the new Soviet weapons were purely defensive.[47]

The first shipment of offensive nuclear missiles arrived at Mariel on September 8 aboard the Soviet freighter *Omsk*. Another shipment arrived shortly thereafter aboard the *Poltava*. Both ships were normally used for carrying lumber and therefore had exceptionally large hatches. Aerial photographs of the two vessels while en route to Cuba showed them riding high in the water, evidence that they were carrying space-consuming cargo—objects of great size and low weight, such as ballistic missiles. Intelligence analysts in Washington saw no particular significance in these facts, however, and assumed the large-hatch ships had been pressed into service to meet the transportation demands of the defensive weapons buildup.[48] On September 19 the CIA's Board of National Estimates released a special national intelligence estimate reviewing the evidence and concluding that the Soviets would not place offensive nuclear missiles in Cuba.[49]

The complacency of the CIA analysts and the Kennedy administration was nurtured by a Soviet campaign of deception and disinformation. On September 4 Khrushchev sent the Soviet ambassador in Washington to Attorney General Robert F. Kennedy with a confidential message promising that he would create no trouble for the United States during the 1962 congressional elections. Two days later he reiterated this claim in a message to presidential counsel Theodore Sorensen: "Nothing will be undertaken before the American congressional elections that could complicate the international situation or aggravate the tension in the relations between our two countries. . . ."

Another message relayed by way of yet another Soviet official with access to the White House was more explicit: "No missile capable of reaching the United States would be placed in Cuba." On September 11 Tass, speaking for the Soviet government, stated that Soviet nuclear weapons were so powerful "there is no need to search for sites for them beyond the boundaries of the Soviet Union." On October 16 Khrushchev told the American ambassador in Moscow that Soviet purposes in Cuba were wholly defensive. Two days later Soviet foreign minister Andrei Gromyko visited the White House and assured President Kennedy that Soviet aid to Cuba was "by no means offensive." By then, however, Kennedy knew better.[50]

The nuclear missiles might have been discovered somewhat earlier had it not been for two unrelated events on the other side of the world. On August 30 a U-2 flying along the periphery of the USSR strayed over Sakhalin Island, a Soviet possession. On September 9 another U-2, this one flown by the Chinese Nationalists, was shot down by SAM missiles over the Chinese mainland. In the wake of these two incidents, the State Department feared that the downing of a U-2 over Cuba would produce the same sort of political crisis that had followed the downing of Francis Gary Powers's flight two years earlier. At State's urging, the Committee on Overhead Reconnaissance, a panel of the United States intelligence community, agreed to modify U-2 flights over Cuba. The planes would not overfly the western end of the island—where the SAM sites happened to be located—but would concentrate on the eastern part of Cuba.[51]

Reports from agents in Cuba and recent refugees from the island arriving in the United States continued to raise suspicions that something more than defensive missiles were being put in place. In the middle of the night of September 12, a CIA subagent observed a truck convoy proceeding in a westerly direction from the vicinity of Mariel. His report, which reached CIA headquarters on the twenty-first, described the trailers as twenty meters long (about the length of the MRBM) and carrying loads concealed by tarpaulins. The CIA analysts doubted the subagent's estimate of length, however, and theorized that the trailers were carrying SAMs, which are about ten meters long. The analysts had heard the cry of wolf too often to take the report seriously. Reports of offensive Soviet missiles had been coming from sources on the island since shortly after Castro came to power. The file of such reports for 1959 alone was five inches thick.[52]

CIA Director McCone, a recent widower, remarried late in August and spent September honeymooning on the French Riviera. He could not get the question of Soviet offensive missiles in Cuba out of his mind, however, and he sent a series of telegrams to CIA headquarters—later dubbed the honeymoon cables—urging that the possibility of offensive missiles be given further consideration. Fortunately, McCone was not the only person in the intelligence community who suspected the Soviets were putting offensive nuclear missiles into Cuba. Another was Colonel John Ralph Wright, Jr., an intelligence analyst at the Defense Intelligence Agency, an organization created a year earlier by Defense Secretary Robert S. McNamara to function as a central military intelligence service.

Studying the U-2 photographs of the SAM sites in western Cuba made late in August, Wright noted a similarity to the clustering of SAM sites in the Soviet Union he had seen in U-2 photographs made in the late 1950s. The Soviet SAM complexes had been arranged to protect offensive missile sites. Wright wondered whether the presence of the same site pattern in Cuba meant they had been placed there for the same purpose. Projecting the geometric pattern formed by the Cuban sites, he found it centered on San Cristobál, a town fifty miles south of Havana. Wright took his discovery to DIA director Lieutenant General Joseph F. Carroll and urged that a U-2 mission be laid on to photograph the San Cristóbal area. McCone, having returned from his honeymoon, added his voice to the plea at a meeting of the Committee on Overhead Reconnaissance on October 4. The flight was approved for October 9, but forecasts of poor weather over the target delayed it until October 14.[53]

Within twenty-four hours of the flight, photo interpreters at the CIA's National Photographic Interpretation Center in Washington had analyzed the pictures and found the MRBM sites. On October 17 another U-2 flight found additional MRBM sites at Sagua la Grande, 135 miles east of Havana, and construction in progress of other sites at Remedios, in central Cuba, and Guanajay, near Havana. At Least sixteen and possibly thirty-two missiles were counted in the aerial photographs, although none was ready to be fired.[54]

Aerial reconnaissance of Cuba became nearly continuous after initial discovery of the missiles in order to monitor progress in readying them for launch. Meanwhile, President Kennedy and his national-security advisers met to consider what action should be taken by the United States. On October 22 Kennedy went on national television to report the situation to the American people and to announce a quarantine of Cuba—that is, a naval blockade to exclude further shipments of offensive weapons to the island. He also stated that the United States would regard any nuclear missile launched from Cuba as a Soviet attack and would respond with a retaliatory attack against the Soviet Union. He called for the "prompt dismantling and withdrawal" of the offensive missiles under United Nations supervision.

Kennedy imposed the quarantine and demanded withdrawal of the missiles in the face of contrary intelligence estimates from the CIA. Three days earlier the Board of National Estimates forecast that the Soviets would neither use the missiles if and when they became operational nor withdraw them if confronted by the United States. Another estimate made the following day forecast that the Soviets would be less likely to retaliate to a swift American invasion of Cuba than to take "more limited forms of military action against Cuba"—for example, air strikes against the missile sites or a naval blockade.[55]

Kennedy held vital intelligence that permitted him to call the Soviets' bluff: he knew not only that Khrushchev did not want a nuclear war but that the Soviet Union was ill prepared to fight one. American knowledge of Soviet strategic nuclear capability was based on overhead reconnaissance of the Soviet Union and also, by many accounts, on intelligence supplied by a high-level Soviet defector in place, Colonel Oleg V. Penkovsky. Penkovsky, a senior officer of the GRU (the Soviet military intelligence service), had volunteered to work for the British Secret Intelligence Service two years earlier. He was debriefed by both SIS and CIA officers during several trips to the West in 1961–62. The information he provided included classified documents relating to Soviet strategic planning and capabilities. According to Dr. Ray S. Cline, the CIA's deputy director for intelligence at the time, his information proved "invaluable" during the missile crisis.[56]

The high-altitude U-2 overflights of Cuba continued, and after the president went public with the crisis on the twenty-second, low-level photoreconnaissance flights by high-speed jet-fighter aircraft began. The increased aerial surveillance of the sites disclosed that they were not in as advanced a state as had initially been supposed but that Soviet crews were now working around the clock to complete them. The CIA estimated that they could not be made ready before December 1. The Cuban overflights were not made without cost, however; on October 27 United States Air Force Major Rudolph Anderson, Jr., was killed when his U-2 was shot down over Cuba by a Soviet SAM.

The death of Major Anderson escalated the crisis to the point of American military action. Kennedy and his advisers had already decided that should a U-2 be shot down, the United States would retaliate against one SAM site; if another U-2 should be attacked, all of the SAM sites would be taken out. After word of the downing of Anderson's plane reached the White House on the evening of the twenty-seventh, there was nearly unanimous agreement among the president's advisers that the air force would attack a SAM site the following morning. Then the president temporized, however, deferring the retaliatory action for a day or so to make certain the reconnaissance plane had actually been shot down and had not crashed because of some mechanical failure.[57]

The day before the downing the administration had received a proposal from Khrushchev through an unofficial channel (newsman John Scali, who had been given the message orally by the KGB chief of station in Washington) offering to remove the missiles in exchange for an American pledge not to invade Cuba. The situation was soon muddled by an official Soviet proposal demanding the removal of American missiles from Turkey as part of the deal. Before the administration could ask for and receive clarification, the U-2 had been shot down. Rather than order the attack on a SAM site, Kennedy decided to accept Khrushchev's first proposal while ignoring the second. This approach defused the crisis. The missiles, together with the I1-28 bombers, were removed; U-2 flights over Cuba during December and January confirmed that Khrushchev had kept his promise. The American noninvasion promise was made, although it was never formalized.[58]

In a very real sense the performance of the United States intelligence community during the missile crisis was the fulfillment of the promises made by Donovan and other advocates of central national intelligence that there would not be another Pearl Harbor. Unquestionably, it was a somewhat tarnished triumph. As in the case of Pearl Harbor, intelligence suffered from an overabundance of information, making it difficult to distinguish the relevant signals from the irrelevant noise. The best minds on the Board of National Estimates were twice proved gravely wrong: first, when they forecast that the Soviets would not put the missiles into Cuba and then when they counseled that they could not be made to withdraw them.

The missile crisis was, in truth, the consequence of failures by both American *and* Soviet intelligence. If the CIA Board of National Estimates failed to foresee the Soviet move, the Soviets obviously did not anticipate the American response to it. Perhaps both sides exceeded the inherent limitations of estimative intelligence in forecasting the actions of national leaders.

It could be argued that the fact that the director of central intelligence— a man with no professional background in intelligence—drew the correct conclusion was simply a matter of dumb luck. But training, experience, and skill—not luck—were the factors that enabled a military intelligence analyst at the Defense Intelligence Agency to look at the U-2 photographs and reach that same correct conclusion.

A failure on the scale of the Pearl Harbor debacle would have meant that the United States government did not learn of the missiles until they were fully operational. But in fact, American intelligence discovered the missiles shortly after they had been delivered to San Cristóbal, the first of the MRBM sites. Even had intelligence analysts paid more attention to the early indications—the agent and refugee reports and the maritime intelligence—and photographed San Cristóbal in mid-September, there would not yet have been missiles to be seen in the photographs. Without such positive and conclusive evidence, the other indications would not have provided a basis for action by the president and the National Security Council.

Based upon what we now know of the options President Kennedy and his advisers considered when the missiles were first detected and the proximity to military action that followed the death of Major Anderson, it seems nearly certain that had the missiles been discovered only after they were operational, air strikes and perhaps an invasion would have been the American response. With the ball then in the Soviet court, the sequel can only be a matter of the grimmest speculation. All that stood in the way of that terrifying scenario was the U-2 pilots and a colonel at the DIA.

The intelligence success of the missile crisis had all the ingredients that characterized postwar American intelligence: the high-tech U-2 over-flights, the traditional human espionage of Oleg Penkovsky, and the Anglo-American liaison that made Penkovsky's disclosures available to the CIA.

"This is the week when I had better earn my salary," Kennedy told an adviser on October 18. It was also the moment in which America's commitment to a massive peacetime intelligence establishment was justified beyond question.

No one who reviews the events of October 1962 can say that it was not a very, very near thing. But neither can one deny that intelligence may have made the difference between a near thing and a nuclear holocaust.

Postscript

The Eagle and
the Sphinx

This narrative closes in October 1962. The full, reliable record of
American intelligence and covert action in the past three decades
will undoubtedly be withheld by the United States government for some
considerable time to come. On the other hand, that which has been disclosed, officially or otherwise, has been so widely disseminated in the flood
of books and other writings of the past dozen years or so that a recounting
here would be redundant. It suffices, then, to review the major events of
this interval that have shaped the present state of the United States intelligence establishment.

It is doubtful that one American in ten had ever heard of the CIA on the
eve of the Bay of Pigs invasion in April 1961. Today, however, the agency
has achieved the dubious distinction of being the world's most famous
secret service. Most of the unsought publicity has been created by the
agency's covert-action operations. Almost all of it has been bad.

During the sixties the unwelcome limelight originated in Southeast
Asia. Despite the unhappy experience of the Cuban invasion, Presidents
Kennedy and Johnson turned repeatedly to the CIA for the quick fix of
covert paramilitary action in trouble spots around the world. One of the
most troublesome such spots was Laos, which the Communist Pathet Lao
forces and the North Vietnamese had been trying to take over since 1954.
In 1962 President Kennedy gave the CIA overall responsibility for American paramilitary operations in that country. A few score officers of the Clandestine Service raised and organized L'Armée Clandestine, a force of some
thirty thousand Meo tribesmen and other Laotians, augmented by some
seventeen thousand Thai mercenaries. Next door, in Vietnam, the agency
and the Green Berets organized and trained the Civilian Irregular Defense

Group, a counterinsurgency militia that grew to a force of seventy-five thousand by 1964. The sheer size of such operations precluded secrecy, and the CIA's role was soon a matter of common knowledge.

"In Saigon," recalls one Clandestine Service officer,

> CIA was a large-scale enterprise, and CIA station chiefs became semipublic figures. Key CIA operators were cited by name and deed in news reporting. Playing its role in a theater of war, the CIA became an all-purpose instrument of action like the Office of Strategic Services in the war with Germany and Japan.[1]

As domestic opposition to the war grew, the CIA came in for its share of criticism by the anti-war movement and was soon the bête noire of the New Left. *The Invisible Government*, a 1964 exposé of the CIA by journalists David Wise and Thomas B. Ross, greatly increased public awareness of the agency and set the sharply critical tone that characterized much of the reporting of the CIA's activities during the sixties. An article in the February 1967 issue of the New Left's *Ramparts* magazine revealed the CIA's covert funding of the National Student Association, an organization of American college students. The revelation triggered a rash of investigative reports on the CIA in which more information was disclosed concerning the agency's covert funding of educational organizations, labor unions, and other groups. These programs, which had been in place since the mid-1950s, were aimed at bolstering the non-Communist Left as an answer to widespread Soviet penetration of similar groups. In the mood of growing distrust of government in the sixties, however, it was popularly supposed to have been done for nefarious and Machiavellian purposes.

The anti-war movement's focus on the CIA was ironic: while demonstrators protested the war in the streets of Washington, CIA intelligence analysts were offering the Johnson administration gloomy forecasts of its outcome. Former DCI John McCone recently recalled in a television interview:

> I disagreed with [Secretary of Defense] McNamara and others who said they could see the light at the end of the tunnel. We in the CIA didn't see any light at the end of the tunnel, and

we had a very pessimistic view which was sharply resented by everyone right up to President Johnson.[2]

As Southeast Asia began to monopolize the attention of the Johnson administration to the exclusion of all other foreign-policy problems, the White House created new layers of national-security machinery—special presidential advisers and task forces—which diminished the role and influence of the CIA and the rest of the intelligence establishment. Unable to affect events, the agency could only endure the unenviable roles of unwelcome messenger to the administration and bogeyman to those who opposed the war.

The dust had not quite settled in Southeast Asia in the seventies when the CIA found itself in another no-win situation, the Watergate affair. The central role played by CIA veteran E. Howard Hunt in the burglary of the Democratic National Headquarters was bad enough in its impact on the agency's public image, but when it transpired that Hunt had received technical aid from the agency for an illegal break-in at a psychiatrist's office, the CIA seemed thoroughly involved in the mess. In fact, the aid had been given to Hunt in ignorance of his illegal activities and was quickly withdrawn when CIA officials became suspicious. Furthermore, DCI Richard Helms blocked President Nixon's attempt to involve the CIA in the Watergate affair as a means of sidetracking the FBI investigation of the matter. This action reportedly cost Helms the directorship in 1973, when it came time for the re-elected Nixon to re-appoint the DCI.

Watergate was not yet done creating troubles for the CIA, however. Upon learning of the agency's unwitting involvement in Hunt's burglary, the new DCI, James R. Schlesinger, ordered a complete internal review of all possible involvement of the CIA in questionable or illegal matters since the first days of the agency. This institutional examination of conscience resulted in a list of nearly seven hundred cases, including such things as assassination plots, warrantless wiretaps and break-ins carried out within the United States, spying on Americans, unauthorized mail opening, and the administration of hallucinogenic drugs to unwitting subjects. This compendium of horrors, dubbed the Family Jewels by CIA insiders, was voluntarily turned over by Schlesinger's successor, William E. Colby, to the congressional committees responsible for oversight of the CIA. Shortly thereafter, several of the items somehow found their way into the pages of the *New York Times*.

Public disclosure of the Family Jewels triggered a full-scale Washington uproar and resulted in the investigation of the CIA by a presidential commission and of the entire intelligence community by special committees of both the Senate and House. The investigations and the inevitable leaks of sensitive information resulting from them created serious internal problems for the CIA.

Disclosure of the secret cooperation the agency had received from many foreigners damaged the sensitive liaison arrangements between the Clandestine Service and the intelligence and security services of many friendly nations. These countries lost confidence in the CIA's ability to protect their secrets, a problem exacerbated by the disclosures made by Philip Agee, a renegade former CIA intelligence officer, in his book *Inside the Company*, published at the height of the investigations. Morale was also seriously damaged. The publication of the agency's past misdeeds, actual and alleged, resulted in personal embarrassment to many staff employees, most of whom had no knowledge of or participation in any of the Family Jewels but were nonetheless presumed to have been involved in all of them by acquaintances and even friends and family. "What shall I tell my children?" became a common lament among those whose children were of a generation already antipathetic toward their parents' government service.

One index of the damage done by Vietnam, Watergate, and the Family Jewels to the public image of American intelligence can be found in reverberations in popular culture. Hollywood, which had traditionally depicted the American secret agent as hero, made an abrupt about-face. The evil CIA official, bent on assassination, torture, drug dealing, or some other unpleasantness, became a staple of films, television dramas, and novels in the seventies, a stock character invoked over and over again by scriptwriters and readily supplied by central casting. In retrospect, James Cagney's OSS officer of *13 Rue Madeleine* seemed like the relic of some species now long extinct. His admonition that in matters of survival there are no rules would have been to post-Vietnam, post-Watergate sensibilities sheer wickedness.

The intelligence establishment achieved a degree of rehabilitation during the eighties in the wake of the foreign-policy failures of the Carter administration. New Soviet subversion in Central America and Africa and new Soviet expansionism in Afghanistan, state-sponsored terrorism against Americans abroad, and especially the Iran hostage crisis all combined to re-acquaint Americans with the harsh reality that the world remains a very dangerous place. For some that seemed a good reason to maintain a strong military and an effective intelligence service. But in others it produced a mood of isolationism that denies both the need for and the propriety of foreign covert operations.

In the continuing debate over American intelligence, espionage, and covert action, it has become fashionable to assert that there is a fundamental incompatibility between such secret activities and a free society. Even an advocate of intelligence such as Roger Hilsman, OSS veteran and one-time chief of State Department intelligence, maintains that "the need for the United States to engage in clandestine activities will continue and so will the tension between this need and the need to preserve the asset of belief in our intentions and integrity." Wise and Ross, in their sharply critical book on the CIA, go further:

> The Invisible Government [i.e., the CIA and the other United States intelligence services] emerged in the aftermath of World War II as one of the instruments designed to insure national survival. But because it was hidden, because it operated outside of the normal Constitutional checks and balances, it posed a potential threat to the very system it was designed to protect.[3]

Those words were written in 1964. The greatly increased congressional oversight of the intelligence community that resulted from the investigations and scandals of the seventies went a long way to silence the charge that it operates outside of the Constitution. But the belief that clandestine activities are inherently incompatible with a free society as epitomized by the United States and that intelligence, espionage, and covert action are recent appendages to the American system, artifacts of the Second World War and the cold war, remains a robust bit of mythology.

In 1923 the War Department chose the Sphinx as the heraldic symbol of intelligence. Today a statue of the mythical beast stands in the courtyard of the United States Army Intelligence Center and School at Fort Hua-chuca, Arizona. Silent and enigmatic, with a human head and the powerful body of a lion, the Sphinx is a fitting emblem of secret service. Yet it is an ancient symbol whose origins are in the Old World, thought by some to be incompatible with the brave, proud, and distinctly American creature that adorns the Great Seal of the United States.

But clandestine activities are as American as apple pie or the bald eagle. Espionage and subversive warfare are part of a venerable American tradition that dates back to George Washington. The vast expansion of covert operations that followed America's assumption of Western leadership in the postwar world may have strained the constitutional mechanism for the management of such activities. However, the thesis that clandestine things are somehow against the American grain, a transplanted organ rejected by the national body, flies in the face of the obscure but demonstrable two-hundred-year history of American intelligence, espionage, and covert action. This account of that history is offered in the hope that it will provide the perspective for a better understanding of such things in our own times.

Notes

FOREWORD

1. Wilson, *A History of the American People.*
2. Sayle, "The Historical Underpinnings of the U.S. Intelligence Community."
3. Constantinides, *Intelligence and Espionage*, p. 11.
4. Stimson and Bundy, *On Active Service in Peace and War*, p. 188.

CHAPTER ONE: LIBERTY BOYS AND BRITISH MOLES

1. Boatner, *Encyclopedia of the American Revolution*, p. 93.
2. Ibid., p. 158.
3. Most of the thirty members of the committee were mechanics, according to Paul Revere (see Forbes, *Paul Revere and the World He Lived In*, p. 225). At the time the word referred to skilled craftsmen such as Revere. The Central Intelligence Agency's booklet *Intelligence in the War of Independence* says the committee was "known as the 'mechanics'" (p. 36). Although I have found no contemporary references to support this assertion, Roger J. Champagne notes that the New York Sons of Liberty styled themselves "the mechanics" to emphasize that they were a working-class group as distinguished from the wealthy merchants of New York City (*Alexander McDougall and the American Revolution in New York*, p. 55). In any case, I have used this term in the text for convenient reference to the Green Dragon group.
4. Davidson, *Propaganda and the American Revolution*, p. 197; Boatner, p. 228.
5. Thompson, "Document Sheds New Light on 'General Gage's Informers,'" p. 8.
6. Ibid.; French, *General Gage's Informers*, chap. 5.
7. Thompson, p. 8; French, chap. 5. See also Van Doren, *Secret History of the American Revolution*, pp. 19–23.
8. Forbes, p. 225. Boatner (p. 228) and Bakeless, *Turncoats, Traitors and Heroes* (p. 26), however, state that Revere did suspect Church.
9. Boatner, p. 627.
10. Higginbotham, *The War of American Independence*, p. 58.
11. French, pp. 10–14, 29–33.
12. Forbes (p. 460) concludes the steeple used was that of Christ Church, the oldest church in north Boston, and not that of the North Square Church, as has often been supposed.

13. Forbes, pp. 267–68.
14. Van Doren, p. 20. Boatner (p. 120) says that the Committee of Safety did not finally decide to fortify Bunker Hill until June 15.
15. Van Doren, p. 20.
16. Montross, *The Reluctant Rebels*, pp. 65–86; Ganoe, *The History of the United States Army*, p. 536.
17. Bakeless (p. 374) notes that the name is sometimes given as Wainwood but states that Wenwood is the spelling in the baker's own newspaper advertisements.
18. For the affair of Church's cipher letter, see French, pp. 183–197, and Van Doren, pp. 20–23.
19. Van Doren, pp. 21–22.
20. Kahn, *The Codebreakers*, pp. 175–76.
21. Bryan, *The Spy in America*, p. 28.
22. Church was also tried and found guilty by the Massachusetts Provincial Congress, but that body decided it could not call the doctor's action—which amounted to loyalty to the king of England—treason; the Declaration of Independence was still nearly a year off, and the Patriots still regarded themselves as Englishmen. On August 21, 1776, the Continental Congress closed the loophole through which Church had cheated the hangman, providing the death penalty for espionage against the United States.
23. Van Doren (p. 22) speculates that Thompson may have been the "confidant" of Dr. Church who purged the doctor's papers of incriminating evidence before General Washington's messenger searched them.
24. John Adams estimated that one third of the colonials were Loyalists (*Dictionary of American History*, s.v. "Loyalists"), while more recent estimates put their number at "between 15 and 36 percent of the *white* population" (Brown, *The Good Americans*, p. 227).

CHAPTER TWO: THE EDUCATION OF AN INTELLIGENCE OFFICER

1. Washington, *Writings*, vol. 3, p. 407n.
2. Boatner, *Encyclopedia of the American Revolution*, p. 523.
3. Flexner, *George Washington in the American Revolution*, p. 65.
4. Ibid., pp. 90–91.
5. General Charles Lee, whom Washington sent to New York in January 1776 to organize the defense of the city, wrote the following month, "What to do with the city, I own, puzzles me. It is so encircled with deep navigable waters that whoever commands the sea must command the town." But he saw New York as an opportunity to inflict a punishing blow on the British: "It might cost the enemy many thousands of men to get possession of it." (Boatner, p. 797.)
6. Boatner, p. 654.
7. Bliven, *Battle for Manhattan*, p. 83; Powe and Wilson, *The Evolution of American Military Intelligence*, p. 5.
8. Washington, vol. 6, pp. 18–19.
9. Ford, *A Peculiar Service*, p. 103.
10. Seymour, *Captain Nathan Hale*, p. 25.
11. Thompson, "Sleuthing the Trail of Nathan Hale."
12. Seymour, p. 25. In some accounts, this is made to seem fortuitous, but it is more likely that Pond and his sloop were waiting by pre-arrangement for Hale or else were regularly used by the Continentals for clandestine crossings to British-occupied Long Island.

13. Pennypacker, *General Washington's Spies*, p. 19.
14. Van Doren speculates that Washington may have owed the survival of the Continental army after White Plains to the unwitting services of a traitor (*Secret History of the American Revolution*, pp. 17–18). William Demont, adjutant to the commander of Fort Washington, defected to the British on the night of November 2, delivering to them the detailed plans of the American fort. Possession of these plans made a British assault on the fort a relatively easy operation. Van Doren suggests (p. 18) that "Demont's treachery affected General Howe's decision to turn back from the pursuit of Washington northward, which might be successful, to the storming of Fort Washington, which was certain to be."
15. An account of Honeyman's service as Washington's agent can be found in Falkner, "A Spy for Washington."
16. Boatner, pp. 911, 1112.
17. Some accounts say four Americans were killed, two from freezing (Boatner, p. 1115).

Chapter Three: Poor Richard's Game

1. Boatner, *Encyclopedia of the American Revolution*, p. 259.
2. Van Doren, *Benjamin Franklin*, pp. 540–41.
3. Although the man's full surname was Achard de Bonvouloir and the proper short way to refer to him is Achard, I have followed the established practice of American writers in calling him Bonvouloir to avoid confusion.
4. Augur, *The* Secret *War of Independence*, pp. 77–78.
5. The Secret Committee, of which Franklin was also a member, controlled all foreign trade. Its covert duties were transferred to the American mission to France in 1777, after which time it was known as the Committee of Commerce, which later evolved into the United States Department of Commerce. See Boatner, pp. 996–97.
6. Beaumarchais has taxed the talents of generations of biographers. Three of the best are Lemaitre, *Beaumarchais;* Grendel, *Beaumarchais;* and Cox, *The Real Figaro.*
7. Lemaitre, pp. 201–2.
8. Morris, *The Peacemakers*, p. 127.
9. Bemis, "The British Secret Service and the French-American Alliance," p. 475.
10. Ibid., p. 474.
11. Edward Bancroft to the Marquis of Carmarthen, September 17, 1784, Public Record Office, Foreign Office Papers, London, England. The full text of this document is quoted in Semis, pp. 492–95.
12. Bemis, p. 477. The British Secret Service expenses nearly doubled during the period of Franco-American negotiations. They increased from £119,560 in 1775 to over £200,000 in 1778, the year the treaty of alliance was signed. See "Account of the Money Issued for His Majesty's Secret and Special Service" in Stevens, *B. F. Stevens's Facsimiles*, no. 2024.
13. Bancroft to Carmarthen, in Bemis, pp. 492–495.
14. Einstein, *Divided Loyalties*, pp. 20–21.
15. These and the other reports Bancroft made to the Secret Service can be found in the Auckland Papers, British Museum, London (William Eden was created Lord Auckland in 1793).
16. Miller, *Triumph of Freedom*, p. 282.

17. Einstein, p. 45.
18. George III, *The Correspondence of King George the Third*, no. 2064.
19. Bemis, p. 490, op. cit. Bemis, p. 491, finds this claim "unbelievable."
20. Bancroft to Carmarthen finds this claim "unbelievable" (in Bemis, p. 491).
21. He was given an additional five hundred pounds per year to stay in France; the sum was doubled in 1780 (ibid.).
22. Boyd, "Silas Deane."
23. Franklin's own loyalty has been called into question in recent years by some revisionist historians who argue that he, too, was working for the British. I have dealt with these allegations at length in "Benjamin Franklin," pp. 45–53.

CHAPTER FOUR: GEORGE WASHINGTON, SPY MASTER

1. This observation was first made by Kahn in *Hitler's Spies*, pp. 528–29. After consultation with Dr. Kahn, I attempted to develop the principle further, especially as it relates to Washington's strategy, in "Kahn's Law," pp. 39–46.
2. Washington, *Writing;* vol. 6, pp. 28–29.
3. Flexner, George *Washington in the American Revolution*, p. 199.
4. Bidwell, *History of the Military Intelligence Division*, pp. 2–3.
5. Bakeless, *Turncoats, Traitors and Heroes*, p. 170.
6. Ibid., p. 171.
7. Russell, *Haym Salomon and the American Revolution*, pp. 44–45. Russell (p. 78) suggests that Salomon was, in fact, a stay-behind agent.
8. Russell, p. 78. Salomon was probably arrested in the general sweep of suspicious New Yorkers conducted by the British forces immediately after the fire of September 20–21 destroyed a large portion of the city. The fire may have been set by the Sons of Liberty to do what the Continental Congress had forbidden Washington to do—burn the city rather than leave it to billet Howe's troops. Some historians suspect that this general roundup of suspects after the fire may have been the reason Nathan Hale was apprehended. See Thompson, "Sleuthing the Trail of Nathan Hale."
9. Russell, pp. 82–83.
10. O'Brien, *Hercules Mulligan*, pp. 88–89.
11. Ibid., pp. 96–97.
12. Bakeless, pp. 177–78.
13. Ibid., p. 173.
14. O'Brien, p. 102. O'Brien offers no specific evidence that the report came from Mulligan, and he writes as though he believed Mulligan was Washington's only New York spy. In several instances, he cites the fact that a report came through Hamilton as proof that its source must have been Mulligan, but as Hamilton was Washington's aide-de-camp, most intelligence reports were probably received by him. Notwithstanding all this, it is not unlikely that Mulligan knew early of Howe's planned expedition to Philadelphia, given his brother's position and that he reported it to Washington.
15. Bidwell, p. 5.
16. The letter, which is in the Pforzheimer Collection of Intelligence Literature (bequeathed to Yale University, New Haven), is quoted in its entirety in the Central Intelligence Agency, *Intelligence in the War of Independenc*, p. 5. At about this time, Colonel Dayton seems to have taken over management of Joshua Mersereau, Washington's

agent on Staten Island, and the other agents of what is now called the Mersereau Spy Ring (Bakeless, pp. 177, 179–181).

17. Washington, vol. 8, p. 499.

18. Boatner, *Encyclopedia of the American Revolution*, p. 109.

19. Washington, vol. 7, p. 462.

20. Bakeless, p. 205.

21. Ibid., p. 207.

22. For example, Lydia Darragh, the wife of a Philadelphia schoolmaster, is said to have often eavesdropped on General Howe (who is supposed to have appropriated some rooms in the Darragh house for his conferences) and reported what she heard to Washington, using her fourteen-year-old son as courier (Bakeless, pp. 206–21). Some historians have questioned this story, however, and one characterized it as "a lie made out of whole cloth" (Bryan, *The Spy in America*, pp. 237–38).

23. Bakeless may overstate matters when he claims that the networks "warned of attacks on Fort Mifflin and Fort Mercer, on the Delaware below Philadelphia, in time for the entire garrisons to get safely away" (p. 197). While the networks may have given advance warning of the attack on Fort Mifflin—Bakeless doesn't say how much warning—the defenders of the fort left half their number behind, dead or wounded, when they fled across the river to Fort Mercer on November 15, after five days of bombardment. Fort Mercer was abandoned on November 20, when General Cornwallis appeared with five thousand troops (Wallace, *Appeal to Arms*, p. 144). If the networks provided any warning of the attacks, it must have been ignored.

24. Boatner, p. 710.

25. Flexner (pp. 284–85) points out that Washington had sound reasons for not making extensive use of cavalry.

26. Boatner, p. 572.

27. O'Brien, pp. 99–100. The second of these kidnapping attempts took place in February 1781 and involved a force of three hundred British troops that secretly left New York, proceeded eastward to some point on Long Island, and was to cross to Connecticut and intercept Washington, who was en route to Newport, Rhode Island (a piece of intelligence apparently collected by Clinton's spies). The incident was mentioned by Washington in a letter to Lafayette, but he did not identify the source of his warning.

28. Tallmadge, *Memoir*, p. 29.

29. Ford, *A Peculiar Service*, pp. 162–65.

30. Pennypacker, *General Washington's Spies*, pp. 32–33.

31. Ford, pp. 165–66, 182–88, 205.

32. A large segment of the Culper code is reproduced in Pennypacker, p. 218.

33. Pennypacker, pp. 51–52. Jay believed he had invented the idea of "sympathetic ink," an invisible ink that requires a special chemical developer to be rendered visible rather than development by such simple means as wetting or heating. He was wrong. Sympathetic ink had been known and used in espionage for centuries. See Kahn, *The Codebreakers*, p. 522.

34. Pennypacker, pp. 58–59.

35. Ibid., p. 246.

36. Ibid.

37. Ibid., p. 49.

38. Ibid., pp. 49–50.

39. Flexner, p. 323.

CHAPTER FIVE: ENDGAMES

1. Washington, *Writings*, vol. 13, p. 231.
2. Pennypacker, *Geoige Washington's Spies*, p. 247.
3. Washington, vol. 14, p. 129.
4. Cummins, "Spanish Espionage in the South," p. 43.
5. Cummins, "Luciano de Herrera and Spanish Espionage," pp. 43–49.
6. McCadden, "Juan de Miralles and the American Revolution," pp. 360–61.
7. Montross, *The Reluctant Rebels*, pp. 384–85.
8. Cummins, "Spanish Espionage in the South," p. 48.
9. Pennypacker, p. 78.
10. Ibid., p. 80.
11. Ibid., pp. 81–84.
12. Ibid., p. 86.
13. Ibid., p. 87.
14. Ibid., p. 84.
15. Ibid., p. 89.
16. Tallmadge, *Memoir,* p. 35.
17. Pennypacker, p. 121. For a somewhat different version of Tallmadge's role, however, see Flexner, *The Traitor and the Spy*, pp. 361–62, 416.
18. Pennypacker, p. 121.
19. Ibid., p. 117.
20. Tallmadge, p. 36.
21. Ibid.
22. Ibid.
23. Washington, vol. 20, p. 173.
24. Hatch, *Major John André*, p. 254.
25. The letter is quoted in its entirety in Van Doren, *Secret History of the American Revolution*, pp. 490–91.
26. Hatch, pp. 268–69.
27. Pennypacker, p. 186.
28. O'Brien, *Hercules Mulligan*, p. 49.
29. Van Doren, p. 380.
30. Ibid., p. 381.
31. Boatner, *Encyclopedia of the American Revolution*, pp. 193–94.
32. Satires and other poetry inspired by the discovery of Arnold's treason began appearing almost immediately (Tyler, *The Literary History of the American Revolution*, vol. 2, pp. 164–65, 181–82). The affair was dramatized upon the New York stage in 1798 in *André* by William Dunlap and thereafter was a perennial theme in nineteenth-century American drama (Bryan, *George Washington in American Literature*, pp. 178–79, 184–87).
33. Thompson, "Intelligence at Yorktown," pp. 26–27.
34. Miller, *Triumph of Freedom*, p. 606.
35. Crary, "The Tory and the Spy." Ford speculates that Rivington's reason for continuing to conceal his wartime espionage after the war was to ensure that the British would make good on the promise of Sir Guy Carleton, Clinton's successor, that the Tory's two sons would receive commissions in the British army and half pay for life, even though they had never seen active service (*A Peculiar Service*, p. 323).
36. Crary, p. 69.
37. Crary thinks it would have been impossible for McLane to travel to Long Island (an

ocean distance of over 250 miles and somewhat longer by land), receive the signals from Rivington, and rejoin de Grasse in the ten-day interval between August 26—the date de Grasse landed near Yorktown—and September 5—when the French fleet sailed forth to meet the British, although Thompson (p. 27) and Ford (pp. 287–88) say this is what happened. It is also possible, however, that McLane rejoined the French fleet during the five-day period subsequent to the battle on September 5, during which time the two fleets were maneuvering for position. But whether or not de Grasse had the British signals on September 5 may be moot: naval historians attribute Admiral Graves's poor performance that day precisely to the inadequacy of the signal system he was using, asserting that his own captains didn't understand his orders (see E. B. Potter and Fredland, eds., *The United States and World Sea Power*, pp. 114–16). If so, it is difficult to see what benefit de Grasse might have derived from possession of the signals.

38. Kahn, *The Codebreakers*, pp. 182–83.
39. Ibid., p. 184.
40. Flexner, *George Washington in the American Revolution*, p. 477.
41. I doubt that this grandiose bureaucratic name was used at the time to describe Haldimand's Secret Service in the Champlain Valley, but I have followed the convention established by Mathews (*Frontier Spies*) and adopted by other writers. In any case, the term does not refer to a northern department of the British Secret Service, but to the Secret Service of the Northern (i.e., Canadian) Department of the British colonial administration in North America.
42. Pemberton, "The British Secret Service in the Champlain Valley," pp. 129–30.
43. Ibid., pp. 130–31; Fryer, *Buckskin Pimpernel*, passim.
44. Pemberton, p. 131.
45. Ibid., p. 132.
46. Ibid., pp. 130, 132.
47. Morris, *The Peacemakers*, p. 459.
48. O'Brien, pp. 49, 85; Ford, p. 314.
49. Ford, pp. 314–15; Crary, p. 62.
50. Boyd, *Number 7*, p. 9.

Chapter Six: Intrigue in the New Republic

1. But at least one deep-cover British agent in New York City, Peter Allaire, reported directly to London, and his role apparently was unknown to the British apparatus run from Canada. See Boyd, *Number 7*, pp. 60–61, n. 121.
2. Boyd, pp. 6–9.
3. Since the population of the United States during the Revolution is estimated to have been more than two million and various estimates of the Tory presence run as high as 36 percent, it seems that most of the Tories remained in the United States after the war, as they were free to do. The peace treaty protected them from prosecution and confiscation of property.
4. Boyd, p. 7.
5. Ibid., p. 7.
6. *Dictionary of American Biography*, first supplement, s.v. "John Connolly." Boatner says Connolly was again involved in a similar scheme in 1798 (*Encyclopedia of the American Revolution*, p. 262).

7. Boyd, p. 24.

8. This account of the Hamilton-Beckwith interview and the quoted dialogue—the eighteenth-century spelling and punctuation having been updated by this author—are from Beckwith's report to Dorchester as quoted in Boyd, pp. 24–25.

9. Washington had not settled on the person to be entrusted with the mission. Dr. Edward Bancroft's name was suggested by John Jay, the former secretary for foreign affairs; Jay, of course, had no idea of Bancroft's wartime service as a British Secret Service agent. At Hamilton's suggestion, Gouverneur Morris, who was then in France on private business, was given the assignment. (Bemis, *Jay's Treaty*, p. 65, n. 16.)

10. In his study of Hamilton's secret diplomatic initiatives, *Number 7: Alexander Hamilton's Secret Attempts to Control American Foreign Policy*, the eminent historian Julian P. Boyd built a persuasive circumstantial case for Hamilton's having schemed behind the president's back and seriously misled him regarding several important matters bearing on British relations. He charges Hamilton with committing "almost the gravest offense of which a cabinet officer can be guilty in his role of responsible advisor to the head of state." But other historians have criticized Boyd's interpretation of the evidence as having an anti-Hamilton bias. As Professor Richard B. Morris wrote in his review of Boyd's book, "In the role of a relentless prosecutor, Dr. Boyd gives foll credence to all the evidence for his side" *(Book Week,* January 3, 1965, p. 3).

11. Boyd, p. 34.

12. Ibid., pp. 143–46.

13. Beckwith's career flourished thereafter, perhaps as a reward for his secret service. He was made governor of Bermuda in 1797, promoted to major general a year later, and commanded British forces in the West Indies and South America. He was knighted in 1809 and promoted to full general in 1814. He commanded the British forces in Ireland from 1816 to 1820 and died in 1823.

14. See Brant's exhaustive analysis, "Edmund Randolph, Not Guilty!"

15. Boatner, s.v. "James Wilkinson"; *Webster's American Military Biographies,* s.v. "James Wilkinson"; Garraty and Sternstein, eds., *Encyclopedia of American Biography,* s.v. "James Wilkinson."

16. Bemis, *Pinckney's Treaty,* pp. 113–24.

17. Ibid., pp. 173–74.

18. Wilkinson's career of treachery continued into the early years of the nineteenth century, when he became a partner in Aaron Burr's conspiracy, then betrayed Burr to President Jefferson and was the principal witness for the prosecution at Burr's trial. Although subsequently court-martialed for his role in the affair, he was not convicted and went on to a disastrous career as a commander in the War of 1812 (a force of seven thousand troops under his command was defeated by two hundred British soldiers at Lacolle Mill in Canada). He survived two more courts-martial and was honorably discharged from the army in 1815. He died in Mexico City ten years later, while preparing a Texas land scheme. The historian Frederick Jackson Turner called him "the most consummate artist in treason that the nation ever possessed" (Garraty and Sternstein, s.v. "James Wilkinson"). Others have been kinder, characterizing him as a mere rascal. It is said of Wilkinson's record as a soldier that "he never won a battle or lost a court-martial" (*The Reader's Digest Family Encyclopedia of American History,* s.v. "James Wilkinson").

19. Bemis, *American Secretaries of State,* vol. 2, p. 224.

20. *Dictionary of American History,* s.v. "Blount conspiracy."

21. Edwards, *Barbary General,* pp. 54–59; Rodd, *General William Eaton,* p. 24.

22. Morison, *The Oxford History of the American People,* p. 353.

CHAPTER SEVEN: ESPIONAGE AND SUBVERSION
IN THE SECOND BRITISH WAR

1. Parker, "Secret Reports of John Howe," p. 80.
2. *Dictionary of National Biography*, s.v. "Herman Witsius Ryland"; Parker, p. 80.
3. Bryan, *The Spy in America*, p. 115.
4. Beirne, *The War of 1812*, p. 78.
5. Wentworth, a native of Portsmouth, New Hampshire, had been royal governor of that colony before the Revolution and was related to Paul Wentworth, the British agent who recruited Dr. Edward Bancroft to the Secret Service.
6. Parker, p. 71.
7. Ibid., p. 75.
8. Beirne, pp. 45–46.
9. Parker, pp. 72–73.
10. Ibid., p. 76.
11. Ibid., p. 79.
12. Ibid., p. 80.
13. Ibid., p. 81.
14. Ibid., p. 349.
15. There are many accounts of the Henry affair, several differing in details. This narrative is based mainly on Beirne, pp. 77–81, and Bryan, pp. 115–16.
16. Bryan, p. 116.
17. In a slightly different account of this amusing affair, Smelser identifies Crillon as "a petty Gascon embezzler named Soubiran, who was wanted by the French police," and states that he was unmasked by "a visiting foreigner" while yet in the United States (*The Democratic Republic*, p. 202).
18. White, *The Jeffersons*, p. 216. Some five thousand additional men were recruited at the outbreak of hostilities but remained temporarily ineffective through their period of training.
19. Bidwell, *History of the Military Intelligence Division*, p. 14.
20. Beirne, pp. 99–101.
21. Coles, *The War of 1812*, pp. 52–53.
22. Howe, *A Journal*. Howe's exploits are not documented elsewhere, but the modesty of his claims lend much credence to his memoirs, which were not written fot publication and were published posthumously. The most interesting episode he recounts is being sent by Gage to Malden, Lynn, Marblehead, and Salem on the night of April 18, 1775, to warn the local Tories of the Concord raid scheduled for the following night, with the request that they "try to restrain the militia" from interfering.
23. Howe, who was in Detroit when it fell, apparently was not recognized by the British conquerors as the man who had recently visited their Ontario garrisons. He was released along with the other American militiamen and moved to Vermont, where he was a smuggler in 1812–13, then went to Mexico and disappeared, at least from surviving record. (Stout, "Excerpts from John Howe's 'Smuggler's Journal,'" pp. 262–63.)
24. Lord, *The Dawn's Early Light*, pp. 22, 47–48.
25. Ibid., p. 25.
26. Ibid., p. 28.
27. Beirne, p. 274.
28. Coles, p. 172.

CHAPTER EIGHT: THE PRESIDENT'S MEN

1. Warner, "Where Secrecy Is Essential," p. 50; Wriston, *Executive Agents in American Foreign Relations*, pp. 122–23, 695.
2. Hamilton, Jay, and Madison, *The Federalist*, p. 419.
3. Warner, p. 46.
4. Wriston, p. 121, n. 27.
5. Sayle, "The Historical Underpinnings of the U.S. Intelligence Community," p. 9.
6. Sayle, "The Déjà Vu of American Secret Diplomacy," p. 400.
7. Tucker, *Dawn Like Thunder*, p. 230.
8. Edwards, *Barbary General*, p. 133.
9. Ibid., pp. 133–34.
10. Allen, *Our Navy and the Barbary Corsairs*, p. 227.
11. Tucker, p. 413.
12. Bemis, *The Latin American Policy of the United States*, p. 29.
13. Ibid., pp. 29–30.
14. Mathews is spelled with a double *t* in many accounts. I have gone with the spelling of the *Dictionary of American Biography* and *Who Was Who in America*.
15. Beirne, *The War of 1812*, p. 83.
16. Wriston, p. 536.
17. Beirne, p. 86.
18. Wriston, p. 536.
19. The task eventually devolved upon Thomas Pinckney, who, while returning East Florida to the Spanish governor, nonetheless ensured that American troops occupied the strategic Amelia Island (upon which Fernandina is located) during the war with Britain (Wriston, p. 537; Beirne, p. 86).
20. Sayle, p. 9.
21. Wriston, pp. 572–73. The specific purpose of McRae's mission was to report on a congress of European powers Adams expected to be held, but no such congress, and no European campaign against the Latin American republics, ever took place.
22. Ibid., pp. 434–35.
23. Ibid., pp. 697–98.
24. Ibid., pp. 698–99.
25. See the introduction and end matter by James H. Pickering in his 1975 reprint edition of Barnum, *The Spy Unmasked*. Pickering notes that after the 1828 publication of this work, Crosby was invited to attend public functions as "the real Harvey Birch" (p. Xa) and on November 27, 1830, participated in a parade up Broadway in the company of James Monroe, Albert Gallatin, and David Williams, the latter one of three militiamen who arrested Major André (p. 207).
26. Wriston, p. 23.
27. Ibid.
28. Ibid., p. 324.
29. Ibid., pp. 324, 703.
30. Ibid., p. 325.
31. Current, "Webster's Propaganda and the Ashburton Treaty."
32. Wriston, p. 265.
33. Warner, p. 51,
34. Sayle, p. 15.
35. Wriston, pp. 446–47, 449–50, 722–24.

36. Ibid., pp. 462–64, 725–26.
37. Ibid., pp. 732–33.

CHAPTER NINE: SECRET SERVICE IN THE WAR WITH MEXICO

1. Subsequent investigation by the American minister to Britain indicated that the information Green reported about such a loan was erroneous (Merk, *The Monroe Doctrine and American Expansionism*, pp. 16–21).
2. Wriston, *Executive Agents in American Foreign Relations*, p. 709.
3. Upshur was killed when an experimental naval gun exploded on the U.S.S. *Princeton* in a demonstration on the Potomac River, February 28, 1844.
4. Wriston, pp. 709–11.
5. Ibid., pp. 714–16.
6. Ibid., pp. 719–20.
7. Herrera had agreed only to meet with an American commissioner to settle the Texas question; Slidell came as an American minister. The technical distinction held an unforeseen importance for Herrera. See Bauer, *The Mexican War*, pp. 24–25.
8. Bidwell, *History of the Military Intelligence Division*, pp. 23–24.
9. Ibid., p. 13.
10. Ibid., p. 24.
11. Wriston, p. 392.
12. Beach, "A Secret Mission to Mexico," pp. 136–37.
13. Ibid., p. 137. Merk, however, says that Beach was motivated by the hope of acquiring the rights to construct an interocean canal across the Isthmus of Tehuantepec in southeast Mexico as a reward for his good offices in negotiating a peace (*Manifest Destiny and Mission in American History*, p. 132; *The Monroe Doctrine*, p. 245).
14. The entire letter is reproduced in Beach, p. 137.
15. Mrs. Storms, together with her father, the New York congressman William T. McManus, had been involved in an attempt to establish a German colony in Texas in the early 1830s. She had been romantically involved with Aaron Burr and was correspondent in Madame Jumel Burr's uncontested divorce suit in 1834. She later worked for Beach's *Sun* as a Washington correspondent and editorial writer. (Merk, *Manifest Destiny*, p. 132.)
16. Beach, p. 138.
17. Ibid., p. 139.
18. Merk, *Manifest Destiny*, pp. 133–34. Bauer says, "To some extent [the Church-sponsored] revolt was fomented by an American agent, Moses Y. Beach" (p. 280).
19. Merk, *Manifest Destiny*, p. 134.
20. Other officers of the Corps of Engineers who carried out such reconnaissance missions in the Mexican War included First Lieutenant P. G. T. Beauregard, First Lieutenant George C. Meade, and Second Lieutenant George B. McClellan (Bidwell, pp. 23, 28, n. 1).
21. Campbell, "Ethan Allen Hitchcock," pp. 13–14.
22. Elliott, *Winfield Scott*, p. 483.
23. Campbell (p. 13) gives the bandit's first name as Juan. Bauer (p. 274) spells his last name Dominquez.
24. Bryan, *The Spy in America*, p. 118.
25. Bidwell, p. 25.
26. Ibid.

CHAPTER TEN: ALLAN PINKERTON AND THE CIVIL WAR

1. The letter is quoted in its entirety in Horan and Swiggett, *The Pinkerton Story*, pp. 92–93.
2. Horan, *The Pinkertons*, p. 64.
3. Fishel, "Myths That Never Die," p. 36; Kenneth P. Williams, *Lincoln Finds a General*, vol. 1, pp. 85–86.
4. Pinkerton, *The Spy of the Rebellion*, pp. 156–57, 252–53.
5. Located on the present site of the main building of the Library of Congress, the notorious Old Capitol Prison was originally the meeting place of Congress while the Capitol was being rebuilt after the British burned Washington in 1814. Later it became a boardinghouse and by a curious coincidence was owned by Greenhow's aunt and had been Greenhow's home during her early teens. It was there Greenhow became acquainted with such prominent Washington figures as John C. Calhoun.
6. Greenhow, *My Imprisonment*.
7. Schmidt, "G-2, Army of the Potomac," p. 48.
8. Horan, pp. 66–68.
9. Boatner, *The Civil War Dictionary*, pp. 632–33.
10. Schmidt, p. 51.
11. Ibid., p. 50.
12. T. Harry Williams, *Lincoln and His Generals*, p. 50.
13. Morn, *"The Eye That Never Sleeps,"* p. 45.
14. Schmidt, p. 51.
15. See, for example, Catton, *Terrible Swift Sword*, p. 270–72. The historian Edwin C. Fishel's most careful and extensive study of Pinkerton's estimates is to be published in his forthcoming *The Secret War for the Union*.
16. T. Harry Williams, p. 50.
17. Horan and Swiggett, p. 113.
18. Ibid.
19. Ibid., p. 114.
20. McClellan, *McClellan's Own Story*, p. 308.
21. Lee's lost orders are discussed at some length in Sears, *Landscape Turned Red*, chap. 4. Sears adds new information and insight to what has generally been known about this matter.
22. Although some of the Confederate movements deviated significantly from Lee's orders, historian Fishel has found that Federal espionage uncovered these variations, thereby preserving the advantage gained through the original discovery. Fishel's findings are detailed in his forthcoming *The Secret War for the Union*.

CHAPTER ELEVEN: CIVIL WAR INTELLIGENCE: SOURCES AND METHODS

1. Pinkerton, *The Spy of the Rebellion*.
2. Baker, *History of the United States Secret Service*, chaps. 1–3 and 8.
3. Baker and others have also referred to the unit as the Bureau of Detective Service, the Bureau of Secret Service, the National Detective Police, the National Executive Police, the National Secret Service Bureau of the United States, and the United States Secret Service Bureau.
4. Fishel, "Myths That Never Die," pp. 30–31.
5. Taylor, "The Signal and Secret Service of the Confederate States," pp. 3–4.

6. The principal source for what is here presented regarding Norris and the bureau is Gaddy, "William Norris and the Confederate Signal and Secret Service."

7. Gaddy, p. 181.

8. Ibid., pp. 180–81.

9. Jones, *J. Wilkes Booth*, pp. 23–36, 65–82; Taylor, pp. 20–22.

10. Gaddy, p. 188.

11. Taylor, p. 3.

12. Canan, "Confederate Military Intelligence," p. 38; Jones, p. 30.

13. Mott, *American Journalism*, p. 329.

14. Ibid., p. 332.

15. Ewing, "The New Sherman Letters," p. 27.

16. Mott, p. 338. For a full discussion of the censorship problem, see Randall, "The Newspaper Problem in Its Bearing upon Military Secrecy During the Civil War."

17. Ewing, pp. 31–32.

18. Mott, p. 337.

19. Ibid., pp. 362–63.

20. Ibid., p. 365.

21. *Washington Star*, June 18, 1861; reprinted in Stepp and Hill, *Mirror of War*, p. 52.

22. Truby, "Pesky Ships of the Air," p. 58.

23. I have not followed a common practice of capitalizing the initial letters of *balloon corps* because the unit was never officially designated as a distinct organizational component of the Army of the Potomac, Lowe and his staff were civilian emptoyees of the army attached initially to the Topographical Engineers and later to other units.

24. Lowe, "The Batloons with the Army of the Potomac," p. 370.

25. Bryan is variously identified as John Randolph Bryan or E. P. Bryan and was either a lieutenant or captain in the Confederate army at the time of his service as a military aeronaut.

26. Longstreet, "Our March Against Pope," pp. 512–13.

27. Ibid., p. 513.

28. MacCloskey, *From Gasbags to Spaceships*, pp. 22–24; Glines, *Compact History of the United States Air Force*, pp. 34–35.

29. Ibid. There is some evidence, however, that Lowe padded his expense reports and indulged in other forms of peculation.

30. Barker, ed., *The History of Codes and Ciphers in the United States Prior to World War I*, pp. 36–44. A cipher-disk device consists of two disks joined at the center and free to rotate with respect to each other. The letters of the alphabet appear around the edge of one disk; numeric codes are printed on the edge of the second. Thus, any particular setting of the disks creates a different monoalphabetic substiturion system. Those readers who were radio listeners during the 1930s or 1940s may remember the "code-o-graphs" of the "Orphan Annie" and "Captain Midnight" serials, which were simple cipher disks.

31. Fishel, p. 47, n. 55.

32. Grant, *Personal Memoirs*, vol. 2, pp. 207–8.

33. Boatner, *The Civil War Dictionary*, pp. 761–62.

34. The veterans were David Homer Bates (see n. 36) and W. R. Plumb, the latter having made this assertion in his *Military Telegraph During the Civil War*. See also Barker, pp. 81–82.

35. The solution was worked out by Friedrich W. Kasiski, a Polish-born officer in the East Prussian infantry. His book was published in Berlin in 1863 (see Kahn, *The Codebreakers*, p. 207).

36. The telegraph office was managed by Major Thomas T. Eckert, who later became president of Western Union. As the hub of Union military communications, it was a prototype of the modern national military-command post. Lincoln visited the office daily and passed much of his time there during the war. Bates published his memoirs of the late president's visits in 1907 (*Lincoln in the Telegraph Office*). Chandler became president of the Postal Telegraph Cable Company, and Tinker was one of the founders of the American Union Telegraph Company.
37. Greely, "The Military-Telegraph Service," pp. 362–64; Bakeless, *Spies of the Confederacy*, pp. 309–10.
38. Bakeless, chap. 15.
39. Ibid., p. 308.

CHAPTER TWELVE: EUROPEAN INTRIGUE IN THE CIVIL WAR

1. Bemis, *A Diplomatic History of the United States*, p. 367.
2. Ibid., pp. 367–68.
3. Spencer, *The Confederate Navy in Europe*, p. 3.
4. Ibid., pp. 3–4.
5. Bulloch, *The Secret Service of the Confederate States in Europe*, vol. 1, p. 41.
6. Ibid., p. 58.
7. Harriet Chappell Owsley, "Henry Shelton Sanford and Federal Surveillance Abroad," p. 212; Sanders, "Henry Shelton Sanford in England," p. 87.
8. Harriet Chappell Owsley, pp. 212–13.
9. Sanders, "Henry Shelton Sanford," pp. 88–89.
10. Sanders, "'Unfit for Consul'?" p. 465.
11. Harriet Chappell Owsley, pp. 214–15.
12. Ibid., p. 214.
13. Ibid., p. 219.
14. Sanders, "Henry Shelton Sanford," p. 90.
15. Ibid.
16. Ibid., p. 91.
17. Ibid., pp. 92–93.
18. Harriet Chappell Owsley, p. 211.
19. Sanders, "Henry Shelton Sanford," p. 93.
20. Harriet Chappell Owsley, pp. 220–22.
21. McMaster, *Our House Divided*, p. 276.
22. Clapp, *Forgotten First Citizen*, p. 166.
23. Butler, *Judah P. Benjamin*, p. 313.
24. McMaster, p. 300.
25. Jordan and Pratt, *Europe and the American Civil War*, pp. 224–26.
26. Butler, p. 313.
27. According to twentieth-century American intelligence jargon, propaganda is white when its official origin is openly acknowledged; gray when its origin is disguised and it is made to appear to have originated with an independent and objective source; and black when it is contrived to appear to have come directly from the enemy—that is, when it is a forgery.
28. Callahan, *The Diplomatic History of the Southern Confederacy*, p. 92, n. 39.

29. Frank L Owsley, *King Cotton Diplomacy*, pp. 155–60; Butler, p. 315.

30. Frank L. Owsley, pp. 159–61; Jameson, "The London Expenditures of the Confederate Secret Service," p. 824.

31. Frank L Owsley, p. 161.

32. Ibid., pp. 169–71.

33. Harriet Chappell Owsley, p. 222.

34. Ibid., p. 223.

35. Ibid., pp. 223–24.

36. Spencer, pp. 82–83.

37. Ibid., p. 395.

38. Monaghan, *Diplomat in Carpet Slippers*, pp. 327–328; Stern, *The Confederate Navy*, p. 160.

39. Bulloch, vol. 1, p. 440.

40. Ibid., vol. 2, pp. 25–36.

41. There are several different versions of the incident: Harriet Chappell Owsley, pp. 225–26; Frank L. Owsley, pp. 422–26; Monaghan, pp. 325–26; Bulloch, vol. 2, pp. 38ff. The best informed as to details, however, seems to be Case and Spencer, *The United States and France*, pp. 437–44.

42. Bulloch, vol. 2, p. 41.

43. Numbers of victories are from individual entries on the ships in the *Dictionary of American History*. Total damage is based on United States claims; *Dictionary of American History*, s.v. "Alabama claims."

44. Long, *The Civil War Day by Day*, p. 720.

45. Graebner, "Northern Diplomacy and European Neutrality," p. 75.

CHAPTER THIRTEEN: CIVIL WAR SUBVERSION

1. Tatum, *Disloyalty in the Confederacy*, pp. 13–14.

2. Ibid., chap. 2.

3. Ibid., pp. 60, 62, 64, 104.

4. Ibid., pp. 57–58, 87.

5. Ibid., p. 108.

6. Ibid., pp. 46n, 93, 95.

7. Ibid., pp. 151–152.

8. Stuart, "Of Spies and Borrowed Names," p. 312. Most of what is known of the Richmond Underground was uncovered through the research and historical sleuthing of Dr. Meriwether Stuart.

9. Stuart, "Colonel Ulric Dahlgren and Richmond's Union Underground," pp. 175–176.

10. Beymer, *On Hazardous Service*, p. 66. Although Beymer's book was written as a popular history, it is based in part on interviews with surviving Civil War spies and those who knew them. The chapter on Van Lew draws on interviews with her physician and one of her neighbors, as well as on her personal papers.

11. Ibid., p. 67.

12. Ibid., p. 86.

13. Johnston, "Disloyalty on Confederate Railroads in Virginia," p. 420; Stuart, "Samuel Ruth and General R. E. Lee," pp. 36–37.

14. Stuart, "Of Spies and Borrowed Names," pp. 319–20.

15. Stuart, "Samuel Ruth and General R. E. Lee," passim.

16. Ibid., pp. 108–9.

17. Beymer, pp. 88–89; Stuart, "Of Spies and Borrowed Names," pp. 310–12.

18. Stuart, "Colonel Ulric Dahlgren and Richmond's Union Underground," p. 159.

19. Dr. Lugo's exploits and evidence that he may have been warned by the Richmond Underground were discovered by Meriwether Stuart and are presented in his "Dr. Lugo."

20. Johnston, pp. 421–22; Stuart, "Samuel Ruth and General R. E. Lee," pp. 102–3.

21. Ibid., p. 81. Ruth's postwar petition to Congress for compensation was denied, however, on the grounds that similar services had been rendered by others without expectation of reward.

22. Corson, *The Armies of Ignorance*, p. 573.

23. Sandburg, *Abraham Lincoln*, vol. 1, pp. 55–56.

24. Horan, *Confederate Agent*, pp. 16–18; Long, *The Civil War Day by Day*, p. 380.

25. The traditional view that the secret societies were a serious threat is well presented by Wood Gray in *The Hidden Civil War*. The revisionist view is argued by Frank L Klement in *The Copperheads of the Middle West* and *Dark Lanterns*. See also Stephen Z. Starr, "Was There a Northwest Conspiracy?" and *Colonel Grenfell's Wars*.

26. Horan, pp. 9–10.

27. Ibid., pp. 30–31.

28. Starr, *Colonel Grenfell's Wars*, pp. 146–50.

29. Klement, *Dark Lanterns*, pp. 28–31.

30. Starr, *Colonel Grenfell's Wars*, p. 155.

31. Headley, *Confederate Operations in Canada and New York*, pp. 223–30; Starr, *Colonel Grenfell's Wars*, pp. 154–77; Starr, "Was There a Northwest Conspiracy?" pp. 332–33.

32. Starr, *Colonel Grenfell's Wars*, pp. 185–87.

33. Dana, *Recollections of the Civil War*, pp. 209–10. Dana does not identify Montgomery by name; his identity was established after David Homer Bates published his memoir, *Lincoln in the Telegraph Office*, in 1907. See Stern, *Secret Missions of the Civil War*, pp. 257–58. Montgomery's own account of his Secret Service work and his Thompson pseudonym can be found in his testimony in Pitman, *The Assassination of President Lincoln and the Trial of the Conspirators*, pp. 24–26.

34. Dana, p. 212.

35. Pitman, p. 25.

36. Dana, pp. 213–15. Dana says the dispatch "was handed over to Mr. Seward for use in London" (p. 215), but there is no reference to it in the published diplomatic correspondence. The intelligence may for some reason have been elaborately "sanitized," however, and presented to the British by Seward in the form of a copy of a letter from the Vermont governor, J. Gregory Smith, to the secretary of state. Seward transmitted to Lord Lyons, the British minister in Washington, an extract of the letter in which Governor Smith stated, "My advices from perfectly reliable sources are that in [the Confederate commissioners'] secret conclaves their plans are being discussed and perfected, and that they threaten that they will destroy the towns of Burlington and St. Albans within thirty days" (Mr. Seward to Lord Lyons, November 22, 1864, in U.S. Department of State, *Papers Relating to Foreign Affairs*, pp. 803–4).

37. Pirman, p. 25.

38. Dana, p. 212.

39. Headley, pp. 274–77.

40. Long, pp. 600–601.

Chapter Fourteen: The Professionals

1. Obituary, John C. Babcock, Mount Vernon (N.Y.) *Argus*, November 21, 1908.
2. Schmidt, "G-2, Army of the Potomac," p. 52.
3. Obituary, George H. Sharpe, *New York Times*, January 15, 1900.
4. Fishel, "Myths That Never Die," pp. 40–41.
5. Ibid, p. 41, n. 32.
6. Ibid.
7. Schmidt, p. 53.
8. Ibid., p. 55.
9. Longstreet, *From Manassas to Appomattox*, pp. 346–47.
10. The mystery of Harrison's identity has engaged Civil War historians since Longstreet first published his memoir of the affair in *Century* magazine in the 1880s. Bakeless offered a plausible and well-documented argument that he was James Harrison, a Shakespearean actor (*Spies of the Confederacy*, pp. 334–36). Stuart, however, found a fatal flaw in Bakeless's case ("Of Spies and Borrowed Names," pp. 314–15). Hall seemed to have settled the matter once and for all, identifying the agent as Henry Thomas Harrison, a native of Yazoo County, Mississippi ("The Spy Harrison"), but some scholars familiar with the question report that the controversy continues.
11. Schmidt, pp. 55–56.

Chapter Fifteen: Intelligence and the Game of War

1. Miller, *The U.S. Navy*, p. 193.
2. Evans, *A Sailor's Log*, 171.
3. Davis, *A Navy Second to None*, p. 33.
4. Dorwart, *The Office of Naval Intelligence*, p. 26.
5. Ibid., pp. 31–32.
6. Ibid., p. 35.
7. Powe, "The Emergence of the War Department Intelligence Agency," p. 17. By one perhaps apocryphal account, the War Department's Military Information Division was established in October 1885 because Adjutant General R. C. Drum had been unable to answer a request from Secretary of War William C. Endicott for information about a foreign country (Powe, p. 16).
8. Ibid., pp. 16–17.
9. Bidwell, *History of the Military Intelligence Division*, p. 54.
10. Powe, pp. 22–25.
11. Hattendorf, Simpson, and Wadleigh, *Sailors and Scholars*, p. 22.
12. Nicolosi, "The Spirit of McCarty Little," p. 74. For a more comprehensive discussion of Little's and Livermore's roles in war-gaming at the Naval War College, see Perla, *The Art of Wargaming*, pp. 63–70.
13. Hattendorf, Simpson, and Wadleigh, p. 41.
14. Ibid., p. 40.
15. Ibid., pp. 42–43.
16. Rickover, *How the Battleship Maine Was Destroyed*, p. 11.
17. Dorwart, p. 53.
18. Ibid., p. 56.
19. Trask, *The War With Spain in 1898*, pp. 74–78.

20. Powe, pp. 28–29.
21. Bidwell, pp. 60–61.

CHAPTER SIXTEEN: ESPIONAGE IN THE WAR WITH SPAIN

1. O'Toole, *The Spanish War,* p. 108.
2. Ibid., pp. 32–33, 207–9; also see O'Toole, "Our Man in Havana," for further details of how the Hellings network was discovered.
3. Most historians have concluded that the United States government had received official Spanish permission for the visit before dispatching the warship, probably because to have done otherwise would seem to have been incredibly reckless. A careful reading of the published diplomatic correspondence (U.S. Department of State, *Papers Relating to the Foreign Relations of the United States, 1898,* pp. 1025–26, 1028) reveals, however, that the Spanish government in Madrid was not advised of the planned visit until after the battleship arrived at Havana. Lee testified to the Navy Court of Inquiry investigating the destruction of the battleship that he was not informed of the visit in advance (U.S. Congress, Senate, *Message from the President of the United States,* document 207, pp. 246-47). Sigsbee's statement that he did not know until after his arrival that the visit had not been announced is in the National Archives, Sigsbee to Long, January 26, 1898.
4. Elsewhere (*The Spanish War,* pp. 104–8, 110, 115–20) I have presented a circumstantial case that the *Maine*'s timetable was suddenly advanced because the McKinley administration feared that the impending visit of German warships to Havana might mean the kaiser planned to intervene in the Cuban crisis, perhaps in the hope of acquiring territory on the island.
5. Rickover, *How the Battleship* Maine *Was Destroyed,* pp. 91, 98–104.
6. Calkins, "The Naval Battle of Manila Bay," pp. 103–4.
7. Healy and Kutner, *The Admiral,* pp. 156–57.
8. Ibid., p. 157; Dewey, *Autobiography,* pp. 198–99.
9. Dorwart, *The Office of Naval Intelligence,* pp. 64–65.
10. O'Toole, *The Spanish War,* p. 227.
11. Trask, *The War with Spain in 1898,* pp. 87–88.
12. O'Toole, *The Spanish War,* p. 227.
13. Ibid., p. 228.
14. Ibid., pp. 232–34.
15. Young, "The Chief of the United States Detectives Tells How He Captured the Spies of Spain," p. 462.
16. Wilkie, "The Secret Service in the War," pp. 426–28; Jefreys-Jones, *American Espionage,* p. 31.
17. Wilkie, pp. 431–32.
18. Ibid., pp. 432–36; Jeffreys-Jones, p. 33.
19. Jeffreys-Jones, pp. 33–34.
20. Powe, "The Emergence of the War Department Intelligence Agency," p. 230.
21. Bidwell, *History of the Military Intelligence Division,* p. 58, n, 11.
22. Foner, *The Spanish-Cuban-American War,* vol. 2, pp. 340–42. Rowan's exploit caught the fancy of businessman-dilettante Elbert Hubbard, who celebrated it as an example of pluck in his essay "A Message to García." The much-reprinted essay gets almost all of the facts wrong.

23. Trask, pp. 340–41; Alger, *The Spanish-American War*, p. 42; O'Toole, *The Spanish War*, pp. 353–54.

24. Dorwart, p. 64; Titherington, *A History of the Spanish-American War of 1898*, p. 332n. It seems likely that the British government also cooperated in the matter of Lieutenant Whitney's cover, perhaps providing official documentation. The relative obscurity of the missions of Whitney and Ward, as compared with that of Rowan, may have been due to the United States government's desire not to embarrass the British unnecessarily by calling attention to the cooperation,

25. O'Toole, *The Spanish War*, pp. 194–95, 209.

26. Mahan, *Lessons of the War with Spain*, pp. 75–85.

27. O'Toole, *The Spanish War*, pp. 208–9.

28. Ibid., pp, 213–14; O'Toole, "Our Man in Havana," p. 3.

29. Blue's own account of his covert reconnaissance and liaison missions is in Bryan, *The Spy in America*, pp. 204–16.

30. O'Toole, *The Spanish War*, pp. 295–96, 305–6, 309–11.

31. On the other hand, the Spanish government might have found it politically impossible to negotiate an end to the war by means of Cuban independence—the minimum American war aim—without first suffering a military disaster, such as the destruction of Cervera's squadron; to have surrendered Cuba without such tangible evidence of resistance would have been deemed dishonorable by the Spanish people (see O'Toole, *The Spanish War*, p. 121). Some, including at least one of Cervera's captains, expressed the belief that Cervera's squadron had been selected for this sacrificial role early on, and this was why the fleet was ordered to sail in such a state of disrepair (Concas, *The Squadron of Admiral Cervera*, pp. 114–16).

CHAPTER SEVENTEEN: ADVERSARIES—BLACK, GREEN, AND ORANGE

1. Dorwart, *The Office of Naval Intelligence*, pp, 72–73.

2. Herwig, *Politics of Frustration*, p. 84.

3. Wandel, *The German Dimension of American History*, p. 3. For a detailed analysis of German immigration in this period, see Rippley, *The German-Americans*, chap. 6.

4. Roosevelt, *Letters*, vol. 1, p. 645.

5. Rickover, *How the Battleship* Maine *Was Destroyed*.

6. See, for example, Challener, *Admirals, Generals, and American Foreign Policy*, p.405, and Dorwart, chap. 9.

7. Herwig and Trask, "Naval Operations Plans Between Germany and the United States of America."

8. Herwig, pp. 42–54, 57–66.

9. Ibid., p. 47.

10. Ibid., pp. 52–53, 57, 58, 60–61.

11. Ibid., pp. 53, 58.

12. Dorwart, p. 77.

13. Edelsheim, *Operationen über See*.

14. Herwig, pp. 85–86.

15. Ibid., p. 85.

16. Dorwart, p. 76.

17. Herwig, p. 102.

18. Dorwart, pp. 80–81.

19. Bailey, *A Diplomatic History of the American People*, pp. 522, 524.
20. Dorwart, pp. 82–85.
21. Bailey, p. 525.
22. Dorwart, pp. 87–90.
23. Tuchman, *The Zimmermann Telegram*, p. 34.
24. Dorwart, p. 90.
25. Challener, pp. 273–74.
26. Tuchman, p. 34.
27. Katz, *The Secret War in Mexico*, pp. 76–77.
28. Goltz, *My Adventures as a German Secret Agent*, pp. 94–110.
29. Katz, citing East German archival documents (p. 586, n. 118), accepts Goltz's claim to have been a German secret agent. Goltz's entertaining account of his picaresque career is replete with facsimile reproductions of documentary evidence supporting the general outlines of his story, and the internal evidence of the book leads one to agree with Katz's estimate that "while many of Goltz's statements cannot be proven and seem exaggerated," his claim to have been a German agent is valid.
30. Tuchman, p. 37.
31. Ibid., p. 25; Katz, pp. 76–80.
32. Challener, pp. 273–74; Perkins, *A History of the Monroe Doctrine*, pp. 271–74.
33. Dorwart, p. 90.
34. Bidwell, *History of the Military Intelligence Division*, pp. 75–84.
35. Challener, pp. 375–78.
36. Dorwart, pp. 93–94.

CHAPTER EIGHTEEN: AMERICA BLINDFOLDED

1. Of course, this brief reference to the Tampico-Veracruz incident oversimplifies events considerably. Some historians have seen the occupation as something Wilson blundered into rather than a considered measure to dislodge Huerta. I have followed the analysis of Wilson's strategy as presented in Haley, *Revolution and Intervention*, chap. 7, and especially pp. 132–40.
2. West, *The Department of State on the Eve of the First World War*, pp. 4–5, 6.
3. Ibid., pp. 132–33.
4. Powe, "The Emergence of the War Department Intelligence Agency," p. 66.
5. Haley, p. 206.
6. Bidwell, *History of the Military Intelligence Division*, pp. 94–95, 102 n. 21. Reed was succeeded in October by Captain Nicholas N. Campanole, who remained in that position until the expedition was withdrawn from Mexico in February 1917 (Bidwell, p. 102, n. 25).
7. Ibid., p. 119, n. 1.
8. Scott, *Some Memories of a Soldier*, p. 512.
9. Tuchman, *The Zimmermann Telegram*, pp. 61–62; Katz, *The Secret War in Mexico*, p. 507.
10. Mashbir, *I Was an American Spy*, pp. 5–9. Sidney F. Mashbir, the young National Guard officer who carried out this secret reconnaissance, was later an intelligence officer in Japan for both army and navy intelligence. During the Second World War he was chief of the Allied Translator and Interpreter Section of General MacArthur's command in the sourhwestern Pacific.
11. Dorwart, *The Office of Naval Intelligence*, pp. 99–100.

12. Ibid., pp. 103–4.
13. Katz, *The Secret War in Mexico*, pp. 509–10.
14. Ibid., p. 350.
15. Ibid., pp. 441–50.
16. Ibid., pp. 348–50.
17. Quirk, *An Affair of Honor*, p. 31.
18. Sayle, "The Historical Underpinnings of the U.S. Intelligence Community," p. 23.

CHAPTER NINETEEN: THE ENEMY WITHIN

1. Landau, *The Enemy Within*, pp. 77–80.
2. Coumbe, "German Intelligence and Security in the Franco-German War," pp. 10–11; Hohne and Zolling, *The General Was a Spy*, pp. 281–82.
3. Landau, pp. 4–8, 23.
4. Papen, *Memoirs*, p. 38.
5. Landau, p. 99.
6. Papen, p. 39.
7. Johnson, *George Sylvester Viereck*, pp. 26–28.
8. Landau, pp. 8–9.
9. Jones and Hollister, *The German Secret Service in America*, pp. 252–54.
10. Millis, *Road to War*, pp. 203–4.
11. The disposition of the American press provides an index of popular sentiment on the war: in November 1914 there were 105 pro-Allied American newspapers, 20 pro-German papers, and 242 neutral papers (H. C. Allen, *Great Britain and the United States*, p. 652).
12. Johnson, p. 31.
13. Bernstorff, *My Three Years in America*, p. 197.
14. Papen, p. 44.
15. Landau, p. 62.
16. Captain Henry Landau, who served as head of the Military Division of the British Secret Service in Holland during the war, later worked as an investigator of claims by Americans before the international Mixed Claims Commission, examining damages done in the United States by German sabotage during the period of American neutrality. His account of these investigations forms Part 2 of *The Enemy Within*.
17. Landau, p. 148.
18. Rintelen. *The Dark Invader*, pp. 73–74.
19. Ibid., pp. 95–96.
20. Ibid., pp. 88–89, 119–20.
21. Ibid., p. 131.
22. Ibid., pp. 166–75; Landau, pp. 47–48; Millis, pp. 205–7.
23. Landau, pp. 10–15.
24. Ibid., p. 17.
25. Papen, p. 40.
26. Sometimes Ghadr (Landau, p. 28) or Gadhr (Jones and Hollister, p. 255), meaning "revolution" or "mutiny" in Urdu.
27. Jeffreys-Jones, *American Espionage*, p. 108.
28. Landau, p. 29.
29. Ibid., pp. 29–32.
30. Papen, p. 40.

31. Landau, pp. 30–31.
32. Ibid., p. 32.
33. Bernstorff, p. 9.
34. Katz, *The Secret War in Mexico*, p. 388.
35. Ibid., pp. 339–42; Haley, *Revolution and Intervention*, p. 212, n. 83.
36. Tuchman, *The Zimmermann Telegram*, p. 66; Jones and Hollister, p. 290; Rintelen, pp. 175–76.
37. Jones and Hollister, pp. 290–91.
38. Voska and Irwin, *Spy and Counterspy*, pp. 192–93. Voska based his assertion on information from a source within the German legation.
39. Landau, p. 48.
40. Tuchman, p. 78.
41. Bernstorff, p. 122.
42. Rintelen, p. 184. Tuchman (p. 83) gives the date of the recall as July 6.
43. Tuchman, pp. 80–81.
44. Ibid., pp. 86–87.
45. Bernstorff, p. 198.

CHAPTER TWENTY: BRITISH INTELLIGENCE AND
AMERICAN COUNTERSUBVERSION

1. Andrew, *Her Majesty's Secret Service*, pp. 3–7.
2. The Intelligence Branch was created in the War Office in 1873. In 1887 the Naval Intelligence Branch was esrablished in the Admiralty (Fergusson, *British Military Intelligence*, pp. 15, 68).
3. Voska and Irwin, *Spy and Counterspy*, pp. 1–22.
4. Ibid., p. 27.
5. Ibid., pp. 32–38.
6. Roetter, *The Art of Psychological Warfare*, pp. 61–64.
7. Voska and Irwin, pp. 25, 75; Millis, *Road to War*, p. 204; Tuchman, *The Zimmermann Telegram*, p. 75.
8. House, *The Intimate Papers*, vol. 2, p. 426.
9. *Dictionary of American Biography*, s.v. "Charles R. Crane"; Voska and Irwin, pp. 20–21.
10. Ibid., p. 198.
11. Jeffreys-Jones, *American Espionage*, p. 46.
12. Voska and Irwin, pp. 192–95.
13. Overstreet and Overstreet, *The FBI in Our Open Society*, pp. 26–27.
14. Jeffreys-Jones, pp. 57–58; Tuchman, pp. 77–78; Beesly, *Room 40*, pp. 225–27.
15. Link, *Wilson: The Struggle for Neutrality*, pp. 650–51.
16. Voska and Irwin, pp. 77–87.
17. Hendrick, *The Life and Letters of Walter H. Page*, vol. 3, pp. 273–78; Link, *Wilson: The Struggle for Neutrality*, p. 651 and n. 24.
18. Link, *Wilson: The Struggle for Neutrality*, p. 563.
19. Goltz, *My Adventures as a German Secret Agent*, pp. 190–211 and passim. Goltz was the German agent who claimed to have stolen a copy of the purported secret Japanese-Mexican treaty.
20. Landau, *The Enemy Within*, p. 70; Jeffreys-Jones, p. 63.
21. Bernstorff, *My Three Years in America*, pp. 262–63.

22. Landau, pp. 92–96.
23. Fowler, *British-American Relations*, pp. 17–18; Andrew, pp. 208–9. The only reference I have found to the Wisdom pseudonym and the W. Wisdom Films cover is in Landau (p. 150), but in view of that author's background as an officer of the British Secret Intelligence Service during the First World War, the information seems reliable.
24. Fowler, pp. 18–19.
25. House, vol. 1, p. 31.
26. Ibid., p. 45.
27. George and George, *Woodrow Wilson and Colonel House*, pp. 124–25.
28. Bernstorff, p. 231.
29. Fowler, p. 13.
30. Link, *Wilson: Campaigns for Progressivism and Peace*, p. 280.
31. Fowler, pp. 21–22.
32. Tuchman, p. 146.
33. The mechanics of Hall's sanitizing the Zimmermann telegram are in Kahn, *The Codebreakers*, pp. 288–91, and Tuchman, pp. 156–58. Nevertheless, Edward Bell, the American liaison officer who was intimately involved in the Zimmermann telegram affair, later claimed that the Mexico City copy of the telegram was the one originally deciphered by Naval Intelligence and that it was this that enabled the Room 40 code breakers to crack the high-level German cipher later on. Bell claimed that the sanitization story was put out by Hall to aggrandize the role of his department and his own ingenuity. See Katz, *The Secret War in Mexico*, pp. 357–59, 613–14.
34. House, vol. 2, p. 452.

Chapter Twenty-one: Intelligence Redux

1. Fowler, *British-American Relations*, p. 24.
2. Ibid., pp. 24–25.
3. Van Deman, *The Final Memoranda*, pp. x–xi; Corson, *The Armies of Ignorance*, pp. 46–47.
4. Van Deman, pp. xii–xiii.
5. Ibid., pp. xiii–xiv; Powe, "The Emergence of the War Department Intelligence Agency," p. 52; Campbell, "Major General Ralph H. Van Deman," p. 13.
6. Powe, p. 70.
7. Ibid., p. 83.
8. Bidwell, *History of the Military Intelligence Division*, pp. 109–10; Powe, pp. 83–84; Van Deman, pp. 22–23.
9. Read and Fisher, *Colonel Z*, p. 103. In his memoirs (p. 22) Van Deman curiously fails to mention Dansey's role in Scott's flip-flop but attributes it to the intercession of an unidentified woman writer and friend of Secretary of War Newton D. Baker whom Van Deman chanced to meet and to the good offices of the Washington, D.C., chief of police.
10. Bidwell, pp. 121–22; Powe, pp. 84–85.
11. Bidwell, pp. 110–11.
12. Ibid., pp. 122–25.
13. Barker, ed., *The History of Codes and Ciphers in the United States Prior to World War I*, pp. 134–36.
14. Barker, ed., *The History of Codes and Ciphers in the United States During World War I*, pp. 10–11.

15. Clark, *The Man Who Broke Purple*, pp. 22–38.
16. Ibid., pp. 41–43.
17. Yardley, *The American Black Chamber*, chap. 1. The official army history of MI-8 points out that in discovering how the diplomatic codes could be broken, Yardley had "the incalculable advantage" of access to the codebooks. "Yardley's achievement may therefore have been much less than he claimed" (Barker, *The History of Codes and Ciphers in the United States During World War I*, p. 13).
18. Yardley, p. 38.
19. Barker, ed., *The History of Codes and Ciphers in the United States During World War I*, pp. 22 and passim.
20. Bidwell, pp. 136–38.
21. Ibid., pp. 139–40.
22. Cave Brown, "C," pp. 103–4.
23. Bidwell, pp. 139, 147, n. 26.
24. Ibid., pp. 138–39.
25. Powe, pp. 91–92.
26. Ibid., pp. 97–99; Bidwell, pp. 127–28.
27. Powe, pp. 95–96.
28. Jessup, *Elihu Root*, vol. 2, p. 368.
29. Fowler, pp. 109–10.
30. Ibid., pp. 110–11.
31. House, *The Intimate Papers*, vol. 3, p. 65; Fowler, p. 75.
32. Fowler, p. 113.
33. Voska and Irwin, *Spy and Counterspy*, pp. 212–14.
34. Maugham, *The Summing Up*, p. 147.
35. Morgan, *Maugham*, pp. 226–28; Voska and Irwin, pp. 214–20; Fowler, pp. 114–15. In "Mr. Harrington's Washing," his Ashenden story based on the Russian assignment, Maugharn has Voska and the other Czechs traveling with him from San Francisco but avoiding any contact en route. This apparently led Morgan (pp. 227–28) to the mistaken conclusion that in fact Maugham crossed the Pacific on the same ship as Voska and crossed Siberia on the same train.
36. Voska and Irwin, p. 229.
37. Ibid., pp. 226–28.
38. Morgan, p. 231; Fowler, pp. 116–17.
39. Maugham, p. 148.
40. Fowler, pp. 123–28.

Chapter Twenty-two: The Secret War in Mexico

1. Landau, *The Enemy Within*, pp. 72–73, 112; Katz, *The Secret War in Mexico*, pp. 411–12.
2. Landau, pp. 46–47, 72; Katz, p. 412.
3. Schellenberg, *Hitler's Secret Service*, pp. 39–40. Landau (p. 34) says Jahnke served in the U.S. Marine Corps.
4. Landau, pp. 34, 84, and passim.
5. Katz, p. 415.
6. Ibid., pp. 414–15; Landau, pp. 171–74.
7. Katz, pp. 431–32.
8. Ibid., pp. 425–27.

9. Ibid., p. 429.

10. Landau, pp. 34–35.

11. Ibid., pp. 117–18.

12. *Dictionary of American History,* vol. 5, s.v. "sabotage."

13. Dubofsky, *We Shall Be All,* pp. 350–51.

14. Ibid., pp. 358–62.

15. Ibid., p. 357.

16. Landau, pp. 114–15, 122.

17. Ibid., p. 117.

18. Ibid., pp. 114–15; Beesly, *Room 40,* pp. 196, 241–42; Katz, p. 625, n. 293. Long before his venture as an intelligence officer, Mason had distinguished himself as the author of the classic tale of cowardice and courage *The Four Feathers* (1902), and as the creator of the fictional French detective Inspector Gabriel Hanaud.

19. Barker, ed., *The History of Codes and Ciphers in the United States During World War I,* pp. 94–95.

20. Landau, pp. 122–23.

21. Ibid., p. 115.

22. Katz, pp. 433, 437–38.

23. Dorwart, *The Office of Naval Intelligence,* pp. 110, 115.

24. Katz, pp. 434, 624, n. 261.

25. Ibid., pp. 436–37.

Chapter Twenty-three: Counterspies and Vigilantes

1. Draper, *The Roots of American Communism,* p. 93.

2. Whitehead, *The FBI Story,* pp. 32, 35.

3. Voska and Irwin, *Spy and Counterspy,* p. 250.

4. Whitehead, p. 35.

5. Jensen, *The Price of Vigilance,* pp. 25, 131, 141. Jensen (p. 141) reports that DeMille also organized an APL aerial observation unit. It is difficult to imagine a role for such a unit in a counterespionage service.

6. Ibid., pp. 154–55.

7. Ibid., pp. 155–56.

8. Dubofsky, *We Shall Be All,* pp. 361–62.

9. Jensen, p. 135.

10. Van Deman, *The Final Memoranda,* p. 30.

11. Ibid., pp. 30–31.

12. Jensen, pp. 122–23.

13. Whitehead, p. 38.

14. Jensen, p. 155,

Chapter Twenty-four: A Gentleman's Profession

1. Powe, "The Emergence of the War Department Intelligence Agency," p. 93; Mashbir, *I Was an American Spy,* pp. 18–21.

2. Bidwell, *History of the Military Intelligence Division,* p. 183; Finnegan, "U.S. Army Counterintelligence in CONUS," p. 18.

3. Bidwell, pp. 190–91; Van Deman, *The Final Memoranda*, pp. 33–34.

4. Bidwell, pp. 190–91.

5. In his memoirs (p. 44) Van Deman recalled:

   Major Biddle had been an official in the New York Metropolitan Police and was selected to head the New York intelligence group on the recommendation of the Police Commissioner of New York City. A better choice could not have been made. Biddle did an excellent job and should be credited with a very large part of the work which was accomplished by the New York office during the war.

   Biddle's connection with the New York City Police Department must have been a minor one, however; no mention is made of it in his entry in *Who Was Who in America* (vol. 1) or in his *New York Times* obituary (February 19, 1923), both of which highlight his roles as manager of the multimillion-dollar estate of Vincent Astor and trustee of several banks and an insurance company. Astor himself served on active duty in the United States Navy during the war; his role as Franklin D. Roosevelt's unofficial intelligence chief lay some years ahead.

6. Read and Fisher, *Colonel Z*, pp. 126–127.

7. Bidwell, p. 193.

8. For a complete account of federal censorship in the First World War, see Mock, *Censorship 1917*.

9. Technical and political difficulties seem to have kept the Germans from constructing an effective transmitter in Mexico City during the war; see Katz, *The Secret War in Mexico*, pp. 416–22. The Mexican government apparently made its own transmitting facilities available to the German legation to some extent, however; see Bidwell, p. 200.

10. Bidwell, pp. 199–200.

11. Ibid., p. 199; Bamford, *The Puzzle Palace*, p. 203.

12. Mock, pp. 115–16.

13. Barker, ed., *The History of Codes and Ciphers in the United States During World War I*, p. 113.

14. Ibid., pp. 117–22.

15. Yardley, *The American Black Chamber*, chaps. 3–5. A secret-ink laboratory in Paris operated by the AEF's G-2 examined a total of 53,658 letters and found only 2 with invisible writing (Barker, p. 110).

16. Van Deman, p. 31.

17. Bidwell, pp. 203–4; Powe, p. 101.

18. Powe, p. 102; Bidwell, pp. 116–17.

19. Van Deman, pp. 54–55, 57, 64; Voska and Irwin, *Spy and Counterspy*, pp. 260–70.

20. Sims, *The Victory at Sea*, pp. 249, 252.

21. Trask, *Captains and Cabinets*, pp. 99–100. Trask's study of Anglo-American naval relations in 1917–18 contains an extensive account of Sims's peculiar situation and indispensable service during the period of American belligerency.

22. Beesly, *Room 40*, pp. 246–47, 269.

23. Ibid., p. 269. Sims may have disguised the source of specific intelligence reports to Washington as Beesly claims, but he did not conceal from the director of the Office of Naval Intelligence the fact that "at the British Admiralty they have a corps of grey-haired Oxford Professors, Egyptologists, Cuneiform Inscription Readers, etc., who break ciphers with great facility, and, I may add, have broken practically every cipher that they have been put up against." (Dorwart, *The Office of Naval Intelligence*, p. 123.)

24. Sims, pp. 253–54.

25. Ibid., p. 254.
26. Ibid.
27. Ibid.
28. Dorwart, p. 124.
29. Ibid., pp. 119–20.
30. Ibid., p. 119. While the MIS/MID seems not to have engaged in similar anti-Semitic acts, Van Deman reportedly held strong anti-Semitic views. See Campbell, "Major General Ralph H. Van Deman," p. 18.
31. Dorwart, pp. 130, 132–34, 136.
32. Ibid., p. 138.

CHAPTER TWENTY-FIVE: THE RUSSIAN MUDDLE

1. Graves, *American Siberian Adventure*, p. 354.
2. But historian and diplomat George F. Kennan has sorted out the facts and composed a coherent account in *The Decision to Intervene* and, more concisely, in chaps. 5–8 of *Russia and the West*.
3. Fowler, *British-American Relations*, p. 170.
4. Ibid., pp. 177, 179; Kennan, *The Decision to Intervene*, pp. 179–81. Kennan's detailed critique of the authenticity of the Sisson documents, published in the *Journal of Modern History* (June 1956, pp. 130–54), was reprinted as an appendix in *Agents of Deceit* by Paul W. Blackstock.
S. Fowler, pp. 167–168.
6. Corson and Crowley, *The New KGB*, pp. 47–49.
7. Graebner, ed., *An Uncertain Tradition*, pp. 116–17.
8. Kennan, *Russia and the West*, pp. 76–77.
9. Kennan, *The Decision to Intervene*, p. 271.
10. Halliday, *The Ignorant Armies*, p. 38.
11. Ibid., pp. 38–39.
12. Kennan, *The Decision to Intervene*, pp. 482–85.
13. Graves, p. 4.
14. Corson and Crowley, p. 52.
15. Kennan, *The Decision to Intervene*, pp. 467–68.
16. Corson and Crowley, pp. 51–63.
17. Halliday, p. 284.

CHAPTER TWENTY-SIX: THE INQUIRY—INTELLIGENCE FOR THE PRESIDENT

1. Steel, *Walter Lippmann and the American Century*, p. 127.
2. Gelfand, *The Inquiry*, p. 27.
3. The full picture of the secret treaties is detailed in Grenville, *The Major International Treaties*, chap. 1.
4. By one account, attributed to Isaiah Bowman, House later stated that Lippmann had been selected to represent the "extreme liberals" of the country, with whom the Wilson administration felt constrained to cooperate (Gelfand, p. 352).
5. Gelfand, pp. 99–100.

6. Ibid., p. 41.
7. Ibid., pp. 103–5.
8. Ibid., p. 108.
9. Ibid., pp. 108–10.
10. Ibid., pp. 126–30; Fowler, *British-American Relations*, p. 200.
11. Gelfand, p. 119.
12. Fowler, p. 200.
13. Gelfand, pp. 119–20.
14. Bidwell, *History of the Military Intelligence Division*, pp. 154–55, 174, n. 14.
15. Steel, pp. 141–43.
16. Gelfand, pp. 94–96.
17. Bidwell, p. 248.
18. Van Deman, The *Final Memoranda*, p. 190.
19. U.S. Department of State, *Papers Relating to Foreign Relations of the United States: The Paris Peace Conference*, vol. 11, pp. 509, 539, 553–54; Bidwell, pp. 248–49; Van Deman, pp. 82–83.
20. Gelfand, pp. 320–21.
21. Ibid., p. 332.
22. Ibid., p. 333.

CHAPTER TWENTY-SEVEN: THE RED MENACE

1. Draper, *The Roots of American Communism*, p. 139.
2. Cook, *The FBI Nobody Knows*, pp. 84–88.
3. Powers, *Secrecy and Power*, pp. 67–68.
4. Overstreet and Overstreet, *The FBI in Our Open Society*, p. 42.
5. Powers, pp. 111–12.
6. Draper, pp. 366–72.
7. Powers, pp. 96–104.
8. Jensen, *The Price of Vigilance*, p. 283.
9. Cook, p. 100.
10. Powers, p. 138; Draper, pp. 202–4.
11. Draper, pp. 366–372.
12. Bidwell, *History of the Military Intelligence Division*, pp. 278–79. The full text of the letter is reprinted in Donner, *The Age of Surveillance*, p. 291n.
13. Bidwell, pp. 277, 279.
14. Alpheus T. Mason, quoted in Overstreet and Overstreet, p. 47.
15. Powers, p. 147.
16. Ibid.
17. Dziak, *Chekisty*, p. 33.
18. Ibid., pp. 47–48. Gaucher, however, states that the Monarchist Association began as a genuine anti-Bolshevik underground but was penetrated and taken over by the Cheka (*Opposition in the USSR*, pp. 127–52).
19. Grant, "Deception on a Grand Scale," p. 53.
20. Ibid., pp. 61, 65–68; Dziak, pp. 49–50.
21. Grant, pp. 68–69, 72.
22. Draper, 422, n. 43; Finder, *Red Carpet*, pp. 12–13.
23. *Current Biography*, 1973, s.v. "Armand Hammer."

24. Carson and Crowley, *The New KGB*, pp. 280–82. For a full discussion of the Hammers' role in Amtorg, see Finder.

25. Within a year after its creation, the Hammers yielded their equity in Amtorg to the Soviet government in exchange for a highly lucrative concession to manufacture pencils in the Soviet Union. Presumably, they were not informed by Lenin or Dzerzhinsky of the company's clandestine functions. In his autobiography, *Hammer,* Armand Hammer makes no mention of his role in founding Amtorg.

26. Carson and Crowley, p. 496.

27. Weinstein, *Perjury,* pp. 61–62; Chambers, *Witness,* p. 32. Both White and Hiss denied under oath that they had worked for Soviet intelligence. Hiss was convicted of perjury in connection with his denial; White died before he could be prosecuted.

28. Lamphere and Schachtman, *The FBI-KGB War,* pp. 25–26, 164–65.

29. Bidwell, pp. 281, 290, n. 33.

30. Corson, *The Armies of Ignorance,* p. 104.

31. *New York Times,* September 7, 1971.

32. I have examined this subject at some length in chaps. 7 and 8 of *The Private Sector.*

33. Kennan, *Memoirs,* p. 84.

34. Ibid., pp. 33–34.

35. Troy, "'Ah, sweet intrigue!'" p. 2.

36. Kennan, p. 84.

37. Bohlen, *Witness to History,* p. 41.

38. Davies, *Mission to Moscow,* p. 550.

39. Kennan, p. 84.

40. Bohlen, p. 43; Kennan, p. 85.

41. Troy, p. 2.

42. Whitehead, *The FBI Story,* p. 159.

CHAPTER TWENTY-EIGHT: OTHER PEOPLE'S MAIL

1. Dorwart, *Conflict of Duty,* p. 39; Dorwart, *The Office of Naval Intelligence,* pp. 137–38.

2. Barker, ed., *The History of Codes and Ciphers in the United States During the Period Between the World Wars,* p. 46.

3. Ibid., pp. 48–49.

4. Kahn, *The Codebreakers,* p. 355. Writing in 1946, the War Department's official historian stated that the reason for the move to New York was unknown and speculates that it was done on Yardley's preference, which seems somewhat unlikely as the whole story (Barker, ed., *The History of Codes and Ciphers in the United States During the Period Between the World Wars,* pp. 49–51). Kahn's explanation is based on further research but fails to explain why so great a move was made instead of to, for example, Arlington, Virginia, or Baltimore, Maryland. Yardley may have hoped that the prospects for intercepting international diplomatic traffic would be better in New York, a major node in the transatlantic cable and radio-telegraph systems.

5. Kahn, pp. 355–56; Barker, ed., *The History of Codes and Ciphers in the United States During the Period Between the World Wars,* pp. 51–53. Barker (p. 53, n. 134) raises a question as to just when the bureau began using the commercial code company cover.

6. Barker, ed., *The History of Codes and Ciphers in the United States During the Period Between the World Wars,* pp. 74–82; Bamford, *The Puzzle Palace,* pp. 28–29.

7. Yardley, *The American Black Chamber,* p. 222.

8. Bailey, A *Diplomatic History of the American People*, p. 634.

9. Yardley, p. 208.

10. Ibid., p. 211.

11. Barker, ed., *The History of Codes and Ciphers in the United States During the Period Between the World Wars*, p. 116.

12. Yardley, p. 208.

13. Layton, *"And I Was There,"* p. 31. The title notwithstanding, Layton does not claim direct knowledge of the affair, and he cites no source for his information.

14. Farago, *The Broken Seal*, pp. 35–36. Farago cites interviews with Admiral Ellis Zacharias as his source. In his memoirs Zacharias confirms the use of women agents against the attaché but makes no mention of the break-ins (*Secret Missions*, pp. 4–5).

15. Farago, pp. 39–40. Layton (p. 31) gives the name as Haworth.

16. Layton, pp. 32–34; Farago, pp. 41–45.

17. Farago (pp. 45–46) identifies the cryptanalyst only as Miss Aggie, Layton (p. 33) gives her name as Agnes Driscoll, née Meyer.

18. *Encode* is to put into code. A code is a devised vocabulary in which words, numbers, or other symbols are assigned to represent the words of a message. *Encipher* is to put into cipher. A cipher is a method of substituting letters or other symbols for the letters comprising the words of a message.

19. Dorwart, *Conflict of Duty*, pp. 39–41.

20. Layton, pp. 31–32.

21. Dorwart, *Conflict of Duty*, p. 45.

22. Layton, p. 33.

23. Farago, pp. 47–48.

24. Zacharias, pp. 104–8; Farago, pp. 50–52.

25. Layton, p. 35.

26. Ibid.

27. Barker, ed., *The History of Codes and Ciphers in the United States During the Period Between the World Wars*, pp.74–79.

28. Jeffreys-Jones *American Espionage*, pp. 158–59.

29. Barker, ed., *The History of Codes and Ciphers in the United States During the Period Between the World Wars*, pp. 129–30.

30. The quotation is cherished by writers of popular intelligence history as a consummate example of dangerous naïveté on the part of a public person regarding the propriety of intelligence operations and is usually incorrectly attributed to Stimson as of the time he closed the Cipher Bureau in 1929.

31. Barker, ed., *The History of Codes and Ciphers in the United States During the Period Between the World Wars*, p. 133.

32. Lewin, *The American Magic*, p. 33; Layton, p. 41. Both authors cite Japanese files as evidence to support the charge.

33. Kahn, p. 363.

34. Ibid., pp. 362–63.

35. Ibid., pp. 364–67. The law, still on the books, is Section 952 of Title 18, United States Code.

36. Ibid., p. 376.

37. Barker, ed., *The History of Codes and Ciphers in the United States During World War I*, pp. 8–9; Clark, *The Man Who Broke Purple*, pp. 64–70.

38. Kahn, pp. 385, 802–14; Willoughby, *Rum War at Sea*, pp. 108, 113.

39. Bidwell, *History of the Military Intelligence Division*, pp. 330, 337, n. 21. Yardley's salary

had been seventy-five hundred dollars; the entire budget of the SIS was seventeen thousand dollars.

40. Bamford, pp. 49–51.
41. Barker, ed., *The History of Codes and Ciphers in the United States During the Period Between the World Wars,* p. 137.
42. Lewin, p. 34.
43. Kahn, pp. 415–19; Clark, pp. 94–97.
44. Farago, pp. 74–75.
45. Layton, p. 79. Layton denies the assertion made by Farago (pp. 78–80) and Zacharias (pp. 180–82) that an ONC analyst got a look at a Red machine during the intrusion into the attaché's apartment.
46. Layton, p. 80.
47. Bidwell, pp. 331–32; Bamford, pp. 52–53.
48. Units of the staff of the Chief of Naval Operations were given the OP prefix; thus the ONI was also designated OP-16, and the ONC was also OP-20. The Research Desk, which had recently become the Communications Security Section of the ONC, was designated the G Section; thus, OP-20-G. OP-20-GX was the subsection responsible for Radio Interception and Direction Finding; OP-20-GY was the Cryptanalysis Subsection; and OP-20-GZ did the Translation and Dissemination of the decoded and deciphered intercepts. See Kahn, p. 11.
49. Bamford, p. 54.
50. Farago, pp. 96–97.
51. Kahn (pp. 21–22) implies that Clark was an employee of OP-20-G. It is not clear whether this is an error or that Clark had transferred to the navy after working for the SIS.
52. Layton, pp. 80–81; Kahn, pp. 21–22; Farago, pp. 98–99.
53. Arcangelis, *Electronic Warfare,* p. 19.

CHAPTER TWENTY-NINE: THE SECRET WAR WITH THE AXIS

1. Dorwart, *Conflict of Duty,* p. 164; Dorwart, "The Roosevelt-Astor Espionage Ring," p. 309.
2. Dorwart, "The Roosevelt-Astor Espionage Ring," p. 310.
3. Cave Brown, "C," pp. 123–124. Cave Brown does not offer a source for Wiseman's membership in the group, and Dorwart ("The Roosevelt-Astor Espionage Ring") makes no mention of him, although he names thirty-two members, citing the Kermit Roosevelt Papers as his source. But whether or not Sir William was a regular member of the group, it is likely that in his role as Wall Street investment banker, he was well acquainted with many, if not most, of the ROOM's members.
4. Jeffes's successors were Captain Henry Maine, Commander H. B. Taylor (Royal Navy), Captain Sir James Paget (Royal Navy), and William Stephenson.
5. Dorwart, "The Roosevelt-Astor Espionage Ring," pp. 310–14.
6. Ibid., pp. 314–15.
7. Ibid. Spy-buff Roosevelt had at least one other private-intelligence service; one was run by foreign-service veteran John Franklin Carter, who wrote a syndicated newspaper column under the pseudonym Jay Franklin and published a number of spy novels under the nom de plume Diplomat. FDR eventually used Carter to watch Astor. See Dorwart, "The Roosevelt-Astor Espionage Ring," p. 321, and Troy, *Donovan and the CIA,* p. 142.

8. Andrew, *Her Majesty's Secret Service*, p. 240; West, *MI6*, pp. 65–66, 120–21; Dorwart, "The Roosevelt-Astor Espionage Ring," p. 316.

9. Dorwart, "The Roosevelt-Astor Espionage Ring," p. 315.

10. Ibid., pp. 316–17. Dorwart cites only letters from Astor to Roosevelt regarding this affair, which was probably not officially documented elsewhere on the American side.

11. Hyde, *Room 3603*, pp. 5–14.

12. Ibid., pp. 2–3; Cave Brown, "C," pp. 262–63.

13. Troy, pp. 34–36; Hyde, pp. 24–27.

14. Sebold's story is in Farago, *The Game of the Foxes*, pp. 322–29, 457–62, and in Kahn, *Hitler's Spies*, pp. 331–33. A longer, journalistic account can be found in the near-contemporary *Passport to Treason* by Alan Hynd. Sebold's story was made into the 1945 docudrama motion picture *The House on 92nd Street*.

15. Riess, *Total Espionage*, p. 288.

16. Kahn, p. 98; Artucio, *The Nazi Underground in South America*, pp. 24–25.

17. Riess, pp. 242–45.

18. Artucio, pp. 191–92, 206–7, 264–67.

19. Rout and Bratzel, *The Shadow War*, pp. 7–15.

20. Ibid., pp. 58–63.

21. Artucio, pp. 266–67.

22. *Current Biography*, 1945, s.v. "Spruille Braden."

23. Braden, *Diplomats and Demagogues*, pp. 229–42; Rout and Bratzel, p. 28. See also Herring, *A History of Latin America*, p. 515.

24. Troy, p. 102. The agency was originally known as the Office for Coordination of Commercial and Cultutal Relations between the American Republics.

25. Ibid., p. 17.

26. Rout and Bratzel, pp. 35, 72–73. Foxworth and another FBI-SIS agent, H. D. Haberfield, were killed on January 21, 1943, in the crash of a United States Army charter transport in Dutch Guiana (Surinam). See the *New York Times*, January 22, 1943, p. 1.

27. Rout and Bratzel, pp. 53–54, 72–73.

28. Ibid., pp. 74–75; Farago, pp. 457–62.

29. Troy, pp. 34–36.

30. Stafford, *Camp X*.

31. Hyde, pp. 135–47. Rout and Bratzel (pp. 112–13) offer a persuasive refutation of the story of the BSC's role in the LATI affair, however.

32. Hyde, pp. 74–79.

33. Ibid., p. 150.

34. Hyde, pp. 148–50; Bryce, *You Only Live Once;* Troy, "Ex-British Agent Says FDR's Nazi Map Faked," pp. 1–3.

35. Stephenson, "The Story of OSS," p. 249; Troy, pp. 29–36.

36. Cave Brown, "C," p. 124. See also Cave Brown's account (p. 264) of the Stephenson-FDR meeting.

37. H. C. Allen, *Great Britain and the United States*, p. 787.

38. Troy, p. 29.

39. Ibid., p. 36.

40. Troy, p. 36.

41. Ibid., pp. 53–54,

42. Ibid., p. 10; Dunlop, *Donovan*, p. 280.

43. Dorwart, "The Roosevelt-Astor Espionage Ring," pp. 317–20; Troy, pp. 47–49.

44. Troy, p. 417.

45. Ibid., pp. 47, 56, 417.
46. Ibid., p. 42.
47. Hyde, p. 152; Troy, pp. 59–61; Stephenson, p. 252.
48. Troy, p. 59; Cave Brown, *The Last Hero*, pp. 163–64; Dunlop, p. 286.
49. Troy, pp. 59, 419–21.
50. Ibid., p. 423.
51. Ibid., p. 77.
52. Ibid., pp. 85, 87, 105.
53. Ibid., pp. 78–80.
54. Ibid.
55. Roosevelt, *War Report of the OSS*, pp. 48–51.
56. Troy, pp. 77, 80.

CHAPTER THIRTY: ANATOMY OF INFAMY

1. Dorwart, *Conflict of Duty*, p. 179.
2. Prange, *At Dawn We Slept*, p. 31. See also Grew, *Ten Years in Japan*, p. 368.
3. Layton, "*And I Was There*," p. 74.
4. Prange, *At Dawn We Slept*, p. 33.
5. Layton, pp. 70–71.
6. Muller, "The Inside Story of Pearl Harbor," pp. 13–17; Roscoe, *On the Seas and in the Skies*, p. 245; King and Whitehall, *Fleet Admiral King*, pp. 228–29.
7. Porter, *Yamamoto*, chaps. 1–5; *Current Biography*, 1942, s.v. "Isoroku Yamamoto."
8. Dull, *A Battle History of the Imperial Japanese Navy*, pp. 6–7.
9. Ibid., p. 9.
10. Prange, *Pearl Harbor*, p. 401.
11. Prange, *At Dawn We Slept*, pp. 70–77.
12. Clark, *The Man Who Broke Purple*, pp. 155–56. Clark cites no sources in his book, nor does he make clear whether Strong made this disclosure with high-level authorization or on his own authority.
13. Ibid., pp. 156–57; Richelson and Ball, *The Ties That Bind*, pp. 1, 137; Lewin, *The American Magic*, pp. 45–46.
14. Farago, *The Broken Seal*, pp. 102–05.
15. Ibid., p. 100; Wohlstetter, *Pearl Harbor*, pp. 75, n. 5, 170.
16. Kahn, *The Codebreakers*, pp. 24–25; Farago, pp. 101–2.
17. Kahn, p. 25; Wohlstetter, p. 181.
18. Kahn, p. 27; Wohlstetter, pp. 178–79. The "fairly reliable source" was German intelligence (Wohlstetter, p. 178).
19. The FBI files contained an intelligence questionnaire prepared by the Abwehr for one of their agents, Dusko Popov, about one third of which contained detailed questions about Hawaii (Prange, *Pearl Harbor*, pp. 660–62). Popov, who was working as a double agent for British intelligence and had the British code name Tricycle, turned over the document to the FBI. There is, however, apparently no substance to Popov's recent claim that he had warned Hoover of Japanese plans to attack Pearl Harbor. See Prange, *Pearl Harbor*, pp. 306–10, and Troy, "'Tricycle' Never Mentioned Pearl Harbor Attack," pp. 1–2.
20. Prange, *At Dawn We Slept*, pp. 158–59.
21. Ibid., pp. 321, 324.

22. Farago, pp. 219–220; Layton, p. 161; Prange, *At Dawn We Slept*, pp. 223–31.
23. Prange, *Pearl Harbor*, p. 656.
24. Prange, *At Dawn We Slept*, pp. 249–51; Farago, pp. 224–26.
25. Prange, *At Dawn We Slept*, p. 355.
26. Ibid., p. 81.
27. Wohlstetter, pp. 187–88.
28. Prange, *At Dawn We Slept*, p. 358.
29. Wohlstetter, pp. 189–90.
30. Ibid., p. 51.
31. Ibid., p. 200.
32. Ibid., p. 201.
33. Ibid., p. 45.
34. Prange, *At Dawn We Slept*, pp. 313–16.
35. Ibid., p. 419.
36. Theobald, *The Final Secret of Pearl Harbor*, p. 45.
37. Prange, *At Dawn We Slept*, p. 357.
38. Ibid., p. 443.
39. Layton, p. 245.
40. Ibid., pp. 229–30.
41. Prange, *At Dawn We Slept*, pp. 443–44.
42. Ibid., p. 485.
43. Ibid., p. 486.
44. Clark, p. 170.
45. Wohlstetter, p. 44.
46. Prange, *Pearl Harbor*, pp. 651–52.
47. Wohlstetter, pp. 213–14, 382–83.
48. Ibid., p. 387.
49. Ibid., pp. 393, 397.
50. Prange, *At Dawn We Slept*, p. 527.
51. Puleston, *The Armed Forces of the Pacific*, pp. 116–17.

CHAPTER THIRTY-ONE: THE EYES AND EARS OF THE ALLIES

1. Holmes, *Double-Edged Secrets*, pp. 53–54.
2. Kahn, *The Codebreakers*, pp. 562–63.
3. Rochefort, "As 1 Recall . . . Learning Cryptanalysis," pp. 54–55.
4. Kahn, pp. 563–64, 565–66.
5. Holmes, pp. 70–73; Layton, *"And I Was There,"* pp. 389–90.
6. Dull, *A Battle History of the Imperial Japanese Navy*, pp. 142–44; Kahn, pp. 566–67; Layton, p. 407.
7. Kahn, p. 567.
8. Layton, pp. 412–13; Holmes, p. 89.
9. Holmes, pp. 90–91; Kahn, p. 569.
10. Holmes, p. 94; Kahn, p. 570.
11. Holmes, pp. 60–61; Dull, p. 141.
12. Dull, p. 141.
13. King and Whitehill, *Fleet Admiral King*, p. 380.
14. More accurately, the SIS and the Special Branch were under direction of the Military

Intelligence *Service*, which was created in a reorganization of the War Department's General Staff in 1942. In an attempt to separate the actual substantive intelligence work from the related policy and planning activities of the General Staff, the MIS was created. Thus the assistant chief of staff for intelligence was to wear two hats: chief of the MID, which was to become a purely policy and planning unit, and chief of the MIS, which was to produce army departmental intelligence. Major General George V. Strong, the MID-MIS chief, considered this arrangement unworkable, however, and therefore it existed mostly in theory. Thus, in the present chapter, reference is made only to the MID, even where it would be technically more correct to say the MIS.

15. Garlinski, *The Enigma War,* pp. 12, 31–38.
16. Lewin expresses some skepticism regarding the story of the walk-in agent and questions the importance of the information supplied by the French to the Polish attack on the Enigma (*Ultra Goes to War,* pp. 36–37).
17. Garlinski, pp. 17–31; Lewin, *Ultra Goes to War,* p. 38.
18. Garlinski, pp. 42–43; Lewin, *Ultra Goes to War,* pp. 39–40; Hodges, *Alan Turing,* pp. 170–75.
19. Hodges, pp. 176–185; Garlinski, p. 71.
20. Lewin, *Ultra Goes to War,* pp. 204–7.
21. Bamford, *The Puzzle Palace,* pp. 394–96.
22. While most accounts state unequivocally that the British did not reciprocate with their Enigma know-how at this time, Lewin, citing "private information," says the British did let the Americans into the Enigma secret at the time but insisted on the tightest controls over the dissemination of the information within the United States government (*The American Magic,* pp. 46, 294, n. 19).
23. Richelson and Ball, *The Ties That Bind,* pp. 137–38.
24. Bamford, pp. 397–98; Richelson and Ball, pp. 138–39.
25. Ambrose, *Ike's Spies,* pp. 39–40.
26. Ibid., pp. 62–64; Lewin, *Ultra Goes to War,* pp. 279–80. 312–18.
27. Lewin, *Ultra Goes to War,* p. 279.
28. Ibid., pp. 207–20; Hodges, pp. 218–19, 222–24, 234–35, 242–44, 259–63. The use of Ultra material by British Naval Intelligence is authoritatively recounted at length by Patrick Beesly, a former senior naval intelligence officer, in his book *Very Special Intelligence.* See also Hughes and Costello, *The Battle of the Atlantic.*
29. Kahn, pp. 503–4.
30. Holmes, pp. 126–129.
31. Blair, *Silent Victory,* pp. 877–78.
32. Lewin, *The American Magic,* p. 10.
33. Ibid., pp. 237–38.
34. Layton, pp. 474–76; Holmes, pp. 135–36; Kahn, pp. 595–601.
35. Layton, p. 476.
36. In his memoirs Layton adds a new detail to the story of the Yamamoto interception. The telltale announcement of the admiral's itinerary was transmitted not only in JN25 but also inadvertently in an army cipher the Imperial Navy regarded as insecure (pp. 474, 476). The Japanese may therefore have attributed the interception to the use of the army cryptosystem.
37. Dorwart, *The Office of Naval Intelligence,* p. 26.
38. Finnegan, *Military Intelligence,* p. 10.
39. Infield, *Unarmed and Unafraid,* pp. 31–42.
40. Goddard, *Overview,* pp. 147–49, 241–45, 308.
41. Babington-Smith, *Air Spy,* pp. 14–28 and passim; Overy, *The Air War,* p. 200.

42. Babington-Smith, p. 71.
43. Ibid., p. 79.
44. Ibid., p. 69.
45. Brugioni, "Naval Photo Intel in WWII," p. 46.
46. Babington-Smith, pp. 147–52.
47. Ibid., pp. 155–56, 162.
48. Ibid., pp. 176–202; Infield, pp. 84–89.
49. Brugioni, p. 51.
50. Babington-Smith, pp. 6, 259.
51. Churchill, *Their Finest Hour,* p. 381.

CHAPTER THIRTY-TWO: CLOAK-AND-DAGGER: THE OSS

1. Troy, "CIA Releases First OSS Papers in 38 Years," p. 1.
2. Thomas F. Troy's *Donovan and the CIA* is the CIA's official account of the roots of that agency in the OSS and contains a comprehensive institutional history of the establishment of both agencies. Kermit Roosevelt's *War Report of the OSS* is the official history of the agency, written immediately after the war.

    R. Harris Smith's *OSS,* published in 1972, is based on Interviews with scores of OSS veterans, as well as a large body of published material, but it lacks the benefit of more recently disclosed information. In writing his 1982 biography of Donovan, *The Last Hero,* Anthony Cave Brown had access to Donovan's private collection of wartime papers, including a considerable amount of official OSS material not previously disclosed. The academic historian Bradley F. Smith combed the archives of the United States and Britain in researching his scholarly and controversial *The Shadow Warriors.*

    Richard Dunlop's *Donovan* is an account of the man and the agency by an OSS veteran. The same author wrote *Behind Japanese Lines,* based on his experiences with the OSS in Burma. *The Secret War Against Hitler* by William Casey is an account of OSS operations in Europe by the former chief of OSS-Europe, later director of central intelligence. The same subject is covered well and at somewhat greater length and detail in *Piercing the Reich* by Joseph E. Persico, who based his account on interviews with Casey and many other OSS veterans, as well as on published materials. Allen Dulles's *Secret Surrender* is a memoir of his OSS service in Switzerland, especially the negotiations leading to the surrender of German forces in Italy. The same subject is covered by the historians Bradley F. Smith and Elena Agarossi in *Operation Sunrise,* based on archival and published materials. *Autobiography of a Spy* by Mary Bancroft is the memoir of an OSS agent and wartime associate of Dulles in Switzerland.

    Sub Rosa by Stewart Alsop and Thomas Braden is a short, readable account of the agency written in 1946 by two veterans. *The OSS in World War II* by Edward Hymoff is another popular account by an OSS veteran. Corey Ford, author of *Donovan of OSS,* was a friend of the subject and served as a liaison officer between the OSS and the United States Army Air Force.

    Of Spies and Stratagems by Stanley Lovell is the popular memoir of the OSS officer who directed the development of special weapons and equipment. *The OSS and I* by William J. Morgan is a memoir of the author's service in the OSS, first as a psychologist and later as a partisan fighting behind enemy lines in France. Carleton S. Coon's *North*

Africa Story is the distinguished anthropologist's memoir of wartime service in the OSS. Peter Tompkins's *Spy in Rome* and Donald Downes's *Scarlet Thread* are two more OSS memoirs. *Wartime Washington: The Secret OSS Journal of James Grafton Rogers* is the diary of a senior OSS official, edited by the intelligence historian Thomas F. Troy.

The CIA contains much material on the OSS, both history and memoir, by Ray S. Cline, a historian and OSS (and CIA) veteran. "The Story of OSS" by William Stephenson is a short memoir of the birth of the OSS by its British intelligence midwife and was published as an appendix to *Secret Intelligence Agent* by H. Montgomery Hyde. Hyde deals with the same subject at length in that book and in *Room 3603*.

William Colby and Peter Forbath's *Honorable Men*, Edmond Taylor's *Awakening from History*, William L. Langer's *In and Out of the Ivory Tower*, and Aaron Bank's *From OSS to Green Berets* all contain important memoirs of the OSS by veterans of the agency.

3. Troy, *Donovan and the CIA*, pp. 129–30.
4. Bradley F. Smith, pp. 116, 119.
5. Cave Brown, pp. 219–22.
6. Troy, *Donovan and the CIA*, pp. 133–53, 427.
7. Dunlop, *Behind Japanese Lines*, p. 84.
8. Taylor, *Awakening From History*, pp. 303–9.
9. Roosevelt, p. 215.
10. The story of Detachment 101 has been recorded at length by four of its members: Dunlop, *Behind Japanese Lines;* Peers and Brelis, *Behind the Burma Road;* and Hilsman, *American Guerrilla.*
11. Roosevelt, pp. 225–28; K. Harris Smith, pp. 145–46.
12. Dorwart, *Conflict of Duty*, p. 123; Cave Brown, p. 175.
13. Ibid., pp. 176–77; Troy, *Donovan and the CIA*, pp. 106–7.
14. Ibid., pp. 140–42.
15. British distrust of Phillips was asserted by his successor, David K. E. Bruce, to Thomas Troy in 1972 (Troy, *Donovan and the CIA*, pp. 107, 497, n. 96). Phillips's subsequent wartime intelligence career is obscure, but his entry in *Who Was Who in America*, vol. 3, lists him as working for the OSS until 1943, long after he had been replaced as chief of secret intelligence,
16. Bruce's membership in the ROOM/CLUB is in Dorwart, "The Roosevelt-Astor Espionage Ring," p. 309.
17. Dulles's role in de-Nazification of the airline is mentioned in his entry in *Current Biography*, 1949.
18. Cave Brown, p. 275.
19. Troy, *Donovan and the CIA*, pp. 162–63; Bradley F. Smith, pp. 171–72; Stephenson, pp. 256–57.
20. Cave Brown, pp. 182–83.
21. Cave Brown (p. 184) writes that Pearson was chosen because he had been a Rhodes scholar at Oxford and while there had become well-known to several senior British intelligence officers. Winks, however, suggests that Pearson may have been recommended, for somewhat obscure reasons, by OSS officer Donald Downes, a Yale graduate, or Charles Beecher Hogan, a member of the Yale faculty (*Cloak and Gown*, pp. 247–48, 257).
22. Cave Brown, p. 185.
23. Roosevelt, pp. 190–91.
24. K. Harris Smith, p. 12; Winks, p. 174.

25. Downes, pp. 65–67.
26. Ibid., pp. 76–77; Roosevelt, pp. 185–86.
27. R. Harris Smith, p. 7.
28. Roosevelt, pp. 76, 241. The OSS Farm should not be confused with a CIA training facility of the same nickname but in a different location.
29. Ford, pp. 141–42.
30. Winks, pp. 175–76; Downes, pp. 81–82.
31. Roosevelt, pp. 157–59.
32. Ibid., pp. 204-5.
33. Ibid., pp. 143–53.
34. Ibid., pp. 66, 200.
35. Ibid., pp. 66, 198.
36. Ibid., p. 199.
37. Ibid., p. 57.
38. Bradley F. Smith, pp. 172–73.
39. Ibid., pp. 175, 372.
40. Ibid., p. 382.
41. Donovan, who returned to private practice after the war, defended Soviet secret intelligence officer Rudolf Abel in 1957 and negotiated the trade of Abel for U-2 pilot Francis Gary Powers in 1962 (see Donovan, *Strangers on a Bridge*). He performed a similar service later that same year in arranging the release of the Cuban freedom fighters captured in the CIA-sponsored Bay of Pigs invasion (see Hayrtes Johnson et al., *The Bay of Pigs*).
42. Ford, p. 134.
43. Cave Brown, p. 173,
44. Casey, p. 17.
45. Ibid., pp. 18–20; Bradley F. Smith, pp. 156–57.
46. Ibid., p. 222.
47. Casey, pp. 39–40.
48. Ibid., p. 39.
49. Bradley F. Smith, pp. 223–24.
50. Persico, pp. 69–70, Since his expulsion from the United States in 1915, Papen had served as German chancellor under Hindenburg and vice-chancellor under Hitler. In 1939 he was made ambassador to Turkey. See Papen, *Memoirs*.
51. Bradley F. Smith, pp. 225–26.
52. Alsop and Braden, p. 227.
53. Ibid., p. 229.
54. Bradley F. Smith, p. 291.
55. Rosiuke, *The CIA'S Secret Operations*, pp. xxiv–xxv.
56. Ibid., pp. 293–94.
57. Alsop and Braden, p. 228.
58. Ibid.
59. Kent, *Strategic Intelligence for American World Policy*, p. 78.
60. Ibid., p. viii.
61. Ibid., p. 74.
62. Alsop and Braden, p. 230.
63. Cave Brown, pp. 15–16.
64. Troy, *Donovan and the CIA*, p. 83.

CHAPTER THIRTY-THREE: FROM OSS TO CENTRAL INTELLIGENCE

1. Troy, *Donovan and the CIA*, p. 218.
2. Ibid., pp. 220–21, 445–47.
3. Ibid., pp. 255–56.
4. Ibid., p. vi.
5. Ibid., pp. 280–81.
6. Braden, "The Birth of the CIA," p. 7; Hymoff, *The OSS in World War II*, pp. 341–42; Bradley F. Smith, *The Shadow Warriors*, pp. 405-6.
7. Hymoff (pp. 341, 342n) states that many of the postwar accounts of the OSS were the result of the personal revelations of former members of the Reports Declassification Section who "managed to leave the OSS with these gems"—files they judged "too good to let go"—as part of Donovan's public relations campaign. In support of this, he lists (p. 389) many magazine articles written by OSS veterans, some of which appeared as late as 1948, three years after the OSS was dissolved.
8. For example, Cave Brown, *The Last Hero*, pp. 790–91.
9. Troy, pp. 303, 309–12.
10. The full text of the letter is in Troy, p. 463.
11. Troy, p. 309.
12. Truman, *Memoirs*, p. 56.
13. Troy, pp. 339–47, 464–65.
14. Ibid., p. 347; Braden, p. 10.
15. Troy, pp. 355–56.
16. Ibid., p. 363; Braden, p. 10.
17. Troy, pp. 362–65.
18. Ibid., pp. 371–75.
19. Rout and Bratzel, *The Shadow War*, pp. 454–56; Troy, p. 365.
20. Kirkpatrick, *The Real CIA*, p. 149. Constantinides identifies the agency Kirkpatrick describes as the Grombach Organization (*Intelligence and Espionage*, pp. 185, 455).
21. Felix, *A Short Course in the Secret War.* See also my *Encyclopedia of American Intelligence and Espionage*, s.v. "John V. Grombach" and "Grombach Organization" (pp. 211–12). For much additional information on the Grombach Organization published since this chapter was written, see Simpson, *Blowback.*
22. Troy, pp. 363–65; U.S. Congress, *Hearing*, p. 49.
23. Ibid., pp. 54–55.
24. Troy, pp. 392, 395, 552, n. 62.
25. Ibid., pp. 318, 363, 538, n. 63.
26. Kirkpatrick (pp. 149–53) says the Grombach Organization (which he does not refer to by name) worked as a contractor to the CIA from about 1950 but proved unsatisfactory, and the contract was terminated. The organization next offered its services to Senator Joseph McCarthy, then at the height of his Red-hunting career, and claimed to the senator that several CIA officers were security risks. What subsequently became of the organization is unclear, but it may have been connected with Industrial Reports, a firm Grombach headed from 1942 until about 1980; he described the latter as providing consulting services in the fields of "security and industrial intelligence" (see *Who's Who in America* and *Who's Who in Consulting*, s.v. "Grombach").
27. The portion of the act pertaining to the creation of the CIA is quoted in full in Troy, pp. 471–72.

28. Cline, *The CIA*, pp. 113, 127, 172.
29. Cave Brown, pp. 677–79.
30. Forrestal, *Diaries*, p. 387.
31. Ibid., p. 395.
32. Donovan, "Stop Russia's Subversive War," pp. 27–30.
33. Karalekas, *History of the Central Intelligence Agency*, pp. 38–40.
34. Kennan, *Memoirs*, pp. 330–31; Corson, *The Armies of Ignorance*, p. 295.
35. U.S. Department of State, *Foreign Relations of the United States*, pp. 848–49. Kennan's words are quoted from his telegram to the State Department sent while he was traveling in the Pacific.
36. Karalekas, p. 40.
37. Powers, *The Man Who Kept the Secrets*, p. 30.
38. Braden, p. 13; Corson, pp. 295–98.
39. Ibid., pp. 298–300.
40. Ibid., p. 298.
41. Cline, pp. 123–24,
42. *Current Biography*, s.v, "Valerian A. Zorin."
43. Forrestal, p. 383.
44. Karalekas, p. 41.
45. Kennan's article is reprinted in Armstrong, ed., *Fifty Years of Foreign Affairs*, pp. 189–205.
46. Kennan details the genesis of the paper in his *Memoirs*, pp. 354–57.
47. Ibid., p. 358.
48. Karalekas, pp. 41–43.
49. Ibid., p. 42.
50. Ibid., p. 43.
51. *New York Times*, June 26, 1950, p. 3.
52. Paige, *The Korean Decision*, pp. 155–56.
53. Corson, p. 318.
54. Ibid., p. 317.
55. Kirkpatrick, p. 87.
56. Montague, *General Walter Bedell Smith*, vol. 2, pp. 1–2, 7.

CHAPTER THIRTY-FOUR: THE CIA TRANSFORMED

1. Kirkpatrick, *The Real CIA*, pp. 88–89; Karalekas, *History of the Central Intelligence Agency*, pp. 28–29; Montague, *General Walter Bedell Smith*, vol. 1, pp. 16–21; vol. 2, pp. 9–11.
2. Kirkpatrick, pp. 101–2; Cline, *The CIA*, pp. 131–32; Prados, *The Soviet Estimate*, pp. 10–11. For an extended account of the estimates problem and Smith's solution, see Montague, vol. 3.
3. Karalekas, p, 30; Ranelagh, *The Agency*, pp. 191–93.
4. Karalekas, pp. 30–31; Cline, pp. 142–45.
5. Ransom, *The Intelligence Establishment*, pp. 149–50; Karalekas, pp. 31–32; Cline, pp. 157–61; Prados, *The Soviet Estimate*, pp. 12–13.
6. Karalekas, pp. 43, 48.
7. Corson, *The Armies of Ignorance*, pp. 313–15; Karalekas, pp. 44–46.
8. Ibid., pp. 48–50; Montague, vol. 4, pp. 60–68; Rositzke, *The CIA's Secret Operations*, pp. 149–50.
9. Montague, vol. 2, pp. 56–58; Karalekas, p. 47, n. 26; Cline, pp. 134–35.
10. Karalekas, p. 47.

11. Phillips, *The Truman Presidency*, p. 306.
12. Infield, *Unarmed and Unafraid*, p. 153.
13. Karalekas, p. 29.
14. Leary, *Perilous Missions*, pp. 124–25.
15. Ibid., pp. 125–26.
16. Ibid., pp. 137–42; Rositzke. p. 173.
17. Leary, pp. 129–32, 195–96.
18. Karalekas, pp. 49–50.
19. Prados, *Presidents' Secret Wars*, p. 34,
20. Ibid., pp. 34–35; Meyer, *Facing Reality*, pp. 110–13.
21. *Current Biography*, 1950, s.v. "Dewitt Clinton Poole."
22. Ibid.

CHAPTER THIRTY-FIVE: HIGH TECH AND DIRTY TRICKS

1. Hohne and Zolling, *The General Was a Spy*, chapter 4; Gehlen, *The Service*, pp. 111–16, 141–45; Powers, *The Man Who Kept the Secrets*, p. 24.
2. Prados, *Presidents' Secret Wars*, pp. 40–42.
3. Ibid., pp. 171–73; Prados, *Presidents' Secret Wars*, pp. 45–52; Bethell, *Betrayed*, passim.
4. Currey, *Edward Lansdale*, pp. 67–77; Smith, *Portrait of a Cold Warrior*, p. 103.
5. Lansdale, *In the Midst of Wars*, pp. 24–30; chap. 3.
6. Smith, pp. 107–8.
7. Roosevelt, *Countercoup*, pp, 107–8, 114–15.
8. Ibid., pp. 1–18.
9. Roosevelt's *Countercoup* is a lengthy, firsthand account of Operation Ajax. Other useful accounts with some additional details may be found in Prados, *Presidents' Secret Wars*, pp. 92–98; Ranelagh, *The Agency*, pp. 260–64; and Treverton, *Covert Action*, passim.
10. Herring, *A History of Latin America*, p. 456; Immerman, *The CIA in Guatemala*, pp. 68–82.
11. Schlesinger and Kinzer, *Bitter Fruit*, p. 102.
12. Immerman, pp. 118–22; Schlesinger and Kinzer, p. 102,
13. Immerman, pp. 133–55; Schlesinger and Kinzer, pp. 108–17.
14. Ibid., pp. 110–14; 147–54; Immerman, pp. 155–60.
15. Leary, ed., *The Central Intelligence Agency*, p. 144.
16. Ranelagh, p. 287.
17. Rositzke, *The CIA's Secret Operations*, pp. 18–22.
18. Ibid., pp. 18–38.
19. Rostow, *Open Skies*, pp. 9, 12, 189–93; Prados, *The Soviet Estimate*, pp. 29–30.
20. Burrows, *Deep Black*, pp. 63–64, 67.
21. Prados, The *Soviet Estimate*, p. 57.
22. Beschloss, *Mayday*, p. 78; Burrows, pp. 66–67; Prados, *The Soviet Estimate*, p. 30, 57.
23. Prados, *The Soviet Estimate*, p. 30; Beschloss, pp. 79–80, 82–83; Burrows, pp. 69–75.
24. Burrows, p. 73.
25. Gunston, *An Illustrated Guide*, p. 36. Burrows (p. 77) states that the craft inadvertently became airborne while taxiing rapidly on July 29. Beschloss (p. 105) says the first intentional flight was made on August 8.
26. Gunston, p. 36.
27. Burrows, pp. 75–76.
28. Ibid., p. 80.

29. Prados, *The Soviet Estimate*, pp. 33–34; Beschloss, pp. 125, 133.
30. Ibid., pp. 146–47.
31. Burrows, p. 80.
32. Ibid., pp. 80–81.
33. Ibid., pp. 104–5.
34. Cline, *The CIA*, p. 185.
35. The full text of the speech can be found in Khrushchev, *Khrushchev Remembers*, pp. 559–618.
36. Cline, pp. 185–86.
37. Ranelagh, pp. 287–88, 308.
38. Carson, *The Armies of Ignorance*, p. 369.
39. Ranelagh, pp. 305–6.
40. Eisenhower, *Waging Peace*, p. 88.
41. Prados, *Presidents' Secret Wars*, p. 125.
42. Colby and Forbath, *Honorable Men*, p. 135.
43. Smith, p. 205.
44. Prados, *Presidents' Secret Wars*, pp. 143–44.
45. Powers, pp. 76–77.

CHAPTER THIRTY-SIX: FAILURE AND VINDICATION

1. Currey, *Edward Lansdale*, pp. 136–37, 142.
2. Ibid., pp. 151–55.
3. Ibid., pp. 182–85; Lansdale, *In the Midst of Wars*, pp. 342–45.
4. Szulc and Meyer, *The Cuban Invasion*, p. 24; Thomas, *The Cuban Revolution*, pp. 433, 544.
5. Agular, ed., *Operation Zapata*, pp. 3–5.
6. Ibid., p. 6.
7. Thomas Powers identifies the task force manager as Jacob Esterline (*The Man Who Kept the Secrets*, p. 106). Referring to Esterline pseudonymously as Jacob Engler, Peter Wyden gives his CIA background and refers to his "working with guerrillas for the OSS in the Far East . . ." (*Bay of Pigs*, pp. 19–20). Jacob D. Esterline is listed in the roster of Detachment 101 veterans published as an appendix to Peers and Brelis, *Behind the Burma Road*.
8. Wyden, pp. 19–20.
9. Ibid., pp. 35–38; Wise and Ross, *The Invisible Government*, pp. 23–27; Johnson et al., *The Bay of Pigs*, pp. 44–45.
10. Wyden, pp. 53–54.
11. Phillips, *The Night Watch*, pp. 90–91, 96–97.
12. Agular, p. 5; Wyden, pp. 55–56; Hunt, *Give Us This Day*, pp. 75–76.
13. Agular, pp. 5–6.
14. Ibid., p. 20.
15. Wyden, pp. 70–71; Agular, pp. 15–16.
16. Phillips, pp. 99–100; Arthur M. Schlesinger, Jr., *A Thousand Days*, p. 233.
17. Ibid., pp. 252–57.
18. Agular, pp. 9–10.
19. Wyden, p, 46.
20. Schlesinger, pp. 257–58.
21. Agular, pp. 11–13; Wyden, pp. 100–01; Schlesinger, p. 243.

22. Wyden, pp. 101–2.
23. Johnson et al., p. 84; Agular, pp. 12–13, 16–17.
24. Wyden, pp. 159–60. (Esterline is called Engler.)
25. Johnson et al., pp. 81–82, 84–85; Kirkpatrick, *The Real CIA*, p. 196.
26. Wyden, pp. 27–28; Agular, pp. 69–70.
27. Agular, p. 17.
28. Ibid., p. 18; Wyden, pp. 175–76.
29. Schlesinger, pp. 271–72; Wyden, pp. 175–76.
30. Schlesinger, pp. 272–73.
31. Narrative of landings and subsequent days of combat on the beachhead is based primarily on Agular, pp. 21–35 and passim, with additional details from Johnson et al., pp. 103–72, and Wyden, pp. 210–88.
32. Johnson et al., p. 179.
33. For example, Hilsman, *To Move a Nation*, p. 33.
34. Kirkpatrick, p. 197; Schlesinger, p. 274; Thomas, *The Cuban Revolution*, p. 578.
35. *New York Times*, August 1, 1961.
36. Agular, p. 39.
37. Phillips, pp. 100 and n., 102.
38. Kirkpatrick, p. 204.
39. Hilsman, p. 86.
40. Divine, ed., *The Cuban Missile Crisis*, pp. 3-4.
41. Allison, *Essence of Decision*, pp. 103–6.
42. Ibid., pp. 118–19.
43. Prados, *The Soviet Estimate*, p. 134.
44. Ibid., pp. 134–35; Hilsman, pp. 170–72.
45. Hilsman, p. 172; Prados, pp. 136–37,
46. De Vosjoli, *Lamia*, pp. 295–97. Note, however, that Constantinides counsels caution regarding de Vosjoli's account of his role in the crisis (*Intelligence and Espionage*, pp. 163–64).
47. Allison, pp. 190–91; Hilsman, pp. 172–73.
48. Allison, p. 103; Hilsman, p. 186.
49. Prados, pp. 136–37.
50. Schlesinger, pp. 798–99; Hilsman, pp. 165–66; Kennedy, *Thirteen Days*, pp. 25–26, 39–41.
51. Prados, p. 136; Allison, p. 121; Hilsman, pp. 173–74.
52. Ibid., p. 169; Allison, p. 119; Prados, p. 137.
53. Abel, *The Missile Crisis*, pp. 15–18; Allison, p. 192; Prados, pp. 137–38.
54. Ibid., pp. 141–44; Hilsman, pp. 214, 216; Schlesinger, p. 815.
55. Prados, pp. 141–42.
56. Ibid., pp. 148–49; Allison, pp. 243, 295, n. 62; Cline, *The CIA*, p. 222.
57. Allison, pp. 224–25.
58. Ibid., pp. 220–23, 227–30; Hilsman, pp. 217–19, 222–24; Schlesinger, pp. 825–30.

POSTSCRIPT: THE EAGLE AND THE SPHINX

1. Rositzke, *The CIA'S Secret Operations*, p. 180.
2. McCone made this statement in the 1989 four-part documentary *Secret Intelligence*, aired on the Public Broadcasting System. See also Karalekas, *History of the Central Intelligence Agency*, p. 93.
3. Wise and Ross, *The Invisible Government*, p. 348.

Bibliography of

Works Cited

Abel, Elie. *The Missile Crisis*. Philadelphia: Lippincort, 1966.

Agular, Luis, ed. *Operation Zapata*. Frederick, Md.: University Publications of America, 1981.

Alger, R. A. *The Spanish-American War*. New York: Harper & Brothers, 1901.

Allen, Gardner W. *Our Navy and the Barbary Corsairs*. Boston: Houghton Mifflin, 1905.

Allen, H. C. *Great Britain and the United States: A History of Anglo-American Relations (1783–1952)*. New York: St. Martin's, 1955.

Allison, Graham T. *Essence of Decision: Explaining the Cuban Missile Crisis*. Boston: Little, Brown, 1971.

Alsop, Stewart, and Thomas Braden. *Sub Rosa: The OSS and American Espionage*. New York: Reynal & Hitchcock, 1946.

Ambrose, Stephen E. *Ike's Spies: Eisenhower and the Espionage Establishment*. Garden City, N.Y.: Doubleday, 1981.

Andrew, Christopher. *Her Majesty's Secret Service*. New York: Viking, 1986.

Arcangelis, Mario de. *Electronic Warfare*. Poole, Dorset, England: Blandford Press, 1985.

Armstrong, Hamilton Fish, ed. *Fifty Years of Foreign Affairs*. New York: Praeger, 1972.

Artucio, Hugo Fernandez. *The Nazi Underground in South America*. New York: Farrar & Rinehart, 1942.

Augur, Helen. *The Secret War of Independence*. New York: Duell, Sloan & Pearce, 1955.

Babington-Smith, Constance. *Air Spy: The Story of Photo Intelligence in World War II*. New York: Harper & Brothers, 1957.

Bailey, Thomas A. *A Diplomatic History of the American People*. Tenth edition. Englewood Cliffs, N.J.: Prentice-Hall, 1980.

Bakeless, John. *Spies of the Confederacy*. Philadelphia: Lippincott, 1970.

———. *Turncoats, Traitors and Heroes*. Philadelphia: Lippincott, 1959.

Baker, Lafayette C. *History of the United States Secret Service*. Philadelphia: Privately printed, 1867. Reprinted as *The United States Secret Service in the Late War*. Revised edition. Philadelphia: John B. Potter, 1889. Several other editions with different titles, publishers, and dates have also been published,

Bamford, James. *The Puzzle Palace*. Boston: Houghton Mifflin, 1982. Revised edition. Harmondsworth, Middlesex, England: Penguin Books, 1983.

Bancroft, Mary. *Autobiography of a Spy*. New York: Morrow, 1983.

Bank, Aaron. *From OSS to Green Berets: The Birth of Special Forces*. Novato, Calif.: Presidio Press, 1986.

Barker, Wayne G., ed. *The History of Codes and Ciphers in the United States During the Period Between the World Wars*. Laguna Hills, Calif.; Aegean Park Press, 1979.

———, ed. *The History of Codes and Ciphers in the United States During World War I*. Laguna Hills, Calif.: Aegean Park Press, 1979.

———, ed. *The History of Codes and Ciphers in the United States Prior to World War I*. Laguna Hills, Calif.: Aegean Park Press, 1978.

Barnum, H. L. *The Spy Unmasked; or, Memoirs of Enoch Crosby, Alias Harvey Birch*. New York: J. & J. Harper, 1828. Reprinted with additional material by James H. Pickering. Harrison, N.Y.: Harbor Hill Books, 1975.

Bates, David Homer. *Lincoln in the Telegraph Office*. New York: Century, 1907.

Bauer, K. Jack. *The Mexican War, 1846–1848*. New York: Macmillan, 1974.

Beach, Moses S. "A Secret Mission to Mexico." *Scribner's Monthly*, vol. 18 (1879), pp. 136–40.

Beesly, Patrick. *Room 40: British Naval Intelligence, 1914–1918*. New York: Harcourt Brace Jovanovich, 1982.

———. *Very Special Intelligence: The Story of the Admiralty's Operational Intelligence Center, 1939–1945*. Garden City, N.Y.: Doubleday, 1978.

Beirne, Francis F. *The War of 1812*. New York: Dutton, 1949.

Bemis, Samuel F. *American Secretaries of State*. New York: Pageant, 1958.

———. "The British Secret Service and the French-American Alliance." *American Historical Review*, vol. 29 (1923–24), pp. 474–95.

———. *A Diplomatic History of the United States*. Revised edition. New York: Holt, 1942.

———. *Jay's Treaty: A Study in Commerce and Diplomacy*. Revised edition. New Haven: Yale University Press, 1962.

———. *The Latin American Policy of the United States*. New York: Harcourt, Brace, 1943.

———. *Pinckney's Treaty*. Revised edition. New Haven: Yale University Press, 1960.

Bernstorff, Count Johann. *My Three Years in America*. New York: Scribner's, 1920.

Beschloss, Michael R. *Mayday: Eisenhower, Khrushchev and the U-2 Affair*. New York: Harper & Row, 1986.

Bethell, Nicholas. *Betrayed*. New York: Times Books, 1984.

Beymer, William Gilmore. *On Hazardous Service: Scouts and Spies of the North and South*. New York: Harper & Brothers, 1912.

Bidwell, Bruce W. *History of the Military Intelligence Division, Department of the Army General Staff: 1775–1941*. Frederick, Md.: University Publications of America, 1986.

Blackstock, Paul W. *Agents of Deceit: Frauds, Forgeries and Political Intrigue Among Nations*. Chicago: Quadrangle, 1966.

Blair, Clay, Jr. *Silent Victory: The U.S. Submarine War Against Japan*. Philadelphia: Lippincott, 1975.

Bliven, Bruce, Jr. *Battle for Manhattan*. Baltimore: Penguin Books, 1964.

Boatner, Mark M., III. *Civil War Dictionary*. New York: McKay, 1959.

———. *Encyclopedia of the American Revolution*. New York: McKay, 1974.

Bohlen, Charles E. *Witness to History, 1929–1969*. New York: Norton, 1973.

Boyd, Julian P. *Number 7: Alexander Hamilton's Secret Attempts to Control American Foreign Policy*. Princeton: Princeton University Press, 1964.

———. "Silas Deane: Death by a Kindly Teacher of Treason?" *William and Mary Quarterly*, third series, vol. 16 (1959), pp. 165–87, 319–42, 515–50.

Braden, Spruille. *Diplomats and Demagogues*. New Rochelle, N.Y.: Arlington House, 1971.

Braden, Tom. "The Birth of the CIA." *American Heritage*, vol. 28., no. 2 (February 1977), pp. 4–13.

Brant, Irving, "Edmund Randolph, Not Guilty!" *William and Mary Quarterly*, third series, vol. 7 (1950), pp. 180–98.

Brown, Wallace. *The Good Americans: The Loyalists in the American Revolution.* New York: Morrow, 1969.

Brugioni, Dino A. "Naval Photo Intel in WWII." *Proceedings of the U.S. Naval Institute,* vol. 113/6/1012 (June 1987), pp. 46–51.

Bryan, George S. *The Spy in America.* Philadelphia: Lippincott, 1943.

Bryan, William Alfred. *George Washington in American Literature, 1775–1865.* New York: Columbia University Press, 1952. Reprinted. Westport, Conn.: Greenwood Press, 1970.

Bryce, Ivar. *You Only Live Once: Memoirs of Ian Fleming.* Frederick, Md.: University Publications of America, 1984.

Bulloch, James D. *The Secret Service of the Confederate States in Europe.* 2 vols. New York: Putnam's, 1884. Reprinted. New York: Thomas Yoseloff, 1959.

Burrows, William E. *Deep Black Space Espionage and National Security.* New York: Random House, 1986.

Butler, Pierce. *Judah P. Benjamin.* Philadelphia: G. W. Jacobs, 1907.

Calkins, C. G. "The Naval Battle of Manila Bay." In *The American-Spanish War.* Norwich, Conn.: Chas. C. Haskell, 1899.

Callahan, James Morton. *The Diplomatic History of the Southern Confederacy.* Baltimore: Johns Hopkins Press, 1901.

Campbell, Kenneth. "Ethan Allen Hitchcock: Intelligence Leader—Mystic." *Intelligence Quarterly,* vol. 2, no. 3 (October 1986), pp. 13–14.

———. "Major General Ralph H. Van Deman, Father of American Military Intelligence." *American Intelligence Journal,* vol. 8, no. 3 (Summer 1987), pp. 13–19.

Canan, Howard V. "Confederate Military Intelligence." *Maryland Historical Magazine,* vol. 59, no. 1 (March 1964), pp. 34–51.

Case, Lynn M., and Warren F. Spencer. *The United States and France: Civil War Diplomacy.* Philadelphia: University of Pennsylvania Press, 1970.

Casey, William. *The Secret War against Hitler.* Washington, D.C.: Regnery Gateway, 1988.

Catton, Bruce. *Terrible Swift Sword.* Garden City, N.Y.: Doubleday, 1963.

Cave Brown, Anthony. *"C": The Secret Life of Sir Stewart Graham Menzies.* New York: Macmillan, 1987.

———. *The Last Hero: Wild Bill Donovan.* New York: Times Books, 1982.

Central Intelligence Agency. *Intelligence in the War of Independence.* Washington, D.C.: CIA Office of Public Affairs, n.d.

Challener, Richard D. *Admirals, Generals, and American Foreign Policy, 1898–1914.* Princeton: Princeton University Press, 1973.

Chambers, Whittaker. *Witness.* New York: Random House, 1952.

Champagne, Roger J. *Alexander McDougall and the American Revolution in New York.* Schenectady, N.Y.: Union College Press, 1975.

Churchill, Winston S. *Their Finest Hour.* Boston: Houghton Mifflin, 1949.

Clapp, Margaret. *Forgotten First Citizen: John Bigelow.* Boston: Little, Brown, 1947. Reprinted. Westport, Conn.: Greenwood Press, 1968.

Clark, Ronald William. *The Man Who Broke Purple: The Life of the World's Greatest Cryptologist, Col. William F. Friedman.* Boston: Little, Brown, 1977.

Cline, Ray S. *The CIA: Reality vs. Myth.* Washington, D.C.: Acropolis, 1982. Revision of *Secrets, Spies and Scholars.*

Colby, William, and Peter Forbath. *Honorable Men: My Life in the CIA.* New York: Simon & Schuster, 1978.

Coles, Harry L. *The War of 1812.* Chicago: University of Chicago Press, 1965.

Concas y Palau, Victor M. *The Squadron of Admiral Cervera.* Washington, D.C.: U.S. Government Printing Office, 1900.

Constantinides, George C. *Intelligence and Espionage: An Analytical Bibliography.* Boulder, Colo.: Westview, 1983.

Cook, Fred. *The FBI Nobody Knows.* New York: Macmillan, 1964.

Coon, Carleton S. *A North Africa Story.* Ipswich, Mass.: Gambit, 1980.

Corson, William R. *The Armies of Ignorance: The Rise of the American Intelligence Empire.* New York: Dial Press, 1977.

Corson, William R., and Robert T. Crowley. *The New KGB: Engine of Soviet Power.* New York: Morrow, 1985.

Coumbe, Arthur T. "German Intelligence and Security in the Franco-German War." *Military Intelligence,* vol. 14, no. 1 (January 1988), pp. 9–12.

Cox, Cynthia. *The Real Figaro: The Extraordinary Career of Caron de Beaumarchais.* New York: Coward, McCann, 1963.

Crary, Catherine Snell. "The Tory and the Spy: The Double Life of James Rivington." *William and Mary Quarterly,* vol. 16 (1959), pp. 61–72.

Cummins, Light. "Luciano de Herrera and Spanish Espionage in British St. Augustine." *Escribano,* vol. 16 (1979), pp. 43–57.

———. "Spanish Espionage in the South During the American Revolution." *Southern Studies,* vol. 19. no. 1 (1980), pp. 39–49.

Current, R. N. "Webster's Propaganda and the Ashburton Treaty." *Mississippi Valley Historical Review,* vol. 34 (1947), pp. 187–200.

Current Biography. New York: H. W. Wilson, 1940–to date.

Currey, Cecil B. *Code Number 72: Ben Franklin: Patriot or Spy?* Englewood Cliffs, N.J.: Prentice-Hall, 1972.

———. *Edward Lansdale: The Unquiet American.* Boston: Houghton Mifflin, 1988.

Dana, Charles A. *Recollections of the Civil War.* New York, 1898. Reprinted. New York: Collier Books, 1963.

Davidson, Philip. *Propaganda and the American Revolution, 1763–1783.* Chapel Hill: University of North Carolina Press, 1941.

Davies, Joseph E. *Mission to Moscow.* New York: Simon & Schuster, 1941.

Davis, George T. *A Navy Second to None.* New York: Harcourt, Brace, 1940.

De Vosjoli, P. L. Thyraud. *Lamia.* Boston: Little, Brown, 1970.

Dewey, George. *Autobiography of George Dewey, Admiral of the Navy.* New York: Scribner's, 1913.

Dictionary of American Biography. New York: Scnibner's, 1928–58.

Dictionary of American History. Second revised edition. New York: Scribner's, 1942–61.

Dictionary of National Biography. London: Oxford University Press, 1922.

Divine, Robert A., ed. *The Cuban Missile Crisis.* Chicago: Quadrangle, 1971.

Donner, Frank J. *The Age of Surveillance: The Aims and Methods of America's Political Intelligence System.* New York; Knopf, 1980.

Donovan, James B. *Strangers on a Bridge: The Case of Colonel Abel.* New York: Atheneum, 1964.

Donovan, William J. "Stop Russia's Subversive War." *Atlantic Monthly,* May 1948.

Dorwart, Jeffery M. *Conflict of Duty: The U.S. Navy's Intelligence Dilemma, 1919–1945.* Annapolis, Md.: Naval Institute Press, 1983.

———. *The Office of Naval Intelligence: The Birth of America's First Intelligence Agency, 1865–1918.* Annapolis, Md.: Naval Institute Press, 1979.

———. "The Roosevelt-Astor Espionage Ring." *New York History,* vol. 62 (July 1981), pp. 307–22.

Downes, Donald. The *Scarlet Thread: Adventures in Wartime Espionage*. New York: British Book Centre, 1953.

Draper, Theodore. *The Roots of American Communism*. New York: Viking, 1957.

Dubofsky, Melvyn. *We Shall Be All: A History of the Industrial Workers of the World*. Chicago: Quadrangle, 1969.

Dull, Paul S. *A Battle History of the Imperial Japanese Navy (1941–1945)*. Annapolis, Md.: Naval Institute Press, 1978.

Dulles, Allen. *The Secret Surrender*. New York: Harper & Row, 1966.

Dunlop, Richard. *Behind Japanese Lines: With the OSS in Burma*. Chicago: Rand McNally, 1979.

———. *Donovan: America's Master Spy*. Chicago: Rand McNally, 1982.

Dziak, John J. *Chekisty: A History of the KGB*. Lexington, Mass.: Lexington Books, 1988.

Edelsheim, Franz von. *Operationen über See. Eine Studie von reiherr von Edelsheim*. Berlin, 1901. Reprinted in translation as *Operations upon the Sea: A Study*. New York, 1914.

Edwards, Samuel. *Barbary General: The Life of William H. Eaton*. Englewood Cliffs, N.J.: Prentice-Hall, 1968.

Einstein, Lewis. *Divided Loyalties: Americans in England During the War of Independence*. Boston: Houghton Mifflin, 1933.

Eisenhower, Dwight D. *Waging Peace, 1956–1961*. Garden City, N.Y.: Doubleday, 1965.

Elliott, Charles Winslow. *Winfield Scott: The Soldier and the Man*. New York: Macmillan, 1937.

Evans, Robley D. *A Sailor's Log*. New York: Appleton. 1908.

Ewing, Joseph H. "The New Sherman Letters." *American Heritage*, vol. 38, no. 5 (July–August 1987), pp. 24–32, 34, 36–37, 40–41.

Falkner, Leonard. "A Spy for Washington." *American Heritage*. vol. 8, no. 8 (August 1957), pp. 58–64.

Farago, Ladislas. *The Broken Seal: The Story of "Operation Magic" and the Pearl Harbor Disaster*. New York: Random House, 1967.

———. *The Game of the Foxes: The Untold Story of German Espionage in the United States and Great Britain During World War II*. New York: McKay, 1971.

Felix, Christopher [pseud.]. *A Short Course in the Secret War*. New York: Dutton, 1963.

Fergusson, Thomas G. *British Military Intelligence, 1870–1914: The Development of a Modern Intelligence Organization*. Frederick, Md.: University Publications of America, 1984.

Finder, Joseph. *Red Carpet*. New York: Holt, Rinehart & Winston, 1983.

Finnegan, John Patrick. *Military Intelligence: A Picture History*. Arlington, Va.: U.S. Army Intelligence & Security Command, 1985.

———. "U.S. Army Counterintelligence in CONUS—The World War I Experience." *Military Intelligence*, vol. 14, no. 1 (January 1988), pp. 17–21.

Fishel, Edwin C. "Myths That Never Die." *International Journal of Intelligence and Counterintelligence*, vol 2, no. 1 (Spring 1988). This is a revised and updated version of "The Mythology of Civil War Intelligence." *Civil War History*, vol. 10, no. 4 (December 1964), pp. 344–67.

Flexner, James Thomas. *George Washington in the American Revolution (1775–1783)*. Boston: Little, Brown, 1968.

———. *The Traitor and the Spy: Benedict Arnold and John André*. New York: Harcourt, Brace, 1953.

Foner, Philip S. *The Spanish-Cuban-American War and the Birth of American Imperialism*. 2 vols. New York: Monthly Review Press, 1972.

Forbes, Esther. *Paul Revere and the World He Lived In*. Boston: Houghton Mifflin, 1942.

Ford, Corey. *Donovan of OSS*. Boston: Little, Brown, 1970.

———. *A Peculiar Service*. Boston: Little, Brown, 1965.

Forrestal, James B. *The Forrestal Diaries*. Edited by Walter Millis and E. S. Duffield. New York: Viking, 1951.

Fowler, W. B. *British-American Relations, 1917-1918: The Role of Sir William Wiseman*. Princeton: Princeton University Press, 1969.

French, Allen. *General Gage's Informers*. Ann Arbor: University of Michigan Press, 1932.

Fryer, Mary Beacock. *Buckskin Pimpernel: The Exploits of Justus Sherwood, Loyalist Spy*. Toronto: Dundurn Press, 1981.

Gaddy, David G. "William Norris and the Confederate Signal and Secret Service." *Maryland Historical Magazine*, vol. 70, no. 2 (Summer 1975), pp. 167–88.

Ganoe, William Addleman. The *History of the United States Army*. New York: Appleton-Century, 1942.

Garlinski, Jozef. *The Enigma War*. New York: Scribner's, 1979.

Garraty, John A., and Jerome L. Sternstein, eds. *Encyclopedia of American Biography*. New York: Harper & Row, 1974.

Gaucher, Roland. *Opposition in the U.S.S.R., 1917–1967*. New York: Funk & Wagnalls, 1969.

Gehlen, Reinhard. *The Service: The Memoirs of General Reinhard Gehlen*. New York: World, 1972.

Gelfand, Lawrence E. *The Inquiry: American Preparations for Peace, 1917–1919*. New Haven: Yale University Press, 1963. Reprinted. Westport, Conn.: Greenwood Press, 1976.

George III. *The Correspondence of King George the Third from 1760 to December 1783*. 6 vols. Edited by Sir John Fortescue. London: Macmillan, 1927–28.

George, Alexander, and Juliette L. George. *Woodrow Wilson and Colonel House*. New York: J. Day, 1956.

Glines, Carroll V. *The Compact History of the United States Air Force*. New York: Hawthorn, 1973.

Goddard, George W. *Overview*. Garden City, N.Y.: Doubleday, 1969.

Goltz, Horst von der. *My Adventures as a German Secret Agent*. New York: McBride, 1917.

Graebner, Norman A. "Northern Diplomacy and European Neutrality." In *Why the North Won the Civil War*, edited by David Donald. New York: Collier Books, 1962.

————. ed. *An Uncertain Tradition: American Secretaries of State in the Twentieth Century*. New York: McGraw-Hill, 1961.

Grant, Natalie. "Deception on a Grand Scale," *International Journal of Intelligence and Counterintelligence*, vol. 1, no. 4 (Winter 1986–87).

Grant, Ulysses S. *Personal Memoirs*. 2 vols. New York: Webster, 1885.

Graves, William S. *American Siberian Adventure, 1918–1920*. New York: Jonathan Cape and Harrison Smith, 1931.

Gray, Wood. *The Hidden Civil War: The Story of the Copperheads*. New York: Viking, 1942.

Greely, A. W. "The Military-Telegraph Service." In *Soldier Life and the Secret Service*, edited by Francis Trevelyan Miller, Part 8 of *The Photographic History of the Civil War*. New York: A. S. Barnes, 1911.

Greenhow, Rose O'Neal. *My Imprisonment and the First Year of Abolition Rule at Washington*. London: Richard Bentley, 1863.

Grendel, Frederic. *Beaumarchais: The Man Who Was Figaro*. Translated from the French by Roger Greaves. London: Macdonald & Jane's, 1977.

Grenville, J. A. S. *The Major International Treaties, 1914–1973: A History and Guide with Texts*. Briarcliff Manor, N.Y.: Stein & Day, 1974.

Grew, Joseph C. *Ten Years in Japan*. New York: Simon & Schuster, 1944.

Gunston, Bill. *An Illustrated Guide to Spy Planes and Electronic Warfare Aircraft*. New York: Arco, 1983.

Haley, P. Edward. *Revolution and Intervention: The Diplomacy of Taft and Wilson with Mexico, 1910–1917*. Cambridge: MIT Press, 1970.

Hall, James O. "The Spy Harrison." *Civil War Times*, vol. 24, no. 10 (February 1986), pp. 18–25.

Halliday, E. M. *The Ignorant Armies*. New York: Harper & Brothers, 1960.

Hamilton, Alexander, John Jay, and James Madison. *The Federalist: A Commentary on the Constitution of the United States*. Introduction by Edward Mead Earle. New York: Modern Library, n.d.

Hammer, Armond, with Neil Lyndon. *Hammer*. New York: Putnam's, 1987.

Hatch, Robert McConnell. *Major John André: A Gallant in Spy's Clothing*. Boston: Houghton Muffin, 1986.

Hattendorf, John B., B. Mitchell Simpson, and John R. Wadleigh. *Sailors and Scholars: The Centennial History of the U.S. Naval War College*. Newport, R.I.: Naval War College Press, 1984.

Headley, John William. *Confederate Operations in Canada and New York*. New York: Neale Publishing, 1906. Reprinted, with accompanying unbound biographical material on Headley. Alexandria, Va.: Time-Life Books, 1984.

Healy, Laurin Hall, and Luis Kutner. *The Admiral*. New York: Ziff-Davis, 1944.

Hendrick, Burton J. *The Life and Letters of Walter H. Page*. 3 vols. Garden City, N.Y.: Doubleday, 1922–26.

Herring, Hubert. *A History of Latin America*. New York: Knopf, 1961.

Herwig, Holger H. *Politics of Frustration: The United States in German Naval Planning, 1889–1941*. Boston: Little, Brown, 1976.

Herwig, Holger H., and David F. Trask. "Naval Operations Plans Between Germany and the United States of America, 1898–1913: A Study of Strategic Planning in the Age of Imperialism." *Militärgeschlichtliche Mitteilungen*, vol. 2 (1970), pp. 5–32.

Higginbotham, Don. *The War of American Independence*. New York: Macmillan, 1971.

Hilsman, Roger. *American Guerrilla: My War Behind Japanese Lines*. Washington, D.C.: Brassey's, 1990.

———. *To Move a Nation: The Politics and Foreign Policy in the Administration of John F. Kennedy*. Garden City, N.Y.: Doubleday, 1967.

Hodges, Andrew. *Alan Turing: The Enigma*. New York: Simon & Schuster, 1983.

Hohne, Heinz, and Hermann Zolling. *The General Was a Spy: The Truth About General Gehlen and His Spy Ring*. New York: Coward, McCann, 1972.

Holmes, W. J. *Double-Edged Secrets: U.S. Naval Intelligence Operations in the Pacific During World War II*. Annapolis, Md.: Naval Institute Press, 1979.

Horan, James D. *Confederate Agent: A Discovery in History*. New York: Crown, 1954.

———. *The Pinkertons: The Detective Dynasty That Made History*. New York: Crown, 1967.

Horan, James D., and Howard Swiggett. *The Pinkerton Story*. New York: Putnam's, 1951.

House, Edward Mandell. *The Intimate Papers of Colonel House*. 4 vols. Edited by Charles Seymour. Boston: Houghton Mifflin, 1926.

Howe, John. "A Journal kept by Mr. John Howe while he was employed as a British spy during the revolutionary war; also while he was engaged in the smuggling business during the late war." *Magazine of History*, vol. 33, no. 4, extra no. 132 (1927), pp. 165–90.

Hughes, Terry, and John Costello. *The Battle of the Atlantic*. New York: Dial Press and James Wade, 1977.

Hunt, E. Howard. *Give Us This Day*. New Rochelle, N.Y.: Arlington House, 1973.

Hyde, H. Montgomery. *Room 3603: The Story of the British Intelligence Center in New York During World War II*. New York: Farrar, Straus, 1963.

————. *Secret Intelligence Agent: British Espionage in America and the Creation of the OSS*. New York: St. Martin's, 1982.

Hymoff, Edward. *The OSS in World War II*. New York: Ballantine, 1972.

Hynd, Alan. *Passport to Treason: The Inside Story of Spies in America*. New York: McBride, 1943.

Immerman, Richard H. *The CIA in Guatemala: The Foreign Policy of Intervention*. Austin: University of Texas Press, 1982.

Infield, Glenn B. *Unarmed and Unafraid*. New York: Macmillan, 1970.

Jameson, John F. "The London Expenditures of the Confederate Secret Service." *American Historical Review*, vol. 35 (1930), pp. 811–24.

Jeffreys-Jones, Rhodri. *American Espionage: From Secret Service to CIA*. New York: Free Press, 1977.

Jensen, Joan M. *The Price of Vigilance*. Chicago: Rand McNally, 1968.

Jessup, Philip C. *Elihu Root*. 2 vols. New York: Dodd, Mead, 1938.

Johnson, Haynes, with Manuel Artime, José Pérez San Roman, Erneido Oliva, and Enrique Ruiz-Williams. *The Bay of Pigs: The Leaders' Story of Brigade 2506*. New York: Norton, 1964.

Johnson, Niel M. *George Sylvester Viereck: German-American Propagandist*. Urbana: University of Illinois Press, 1972.

Johnston, Angus J., II. "Disloyalty on Confederate Railroads in Virginia." *Virginia Magazine of History and Biography*, vol 63, no. 4 (October 1955), pp. 410–26.

Jones, John Price, and Paul Merrick Hollister. *The German Secret Service in America, 1914–1918*. Boston: Small, Maynard, 1918.

Jones, Thomas A. *J. Wilkes Booth*. Chicago: Laird & Lee, 1893.

Jordan, Donaldson, and Edwin J. Pratt. *Europe and the American Civil War*. Boston: Houghton Mifflin, 1931.

Kahn, David. *The Codebreakers: The Story of Secret Writing*. New York: Macmillan, 1967.

————. *Hitler's Spies: German Military Intelligence in World War II*. New York: Macmillan, 1978.

Karalekas, Anne. *History of the Central Intelligence Agency*. Laguna Hills, Calif.: Aegean Park Press, 1977. Reprinted in *The Central Intelligence Agency: History and Documents*, edited by William M. Leary. University: University of Alabama Press, 1984.

Katz, Friedrich. *The Secret War in Mexico: Europe, the United States, and the Mexican Revolution*. Chicago: University of Chicago Press, 1981.

Kennan, George F. *The Decision to Intervene*. New York: Atheneum, 1967.

————. *Memoirs, 1925–1950*. Boston: Little, Brown, 1967.

————. *Russia and the West*. New York: Mentor, 1962.

Kennedy, Robert F. *Thirteen Days: A Memoir of the Cuban Missile Crisis*. New York: Norton, 1969.

Kent, Sherman. *Strategic Intelligence for American World Policy*. Princeton: Princeton University Press, 1949, 1966.

Khrushchev, Nikita. *Khrushchev Remembers*. Translated and edited by Strobe Talbott. Boston: Little, Brown, 1970.

King, Ernest J., and Walter Muir Whitehill. *Fleet Admiral King: A Naval Record*. New York: Norton, 1952.

Kirkpatrick, Lyman B., Jr. *The Real CIA*. New York: Macmillan, 1968.

Klement, Frank L. *The Copperheads in the Middle West*. Chicago, 1960.

————. *Dark Lanterns: Secret Political Societies, Conspiracies, and Treason Trials in the Civil War*. Baton Rouge: Louisiana State University Press, 1984.

Lamphere, Robert J., and Tom Schachtman. *The FBI-KGB War: A Special Agent's Story*. New York: Random House, 1986.

Landau, Henry. *The Enemy Within: The Inside Story of German Sabotage in America*. New York: Putnam's, 1937.

Langer, William L. *In and Out of the Ivory Tower*. New York: Random House, 1977.

Lansdale, Edward Geary. *In the Midst of Wars: An American's Mission to Southeast Asia*. New York: Harper & Row, 1972.

Layton, Edwin T. *"And I Was There": Pearl Harbor and Midway—Breaking the Secrets*. New York: Morrow, 1985.

Leary, William M. *Perilous Missions: Civil Air Transport and CIA Covert Operations in Asia*. Tuscaloosa: University of Alabama Press, 1984.

———, ed. *The Central Intelligence Agency: History and Documents*. Tuscaloosa: University of Alabama Press, 1984.

Lemaitre, Georges. *Beaumarchais*. New York: Knopf, 1949.

Lewin, Ronald. *The American Magic: Codes, Ciphers and the Defeat of Japan*. New York: Farrar, Straus & Giroux, 1982.

———. *Ultra Goes to War: The First Account of World War II's Greatest Secret Based on Official Documents*. New York: McGraw-Hill, 1978.

Link, Arthur S. *Wilson: Campaigns for Progressivism and Peace, 1916–1917*. Princeton: Princeton University Press, 1965.

———. *Wilson: The Struggle for Neutrality, 1914–1915*. Princeton: Princeton University Press, 1960.

Long, E. B. *The Civil War Day by Day: An Almanac, 1861–1865*. Garden City, N.Y.: Doubleday, 1971.

Longstreet, James. *From Manassas to Appomattox*. Philadelphia: Lippincott, 1896.

———. "Our March Against Pope." In *Battles and Leaders of the Civil War*. Vol. 2, pp. 512–26. New York: Century, 1884, 1886.

Lord, Walter. *The Dawn's Early Light*. New York: Norton, 1972.

Lovell, Stanley. *Of Spies and Stratagems*. Englewood Cliffs, N.J.: Prentice-Hall, 1963.

Lowe, T. S. C. "The Balloons with the Army of the Potomac." In *Soldier Life and the Secret Service*, edited by Francis Trevelyan Miller. Part of *The Photographic History of the Civil War*. New York: Castle Books, 1957.

MacCloskey, Monro. *From Gasbags to Spaceships: The Story of the U.S. Air Force*. New York: Richards Rosen Press, 1968.

McCadden, Helen Matzke. "Juan de Miralles and the American Revolution." *Americas*, vol. 29, no. 3 (1973), pp. 359–75.

McClellan, George B. *McClellan's Own Story*. New York: Webster, 1887.

McMaster, John Bach. *Our House Divided*. New York: Premier Books, 1961. Reprint of *History of the People of the United States During Lincoln's Administration*. New York: Appleton-Century, 1927.

Mahan, Alfred T. *Lessons of the War with Spain*. New York, 1899. Reprinted. Freeport, N.Y.: Books for Libraries, 1970.

Mashbir, Sidney Forrester. *I Was an American Spy*. New York: Vantage, 1953.

Mathews, Hazel C. *Frontier Spies: The British Secret Service, Northern Department During the Revolutionary War*. Fort Myers, Fla.: Ace Press, 1971.

Maugham, W. Somerset. *The Summing Up*. New York: Literary Guild, 1935.

Merk, Frederick, *Manifest Destiny and Mission in American History: A Reinterpretation*. New York: Knopf, 1963.

———. *The Monroe Doctrine and American Expansionism, 1843–1849*. New York: Knopf, 1966.

Meyer, Cord. *Facing Reality: From World Federalism to the CIA*. New York: Harper & Row, 1980.

Miller, John C. *Triumph of Freedom, 1775–1783*. Boston: Little, Brown, 1948.

Miller, Nathan. *The U.S. Navy: An Illustrated History*. New York: American Heritage and Bonanza Books, 1977.

Millis, Walter. *Road to War: America, 1914–1917*. Boston; Houghton Mifflin, 1935.

Mock, James R. *Censorship 1917*. Princeton: Princeton University Press, 1941.

Monaghan, Jay. *Diplomat in Carpet Slippers: Abraham Lincoln Deals with Foreign Affairs*. Indianapolis: Bobbs-Merrill, 1945.

Montague, Ludwell Lee. *General Walter Bedell Smith as Director of Central Intelligence, October 1950–February 1953*. 5 vols. Langley, Va.: Historical Staff, Central Intelligence Agency, 1971. A slightly abridged edition of this internal document was declassified and released to the author under the terms of the Freedom of Information Act.

Montross, Lynn. *The Reluctant Rebels*. New York: Harper & Brothers, 1950.

Morgan, Ted. *Maugham*. New York: Simon & Schuster, 1980.

Morgan, William J. *The OSS and I*. New York: Norton, 1957.

Morison, Samuel Eliot. *The Oxford History of the American People*. New York: Oxford University Press, 1965.

Morn, Frank. *"The Eye That Never Sleeps": A History* of the *Pinkerton National Detective Agency*. Bloomington: Indiana University Press, 1982.

Morris, Richard B. *The Peacemakers: The Great Powers and American Independence*. New York: Harper & Row, 1965.

Mott, Frank L. *American Journalism: A History* of *Newspapers in the U.S. Through 260 Years*. New York: Macmillan, 1950.

Muller, Edwin. "The Inside Story of Pearl Harbor." In *Secrets & Spies: Behind-the-Scenes Stories of World War II*, pp. 13–17. Pleasantville, N.Y.: Reader's Digest, 1964.

National Archives. Area File of the Naval Records Collection, 1775–1910. Microcopy M625, reel 225.

Nicolosi, Anthony A. "The Spirit of McCarty Little." *Proceedings of the U.S. Naval Institute*, vol. 110/9/979 (September 1984), pp. 72–80.

O'Brien, Michael J. *Hercules Mulligan: Confidential Correspondent of General Washington*. New York: P. J. Kennedy, 1937.

O'Toole, G. J. A. "Benjamin Franklin: American Spymaster or British Mole?" *International Journal of Intelligence and Counterintelligence*, vol. 3, no. 1 (Spring 1989).

———. *Encyclopedia of American Intelligence and Espionage*. New York: Facts on File, 1988.

———. "Kahn's Law: A Universal Principle of Intelligence?" *International Journal of Intelligence and Counterintelligence*, vol. 4, no. 1 (Spring 1990).

———. "Our Man in Havana: The Paper Trail of Some Spanish War Spies." *Intelligence Quarterly*, vol. 2, no. 2 (July 1986), pp. 1–3.

———. *The Private Sector*. New York: Norton, 1978.

———. *The Spanish War: An American Epic, 1898*. New York: Norton, 1984.

Overstreet, Harry, and Bonaro Overstreet. *The FBi in Our Open Society*. New York: Norton, 1969.

Overy, R. J. *The Air War, 1939–1945*. Briarcliff Manor, N.Y.: Stein & Day, 1981.

Owsley, Frank L. *King Cotton Diplomacy: Foreign Relations of the Confederate States of America*. Second edition. Chicago: University of Chicago Press, 1959.

Owsley, Harriet Chappell. "Henry Shelton Sanford and Federal Surveillance Abroad, 1861–1965." *Mississippi Valley Historical Review*, vol. 48 (1961), pp. 211–28.

Paige, Glenn D. *The Korean Decision (June 24–30, 1950)*. New York: Free Press, 1968.

Papen, Franz von. *Memoirs*. New York: Dutton, 1953.

Parker, David W. "Secret Reports of John Howe, 1808." *American Historical Review*, vol. 17 (1911–12), pp. 70–102, 332–54.

Peers, William, and Dean Brelis. *Behind the Burma Road*. Boston: Little, Brown, 1963.

Pemberton, Ian Cleghorn Blanchard. "The British Secret Service in the Champlain Valley During the Haldimand Negotiations, 1780–1783." *Vermont History*, vol. 44, no. 3 (1976), pp. 129–40.

Pennypacker, Morton. *General Washington's Spies on Long Island and in New York*. Brooklyn, N.Y.: Long Island Historical Society, 1939.

Perkins, Dexter. *A History of the Monroe Doctrine*. Boston: Little, Brown, 1955.

Perla, Peter P. *The Art of Wargaming*. Annapolis, Md.: Naval Institute Press.

Persico, Joseph E. *Piercing the Reich: The Penetration of Nazi Germany by American Secret Agents During World War II*. New York: Viking, 1979.

Phillips, Cabell. *The Truman Presidency*. New York: Macmillan, 1966.

Phillips, David Atlee. *The Night Watch: 25 Years of Peculiar Service*. New York: Atheneum, 1977.

Pinkerton, Allan. *The Spy of the Rebellion, Being a True History of the Spy System of the United States Army During the Late Rebellion*. New York: G. W. Dillingham, 1888.

Pitman, Benn. *The Assassination of President Lincoln and the Trial of the Conspirators*. Cincinnati: Moore, Wilstach & Baldwin, 1865.

Plumb, W. R. *The Military Telegraph during the Civil War in the United States, with an exposition of ancient and modern means of communication, and of the Federal and Confederate cipher systems; also a running account of the War between the States*. Chicago: Jansen, McClurg, 1882.

Potter, E. B., and J. R. Fredland, eds. *The United States and World Sea Power*. Englewood Cliffs, N.J.: Prentice-Hall, 1955.

Potter, John Deane. *Yamamoto: The Man Who Menaced America*. New York: Viking, 1965.

Powe, Marc B. "The Emergence of the War Department Intelligence Agency: 1885–1918." Master's thesis, Department of History, Kansas State University, Manhattan, 1974.

Powe, Marc B., and Edward E. Wilson. *The Evolution of American Military Intelligence*. Fort Huachuca, Ariz.: U.S. Intelligence Center & School, 1973.

Powers, Richard Gid. *Secrecy and Power: The Life of J. Edgar Hoover*. New York: Free Press, 1987.

Powers, Thomas. *The Man Who Kept the Secrets: Richard Helms and the CIA*. New York: Knopf, 1979.

Prados, John. *Presidents' Secret Wars: CIA and Pentagon Covert Operations Since World War II*. New York: Morrow, 1986.

———. *The Soviet Estimate: U.S. Intelligence Analysis and Russian Military Strength*. New York: Dial Press, 1982.

Prange, Gordon W. *At Dawn We Slept: The Untold Story of Pearl Harbor*. New York: McGraw-Hill, 1981.

———. *Pearl Harbor: The Verdict of History*. New York: McGraw-Hill, 1986.

Puleston, W. D. *The Armed Forces of the Pacific: A Comparison of the Military and Naval Power of the United States and Japan*. New Haven: Yale University Press, 1941.

Quirk, Robert E. *An Affair of Honor: Woodrow Wilson and the Occupation of Veracruz*. New York: Norton, 1962.

Randall, James G. "The Newspaper Problem in Its Bearing upon Military Secrecy During the Civil War." *American Historical Review*, vol. 23 (1918), pp. 303–23.

Ranelagh, John. *The Agency: The Rise and Decline of the CIA*. New York: Simon & Schuster 1986.

Ransom, Harry Howe. *The Intelligence Establishment*. Cambridge: Harvard University Press, 1970.

Read, Anthony, and David Fisher. *Colonel Z: The Secret Life of a Master of Spies*. New York: Viking, 1985.

The Reader's Digest Family Encyclopedia of American History. Pleasantville, N.Y.: Reader's Digest, 1975.

Richelson, Jeffrey T., and Desmond Ball. *The Ties That Bind*. Boston: Allen & Unwin, 1985.

Rickover, H. G. *How the Battleship* Maine *Was Destroyed*. Washington, D.C.: U.S. Government Printing Office, 1976.

Riess, Curt. *Total Espionage*. New York: Putnam's, 1941.

Rintelen, Franz. *The Dark Invader: Wartime Reminiscences of a German Naval Intelligence Officer*. London: Lovat Dickson, 1933.

Rippley, La Vern J. *The German-Americans*. Boston: G. K. Hall, 1976.

Rochefort, Joseph. "As I Recall . . . Learning Cryptanalysis." *Proceedings of the U.S. Naval Institute*, vol. 109/8/966 (August 1983), pp. 54–55.

Rodd, Francis Rennell. *General William Eaton: The Failure of an Idea*. New York: Minton, Balch, 1932.

Roetter, Charles. *The Art of Psychological Warfare, 1914–1945*. Briarcliff Manor, N.Y.: Stein & Day, 1974.

Rogers, James Grafton. *Wartime Washington: The Secret OSS Journal of James Grafron Rogers, 1942–1943*. Edited by Thomas F. Troy. Frederick, Md.: University Publications of America, 1987.

Roosevelt, Kermit. *Countercoup: The Struggle for the Control of Iran*. New York: McGraw-Hill, 1979.

———. *War Report of the OSS (Office of Strategic Services)*. New York: Walker, 1976.

Roosevelt, Theodore. *The Letters of Theodore Roosevelt*. 8 vols. Edited by Elting E. Morison. Cambridge: Harvard University Press, 1951–54.

Roscoe, Theodore. *On the Seas and in the Skies: A History of the U.S. Navy's Air Power*. New York: Hawthorn, 1970.

Rositzke, Harry. *The CIA's Secret Operations: Espionage, Counterespionage and Covert Action*. New York: Reader's Digest Press, 1977.

Rostow, W. W. *Open Skies: Eisenhower's Proposal of July 21, 1955*. Austin: University of Texas Press, 1982.

Rout, Leslie B., Jr., and John F. Bratzel. *The Shadow War: German Espionage and United States Counterespionage in Latin America During World War II*. Frederick, Md.: University Publications of America, 1986.

Russell, Charles Edward. *Haym Salomon and the Revolution*. New York: Cosmopolitan, 1930.

Sandburg, Carl. *Abraham Lincoln: The War Years*. 4 vols. New York: Harcourt, Brace, 1939.

Sanders, Neill F. "Henry Shelton Sanford in England, April–November, 1861: A Reappraisal." *Lincoln Herald*, vol. 77, no. 2 (1975), pp. 87–95.

———. "'Unfit for Consul'?: The English Consulates and Lincoln's Patronage Policy." *Lincoln Herald*, vol. 82, no. 3 (1980), pp. 464–74.

Sayle, Edward F. "The Deja Vu of American Secret Diplomacy." *The International Journal of Intelligence and Counterintelligence*, vol. 2, no. 3 (Fall 1988).

———. "The Historical Underpinnings of the U.S. Intelligence Community." *The International Journal of Intelligence and Counterintelligence*, vol. 1, no. 1 (Spring 1986).

Schellenberg, Walter. *Hitler's Secret Service*. New York: Harcourt Brace Jovanovich, Jove, 1977.

Schlesinger, Arthur M., Jr. *A Thousand Days: John F. Kennedy in the White House*. Boston: Houghton Mifflin, 1965.

Schlesinger, Stephen, and Stephen Kinzer. *Bitter Fruit: The Untold Story of the American Coup in Guatemala*. Garden City, N.Y.: Doubleday, 1982.

Schmidt, C. T. "G-2, Army of the Potomac." *Military Review*, vol. 28 (July 1948), pp. 45–56.

Scott, Hugh Lenox. *Some Memories of a Soldier.* New York: Century, 1928.

Sears, Stephen W. *Landscape Turned Red: The Battle of Antietam.* New Haven, Conn.: Ticknor & Fields, 1983.

Seymour, George Dudley. *Captain Nathan Hale, Major John Palsgrave Wyllys: A Digressive History.* New Haven, Conn.: Privately printed, 1933.

Simpson, Christopher. *Blowback: America's Recruitment of Nazis and Its Effects on the Cold War.* New York: Collier Books, 1988.

Sims, William Sowden. *The Victory at Sea.* Garden City, N.Y.: Doubleday, Page, 1920.

Smelser, Marshall. *The Democratic Republic, 1801–1815.* New York: Harper & Row, 1968.

Smith, Bradley F. *The Shadow Warriors; OSS and the Origins of the CIA.* New York: Basic Books, 1983.

Smith, Bradley F., and Elena Agarossi. *Operation Sunrise: The Secret Surrender.* New York: Basic Books, 1979.

Smith. Joseph Burkholder. *Portrait of a Cold Warrior.* New York: Putnam's, 1976.

Smith, K. Harris. *OSS: The Secret History of America's First Central Intelligence Agency.* Berkeley: University of California Press, 1972.

Spencer, Warren F. *The Confederate Navy in Europe.* Tuscaloosa: University of Alabama Press, 1983.

Stafford, David. *Camp X.* New York: Dodd, Mead, 1986.

Starr, Stephen Z. *Colonel Grenfell's Wars.* Baton Rouge: Louisiana State University Press, 1971.

———. "Was There a Northwest Conspiracy?" *Filson Club History Quarterly*, vol. 38 (1964), pp. 323–29.

Steel, Ronald. *Walter Lippmann and the American Century.* Boston: Little, Brown, 1980.

Stephenson, Sir William. "The Story of OSS." Appendix to *Secret Intelligence Agent: British Espionage in America and the Creation of the OSS*, by H. Montgomery Hyde, pp. 247–61. New York: St. Martin's, 1982.

Stepp, John W., and I. William Hill. *Mirror of War: The Washington Star Reports the Civil War.* Washington, D.C.: Castle Books, 1961.

Stern, Philip Van Doren. *The Confederate Navy: A Pictorial History.* Garden City, N.Y.: Doubleday, 1962.

———. *Secret Missions of the Civil War: First-hand Accounts by Men and Women Who Risked their Lives in Underground Activities for the North and the South.* Chicago: Rand McNally, 1959.

Stevens, Benjamin Franklin. *B. F. Stevens's Facsimiles of Manuscripts in European Archives Relating to America, 1773–1783.* 25 vols. London, 1889–98.

Stimson, Henry L., and McGeorge Bundy. *On Active Service in Peace and War.* New York: Harper & Brothers, 1947.

Stout, Neil R. "Excerpts from John Howe's 'Smuggler's Journal.' "*Vermont History*, vol. 40, no. 4 (1972), pp. 262–70.

Stuart, Meriwether. "Colonel Ulric Dahlgren and Richmond's Union Underground, April 1864." *Virginia Magazine of History and Biography*, vol. 72, no. 2 (April 1964), pp. 152–204.

———. "Dr. Lugo: An Austro-Venetian Adventurer in Union Espionage." *Virginia Magazine of History and Biography*, vol. 90, no. 3 (July 1982), pp. 339–58.

———. "Of Spies and Borrowed Names: The Identity of Union Operatives in Richmond Known as 'The Phillipses' Discovered." *Virginia Magazine of History and Biography*, vol. 89, no. 3 (July 1981), pp. 308–27.

———. "Samuel Ruth and General R. E. Lee: Disloyalty and the Line of Supply to Fredericksburg, 1862–1863." *Virginia Magazine of History and Biography*, vol. 71, no. 1 (January 1963), pp. 35–109.

Szulc, Tad, and Karl E. Meyer. *The Cuban Invasion: The Chronicle of a Disaster.* New York: Praeger, 1962.

Tallmadge, Benjamin, *Memoir of Col. Benjamin Tallmadge.* New York, 1858. Reprinted. New York: New York Times and Arno Press, 1968.

Tatum, Georgia Lee. *Disloyalty in the Confederacy.* Chapel Hill: University of North Carolina Press, 1934. Reprinted. New York: AMS Press, 1970.

Taylor, Charles E. "The Signal and Secret Service of the Confederate States." *North Carolina Booklet,* vol. 2, no. 11 (1903).

Taylor, Edmond. *Awakening from History.* Boston: Gambit, 1969.

Theobald, Robert A. *The Final Secret of Pearl Harbor.* Old Greenwich, Conn.: Devin-Adair, 1954.

Thomas, Hugh. *The Cuban Revolution.* New York: Harper & Row, 1977. This is the final half of *Cuba: The Pursuit of Freedom.* New York: Harper & Row, 1971.

Thompson, Edmund R. "Document Sheds New Light on 'General Gage's Informers.'" *Intelligence Quarterly,* vol. 4, no. 3 (August 1989), pp. 8–10.

———. "Intelligence at Yorktown," *Defense 81,* October 1981, pp. 25–28.

———. "Sleuthing the Trail of Nathan Hale." *Intelligence Quarterly,* vol. 2, no, 3 (October 1986), pp. 1–4.

Titherington, Richard H. *A History of the Spanish-American War of 1898.* New York: Appleton, 1900.

Tompkins, Peter. *A Spy in Rome.* New York: Simon & Schuster, 1962.

Trask, David F. *Captains and Cabinets: Anglo-American Naval Relations, 1917–1918.* Columbia: University of Missouri Press, 1972.

———. *The War with Spain in 1898.* New York: Macmillan, 1981.

Treverton, Gregory F. *Covert Action: The Limits of Intervention in the Postwar World.* New York: Basic Books, 1987.

Troy, Thomas F. "'Ah, sweet intrigue!' Or Who Axed State's Prewar Soviet Division?" *Foreign Intelligence Literary Scene,* vol. 3, no. 5 (October 1984), pp. 1–2.

———. "CIA Releases First OSS Papers in 38 Years." *Foreign Intelligence Literary Scene,* vol. 3, no. 4 (August 1984), p. 1.

———. *Donovan and the CIA: A History of the Establishment of the Central Intelligence Agency.* Frederick, Md.: University Publications of America, 1961.

———. "Ex-British Agent Says FDR's Nazi Map Faked." *Foreign Intelligence Literary Scene,* vol. 3, no. 6 (December 1984), p. 1.

———. "'Tricycle' Never Mentioned Pearl Harbor Attack, Says FBI Review of His File." *Foreign Intelligence Literary Scene,* vol. 3, no. 2 (April 1984), p. 1.

Truby, J. David. "Pesky Ships of the Air." *Military History,* vol. 4, no.4 (February 1988), pp. 8, 58, 60–61.

Truman, Harry S. *Memoirs.* Vol. 2, *Years of Trial and Hope.* Garden City, N.Y.: Doubleday, 1956.

Tuchman, Barbara W. *The Zimmermann Telegram.* New York: Viking, 1958.

Tucker, Glenn. *Dawn Like Thunder: The Barbary Wars and the Birth of the U.S. Navy.* Indianapolis: Bobbs-Merrill, 1963.

Tyler, Moses Coit. *The Literary History of the American Revolution, 1763-1783.* 2 vols. Reprinted. New York: Burt Franklin, 1970.

U.S. Congress. House. Committee on Expenditures. *Hearing Before the Executive Departments on H.R. 2319 (National Security Act of 1947), June 27, 1947.* 80th Congress, 1st session. Washington, D.C.: U.S. Government Printing Office, 1982.

U.S. Congress. Senate. *Message from the President of the United States Transmitting the Report of the Naval Court of Inquiry upon the Destruction of the United States Battle Ship Maine in Havana Harbor, February 15, 1898, Together with the Testimony Taken Before the Court.* 55th Congress, 2d session. Washington, D.C.: U.S. Government Printing Office, 1898.

U.S. Department of State. *Foreign Relations of the United States, 1948.* Part 3. Washington, D.C.: U.S. Government Printing Office.

———. *Papers Relating to the Foreign Relations of the United States, 1898.* Washington, D.C.: U.S. Government Printing Office, 1901.

———. *Papers Relating to the Foreign Relations of the United States: The Paris Peace Conference, 1919.* Washington, D.C.: U.S. Government Printing Office, 1945.

Van Deman, Ralph H. *The Final Memoranda: Major General Ralph H. Van Deman, USA Ret., 1865–1952, Father of U.S. Military Intelligence.* Edited by Ralph E. Weber. Wilmington, Del.: Scholarly Resources, 1988.

Van Doren, Carl. *Benjamin Franklin.* New York: Viking, 1938.

———. *Secret History of the American Revolution: An Account of the Conspiracies of Benedict Arnold and Numerous Others, Drawn from the Secret Service Papers of the British Headquarters in North America, now first examined and made public.* New York: Viking, 1941.

Voska, Emanuel Victor, and Will Irwin. *Spy and Counterspy.* Garden City, N.Y.: Doubleday, Doran, 1940.

Wallace, Willard M. *Appeal to Arms: A Military History of the American Revolution.* New York: Harper & Brothers, 1951.

Wandel, Joseph. *The German Dimension of American History.* Chicago: Nelson-Hall, 1979.

Warner, John S. "Where Secrecy Is Essential." *Extracts from Studies in Intelligence to Commemorate the Bicentennial of the United States Constitution.* Washington, D.C.: Central Intelligence Agency, 1987.

Washington, George. *Writings.* Edited by John C. Fitzpatrick. 39 vols. Washington, D.C.: U.S. Government Printing Office, 1931–44.

Webster's American Military Biographies. Springfield, Mass.: G. & C. Merriam, 1978.

Weinstein, Allen. *Perjury: The Hiss-Chambers Case.* New York: Knopf, 1978.

West, Nigel. *MI6: British Secret Intelligence Service Operations, 1909–45.* New York: Random House, 1983.

West, Rachel *The Department of State on the Eve of the First World War.* Athens: University of Georgia Press, 1978.

White, Leonard D. *The Jeffersonians.* New York: Macmillan, 1951.

Whitehead, Don. *The FBI Story: A Report to the People.* New York: Random House, 1956.

Who Was Who in America. Chicago: A. N. Marquis, 1963–2013.

Who's Who in America. Forty-second edition. 2 vols. Chicago: A. N. Marquis, 1982–83.

Who's Who in Consulting. Second edition, Detroit: Gale Research, 1973.

Wilkie, John E. "The Secret Service in the War." In *The American-Spanish War.* Norwich, Conn.: Chas. C. Haskell, 1899.

Williams, T. Harry. *Lincoln and His Generals.* New York: Knopf, 1952.

Willoughby, Malcolm F. *Rum War at Sea.* Washington, D.C.: U.S. Government Printing Office, 1964.

Wilson, Woodrow. *A History of the American People.* 5 vols. New York: Harper & Brothers, 1901–2.

Winks, Robin W. *Cloak and Gown: Scholars in the Secret War, 1939–1961.* New York: Morrow, 1987.

Wise, David, and Thomas B. Ross. *The Invisible Government.* New York: Random House, 1964.

Wohlstetter, Roberta. *Pearl Harbor: Warning and Decision*. Palo Alto, Calif.: Stanford University Press, 1962.

Wriston, Henry Merritt. *Executive Agents in American Foreign Relations*. Baltimore: Johns Hopkins, 1929. Reprinted. Gloucester, Mass.: Peter Smith, 1967.

Wyden, Peter. *Bay of Pigs: The Untold Story*. New York: Simon & Schuster, 1979.

Yardley, Herbert O. *The American Black Chamber*. Indianapolis: Bobbs-Merrill, 1931. Reprinted. New York: Ballantine, 1981.

Young, Louis Stanley. "The Chief of the United States Detectives Tells How He Captured the Spies of Spain." In *The Life and Heroic Deeds of Admiral Dewey*. Springfield, Mass.: Hampden, 1899.

Zacharias, Ellis M. *Secret Missions: The Story of an Intelligence Officer*. New York: Putnam's, 1946.

Index